Geo. Peabody *was built in 1867 by Readhead,Softley on the Tyne. Registered length 100.4 feet, 115 tons gross, 55 n.h.p. She was broken up in 1924.*

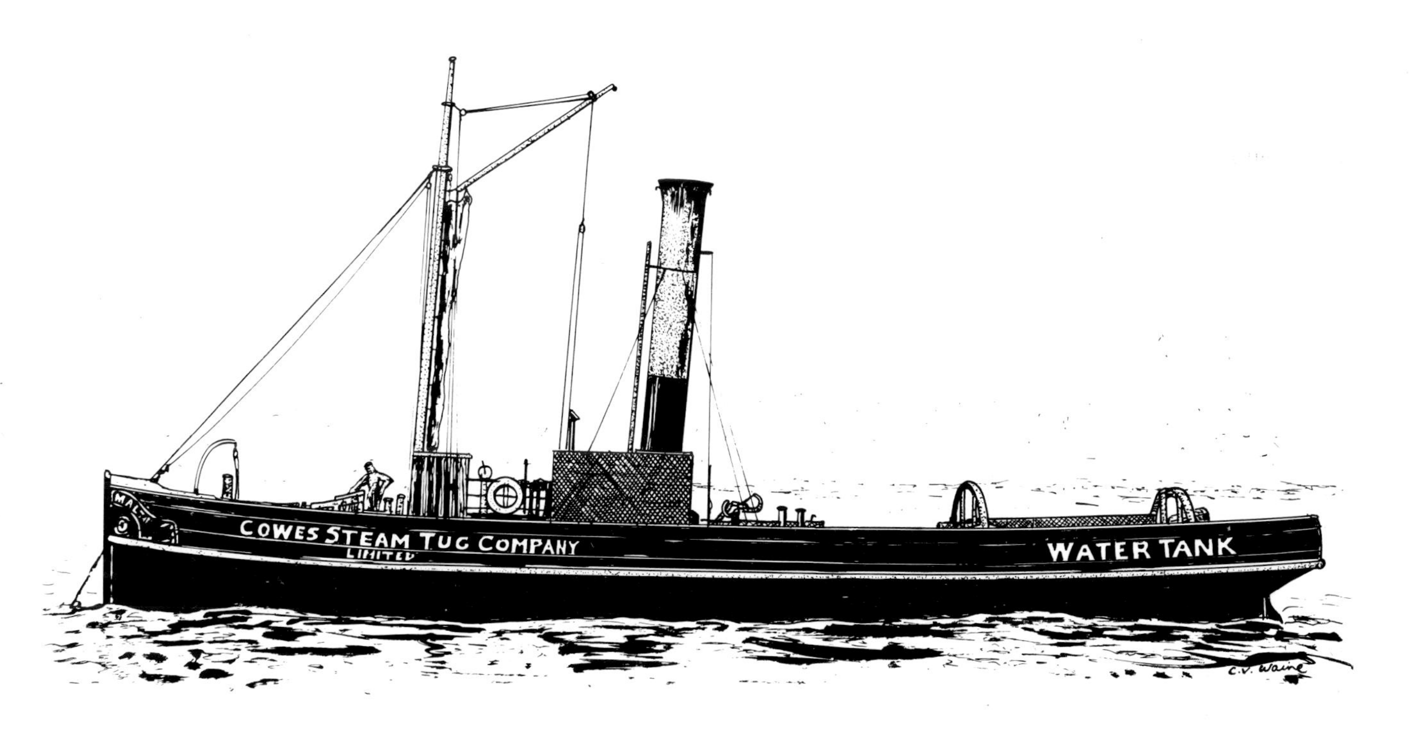

Malta *of 1883 was originally a Watkins tug which was acquired by the Cowes Steam Tug Company. She looks rather 'old fashoned' with her bell-topped funnel and gaff rigged mast.*

Also in this Series

British Ocean Tramps. Volume 1. Builders & Cargoes.
by P.N.Thomas *ISBN 0 905184 13 0. 158 pages.*

A major study of the ships which were the backbone of British commerce, this first volume defines the tramp steamer and looks at construction and builders, including short histories of the main builders. The different designs are fully illustrated including those for world war one and two. The cargoes, coal, grain, ore, timber etc, and how they were carried. Shipbroking: how the ships got their cargoes; chartering, freight rates and unseaworthiness. Steam tramps in world events, particularly in wars great and small. With 48 detailed plans and colour plates, 54 photos, maps and diagrams.

British Ocean Tramps. Volume 2. Owners & Their Ships.
by P.N.Thomas. *ISBN 0905184 14 9. 182 pages.*

The second volume in a major study of the ships which were the backbone of British commerce. Owners and Crews. Histories of the major and minor owners, some 1,300 companies in all, including the early companies active in the 19th century. Notes on some 2,400 ships and typical voyage patterns. Characteristic naming patterns used by the companies. Illustrated with 56 photos from the 1890s to the 1950s, 22 colour profiles and 34 plans.

The Steam Collier Fleets
by J.A.MacRae & C.V.Waine. *ISBN 0 905184 12 2. 226 pages.*

This book was begun by Captain Jim MacRae aboard the Thames up-river collier HACKNEY and with Dr. Charles Waine produced this companion volume to **Steam Coasters & Short Sea Traders.** *A book to delight the coaster enthusiast, model-maker or just about anyone who likes pictures of ships...The result must surely deserve the accolade of a definitive work, something which will be referred to time and again...*SEA BREEZES. A full history of the colliers and coasters in the coal trade of the British Isles and near Continent covering over 800 owners, 1200 ships and the harbours built to serve them. Illustrated with 93 ship plans and coloured profiles, 55 photos, some in colour and 53 sketches, harbour maps and charts.

British Steam Tugs
by P.N.Thomas. *ISBN 0 905184 07 6. 222 pages.*

This book is beautifully produced and a must for anyone at all interested in these fascinating craft..MODEL BOATS. A full history covering early tugs, wood iron and steel paddle tugs; harbour, seeking and coastal screw tugs, and ocean tugs. Thames craft tugs, tenders and passenger carrying tugs, naval and wartime tugs. Tug owners and builders. Tug construction, engines and deck gear. Over 1000 steam tugs, 100 builders and 400 owners are covered. The tug plans range from 1833 to 1956, and 29 colour profiles will be of interest to modellers. More than 90 photographs (some colour), sketches, and colour diagram of 88 funnel colours.

Old Time Steam Coasting
by O.G.Spargo & T.H.Thomason. *ISBN 0 905184 07 6. 138 pages.*

An eye witness acount of life in Liverpool steam coasters in the 1920s and 1930s. *Between them the authors have made a tremendous contribution to the field of both maritime and social history, for their sharp and detailed accounts provide us with a wealth of important information of the kind which is far too often omitted from shipping histories...*SHIPS MONTHLY. The operation of the coasting trade, vessels, crews and cargoes are fully described. Six colour plates, 5 plans and numerous sketches, photos and voyage charts.

Estuary & River Ferries of South West England
by Martin Langley & Edwina Small. *ISBN 0 905184 08 4. 148 pages.*

The many creeks and rivers of the area had rowing and sailing ferries which were later replaced by paddle and screw steamers or steam chain ferries in a number of cases. Full histories of some 139 ferries and over 300 boats are supported by sketch maps, plans (some in colour), and photographs from the River Severn in the north around the coast to the River Stour, Christchurch and Poole in the south.

Steam Coasters & Short Sea Traders ***3rd Edition, 1994***
by C.V.Waine & R.S.Fenton *ISBN 0 905184 15 7. 182 pages.*

The history of the British steam coaster covering building, repairing, machinery, early designs, Clyde 'puffers' and the various engines-aft types, including the big east coast colliers. Also covered are those with engines amidships and coastal tankers. This new edition has a much expanded text with 25 extra pages concentrating on the smaller coasting shipowners, as those owners mainly in the coal trade are covered in the companion volume, **The Steam Collier Fleets.** Illustrated with 76 plans and 29 colour profiles selected with the modelmaker in mind plus 97 black and white sketches and photos.

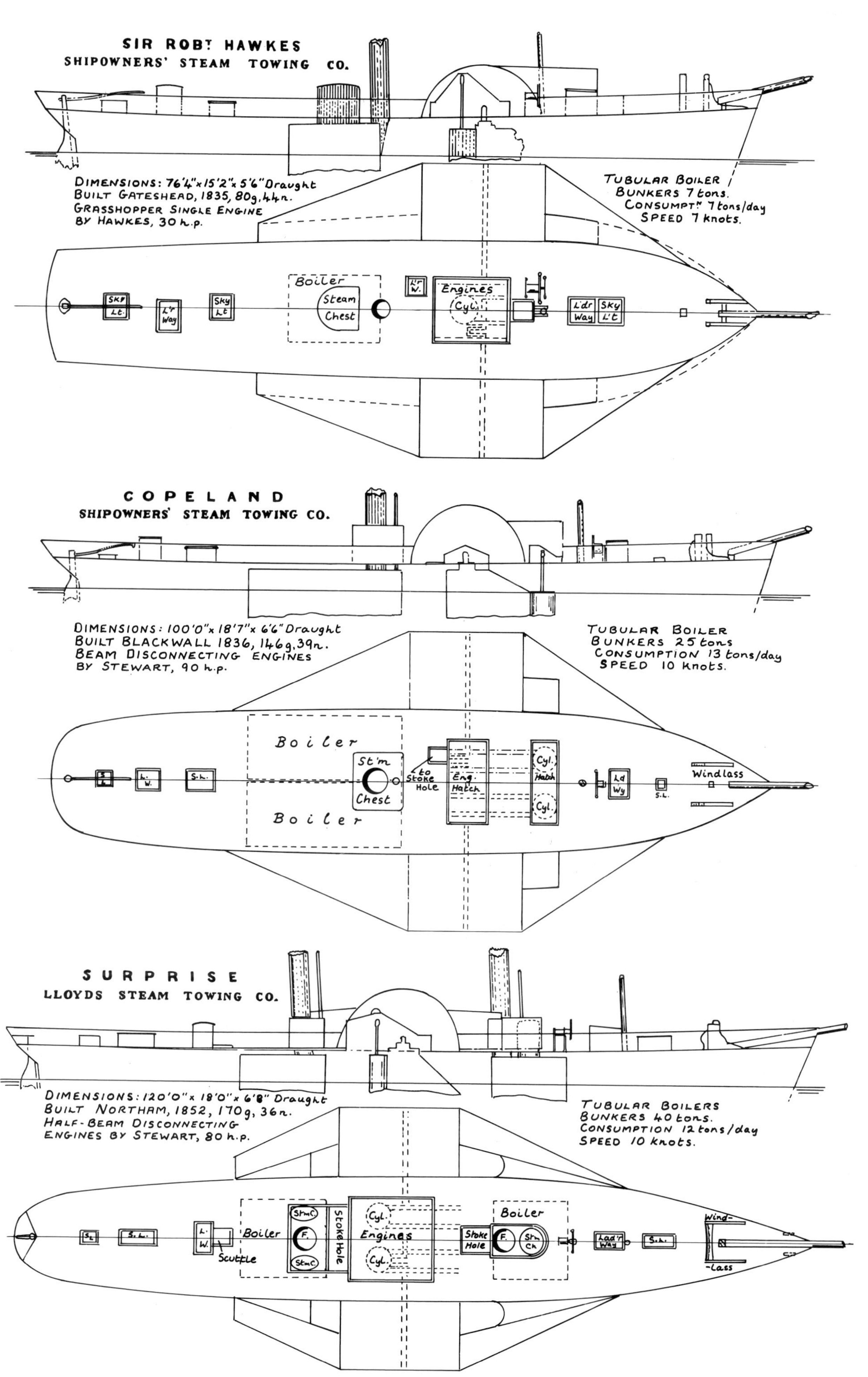

1. Sketches of wood paddle tugs from a Royal Navy survey of 1852, see also page 4.

Plate 2 The Paddle Tug GEORGE BROWN was built in 1887 for Irvine Harbour.

BRITISH STEAM TUGS

P. N. THOMAS

(3) **Conqueror** *built 1897.*

Illustrated by C. V. Waine

WAINE  Research

Publications

This book is dedicated to my wife Jean who encouraged me in my researches into the history of steam tugs.

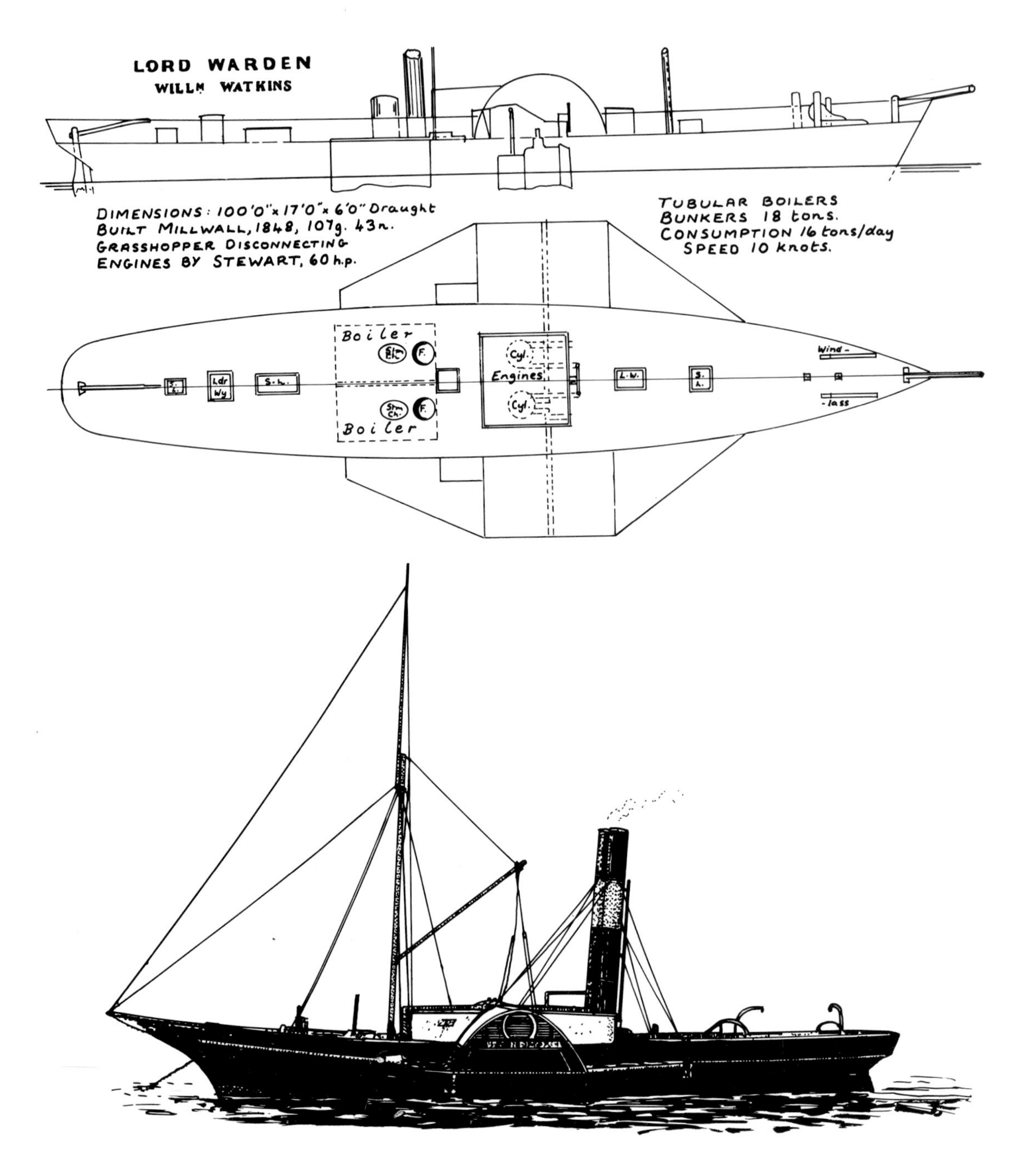

(4) *Iron Paddle Tug Wonder of 1857 was completed with a clipper bow and figurehead.*

Waine Research,
Mount Pleasant,
Beamish Lane,
Albrighton,
Wolverhampton WV7 3JJ.

First Published 1983.

Reprinted 1997.

ISBN 0 905184 07 6.

Printed & Bound in England.

Foreword

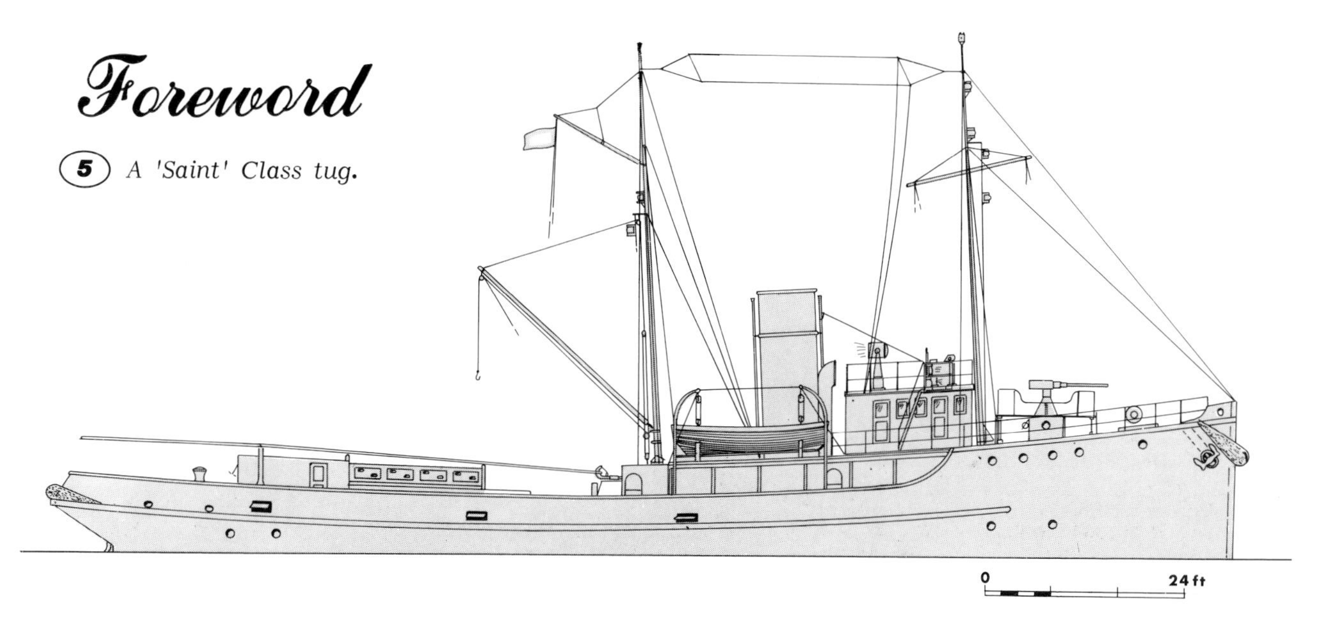

(5) *A 'Saint' Class tug.*

This book happened because the Irvine Harbour Board decided to scrap their old paddle tug, the **George Brown**, in 1956. For years I had passed her lying alongside the quay, but never had I given her much thought. However, her scrapping meant the disappearance of a part of maritime history. She had been built in 1887, and the arrival of the new motor tug, the **Garnock**, left me wondering how tugs had developed over those 69 years. During the years which followed, my interest in tugs blossomed. I made many friends by letter and made the acquaintance of many of the men who worked on tugs. They are a good crowd of lads who make you welcome and explain the mysteries of their trade. The older men had a fund of anecdotes and memories of earlier days when there were characters aboard the boats- "The Councillor", "Cowboy Dan", "Gentleman Jim", and "Hurricane Jack". The tug owners themselves have patiently helped me in my search for photographs and information and I have never been made to feel that I was making myself a nuisance.

My interest was strengthened by the feeling that British tugs were a very neglected aspect of maritime history. Nobody had written a book about them except for the Watkin's history by F.C. Bowen. Articles were few and far between and the half-crown Ian Allan books were the first real publicity that British tugs received. My book is an attempt to remedy the situation.

The information for this book has been gleaned over many years from a wide variety of sources, registers, directories, magazines, books, owners and official reports. The detailed information about a given vessel can vary depending on the source and the date of the report. The tonnage frequently alters and so does the power of the engine, and in the early days even the dimensions change to meet new rules for classification. Some general comments regarding the dimensions given against the names of tugs are included on the contents page. As regards horsepower, the registers quote a figure based on certain characteristics of the engine worked into a formula (see page 200).

The illustrations selected endeavour to show the development of the tug over as long a period as possible. The plans and photographs include tugs from all parts of the country, from a wide range of shipyards with a variety of shapes and sizes. My thanks are due to those friends and firms who have allowed me to reproduce their pictures and plans; tug history is indebted to Thomas McLaren & Co. (Glasgow) Ltd., a firm of ship sales brokers who, over the years, built up a unique collection of old tug photographs and plans. Also to the Forth Port Authority, one of whose employees had a remarkable collection of old photographs of tugs which had sailed on the Firth of Forth, a collection which was unfortunately lost during a reorganisation.

It must be pointed out that the drawings reproduced in this book are, in almost every case, the original builders' plan which may not necessarily represent the tug 'as built', though differences between the office plan and the 'as fitted' vessel are usually, though not always, fairly minor. A case in point is the **Flying Scotsman** (42); in the plan the house on the sponson is shown with a sloping roof, while in the trials photographs the roof is clearly parallel to the waterline.

Acknowledgements: I wish to thank the various shipbuilders and the holders of builders' drawings for granting me permission to reproduce the tug plans in this book. My thanks are also due to the individuals and authorities who have allowed me to use photographs from their collections. I wish to thank also the North East Coast Institution of Engineers and Shipbuilders for information extracted from a paper on engines and boilers read before the N.E.C.I.E.S. during the 1935-36 session by Mr.Baird and Smith's Dock Co. Ltd., for drawings and information obtained from their Journal of May 1933 describing wood tug construction.

Thanks are also due to Mr. Ken Troup, C.Eng., F.R.I.N.A., F.I.Mar.E. and Captain Jim Nelson for reading the final draft, the ladies of the photocopying department who have had to put up with my 'dirty old tracings' over the years, Mrs. Sheila Muir who typed the final script and last, but most important, my wife who has lived with my 'tug fever' for all these years.

P. N. Thomas,
Thornliebank, 1983.

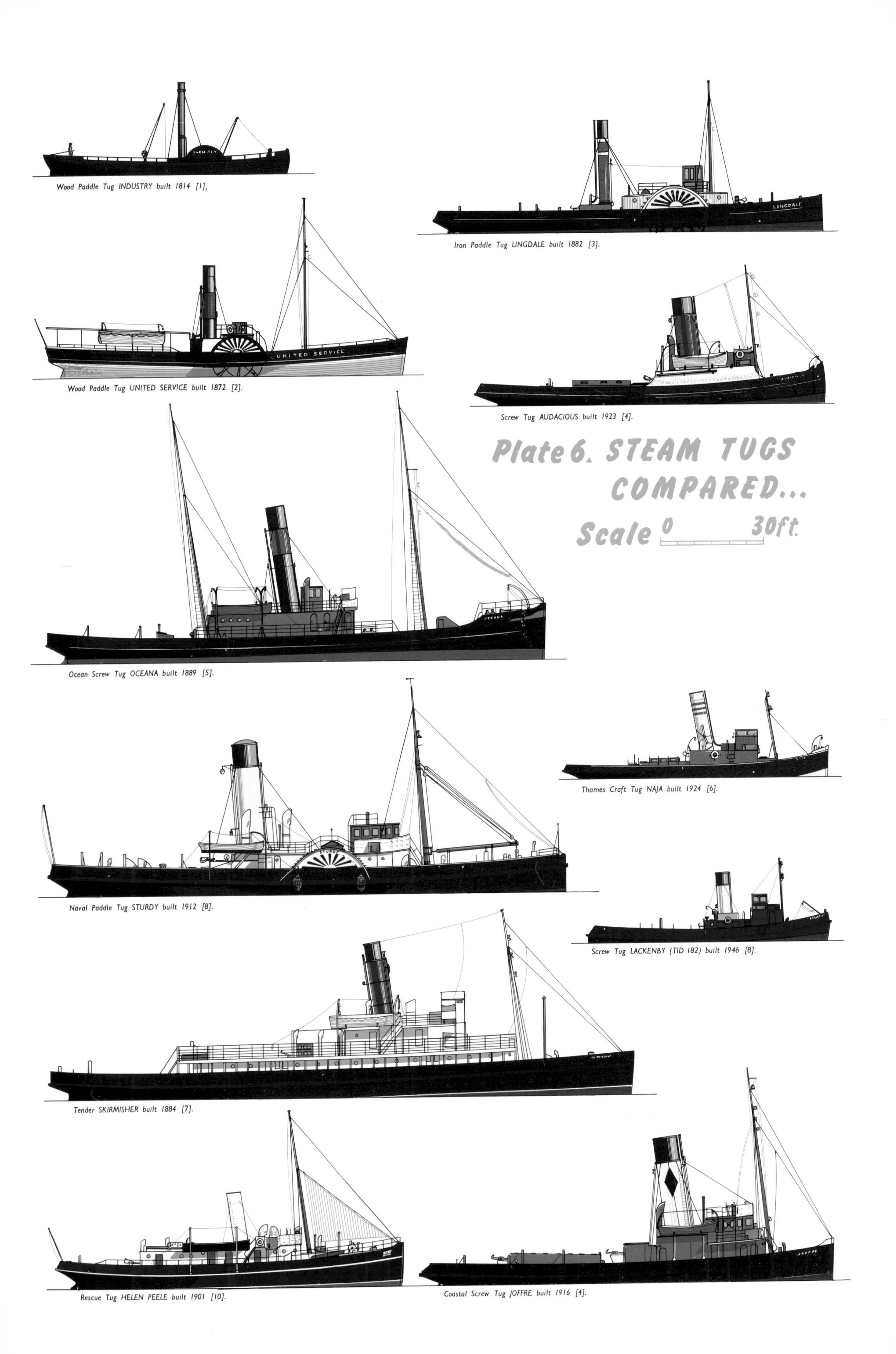

Plate 6. STEAM TUGS COMPARED...

Wood Paddle Tug INDUSTRY built 1814 [1],

Iron Paddle Tug LINGDALE built 1882 [3].

Wood Paddle Tug UNITED SERVICE built 1872 [2].

Screw Tug AUDACIOUS built 1923 [4].

Ocean Screw Tug OCEANA built 1889 [5].

Thames Craft Tug NAJA built 1924 [6].

Naval Paddle Tug STURDY built 1912 [8].

Screw Tug LACKENBY (TID 182) built 1946 [8].

Tender SKIRMISHER built 1884 [7].

Rescue Tug HELEN PEELE built 1901 [10].

Coastal Screw Tug JOFFRE built 1916 [4].

CONTENTS

(7) **Lion** was built by Geo. Brown of Greenock for Associated Portland Cement Co. When towing lighters with 1500 tons aboard she used three tons of coal in 24 hours. She measured 74.5 x 19.2 x 9.4 feet.

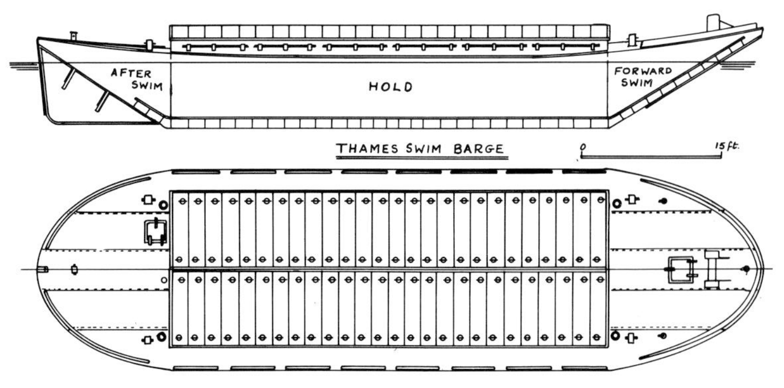

NOTES. ***Date:*** *This is the year in the registers and not necessarily the year of launching.* ***Length:*** *Where the figure is decimal e.g. 80.5 ft., the length is that between perpendiculars (fore side of stem at the waterline to the aft side of the stern post). Feet and inches (80'6") the length is overall.* ***Tonnage:*** *Tugs are registered in gross tons, a volumetric measure (the total enclosed space in cubic feet divided by 100 and called tons). This gives an idea of the tug's size. Naval tugs are specified in displacement tons (the weight of the tug loaded to its normal waterline).*

Figure numbers correspond with page numbers.

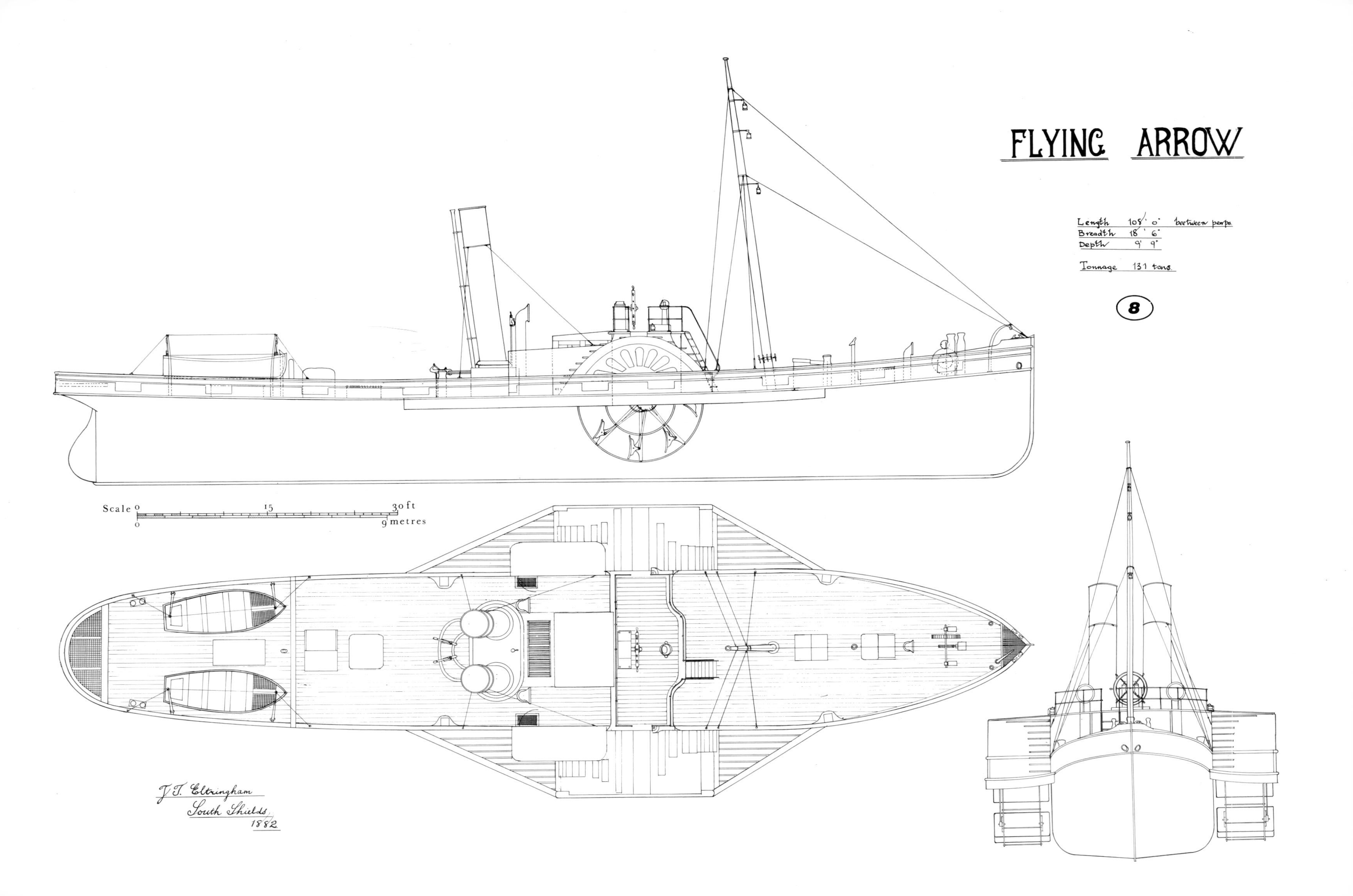
FLYING ARROW
Length 108' 0" between perps
Breadth 18' 6"
Depth 9' 9"
Tonnage 131 tons
8
Scale 0 15 30 ft
0 9 metres
J. T. Eltringham
South Shields
1882

Introduction

(9) *Charlotte Dundas.*

Since the early days of the nineteenth century tugs have been employed in assisting large vessels into and out of port. In both press and sea stories, tugs are generally described as 'fussy, bustling little craft'. Many people do not pay much heed to the tugs as they do not realise how helpless large ships are when in confined waters where they are unable to move at speeds sufficient to maintain steerage way. Not only that, but in shallow water it is difficult to control a deep draughted ship. If people were to watch closely they would see an exhibition of seemingly effortless shiphandling as the tugs work as a team. Sometimes there is complete silence as the tugmasters go about their business, knowing when and where to apply the pull, whilst at other times the air is rent by shrill whistles from the pilot on the tow and answering blasts from the sirens of the tugs. Towing looks an easy operation free from danger. How wrong! It is quite the reverse. Those experts make it look easy, but a small error of judgement on someone's part and there is another headline - "The tug sunk while towing S.S.........etc." The **Kenia** is shown grounded after a collision in August 1964(10) with a great gash where the stem of the ship has struck her. Just look round a tug and see the dents in her bulwarks and rubbing strake. Tugs are very heavily built, they have to be!

At the end of the steam era,tugs could be classified under six general headings, though it was not always easy to place a tug under a given heading as their uses overlapped. The classes and approximate range of dimensions were as follows:

1. Harbour or dock tugs.	(Up to 80 ft.)
2. River tugs	(80 ft. to 105 ft.)
3. Coastal tugs.	(100 ft. to 130 ft.)
4. Ocean-going tugs.	(120 ft. upwards)
5. Thames craft tugs.	(50 ft. to 100 ft.)
6. Tenders.	(Around 130 ft.)

The following are brief descriptions of the steam tugs as they were in the 1950s when they faced replacement by the new motor tugs.

Harbour tugs: In general the dimensions of these small craft were limited by the features of the port in which they operated. The machinery took up most of the space below deck and as they had only day accommodation, the superstructure was minimal. The hull had a generous beam, for, whatever size a tug might be she had to be stable. The draught was as deep as local conditions would allow as a propeller exerts its greatest thrust when it is deeply immersed. In common with most types of tug the towing hook was placed at the rear end of the superstructure, on the centreline and just aft of amidships. Engine skylights and companionways on the after deck were protected by steel towing bows to guide the towrope freely over them. Generally a small lifeboat was carried but permission was often granted to carry a life raft if the tug was restricted to docks.

River Tugs: The size of these vessels was not restricted to the same extent as the harbour tug, but in most ports the river tug also had to work in the dock areas and it was here that the restriction arose. In many of the larger rivers there was a regular traffic of tugs towing hopper barges from the dredgers or town refuse to dumping ground beyond the river mouth. The tugs were again beamy and as the seas which they encountered were quite rough at times they had a good sheer forward while keeping their low freeboard aft. The wheelhouse often had a flying bridge above it to give better visibility during docking. In some ports the tug's job was finished after they towed the ship into the river estuary. In other ports such as Glasgow they took their tow along many miles of narrow winding river before casting off the towline. They also attended the launching of large vessels and berthed them alongside the fitting out quays.

Usually the full equipment of a tug was fitted; full width towing beams, spring hook, lifeboats and radar. Sometimes fire monitors were installed in order that they might tackle fire aboard ships especially where they were often employed berthing tankers at oil terminals.

Coastal Tugs: : Although these larger tugs were designed for coastal work there was not enough business to keep them gainfully employed in this particular field and they had to be capable of operating in the rivers and even in the larger docks. They had the usual tug feature of ample beam and deep draught aft. They had a high sheer forward with a heavy flare to the bows to prevent the seas in bad weather from breaking over the deck. Any water which came aboard was shed through large freeing ports along the bulwarks. The accommodation was generous as they frequently had to remain away from their home ports for protracted periods. A few had raised forecastles like the ocean-going tugs but this was not a common feature on British coastal tugs. Their speed was quite high as they had to answer distress calls when no time could be wasted, though of course it was the weather conditions which determined the rate of progress when answering a call for assistance. Coastal tugs were fitted with all the latest navigational aids - Decca navigation, radio direction finding, radio telephone and wireless telegraphy. All coastal tugs had to carry lifeboats and buoyant rafts.

Ocean - going Tugs: There was no restriction on the size of these tugs except initial cost and running costs. Steam tugs went up to around 175 ft. but the modern motor driven deep sea tugs have reached sizes of 200 ft., though foreign tugs had well exceeded this. With a deep sea tug which was dependent on salvage work for large profits, a high free running speed was essential, though this introduced problems, setting a compromise in the design of the propeller between free-running and towing conditions.

The usual features of broad beam and deep draught were still required and almost universal was the continuous raised deck forward extending aft to nearly amidships. The bridge was high, built with wings extending to the side of the hull. The accommodation was generous, and as far as possible access to all parts was by internal passageways. Because the tugs had to operate anywhere in the world from the tropics to the icy seas of the North Atlantic, air conditioning and refrigerated food stores were not uncommon. Range was important and huge bunkers had to be provided. This was where oil scored over coal as, for a given weight of fuel carried, the oil fired tug had a range 50% greater than her coal fired rival. As salvage work was the most lucrative source of income those large tugs were well equipped for carrying out all manner of salvage, on the high seas or where the casualty had gone ashore. Pumps, compressors, anchors, electric generators and even steam generating plant were carried. Their lifeboats were large and at least one would be motor driven to be used for ferrying salvage gear across to the casualty. The towing beams spanned from bulwark to bulwark, high enough to walk below. An automatic towing winch was commonly fitted, designed to operate on a set strain on the towing gear, paying out the hawser if the strain was exceeded and winding in again as the strain relaxed. Heavy lifting derricks were an essential item to handle the salvage gear and it goes without saying that the most modern navigational aids were carried.

Thames Craft Tugs: Because of the congested conditions on the River Thames the size of the craft tugs was kept to a minimum, and she was, for a tug, rather narrow in the beam. As these tugs went well up the river and up the creeks which fed into the river the draught was kept as shallow as was consistent with maintaining propeller thrust. The typical Thames lighter had a very pronounced overhang at bow and stern and to avoid damage the tug's bulwarks were sloped sharply inwards and sheathed with timber at the stern, the bulwarks often being set inboard from the edge of the deck. For the same reason the casing was kept as low as possible and such casings as there were were spanned by simple steel towing bows; full width towing bows were seldom used. As the river is crossed by many bridges the height of the tug's wheelhouse had to be kept low. Frequently the wheel was protected only by a waist-high screen, sometimes with glass windscreens above which were collapsable. In many 'toshers' the skipper and helmsman's only protection was a canvas dodger.

Tenders: The tender or passenger carrying tug had all the design features of the coastal tug, but a promenade deck was built from the front of the bridge right to the stern. No extra boats were carried but there was a large number of buoyant seats and lifejacket boxes upon which the passengers sat. Usually a small saloon was provided below deck with toilets and possibly a ladies' room was included. When passengers' baggage was carried there was a small hold with a derrick above it. As the tender had to go alongside the liner an extra heavy wooden belting was fitted along the hull.

__Kenia__ beached after a collision on 25th August 1964 at Tilbury dock with M.V. Maashaven. __Kenia__ was built in 1927 by Cochrane & Sons for William Watkins of London. PHOTO: J.E. Evans.

1. Early Days

(11) *Perseverance* built 1849

The towing of one vessel by another smaller one did not start with the advent of the steam tug. The Romans had an organised fleet of ships bringing grain from Alexandria and to manoeuvre them when they arrived in harbour small oared galleys were used. The rowers in these towing vessels were not slaves but freemen who enjoyed the same high social status as athletes. The barges carrying blocks of stone for the Pyramids were towed along the Nile by small galleys. Warships becalmed or badly damaged after a battle at sea, would commonly hoist out their boats for towing. This method of pulling boats could only be used for a short period of time, the length of which was dictated by human endurance. To move a ship within a harbour, teams of men would be used pulling on a rope attached to the vessel or else the crew would set up a tackle to the pierhead and with the other end of the rope round the capstan, they would tramp around the capstan pushing on the capstan bars until they were at the harbour mouth. Where they had penetrated up a river or creek they would warp the vessel to the river mouth themselves or purchase the services of a horse to provide the pulling power. The answer to the problem was to replace man by machine!

It has been recorded that in 1682 a towing vessel was constructed, propelled by paddle wheels which were driven in some way by horses within the hull. Some sources say that this contraption actually worked in Chatham Dockyard. In 1736 Jonathan Hulls of Campden, Gloucestershire applied for a patent to cover 'a newly invented machine for carrying vessels or ships against wind and tide or in a calm.' He planned to strip a small merchant ship of her masts and spars and to install a Newcomen atmospheric engine driving the paddle wheel in the stern through a ratchet mechanism. There is no record that the vessel was actually built, but it is highly unlikely, as an engine of the Newcomen type would have been so heavy that the boat would probably have sunk under the weight. Around 1787 experiments were carried out by Patrick Miller of Glasgow working in conjunction with William Symington, but he was basically interested in steam and paddle purely as a means of propulsion. His boats did function, one being 25 feet in length and capable of 5 miles per hour. On the Bridgewater Canal a stern paddle wheeler was built in 1798/9 and was applied to coal laden barges. The trials were satisfactory though the speed achieved was barely that of a horse. No one seems to have been very impressed, and there were fears that the wash generated by the paddles would damage the banks of the canal, the **Bonaparte** as she was called, was dismantled and the engine used to drive a pump in a coal mine.

In 1802 Lord Dundas who owned the Forth and Clyde Canal engaged William Symington, who had worked on Miller's steamboats, to undertake the construction of a steamboat to tow coal barges on the canal. The vessel, which was called the **Charlotte Dundas**, 56 feet long by 18 feet beam made her trial trip in March 1802 with a party of gentlemen on board, towing two barges of 70 tons burden, accomplishing the trip from Lock 20 to Port Dundas, Glasgow (a distance of nineteen and a half miles) in six hours against a strong headwind which impeded all other traffic on the canal. Lord Dundas was very impressed and decided he would operate a fleet of 9 towing vessels on the canal, but before any move could be made he died and unfortunately the Canal Company lacked his Lordship's foresight. They cancelled the order and laid up the **Charlotte Dundas**, using the excuse that the excessive wash from a steamboat would damage the canal banks. The old steamer was finally broken up in 1861. The next proposal came from the famous Cornish engineer Richard Trevithick. While Britain was at war with France, Trevithick broached the idea of using a steam vessel to tow a fire-ship into the anchorage at Boulogne where the French invasion fleet was assembling. Before any action could be taken the French fleet moved from Boulogne and Trevithick changed his plan to cover the building of a tugboat; the **Nautical Labourer**, for towing boats in and around the London docks. She was to have a steam powered crane to assist with the unloading of cargoes, and a steam driven fire pump for tackling fires on ships or in dock establishments. His ideas were strongly opposed by all employed in the docks who saw the **Nautical Labourer** as a threat to their livelihood and so Trevithick gave up the idea.

In 1812 Henry Bell introduced his history-making paddle steamer *Comet*, the first successful passenger carrying steamboat in the United Kingdom. She was 40 feet long by 10 feet 6 inches beam and was capable of about 7 miles per hour. In the following year Marc Brunel who was engaged to work on the naval installations at Chatham proposed to the Admiralty that a steam powered towing vessel would provide an inestimable service to warships attempting to sail against unfavourable winds and tides. However, their Lordships showed great shortsightedness and felt that it was their duty to discourage the employment of steam vessels as they considered that steam would strike a fatal blow at their naval supremacy.

In 1814 (two years after the *Comet*'s first voyage), J.& W.Fyfe of Fairlie on the Firth of Clyde built the **Industry**, a steamer intended for the passenger trade. Built to the orders of Mr.Cochrane, a Glasgow tanner, she was engined by J.Thompson of Glasgow, and was 68'4" long by 16'6" beam being 83 registered tons. After two trips with passengers she was converted into a luggage boat. Up to this time all goods destined for Glasgow had to be off-loaded at ports on the Clyde coast and conveyed to the city by packhorse or alternatively transferred to lighters at Port Glasgow and pulled by horses walking along a towpath on the river bank up to Glasgow taking as long as three days on the journey. The **Industry** as a luggage boat, could carry passengers and cargo, and in 1815 she was bought by the Clyde Shipping Company for that purpose. Soon after she began to tow barges, thereby increasing her usefulness. The exact date is unknown and although she is generally regarded as the first tug, the claim cannot be substantiated. The **Industry** was in form like the small sailing ship of the day with a very bluff bow and a hull which tapered to a square stern. The paddles were placed very far forward as if to pull the vessel rather than push her. In common with many paddle steamers of the day, the deck overhung the hull to the width of the paddleboxes. This design feature was resurrected for the paddle tugs of the Manchester Ship Canal Company 80 years later. The funnel is tall and slender and in prints and photographs she is shown as having no mast but instead two cranes for cargo handling are fitted, one forward and one aft (6). She was laid up in the 1870s and the hulk was still in Bowling Harbour in the 1890s. The plan of the **Industry** which is reproduced here was published in 1909(13), but its origins are not stated.

As is common with inventions and new ideas, men in different places often arrive at the same conclusion at nearly the same time and it is not easy to credit one particular man with being the first in the field and so it was with towing. On the Tyne, steamboats made an appearance soon after the *Comet* sailed on the Clyde. The **Tyne Steamboat** was launched on the Tyne in 1814 and greatly impressed the populace. In 1815 a Mr. Joseph Price of Gateshead became a shareholder in a steamboat speculation on the Tyne which lasted about two years before it got into financial difficulties. Mr. Price purchased from the company the **Eagle** and the **Tyne Steamboat** which he renamed the **Perseverance**, repaired them and ran them between Newcastle and Shields, still at a loss. In July 1818 Joseph Price conceived that "good might be done by towing vessels to sea." Accordingly he arranged with the owner of the Hull trader *Friends Adventurer* to have his vessel ready an hour and a half before high tide. For the first three miles the tide was against the tug and her tow, but the vessel was towed two miles over the bar before being cast off, covering a distance of 13 miles in 2 hours 10 minutes against a contrary wind. Mr. Price claimed that this was the first time that a sailing vessel was ever towed by a steamboat.

At first no one was impressed by the performance of his 'tugboat' but as time went on he and other steamer owners succeeded in establishing towing as part of the operation of the River Tyne, both towing colliers clear of the bar and towing keels out to complete their loading on to colliers outside the river. Two main advantages soon became clear, firstly no vessel larger than 240 tons had ever attempted the passage of the River Tyne as far as Newcastle but, by 'taking steam', vessels up to 400 tons were regular visitors to the Newcastle quayside. Secondly due to the vagaries of wind and weather, delays at the port restricted the colliers to only eight voyages per year, but by 1833 with the help of tugs thirteen voyages per year were now possible. No longer were there holdups when hundreds of colliers were windbound at the mouth of the river and thus a more regular supply of coal found its way south to London. Mr. Price was honoured with a dinner and a silver tankard but was somewhat disappointed at the lack of appreciation as is evident from his open letter which he wrote in 1838 (hoping, apparently, for a more tangible vote of thanks in monetary terms). In this he claimed that his speculation in the towing system had cost him upward of £3000.

On the Thames the steamer **Majestic** appeared in 1816 and was 'thought to have been the first steamer employed in towing ships', as, on August 28th, 1816 she towed the *Hope* an East Indiaman from Deptford to Woolwich at a rate of 3 miles per hour against the wind. Then Liverpool made her claim that 'the first application of steam for the towing of vessels was made in October 1816 when the *Harlequin* was towed out of the Mersey by the **Charlotte**, a steamer which in the summer of the same year had been placed as a ferry boat to run between Liverpool and Eastham.' Now that the claimants had shown that towing by steamboats was a feasible proposition in each of their own ports the idea spread slowly to the other ports in the United Kingdom. The word 'tug' would appear to have been first used for a towing vessel when a steamboat was built at Dumbarton in 1817 for the specific purpose of towing ships from Leith to Grangemouth; she was called the **Tug.** The **Tug** worked as a tug until 1838 when she was sold and converted into a sailing ship. The Clyde makes a counter-claim that the first true tug came from her shipyards when in 1818 the Clyde Shipping Company "being sensible of the uncertain, inconvenient mode of carrying goods up the Clyde to Glasgow, resolved to have built and fitted up in an elegant fashion, a handsome and stout steam vessel called the **Samson** with accommodation for passengers and for towing lighters laden with goods." No mention is made of carrying goods in the **Samson** and she may presumably be regarded as a true tug although she did carry passengers. The **Samson** was 82'0" long x 16'11" beam built of wood, 54 tons register, with two engines having a total horsepower of 40 nominal.

In the south of England the **Earl of Egremont** went into service in April 1821 towing barges from Portsmouth to Milton for the Portsmouth and Arundel Canal Co. It would appear that, for a time at least, towing generally was left to the local packets and ferries which undertook this work when they encountered vessels prevented by contrary winds from entering or leaving harbour. Towing was introduced between Hull and Gainsborough in 1821 and on the River Tees in 1824 when, on Christmas Eve "one of these new-fangled toys, the **Albion**, towed the collier *Cumberland* from the river mouth to Stockton in grand style". It is almost certain that this vessel, the **Albion,** was designed by George Stephenson for the purpose of hastening the despatch of coal from the new staithes which local Quakers had built the previous year. The **Albion** worked as a tug for ten years before she was laid up, her engines removed, and she was re-rigged as a brigantine. In Liverpool the first mention of a tug is in 1821 when the **Hero** was built. It is probable that she was really a ferry as she was 130.5ft. long, but she became a tug eventually when bought by the Liverpool Steam Tug Co. in 1839. In 1823 the **Druid** was referred to as a tug - as she was 84'5" long this is quite possible. In Liverpool there is a painting of the tug **Eagle** built in 1824, which claims that she was the first true tug on the river, showing her with four paddle wheels.

The main feature which these early vessels seem to have had in common is that they were employed both as tugs and passenger steamers. Shore labour was very cheap and although taking a ship out of dock manually was hard slow work it cost less than taking a tow from a steamer. As a result the owners of the steamboats had to cover their losses by providing a passenger ferry service. Unfortunately for all concerned the tug captain, who was generally the owner as well, took whichever form of employment looked most remunerative at the time, and a ship could be left without a tug while the ferry became a tug. The other feature which they had in common was that they were small and underpowered, barely able to make headway themselves against a strong current and sometimes forced to give up a tow in any other than calm weather. It is almost certain that the tugs of the Tyne served the dual function of tug and ferry until the Tyne General Ferry Company was formed in 1862 to provide permanent services on the river.

Surprisingly enough the Thames seems to have been about the last river in the country to introduce steam tugs as it was not until 1832 that the **Lady Dundas** arrived from the Tyne and **Wear** from Sunderland. The **Wear** was built in 1825 and was 67.7' long x 16.0' beam with a draught of 5'6" and a registered tonnage of 33 tons. The **Lady Dundas** was back on the Tyne by 1835 - the only detail which survives of her is that her tonnage was 18. The London owners of these two vessels soon discovered that they had bought a pig in a poke and that they were so underpowered that they could not tow any size of ship. However, the following year Mr. John Watkins went to the Tyne himself to H.S. Waite of North Shields and had a tug built to suit his own specifications. The **Monarch** was a wooden paddle tug 64'10" long x 13'11" beam and a draught of 4'6". Turner portrayed her in his famous painting 'The Fighting Temeraire' but she looks like a small black beetle and he gives no real idea of her true appearance. However in the museum at Newcastle there is a

13 *This plan of **Industry** (1814) was published in 1909, but its origins are not stated. The bow appears sharper in photographs with deck and sponsons less rounded and paddle-boxes further aft.*

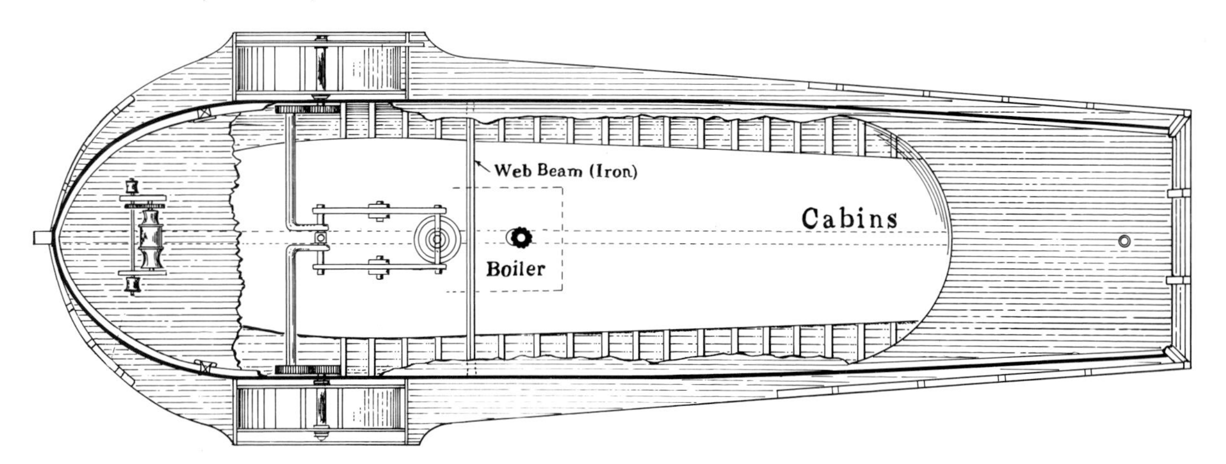

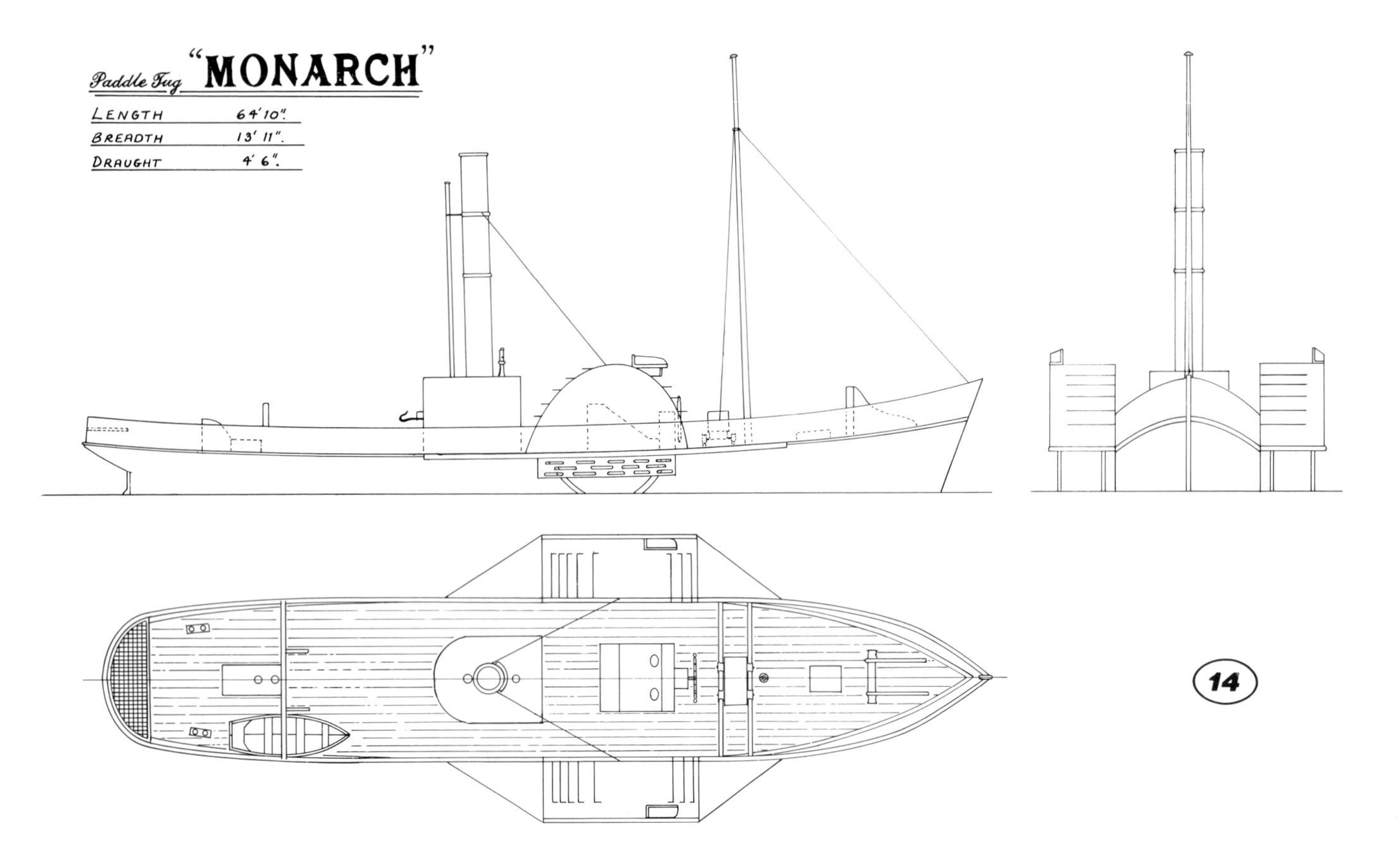

small model which looks as though it is reasonably accurate (14). It shows a clinker built hull with slight sheer, a raked stem and a counter stern. There is a pole mast and a tall thin funnel aft of high paddle boxes. She has only a few structures on the deck, a companionway to the accommodation, a hatch to the bunkers, and a cover over the crosshead slides of her side lever engine. On the foredeck is a strange contraption; a wheeled bogie filled with scrap iron running on rails arranged athwartships across the deck. The early tugs had a single engine and were difficult to manoeuvre using their rudder only. When the loaded bogie was run to one side the tug heeled over dipping one paddle further into the water and enabling it to exert more thrust than the other which was barely touching the water. The idea worked but often resulted in a broken paddle shaft. Despite the awkwardness in handling paddle tugs with a single engine, they were still being built as late as 1898 when the **Flying Scotsman** (43) was delivered to the Clyde Shipping Company of Glasgow. It has been asserted that the single engined paddle tug could exert a stronger pull than a double engined paddle tug of the same horsepower.

In Bristol the local Chamber of Commerce urged the use of steam tugs on the Avon, following the example of the other major rivers in the country. They first raised the matter in 1824 but another twelve years went by before they had any success, as it was 1836 before the tug **Fury** went into service. The name was most appropriate as it raised the anger of the labourers and the boatmen on the river who foresaw the vessel as a threat to their livelihood, the pulling of ships seven miles from Pill to Bristol. A party of them went on board the tug, set her adrift and tried to scuttle her in the river. She was raised and returned to service ending her career in 1859 when her boiler exploded in Kingroad. The explosion occurred on 23 September as she was lying at her moorings and she was completely destroyed; the engineer and the fireman were killed and the ship's boy was injured. The date of build of the **Fury** was 1835 and it is of interest to note that she was built on the Thames at Deptford and was 57.3' long x 13.4' beam with a draught of 3' 0". Another Bristol tug, the **Black Eagle**, blew up in the Avon in November 1866; the vessel was only five years old and the boilers three years old. The picture shows how complete the devastation was when one of these wooden paddle tugs suffered a boiler explosion (15). At the same time that the **Fury** was introduced in Bristol, the Aire and Calder Navigation started a steam towing service on the East Coast using double engined paddle tugs. Much later the Commissioners for the River Severn purchased two paddle tugs from the River Thames, the **Enterprise** and the **Perseverance**, the latter being lost on the passage round the coast. The tugs had been employed in towing coal barges on the Thames from London to Windsor and were fitted with 'reefing' paddle wheels: presumably this meant feathering floats. The **Enterprise** answered well and towed trains consisting of twelve vessels carrying cargoes of 30 tons each at a rate of $2\frac{1}{2}$ to 3 miles per hour against a stream running at 2 miles per hour. Soon after, in 1860, tugs were placed on the Gloucester and Berkeley Canal to tow sea-going vessels. There were three tugs, all being of iron, two 65' x 12' drawing 6'3", the third was 55' x 9'6" x 5' draught and the three cost a total of £3,000. Previously the incoming ships had been towed by horses the number of horses being regulated in accordance with a fixed scale:

Vessels up to 40 tons (1 horse), 40 to 80 tons (2 horses), 80 to 130 tons (3 horses), 130 to 180 tons (4 horses), 180 to 250 tons (5 horses), 250 to 300 tons (6 horses), 300 to 350 tons (7 horses), 350 to 420 tons (8 horses), 420 tons upwards (9 horses).

All the time that the paddle steamers were developing and the paddle tugs were gaining ground, the inventors of the screw propeller were busy. In July 1836 Captain Ericsson, a Swede, a partner in the firm of Braithwaite and Ericsson, after experiments with a model, built a 45 ft. screw tug, the **Francis B. Ogden.** She was built of wood and had two propellers contra-rotating on the same shaft. Trials were organised in the presence of the Royal Navy but they were not impressed. The **Francis B. Ogden** even towed their barge at ten miles per hour for a considerable distance, but to no avail. The scientific experts had advised the Admiralty representatives that 'the screw propeller was designed on erroneous principles, and would be unsteerable, while its vast loss of mechanical power would prevent it from being employed as a substitute for the now old established paddle wheel.' However, inventors take a lot of stopping and in 1840 an experiment was organised to test the Archimedian screw as compared with the common (fixed float) paddle wheel in the presence of Mr. Fawcett, the eminent steam engine builder from Liverpool, Mr. Barnes and others. The two contestants were the **William Gunston** and the **Archimedes.** The **William Gunston** was a wooden paddle tug which had been built in Gateshead in 1837, 90.0' long x 17.0' beam, with two engines of 20 n.h.p. each. (The register gives 60 n.h.p. total.) The **Archimedes** was a wooden built screw steamer launched in Poplar in 1839, 105.0' long x 20.2' beam, with a draught of 9'2" with two engines of 25 n.h.p. each. (The register gives 80 n.h.p. total.) The **Archimedes** first towed the **William Gunston** to ascertain that the screws were not affected by the relative positions of the vessels. When the trials proper started, the **Archimedes** was seen to have lost all power over her rival and the paddle tug was towing her in spite of her superior engine power and the much praised screw propeller. At first slowly and then faster until the usual speed of 8 to 9 miles per hour was reached. The paddle enthusiasts were ecstatic but the proponents of the screw fought back with letters to the Press protesting about inequality of power, that the horsepower figures quoted were fallacious, the disparity between the two vessels; the verbal battle went on for months. Possibly the most reasonable claim was that the paddle steamer had started first and the screw of the other boat could not operate in the disturbed water from the paddles.

Five years later the Admiralty arranged a trial between the *Rattler,* screw propeller, and the *Alecto,* a paddle steamer. The *Rattler* was a wood built screw sloop 176' long x 32'6" beam, built in 1843. The *Alecto* was a wooden paddle sloop 164' long x 32'6" beam, built in 1839, and so on the face of it the two vessels would appear to have been evenly matched. On 30th March 1845 the *Rattler* beat the *Alecto* in a race from the Little Nore to Yarmouth Roads, a distance of 80 miles, by a margin of 23 ½ minutes despite a shortage of steam. They raced again from Yarmouth to Cromer Light, 34 miles, when the *Rattler* won again by a margin of 13 minutes. Next day they raced to the Spurn Light, 60 miles, when the *Rattler* arrived 40 minutes ahead of her rival. Trial after trial showed the superiority of the screw in free running, but the most telling trial was a straight tug-of-war, when *Rattler* towed the *Alecto* at 2½ miles per hour in spite of her every effort. Again the arguments started, the supporters of the paddle wheel claiming that the *Alecto's* engines were designed for 390 h.p. indicated, but were old and worn out, while the *Rattler* had new engines of 460 h.p. indicated. Whatever the truth the result convinced the Admiralty, and it is generally accepted that this trial was the turning point for screw propulsion. While all this publicity was being given to this contest a fact that was not mentioned was that the *Rattler* had already been in competition with the paddle yachts *Black Eagle* and *Victoria and Albert* and had come off second best on both occasions. In the latter case it is hardly surprising as the *Victoria and Albert* was a much larger vessel. Later in the same year a most peculiar vessel was constructed to take these tests further. The **Bee,** as she was called, was fitted with both screw propeller and paddle wheels and tests were carried out with the screw and paddles working in opposition to one another both ahead and astern. In each case the paddles overcame the screw. In a dynamometer test the screw gave 583 lb. and the paddles 627 lb. The results of these tests received little publicity and were overshadowed by the *Alecto/Rattler* trials. Another pioneer of screw towing was the **Liverpool Screw,** a steamer 65' x 12'6" with a 3'9" draught, which was reputed in 1844 to have excelled all other steamers of the port of Liverpool in towing out vessels in a rough sea.

The contest between the *Alecto* and the *Rattler* may have convinced the Admiralty but had little effect on the tug-owning fraternity as it was many years before the screw tug was built for general ship handling work. Some went into service on canals and on the River Thames towing lighters but on most of the rivers and in the ports of the United Kingdom the paddle tug reigned supreme. The owners of the small tugs were cautious men and preferred to keep to a tried means

Wood Paddle Tug ***Black Eagle*** *Destroyed by a boiler explosion 1st November 1866. She measured 87.4 x 18.3 x 9.5 feet.*

of propulsion, though they accepted the various improvements in engines and paddles as they were introduced. Generally the tugs were owned as single units rather than in fleets, with shares on the 1/64th. basis as was common with the cargo carriers of the period. Here the value of the ship was divided into 64 equal shares which were purchased by local tradesmen, gentlemen, and harbour officials, though in some ports the latter were often specifically precluded from owning shares in tugs where this might lead to irregularities in the hiring of the tug's services. This system survived until the end of the century and even in ports where fleets did exist a fleet owner might have shares in a tug outside his own fleet.

The tugs of the 1840s had progressed somewhat from the basic simplicity of Watkin's **Monarch.** They were fine lined vessels with a slight sheer, often with a clipper bow and a bowsprit and sometimes with a figurehead. They had a single mast and had a full set of sails with a gaff mainsail and a jib which they set at sea to help economise on their supply of coal while they sought a tow. The engines were greedy on coal and tugs could hardly keep at sea for three days without running short of coal. The **Monarch** was a notorious coal eater and on more than one occasion had to borrow fuel from her tow.

The sketch of the **Perseverance** shows a typical wooden paddle tug with a clipper bow and cutter rig (11). The picture is deceptive and makes the tug look smaller than she was - 97.0 ft. x 17.7 ft. x 10.8 ft. 156 tons gross, she was built in 1849 for Thos. Petley of London, one of the 'big names' in towing between London and the English Channel. Thirty years later she was relegated to working in the docks in the Port of London. The tugs were still low powered and were frequently forced to slip their tow if the weather turned foul, to save themselves from being driven ashore, a fate which befell their helpless tow. They were uncomfortable vessels on which to work, with no shelter on the deck, even the engineer stood in the open beside his control levers and the helmsman stood by the tiller in the stern. Not only was he exposed to the elements but he had to dodge the tow rope should the tow take a sheer off to one side. On the 24th March 1860 the tug **Tiger** of Bristol was towing the ship *Juno* to Cardiff when, off Blackmore, a gale came on and the tug was unable to tow. She gathered sternway so that the helm shifted suddenly and the tiller knocked the unfortunate helmsman overboard. Even on their own, should one of the small tugs be caught at sea when the weather broke, they were frequently driven ashore as they made for harbour and were wrecked. Some were overwhelmed while still at sea. In December 1867 the tug **Pearl** put to sea from the River Tyne in comparatively fine weather but when she returned about five hours later the seas had become rough. As observers on the shore watched a heavy sea struck her and she overturned. Witnesses commented that it was a common thing for tugs to go out in rough weather in search of vessels. The gale in which the **Pearl** was lost, destroyed 250 ft. of the South Pier at the river mouth.

Another comment in the report was that the **Pearl** was fitted with a wheel in the middle in place of the usual tiller at the stern. The **Pearl** was quite a new tug having been built in 1866 and was of a fair size being 79.1' long. However, no matter how bad the weather, the tugmen were seamen and were prepared to take risks to help ships in distress. On 6th January 1839 a terrible storm broke in the Irish Sea shortly after the departure of three sailing packets bound from Liverpool for New York. All three were driven ashore, one of them the *Lockwoods* carrying 168 emigrants. The tug **Victoria** built in 1837 and 111 ft. long towed out the lifeboat to the wrecks. After an unsuccessful attempt to approach the *Lockwoods* the lifeboat was forced to run for shelter. In spite of the gale the **Victoria** pushed closer, dropped her anchor and slacking out her cable she dropped down to the ship to take off some of her passengers. She returned next day with another tug and rescued more people from the three vessels which had been stranded. Their heroic action was well rewarded with £400 to the owners of the **Victoria,** £100 to the master, £10 to the mate and £5 to each of the crew.

During the 1830s the tugs which came from the slips on the banks of the Tyne were generally small, most of them between 50 and 70 ft. in length. A few tugs were built in other shipyards throughout the country and these tended to be somewhat larger mostly between 80 and 100 ft. Other larger boats were built but these were usually ferries which at a later date were taken over by towing companies, vessels such as the **Mona** built for the Isle of Man Steam Packet Co. and transferred to the Liverpool Steam Tug Co. in 1839. During the 1840s the tugs from the Tyne still tended to be in the 50/70 ft. range though wooden tugs up to 110' had entered into service. An increased number of tugs came from yards outside the Tyne ranging from 60 to 110 ft. in length. The practice in the North-East seemed to have been to build a tug for a local owner who kept the vessel for a year or two and then sold it to owners elsewhere. The style of the wooden paddle tug had changed little since the **Monarch** except that the overall length was greater. They had little sheer, the bow was raked forward and they still had that somewhat 'fragile' appearance.

The plan of the **Vanguard** (17) was published in the Smith's Dock Journal and gives an impression of the earlier form of the wooden paddle tug with a heavily raked stem and tiller steering. There is no bridge deck but there is quite a high boxlike casing over the engine room. The placing of the forward companionway to the port side seems odd but is confirmed by photographs of similar tugs. Right aft she appears to have two heavy knees, one on either side of the tiller flanked by a samson post. The nearest tug of the same dimensions which can be found in the records was built in 1858 for Shields owners. She was sold to Cardiff in 1864 and returned to the Tyne in 1876 where she remained until broken up in 1890.

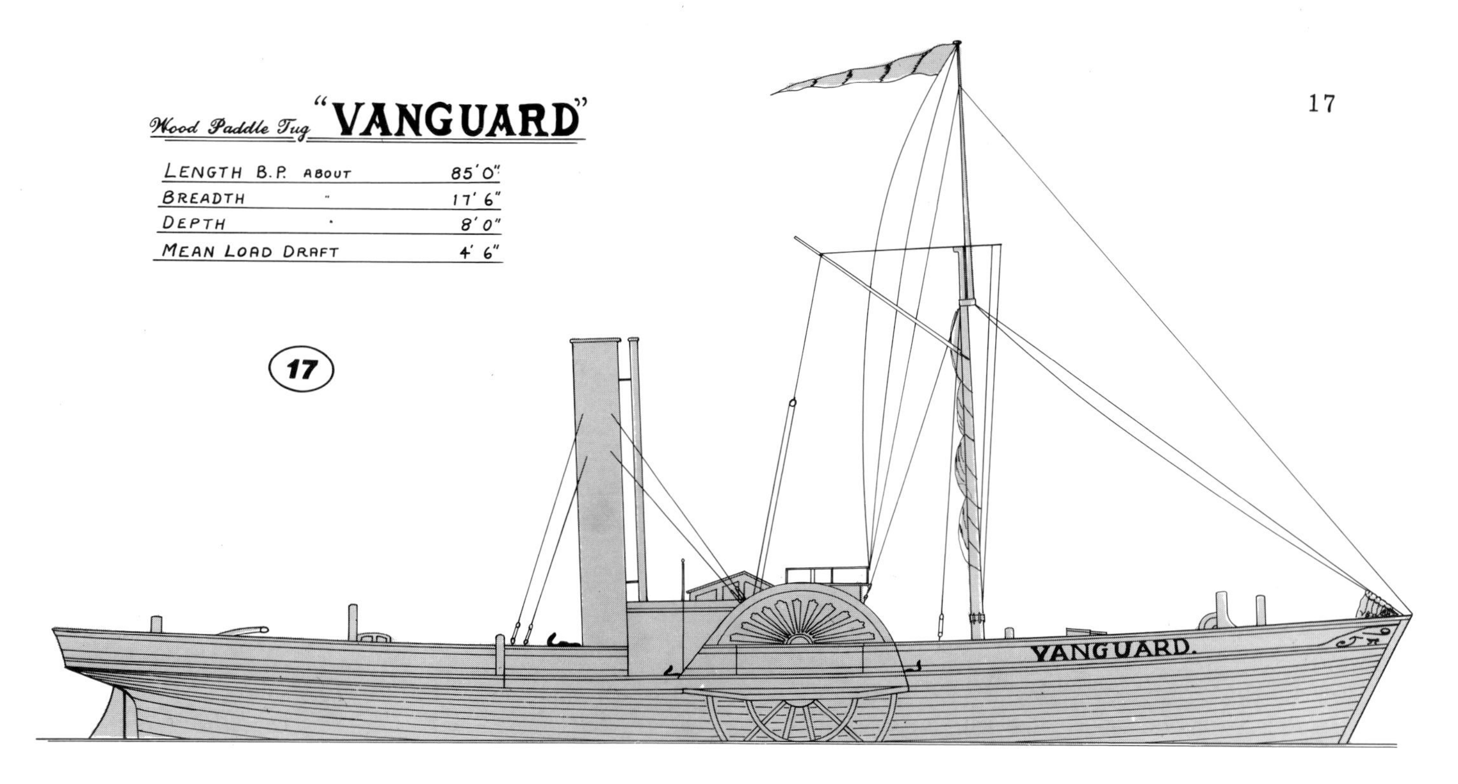

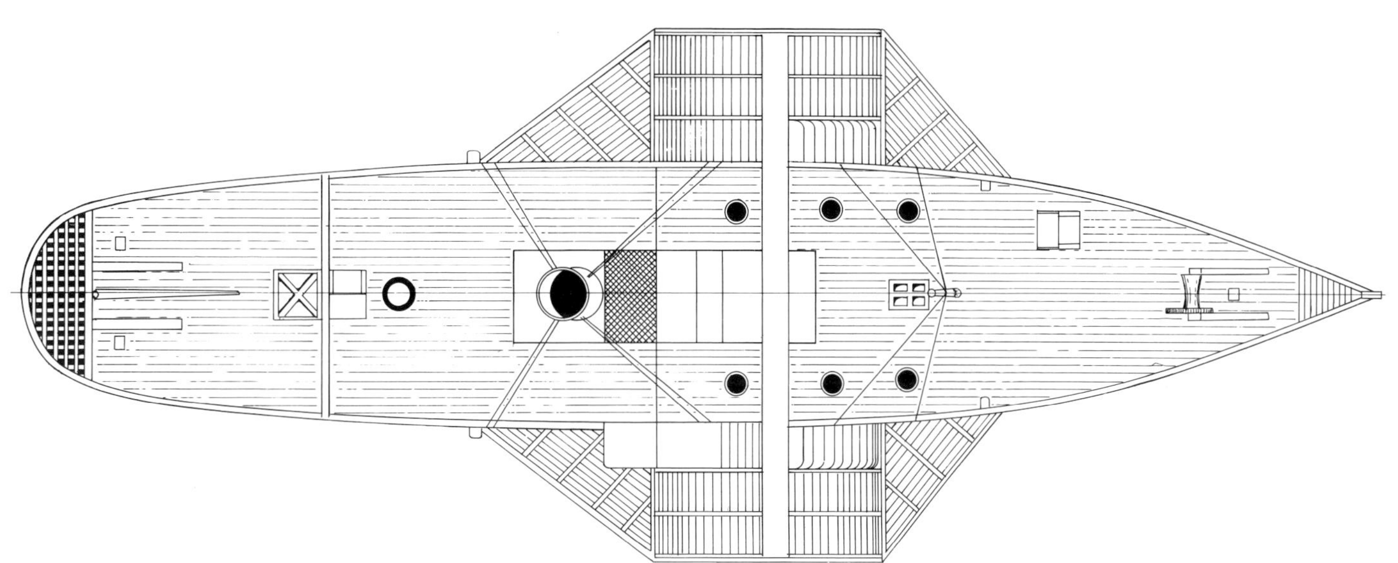

The photograph(17) shows two typical 'old stagers' on the River Tyne at Newcastle. The **Judith** was the older of the two, having been built in 1847 for owners in Goole, returning to Newcastle in 1872. She was a small tug 62.5 ft. x 15.1 ft. x 7.4 ft. with a gross tonnage of only 43 and having an engine of 18 n.h.p. She had the quaint 'crown' sometimes seen on those early funnels. There was no bridge, not even a plank between the paddle boxes which were supported by the characteristic iron stays. The other tug is the **Heather Bell**, built in 1861 and spending all her life with Tyne owners. She was only a little larger, 73.4 ft. x 15.1 ft. x 7.5 ft., 45 gross tons and 20 n.h.p. She was rather similar in appearance to the **Judith** but she had the arched plank helping to stiffen the paddle boxes. They both had tillers.

Wood Paddle Tugs ***Heather Bell*** *(left) and* ***Judith*** *(right). The picture was taken before 1893, the year that* ***Judith*** *was lost by stranding. PHOTO: W. Featherstone.*

Ignoring some of the larger iron vessels which were probably built as passenger vessels though they later belonged to tug companies, it is possible that the **Defiance** of 1841 was the first iron paddle tug; she was 112.3' long x 20.3' beam with a tonnage of 124. Her earlier owners are not known, but in 1853 she entered the fleet of J. Tyrer of Liverpool. In the same year the **Satellite** was launched for John Watkins of Liverpool who was the son of John Watkins of London, the well-known tug owner. It is possible that the **Satellite** was a tender when built.

The Parliamentary Reports first gave owners' names in 1848 and from these emerge the fact that in some ports substantial fleets of four or more tugs had been formed:

London: Caledonian Steam Towing Co. (9 tugs), Shipowners Towing Co. (8 tugs), Thames Steam Towing Co. (8 tugs), Thos. Petley (4 tugs), William Watkins (4 tugs). **Cardiff:** William Bird and others (6 tugs), **Liverpool:** Liverpool Steam Tug Co. (9 tugs), William Willoughby & Son (6 tugs), **Stockton:** J. & A. Strong (7 tugs). **Glasgow:** Clyde Shipping Co. (7 tugs), New Clyde Shipping Co. (4 tugs).

In the majority of cases the tugs were still in the hands of individuals though these men did not hesitate to give themselves grandiose titles to impress prospective customers. Names such as The Independent Steam Tug Company and the Original Steam Tug Company. The tugs' names too, played a big part with **Hercules** and **Samson** being very popular, and names such as **Defiance** and **Champion** aimed at giving the right impression. The name **Sea Horse**, although very appropriate appears only three times. It was given to two very early tugs, one in Aberdeen built in 1838, the other in Middlesbrough built in 1840. A naval tug bearing this name was launched in 1880.

However the tug was at last making its mark and the industrialists were beginning to realise that it was a versatile type of vessel. The **Goliath** was chartered in 1850 for the laying of the first telegraph cable across the English Channel. A large drum weighing 2 tons was erected on her after-deck, it was 15 ft. long and 7 ft. in diameter, and on it the cable weighing 5 tons was wound. On 28th August 1850 the **Goliath** left Dover harbour paying out the cable as she went, following a track indicated by flag buoys. The laying of the cable was completed in a single day. Unfortunately, the cable did not remain in service for long, as a French fisherman fouled the cable with his anchor and when he hauled it up he thought the cable was a new sort of seaweed and he chopped off a piece to show to his friends on shore. The **Goliath** was a big new wooden paddle tug 103 ft. long. In 1852 a new tug called the **Bishop** 70.8 ft. long was used for towing the barges of stone needed for the building of the lighthouse on the Bishop Rock. There were still plenty of old wooden paddle tugs in service; in 1852 the **Rob Roy**, quoted as 35 years old, i.e. built in 1817, was driven ashore and wrecked at Warkworth when seas broke over her and put out her fires. One wonders how she had survived so long! But the winds of change were about to blow!

The foregoing has been a brief history of how steam towing began, brief because of the lack of information about tugs and towing in those early days. The learned gentlemen of the period were still discussing the ability of a sailing warship to tow a disabled comrade at a time when there were steam tugs in every important port in the country. As is so common the tug was a part of their everyday life and was not worth commenting on. Information on the tugs themselves is equally difficult to find as the Lloyds Registers of the day ignored small vessels completely and even many of the steamers received no mention. Fortunately reports regarding steam vessels were submitted from time to time to Parliament and it is possible to glean some facts from these. Even then the information varies from report to report. Sometimes no date of build is given, sometimes no dimensions, only in later reports are owners names mentioned. Worse still, the basic facts change as rules for measurement changed and the same vessel may have as many as three sets of dimensions and varying tonnages. **Favourite** official number 24414. Built North Shields 1828. Wooden paddle tug. She was remeasured as follows:

1845: 52.2' x 11.0' x 3'0" draught, 10 tons register, 8 n.h.p. **1848:** 52.2' x 11.0', 27 tons gross. **1855:** 52.2 x 11.0' x 6.2', 25 tons gross. **1878:** 54.3' x 12.0' x 6.1', 24 tons gross, 9 n.h.p. **Favorite** had a long life as it was not until 1890 that she was noted 'not sea-going' and her register closed in 1891.

Since this book was first published, Royal Navy surveys of merchant ships to assess their suitability for carrying guns have come to light. In 1852 they surveyed London, Bristol and Liverpool tugs in some detail (1,4). Other ports were not visited as they found that the vessels generally had large cylindrical boilers, no room for extra coal, steam chests above deck and in some cases the starting gear also. Only the larger tugs of the Liverpool Steam Tug Co., such as **Dreadnaught** (113'7" x 20'4" x 9'3" draught) built in Liverpool 1844 with side lever engines could carry two days extra coal in their holds. Daily consumption was 23 tons, bunkers 24 tons, speed 8 knots. The Thames tug **Newcastle**, built at North Shore in 1824, with a 45 h.p. grasshopper engine by Hawkes was more typical. She measured 86'0" x 14'6" with a flue boiler burning 7 tons daily for a speed of 7 knots; bunkers 18 tons.

Of the tugs surveyed the places of building were: River Tyne (40), London (11), Liverpool (10), Southampton (3), Bristol (3), Glasgow (2), Middlesbrough (2), Sunderland (2).

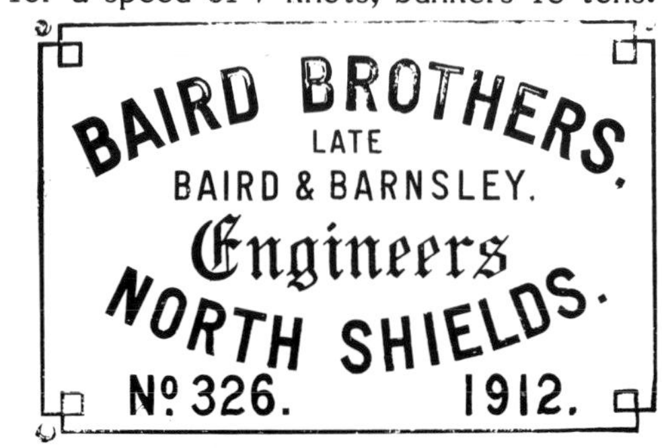

Right: The engine builders plate of the paddle tug ***Elie*** *illustrated on the opposite page.*

Plate 19

Steel Paddle Tug ACTON GRANGE
Manchester Ship Canal Company.
She was completed in 1907.

Steel Paddle Tug EPPLETON HALL
In the colours of her last owners, the Seaham Harbour Dock Co. From a plan by H.G.Raffay.

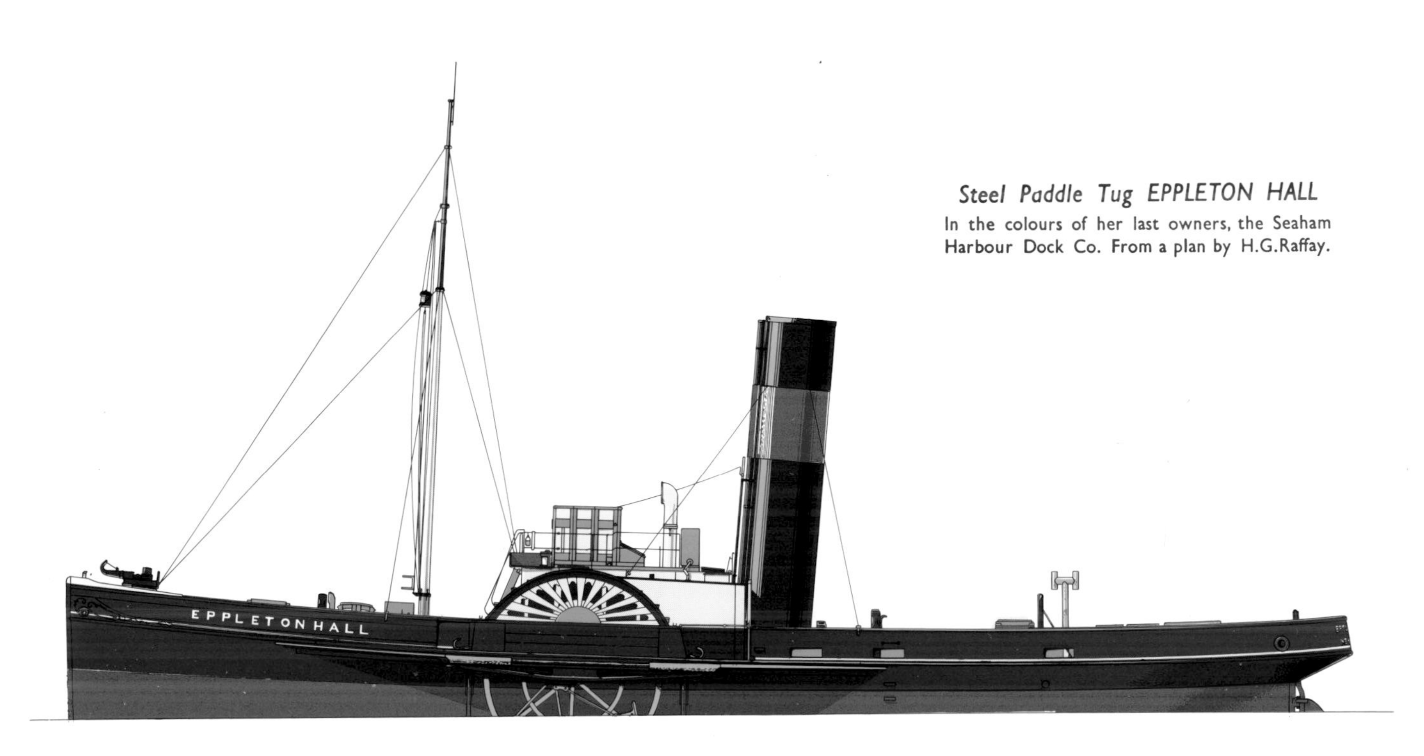

Steel Paddle Tug ELIE
Grangemouth & Forth Towing Co.
From a plan by P.N.Thomas (1960).

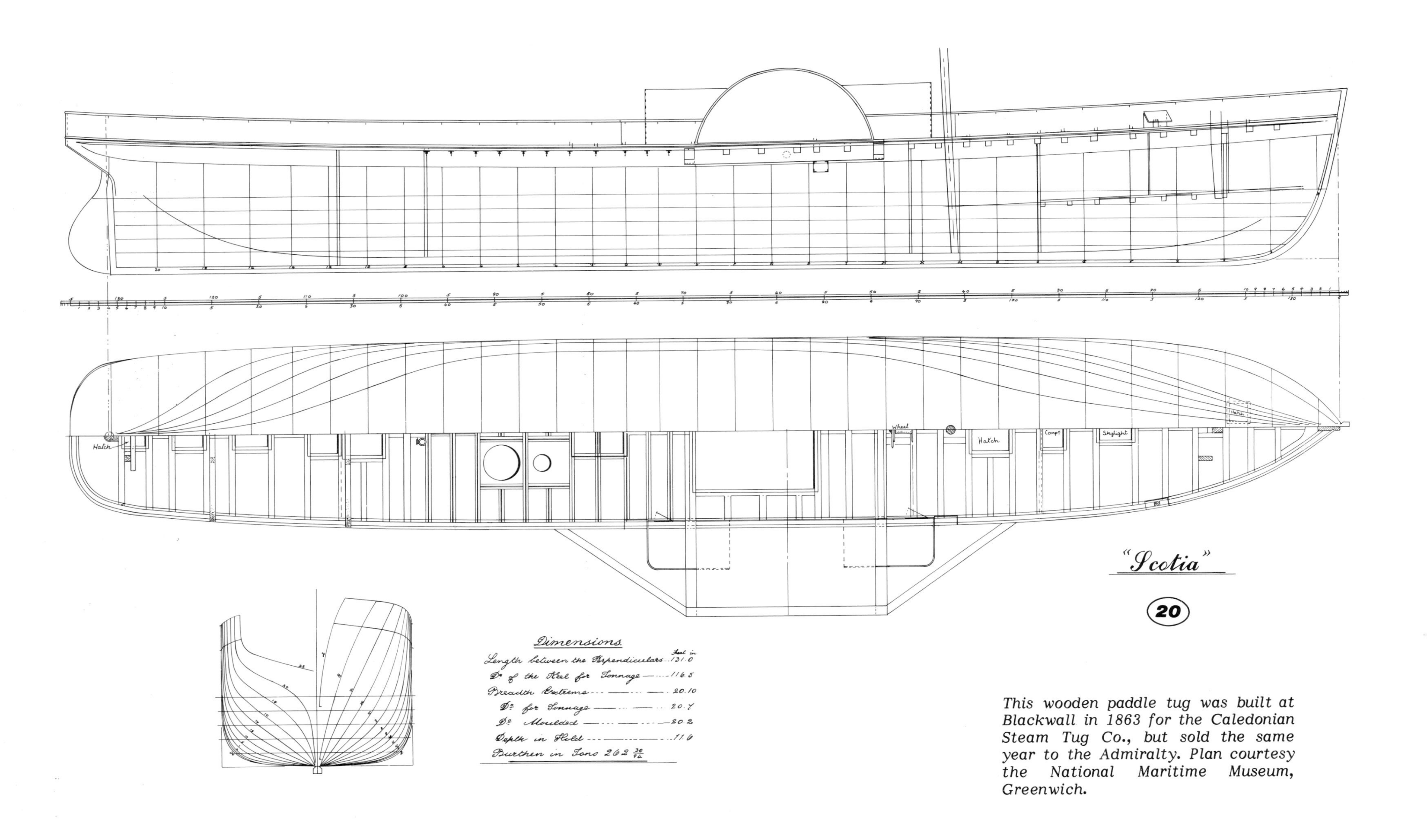

"Scotia"

20

This wooden paddle tug was built at Blackwall in 1863 for the Caledonian Steam Tug Co., but sold the same year to the Admiralty. Plan courtesy the National Maritime Museum, Greenwich.

2.

(21) *North Shields, 1882 from the 'Tyne & Its Tributaries' (Palmer).*

Wood Paddle Tugs

There now occurred two events which were to change considerably the towing industry. In 1851 gold was discovered in Australia and when the news reached England there was an unprecedented demand for passages to Australia. Shipowners advertised 'taking steam to the Nore' as a proof of their desire to give a fast passage by cutting out any possibility of delay at the start of the outward voyage, hoping thereby to encourage emigrants to take passage on their vessels. During the next few years several new powerful tugs joined the 68 tugs already registered in London:

1851:	**Friend to All Nations**	Newcastle. 107.6 x 20 ft, 152 tons. 240 n.h.p. Iron. Thomas Petley.
1852	**True Briton**	Poplar. 78.0 x 16.0 ft. 95 tons. 120 n.h.p. Thomas Petley.
1852	**Mystery**	96.1 x 16.6 ft. 105 tons. R.D. Ross.
1852	**Surprise**	111.4 x 16.6 ft. 132 tons. R.D. Ross.
1852	**Sir Walter Scott**	103.4 x 16.0 ft. 76 tons. 70 n.h.p. Caledonian Steam Towing.
1853	**Cock of the North**	Grangemouth. 93.7 x 19.1 ft. 136 tons. 120 n.h.p. Shipowners Towing Co.
1853	**Victoria**	Southampton. 116.0 x 17.1 ft. 147 tons. 180 n.h.p. William Watkins.
1854	**Caledonia**	Blackwall. 102.0 x 16.4 ft. 124 tons. 70 n.h.p. Caledonian Steam Towing Co.

In addition a further 8 second-hand tugs were purchased and registered in London. It is of interest to note that only one of the above new tugs was built of iron making a total of two in service on the Thames by 1854. In Liverpool the other main passenger port, 6 new big tugs were registered together with 6 second-hand tugs:

1853	**Tiger**	Liverpool. 91.6 x 16.0 ft. 107 tons. 40 n.h.p. Iron. Liverpool Steam Tug Co.
1853	**Rattlesnake**	101.0x 15.5 ft. 99 tons. Iron. George Booker.
1853	**Constitution**	Northumberland. 132.9 x 22.3 ft. 262 tons. 120 n.h.p. Iron. Peter Maddox.
1852	**Invincible**	Warrington. 105.0 x 16.6 ft. 111 tons. 70 n.h.p. Iron. John Rigby.
1854	**Iron King**	Northumberland. 123.0 x 18.3 ft. 172 tons. 100 n.h.p. Iron. H.J. Ward.
1854	**Pilot**	109.3 x 17.6 ft. 112 tons. 60 n.h.p. Iron. Liverpool Steam Tug Co.

By comparison with the London owners the tugowners in Liverpool were now changing to the new-fangled iron hulled paddle tugs.

All this time shipbuilding techniques were improving and larger ships were being built, and to tow these ships the tugowners had either to use more tugs on each tow or to start employing more powerful tugs. The bigger engines which were required needed bigger hulls to accommodate them together with bigger boilers. In London the boost came when the Crimean war broke out in 1854. Most of the supplies for the theatre of war were channelled through the Woolwich Dockyard and the Deptford Victualling Yard and were carried entirely by sailing ships. The demand for shipping space caused a shipping boom but in order to avoid 'traffic jams' it was essential to keep the vessels moving independent of winds and tides. There was still a shortage of good quality tugs with adequate power, but the prospect of profitable Government towing contracts acted as a spur and during the next three years thirty new tugs of 80 ft. and over were put into service on the River Thames by William Watkins, Caledonian Steam Towing Co, Daniel Barker and others. Most of these tugs had two engines allowing independent control of the paddle wheels, increasing the manoeuvrability of the vessel and many had adopted the practice of having two boilers arranged side by side, each with its own funnel, an arrangement which was continued into the 1880s.

The two boilers were of a size already tried and proved reliable and gave the advantage of economy in that the engineer could lightly bank one of the fires when running free, i.e. could close off the supply of air to the fire and reduce the rate of burning of the coal. When additional power was required for a tow he opened the air inlets, raked the fire and added more coal. To allow them to remain at sea for longer periods the bunker capacity of these tugs was also increased and they were now capable of a tow from the centre of London to the Downs. Having cast off their tow they took to anchoring there or off Dungeness offering their services to incoming ships and with this the practice known as 'seeking' was established. 'Seeking' was the most interesting aspect of towing and was to survive until World War I. The tow out was a dull business with all the arrangements being made in the office ashore with a note received from a messenger giving the tug captain the time, place and name of his tow. 'Seeking' developed into an art which changed little even though the tugs themselves changed over the years. It was a battle of wits between experts.

Incoming steamers which had 'spoken' sailing ships, reported on arrival the date and position of the meeting and these were printed in the shipping papers which were studied by the tug captains. Wind and weather were assessed and adding some knowledge of the ships and their captains, a tug skipper would make up his mind where to look for his prize. He would conceal his intentions from his rivals by trying to slip away unseen, but if there was any chance that he had been spotted he would steer a false course, doubling back as soon as visibility made it safe to do so, or if night had fallen he might reverse his navigation lights, douse them altogether, anything to throw his rivals off the scent. All this to ensure that should he find the ship of his choice he would have the field free. The basic rule of seeking was that the first tug to hail the ship should have the right to bargain for the tow and that any other tug must stand off until it was clear that the first tug was not going to take the ship in tow. It was a game of chance for, even should he find his ship there was no guarantee that his rope would be accepted. The argument over the price of the tow could go on for hours or even days (especially if the ship were British owned). The two captains bargained like Arabs in the market, haggling until agreement was reached. The price would drop as the distance home decreased and the chance of a rival tug appearing increased, the tension would mount, and then at last the terms would be agreed or the tug would sheer off in disgust to look for a better proposition. The whole proceeding was followed intently by two crews: for those on the sailing ship it could mean less days spent at sea and no more 'pulley-hauley', to those on the tug it could mean a bonus and the return to port after fruitless days scouring the seas. The wise tug captain always had a bundle of newspapers and some fresh vegetables to hand over to the ship when the bargain was clinched.

Seeking was not always carried out in a spirit of good will and sometimes tempers were lost. In a court case being heard in Liverpool in the 1860s, the judge is quoted as saying:- "I remember a case which occurred in the Mersey where the master of a tug having been disappointed by the refusal of employment, absolutely went straight for the vessel in question and ran her down purposely." Unfortunately no further information was printed. Another example of unethical behaviour occurred in 1864 in Sunderland. The tug **Nimrod** (1857. 85.1 ft, 73 tons, 40 n.h.p.) had been waiting outside the port when she saw a small sailing ship approaching. She went alongside, agreed the terms for the tow and as she went ahead to pass the towrope she was struck in such a way that she was driven away from her tow by the tug **Marco Polo** (1858. 77.6 ft, 58 tons, 28 n.h.p.) which had followed her out. The offending tug immediately passed her towrope and took the ship into the port. The captain of the **Marco Polo** claimed that he had acted according to the local rule that 'the tug which first hailed a ship should have the towage' and that the **Nimrod** had deliberately gone in after he (in the **Marco Polo**) had made contact.

On the North-East Coast there was a lot of trade with foreign shipping and the tug captains had their own mode of address; a Frenchman would be "Moundseer", while a vessel from the Baltic would be greeted with "Steerman". The Newcastle tugs used to lie 'driving', that is barely making headway against the wind with the fires well down to conserve coal, while the men from Sunderland could

*W.P.T. **Ruby** (below left) stranded in the Forth August 1885. Built in 1862 she measured 75.3 x 15.7 x 8 feet, 56 tons. PHOTO: Corporation of Glasgow Archives.*
*W.P.T. **Australia**, built 1885, in the colours of the Sunderland Towage Co. (below right).*

Plate 23

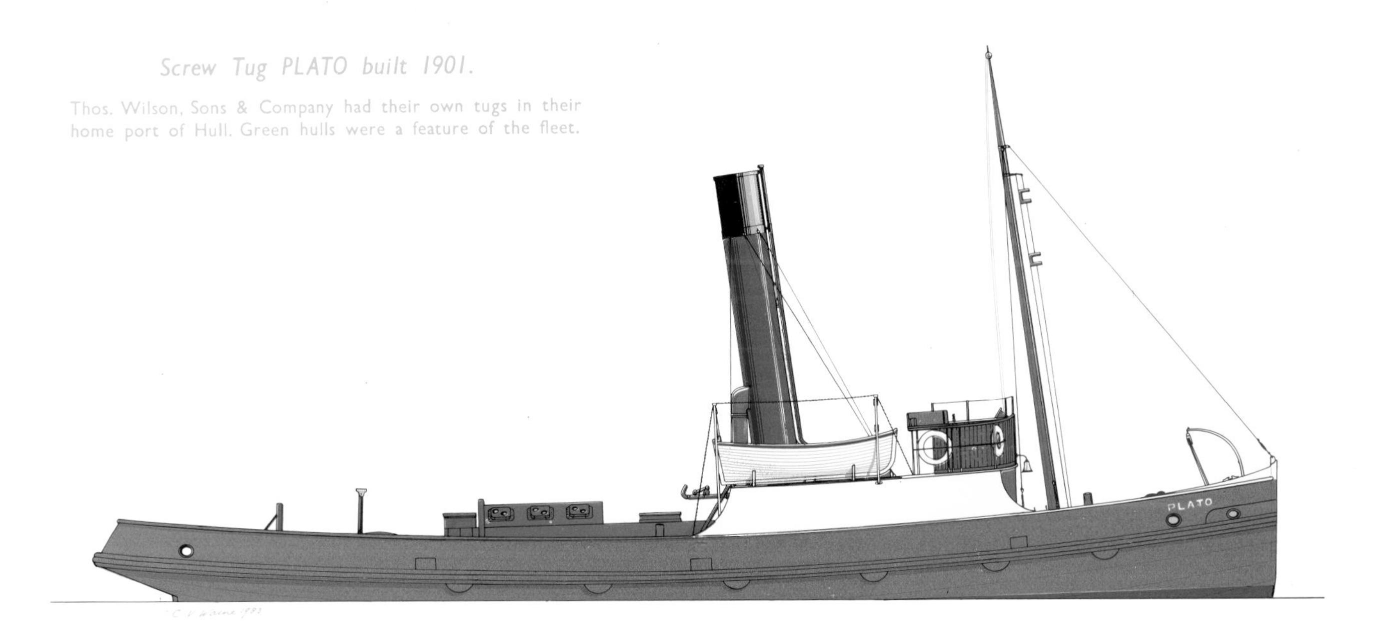

Screw Tug PLATO built 1901.

Thos. Wilson, Sons & Company had their own tugs in their home port of Hull. Green hulls were a feature of the fleet.

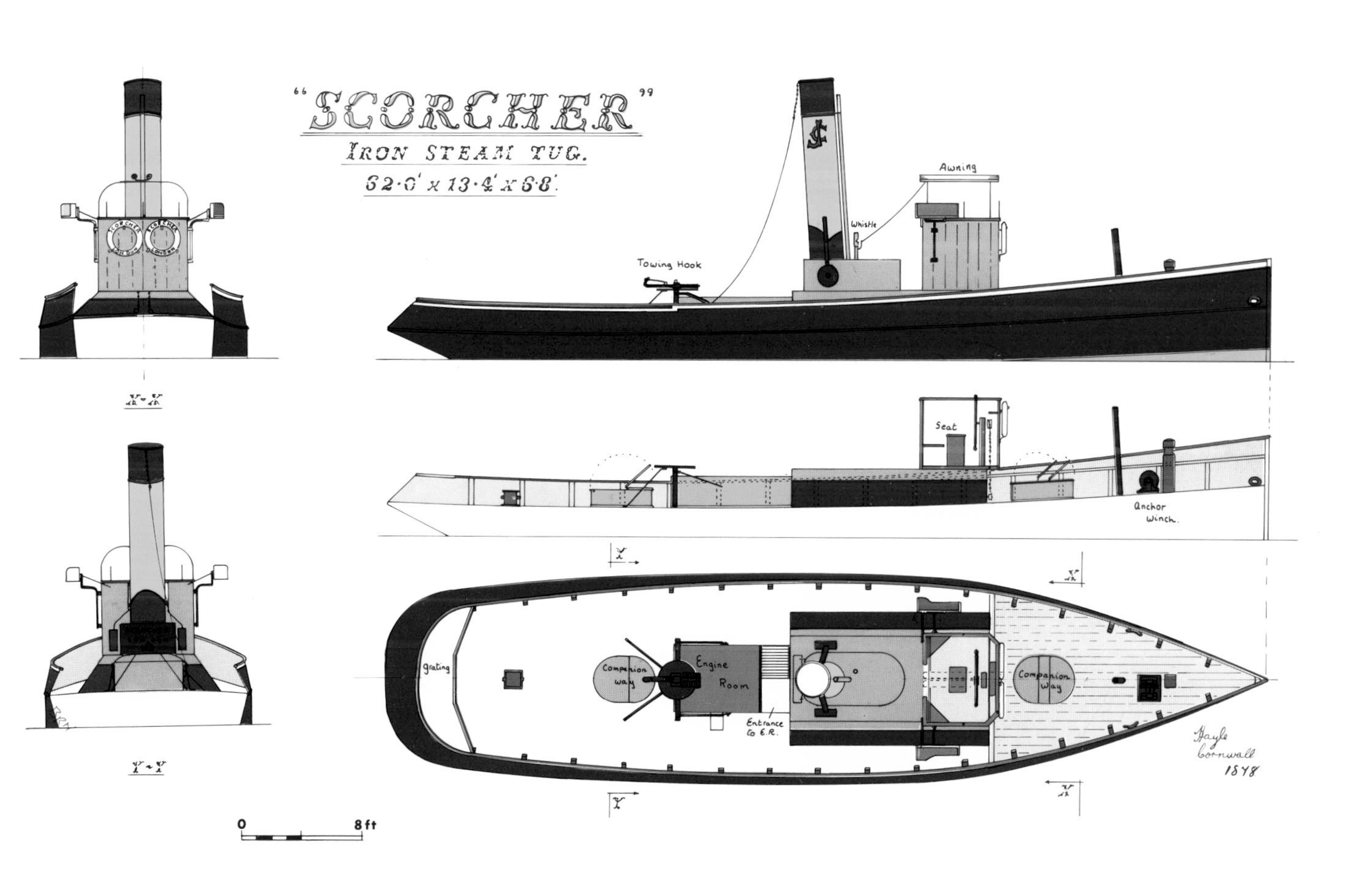

be recognised by the plume of steam from the steampipe as they kept up a full head of steam, ready for instant action should a ship be sighted. Ashore the tugmen were the best of friends but once at sea they would behave like bitter enemies.

On 30th April 1861 the Clyde Shipping Company took delivery of the paddle tug **Flying Dutchman** (106.3 ft. 126 tons. 50 n.h.p.) One source says she was wooden, the owner's records say 'iron frames', Lloyds and the nautical press say she was iron built. If she was composite built, i.e. iron frames and wooden planking, then she was unusual, as this system of construction was not common in tugs. Her new owners did not waste the delivery voyage as she had in tow the ship *Vesta* of London, having brought her round the north of Scotland through the treacherous Pentland Firth taking 88 hours for the trip, an average speed of 7 kts. which seems to have been normal for this size of paddle tug. Her owners did not keep her for very long giving her in part exchange for a new **Flying Dutchman** in 1867, this time definitely an iron paddle tug. This kind of trade-in happened quite often and the builder usually found a ready buyer for the older craft. The new **Flying Dutchman** had already had two names during the year when she was built, but Clyde Shipping seem to have been happy with her as they kept her for 13 years.

Generally the wooden paddle tug did not exceed 100 ft. in length, though amongst the bigger paddle tugs built during the Crimean War was **Scotia** (20), built at Green's yard at Blackwall in 1863, one of the largest of the wooden paddle tugs. She was 131.9 ft. x 21.0 ft. x 8.8 ft. and her gross tonnage was 199. She was sold in the same year to the Admiralty for £17,500 and replaced by another **Scotia** in 1864 which was almost identical. She was built for the Caledonian Steam Tug Co. whose tugs went seeking down the English Channel. She had wheel steering but the wheel was on the deck between the paddle boxes and the helmsman could have had no view astern because of the casing over the engine. The hull was narrow and her lines were fine as if built for speed. She represents an early two funnelled paddle tug with the funnels athwartships. The bow had the slight rake which all wooden paddle tugs seemed to have, but her forefoot was very rounded unlike the small paddlers which had a sharp forefoot as can be clearly seen in the picture of the **Ruby** stranded on rocks (22) in the Forth. The **Scotia** had two boilers with two funnels side by side behind the paddle boxes. In the early days the wooden paddle tugs ranged in size from 50 ft. to 100 ft. but as the years passed it was mainly the larger size that went into service. Also with time the rake of the bow was reduced though this can by no means be taken as a feature by which to date a wooden paddle tug. The majority of them retained the supporting ironwork for the paddle box beams. Most of the wooden tugs survived for a good many years but there was a steady loss amongst them. Sometimes they foundered at sea through stress of the weather, sometimes they just sank at their moorings. On 11th October 1876 the Glasgow papers reported such an incident in typically quaint Victorian terms: "A Greenock tug steamer, namely the **Daisy**, a venerable craft noted for her antiquated build and leisurely dignity of pace, whose figurehead has for years been familiar on the lower reaches of the Clyde, quietly sank at her moorings in Victoria Harbour, Greenock yesterday morning. No one was aboard her at the time and the cause of the subsidence is not exactly known, but it is supposed that the infirmities of her great age and the increasing tenderness of her ancient timbers coupled with the rain of the previous evening proved too much for the **Daisy**."

The **St. Vittorio** was the first tug built by Wm. Simons who at that time (1853) had a yard at Whiteinch in Glasgow. She was somewhat anachronistic, being reminiscent of tugs built ten to fifteen years earlier, with her clipper bow and bowsprit (25) and slender hull with very hollow waterlines. She is shown fully rigged for her delivery voyage and her mizzen mast would be removed before she went into service. Very little deck detail is shown but she was almost certainly tiller steered and would have had a cover over the engine crosshead slide. There is no record of her owner though it may have been a Mr. A. Gabrielli of London who owned a tug of this name built in 1862.

Many of the wooden tugs were lost when they were stranded, unable to battle against wind and seas. Not all were total losses. Take the **Ruby** for instance which is shown well and truly ashore in the Forth (22). She was a typical clinker built wooden paddle tug with the extreme rake of stem and lovely sweep of stern so typical of the breed. She was still tiller steered, had no bridge, just a plank spanning the paddle boxes. The hand anchor windlass looks overlarge, probably because the **Ruby** was a small vessel. She survived this stranding and went back into service, lasting until 1898 when she was sold to Newcastle owners, but sank due to leaks in her hull, while being towed along the coast.

It was not only on the Forth that bridge builders found work for the old paddle tugs like the **Ruby** (22). In 1889 while the London Bridge was being built the contractors Messrs. Wm. Arrol hired an ancient wooden paddle tug, the **John Bull** (1849. 96.0 ft. 114 tons, 60 n.h.p.) to work between Shadwell and the new bridge at a fee of £5 per day. The construction of the second railway bridge over the River Tay required the services of a considerable number of tugs including several wooden paddle tugs. Each section of the bridge was built on a special quay and as each was completed two pontoons were pushed into slots cut into the quay and the hydraulic jacks on the pontoons raised the section clear of the ground. The tugs then towed the pontoons out to the bridge and held them in position while the jacks raised the ironwork into its final resting place.

There was, however, another side to the coin. Despite the small size of the wooden paddle tugs in general, built as they were for work in sheltered waters, money was money and the owners

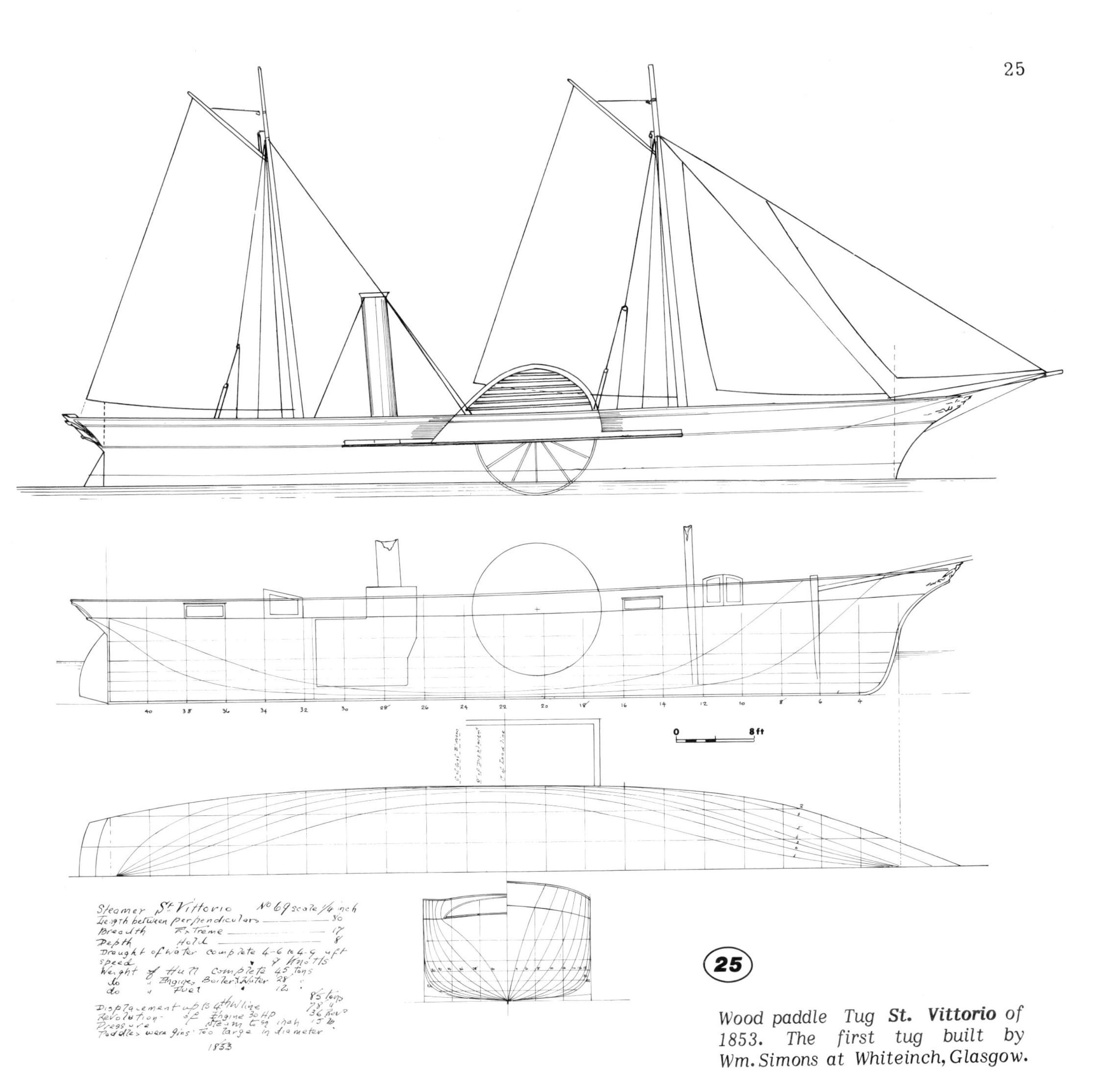

Wood paddle Tug **St. Vittorio** *of 1853. The first tug built by Wm. Simons at Whiteinch, Glasgow.*

and captains were prepared to fight for it, ready to fight the sea as well as each other. They were to be found cruising up and down the coast off their home ports ready to offer their services to the inbound sailing ships in fair weather and in foul. On 25th October 1851 the **Britannia** of Middlesbrough was out looking for a tow when a gale suddenly got up and the tug was wrecked half a mile north of Coatham, Redcar. The **Britannia** had been built in 1831 and was only 62.2 ft. long x 11.6 ft. beam. Her draught was a mere 4 ft. and her tonnage 39 tons: hardly a seagoing tug! If a ship got into trouble and a tug was able to help, the reward could be high compared with the remuneration from a simple tow. The **Vigilant** and the **Heather Bell**, both of Sunderland, at great risk to themselves, went to the assistance of the *Lord Collingwood* which had been driven ashore in gale force winds on 29th October 1867. The grounding occurred on a lee shore but the tugs went in, succeeded in passing towlines, took her off and towed her to the Tyne. Each tug was awarded £100 and an additional £5 was granted to the **Vigilant** for the loss of her tow rope. Both the tugs were quite new vessels, the **Vigilant**, 1860, was 90.6 ft. long and 40 n.h.p., the **Heather Bell**, built 1862 was 79.1 ft. long and 30 n.h.p. (photograph, page 17).

On the North-East Coast where literally hundreds of paddle tugs worked, life was hard and the returns were small. By 1868 there were 236 tugs and ferries on the Tyne of which only 12 were iron built. One such tug was the **Prince of Wales** built in 1861 at the time when the forward rake of the bow of the wooden paddle tug was still marked. The plank between the paddle boxes was well clear of the small cover over the engine, and she had no sidehouses on the sponsons, not uncommon with those smaller tugs. She had a steering wheel forward of the engine housing, but retained the tiller aft, again not an uncommon feature. The tiller was used when the tow was to be manoeuvred with the helmsman pushing the rope across the well greased towrail to ensure accurate placing of the tow, often a timber raft. For a long run down the river the steering was done from the wheel amidships (26).

The change over from the wheel to the tiller sometimes led to confusion.With a tiller a 'helm order' was given, e.g. port your helm meant push the tiller to port which turned the tug to starboard. On one tug the skipper was from the Tyne and used to giving 'helm orders'. One day when another vessel was crossing his path he gave the order "port your helm", forgetting that the tug was equipped for wheel steering. The man at the wheel put the wheel hard over to port and only the skipper's quick reaction prevented a collision.

On the Wear, at Sunderland 48 tugs were registered by 1860, but among them only one tug was of iron. On the Tees between Stockton and Middlesbrough there were 22 tugs including 2 iron boats. The skippers snatched at any chance to get an extra pound or two. In February 1865 the **Victoria** of Sunderland went to the assistance of a brig, the *Tartar*, which appeared to be in difficulties due to the heavy seas. The rate for towage was £1.10.0 but the **Victoria**'s skipper managed to squeeze an extra £1 out of the tow to compensate for the hard job they had in making port, and he went to court to get it! Constant mention is made of the low power of the majority of the wooden paddle tugs on the North East coast and an example can be quoted, again involving tugs from Sunderland. In March 1866 the tug **Seaflower**, unable to control the barque *Hubert* which she was towing, was forced to slip the tow rope and the barque went ashore. The tugs **Belmont, Waterlily, Diamond** and **Gently** tried to tow her off but without success, and the attempt was abandoned until the following day when the **Diamond, Waterlily, Gently, Ryhope** and **Marco Polo** were more successful. The tug owners claimed salvage and demanded £445, but had to be content with the £110 awarded by the court. The award was split up as follows: **Belmont** £15, **Diamond** £25, **Gently** £20, **Ryhope** £20, **Marco Polo** £10 and the **Waterlily** £20. These sums of money may not sound much but they were equivalent to a fair number of tows. The details of the tug were: **Belmont** (1841) 72.4 ft. 48 ton, **Diamond** (1859) 70.3 ft. 43 ton. 24 n.h.p., **Gently** (1846) 70.0 ft. 58 tons, **Marco Polo** (1858) 77.6 ft. 58 ton. 28 n.h.p., **Waterlily** (1857) 80.3 ft. 65 ton. 20 n.h.p., **Seaflower** (1860) 74.0 ft. 55 ton. 25 n.h.p., **Ryhope** (1860) 85.4 ft. 81 ton. 40 n.h.p. At any time there was little more than about 120 n.h.p. available, about 600 h.p., equal to that provided by a medium sized screw tug 30 years later!

Because all these examples are drawn from the North East coast it does not indicate that the tugmen there were unscrupulous and those in the rest of the country were angels; certainly not! Similar situations will be commented on in the chapter on owners, which will show that the same type of incident occurred elsewhere. It is only that with smaller numbers of tugs involved, the battles, losses, etc. were fewer in number. The events have been chosen to illustrate the wide variety of happenings in the life of the tugmaster in those early days.

The men who manned these tugs had to be a tough bunch and the reports from the law courts give a vivid picture of the rougher side of their lives. While one of the Tyne hoppers was proceeding to sea on 24th February 1867, the tug **Vigilant** (1860 77.0 ft. 56 tons. 25 n.h.p.) came inwards round the South Pier and set a course which was bound to result in a collision. The hopper altered course to the south but the tug kept the helm down resulting in the hopper striking the tug just forward of the paddleboxes. All but the captain of the tug leapt aboard the hopper, but the captain put the tug's engines astern and on pulling free the tug sank. It transpired that the crew of the tug had bought spirits from a foreign vessel which they had towed from the Tyne to the Wear and had then all become drunk apart from the cabin boy. At the time of the collision the fireman was sitting on the fiddley grating, the engineer was lying on top of the engine housing, and the master

26

*Wood Paddle Tug **Prince of Wales**. Her dimensions were 75.3 x 15.3 x 8.1, 50 tons gross. She was built at Low Walker on the Tyne for C. Carr, Newcastle and was eventually broken up in 1915. Beyond the **Prince of Wales** is the **Pride of Scotland** built at North Shields for W. McKinnon, Peterhead. Her dimensions were 76.4 x 16.0 x 7.5 feet, 57 tons gross. PHOTO: G.E. Langmuir.*

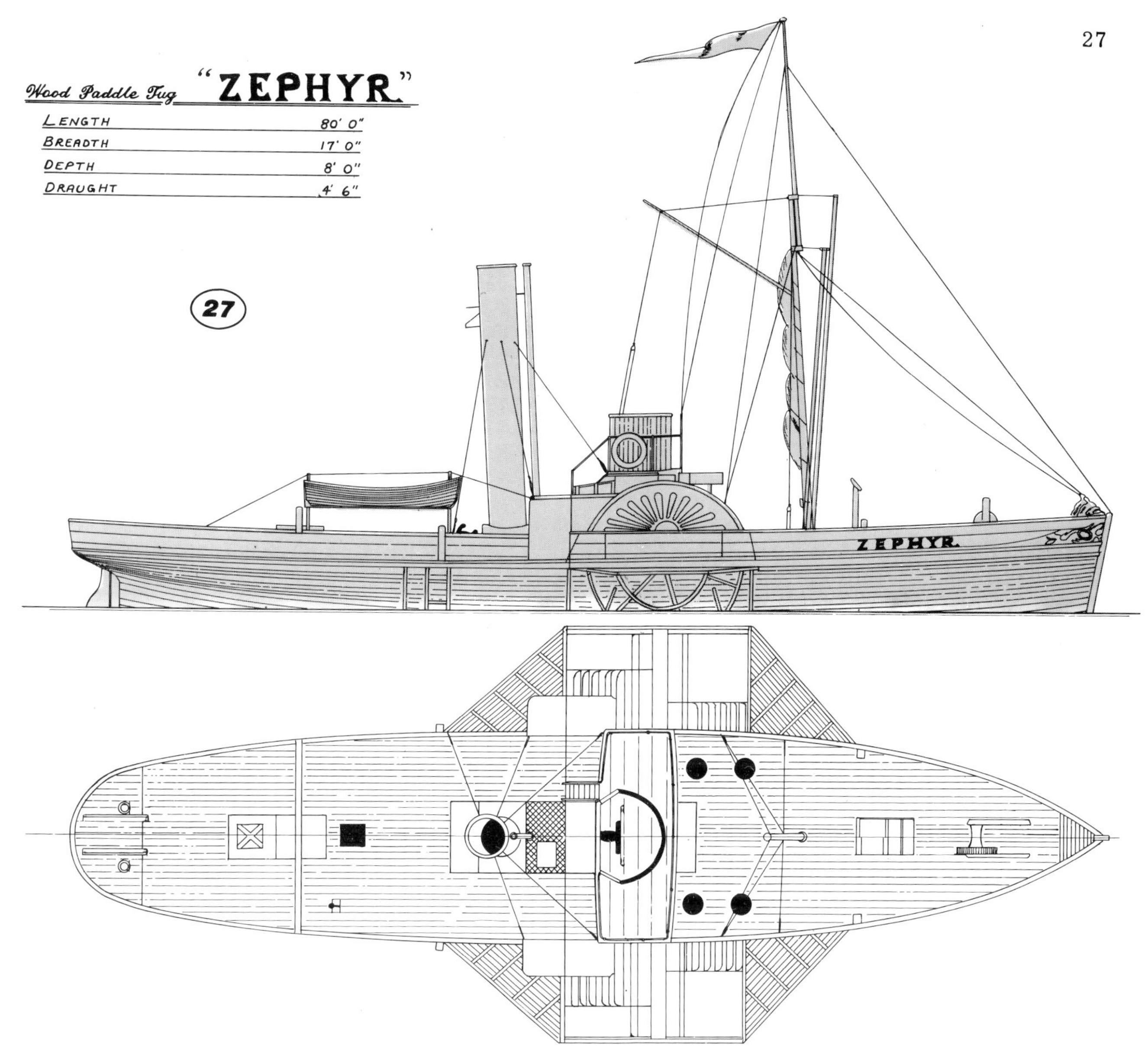

was steering from a position behind the funnel with ropes led aft to the tiller. This idea of steering the tug from a warmer and less exposed position behind the funnel was not uncommon, and it was only a matter of time before a wheel was fitted amidships between the paddle boxes and the tiller steering was abandoned. However tiller steering was retained on the Tyne on tugs which towed keels as their everyday task.

The rules for 'seeking' for a tow were faily clearly defined. On the North East coast it was the custom that when one steam tug was ahead of another by 100 yards in making for a vessel the last had to give in, but the difficulty seemed to be as to who was the best judge of the distance between the two rival boats. A case came before the South Shields magistrates in 1866 in which George Whale, captain of the steam tug **Scottish Maid** (1851. 63.0 ft. 37 tons. 20 n.h.p.) was charged with assaulting Thomas Atkin master of the steam tug **Adur** (1855. 79.4 ft. 64 tons. 35 n.h.p.) In the course of the enquiry it transpired that a most dangerous practice was indulged in by the commanders of the steam tugs while out at sea looking for ships making for the harbour, by exciting competitions of who should get to the vessel first. In this case the **Adur**, steam tug, was knocking about off Tynemouth Castle in search of ships and happened to descry a brig bearing for the Tyne, so made for her. The **Scottish Maid** which was also on the lookout, made for the vessel at the same time. The **Adur** was ahead, but the **Scottish Maid** being the swifter boat came up to her. Both steamers, however, got alongside pretty much at the same time. During the time they were running towards the vessel the captain of each steamer got to high words. One threatened to run the other down, and in the dispute the **Scottish Maid** ran across the bows of the **Adur.** The captain of the **Scottish Maid** (Whale) then threw a bottle at Atkin which luckily missed him. Next he threw a number of iron nuts, which were produced in court and certainly would have inflicted serious injuries had they struck anyone, being nearly 2" across.

The **Zephyr** is the second of the two drawings which appeared in the article in the Smith's Dock Journal (27) and represents the later form of the wooden paddle tug. The rake of the stem has been reduced and a small bridge deck spans the paddle boxes. The dimensions are given as 80'0" x 17'0" x 8'0" and the nearest vessel which can be found in the directories is that built in 1876 for Newcastle owners, 69 tons gross and 30 n.h.p. She was wrecked in 1891. According to the author the **Zephyr** was built with 24 planks on each side instead of the traditional 22 planks.

Shipowners used the tugs but regarded them as a necessary evil and never ceased to complain about irregularities and excessive charges. In 1864 the pilots were accused of being in the pockets of the tug men, accepting bribes to ensure that one owner's tugs were used in preference to another's, or insisting on 'taking steam' when it was not really necessary. In some areas local harbour regulations forebade any pilot to have any interest in a tug in an effort to ensure that such accusations might be unjustified. At a special meeting of the Sunderland Pilotage held to investigate the groundings of the *Grootmeister National* on 8th October 1867 the Chairman stated that there had been too many incidents like the following in recent years and that the pilots of the port were getting a bad name abroad. The captain of the *Grootmeister National* described how, when off Hartlepool, the steam tug **Bulldog** (1858. 78.9 ft. 61 ton) was engaged to tow the vessel to Sunderland for the sum of £9. Off Seaham the tug **Telegraph** (1857. 79.5 ft. 62 ton. 30 n.h.p.) came alongside and offered to assist as there was a strong tide running. He refused, but the **Bulldog** engaged the **Telegraph** to assist her. Near Seaham the pilot requested the tugs to keep the ship further offshore or she would go aground, but the tugs did not appear to hear. Shortly afterwards the ship went on the Blue House canch, suffering £800 worth of damage. The **Telegraph** immediately cast off and ranged alongside asking £40 to tow the ship off, but on being refused, the offer was reduced to £20. This was again refused and as the tide was making the **Bulldog** was able to pull the ship off. Although the pilot admitted that he had been negligent in allowing the tugs to take the ship so far inshore, he said that the two tugs belonged to Shields and had behaved very badly. He added that the Tyne tugboat men were addicted to this sort of thing and were bad men when towing. The committee stated that the pilot could easily have prevented the whole thing by simply casting off the tow rope.

Life on the small tugs in Victorian times was anything but monotonous especially in the large ports which lay on or up rivers - ports such as Newcastle, London, Liverpool and Glasgow which all had considerable fleets of tugs, passenger steamers and ferries as well as a huge seaborne trade. It is small wonder that the Victorian newspapers which revelled in disaster were able to make constant reference to accidents involving tugs. After the weary time patrolling the shipping lanes and finding a tow, the tug had to take her into the river, weaving in and out of the stream of ships making their way up and down and across the river between various calling points. It was inevitable that every now and again a tugmaster would be unlucky and make a mistake or be the victim of someone else's error. The resulting collision could land him in court at best, or at the bottom of the river at worst. An incident which must have been typical occurred in November 1860 when the paddle tug **Cruiser** (no details known) was coming down the Tyne with the brig *Miner* in tow and a large number of vessels were passing through the harbour from the dock. A vessel called the *Clemintina* ran aground and in the confusion the *Miner* fouled the **Cruiser**, cutting her nearly to the waterline. She was a new tug owned by Mr. Chisholm of North Shields and she had made her trial trip only a few days previously.

The casualty rate among the wooden paddle tugs was quite high as shown in the following table which lists total losses. In fact collisions with 'damage only' occurred about five times as frequently. Under the heading 'sank' are losses due to damage received in serious collisions and losses where the tug foundered either at sea or in harbour.Under 'wreck' the loss is simply due to stranding but the official reports seldom give the reason. Occasionally there is a clue usually indicating that the weather was the cause - "**Iron Duke** (1873, wood, 32 tons reg.) registered Greenock. Owned William Park & Co., Greenock. Builders J.T.Eltringham, South Shields. Sailed from Greenock for cruising (i.e. seeking) 11th December 1883, stranded $\frac{1}{4}$ mile north of Dunure, Ayrshire. Wind Force 10 NW." On the Beaufort Scale this is classed as a storm with very high waves with foam blowing off the crests, the tumbling of the sea becomes heavy and shocklike! It is hardly surprising that the **Iron Duke** succumbed in these conditions. The heading 'machinery' covers losses caused by boiler explosions which were all too common, and cases where part of the engine broke loose causing damage to the hull resulting in the foundering of the vessel. "**Conquest** 1866, reg. North Shields, wooden paddle tug. 8 tons reg. 4 crew. Owner T. Johnston. North Shields. Left North Shields seeking. Bottom of hotwell fell out, vessel sank 10 miles ENE of Tyne - 30th May 1900." Less than two months earlier the same thing happened to another Shields tug the **Knight Templar** of 1875.

Losses of wooden paddle tugs due to various causes (and as a percentage of those in service)

	Sank	Wreck	Machinery	Total losses	Total number of wooden paddle tugs in service
1880 - 1889	41 (8%)	13 (3%)	9 (2%)	63 (13%)	494 (1885)
1890 - 1899	25 (12%)	8 (4%)	9 (4%)	42 (20%)	215 (1895)
1900 - 1909	15 (14%)	3 (3%)	6 (6%)	24 (23%)	105 (1905)

As would be expected the losses increase as the age of the wooden tug fleet increased. The losses reported in the marine press were not always as total as the report claimed. "**Rescue** built 1869. Reg. Sunderland. Wood paddle tug. 8 tons reg. 4 crew. Owner R.L. Cook, Sunderland. Left Sunderland seeking, lost in collision off Sunderland with *S.S.Trevithick* of Newcastle 2nd September 1897." It could not have been a ghost which took part in a rather simple salvage case in 1931 when the same tug towed the *Olavus* to a safe position after a collision, collecting a £450 award.

The **Robert Airey** (1858. 80.7 ft. 64 tons. 30 n.h.p.), a wooden paddle tug had a fairly short

(29)

W.P.T. ***Moselle.*** *Built at Low Walker (Tyne). In the colours of G.Robson, Newcastle. Dimensions were 88.7' x 18.1' x 9.8'. PHOTO: South Tyneside Central Library.*

and troubled life. In February 1865 she ran out of coal off the Durham coast and was towed into the Tyne half full of water by another tug. In October of the same year she left the Tyne with a lighter in tow and was never heard of again. Although many wooden paddle tugs were lost off the North East coast someone usually survived to report the cause of the loss. The tugmen in London had another hazard to contend with; the Smoke Nuisance Abatement Act of 1851 under which they were continually being prosecuted. In 1860 one of the offenders was Watkin's old tug **Monarch,** now 28 years old. Even with her third new boiler she still made too much smoke to meet the requirements of the Act.

There is a shortage of plans of wooden tugs and so we must rely on photos (29) for our information. The **Moselle** (1861, 88.7 ft. 92 tons, 40 n.h.p.) is taken from an unusual angle and gives us some idea of the deck layout of a wooden paddle tug. In the bow she had a hand windlass for the anchor, and aft of that the companionway to the crews quarters. The mast was stepped in a tabernacle for lowering and the counterweights for the lowering funnel can just be seen. This enabled her to work higher up the river beyond the bridges. A very narrow bridge deck spanned between the paddleboxes and on it were the wheel and a waist high shelter. Below it was the structure which covered the crosshead slides of the side lever engine, built up high enough at the sides to support the bridge deck, open at the front to give a view forward and open at the back for the engineer. Her name was carved on the inside of the stern as was customary with the paddle tugs. She had small cowl vents to the engine room, a feature which was seldom seen on this type of vessel. The **Sir George Elliot** was built in 1875, 92.7 ft. 98 tons, 38 n.h.p. and she shows that little had changed in the 14 years since the **Moselle** had been launched. The inside of her bulwarks was elegantly panelled between the stanchions while outside the hull a number of vertical straps had been fitted which help to protect the hull and, it has been suggested, to help keep the hull watertight by holding the planks together in the vicinity of the boiler. On the **Moselle** the cock boat was stowed on the deck aft, but on the **Sir Geo. Elliot** it was precariously balanced on a strut and on a chock on the side house, with only a single davit for handling it.

The latter day wooden tugs were well built vessels quite capable of carrying out coastal tows. The **England** (1876. 100.6 ft. 115 tons. 60 n.h.p. 350 e.h.p.) belonging to South Shields secured a contract for the towing, on a regular basis, of a 168 tons gross barge loaded with pig iron from Middlesbrough to Grangemouth and back empty for the sum of £36 per trip. This tug is an excellent example of the 64ths. division of ownership referred to earlier as she belonged to no less than fifteen partners: T. Henderson -1, L. Wright -1, W. Ramsay - 1, W.T. Grahamsley - 1, W. Wright - 12,

(29)

W.P.T. ***Sir Geo. Elliott*** *was built in South Shields and owned most of her career by Andrew Bain of North Shields, passing to Geo. Robinson of Middlesborough around 1900. She was run down by a steamer at her moorings on the 15th of January 1905.*

L. Wright - 4, H. Nelson - 8, C. Dyble - 4, T.F. Tully - 2, G.E.Henderson - 18, W. Harrison - 2, T. Emmerson - 4, R.S. Donkin - 4, Geo. Fenwick - 1, C.F. Jackson - 1. On one of these voyages in 1901 she had some trouble when the towrope parted in rough weather and she had a bit of difficulty in reconnecting the tow. She was awarded £200 in salvage fees. Her owners were lucky for, as has been said elsewhere, the courts usually regarded it as the duty of a tug to complete an agreed contract without any extra payment for an occurrence such as this. A few months later her owners were less fortunate as the **England** was badly damaged by a fire which broke out on board.She was declared a total loss with a value of £1,500, but when her owners went to the insurance company they refused payment as their assessor claimed that repairs could be carried out at less than 80% of the £1,500, under which circumstances no 'total loss' was allowed. At this point she disappears from the register so apparently she was not repaired.

During the ten years which followed the launch of the **Sir Geo. Elliot** the number of wooden paddle tugs built each year dropped, but with a final flourish in 1885 the last 9 but one of the wooden paddle tugs were built, all on the Tyne and all but two for North East Coast owners. The tugs are listed below, giving their first owner but indicating the areas to which they went later:

Australia 90.5' x 18.4' x 9.7'. 97 tons. Built Rennoldson. 36 n.h.p. for Sunderland Towage Co. (Later went to Tyne)

General Gordon 92.0' x 18.4' x 9.8'. 97 tons. built Rennoldson. 40 n.h.p. for Irwing Steam Tug Co., Sunderland. (Later to Blyth)

General Gordon 90.0' x 18.0' x 9.5'. 88 tons. built Rennoldson. 32 n.h.p. for James C. Bridges, Leith.

Gleaner 89.1' x 18.1' x 9.6'. 87 tons. built South Shields. 54 n.h.p. for George Nicholson, Great Yarmouth. (Later to North Shields)

Norman Prince 89.8' x 18.6' x 9.5'. 91 tons. built South Shields for William H. Storey, North Shields. (Later renamed **Hetton**)

Pera 99.0' x 18.6' x 9.9'. 107 tons. built Wouldhave & Johnston, North Shields. 42 n.h.p. for J. Smart, North Shields.

St. Giles 89.6' x 18.5' x 9.6'. 90 tons. built South Shields. 35 n.h.p. for Ralph Pigg, North Shields

Stag 100.0' x 19.5' x 10.5'. 123 tons. built J.R. Maxwell, South Shields. 45 n.h.p. for Anderson, North Shields. (Later to Sunderland) 450 e.h.p.

William Dodds 89.0' x 18.6' x 9.5'. 87 tons. built South Shields. 34 n.h.p. for William Dodds, North Shields

Four years later a single wooden paddle tug was launched, the last of her kind:

Tyne Dock No.4 76.3' x 19.0' x 9.6'. 98 tons. built J.T. Eltringham. 50 n.h.p. built 1889 for North Eastern Railway Co., Grimsby. 1911 to Axel H. Anderson, North Shields, renamed **Enable.**

The **Australia** (22) was one of the last wooden paddle tugs to be built. When compared with the **Rapid** built 17 years earlier, it is evident that little change had been made to their design. The **Australia** had sidehouses and the iron stays are not fitted. With the engine house full depth between the deck and the bridge there was no need for stiffeners. She has a nice bit of scrollwork on her bow. The typical construction of the bulwarks can just be made out; three planks high with the centre plank thicker and rounded on the outer face.

One of the ports which held on to its wooden paddle tugs was Great Yarmouth, and these tugs keep cropping up again and again in salvage actions along the coast nearby where plenty of opportunities presented themselves, earning handsome awards for their owners. Most of the cases were fairly straightforward but in 1905, when the steamer *Newburn* ran aground at full speed on the Haisborough Sands matters became a little more complex. The crew of the steamer began to jettison some cargo and when the wooden paddle tugs **Cruiser** (1880. 88.2 ft. 84 tons, 340 e.h.p.) and **Yare** (1883. 97.1 ft. 104 tons. 250 i.h.p.) arrived on the scene, their ropes were made fast and they commenced towing, but to no avail. They were joined by the wooden paddler **Meteor** (1875. 94.0 ft., 98 tons. 250 i.h.p.) but the *Newburn* stuck fast. Next day the iron paddle tug **King Edward VII** (1901. 100.0 ft. 138 tons. 280 e.h.p.) and the wooden paddle tug **Gleaner** (1885. 89.1 ft. 87 tons. 54 n.h.p.) were ordered to assist while more cargo was thrown overboard. Eventually two London screw tugs **Champion** (1892. 89.1 ft. 116 tons. 500 i.h.p.) and **Victor** (1895.96.2ft.133tons.650a.h.p.) came on the scene and lent a hand, and the *Newburn* slid off the sandbank. Again we can see how ineffective these low powered paddle tugs could be. The captain of the *Newburn* was concerned about the damage to his vessel's hull and requested that the **Cruiser** and the **King Edward VII** accompany him to the Tyne where he could have repairs carried out. This was somewhat unusual but the tugs had to oblige. Before they could do so, however, they had to borrow coal from the *Newburn* as they were running low on bunkers. To save money the *Newburn* refused to take a tow but proceeded under her own steam at a very slow pace, and off the Humber the tugs had to persuade the captain to go into Hull while they replenished their coal supply, a request to which he agreed most unwillingly. Eventually the little convoy reached the Tyne much to the tug captains' relief. The effort was worth all the trouble as the awards were generous - **Cruiser** £700, **King Edward VII** £500, **Gleaner** £300, **Meteor** £300, **Yare** £450. The London tugs **Champion** and **Victor** shared £1,000 between them.

The **United Service** (Plate 6) was a well known wooden paddle tug in the port of Great Yarmouth where she spent all her working life. Built in 1872 she was fairly large being 98.6 ft. long and fairly powerful having a single cylinder side lever engine of 44 n.h.p. (300 e.h.p.). She was familiar to the holiday makers as she carried them on pleasure cruises and well known to the shipping fraternity many of whose ships she helped to salvage. She was a goldmine to her owners who had a steady income both summer and winter; she shared awards for salvage ranging from £200 up to £5,000.

3.

(31) *Iron Paddle Tug **Iona***

Iron & Steel Paddle Tugs

As mentioned in Chapter I the **Defiance** was probably the first iron paddle tug to go into service. There is a reference in one source that in 1839 two iron tugs were operating on the Thames, the **Enterprise** of 92 tons and 40 n.h.p. and the **Alice** of 170 tons and 60 n.h.p., but the official records of the period do not mention either of these vessels. By the start of the Crimean War in 1854 only about 25 iron paddle tugs had been built. They were accepted very slowly, being introduced in various ports around the country in ones and twos. From the official records the following was the pattern for the introduction of the iron paddle tug:

Lowestoft:	**Lowestoft** (1846 Blackwall) 93.0 ft. x 16.4 ft. 103 tons. 60 n.h.p. Lowestoft Railway and Harbour Co.
Liverpool:	**Prince of Wales** (1849) 99.0 ft. x 13.8 ft. 84 tons.J.H. Humphrey.
Swansea:	**Tartar** (1850 Shields) 86.0 ft. x 16.7 ft. 110 tons. 50 n.h.p. W. Jenkins.
South Shields:	**Lioness** (1851 South Shields) 94.1 ft. x 17.6 ft. 87 tons. 60 n.h.p. T. Jolliffe.
London:	**Friend to all Nations** (1851 Newcastle) 107.6 ft. x 20.0 ft. 152 tons. 64 n.h.p. 240 i.h.p. Thomas Petley.
Leith:	**Lioness** (above) H.F. Caldwell and in service from 1853.
Cork:	**Powerful** (1854 Cork) 108.2 ft. x 18.1 ft. 146 tons. 70 n.h.p. Abraham Sutton.
Newcastle:	**Dragon** (1855) 85.6 ft. x 16.6 ft. 93 n.h.p. H.W. Powell.
Cardiff:	**Iron Duke** (1857 Glasgow) 108.3 ft. x 19.2 ft. 140 tons. 38 n.h.p. Cardiff Steam Towing Co.
Sunderland:	**Harry Vane** (1857 Northumberland) 73.2 ft. x 16.2 ft. 77 tons. 40 n.h.p. Dowager Marchioness of Londonderry.
Belfast:	**Wonder** (1857 South Shields) 112.6 ft. x 18.9 ft. 127 tons. 60 n.h.p. Robert Alexander
Hull:	**James Watt** (1858 Hull) 80.4 ft. x 17.2 ft. 90 tons. 40 n.h.p. Stephen Gray.
Falmouth:	**Pendennis** (1863 London) 79.4 ft. x 16.9 ft. 73 tons. 40 n.h.p. R. Taylor
Glasgow:	**Wizard** (1848) 76.0 ft. x 17.7 ft. 80 tons. 40 n.h.p. Clyde Shipping Company.
Dundee:	**Atlas** (1865 Dundee) 85.5 ft. x 18.6 ft. 102 tons. 50 n.h.p. Dundee, Perth and London Shipping Co.

The dates given above are both the date of build and the date on which the tugs took up station in the port unless otherwise indicated.

There was nothing standard about the appearance of the iron paddle tugs. The **Clyde** was a rather unlovely vessel built for the Clyde Navigation Trustees for towing barges of spoil down the river (32) to the dumping grounds in the Firth of Clyde and to assist the dredging plant whenever necessary. The two side-lever engines from this old tug can still be seen on the river bank at Renfrew where they stand as a memorial to her builders. Although she was iron hulled, she had wooden bulwarks, a feature which was common on iron paddle and screw tugs for many years to come.Tugs were frequently involved in collisions and timber bulwarks were easily repaired by a carpenter, whereas for a repair to iron bulwarks the tug would have had to be taken out of service. The **Clyde** lasted until 1912 when she was replaced by a screw tug of the same name. The **Wonder** of 1857 also had a pair of side-lever engines but she had two funnels side by side (4) unlike the **Clyde** which had but one. The outstanding feature of the **Wonder** is the beautiful clipper bow complete with figurehead. Despite her size she had no bridge deck and so must have had her wheel on the deck between the paddle boxes. Note how the galley funnel was led into one of the main funnels.

In the Glasgow City Archives is a bundle of drawings marked "Tug for the Clyde Navigation Trust 1851". There are several lines plans but no general arrangement and no indication of which set of lines was used for the building of the tug **Clyde.** The best of the selection is reproduced here (32) though it is not fully detailed. However, the drawing does give a comparison between the early iron paddle tug and its wooden contemporary (**St. Vittorio**). The impression is one of clumsiness and bluffness at the bow and stern. It should be borne in mind though, that she was built for towing dredgers, hoppers and lighters loaded with stone, a task where speed and manoeuvrability was of no account. Three years after she was launched the **Clyde** was lengthened forward by about 15 ft. being given a finer entry and a sharper bow.

The **Vanguard** (1868. 114.6 ft. 139 tons. 50 n.h.p.) was the first iron paddle tug to go into service in the fleet of J. Steel of Glasgow, later Steel and Bennie. The **Vanguard** was built by Robertson of Greenock, a yard more accustomed to producing Clyde steamers which accounts for the long sweep up of the keel at the bow. The timberheads on the fore deck were doubled and had a 'cavil' for securing ropes. The sidehouses had an unusual shape of sloping aft and rounded at the after end. The lines were fine as she was intended to be a fast boat, there was a fair rise of floor and the bilges were quite rounded. The drawing was prepared from the original builders' half model with additions picked out from photographs, but detail is not complete (33). The **Vanguard** served on the Clyde for the same owner from 1868 until she sank in Glasgow on 19th November 1916 when the bottom of her hotwell gave way. She was raised and broken up.

To make them effective the big paddle tugs had to be provided with large bunkers to enable them to operate over longer distances than before. The more enterprising shipowners were prepared to have their sailing ships towed right down the channel if necessary if the wind were contrary. Unfortunately for the tugowners, the shipowners were not all farsighted and many of them fought shy of using tugs and instructed their captains to think likewise. The tugs from London ranged far away from the Thames first to the Downs and then, as their range increased, to the Isle of Wight where the heights above the Blackgang Chine were used as a vantage point where a contact on shore

32

Lines Plan; believed to be that of the iron paddle tug ***Clyde****, courtesy Glasgow City Archives. The* ***Clyde*** *was lengthened forward by about 15 feet three years after she was launched. She was almost not built as A. & J.Inglis were the only yard to tender. The hull was sub-contracted to J. Henderson of Renfrew. After lengthening she measured 103.0 x 20.1 x 8.4 feet.*

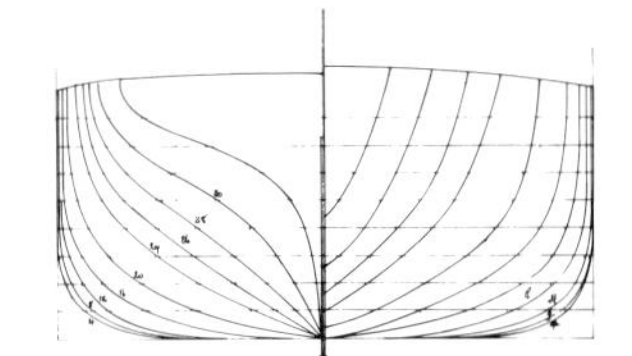

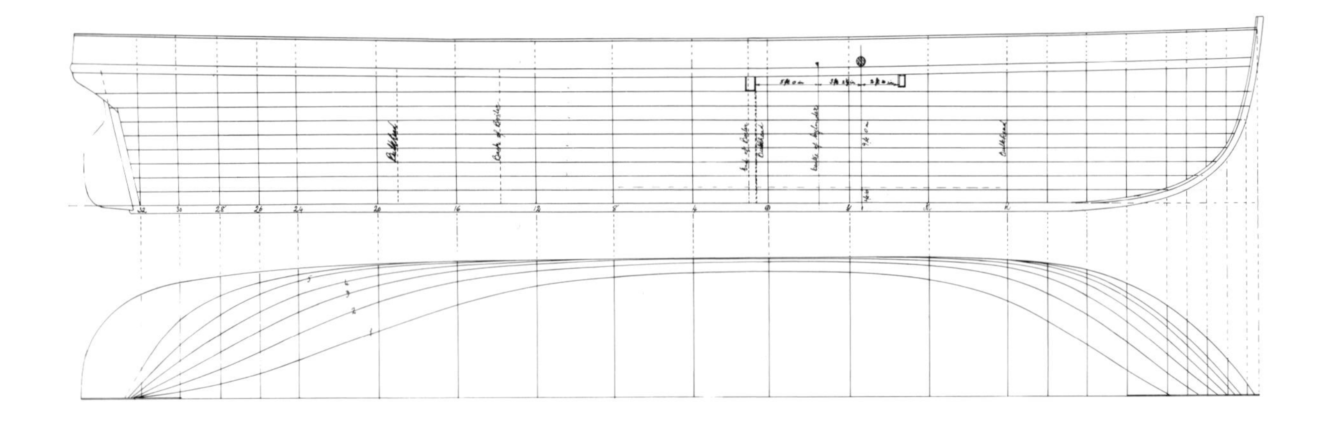

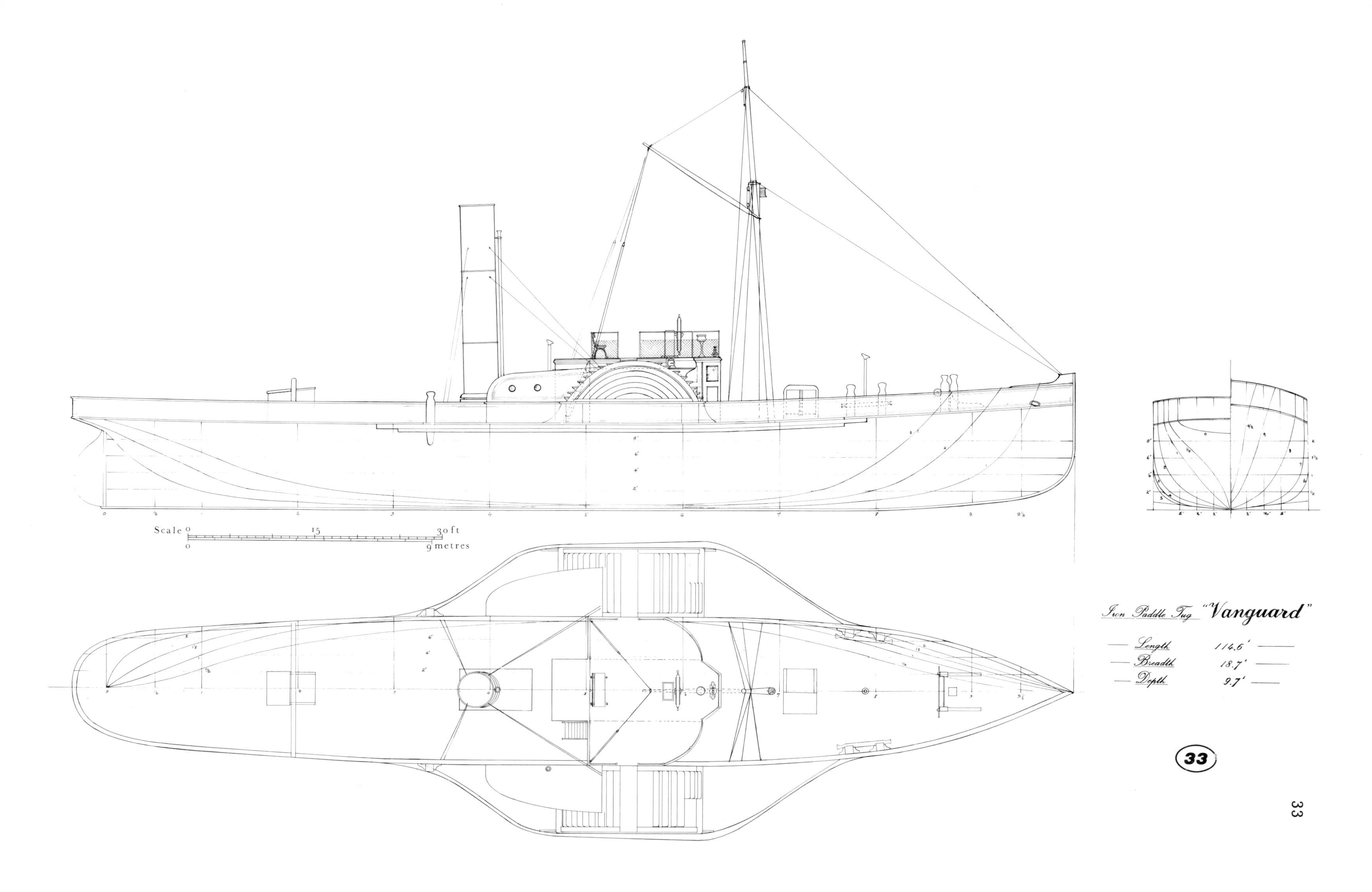

Scale 0 15 30 ft
0 9 metres
Iron Paddle Tug "Vanguard"
Length 114.6'
Breadth 18.7'
Depth 9.7'
33

or even one of the crew would scan the Channel for sight of a sail. The tug crews catered for themselves putting money into a kitty which one of their number was elected to administer. Whenever the food store ran low he was sent ashore to replenish it and needless to relate he picked up at the same time every scrap of information which might lead to finding the much wanted tow. As their operating range increased, the London tugs were to be found down Channel as far as the Lizard. Sometimes seeking produced surprises and things did not always go smoothly. In March 1865 the ship *White Star*, from Port Philip with passengers and cargo for London, when off Newhaven engaged the I.P.T. **Alexandra** (1863. 94.2 ft. 124 tons. 120 n.h.p.) valued at £4,000, to tow her to Gravesend for the sum of £75 if no assistance was taken, and £67.10.0 if another tug were required. After three hours the **Nelson** (1858 W.P.T. 99.0 ft. 99 tons. 90 n.h.p.) valued at £3,000 was engaged to help the **Alexandra** for the sum of £35. Off Hastings the tugs were cast off and the ship anchored. A gale blew up and the ship was forced to slip her cables with the loss of her anchors. She was picked up again by the same tugs and they were joined by the **Enterprise** (1859 I.P.T. 113.1 ft. 147 tons. 120 n.h.p. Value £5,000) as the pilot insisted that the **Enterprise** be engaged as well. The master of the **Enterprise** was the brother of the master of the **Alexandra.** The tugs soon discovered that the ship had no anchors and immediately slapped in a claim for salvage on the grounds that the ship was in danger due to the gale and that without their help she could not have survived. The court decided that when a tug was engaged to carry out a tow, she must complete that tow doing all in her power to keep that tow from danger. It was agreed that services had been rendered beyond that of an ordinary towage and therefore an additional sum was granted amounting to £295. It must have been a severe disappointment to the tugmen who had been reckoning on a salvage award based on the value of the *White Star* which totalled £218,000.

The **Warrior** was a typical 'down channel' paddle tug from London with her two funnels set athwartships (35). The curious sweep of the rubbing strake at the bow can be seen in the plan of the **Great Britain** (76), another big tug with wooden bulwarks. The heavy protection for the paddle-wheels is seen on other drawings. Clearly visible are the doors in the bulwarks which paddle tugs had, to give access to the sponsons.

To appreciate what these seeking tugs were doing it is interesting to consider the distances which they were covering. The following table shows the distance of various landmarks and lighthouses from Gravesend and the time required to carry out a tow assuming a towing speed of 6 kts:

Gravesend to:	Nautical miles	Hours
Beachy Head	116	19
St. Catherines Point	176	29
Eddystone Light	292	48
Bishop Rock	380	63

Life for the men of the big tugs was not all one of excitement, there were other ordinary jobs to be done such as coastal tows as it was quite common for sailing ships to be towed from one port to another with only a skeleton crew aboard, but even the most ordinary job can go awry. During 1864 the owners of the ship *Western Empire* arranged for the Liverpool New Steam Tug Co. to tow their vessel from Blackwall in London to Liverpool. It so happened that their tug **Retriever** (1857, 158.8 ft. 300 tons, 140 n.h.p.) was engaged at Dover in laying telegraph cable and a telegram was despatched giving her captain instructions to proceed to London to tow the *Western Empire* round the coast. Unfortunately the telegram was not delivered and the ship's captain, being unable to obtain a seagoing tug in London hired additional hands to sail the vessel to Deal. There he found tugs a plenty waiting for incoming vessels and he had to pay over the odds to persuade one of them to undertake the tow to Liverpool. The fee for the **Retriever** was to have been £200, instead of which he had to pay out £15 for a tow from Blackwall to Deal, £12 for pilotage, £18 for extra hands and then to cap it all £250 for the coastal tow. The Liverpool New Steam Tug Co. were taken to court and had to pay out £176 for defaulting. Quite a blow!

In these early days there was no distinction between harbour, river or coastal tugs. Regardless of size they were prepared to undertake any kind of tow. All around the coast the local tugs were prepared to go to the assistance of vessels in distress, frequently with the lifeboat in tow. Indeed in Liverpool there was considerable rivalry between the tug companies for the honour of performing this service. The reward was small, about £15, the risks great, but the privilege was jealously guarded and there was trouble if the tug on duty was 'robbed' of her turn. In February 1867 the *Coquimbo* went aground on the Jordan Flats at the entrance to the River Mersey when her tow rope broke and the tug proceeded to Liverpool to call out the lifeboat. The **Rover** (1861. 115.6 ft. 156 tons. 70 n.h.p.) of the New Steam Tug Company, being the first to receive the news, set out at once (although she was not the duty tug for that day) and picked up the New Brighton lifeboat. She towed the lifeboat to the stranded vessel picking up 5 men herself and the lifeboat a further 10. The duty tug, the **Slasher** (1861. 133.3 ft. 196 tons. 90 n.h.p.) of the Old Steam Tug Company arrived too late to be of service. Her owners went to court, claiming that the **Rover** should receive no payment, it not being her turn for lifeboat duty. It may sound rather a harsh attitude, but in fact the **Slasher** was allocated to lifeboat service for that day, not undertaking any other work. The **Rover** still received £15 from the Mersey Dock Board and a further £25 from the owner of the *Coquimbo*. Some years later in September 1875 a somewhat similar event occurred but in rather tragic circumstances. The American ship *Ellen Southard* was in tow for Liverpool but the wind

(35)

Iron Paddle Tug **Warrior**, *built 1871 by Readhead, Softley of South Shields. Her dimensions were 100.8 x 18.1 x 9.1 feet, 112 tons gross, 70 n.h.p. She is seen here on the Tyne where she worked from 1884 until broken up in 1932.*

was rising, the tug was forced to slip the tow and the ship anchored. The wind increased further and, dragging her anchors, the *Ellen Southard* went ashore, once more on the Jordan Flats. In answer to her distress signals both the New Brighton and the Liverpool lifeboats were called out and both were taken in tow by Liverpool tugs. The **Rattler** (1862, 139.2 ft. 244 tons.120 n.h.p.) having the Liverpool lifeboat in tow and being the faster vessel, reached the casualty first. The lifeboat was drifted down to the wreck, taking off 17 people, but as she drew clear a monstrous wave overturned her, throwing all the occupants into the water. Meanwhile the New Brighton lifeboat in tow of the **Spindrift** (1869, 121.0 ft. 175 tons. 70 n.h.p.) arrived on the scene and was successful in rescuing 19 people, 12 lives being lost including the local Pilot and three people from the other lifeboat. The American Government awarded gold medals to the crews of the lifeboats, but no mention is made of an award to the tug crews who must also have taken great risks.

The **Lion** in photograph (35) is just the type of paddle tug which would have been involved in these events on the Mersey. She was at least 40 years old when this picture was taken and she had lost the bowsprit from her shapely clipper bow. The enormous boiler stuck right above the deck with the uptake and steam dome clearly visible. The elegant wooden companionways can be seen on the decks fore and aft.

In the south of England the name of the paddle tug **Aid** crops up regularly (36) in connection with salvage and rescue operations, frequently in co-operation with the lifeboat from Ramsgate where the tug was stationed by the Board of Trade. Built in 1889 by Allsop of Preston (126.1 ft. 194 tons. 950 i.h.p.) she replaced an old wooden paddle tug of the same name which had performed similar duties. The new **Aid** was an unusual looking vessel being double-ended, i.e. she was "sharp" at both ends, and had bow and stern rudders, all of which meant that she was equally manoeuvrable going ahead or astern. So that she could tow astern, she had two sets of towing hooks and towing beams and duplicate sets of navigation lights were fitted so that the correct arrangement of lights could be displayed by covering one set with shutters and raising shutters on the other set. As she had no mast the masthead lights were carried on the funnels. Normally she carried out the duties of the average harbour tug, but when the storms began to blow she prepared for the almost inevitable shipwreck on the notorious Goodwin Sands. Sometimes she worked on her own: "January 1898, casualty *Kommander Svend Foyn*, award £850, (value of tug £8,000, crew 8)". At other times she was assisted by some of the many tugs to be found 'cruising' in the area: "May 1902, casualty *Rion;* salvage by the **Aid**, I.P.T. **Conqueror** (3) (950 e.h.p., value £9,000), I.S.T. **Burma** (1889. 85.8 ft. 94 tons 70 n.h.p., value £4,500), and I.P.T. **Lady Vita** from Dover (1882, 107.7 ft. 174 tons. 75 n.h.p.)". The first three named received awards of £350, £500 and £250 respectively.

The **Aid** certainly earned her keep regularly receiving awards ranging from £400 to £1,000. Her value is given variously between £8,000 and £13,000 and her crew is quoted from 8 to 13 hands. The **Conqueror** mentioned above was another tug which was regularly in the news; being owned by

(35)

Iron Paddle Tug **Lion** *built 1859 at South Shields for W. & T. Jolliffe of Liverpool. She is seen here at Leith circa 1912. Registered length 106.2 feet, 121 tons, 60 n.h.p.*

W. Sandford of Gravesend she was used as an excursion steamer during the summer months, but during the winter she attended one casualty after another, year after year, earning for her owner anything from £350 to £650. In the accounts her power varies from 650 to 1000 e.h.p., another example of the exaggeration which it was hoped would affect the salvage awards. The **Conqueror** was quite a large tug with widely spaced funnels (3). In common with most tugs from the South coast there was no wheelhouse over what was a very large steering wheel. The towing bows have arms at each side which fold down to leave a clear deck for passengers when the **Conqueror** was engaged in excursion work.

We have jumped ahead a bit in time, but a word about salvage, a subject which occupied the mind of every tugmaster and his crew. Performing the actual salvage operation itself was often difficult and fraught with danger, but the legal battle was quite another matter. In the calm and quiet of the courtroom it was not easy for the tug captain to put over to the court the terrible battle which he had fought against the sea and the wind, and it was much easier for the owner of the salvaged vessel to belittle the risks taken by the tug in carrying out the rescue. The verdicts given for apparently similar cases were often conflicting and were discussed at length in the nautical press, but most verdicts where the salvage claim was dismissed were based on the premise that when a tug contracted to tow a vessel she was bound to carry through that tow and that 'unforeseen difficulties and interruptions did not release the tug from the obligation to fulfil her contract.' If a ship met bad weather and, on the towrope breaking under the strain that ship got into difficulties, the tug had to do all in her power to rescue that vessel. Even though in other circumstances that effort might have constituted salvage. In such a case the court might well have thrown out a claim for salvage money. On the other hand the rule did work to one tug's advantage. In 1900 the Troon tug **Titchfield** was towing a small sailing vessel which sank while in tow forcing the tug to cut the hawser. Her owners claimed successfully in court for her towing fee and for recompense for the loss of her towrope as she had lost the tow through no fault of her own and the towage contract was still valid.

Odd items of news give us some idea of the capabilities of the iron paddle tugs. In 1864 the **Conqueror** (126.4 ft. 232 tons. 2 x 95 n.h.p.) built for the Clyde Shipping Company but sold to

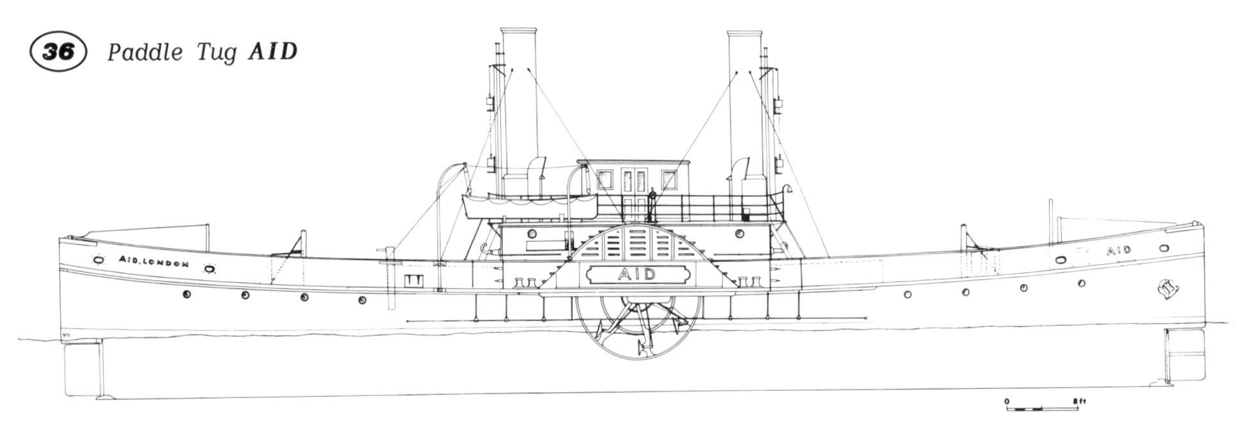

(36) *Paddle Tug* ***AID***

Calcutta to replace local tugs lost in a cyclone was credited with a speed of 14.312 kts. on her trial trip. The **Flying Meteor** (1864. 111.5 ft. 127 tons. 65 n.h.p.) again belonging to the Clyde Shipping Company towed a sailing ship from Liverpool to the Clyde in 30 hours despite gales. This gives an average speed of 6.67 knots which compares favourably with the screw tug **Cruiser**, also from the Clyde which in 1904 towed a sailing ship from the Clyde to Port Talbot in 48 hours, an average speed of 6.12 knots. The **Conqueror** was an example of the bigger paddle tug with two funnels placed fore and aft of the paddleboxes. Fully half of the length of the vessel was taken up with the engines and boilers (37,38). The companionways to the accommodation were very ornate as was usual in those days, but compare the space provided for the officers with that provided for the crew. One wonders why all that saloon area was needed. The hook was braced back to the main after paddle beam. For a tug of this size the sponsons were somewhat small as are the sidehouses. The body plan shows a hull with a sharp entry but a full body amidships. She was built to replace the tug of the same name which was sold to India in 1864. She was built in 1865 by Simons of Renfrew- 136.5 ft. 199 tons. 120 n.h.p. and after working for five years carrying out coastal tows for the Clyde Shipping Co. she was sold to owners in Quebec.

The **Bulldog** (1863, 160 ft. 378 tons. 240 n.h.p.) had a range equivalent to 14 days steaming presumably without a ship in tow. In 1868 the **Castrina** (no details available) arrived at Gibraltar 180 hours from the Tyne (average 8.89 kts.) with two days of coal in her bunkers, the first time a tug had reached the Straits of Gibraltar without refuelling. There was a constant striving to increase the duration of the paddle tugs, partly because the longer they could remain at sea the less time was wasted in transit, and partly because coal bought at a port away from home was usually more expensive, this being true especially if a tug had to refuel in any of the ports on the south coast of Ireland. Tugs which went seeking, frequently carried extra coal on the deck which impaired their stability until it was consumed. One wonders if some of the unexplained casualties were due to this practice. When the tug **Ovington** 'overbalanced with coal' in 1865 and sank

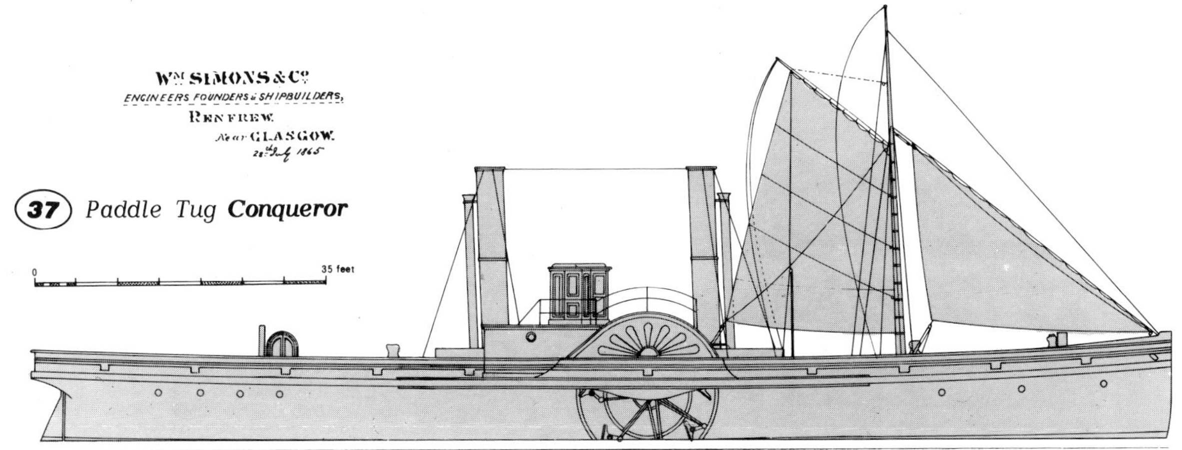

(37) *Paddle Tug* ***Conqueror***

below the coaling staithes of Sunderland, was it that the captain was trying to take that extra ton or two on board?

The number of iron paddle tugs in service increased steadily, both double engined and single engined, the latter retaining its popularity as the tugmen swore that the single engined tug had a greater pull than a double engined tug of the same power. As with the wooden tugs two boilers were fitted, usually each with its own funnel, generally side by side but occasionally the funnels were fitted fore and aft of the paddle boxes. One of the finest examples of this was Watkins' **Iona.**

The **Iona** had her two tall funnels arranged fore and aft with a rake that gave her an air of grace. She had a very large skylight over the aft saloon which made her suitable for excursion work. The bridge deck was large and uncluttered and as was usual with London tugs the wheel was open. The **Iona** started life as the **Ben Nevis** built in 1876 by Hall Russell of Aberdeen (121.7 ft. 203 tons. 138 n.h.p.) for J.F. Gibb of Ratcliffe, London. She was acquired in 1886 by Wm. Watkins who had to give her a thorough overhaul before she was fit to go into service on the Thames and to undertake seeking in the Channel. She went to G. Alder of Middlesbrough in 1920 and was finally scrapped in 1928 **Iona** (31).

Over the years there was little change in the outward appearance of the iron paddle tug except that some, like the screw tugs, had bulwarks with pronounced tumblehome aft. The tugs themselves varied in shape and size and it is difficult to date an iron paddle tug from her appearance. As the nineteenth century drew to a close the big paddle tugs of the 1860/70s were scrapped and replaced by screw tugs of smaller size and the size of the iron paddler decreased until 100 to 120 ft. was the average for the upper end of the size range. The smaller iron paddle tugs replaced the aged wooden paddle tugs which were being lost and scrapped quite rapidly.

Many of the paddle tugs had two funnels arranged side by side and on the **Lingdale** the funnels and the mast were absolutely vertical. She had a very extensive bridge deck and there were side-houses both fore and aft on the paddleboxes. The towing hook on the foredeck was frequently found on paddle tugs operating on the North East Coast though not usually as far back as shown on the **Lingdale.** It was set on a massive timber post heavily braced to take the strain. Just ahead of this hook was a capstan for handling the tow rope. Shown on the drawing is the arrangement for transmitting the strain from the after hook - a chain which was shackled to the keelson. The drawing was prepared from the model of the tug which was in the offices of the Tees Towing Company and photos taken aboard show her as she was in later years (39). The **Lingdale** was built by Westwood, Baillie & Co., London in 1882 (174 tons. 75 n.h.p.) as the **Lady Vita** for the Dover Harbour Board. She served them well for 32 years, being involved in numerous salvage jobs in the English Channel and the Goodwin Sands. In 1914 she was sold to the Tees Tug Co. (Crosthwaite) of Middlesbrough, spending some time on requisition to the Admiralty, and joining the fleet of the Tees Towing Co. in 1920. She was broken up in 1954 at the ripe old age of 72.

In contrast to the **Lingdale** the funnels of **Flying Arrow** (8) had a rake which makes her look less stiff. The boilers were entirely below deck and only the covers over the steam dome protruded just enough to carry the fixings for the towing hooks. The boats are shown on davits but in practice they were stowed on deck and the davits were demountable. She had a simple hand windlass for the anchor but on the Clyde there would be little reason for using an anchor as the tug would tie up in a dock at the end of a working day. It was usual to put a grating on the deck outside a door so that the deck would not be worn by the boots of the crew as they stepped out on deck. The drawing is based on the model in the Liverpool Maritime Museum. The **Flying Arrow** was a product of the South Shields yard of J.T. Eltringham, one of the main builders of paddle tugs. She was built in 1882 (108.0 ft. 131 tons. 80 n.h.p.) with a single side lever engine and was kept by the Clyde Shipping Co. for 10 years before her sale to Wm. Taylor of Grangemouth. About five years later she was again sold, this time to Russian owners.

In Chapter 2 mention was made of the work of the wooden paddle tugs during the construction of various bridges. The iron paddle tugs were also involved and the picture shows the **Iron King** assisting in towing out pontoons with (164) a new span for the Tay Bridge resting on them. It was quite common to paint the bottom of the funnel white with lime as this reduced the radiation of heat on to the back of the engineman who was working just in front of the funnel (the housing over the engine had no back to it!) When the **Roker** arrived in Methil in 1962 the first thing they did was to extend the shelter and put canvas drapes at the after end to cut down the icy draughts.

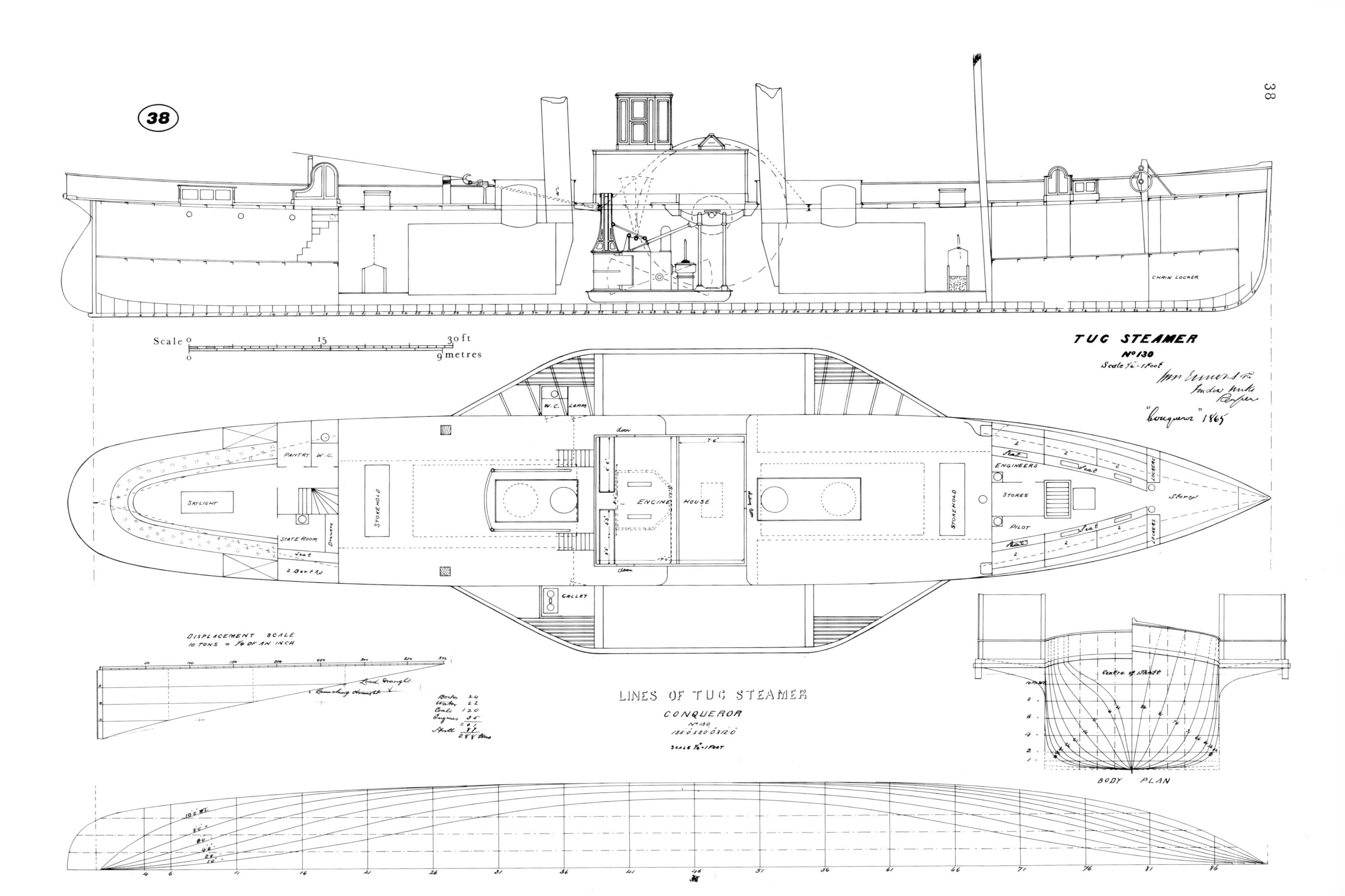

38
CHAIN LOCKER
Scale 0 15 30 ft
0 9 metres
TUG STEAMER
No 130
Scale 1/4"-1 foot
"Conqueror" 1865
PANTRY W.C.
SKYLIGHT
STATE ROOM
Drawers
Seat
2 Berths
STOKEHOLD
W.C. LAMPS
door
ENGINE
HOUSE
sliding door
GALLEY
STOKEHOLD
ENGINEERS
STORES
PILOT
Seat
LOCKERS
Stores
DISPLACEMENT SCALE
10 TONS = 1/4 OF AN INCH
Load Draught
Launching Draught
Boiler 24
Water 22
Coals 120
Engines 35
201
Hull 87
288 tons
LINES OF TUG STEAMER
CONQUEROR
No 130
135'0" x 20'0" x 12'0"
SCALE 1/4"-1 FOOT
Centre of Shaft
BODY PLAN

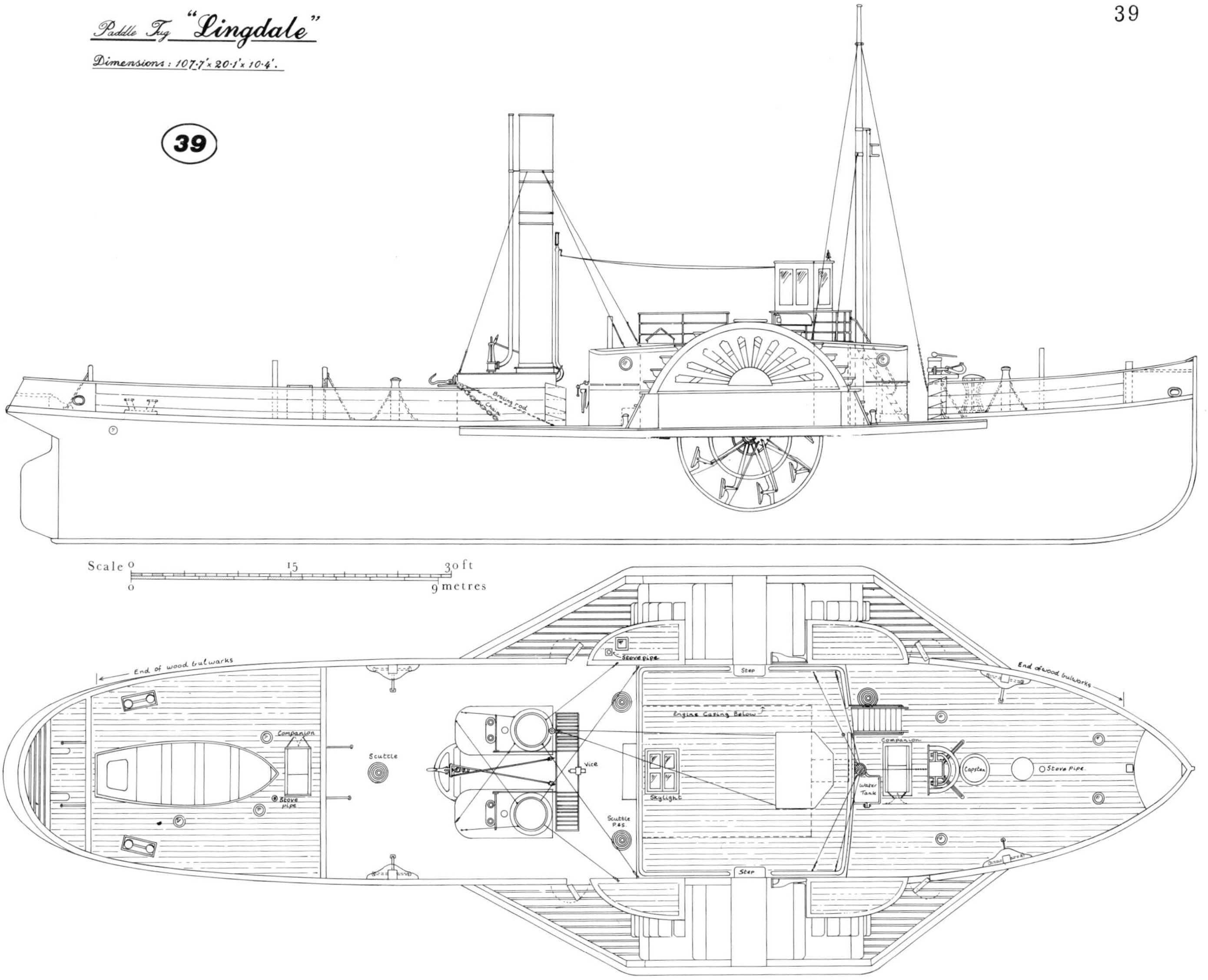

Paddle Tug "Lingdale"

Dimensions: 107·7' x 20·1' x 10·4'.

(39)

Scale 0 15 30 ft
0 9 metres

The **Rover** was so typical of the paddle tugs built on the Tyne that it is almost impossible to comment. However a look at the hull shape will dispel the idea that the paddle tugs had hulls with parallel sides. There was hardly a straight line along the **Rover**'s hull. The composite companion-ways and skylights for the accommodation are very attractive features. As on most paddle tugs there was a large saloon (40), aft for the officers and passengers, but the space forward for the crew was somewhat cramped. The sidehouses contained the W.C.s and galley, with a lamp and oil store. In common with many other Clyde paddle tugs the **Rover** had only a single side lever engine. Although only one year separated the **Rover** from the **Flying Scotsman** (43) the **Rover** was more old fashioned having a vertical bulwark at the stern and wood decks throughout her length. The **Rover** was another Eltringham tug built in 1897 for Steel & Bennie of Glasgow (108.0 ft. 152 tons. 99 n.h.p.) On trials the single side-lever engine produced 500 i.h.p. and a speed of 11 kts. Although she was a seeking tug normally restricted to the Firth of Clyde she was despatched in December 1914 to Southampton only to be driven ashore as a total loss on the Irish coast. She had been stranded before in 1901 on which occasion she had been described in the report as a paddle trawler. As paddle trawlers were not used on the Clyde it is more probable that she had been working as a fish carrier.

To gain some idea of the lines of a paddle tug of the turn of the century the lines of the **Troon** were taken off the builders block half model. They show quite a full hull amidships with an almost flat bottom and a sharp turn on the bilges. J.P. Rennoldson of South Shields built the **Troon** in 1902 (100.0 ft. 130 tons. 70 n.h.p.) for the Glasgow & Southwestern Railway Co. to be based in Troon harbour on the Ayrshire coast. In 1930 she was sold to Middlesbrough Towage Co. and in 1934 resold to Wm. Lamey of Liverpool, being scrapped in 1948.

The **King Edward VII** was one of the last of the paddle tugs and is a typical example. She was a money spinner for her Yarmouth owners as she gained no less than eleven salvage awards in under five years soon after she went into service. She is shown here in the unusual funnel colours of the Irwing Steam Tug Co. of Sunderland. Two "Cs" placed back to back in a shield with a twist of rope in a figure of eight - this indicated a connection with Culliford and Clarke whose ships these tugs attended. (1901. 100.0 ft. 138 tons. 280 e.h.p.). See photograph (41).

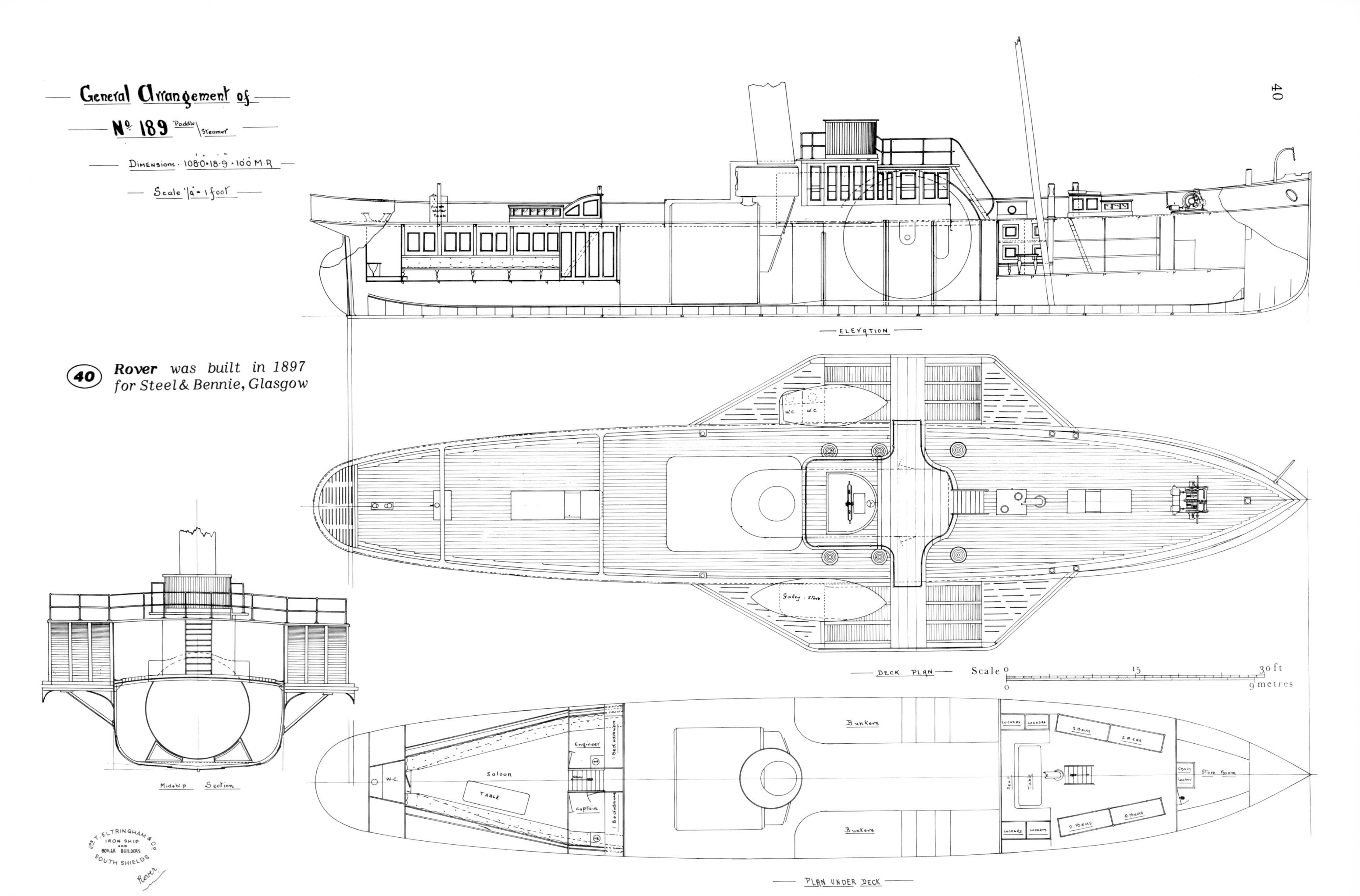

40 ***Rover*** *was built in 1897 for Steel & Bennie, Glasgow*

41

I.P.T. ***King Edward VII*** *was built in 1901 by J.P. Rennoldson for Nicholson Towage, Great Yarmouth passing to the Irwing Steam Tug Co., Sunderland whose colours she wears in this photo.*

It may be thought that by 1900 the paddle tug finished, but far from it! Surprisingly, no less than 3 iron hulled and 21 steel hulled paddle tugs were built between 1900 and 1914, the last being the **Sir Hugh Bell**, built 1913, steel, described in the chapter on tenders and the **Eppleton Hall** (1914, 100.5 ft. 166 tons. 80 n.h.p.) Quite out of the blue, the Tees Commissioners ordered a paddle tug in 1930, the **John H. Amos** for duty as a tender and for towing dredging plant. She is dealt with more fully in the chapter on owners. With the building of the **John H.Amos** the civilian paddle tug died, but among the proposal drawings of Ferguson Bros., Port Glasgow are three drawings of 1937 for the Manchester Ship Canal Co of 106' paddle tugs, one with two single cylinder diagonal engines, one with similar, but compound engines and finally a diesel driving paddles through clutches, and gear boxes with chain or belt final drive. All were very ugly looking vessels.

During the First World War a large number of iron paddle tugs saw service with the Navy and the Army transport corps, returning after the cessation of hostilities to their civilian owners to face a much more mundane existence. After the war 'seeking' was finished, destroyed partly by the huge losses of the sailing craft which had been their bread and butter, partly by the drive for efficiency where the tows were organised in the office ashore, the tug being instructed what boat she was to tow and where she would pick up her tow. The steam coasters had mostly taken over from the schooners and ketches (which often had engines too) and they were more or less independent of the tug, except in some small harbours which were tight for space. London's last paddle tug was the **Iona** described previously (31). In Liverpool the paddle tug disappeared when the **Enterprise** (1885, 118.4 ft. 157 tons. 480 i.h.p.) was sold in the 1920s, but the paddle tug served again on the Mersey in the form of **Troon** *(41)*. She was purchased by W.H. Lamey in 1934 and proved very useful for work up river. She gave valuable service during the second war including a spell in North Wales in connection with the towing of the sections of the Mulberry Harbour. She was finally scrapped in 1948. In Glasgow the paddle tug survived until the last of the Clyde Shipping Company's paddle tugs was sold. The **Flying Scotsman** (1898, 118.0 ft. 177 tons. 90 n.h.p.) although built so late she still had a single side-lever engine as had most of her predecessors (43). She showed several characteristics of the screw tug i.e. the tumblehome of the bulwarks aft, the wood sheathing over the crew spaces instead of covering the whole deck and the circular skylights with vents. As she had a single engine, the casing was quite narrow but it had been raised aft to clear the big boiler. She was provided with a wheelhouse when built, which was a bit of a luxury. With her clear decks she came in useful for attending trials, carrying technicians and officials and even equipment out to

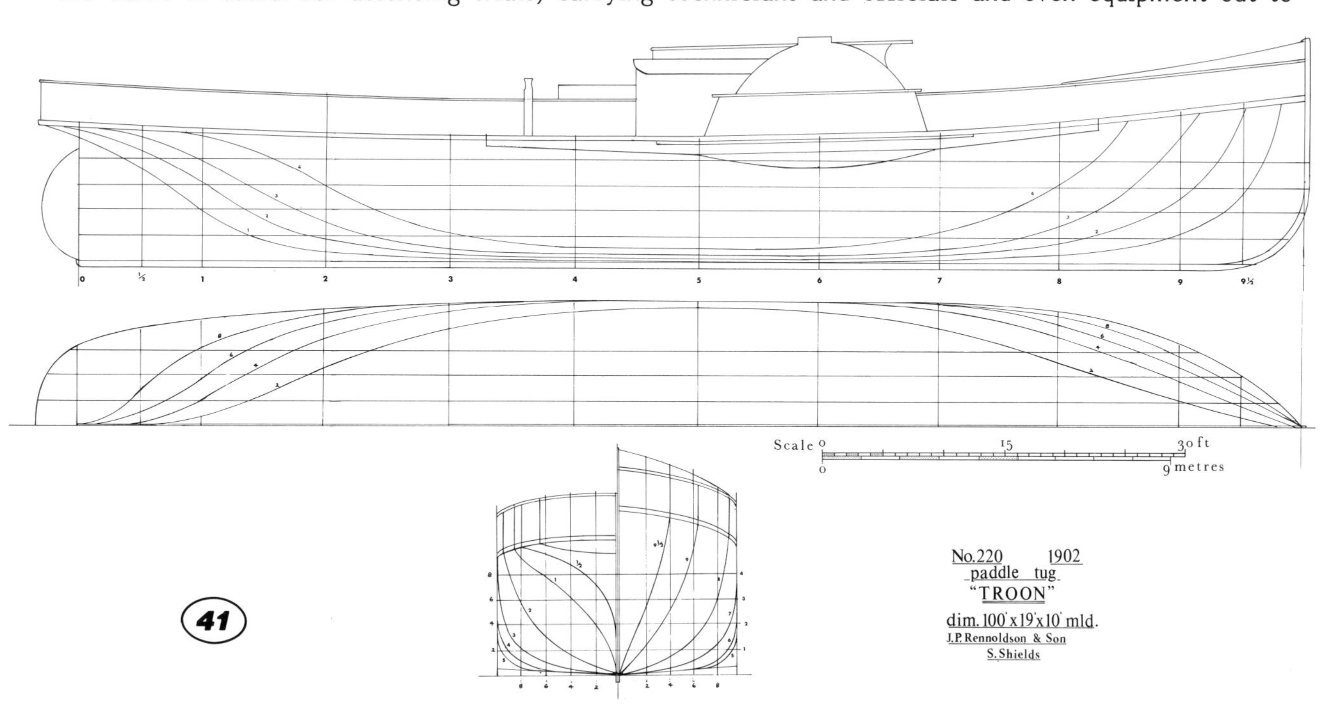

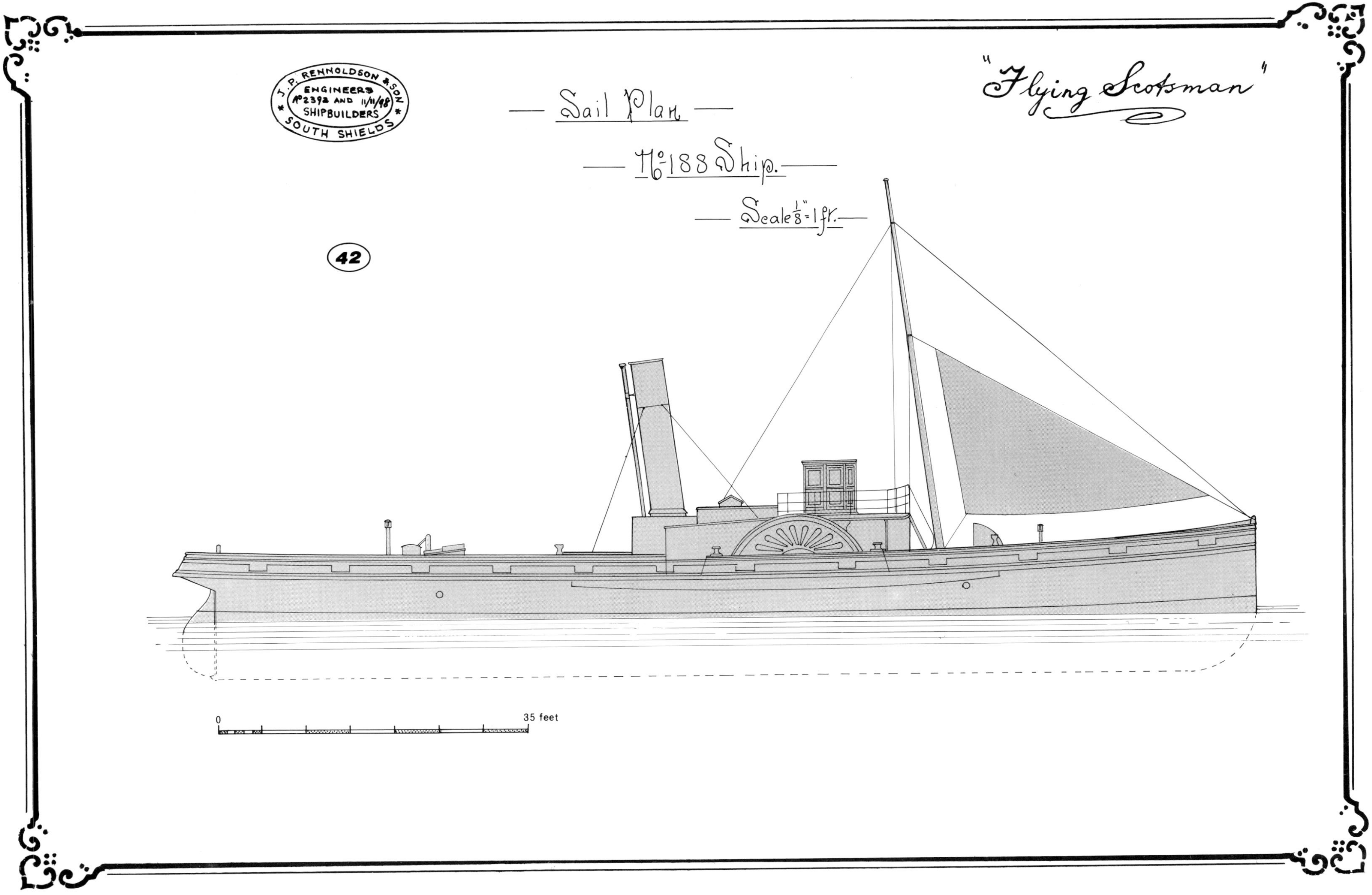

"Flying Scotsman"

— Sail Plan —

— No 188 Ship. —

— Scale 1/8" = 1 ft. —

J. P. RENNOLDSON & SON
ENGINEERS
No 2392 AND 11/11/98
SHIPBUILDERS
SOUTH SHIELDS

42

0

35 feet

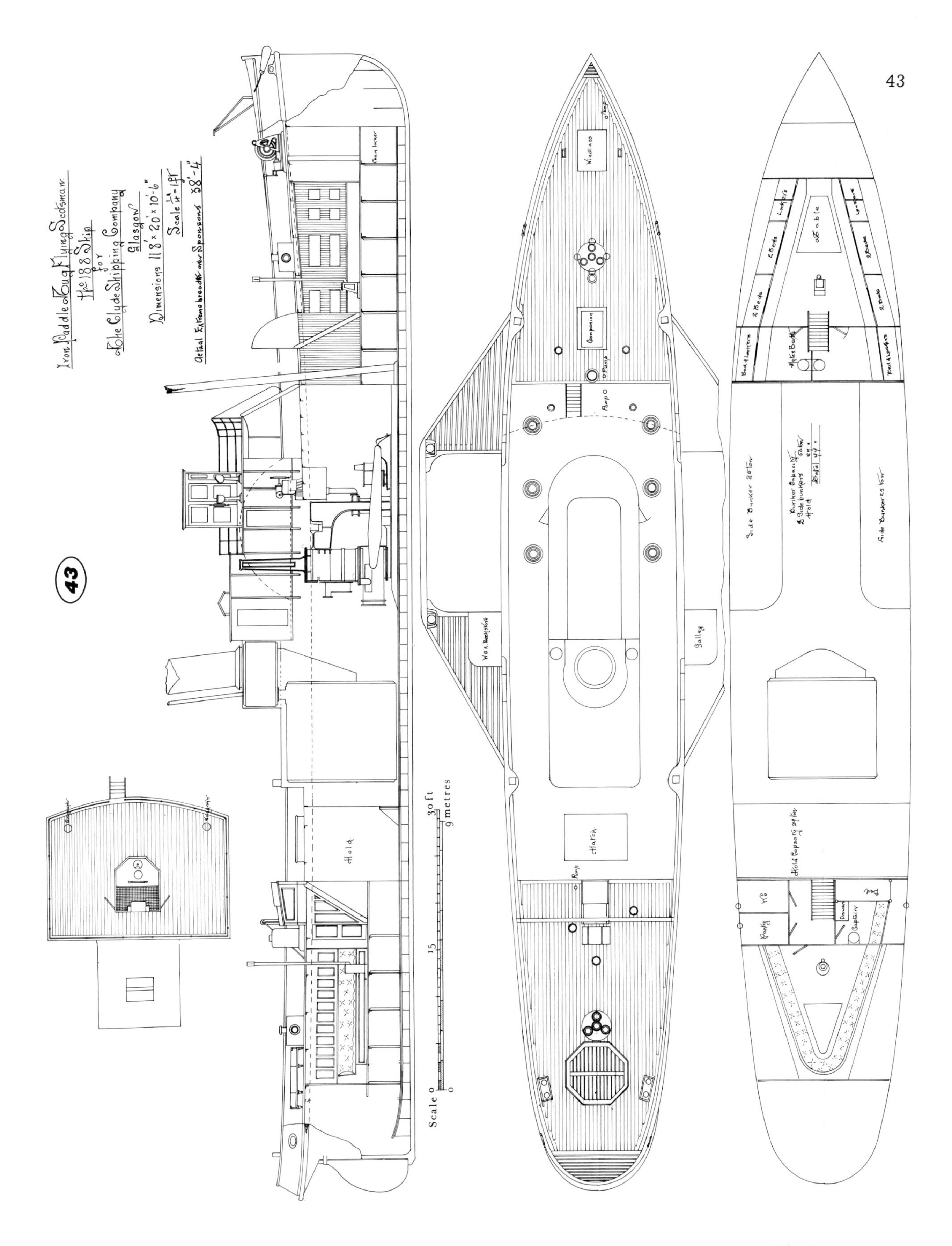

vessels lying off Greenock. Surprisingly enough all the paddle tugs purchased new by the company had been single-engined, though some of their second-hand purchases were double-engined. The **Flying Scotsman** came from the Rennoldson yard and was somewhat larger than her contemporaries. She served the Clyde Shipping Co. uneventfully for 50 years and in 1948 was sold for conversion to a yacht to be called **Cambrian.** She lay off Oban for some time, the whole idea was abandoned and the tug went to the breaker's yard. In the Firth of Clyde itself the last paddle tug in service was the iron and steel **George Brown** which served the Irvine Harbour Company from 1887 to 1956 (93.0 ft. 99 tons. 300 i.h.p.)

The **George Brown** was built by S. McKnight & Co. of Ayr on the Clyde, not in the traditional home of the paddle tug builders, the Tyne. She was a smallish tug but she had a pair of single cylinder diagonal engines, a rare type for a civilian paddle tug of her size and power. They were generally confined to large civilian or naval tugs. The boiler was large and protruded right above

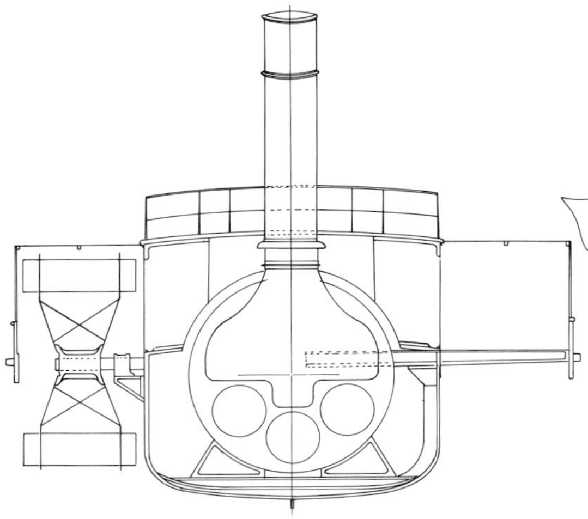

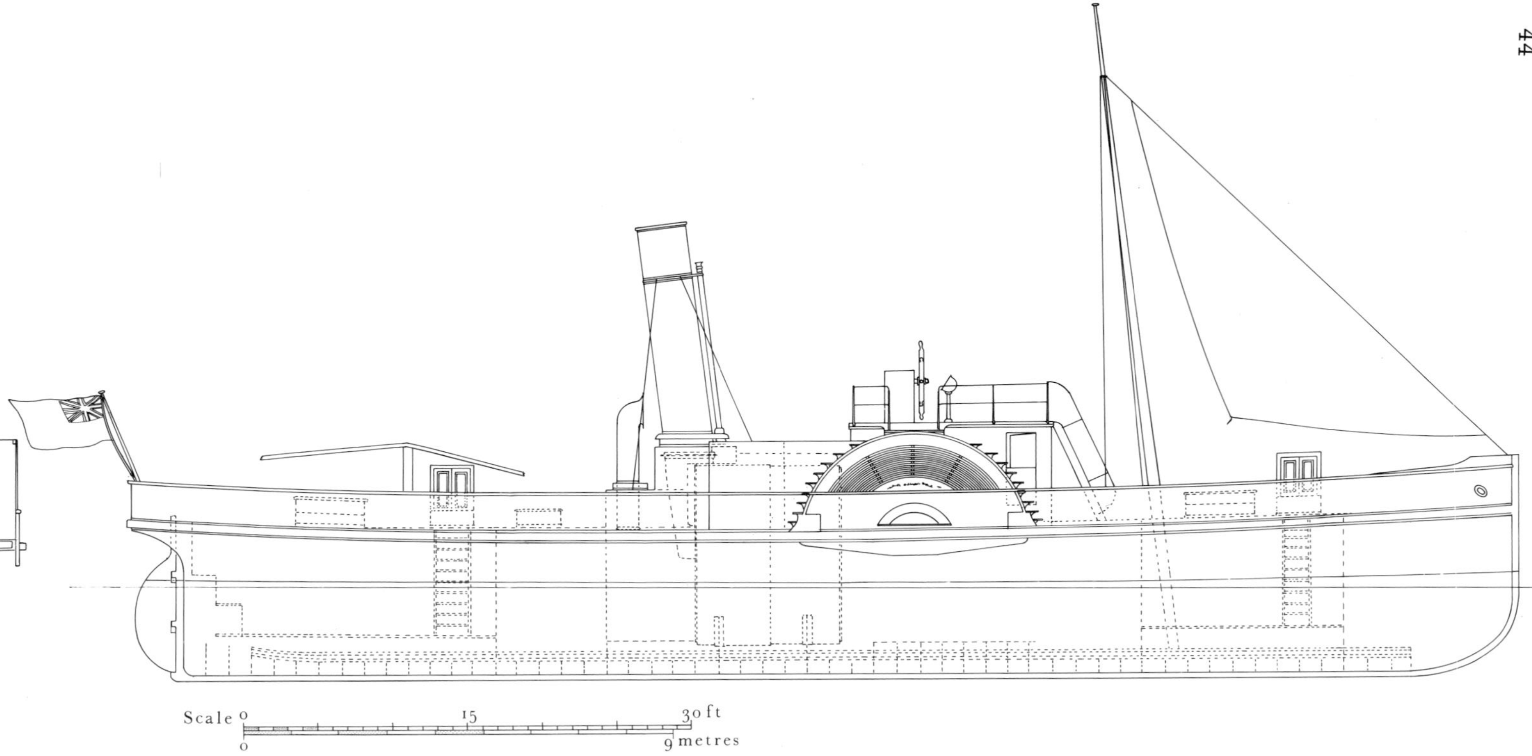

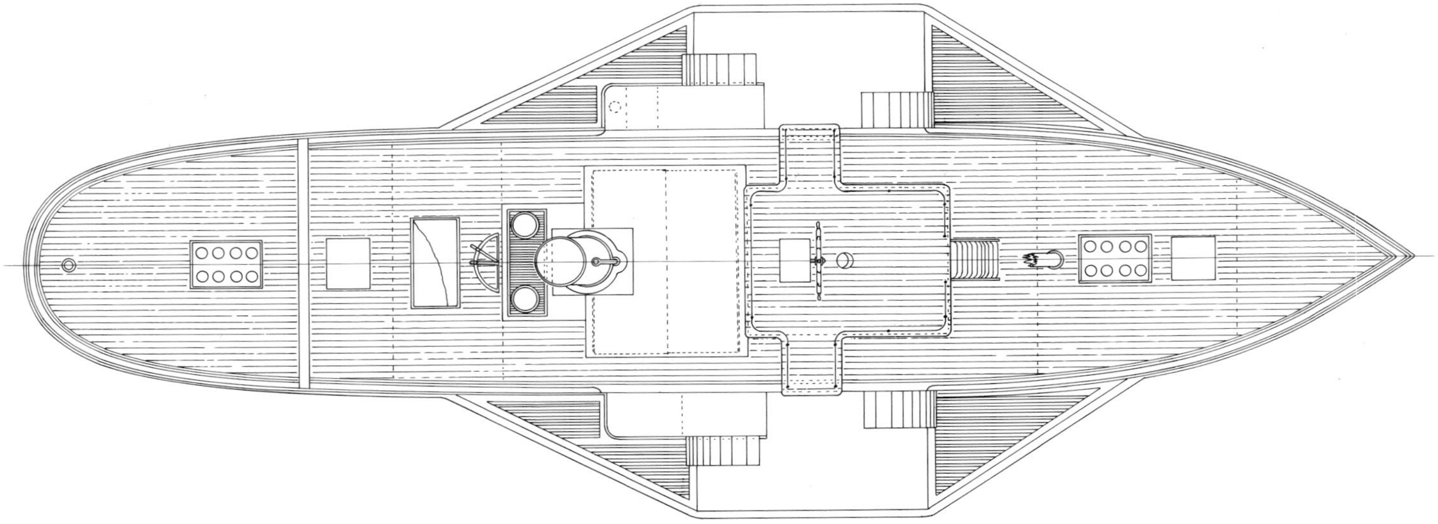

44

Iron Paddle Tug
George Brown
of Irvine

the deck with the funnel perched on it (44). The coaling hatch aft of the boiler was an unusual feature. When built she had two sidehouses aft but at a later date the port one was cut down to the level of the bulwark and the lifeboat was placed on it. Someone obtained an old seat from a tramcar and this was placed in front of the steering shelter.

On the North-East coast of England after World War II there was still a large though ageing fleet of paddle tugs. Even in 1957, 13 were spread between Blyth, Sunderland, Seaham Harbour and Middlesbrough. The **Earl of Beaconsfield** of Blyth (1889. 95.0 ft. 114 tons. 75 n.h.p.) was finally broken up in 1958. The **Eppleton Hall** was one of the last paddle tugs to be built for British owners and her large funnel gave her quite a heavy appearance. The hook on the samson post in the bow was typical North-East Coast practice, though the actual position of the hook varied from tug to tug. The main towing hook rested on the boiler casing, which had to be kept well greased, and was of the spring loaded type,unusual on a paddle tug (45). Compare the position of the forward hook with that of the **Lingdale** (39). Although she had two engines she still had cant hooks on the sponsons both before and aft of the paddle boxes. It is interesting to note the wooden ash chute on the starboard after sponson. This drawing was prepared by Helmut Raffay of Vienna who spent three weeks in Seaham Harbour measuring up the tug. Another of the well known Tyne tug builders, Hepple & Co. built the **Eppleton Hall** in 1914 (100.5 ft. 66 tons. 80 n.h.p.) for the Lambton & Hetton Collieries Ltd. of Newcastle. This fleet was absorbed by France Fenwick, Tyne & Wear Co. in 1945 and the tug went into service in Sunderland until sold to the Seaham Harbour Dock Co. in 1964 (Plate 19). They disposed of her in 1967 for demolition but she was rescued, overhauled, sailed across the Atlantic and now sails in San Francisco Harbour as a working museum piece.

The **Reliant** left Seaham Harbour in 1969 for the National Maritime Museum. On the East coast of Scotland a paddle tug had been stationed at Methil for many years, the last being the **Roker** (1904. 95.0 ft. 119 tons. 70 n.h.p.) which had a short-lived service in the port from 1962 to 1966. She was in a poor way when she arrived there and had very little power, the owners even had to fit a diesel air pump to take some of the load off her ancient engines.

The **Elie** was the last but one of the paddle tugs which worked out of Methil on the Fife coast. In profile she might be mistaken for a screw tug with her funnel placed forward of the paddles and the tumblehome of her bulwarks. Even the stowing of her lifeboats was in keeping with the appearance of a screw tug. The old skipper of the **Elie** used to stand by the engine telegraph behind the funnel with no one at the wheel, guiding the tug round the dock on engines only, a sight to watch with awe. The two 'horns' sticking above the bulwarks by the hook were the guards which prevented the rope catching the superstructure should the tug swing too far round across the rope. J.T. Eltringham built the **Elie** in 1912 (105.1 ft. 168 tons. 68 n.h.p.) as the **Pen Cw** as a tender for the Great Western Railway at Fishguard, equipping her with two diagonal engines instead of the conventional side-lever type. Tees Towing Co. acquired her in 1927 renaming her **Ingleby Cross**, selling her in 1934 to the Grangemouth & Forth Towing Co. (Plate 19). She worked on the Forth for the next 29 years being scrapped locally in 1963 by J.A. White.

In the chapter on wooden paddle tugs an indication was given of the numbers of casualties and the causes for the period 1880 to 1909. The same definitions of causes apply.

Losses of iron paddle tugs due to various causes:

	Sank	Wreck	Machinery	Total losses	Total number of iron or steel paddle tugs in service
1880 - 1889	8 (2%)	8 (2%)	none (0%)	16 (4%)	339 (1885)
1890 - 1899	13 (5%)	6 (2%)	3 (1%)	22 (8%)	228 (1895)
1900 - 1909	5 (2%)	4 (2%)	1 (0.5%)	10 (5%)	220 (1905)

The comparison of this table with that for wooden tugs (page 28) shows how vulnerable were the wooden tugs partly due to their age and partly due to their construction.

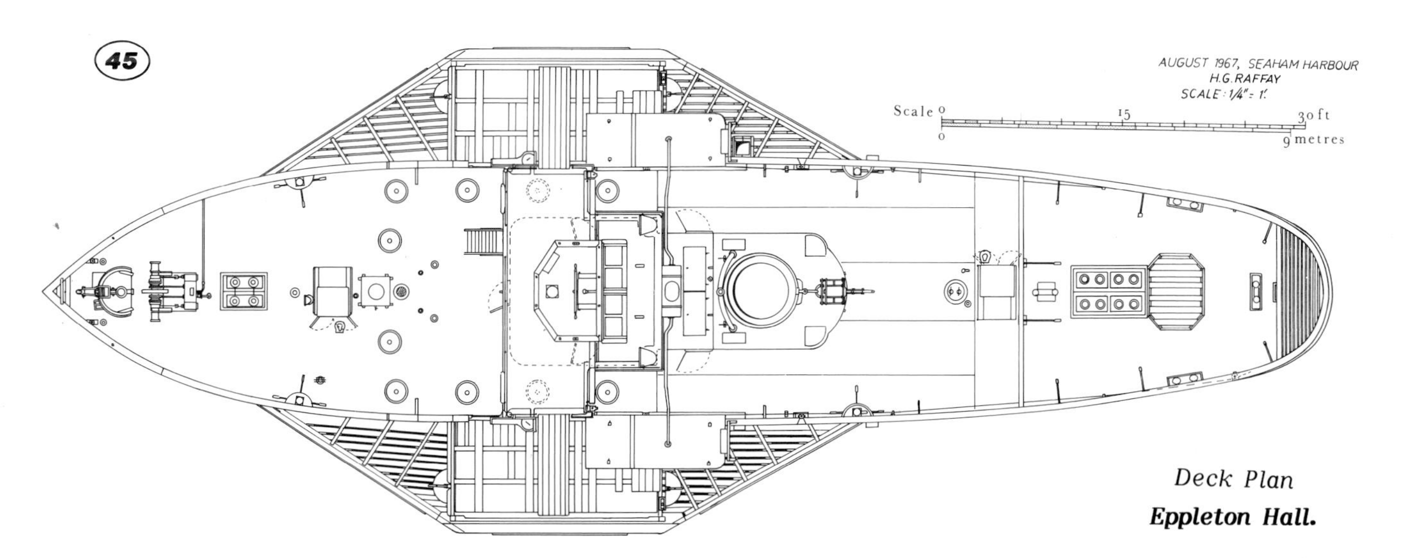

Deck Plan
Eppleton Hall.

***Dunrobin** was built by J.& W.Gunn, Cardiff for White, Edwards & Jenkins of Cardiff, (later J.Jenkins). She is seen here at Scarborough where she was owned by G.A.Smith & J.Douglass who had a big fleet of paddle trawlers.*

For those interested in statistics the following table shows the numbers of paddle tugs in service in 1929 and their distribution round the ports of the U.K. The number in service by 1940 had changed considerably and is indicated by the numbers in brackets below:

	Wood	Iron	Steel	Total
	1929 (1940)	1929 (1940)	1929 (1940)	1929 (1940)
South Coast	0 (0)	1 (0)		1 (0)
West Coast	0 (0)	4 (1)	5 (7)	9 (8)
West Scotland	0 (0)	6 (1)	3 (1)	9 (2)
East Scotland	0 (0)	6 (2)	1 (1)	7 (3)
North-East Coast	6 (0)	41 (17)	12 (9)	59 (26)
East Anglia	1 (0)	1 (0)		2 (0)

As the number of steam coasters grew, so the need for tugs declined. The Tyne suffered badly, as the tugs were small and it took three and sometimes more tugs to bring a ship in from or out to sea. Up until 1865 each tug charged the full rate of 2/- for each 13 tons registered of the ship for one mile or less, and 1/- extra per 13 tons registered ton if the ship were taken to sea or brought in from the sea. After 1865 the rates were altered to $1\frac{7}{8}$d. per ton maximum for dock to sea and vice versa. The towage distances were about 4 miles and took $\frac{3}{4}$ of an hour to complete and it was reckoned that at that time the Tyne had the most expensive rate of towage in the U.K. and so the ships were loath to use their services. In 1873 a survey was conducted which showed that there were about 145 tugs operating on the river and it gave the following figures. "Three tugs had engines of 45 nominal horsepower. These were the only ones equal to towing requirements of the shipping of the day. A further 10 had engines of 36 to 40 n.h.p. The remainder were from 35 n.h.p. down to 8 n.h.p. and were wholly unfit for towing."

These small tugs haunted the shipping lanes for any tow they could find and they were not averse to towing the sailing trawlers which were often becalmed or held up by headwinds on their way to market with their catch. The trawling smacks would sometimes put over the trawl to take advantage of the tow to add a few more fish to their haul. In 1877 Mr. Purdy of North Shields had a notion that he might tow the trawl himself and earn himself the money. He equipped his little wooden paddle tug **Messenger** (then 34 years old, 71.5 ft. and 25 n.h.p.) with a beam trawl and a derrick to recover it, and set out amid the jeers of the local tugmen and fisherfolk. To their chagrin he made £7.10.0 from his first catch and took a ship in tow into the bargain. On his second trip he made £9, a fact which did not escape the attention of his critics, and without further ado many of the other tugowners converted their own tugs for trawling or sold them to speculators looking to make easy money. Two of the paddle trawlers visited Aberdeen in 1882 and the incident stimulated the interest of some of the businessmen in the city in the possibilities of the new method of fishing. In the spring of 1882 a Mr. Brown took the initiative and along with some others purchased the **Toiler** from Dublin at a cost of £1550. The **Toiler** (1873) was quite a large wood tug 101.4 ft. long, and 50 n.h.p. which had originally worked on the Tyne. She was fitted with a derrick and beam trawl and she went to sea on 22nd March, viewed with distrust by the local fishermen. Her career was spectacular; during the first month her daily trips realised over £200 and at the end of the first year the syndicate declared a dividend of 100% in addition to dividing bonuses totalling £520 among her crew. Though the **Toiler** paid for herself during those first twelve months the strain had told on her timbers and she was worn out, but she had paved the way for others.

Many of the paddle tugs which were put into service as trawlers were old wooden vessels from the Tyne and many were not fit for the daily grind of towing the heavy beam trawl along the seabed. The casualty rate was high; during the second six months of 1880 eight paddle trawlers were lost, the oldest being the **Apollo** of 1857, the newest being the **Nation's Hope** only four years old, built 1876. However the success of the new industry prompted responsible owners to have built new paddle trawlers suitably strengthened for the job; tugs such as the **Constance** built in 1882 for Scarborough owners.

In 1881 the first screw propelled trawler had been built and once it had been accepted by the fishing fraternity the number of screw trawlers grew rapidly. However there was a body of opinion which held that the propeller was likely to cause a lot of trouble by fouling the warp or line which pulled the trawl and this fear gave a new lease of life to the paddle trawler. Once this worry had been overcome the paddle trawler was doomed but, since the design was based on the paddle tug it was a simple matter to strip off the trawling gear and put the vessel into service towing. Another fact which saved the paddle trawler and prolonged her use was that many second-hand boats were used, purchased at low prices. The photograph shows the **Dunrobin** (46) at Scarborough. She was an iron paddle tug built in 1876 at Cardiff for local owners, sold in 1892 to Belfast and wrecked on the 23rd December 1894, being written off as a total loss. However, she was salvaged, repaired and in the following year she arrived in Scarborough as a paddle trawler and she was still operating out of that port in 1904. The beam trawl and the derrick are clearly seen and in the bulwark below the trawl a special fairlead has been fitted for the trawl warp. Not visible is the steam capstan, usually installed on the starboard side abaft the boiler casing and used for hauling in the trawl warp.

The question of tug/trawler remained somewhat mixed for several years. In 1885 the screw trawlers **Bonito** and **Lamberton** were launched at Dundee and were provided with towing hooks and a towing rail so that they could operate as tugs if required. In 1893 the screw tug **Dragon** was built in Falmouth, in outline a pure tug but she was fitted with trawling gallows (on the starboard side only) As she was employing otter boards it was not necessary to have a derrick. The **Dragon** was quite large (47), being 120 ft. long x 20 ft. beam. She was constructed by Cox of Falmouth who had built 13 other vessels for Falmouth in the 25 years for which they had been shipbuilders. One owner covered all possibilities; in 1882 W. & R.H. Strong of Cardiff ordered the **Advance**, the first screw tug in Cardiff, to be equipped for passenger carrying, towing and trawling. One wonders how he got rid of the smell of the fish!

Although the story of the paddle trawler started in 1877, tugs had been involved with the fishing industry for many years before. The sailing trawlers used to operate alone, returning with their catch as they filled their holds, but in about 1850 the 'fleeting' system was introduced where a fast sailing vessel would collect the catches from a group of trawlers enabling them to remain on the fishing grounds and not waste time on the run into port. Every now and again a paddle tug would perform this task, one, the **British Dominion** (1840, 69.0 ft. 58 tons. 30 n.h.p.) a wooden paddler from Shields, was lost in 1856 as she approached Hauxley Harbour, north of the Tyne, loaded with herring. The weather was hazy, a proper watch was not being kept and she struck a rock 500 yards offshore. In the Firth of Clyde the paddle tugs picked up the occasional cargo of herring for the market, carrying the cargo on their decks. The iron paddle tug **Flying Cloud,** (built 1866, 80.5 ft. 61 tons. 30 n.h.p.) struck Helensburgh Pier as she tried to come alongside and sank, losing most of her deck cargo of fish, but she was raised eleven days later and taken to Greenock for repair.

Screw tug / trawler ***Dragon*** *of the Falmouth Towage Company.*

(48) ***Lady Brassey***, *built 1913 by J.P. Rennoldson, South Shields for Dover Harbour Board. Dimensions 130.1 x 28.1 x 13.8 feet. Scrapped 1958. PHOTO: Skyphotos Ltd.*

4. Screw Tugs

The development of the screw tug is somewhat more complex than that of the paddle tug since the approach to the use of the screw tug varied in each area of the country. The way this is tackled is to consider each main area and to see how the screw tug was adopted, starting in London and working clockwise round the coast. Some part of the country used almost entirely second-hand tugs and therefore the word 'development' can hardly be used.

River Thames.

Despite the successful trials run by Captain Ericsson in 1836 with his screw tug **Francis B. Ogden** and later the **Robert F. Stockton**, there was little enthusiasm shown by the tugowners of the day. They can hardly be blamed for not taking to this new-fangled invention; the screw tugs were small and low powered to say the least. The paddle tugs themselves had only recently been accepted and most men's capital had been sunk in them. In the thirty years following the exploits of Ericsson's tugs, about twenty screw tugs were built for the Thames, all of iron, of which seventeen were craft tugs. It has been said that the early screw tugs were not very successful because they were straight adaptations of the paddle tug, retaining the slim hull and shallow draught which did not give the 'grip' on the water which the screw tug needs to exert pull. Unfortunately no drawings of the early screw tugs have survived to confirm this, though the dimensions of those early vessels show a length to breadth ratio of 5:1 or greater which is comparable with paddle tugs. It is probably true enough, as most changes are made by adapting an existing 'vehicle'; take the first car for instance, just a horseless carriage with an internal combustion engine fitted.

In London, apart from the craft tugs, the screw tug was accepted only slowly. R.D. Ross introduced the **Triumph** in 1856 (89.8 ft. x 18.6 ft. 81 tons. 80 n.h.p.) William Watkins tried the **Era** in 1869 (65 ft. 30 tons. 24 n.h.p.) but she was too small to be effective for towing large ships, and her draught was only 5 ft. She could make 13 kts. running free with a coal consumption of $1\frac{3}{4}$ lb. of coal per H.P. per hour, which was all very well, but a tug needs performance while towing! His next screw tug was the **Albion** (1870, 118.0' x 18.0'. 109 tons. ? n.h.p.). Although she also was reputed to suffer from the defect of shallow draught she nevertheless impressed the nautical papers of the day. On one occasion she left the Mouse Lightship at 5 am. with the 1400 ton ship *Knight Commander* in tow and took her as far as the North Foreland. She ran back free to the West India Dock and from there towed the 1200 ton *Hindoostan* to Gravesend arriving at 5 p.m. In 12 hours she had covered 130 miles, averaging 11 m.p.h. between towing and running free. It was 1877 before he bought another screw tug, this time the **Bristol** (1876, 76.7 ft. 59 tons. 45 n.h.p.) and from then on all his new tugs were screw propelled. They were of average size 90 ft. to 110 ft. and they were used extensively for seeking and coastal towing. Two of his tugs, built in Holland, the **Australia**

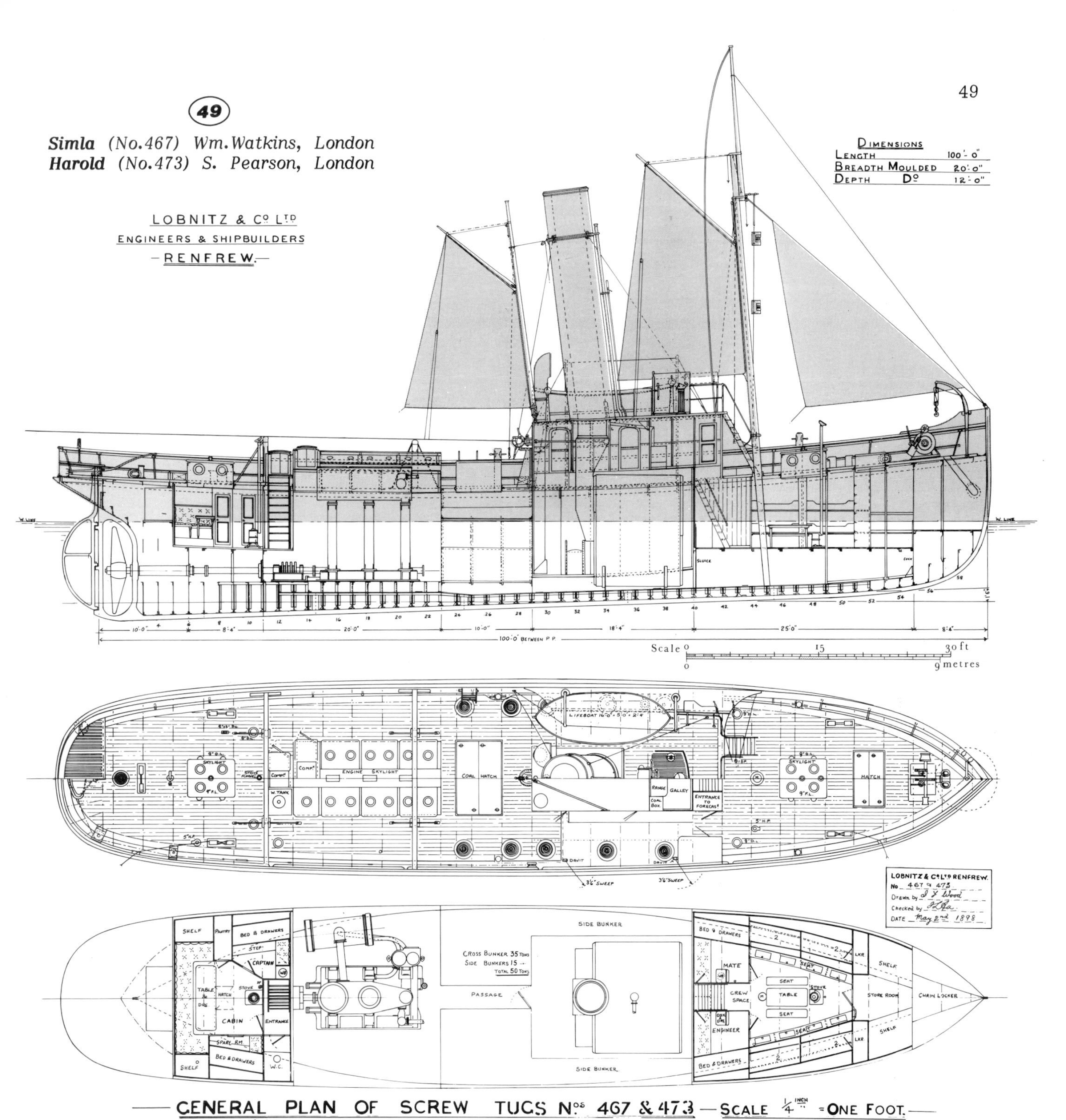

GENERAL PLAN OF SCREW TUGS Nos 467 & 473 — SCALE 1/4 INCH = ONE FOOT.

and the **Zealandia** (1882, 90.4 ft. 128 tons. 70 n.h.p.) had two funnels side by side, an arrangement which was common with the paddle tugs but rarely seen on a screw tug. In their case the arrangement resulted in very ugly vessels. These early tugs were fairly low powered and it always seemed to take a number of them to effect a salvage. In 1899 the steamer *Amiral Aube* drove ashore on the Great Sunk with a strong wind blowing and in a choppy sea. A strong tide scoured away the sand around her and she began to embed herself. She called over a pilot cutter and offered her £50 if she would go and fetch a tug. The cutter brought two Ipswich screw tugs, the **Spray** (1897, 69.9 ft. 58 tons. 350 i.h.p.) and the **Garnet** (1881, 63.0 ft. 34 tons. 20 n.h.p.), but they could not move the steamer. These two were joined by the iron paddle tug **Merrimac** (1883, 91.0 ft. 96 tons. 350 i.h.p.) and the screw coaster **Seagull** (1893. 100.0 ft. 144 tons), with no more success than before. Next upon the scene were the three Watkins tugs I.P.T. **Cambria** (1870. 138.8 ft. 209 tons. 600 e.h.p.) and the screw tugs **Burma** (1889, 85.8 ft. 94 tons. 70 n.h.p.) and **Columbia** (1884, 121.0 ft. 214 tons. 960 e.h.p.), but despite all this assembly of tugs the *Amiral Aube* just refused to budge., Next day some of the cargo was jettisoned and further attempts were made to refloat the steamer. The tugs in attendance being the **Columbia, Cambria, Burma, Merrimac** and **Spray** which had now been joined by another screw tug from London, the **Warrior** (1895, 106.0 ft. 192 tons. 650 e.h.p.) Together these six tugs pulled the *Amiral Aube* into deep water, their combined effort producing about 3,600 i.h.p.

The **Simla** was a typical seeking tug with fine lines and a slender hull built for speed and provided with good accommodation for her crew who had to spend several days aboard **(49).** She had large

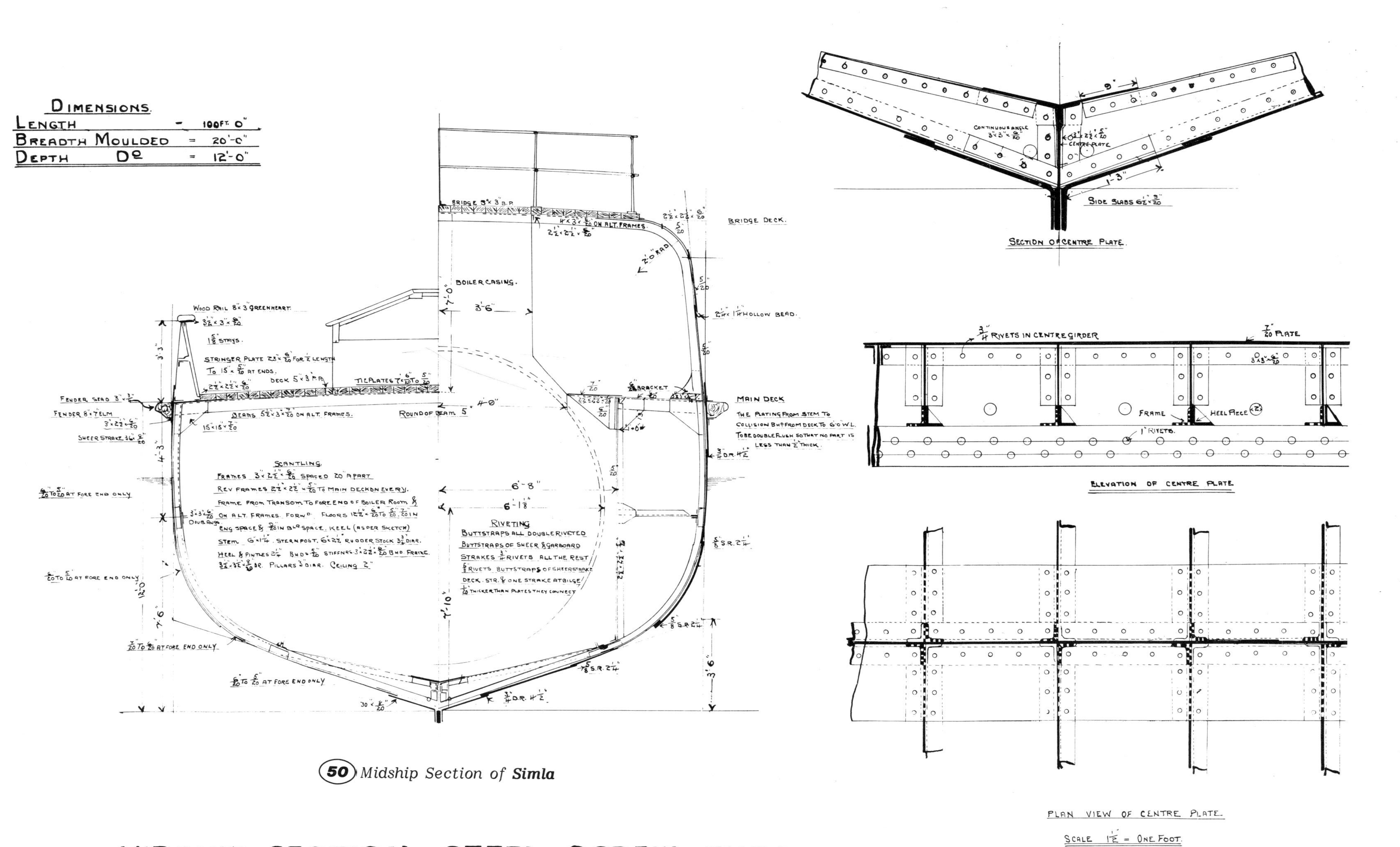

50 *Midship Section of* ***Simla***

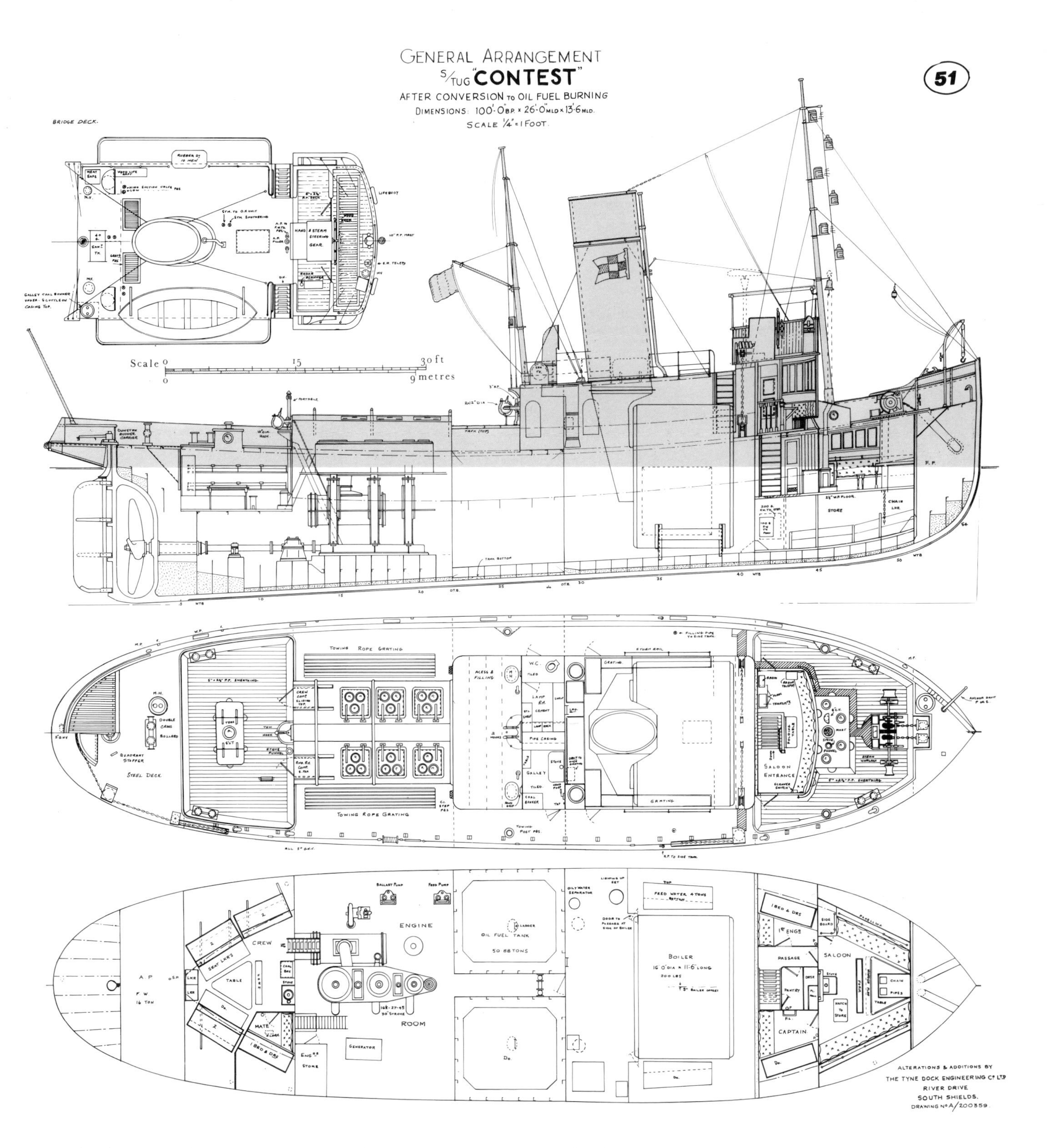

bunkers to give her the chance to remain on station and a full set of sails to eke out the coal. The lead of the steering chains is interesting, running along the round-down of the deck and then through two diverter pulleys to the waterway. The midship section (50) had all the features of the seeking tug, the pronounced rise of floor and very rounded bilges, sacrificing some stability for speed. The **Simla** was built in 1898 for Wm. Watkins of London and was 144 tons and 99 n.h.p. She remained with the Watkins fleet until 1964 apart from a period of service with the Navy and the Army in 1914/15. Her sister was the **Harold** built for S. Pearson of London.

At first there was little competition from the other tugowners whose fleets were small compared with the Watkins 'navy'. One of the opposition was T.W. Elliott whose first screw tug was the iron built **Contest** (1883, 81.0 ft. 82 tons. 80 n.h.p.) followed by the larger **Challenger** (1884, 100.0 ft. 137 tons. 95 n.h.p.) This set the pattern for their future tugs which were normally around the 100 foot mark. Once again their tugs were deeply involved in seeking, coastal towage and in salvage. These London tugs operated over a wide range; the **Contest** managed to involve herself in a salvage operation off Swansea in 1899.The **Warrior** mentioned earlier was one of the larger tugs which seemed to spend most of its time away from home and keeps on cropping up in operations in various parts of the country. In 1901 she was hired to tow the ship *Superb* from Gibraltar to Middlesbrough (although she was not classed as a deep sea tug) for a fee of £700 on a no cure, no pay basis, with the added rider that there was to be no salvage charge. The *Superb* was unseaworthy but her owners were making sure that whatever happened they would not be the losers. Things were so bad that the tug had to take her into Vigo for essential repairs which involved a delay of 21 days, but she was not paid demurrage, as it was claimed she had to go in anyway for coal. In 1903 she was up at Sunderland helping four local paddle tugs which were having a hard job with the salvage of the *D.H.Watjen.* In 1904 she towed the ship *Bay of Biscay* from the Eddystone Light round the coast to Leith having picked her up at midnight on the 24th July and arriving Leith at 7 a.m. on the 31st. She had had a bad time on the journey and had broken two 13" hawsers, one of which was brand new.

The **Contest** shown in the plan is the last of the steam tugs to join their fleet (51), surviving until 1972. She was built by A. Hall of Aberdeen (213 tons gross. 1150 i.h.p.) in 1933 to replace a similar tug built in 1931 and sold the following year to Italian owners. In plan she shows the typical elliptical Hall stern and two unusual deck details; the skylight aft which was elongated athwartships, and the anchor windlass with the warping drums set wide apart each with its own bearing pedestal. The main towing hooks were set side by side, each on its own pivot rather than on a common rail and on the after end of the engine casing was another hook position for towing barges close up to the stern. The mainmast was set so far back on the boat deck that special brackets had to be provided for the stays, but the brackets also served as rope stops. The wheel was open as was common practice on the Thames ship-handling tugs of the period and it is interesting to note the doubling of the planking in front of the wheel carried right to the wings of the bridge to safeguard against wear. There was generally a lot of walking from side to side during a complicated docking manoeuvre.

Apart from the **Oceana** which is described in the chapter on ocean-going tugs, the London owners did not go in for big screw tugs for deep sea work. With the volume of shipping arriving in the Thames they had their hands full and the medium sized screw tugs were adequate for towing sailing ships from anywhere in the English Channel. They made do with the tugs they had and sent them coastwise as required. It is interesting to compare the different approach of the Liverpool and Glasgow owners. The average London shiphandling screw tug remained around 90 foot to 110 foot in length with the beam and the draught increasing slowly as more powerful engines were installed, with a resultant rise in the gross tonnage.

1883	**Tasmania**	80.0 ft. x 16.6 ft.	Ratio Length/Breadth	4.82	81 tons
1888	**Mercia**	85.8 ft. x 18.1 ft.	Ratio Length/Breadth	4.72	94 tons
1909	**Badia**	96.2 ft.x 20.6 ft.	Ratio Length/Breadth	4.67	150 tons
1927	**Gondia**	100.0 ft. x 25.1 ft.	Ratio Length/Breadth	3.98	200 tons
1943	**Napia**	105.8 ft. x 30.1ft.	Ratio Length/Breadth	3.51	261 tons

(52) *The **Sun IV** was built by Earles of Hull in 1915 for W.H.J. Alexander of London. (105.0' x 25.5' x 12.4', 200 gross, 80 n.h.p.)*

53

***Canute** of the 'Red Funnel Fleet' was built in 1923 by J.I. Thornycroft and worked in Southampton until 1965 when she was sold to Greek owners.*

W.H.J. Alexander's **Sun** tugs were always very smart in appearance and had a jaunty look about them. The **Sun IV** was one of their larger tugs which they used for ship handling (they also maintained a fleet of smaller tugs to handle the Thames lighters). Her bridge deck was built up above the level of the boiler casing giving the skipper a clear view aft over the top of the lifeboats. She had towing bows over the engine casing but none between the two bulwarks. Very prominent were the two stove chimneys; even in the 1950s diesel tugs sometimes had them (52).

Except for dock work, undertaken mainly by the Port of London Authority, twin-screw tugs were seldom used on the Thames. Each dock system in London owned its own fleet of tugs, but until the arrival of the twin screw tug **Hotspur** (143) in 1897 the ship-handling work in the docks had been carrried out by big iron paddle tugs. The numerous screw tugs which were to be found in London's dockland were small vessels between 50 and 70 ft. long similar to the craft tugs which worked on the river itself. The new twin screw tugs which rapidly replaced the old paddle tugs from 1897 onwards had powerful engine installations totalling from 800 to 1000 i.h.p., quite a power to pack into the still quite narrow hulls. The twin screw arrangement was adopted because of the extra manoeuvrability which it afforded for working in the narrow confines of the docks. A feature common to many of these tugs was the raised deck amidship in way of the casing, sometimes with an open rail (**Hotspur** 143), sometimes with the bulwarks raised. Although the **Hotspur** was 109.5 ft long, the later tugs were smaller, the twin-screw tugs being 86 to 90 ft., while the single-screw tugs which were used in connection with the dredging plant were around 90 to 96 ft. long.

In the south-east corner of England the major port was Dover just round the corner from the notorious Goodwin Sands. The tugs which worked out of Dover had to be capable of providing salvage facilities for casualties on that death-trap under all weather conditions and the tugs had to be big and powerful. When the first screw tug arrived in Dover she was just such a vessel; the **Lady Curzon** (1904, 120.2 ft. 253 tons. 138 n.h.p.). She and the other large tugs which followed were kept busy earning considerable awards for their services. The **Lady Brassey** (1913, 130.1 ft. 362 tons. 1600 i.h.p.) illustrated in the photograph as performing a somewhat more menial task, towing an empty hopper back from the dumping ground (48). The two funnels made her look rather larger than she really was and their close spacing spoilt her appearance. This was quite a common fault with most of the early two funnelled tugs. In one case the after funnel served a donkey boiler for the salvage pump and again made the tug look large, while she was in fact only 100.0 ft. long (**Moonfleet** 1918, 145 tons. 92 n.h.p.); on the **Lady Brassey** the full width wheelhouse is unusual for a tug, but she was also a tender and had a raised landing platform forward of the funnels. She was hired by the Admiralty in both world wars and among her salvage jobs was the rescue of the *Surrey* in 1915 when she and her near sister **Lady Crundall** (1906. 130.0 ft. 366 tons. 275 n.h.p.) had to enter the very minefield which had damaged the *Surrey*.

Southampton saw the arrival of the screw tug in 1851 when the P. & O's **Mary** (1851. 78 ft. 25 tons. 12 n.h.p.) was the first vessel to enter the new inner dock. With that size and power the **Mary** was little more than a large steam launch rather than a true tug. The **Alexandra** (1876, 110.0 ft 120 tons. 60 n.h.p.) set the pattern for the fairly large screw tugs which were to be the mainstay of the port's towing fleets. In 1890 even larger tugs arrived on the scene starting with the **Hercules** (1890. 135'5". 316 tons. 1200 i.h.p.), big tugs capable of handling the large ocean liners which were now using the port and designed to carry the passengers and their luggage when called on. The **Canute** (1923, 111.5 ft. 271 tons. 1200 i.h.p.) shows a typical twin screw tug from the "Red Funnel Fleet". Two features to note are the raised bridge with wings reaching to the breadth of the vessel and the way in which brackets had been fitted to carry the foot of the quadrant type davits rather than have the boat deck extended to the full beam. This helped to keep the boats inboard where they were less exposed to damage when coming alongside liners (53).The very square stern was a feature of these tugs. At the same time there were always small tugs working in the waters around Southampton and among the earliest examples of these was the **Beaulieu** (1901, 70.0 ft. 58 tons. 35 n.h.p.) and a second-hand tug, the **Ada** (1885, 55.0 ft. 22 tons. 14 n.h.p.). R.E.V. James (James Dredging, Towage and Transport Co. Ltd.) began to order new tugs in 1924, firstly from Holland and then from A. Hall of Aberdeen, but these tugs were generally sold within the year. Among these tugs all prefixed **Foremost** was the **Battleaxe** (154) ex. **Foremost 43.**

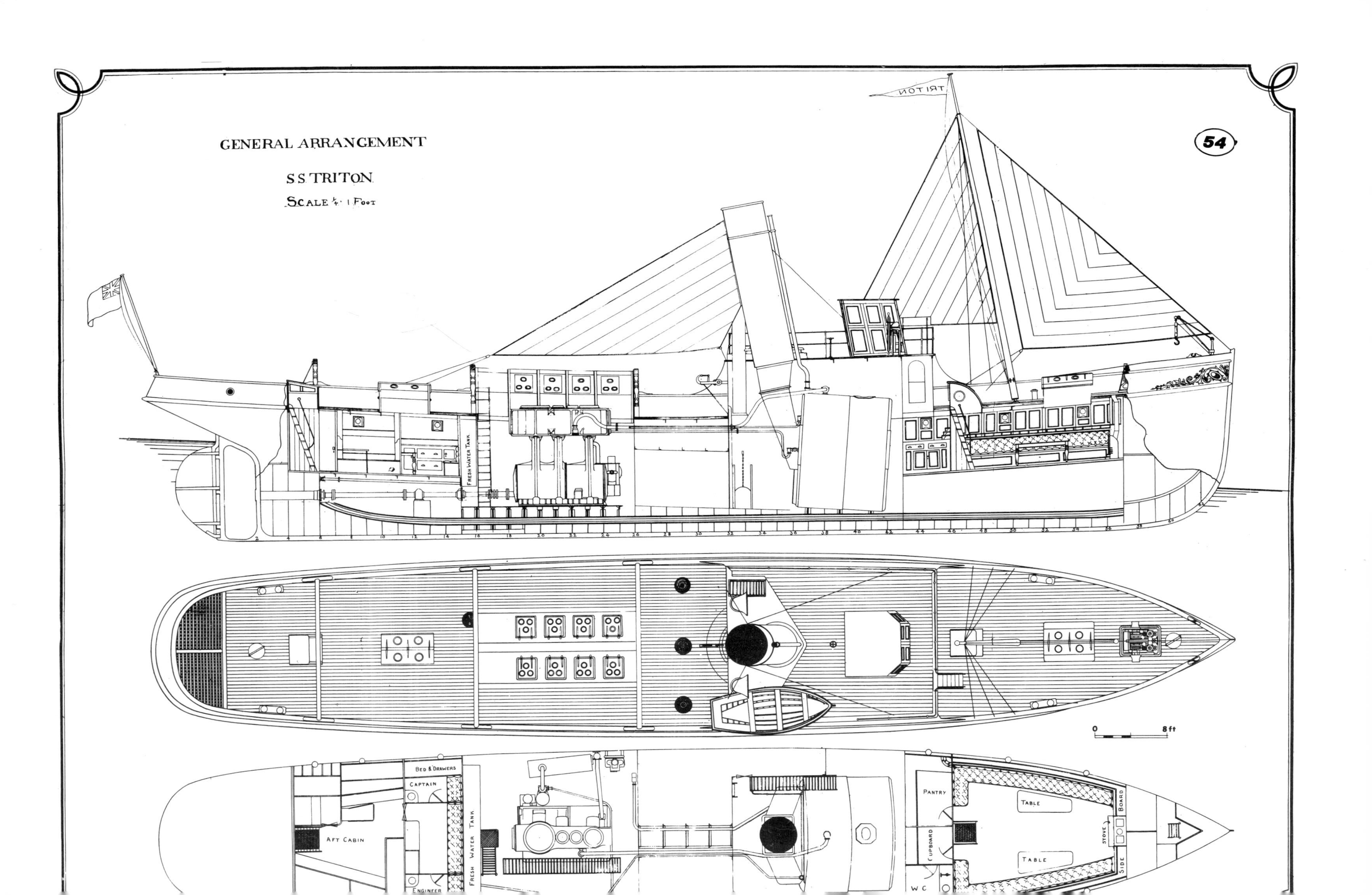
GENERAL ARRANGEMENT
S.S. TRITON
SCALE ¼" : 1 FOOT
54
TRITON
FRESH WATER TANK
0
8 ft
BED & DRAWERS
CAPTAIN
AFT CABIN
ENGINEER
FRESH WATER TANK
PANTRY
CUPBOARD
W C
TABLE
TABLE
STOVE
SIDE
BOARD

Southwest England

In this area the ports were small and the trade was mostly coastal with cargoes carried by schooners and ketches. Their owners had a hard enough time making ends meet without paying for towage and so their captains usually managed without the services of a tug. The first screw tug in Falmouth was the **Briton** (1861, 79.8 ft. 139 tons. 60 n.h.p.) and she was followed by many others which in the main were of a small size. Many of them were neat looking vessels with the appearance more of a steam yacht than of a tug, with an elegant counter stern.

The **Busy Bee** is a delightful name for a tug and the picture shows a dainty vessel(189), almost too yachtlike, and yet she had iron hoop towing beams and a hook on a little framework bolted to the casing. Between the mast and the bridge was a companionway cum skylight, the sides of which were made of glass protected with closely spaced brass rods. She was built at Falmouth in 1889, only a mere 25 tons. Around 1900 she was sold from the South coast to owners in Birkenhead. Most of the tugs did not remain in the area for long, finding ready buyers in all parts of the country. Falmouth was an excellent anchorage and was used as a port of call for sailing ships looking for 'orders', that is instructions regarding the destination of their cargoes which was frequently decided while they were still at sea. The 'seeking' tugs from London and Liverpool were in the habit of looking in while passing and even the odd Glasgow tug might be found there on the off-chance of picking up a tow. The coastline of Cornwall was a rocky one and in bad weather ships were glad of assistance when caught on a lee shore and there was plenty of opportunity for salvage. When the weather was bad the small local tugs were not sufficiently seaworthy or powerful to render assistance and reliance had to be placed on outsiders. In 1901 the barque *Albatross* got into trouble off Falmouth but lying in Falmouth was the big Liverpool paddle tug **Pathfinder** which had called in for shelter while on a voyage from Liverpool to Vigo to bring back a disabled steamer. The **Pathfinder** carried out a successful salvage and collected an award of £700.

It was evident that if local tugs were to compete in salvage jobs in foul weather, then larger more powerful vessels would be required, and these began to appear in the 1880s, tugs such as the **Briton** (1880. 84.8 ft. 66 tons. 46 n.h.p.). This may not sound large but she was big compared to the 24/30 ton tugs in service at the time. By 1900 the **Triton** was the largest tug in the area and was a vessel which featured in many salvage cases although a lot of them involved the rescue of ships which had run aground in calm conditions in the mists and fogs which plagued the area.

Like the **Conqueror** of Swansea (57) the **Triton** had a low profile giving a false impression of her size; although she was 114 feet long her beam was only 20.7 feet(54). She had a sloping wheelhouse which matched the rake of the mast and funnel, all to give the impression of speed. Note the elegant bow decoration, and the full suit of sails which the tugs of the period frequently carried. She was nicely fitted out with her comfortable saloon forward with all its upholstery and the turned wooden legs which support the towing bows. It is unusual to find a gap between the two casings down to deck level. It was more common to continue the engine casing through, giving more headroom in the cross bunker. She was built in 1900 by Cox & Co. of Falmouth with a tonnage of 173 and engines for 99 n.h.p. She was originally employed by Falmouth Towage Co. and went to Bristol (Commonwealth Steam Tug Co.) in 1936. The **Triton** was taken over by the Admiralty in 1918 and for a year was known under the name of **Plunger.**

An incident of the kind which got tug skippers a bad name occurred in 1916 when the four-masted barque *Medway* arrived off Falmouth to await further orders. As she approached the harbour the wind fell away and she was in danger of drifting ashore. The tug **Triton** came out to her about two miles from the harbour entrance and demanded an exhorbitant fee of £40 to tow her in, a demand which the ship's captain had no alternative but to accept or drive ashore.

Following the First World War larger tugs joined the local fleets but they were mainly second-hand tonnage. One or two of these are worth mentioning, tugs such as the **Tactful** (1909, 75.2 ft. 112 tons. ? n.h.p.), built originally for Canadian owners and having the long central superstructure associated with the American tugs. Another tug of similar appearance was the **Helen Peele** used by the Royal National Lifeboat Institution for towing their pulling lifeboat at Padstow. The **Helen Peele** was involved in a salvage case off Newquay in 1902 together with two Falmouth tugs and after giving assistance to the ship, the **Helen Peele** was asked to tow her to Cardiff, thus performing her function as a true tug. (See plate 6, and pages 147-149).

Bristol Channel

In the Bristol Channel area the main ports were Bristol, Cardiff and Swansea. Lying at the end of the narrow winding Avon Gorge, Bristol attracted the smaller size of ship and so when the screw tugs appeared they too were small, the **Merrimac** (1859, 45.7 ft. 11 tons. 14 n.h.p.) was constructed of wood and was C.J. King's first tug. Bristol Steam Navigation Co. responded with the iron screw tug **Alarm** (1862, 59.3 ft. 22 tons. 24 n.h.p.). These early screw tugs were very basic with the boiler sticking up through the deck, a small casing over the engine and the wheel completely open in front of the funnel. Despite their size these little tugs were sent 'seeking' in the Bristol Channel. Occasionally they managed a piece of salvage but they seem to have been in collision themselves at frequent intervals. The **Sea King** (1875, 45 tons. 25 n.h.p.) had quite a record; 1892 collided with the light vessel on the English and Welsh Grounds, 1898 in collision with the *Britannia* in

Sea King *(68.4 x 13.0 x 7.8 feet, 45 tons, 25 n.h.p.) belonged to C.J. King of Bristol where she was built in 1875.*

the Avon, 1899 in collision with the *Talbot* in the Avon, in 1903 sank after colliding with the hopper *Frome* while 'seeking' in the Bristol Channel. The **Sea King** is shown in what was not an uncommon situation in the River Avon with its shelving mud banks. Her decks look bare, the wheel was open and in this case in front of the mast (not usual), the casings were low and the rope cradle filled almost all the open area of the deck. The anchor hanging at her bow looks almost too large for the size of tug (56).

The River Avon saw plenty of accidents. In 1913 the steamer **Hero** ran ashore in the fog and refloated herself, in the process running into the tug **Volunteer** (1875, 54.0 ft. 24 tons. 16 n.h.p.) and the steamer *Clifton*. The **Volunteer** which had been going to the assistance of the **Hero** was so badly damaged that she sank at once and the *Clifton* was only saved from a like fate by being run aground. This was the second time the **Volunteer** had been sunk, she had capsized and sunk in calm weather off Sharpness Pier in 1901.

In the South Wales ports where there was considerable coming and going of big sailing ships laden with coal and ore, there was a need for big tugs to handle them. The Cardiff Steam Towing Company tug **Iron Duke** (1857, 108.3 ft. 140 tons. 38 n.h.p.) was followed by a smaller tug the **Lady Bute** (1857, 76.4 ft. 67 tons. 45 n.h.p.), a wooden screw vessel. In 1866 Young of Cardiff built the **Lanercost** (111.7 ft. 132 tons. 70 n.h.p.) The Welsh ports were frequently named as ports of call for sailing ships in tow of big deep sea and coastal tugs from Liverpool and Glasgow and it was not unusual to find these assisting local tugs whose low power had prevented them from completing a salvage. In 1900 the **Flying Eagle** (1890, 145.0 ft. 393 tons. 650 i.h.p.) arrived off Cardiff with the ship *Pinmore* which she had towed from Hamburg. As the weather was bad the ship anchored and the tug went into Cardiff. The weather grew worse and the ship's anchors began to drag so the local tug **Bantam Cock** (1882, 75.8 ft. 70 tons. 40 n.h.p.) took her in tow but was quite unable to hold her. Fortunately the **Flying Eagle** returned and took the *Pinmore* safely in tow. Shortly after, another ship the *Zinita* was towing out of Cardiff behind the **Flying Serpent** (1886, 134.9 ft. 262 tons. 98 n.h.p.) when an explosion occurred aboard the ship followed by clouds of smoke. Nearby was the **Nelson** of Cardiff (1882, 58.4 ft. 26 tons. 35 n.h.p. 250 i.h.p.), which, despite her small size was equipped with a Worthington fire pump and a fire hose, giving 2700 gallons of water per hour. She immediately closed with the *Zinita*, put her hose aboard and started to pump water into her hold. For some strange reason the crew of the *Zinita* tried to resist the efforts to help and a minor skirmish ensued. At the subsequent enquiry it transpired that despite the explosion there had been no fire aboard the *Zinitia* and all that the **Nelson** had succeeded in doing was to spoil several tons of cargo. However, the claim for salvage and the counter-claim for water damage were both dismissed.

The **Prairie Flower** was built at Falmouth in 1883 for J.H. Dunn of Cardiff (56) and shows the typical small tug in use in South Wales ports. The superstructure was minimal with very low casings. She had bitts on the foredeck supporting the old hand windlass but just aft there was a cargo winch and even more peculiar was the stockless anchor suspended over the bows. It looks as though her owners had equipped her for salvage work. Indeed her last owners were J. Davies Towage and Salvage Ltd. She had a very nice cast scroll round the original hawse hole.

Prairie Flower *built 1883 for J.H. Dunn, Cardiff (76.1 x 15.4 x 9.1 feet, 64 tons). Sank in 1919 off Cardiff.*

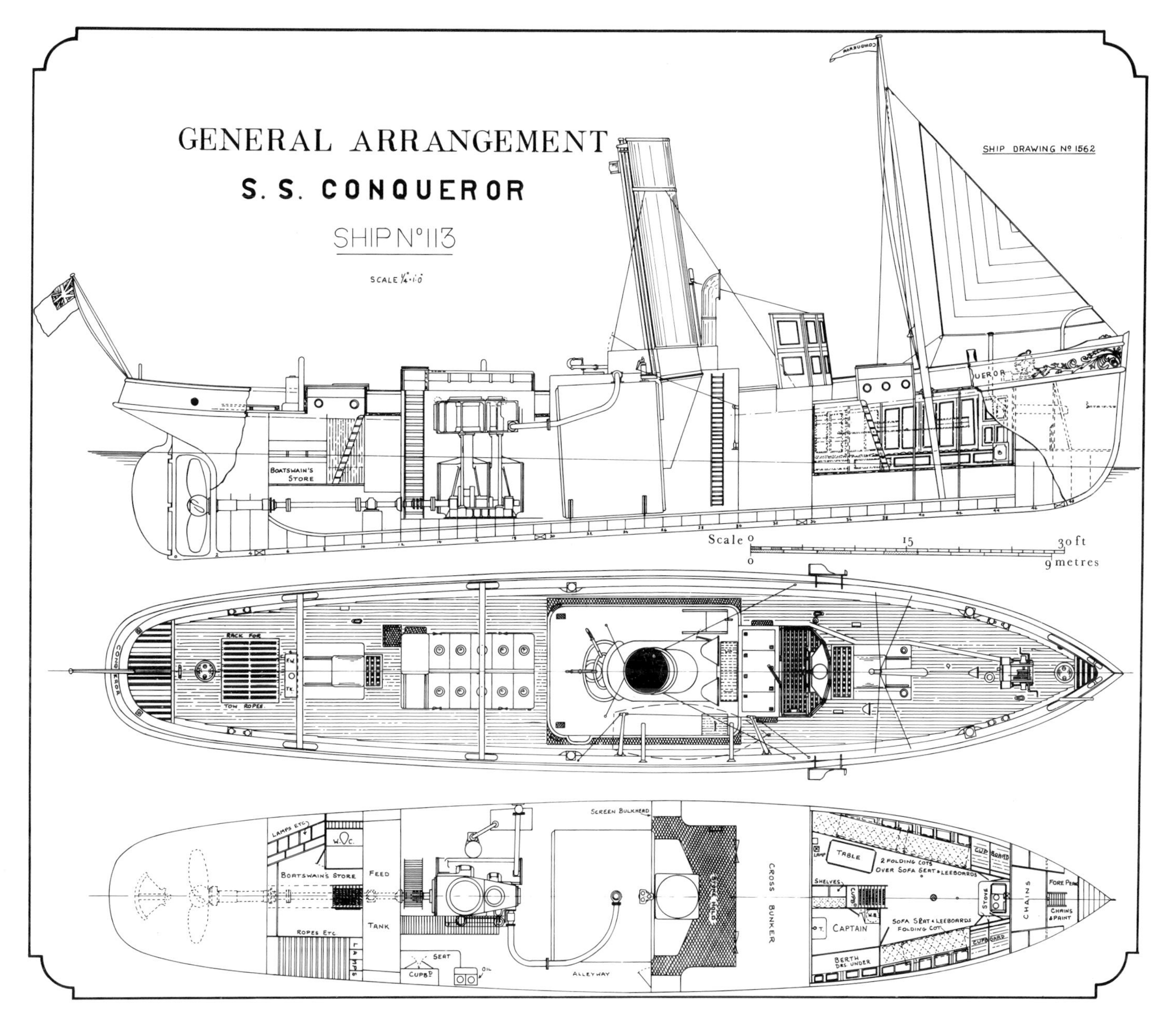

57 *The* ***Conqueror*** *was built in 1905 by Cox of Falmouth for the Steam Tug Conqueror Co. Ltd. (William Jones, Managing owner). Her dimensions were 90.4 x 17.9 x 9.8 feet, 102 gross tons, 75 n.h.p.)*

In 1885 a big new tug was built for Cardiff, the **Red Rose** (115.5 ft. 215 tons. 99 n.h.p.) but within a year she had been sold to London owners. Other big tugs came and went within a few years; large tugs just did not seem to fit that area. The **Furet** (1890, 111.5 ft. 135 tons. 53 n.h.p.) sold 1895, **The Rose** (1889, 100.7 ft. 142 tons. n.h.p.) bought 1903, sold 1906.

At first the **Conqueror** looks to be quite a small (57), but she was 90 feet long, although she was narrow and shallow. Her boiler casing was small and low and even the wheelhouse was only raised the height of the bulwarks (note how it slopes back, a very common feature on the early screw tugs). The coaling hatch was placed between the bridge and the funnel but this was not as obvious as it was on the **Flying Eagle** (67). She had a beautiful cast bow scroll around the hawse-pipe, an ornamental feature which was still being fitted in the early 1920s. Built in 1905 and of 75 n.h.p. (500 i.h.p) she was owned by The Steam Tug Conqueror Ltd. of Swansea. This mode of title was frequently used and sometimes each tug in a fleet would have its own registered company. She was sold in 1920 to France Fenwick Tyne & Wear Co. of Sunderland and renamed **Criccieth** in 1922. Although comparatively small, she had her fair share of salvage awards while working out of Swansea.

The Welsh tugs were often found 'dodging', another word for 'seeking', a word which aptly describes the methods used to avoid the attentions of other tugs; in 1896 the **Britannia** of Swansea (1894, 80.1 ft. 63 tons. 36 n.h.p.) and the **Cruiser** (1881, 76.3 ft. 58 tons. 40 n.h.p.) were both caught sailing without navigation lights, a favourite trick which had its dangers.

After the First World War tugs of larger tonnage were purchased secondhand to provide the greater towing power required to meet the needs of the shipping now using the ports. The need for speed ended when owners began to fix towage contracts from an office desk. The call now was to provide a more economical service by using fewer tugs of greater power. Shipowners had long ago become disenchanted about paying for the services of several tugs.

England, West Coast

In Liverpool some screw vessels went into service quite early on, the **Victoria** (1855, 92.0 ft. 89 tons. 30 n.h.p.) which might not have been a tug, and the **Maggie Lauder** (1863, 90.4 ft. 130 tons. 60 n.h.p.) which was a tug. There is however no indication of their appearance or the type of work on which they were employed. The majority of the screw tugs used on the Mersey were the big deep sea vessels described in the chapter on ocean towing, tugs which appeared from 1877 onwards. There was however, traffic in Liverpool with barges and coastal sail, and a few small tugs were employed here, such as the **Bantam Cock** (1878, 68 ft. 36 tons), the wooden **Seagull** (1871, 66.7 ft. 30 tons. 21 n.h.p.) and the wooden **Estella** (1866, 54.6 ft. 28 tons. 16 n.h.p.) It is almost laughable to read the advertisement in 1900 when the "well known and powerful iron screw tug **Bantam Cock**" was offered for sale, while in the next line she is described as "too small for her owners' requirements."

As ships became more reliable and the call for deep sea tugs fell off, the number of big tugs built for Liverpool decreased. Engines were also becoming more efficient giving the same power from a smaller plant. As a result more tugs around 90 ft. to 100 ft. in length joined the fleets on the river, concerned now with towing ships within the confines of the Mersey itself. G.B. Cowl bought tugs from the Clyde - **Clyde, Tay, Forth** and **Narwhal,** which are described later, tugs which formed the nucleus of the Alexandra Towing Co. The Liverpool Screw Towing and Lighterage Co. also built small tugs like the **Woodcock** (1884, 64.6 ft. 32 tons. 18 n.h.p.), and bought secondhand larger boats such as the **Prairie Cock** (1884, 90.7 ft. 125 tons. 90 n.h.p.). Towing on the river was rather humdrum, but was not without its drama of collisions and sinkings. There were still opportunities for salvage though these happened mainly in the river itself. In 1897 the full rigged ship *Majestic* was entering Canning Dock in tow of the paddle tug **Pathfinder**, using a check rope to help her to turn. The rope broke, her anchor flukes fouled the lock gate, she swung round and there she was, jammed in the lock entrance. The paddle tugs **Reaper** (1869, 121 ft. 188 tons. 400 a.h.p.) **Great Britain** (76) (1876, 154.1 ft. 300 tons. 130 n.h.p.) and **Sea King** (1864, 133.3 ft. 207 tons. 500 i.h.p.) came up and put tow ropes aboard. They made an impressive array, but could not budge the *Majestic*. Things were getting desperate so the screw tugs joined in; the **Andrew Jolliffe** (1894, 102.0 ft. 180 tons. 600 e.h.p.) followed by the **Pea Cock** (1876, 80.4 ft. 75 tons. 70 n.h.p.), the **Sea Cock** (1877, 76.9 ft. 101 tons. 60 n.h.p.) and the **Weather Cock** (1885, 78.1 ft. 68 tons. 55 n.h.p.) Still nothing happened until the twin screw tug **Conqueror** (1879, 122.0 ft. 206 tons. 98 n.h.p.) threw her weight into the battle and the *Majestic* was pulled free. What a sight that must have been nine tugs close together in the approaches to the dock with smoke pouring from their funnels. The weather was fine, the risks taken small, apart from the risks of collisions in the melee, but the award was quite generous. Despite the fact that nine tugs were involved, the total horsepower available was only about 5000 i.h.p., 1200 of which was provided by the **Pathfinder.** Nowadays two motor tugs could produce as much, and with their Kort rudders the effective bollard pull would have been greater.

Although by the 1900s the screw tugs in the Mersey were medium sized they did occasionally range away from home. Indeed one of them, the **Clarence** (1904, 92.0 ft. 149 tons. ? n.h.p.) of the Alexandra Towing Co. was lost in the Irish Sea. In 1905 she towed the sailing ship *Marathon* as far as the Tuskar rock where she cast off the tow. That same night a strong gale sprang up and the tug **Clarence** vanished with her eleven man crew, an unusually large number for a tug of her size.

Most of the tug owners in the area followed the same pattern with some small tugs for lighterage work and larger ones for the shipping work. However, only the big companies built new tonnage, the rest bought secondhand. In the 1900s the ship tugs were quite slender vessels built with an eye on speed, their funnels were long and thin to achieve the natural draught to keep the boilers going at full output.

The **East Cock** was built by Cammell Laird & Co. of Birkenhead in 1909 for G.R. Nicholson (Liverpool Screw Towing Co.), a typical ship-towing tug for the Mersey (95.1 ft. 139 tons. 99 n.h.p).

East Cock *of Liverpool, working there from 1909 to 1960 when she was broken up.*

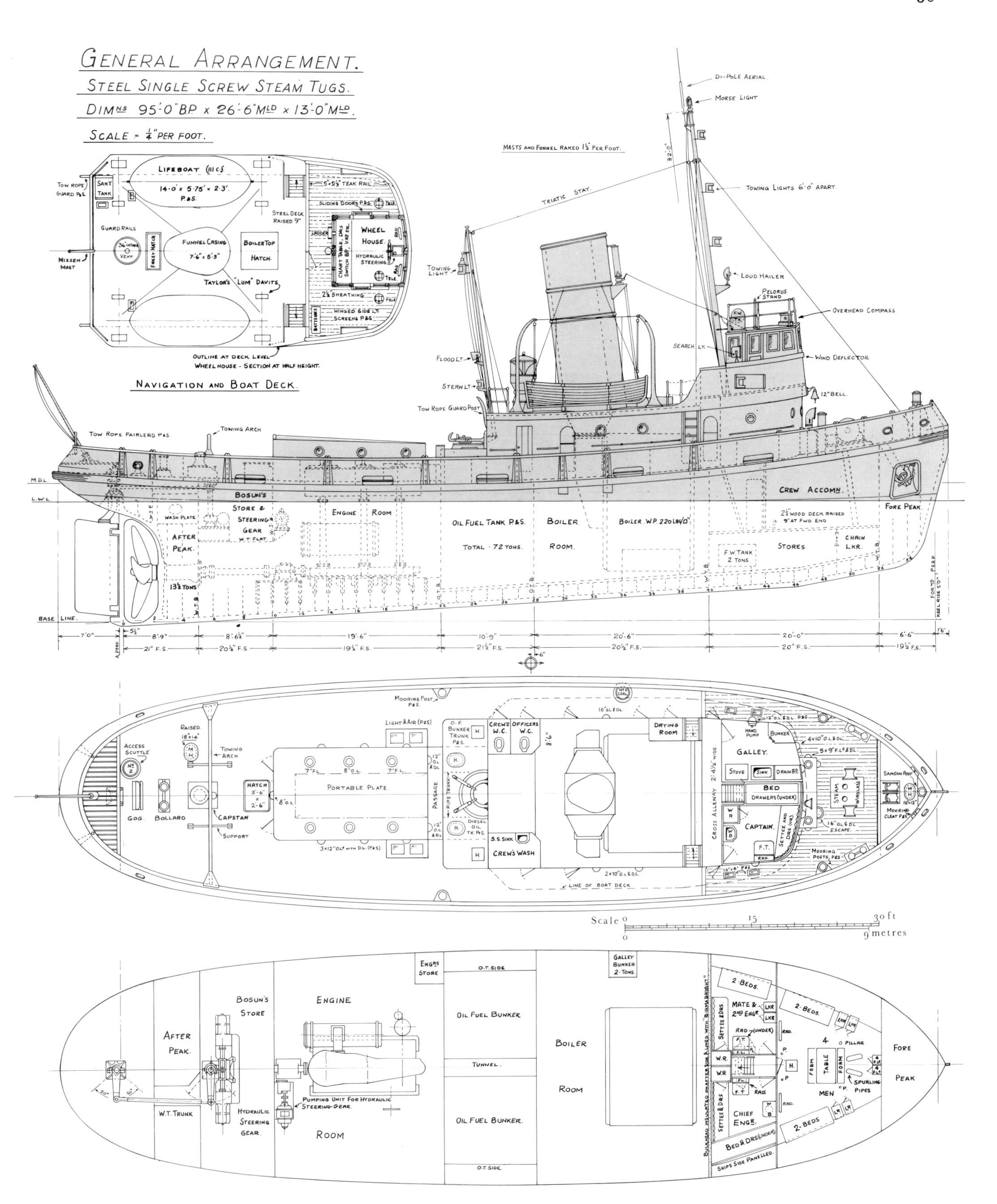

59 ***North Light*** *and* ***North Rock*** *were built in 1956 for the Alexandra Towing Co. Ltd., Liverpool. They were of 206 tons gross with an engine of 56 nominal horse-power (1000 indicated horse-power) by C.D. Holmes & Co. Ltd. of Hull.*

She had the usual row of stanchions supporting the overhang of the boat deck and even late in life still had an open wheel. On the after deck there was only a single towing bow and there was no capstan. The Mersey tugs were seldom fitted with one. The cowl top to the funnel was a feature of the 'Cock' tugs and if the photograph had only gone slightly higher the characteristic metal cock emblem on the top of the mast would have been evident (58).

Between the Wars the tugs had noticeably increased in beam and the funnels were of greater diameter. After the Second World War the funnels were not so high, as forced draught fans provided the air that was necessary to achieve good combustion. Another feature which distinguished the tugs of the 1940s from the earlier vessels was the absence of stanchions supporting the boat deck. All early tugs had either a row of stanchions or in some cases a rounded casing level with the wheelhouse. The later Rea tugs were unusual in the way that the space between the bulwarks and the boatdeck was sheeted in solid, with the expanse of metal broken by several portholes as in **Rosegarth**(153). The tugs of the Rea fleet were in great demand for jobs in Barrow and this fairing made them more seaworthy for the short but often stormy passage to Barrow.

The Mersey tugs were hard worked during the war and after the cessation of hostilities there was a general renewal of tonnage, still with steam tugs. However, the diesel engine was on its way, in the form of the **John Lamey** ex **Geertruida XV** ex **Lady Elizabeth** (1927, rebuilt and re-engined 1957, 94.6 ft. 165 tons) which had been converted after her purchase in 1956.

The **North Light** and the **North Rock** were among the last of the steam tugs to be built for Liverpool or for that matter any other port. About the only concession to modernity was the odd ventilator behind the funnel, oil firing and the close stowing anchor. There was a conspicuous lack of towing bows over the engine room but as most of their towing was carried out on a short tow rope rising at a steep angle to the tow, this lack of protection would raise little difficulty. They were built in Greenock by George Brown & Co. Ltd. for the Alexandra Towing Co. Ltd. of Liverpool in 1956 (59).

Next door to Liverpool is Manchester which had been connected to the River Mersey by its famous Ship Canal since 1894. The nucleus of the newly formed Manchester Ship Canal Company was a motley collection of old paddle tugs formerly owned by the Bridgewater Navigation Co. The new company immediately began a programme of replacement purchasing new tugs both paddle and screw, the screw tugs being medium sized vessels with a single screw, tugs such as the **Old Quay** (1907, 85.4 ft. 119 tons. 75 n.h.p.) After the First World War a number of secondhand ex-Government twin-screw H.S. tugs (129) were bought along with other single-screw tugs. In the 1930s four more single-screw steam tugs were built and these were followed in 1940 by the first of a long line of twin-screw diesel tugs. A number of the Ship Canal tugs were equipped with fire pumps and monitors to enable them to fight fires on board ships or in warehouses.

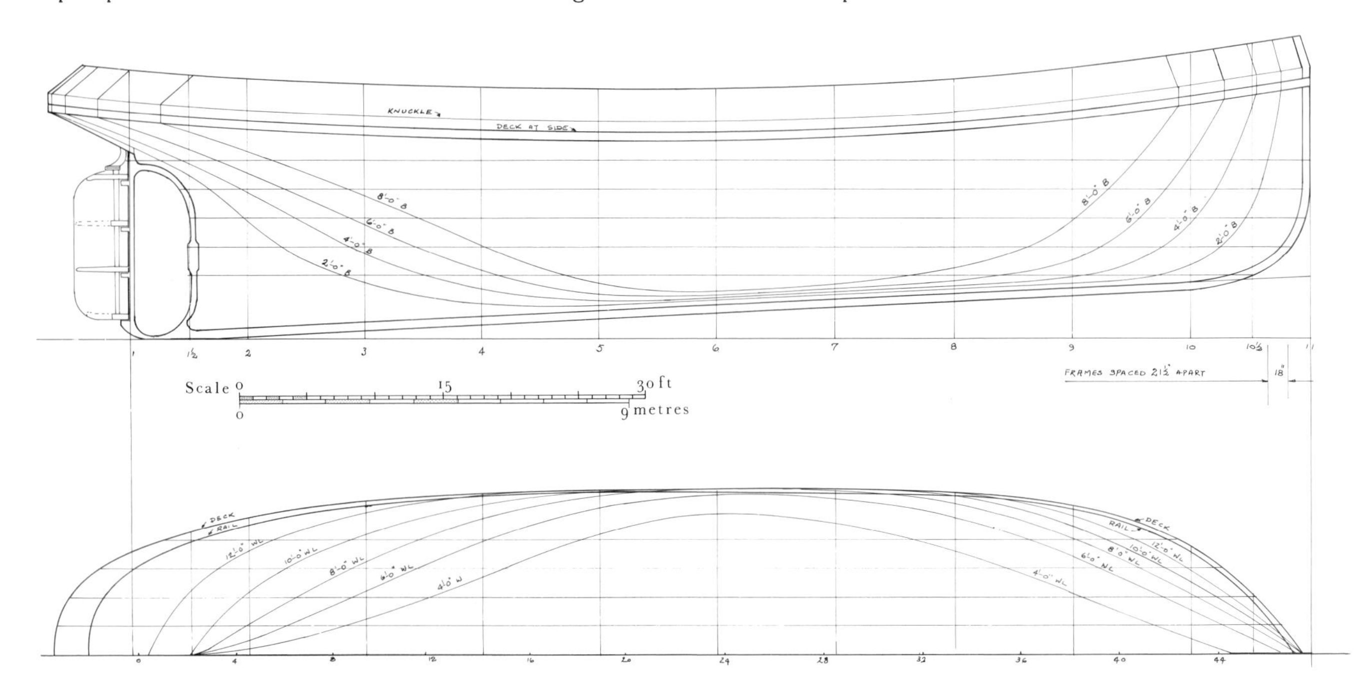

MSC ARROW

Nº 266

DIMNS 86'0" 23'0" 12'0" mld

SCALE ¼" = 1 FOOT

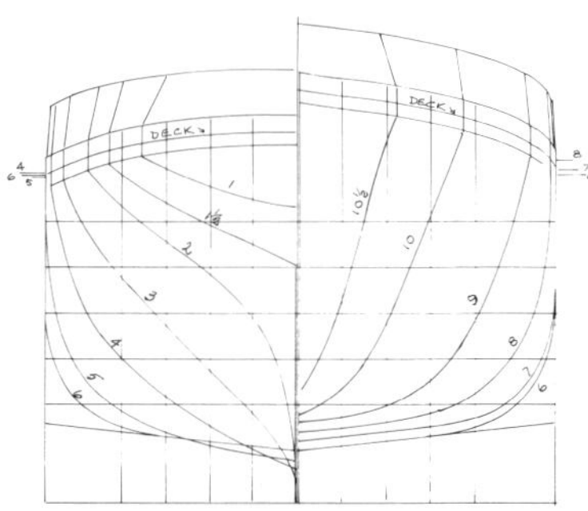

61

M.S.C. **Badger**, *built 1939 for the Manchester Ship Canal Co.*

The M.S.C. **Badger** (61) had on her foredeck the cruciform bollard peculiar to the Manchester Ship Canal tugs and the occasional Tyne tug. Not built for speed the hull was bluff and stubby, her length/breadth ratio very low: 3.7. Working in a canal she was not required to carry lifeboats and there was no overhanging boatdeck. The square vents look a bit odd and may not be original. The tug was built by Henry Robb of Leith in 1939. (85.0 ft. 144 tons. 850 i.h.p.) When this photograph was taken she and a motor tug had just laid the tow across the corner of a dock which acted as a fulcrum while they canted her. Here the **Badger** was making a fine adjustment to the position of the tow by going astern and giving the ship a nudge with her well padded stern. For the lines of the M.S.C. **Badger** see the plan of the M.S.C. **Arrow** (60) which was built to the same plans. Although the M.S.C. **Arrow** was built for canal work it was a ship canal and it is hardly surprising that her general lines were those of a normal ship-handling tug. A fairly beamy hull with not much rise of floor and with a moderate radius to her bilges.

One of the 'oddities' on the canal was the **Clarendon** built 1909 as the **J.O. Gravel** for Canadian owners (94.5 ft. 197 tons. 54 n.h.p.). She looked quite out of place with her long American type superstructure. She was purchased specially for towing silt laden barges belonging to the canal's dredging department out to the dumping grounds off Hoylake. Even in the Ship Canal there were moments of excitement which in one case involved a considerable number of tugs. In 1900 the steamer *Sidney Thomas* was leaving Eastham Locks and her steering failed. She sheered hard to port and ran aground at speed. The lockmaster at once sent out six canal tugs to assist: **Eastham** (1899) 80.3 ft. 103 tons. 460 a.h.p. Value £4,500, **Partington** (1899) 80.3 ft. 103 tons. 460 a.h.p. Value £4,500, **Mercia** (1888) 85.8 ft. 94 tons. 330 a.h.p. Value £4,500, **Agnes Seed** (1892) 86.1 ft. 93 tons. 300 a.h.p. Value £2,700, **Pomona** (1896) 86.0 ft. 99 tons. 250 a.h.p. Value £4,500, I.P.T. **Gower** (1868) 119.8 ft. 145 tons. 350 a.h.p. Value £3,100.

After numerous towropes had broken it became evident that, with the tide falling, nothing more could be achieved for the moment. The next day the big paddle tug **Pathfinder** (which features in many Mersey salvage jobs) arrived and offered her assistance which was refused at the time, but accepted four hours later. The paddle tug **Sea King** was also asked to assist and she and the **Pathfinder** together with the **Eastham, Partington** and **Mercia** pulled the steamer off. In court the owners claimed that their vessel was never at any time in danger, and although she was badly placed her hull would never have broken, and that as her own engines were still operational she would have got herself off. The Court did not share their optimistic view and awarded a total of £1,700.

It possibly surprises some people that Preston had been a port in its own right for many years, busy enough to warrant its own tug fleet. The first screw tug was introduced in 1896, the twin screw **Perseverance** (120.8 ft. 212 tons. 98 n.h.p.) and apart from the **Energy** (79 tons, 48 n.h.p.), the tugs were quite large in size. The early tugs were quite sleek and looked as though they had a fair turn of speed.

The **Energy** of Preston was not a large tug (81.1 ft. x 17.2 ft. x 8.6 ft.) though in the photo (61)

Energy, *built in 1899 by Allsup & Co, Preston for Preston Corporation. She was sold in 1927 to Workington Harbour & Dock Board.*
PHOTO: John Clarkson.

she looks bigger. Her hull has very slender lines; see the way she cuts through the water instead of pushing up a huge bow wave. Her casings had been kept low and her bearded captain stands in a low wheel shelter balanced on the front end of the boiler casing. Unlike most tugs her anchor was kept lashed on the bulwarks at the bow ready for dropping, in fact the stock was not even designed for folding.

Scotland

On the Clyde the Screw Tug Company was formed in 1874 with the first of four twin screw tugs, the **Clyde** (1874), **Forth** and **Tay** (1875) and the **Tweed** (1877, 87.7 ft. 88 tons. 75 n.h.p.). The **Clyde** was a queer looking craft with her rounded ends, together with propellers and rudders at each end (67). Two boilers had to be fitted to leave room for the central propeller shaft and only a narrow casing was needed over the steam collecting cylinder. The high panelled casing over the engine gave her an odd profile. The original drawing was incomplete but it looks as though she had only a single hook and towing bow at the 'stern', while forward there were twin posts as if for the old fashioned hand wound anchor windlass. As with most Victorian innovations a lot of thought had gone into the design of the **Clyde.** It was generally agreed that a shallow draughted twin-screw tug did not perform as well as a single-screw tug with a large deeply immersed propeller. The **Clyde** had a relatively shallow hull to cut down her displacement and therefore the power required to drive her, but the keel was deepened at the stem and stern frames to allow a large diameter screw to be used, immersed deeply for efficient operation. Experiments had been carried out by other inventors with vessels of similar design which had showed that the pulling power of the bow propeller was greater than the pushing power of the one at the stern. It was claimed,

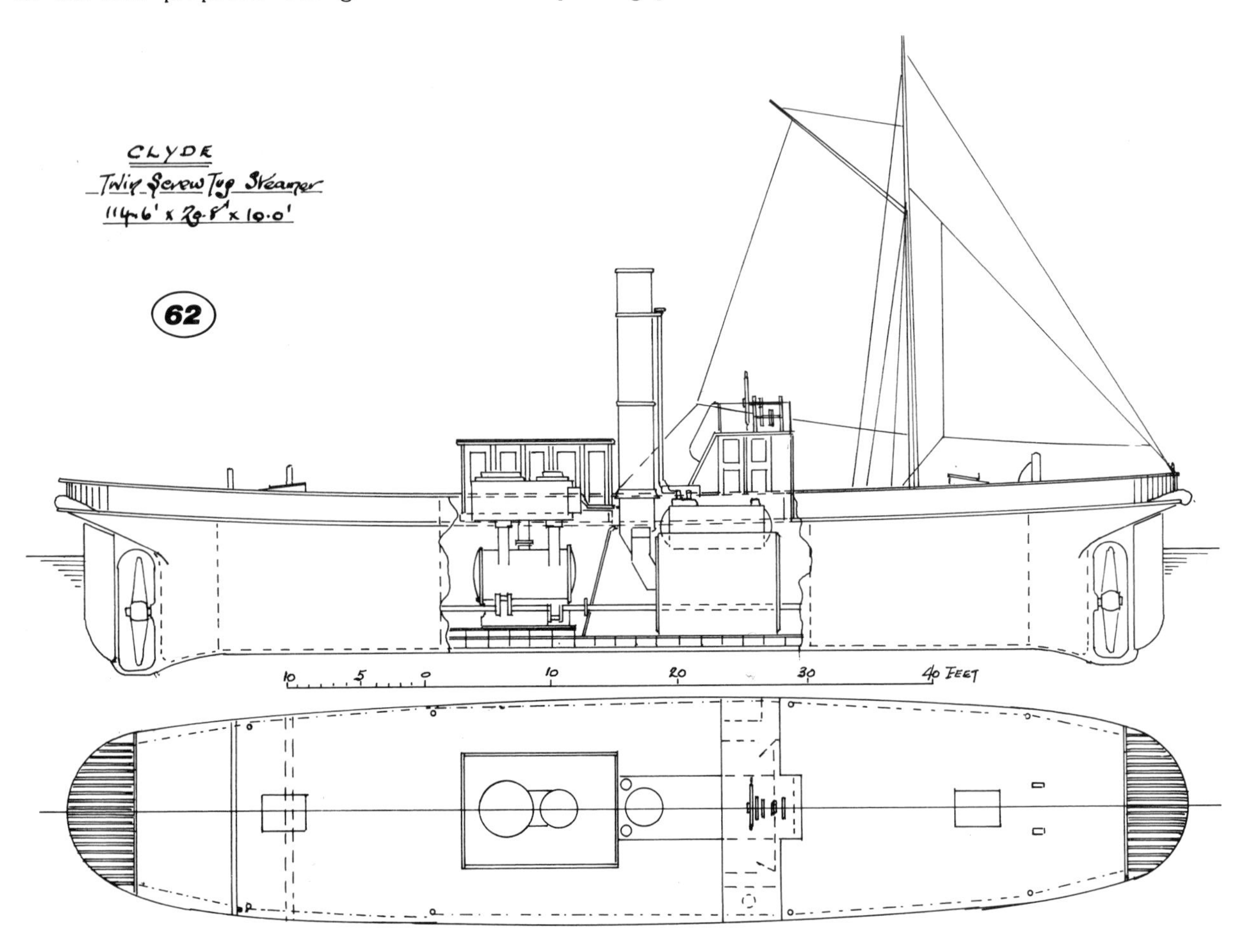

though not proved by dynamometer tests, that with the two screws working together, almost twice the 'pulling power' (i.e. bollard pull) would be available from the engine, compared with a conventional tug of the same power. The **Tay, Forth** and **Tweed** were also fitted with a screw at each end but they had bows of almost normal design with an extended fender to protect the propeller. The directors of Screw Tug Company were delighted with the performance of their tugs and would have ordered more, but they were bought over by the Clyde Shipping Company who apparently did not share their enthusiasm and sold the tugs to Liverpool owners shortly after for £13,000.

On the Clyde there were extensive 'timber ponds' where logs were stored to season, drying out at low tide, floating at high tide, penned in by thousands of stakes driven into the sand or mud. When timber was required the logs were made up into rafts and towed to the shipyards. In 1876 the first twin-screw aft tug was put into service by Laird of Port Glasgow to undertake the towage of the timber rafts. The tug, the **Otter** (80.0 ft. 61 tons. 25 n.h.p.) was followed by the **Seal** in 1877 and the **Narwhal** in 1878. The tugs were also bought by the Clyde Shipping Company in 1880 and disposed of before six years had passed as they were too small and underpowered for shipping work. From then on the towing of the rafts was taken over by a miscellaneous collection of old paddle tugs and converted steam yachts.

63

The **Huskisson** (right) is obviously an elderly tug with her tall funnel and the stanchions supporting the boat deck. She was built by J. Crichton of Chester in 1934, 103'0" o.a., 201 tons, 1000 i.h.p. and she still has an open bridge at the late date when this picture was taken. The application of the 'gogrope' or 'bridle' can be seen clearly.

The **Formby** (below) was a late addition to the fleet of Alexandra Towing Co. of Liverpool built 1951 by Cochrane of Selby (108'10" o.a., 237 tons, 1200 i.h.p.), replacing the **Formby** of 1905. She is somewhat similar to the **North Light** (59) but still has open rails round the boat deck. The enclosed flying bridge was not often seen outside Liverpool.

The **Sylvia** was typical of the converted steam yacht, built 1882, she was quite large (80.6 ft. x 16.0 ft. x 7.2 ft., 56 tons) but had an engine of a mere 15 n.h.p., just enough for the towing of the timber rafts. She retained her general appearance of a yacht with the addition of the hook and the towing bow (65). The hook was at the after end of the engine casing which was in fact not all that far aft. Four samson posts were added along the bulwarks as on a normal tug.

The first single screw tug was the **Flying Foam** (1877, 109.2 ft. 126 tons, 70 n.h.p) for the Clyde Shipping Company's fleet. She was an odd looking vessel with the steering wheel placed aft of the funnel on the top of a long superstructure which covered the boiler and engine. The helmsman could thus keep an eye on his tow but depended on orders from the captain regarding what was going on ahead (66).

In 1880 the Clyde Shipping Company began building big twin-screw tugs to undertake the towing of large sailing ships from the Clyde to the south of Ireland, the cost of the tow outweighing the cost of battling down the Irish Sea against head winds. Farseeing shipowners also engaged the big tugs to tow their ships on the northward journey. The first was the **Conqueror** (99)(1879, 126.6 ft. 184 tons, 550 i.h.p.) and she was followed by the **Gulliver** in 1884 and the **Hercules** in 1885.

The **Conqueror** of 1879 bears out the suggestion that the early screw tugs were just paddle tugs stripped of their paddles. She had a shallow hull which had constant beam for much of its length. The deck was very bare and it seems ridiculous that in a tug of her size it was necessary to put the W.C. in a side house on the foredeck. Both the towing hook and the samson posts were very strongly braced to withstand strain. The hold forward could be used to carry an extra 70 tons of coal. With all that empty space on the upper deck it was strange that the lifeboat should be carried aft where it had to be stowed on deck to clear the tow rope, a practice found on paddle tugs. The twin screws were arranged so that their "discs" overlapped through the hole in the stern, an arrangement which was called for by the Rankin & Blackmore engines which were fitted on this and later tugs. The **Conqueror** was built in 1879 by Napier, Shanks and Bell of Yoker in Glasgow and she was 126.6 x 20.9 ft. x 11.0 ft. She was 184 tons gross when launched, later increased to 208, and her engines were rated at 98 n.h.p. total. She changed hands so often that it is simpler to make a list of her owners:- **Conqueror**, Clyde Shipping Company, Glasgow (1879-89), Alexandra Towing Co., Liverpool (1889-1905). Went ashore at Ramsay, Isle of Man, salvaged and sold 1905 to J.P. Purcell, Ramsay. Resold 1907 to Furness, Withy, West Hartlepool. Renamed **Recovery** by Irvine's Shipbuilding and Dry Dock Co., West Hartlepool. Sold 1916 Charlton & Co., Grimsby for £5,500 and in 1935 sold to shipbreakers. The **Conqueror** was not a very impressive looking vessel, she was narrow and too shallow draughted for the trade in which she was employed.

Tugs from the fleets of Clyde Shipping Co., Steel & Bennie and others were used for 'seeking' but these tugs were paddle driven and their activities were restricted to the Firth of Clyde. The three big screw tugs were not retained long and a new series of twin-screw tugs was started, the first being the **Flying Serpent** (1886, 134.9 ft. 262 tons. 98 n.h.p.). The biggest coastal tug was the **Flying Buzzard** (1895, 150.0 ft. 380 tons. 127 n.h.p.). Despite their size these tugs were not used for ocean towing although some of them like the **Flying Buzzard** undertook deep sea work after they had been sold away from the Clyde. **Flying Buzzard** (65) became **Cruizer** of the Liverpool Screw Tug Co. They were frequently used for coastal tows, on one occasion three steam ships lying at Dundee were required in Liverpool and three tugs were engaged to tow them, the **Flying Vulture** of Glasgow (1890, 135.0 ft. 291 tons, 98 n.h.p.) with the *Maulesden*, the **Blazer** of Liverpool (1888, 130.0 ft. 283 tons. 130 n.h.p.) with the *Balmoral*, and the **Columbia** of London (1884, 121.0 ft. 214 tons. 120 n.h.p.) with the *Brabloch*. The three tows went north-about through the Pentland Firth and the **Flying Vulture** won the unofficial "race".

These big tugs were designed with a hold forward of the bridge which served as additional bunker capacity. This hold could be used also to carry salvage equipment and on occasion cargo could be carried. During the fishing season catches were transferred by fish carriers, small specially designed cargo vessels. However some of the Clyde Shipping Company's big tugs were chartered to transport fish from Kinsale in Ireland to Milford Haven where they could be transported by train to London. The **Flying Serpent** in 1897 and the **Flying Cormorant** in 1900 and 1903.

The **Flying Buzzard** was typical of this group of tugs with her long central island and tall funnel amidships, identical in appearance to the American deep-sea tugs of the period. The two masts were fore and aft rigged and a heavy derrick was provided on the foremast. However, unlike her predecessors, this tug was single screw. The orange and black 'gunports' of the Clyde Shipping Company made a very attractive colour scheme (See Plate 140).

Steel & Bennie did not go in for the big coastal tugs but they were the first with a workable single-screw tug for use in the river when they built the **Neptune**. Here is Steel & Bennie's **Neptune** under a coaling crane (66). Having a large coaling hatch between the two casings a wagon tip could be used, much easier than humping bags of coal and emptying them through scuttles in the deck. She had the fine lines of the seeking tug with a considerable flare at her bow, while aft, the three towing beams arched high above the large engine casing. She was built by Barclay Curle in Glasgow in 1893 (100.0 ft. 167 tons. 84 n.h.p.). The Clyde Shipping answered some years later with the **Flying Scout** (1902, 106.0 ft. 168 tons. 98 n.h.p.) followed in rapid succession by similar vessels with a lean greyhound look, obviously designed for speed. The **Flying Scout** was lost on her way to Aust-

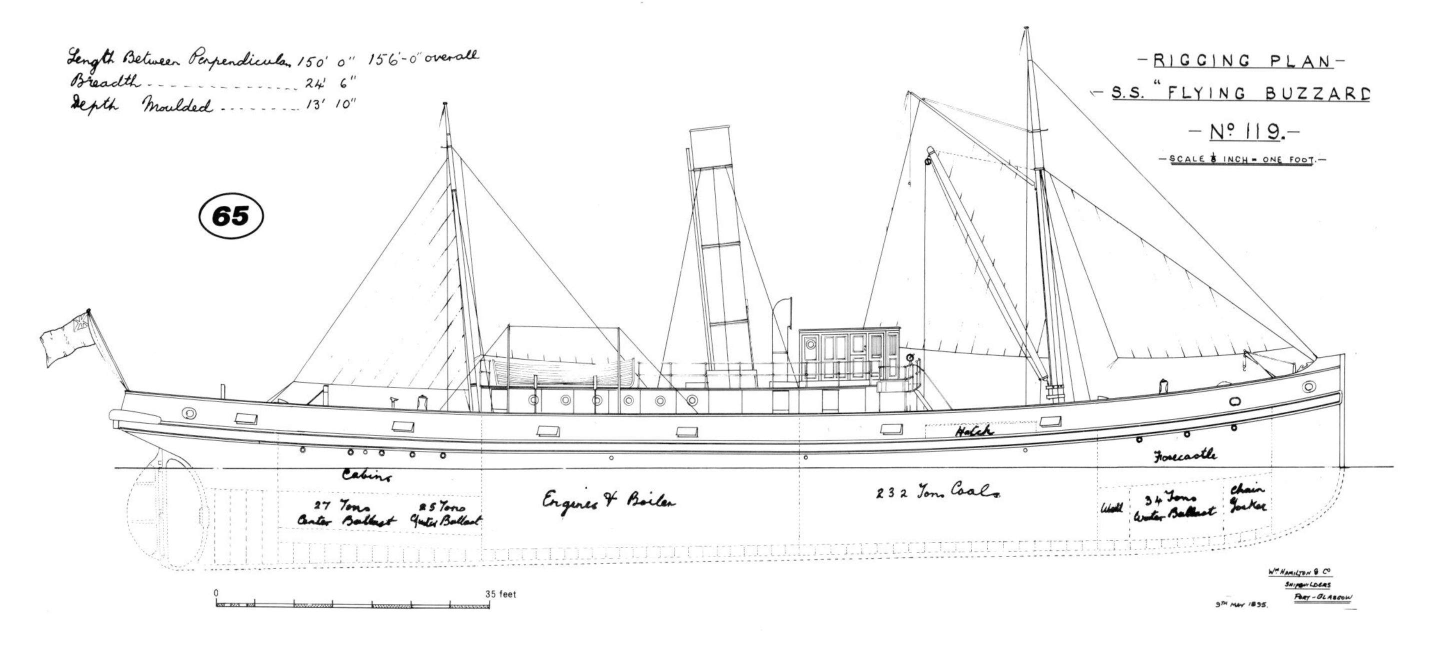

ralia having been sold to Sydney owners, when she sank in the Red Sea having overturned due to being top heavy with about 50 tons of coal on her deck. The two companies dominated the river and were great rivals, their screw tugs carried on the tradition of 'seeking' as the paddle tugs left the scene. Their captains did not always play the game according to the rules; in 1911 the **Flying Linnet** (1904, 107.0 ft. 185 tons. 99 n.h.p.) and the **Cruiser** (1904, 104.8 ft. 167 tons. 99 n.h.p.) were out seeking when the *Orsova* was spotted about ten miles distant. During the ensuing race the tugs 'came in contact', each blaming the other for the collision. In the ensuing litigation, in the absence of unbiased witnesses, the court decided in favour of the **Cruiser**, she being acknowledged the fastest tug on the river, and therefore in no need of resorting to underhand tricks.

World War I saw the end of seeking but the new tugs retained their slender hull although the need for speed had lessened, until the **Flying Eagle** (1928, 105.0 ft. 260 tons. 950 i.h.p.) was built with an extra three feet on her beam. The **Flying Eagle** is in appearance the very essence of the old steam tug, heavy and 'broad shouldered'. She contrasts starkly with the **Flying Foam** of 1877 having a similar length but with a beam of 27.1 ft. against the earlier tug's 18.1 ft.

The **Flying Eagle** was built with coastal towing in mind and she was given a big coal bunker capacity which was loaded through a hatch located between the wheelhouse and funnel (67). A sturdy mast was stepped on top of the wheelhouse and the stays were kept to a minimum. The boats were swung well inboard on davits with very long arms, davits which were stepped in large castings on the boat deck instead of on the main deck thus leaving the side of the deck clear of obstructions. She had a steam steering engine aft of the engine casing and heavy chequerplate covers over the

Converted Steam Yacht ***Sylvia*** *of 1882 used for towing timber rafts.*

(66)

__Neptune__ of 1893 about to get a truck-load of coal down her coaling hatch!

chains. Note the massive samson post in the bow bolted on a plate across the gunwale. This tug was built by Bow MacLachlan of Paisley for the Clyde Shipping Company. She was bought in 1958 by J.H. Lamey of Liverpool who changed her name to **James Lamey** and added a flying bridge. This addition and the change of colour scheme altered her appearance somewhat. She was a useful addition to their fleet and did good work outside the bar at Liverpool. In 1966 she was purchased by Chas. Brand Ltd. and put to work in Belfast as the **Lilias.** The Second World War saw the Clyde tugs subjected to very hard usage as the Clyde became a very important part of the war effort. When the war was over many of the **Empire** class of tugs which had been stationed in the river and managed locally, were bought to replace the older worn out tugs. These gave valuable service for many years until replaced by new diesel tugs. The last steam tugs built for Clyde use were the **Flying Buzzard** and the **Flying Merlin** (1951, 114'11", 261 tons, 1150 i.h.p.) and their near sister **Flying Petrel** (1951, 119'2", 278 tons, 1500 i.h.p.). Most of the steam tugs used on the Clyde were capable of undertaking coastal tows although they worked mainly in the confines of the river itself. Surprisingly enough the **Merlin** and the **Buzzard** were equipped with compound engines, a rather old-fashioned move which in no way affected their performance as tugs except in terms of fuel consumption, but did impart to them a particular "wag" which was very noticeable when one stood right in the stern.

Scotland-East Coast

On the east coast of Scotland the owners of paddle tugs replaced them with second-hand tugs purchased from other ports of the United Kingdom or from the Continent. In Aberdeen after the departure of the paddle trawlers, there was work for screw tugs to assist the host of trawlers now using the port. Most of the tugs bought were on the small side such as the **Chester** which

__Grangeburn__ (left) in drydock showing her Kort nozzle. __Flying Foam__ (right). The first single screw tug built for the Clyde Shipping Co.'s fleet in 1877.

(66)

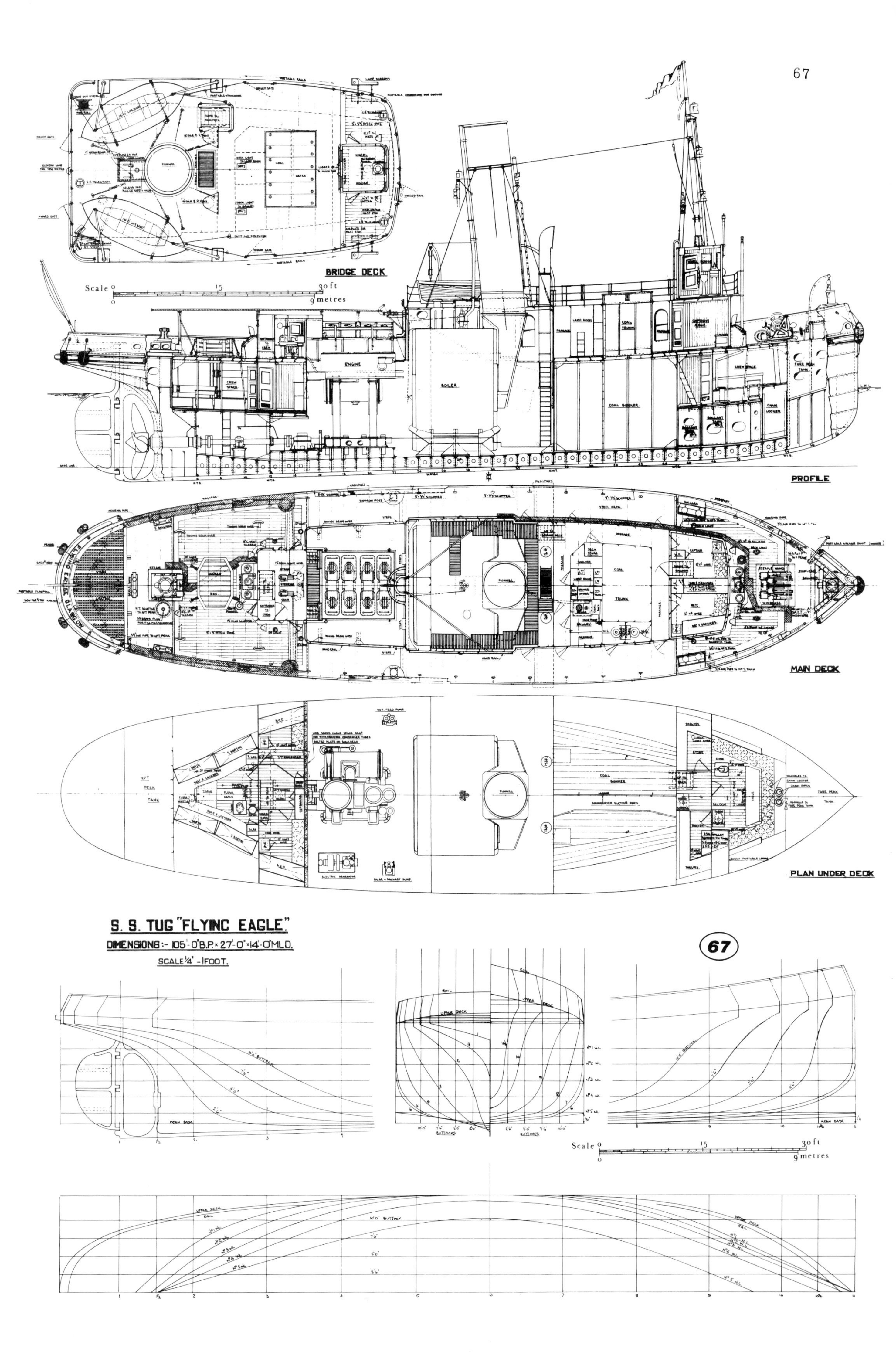
BRIDGE DECK
Scale 0 15 30 ft
0 9 metres
PROFILE
MAIN DECK
PLAN UNDER DECK
S. S. TUG "FLYINC EAGLE."
DIMENSIONS:- 105'-0" B.P.× 27'-0"×14'-0" MLD.
SCALE 1/4" = 1 FOOT.
67
Scale 0 15 30 ft
0 9 metres

was purchased from Hull in 1921 (1900, 80.0 ft. 90 tons, 400 i.h.p.) and the **Danny** (165) which was bought much later in 1948, (built 1918 as the **Mary Tavy** for the Navy (93.5 ft. 182 tons. 800 i.h.p) which was a larger tug for ship handling. Dundee was a late starter and did not see the screw tug until 1921 when Victor Cappon bought the **Vict** (1889, 80.2 ft. 73 tons. 35 n.h.p.). Later tugs reached 115 ft.

On the Forth the paddle tug reigned supreme until 1901 when the small tug **Renown** arrived, (1879, 70.1 ft. 54 tons. 22 n.h.p.) an old London craft tug. Once the Leith Salvage & Towage Company started business in 1919 there was no telling what might appear on the river as their fleet covered the whole range from ex-London craft tugs to big deep sea tugs converted for salvage which included the **Stormcock** (79) of 1883, now the **Bullger** which was replaced, when she was wrecked, by a second **Bullger** (ex **Cartmel**) (1907, 128.0 ft. 270 tons. 184 n.h.p.) One of their salvage steamers was the Old Mersey ferry *Storeton* stripped and fitted with heavy lifting gear. Further upriver, Grangemouth too clung to the paddle tug but in 1911 the **Jumbo** went into service, a smallish tug suitable for working in the restricted waters of Grangemouth Docks (1888, 85.0 ft. 95 tons. 48 n.h.p.). The screw tugs which followed were second-hand varying from 90.0 ft. to 103.2 ft. Two new tugs were purchased the **Kerse** (1923, 100.1 ft. 215 tons 800 i.h.p.) and the **Grangeburn** (1937, 100.0 ft. 196 tons, 900 i.h.p.) the latter being one of the earliest screw tugs to be fitted with the Kort nozzle. Although this improved the bollard pull, it impaired the handling qualities of the tug.

The **Grangeburn** is shown here in the dry dock where the fixed Kort nozzle can clearly be seen (66). Since the nozzle was fixed and the rudder was partly inside it, the hull continued in a fuller form without the usual cast stern post. This picture gives some idea of the large size of the propeller compared with the size of the tug itself. The **Grangeburn** was built by the Grangemouth Dockyard in 1937 (100.0 ft. 196 tons, 95 n.h.p.).

The North-East coast was the home of the paddle tug and for a long time it looked as though only paddle tugs would be found there. True, the shipyards built screw tugs but these were for owners in other parts of the U.K. and abroad. However in 1883 the **Africa** (100.0 ft. 122 tons, 80 n.h.p.) was launched for service on the Tyne, though she remained there only eight years, (68).

The photograph shows the **Nestor** which had originally been the **Africa**. She was unlike the later Tyne screw tugs. Her superstructure was cramped up amidships and her hook was placed on the after end of the engine casing, placing it further aft than the ideal position of 2% of the vessel's length aft of amidships. The casings were so low that the bridge stood on stilts and the boats had a curved framework to support them. The curved sternboard was reminiscent of the old paddle tugs. The scrollwork on the bow was disappointing - it was painted on, not a casting.

From then on for about thirty years the screw tugs joining the local tug fleets were secondhand, mostly small to medium sized river tugs. The Tyne tug owners were enterprising men and despite the small size of their tugs they were frequently found well away from home.

By 1904 the **Africa** was back on the Tyne but still worked away from home from time to time. In 1905 she was returning to the Tyne from a towing contract and when a fog enveloped her off Yarmouth she anchored for safety. When the fog lifted the next morning she saw the steamer *Rockcliffe* aground and offered her services to tow her off. The offer was refused but the tug was asked to stand by the stranded ship. She could not approach her in any case, as she drew 11'8" aft. She was later asked to make fast which she did by passing her rope via local boatmen who had come on the scene, but she was unable to move the *Rockcliffe*. She was joined by the local wooden paddle tugs; the **Yare** (1883, 97.1 ft. 104 tons, 250 i.h.p.), **Gleaner** (1885, 89.1 ft. 87 tons, 54 n.h.p.0, **Meteor** (1875, 94.0 ft. 98 tons, 250 i.h.p.), and **Cruiser** (1880, 88.2 ft. 84 tons 340 e.h.p.). Due to the position of the stricken ship the tugs were compelled to pass tows from one to the other to form a chain, a very unusual arrangement which must have thrown quite a strain on the towing gear of the tugs nearest the casualty. The *Rockcliffe* still would not move and some of her cargo was jettisoned. With further assistance from two more local tugs, the wooden paddler **United Service** (6) (1872, 98.6 ft. 110 tons, 300 e.h.p.) and the iron paddle tug **King Edward VII** (41) (1901, 100.0 ft. 138 tons,

68

Nestor *(ex.Africa) built 1883. Seen here when owned by the Lawson Steam Tug Co.*

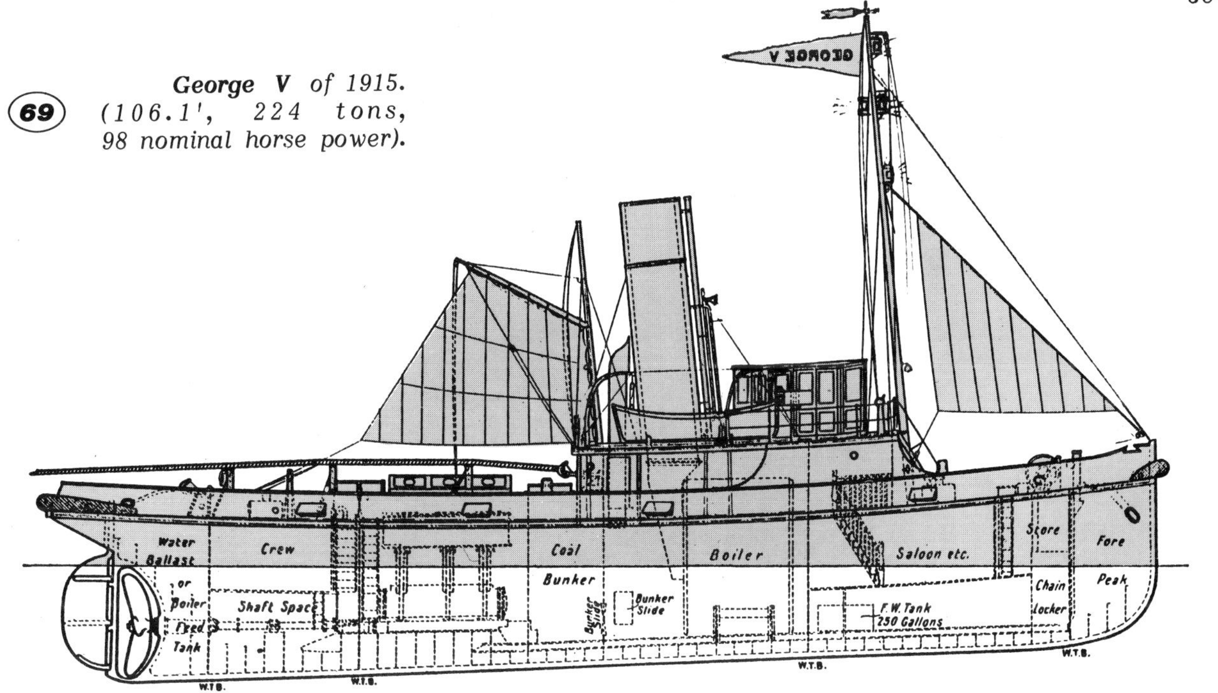

(69) *George* **V** *of 1915. (106.1', 224 tons, 98 nominal horse power).*

280 e.h.p.) the **Rockcliffe** slid off the sands. All those seven tugs together could produce only about 2000 i.h.p. For this straightforward piece of salvage the Yarmouth tugs shared £1,000 while the **Africa** came away with £400, quite a bonus for what would otherwise had been a run home without income.

In 1910 a new large tug, the **George V,** (100.0 ft. 188 tons, 750 i.h.p.) began working in the Tyne towing hoppers in connection with the clearing of the site for the Walker Naval Yard, a job which occupied her and other tugs for three years. Although she was a coastal tug and her crew had no deep sea experience, her owners sent her out to Vigo in Spain in 1913 to assist the Dutch ocean-going tug **Poolzee** which was to tow home to the Tyne the *Glenmorven*, a ship laden with iron ore which had been ashore and had damaged her rudder. The **Poolzee** towed while the **George V** assisted in steering. Heavy weather blew up and the "runners" from the *Glenmorven* abandoned the ship and boarded the Dutch tug which left the scene. When the storm passed the **George V** found herself alone, but nothing daunted she put a rope aboard the casualty and made for Falmouth, where the local tug **Dragon** (1893, 114.7 ft. 163 tons, 530 e.h.p.) gave assistance and tried to claim salvage, without success. The crew of the **George V** had had a most uncomfortable time as their tug did not have the accommodation, water, food or fuel for a long sea trip. The tug stocked up at Falmouth and completed the tow to the Tyne. The owners of the tug, R. Redhead & Sons, received the original contract price of £400, and, despite the salvage, the time consumed, the dangers and the discomforts endured, only an additional £1,850 was granted by the court. Every now and again you come across a tug with some peculiarity and the **George V** was such a one. She had not much sheer forward and did not have covers over the hawse pipes where they came through the deck and as a result, when she was travelling at full speed the water came streaming up on to the fore-deck. The Clyde tug **Thunderer** ex **Empire Dolly** was another very 'wet' boat which was nicknamed "The Flat Iron" because of her lack of sheer. The **George V** was sold to Russia in 1914 and replaced by an almost identical vessel in 1915 (69) which during her career carried out many coastal tows. In 1954 she was modernised and converted to diesel propulsion with a completely different profile (Photo page 175).

As the old paddle tugs reached the end of their useful life they were replaced by secondhand screw tugs, though a few new tugs capable of coastal tows were put into service, tugs such as the **Hendon** (1924, 105.0 ft. 241 tons. 950 i.h.p.) for France, Fenwick, Tyne & Wear Co. The River Tyne Commissioners generally bought new tugs while the private owners bought old tugs from other areas. (For **Hendon** see page 171).

The Lawson Steam Tug Company, despite the relatively small size of their tugs, was very active in the field of coastal towing. So much so that at last in 1916 they had built at Ardrossan a large tug specially for that purpose. The **Joffre** nearly came to grief far away from home in 1925 when she went ashore off Start Point in the English Channel on a voyage from Falmouth to Antwerp. The casualty report at the time said "Likely to be a total loss", and judging from the photographs which showed her almost submerged with the seas breaking over her, it looked as though they might be right. However, her builders had done a good job and she survived until 1966 when she went to the breakers yard. The **Joffre** was salvaged by the **Trover**, an ex-German tug owned by the Liverpool Salvage Association which was later purchased by Ridley Steam Tugs Ltd. of Newcastle. The **Trover** (1920, 99.8 ft. 156 tons. 500 i.h.p.) had an icebreaker bow and she was fitted with an impressive array of salvage pumps on her after deck.

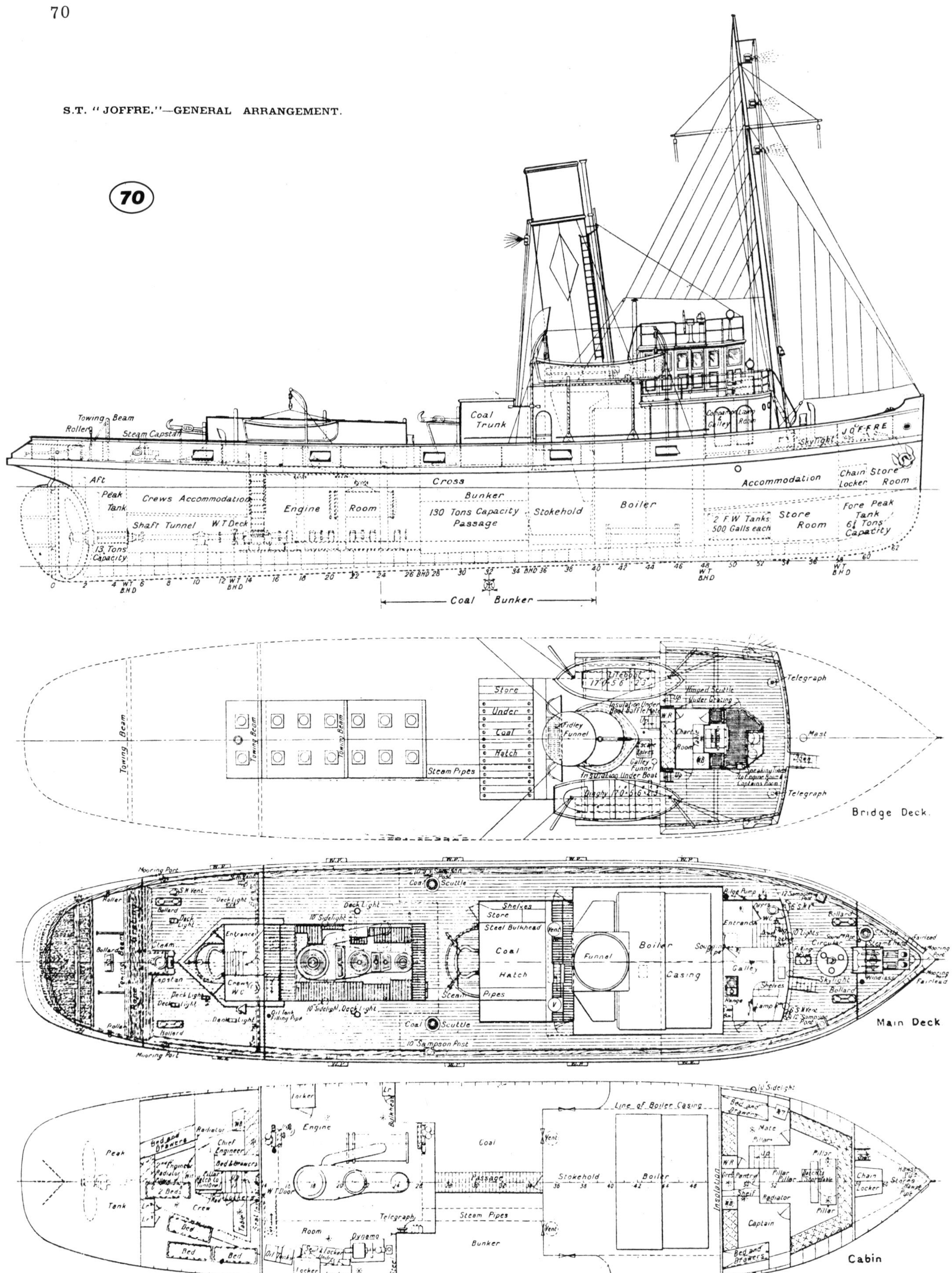

Like the **Flying Eagle** the **Joffre** was built specifically for the coastal towing business. She was big and heavy looking with a deep beamy hull, little rise of floor and moderately rounded bilges. The arrangement of the wheelhouse was odd as the boiler casing stepped up behind it. The casing was made flush at a later date when she was being refitted. The dinghy on the after deck was used to take the crew ashore when the **Joffre** was moored in the river. She had a very large bunker capacity with a trunk to give extra space. Instead of a rope cradle for the wet tow ropes she had a grating arranged across the deck aft of the capstan which was used for handling the 'gog rope'. As befits a tug which spent much time away from her home port, she had what was better than average accommodation. The two sets of hooks were unusual for a tug her size, but the after one came in useful for towing lighters in the river Tyne. Tug owners could not afford to be choosy about contracts! The **Joffre** was built in 1916 in Scotland by the Ardrossan Dry Dock and Shipbuilding Company. She was 115.0 ft. x 26.1 ft. x 11.7 ft. and had a gross tonnage of 260. Her engine was 177 n.h.p. (1,140 i.h.p.), quite a high power for the tugs of the day. She was owned for the whole of her career in Newcastle by Lawson-Batey Tugs Ltd, (70).

Further south in Sunderland the tug fleets were mainly composed of paddle tugs but from 1910 the Sunderland Towage Company began to build new screw tugs like the **Souter** (1910, 85.0 ft. 123 tons, 380 i.h.p.). After the Second World War the leading tug owners of the Wear were France, Fenwick, Tyne & Wear Co.

In Middlesbrough the screw tugs joining privately owned fleets were almost entirely secondhand and varied in size from the **Storm Cock** (1891, 83.5 ft. 64 tons. 48 n.h.p.) bought 1910, to the **Samphire Batts** (1893, 112.0 ft. 174 tons. 75 n.h.p.) bought 1913. She had an unusual history having begun life as the trawler **Sea King** on the Firth of Forth, but after her conversion no-one would have guessed, the change in appearance was so extensive. As on many other rivers the local river commissioners were the ones who built new tugs while the other owners bought old tugs.

Although river commissioners usually employed quite large tugs, from time to time they had in their fleets small tugs for towing lighters and dumb barges. On one river a small tug used to carry the wages clerk as he visited each of the commissioners' vessels to hand over the week's pay. Such a tug was the **C.J. Archer** (72). She had two long casings which occupied nearly two thirds of her length, and the forward one had a little saloon to make the passengers comfortable. Although built in 1913 she had wood sheathing over almost her entire deck, a practice which had been abandoned by commercial owners. The wheel was raised to give a clear view over the deck saloon which provided locker space below for lamps, etc. She was a fairly small tug being only 64 tons. She spent her whole life on the Tees in the fleet of the Conservancy Commissioners. At one time there was a dumping ground off the mouth of the River Tees where hoppers emptied loads of slag from the ironworks and domestic rubbish from the households along the riverside. The Commissioners decided where the waste was to be disposed of and the tug **C.J. Archer** was despatched to act as a marker vessel at the dumping ground. The slag dropped from the hoppers quite rapidly and a wide swing round the tug was usually enough. However, the domestic rubbish was another matter and the hoppers had to circle the tug while a gang of men had to push the rubbish through the open doors with long rakes. While she was carrying out this undignified but necessary task the **C.J. Archer** would fly a single flag from her mast to indicate that dumping could be carried out.

Hull was a busy port, but in the main the traffic consisted of small ships. The tugs therefore were correspondingly small, both paddle and screw. The early screw tugs were secondhand but in the 1880s the leading tug owner T. Gray began to build new tugs starting with the **Welshman** (1889, 169 tons) which he sold the same year to the French. His next big tug was the **Scotsman** (1894, 120.4 ft. 204 tons. 95 n.h.p.), but most of his new screw tugs were small ones like the **Norman** (1897, 60.3 ft. 32 tons, 25 n.h.p.) for which he could find plenty of work handling the barges in the docks of Hull and in the rivers in the surrounding areas.

The **Krooman** was used for towing in and around the docks of the River Humber and up the rivers leading into that river. She was therefore a fairly shallow draught. She had a long low casing which could not accommodate a W.C. or galley and so these were placed forward in sidehouses one on either bow. These erections were a common feature on small screw tugs. The towing hook was secured, not to the boiler casing, but to the forward end of the engine casing on a framework of channels and angle irons. The steering chains were led down to deck level through tubes inside the boiler casing. She was built in 1905 in South Shields for T. Gray of Hull to be taken over with that fleet by the United Towing Company in 1921. She was a smallish tug intended for river and canal work, 61 tons, 30 n.h.p., (73).

Hull was one of the ports where 'seeking' was practised and even the small tugs could be found well down the Humber looking for a tow. In 1894 the barque *Samanco* of Liverpool was twelve miles east of the Spurn Lightship when the little **Pendragon** (1870, 73.0 ft. 59 tons, 45 n.h.p.) came alongside. The wind was light and against the ship so the **Pendragon** asked £35 for the tow to Hull. The ship's captain declined the offer but the tug captain said he would stay alongside the ship and as long as he was there no other tugs would come near. Eventually the wind died leaving the ship helpless and a compromise was reached for £22.10.0 which the *Samanco's* captain still thought exorbitant. In the main the tugs on the Humber remained on the small side rarely exceeding 100 tons, those that did were seldom retained for more than four or five years before being sold away from the river. The **Scotsman** of 1894 was sold in 1899, the **Scotsman** of 1903 (98.5 ft. 141 tons, 420 i.h.p.) was sold in 1908. The screw tugs were very active in the numerous salvage opportunities which occurred in the area but occasionally they were found away from home. In 1910 the **Roman** (1906, 90.2 ft. 108 tons. 420 a.h.p.) and the **Diplomat** (1909, 83.0 ft. 91 tons. 460 a.h.p.) salvaged the *Aislaby* off Yarmouth. Their award was £1,000. Mention has already been made of the low power of the old paddle tugs and sometimes the same thing applied to the small screw tugs. The **Burman** (1900, 80.5 ft. 75 tons, 300 e.h.p.) was seeking off Spurn Point in 1903 when she fell in with

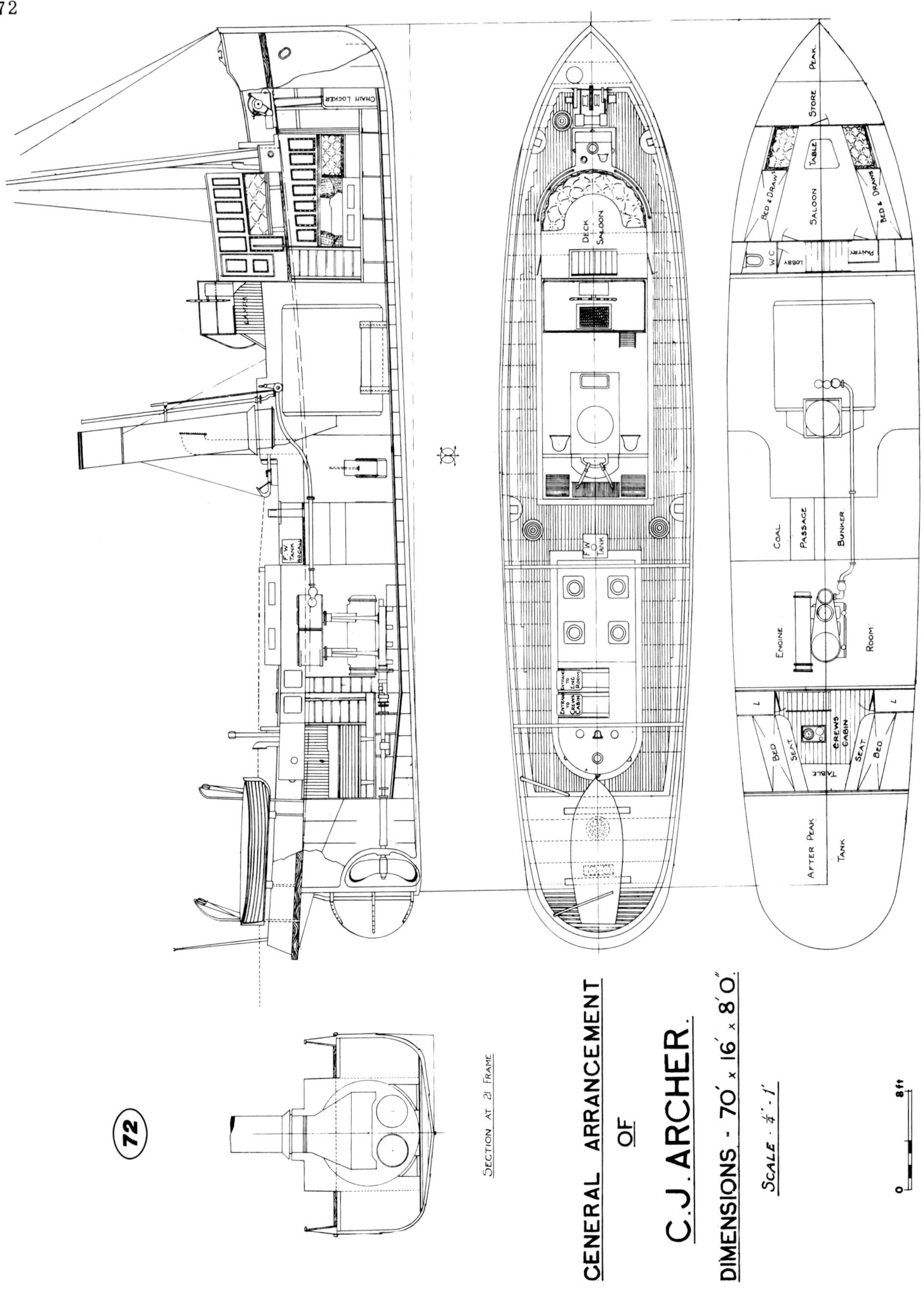

the sailing ship *Biarritz* and contracted to tow her to Hull. A second tug was needed so she engaged the wood screw tug **Lady Bute** (1857, 76.4 ft. 67 tons, 315 i.h.p.) to assist. The wind became wild and although the two tugs worked at full power they were unable to prevent the ship from being driven ashore dragging her tugs, both on their beam ends with their rails under the water. Fortunately the big London tug **Oceana** which had been towing a ship up the Humber saw their plight. She and her tow had anchored to weather the storm and she was in a position to render assistance in refloating the ship. The power of the **Burman** may have been small and the tug herself of no great size but her owners used her for coastal towing. In December 1901 while she was en route from Kings Lynn to Hebburn-on-Tyne she encountered winds of force 10. (Storm, speeds 48 to 55 knots) as she passed off Hartlepool. Her wheelhouse was washed overboard and one man lost his life.

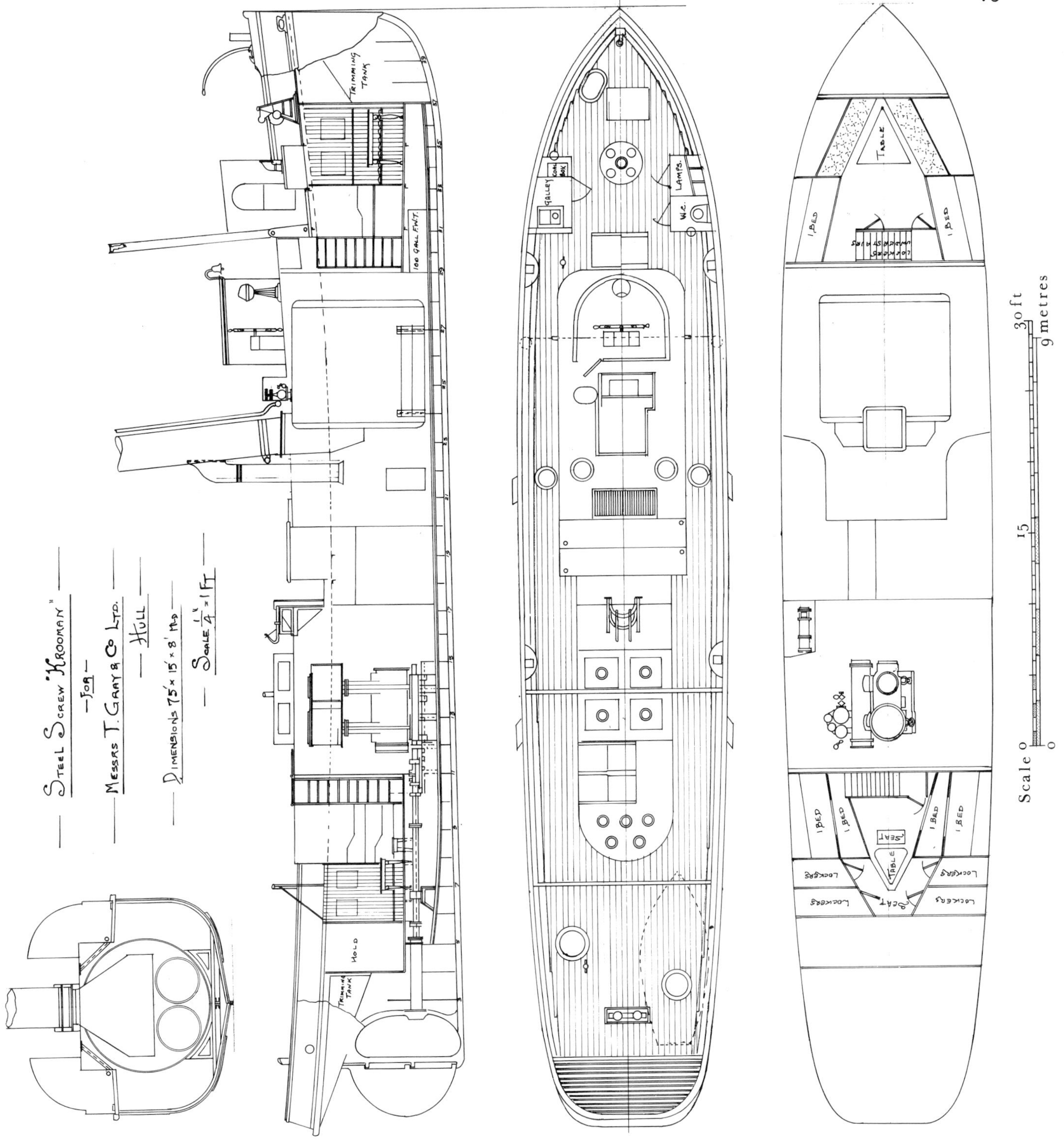

The **Southern Cross** was not a large tug but she was designed for coastal work. The foredeck was raised to bulwark level between the bow and the bridge where a hull width bulkhead prevented the sea from sweeping along her deck (74). She had a small hand windlass for raising the anchor and behind it a breakwater. The captain had a waist high shelter that spanned the hull but behind him the structures were very plain and spartan. The mizzen mast had a sail for steadying purposes. The **Southern Cross** had an engine of only 38 n.h.p. (300 i.h.p.) which was not very powerful for coastal work. She was built at Beverley in 1896 and remained in Hull for all of her working life except when she served with the Navy in 1917.

Following World War I the newly formed United Towing Company began to scrap the small tugs in their fleet and to replace them with larger tugs capable of coastal and even ocean towing the first being the **Masterman** (1923, 96.6 ft. 171 tons. 106 n.h.p.). At the same time they still put new tugs into service to deal with the river traffic including one of the early motor tugs appropriately named the **Motorman** (1925, 56.9 ft. 35 tons. 15 n.h.p.). In the Humber ports the trawling industry gave a lot of work to the tugs. As the trawlers came in from the fishing grounds their crews were sent home and the vessels were moved around the docks as required by the numerous small tugs which were available. As the years passed, the size of the trawlers increased and to meet this, the tugs used had to be improved, though the majority were purchased secondhand.

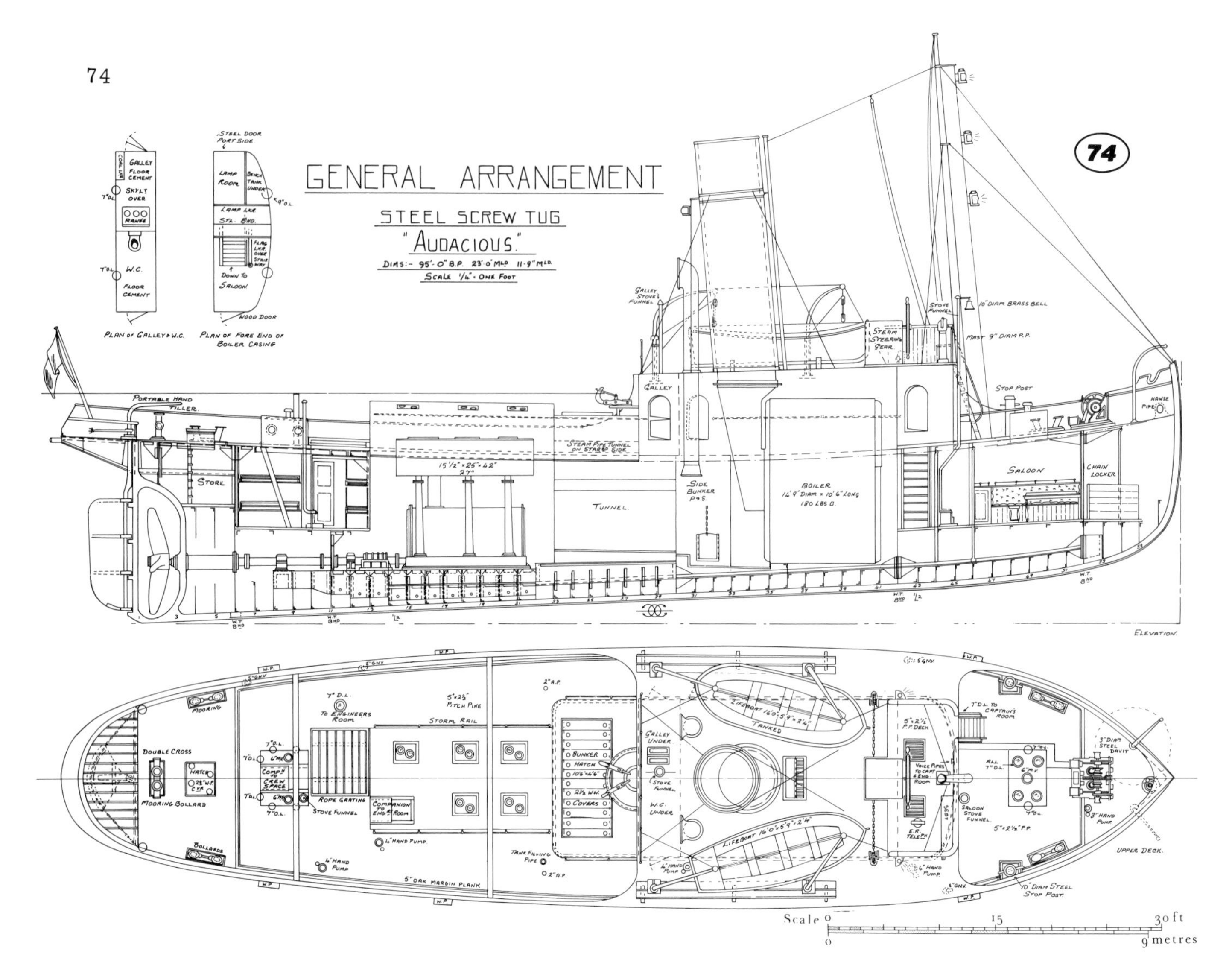

The **Goole No.3** epitomises the 'fussy little tug' which writers are so fond of referring to in their articles, as she ploughs through a sea of liquid mud (75). The two sidehouses on the foredeck for the W.C. and store are clearly visible. The captain stands in a neat wheel shelter which bears the builders' plate. The shape of the towing bows is interesting as they are not curved over their length but straight at the ends. The sidelights are set very low, just above the bulwarks. The **Goole No.3** was built in South Shields in 1899, 75.0 ft. x 15.1 ft x 6.8 ft. 56 tons and 30 n.h.p. Although she was small she was sufficiently useful for the Navy and Army to keep her requisitioned for three years during World War I.

Norfolk Coast

In this area the ports were small and the tugs which served them were restricted in size. In 1901 the **Bulldog** (1884, 77.0 ft. 72 tons. 40 n.h.p.) was purchased from London owners for service in Boston while round the coast in Great Yarmouth the **George Jewson** was bought new by the harbour authorities (1908, 70.3 ft. 57 tons. 40 n.h.p.). As the ships which used the port were coastal sailing

Southern Cross *(1896) measured 82.0' x 16.1' x 9.0', 78 tons gross which was not very large for coastal work. PHOTO: M. Barnard.*

Richard Lee Barber *was built by Fellows & Co., Great Yarmouth in 1940 for the Port and Haven Commissioners. PHOTO: Ken Turrell.*

vessels and fishing boats there was no call for larger tugs. The **Richard Lee Barber** (1940, 83.0 ft. 122 tons, 50 n.h.p.) was the last steam tug to enter service there and as can be seen from the photograph (75) she was a fairly typical screw tug, although the bulwarks at the stern have little or no sheer, giving her a rather flat appearance which contrasts with the very high bow. She was fitted with firefighting and salvage equipment.

Ireland

The Belfast Harbour Commissioners first screw tug was the **Musgrave** (1897, 115.0 ft. 253 tons, 147 n.h.p.) which they used also as a tender having designed her with a fair sized saloon forward. The screw tugs which followed were however of a much smaller size the next being the **Lagan** (1900, 58.3 ft. 24 tons. 21 n.h.p.). This kind of size was maintained when they purchased two of the wartime TID tugs in 1946/7. The **Harbour Light** (1892, 64.0 ft. 45 tons. 30 n.h.p.) was built for J. Waterson who also had the big tug **Hercules** (1885, 125.0 ft. 225 tons. 98 n.h.p.) which had been bought from the Clyde in 1899.

The old story of underpowered tugs was repeated here in Belfast in 1902 when the **Harbour Light** was not able to complete a tow because of bad weather and had to be helped out by the now rival tug **Hercules** which had been sold the year before. J. Cooper took over around 1908 with a variety of secondhand tugs until in 1923 the **Audacious** was built for his fleet (94.9 ft. 160 tons. 99 n.h.p.) in its day a modern shiphandling tug. After this more medium sized tugs were bought-in until 1946/7 when two ex-**Empire** type tugs were added to the fleet, the last of the steam tugs.

Although she was built in 1923 the **Audacious** had a number of features which were somewhat out-dated. The rounded fairing over the side passage had been common in the early days but had hardly been used since the early 1900s. The deck was sheathed in 5" x 2 ½ " pitch pine over almost the whole length when the contemporary tugs had wood 'deadening' only over the accommodation. She had samson posts on the foredeck only, having none abreast of the hook. The davits did not go down to the main deck but pivotted in heavy castings fixed on the fairing. The **Audacious** was built by A. Hall in Aberdeen (75).

Further south the port of Dublin saw a succession of quite large secondhand screw tugs come and go. The **Energy** (1884, 123.5 ft. 203 tons. 55 n.h.p.) was bought in 1899, though the largest was the **Dainty**, an ex-Admiralty tug (1918, 141.7 ft. 468 tons. 204 n.h.p.). After that the tugs were of the usual ship tug size around 105 ft. long.

Goole No.3 *of the Goole & Hull Steam Towing Co. was mainly intended to work between the ports in the title. The finishing touch to the photo is the inset of the Captain.*

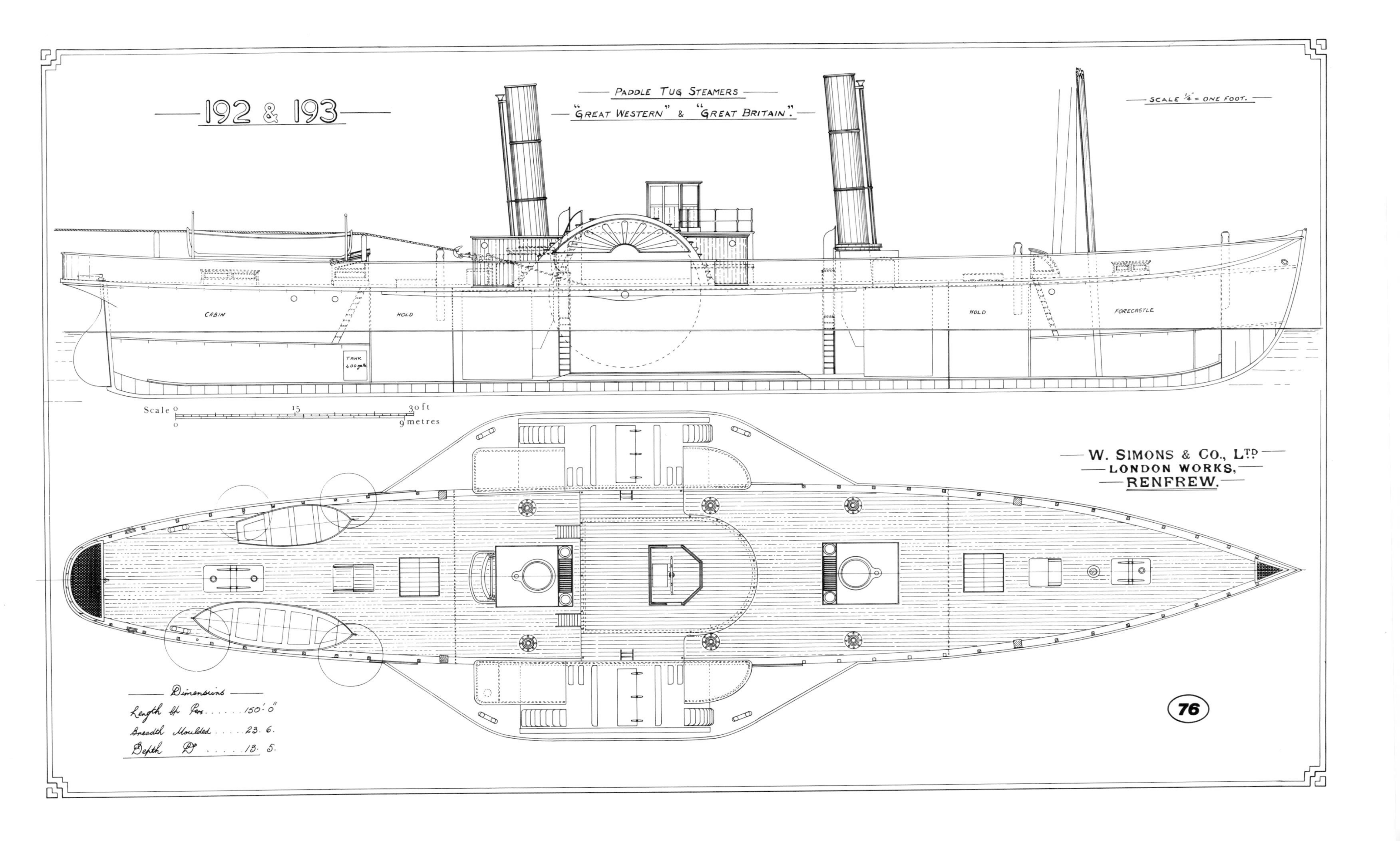
192 & 193
Paddle Tug Steamers
"Great Western" & "Great Britain".
Scale 1/4" = one foot.
Cabin
Hold
Hold
Forecastle
Tank 400 gals
Scale 0 15 30 ft
0 9 metres
W. Simons & Co., Ltd
London Works,
Renfrew.
76
Dimensions
Length bp Pers . . . . . 150' 0"
Breadth Moulded . . . . 23. 6.
Depth Do . . . . . 13. 5.

5.

Ocean-going Tugs

(77) *I.P.T. Anglia (1866)*

With the coming of the big tugs and their ability to tow long distances, new avenues were opened for their use. Larger and larger ships were being built and all over the world ports were beginning to find that they could not berth such large craft. The demand grew for dredgers and to meet this demand dredgers were built in Great Britain, stripped down, transported on board ship and re-assembled abroad. There were difficulties due to local labour being unskilled, delays through lack of engineering facilities, altogether an unsatisfactory state of affairs. In 1859 William Watkins of London, who already had a fair sized fleet of smallish tugs, transferred from his son's fleet in Liverpool the iron paddle tug **Victor** (1857, 136.3 ft. 219 tons, 100 n.h.p.) and in 1860 the tug was engaged to tow the dredger *Navigator* from Gravesend to Cadiz for £752.10.0. The awkward bucket dredger was delivered successfully to be followed by others. The tows did not always go smoothly. In November 1860, with the dredger *Industrious* in tow, the **Victor** was damaged in a collision in the Thames and there was a delay while repairs to the tug were carried out. The tow eventually arrived at Ferrol on 21st December, four days out from Plymouth, a distance of 500 miles and the towage fee of £785.5.0. was paid. In the following year there was another tow from London to Cadiz with the dredger *Excavator*, the **Victor** covering the distance of 1,150 miles in eight days. In March 1861 she was again on the same route from London to Carthegina with the dredger *Diligent* receiving £1,800 for the tow. Although the money paid for these delivery tows was high, the Watkin's tugs seem to have the monopoly despite the fact that other more powerful and larger tugs were in service on the River Thames. Other tug owners did in fact try their hand at deep sea towing but after several losses in tow had been suffered, the underwriters used their influence to encourage the use of Watkin's tugs and expertise. The large deep sea tugs from Liverpool seemed content with towing back to the U.K. ships rendered helpless by engine failure, lost propellers, broken crankshafts or broken rudders. Generally the casualty was taken in tow by a passing steamer and was taken to the nearest convenient port. News would be sent to Liverpool and a large tug would be sent out to tow the crippled ship home. One of the earliest big tugs in Liverpool was the **Resolute** (I.P.T., 1857, 161 ft. 375 tons, 700 i.h.p.). She carried 200 tons of coal which she burned at the rate of 36 tons per day when running free at 12 kts., equal to a range of 1,600 miles. In 1859 a derelict was reported abandoned in the Atlantic and after a search of four days the **Resolute** located her at 48 30' N.16 W., 300 miles off the southwest tip of Ireland, waterlogged and without a rudder. The towing gear was attached to the ship's anchor cable and after five days of towing in foul weather the ship, the *Marianne*, was towed into Queenstown. In 1865 the **Brother Jonathan** (1857, 140.8 ft. 283 tons, 150 n.h.p.) towed a steamer from Ferrol in northern Spain to Liverpool, the steamer having received damage to her machinery. Despite the power of these tugs even the weather was sometimes too much for them. The **Prince Arthur** (1864, 143.7 ft. 253 tons, 100 n.h.p.) also of Liverpool had to turn back twice as she attempted to tow out a large ship against adverse winds.

In 1866 William Watkins placed an order for a new iron paddle tug intended for very long distance towing, with very powerful engines, capable of towing the biggest ship afloat. She was originally conceived with four boilers each with its own funnel, but the designers could not find enough room for the extensive coal bunkers and they had to sacrifice one boiler forward. Her unusual appearance with one funnel forward and two funnels aft earned her the nickname of 'Three Fingered Jack'. She was 144.4 ft. long, 275 tons and had engines of 700 i.h.p. (77). She was quite a coal eater, consuming about one ton of coal for every four miles which she covered. For several years she was used mainly in 'seeking' or in coastal towing, interspersed with special charters such as the repair of Reuter's private telegraph cable across the North Sea at a rate of £20 per day, followed by a charter to assist in the laying of the telegraph cable to Belfast. She towed a paddle steamer the *Monarch* to Belfast for the sum of £300 which more than paid for her coastal trip. The other Watkins tugs were kept busy with tows as far afield as Lisbon (**Victor**) and Corunna (**Anglia** and **Scotia**). The latter tow paid £1,400, not bad for a straightforward towing job. In 1875 news was delivered that the Union Liner *Syria* had broken down and had been taken to St. Helena. The **Anglia** was despatched to bring her home and undertook what was at the time the longest tow to date, bringing the liner home to Southampton for a fee of £4,800, covering a distance of 4,300 miles. Some years later the **Stormcock** (1877, 155.5 ft., 325 tons, 220 n.h.p.), a screw tug owned by the Liverpool firm of W.B. Hill, was ordered to proceed to Fernando Noronha, off the coast of Brazil, where the 2,000 ton sailing ship *Ardencaple* was lying, and to tow her to Greenock 4,000 miles distant. She covered the distance in 30 days including stops for coaling at St. Vincent, the Cape Verde Islands, and at Las Palmas in the Canary Islands. It was not always as easy as that, when the screw tug **Knight of St. John** (1884, 147.2 ft., 275 tons, 106 n.h.p.) belonging to Prendeville of Liverpool was towing a dismasted barque, the *Royal Alexandra*, from Rio de Janiero, she was compelled to leave the tow 400 miles from St. Vincent where she went to take on coal to complete the voyage. When she returned to resume the tow the barque was nowhere to be seen and after a search the tug had to give up. It transpired that the crew of the sailing ship had managed to make a jury rig and had sailed her to the Barbados where she was refitted and returned home under sail.

The **Knight of St. John** (78) and the **Knight of the Cross** were typical of the large, twin-screw tug used by the Liverpool tug owners with their long central casing, the two close set funnels and the row of stanchions supporting the edge of the boat deck. Some of them had a small anchor deck on which the two folding stock anchors were lashed down while the tug was at sea. The **Knight of the Cross** was built in 1883 by W. Stevens of Birkenhead, 135.7 x 22.7 x 12.2 ft., 245 tons gross and 99 n.h.p. She was sold in the same year to the Admiralty and renamed **Magnet**, and resold to Spain in 1920 where she became the **San Antonio.** One of the last of the big Liverpool paddle tugs was the **Great Britain** (76). She had a bow which might almost be called a 'canoe bow' and it could be found on a number of deep sea tugs. The way in which the rubbing strake swept up at the bow was less characteristic but nevertheless did appear on other paddle tugs with timber bulwarks. What is striking is the vast expanse of deck with only a few companionways, hatches and casings upon it. She was provided with an enclosed wheelhouse, a luxury which was denied to her smaller sisters. The towing hooks were mounted on two posts strongly stayed back to the after casing and the deck beams. The **Great Britain** and her sister **Great Western** (93) were built by Wm. Simons of Renfrew for the Liverpool fleet of W. & T. Jolliffe in 1876. They were 154.1 ft. x 23.7 ft. x 12.7 ft. with a gross tonnage of 300 tons and engines of 130 n.h.p. The engines were of the diagonal type, not the more usual side lever engines. On the other paddle tugs illustrated it will be noticed that the paddle boxes were forward of amidships but those on the **Great Britain/Great Western** were set much further aft in a position more typical of the passenger steamers of the day. This can only have been of assistance when she was being driven at full speed as, while towing, there was only a small moment between the paddles and the hook and this would affect her directional control of the tow.

In 1878 the **Anglia** was in the news again. The famous obelisk Cleopatra's Needle was being towed from Egypt to London by a steamer called the *Olga* for a fee of £900, when after twenty days, in the Bay of Biscay, a storm got up and the towline broke. The ship lost contact with her tow which was a big iron cylinder about 90 ft. long by 16 ft. diameter with a small cabin mounted on it to accommodate the crew of six. Another steamer called the *Fitzmaurice* came across her and towed her to Vigo, earning a salvage fee of £2,000. After a few weeks delay the **Anglia** arrived to take it on to London. Despite its small size the Needle's container gave the **Anglia** more trouble than a ship might have done as the following extracts from the tug's log show:

16.1.1878. Ferrol: Anchor hove up at 7.35 pm. Cleopatra steers badly, sheering to port then to starboard. 100 fathoms paid out. Engines $17\frac{1}{2}$ r.p.m., tow pitches heavily. 24 hrs. $115\frac{1}{4}$ miles.
17.1.1878 Sea smoother. $19\frac{1}{2}$ r.p.m. 24 hrs. 134 miles.
18.1.1878 Cleopatra signalled 'Stop for repairs', shortened wheel chains, 20 mins., improved steering but out on port quarter. $18\frac{1}{2}$ r.p.m. wheel amidships.
19.1.1878 8 am. sighted Portland. Cleopatra tending to drag broadside on.
4 pm. passed the Needles.
20.1.1878 4 am. passed Beachy Head. 10.30 am. anchored Chapman Light.
21.1.1878 Under way 7.30 am. Off buoy at Gravesend at 10 am.

Knight of St. John *built in 1884 for Prendeville of Liverpool.*

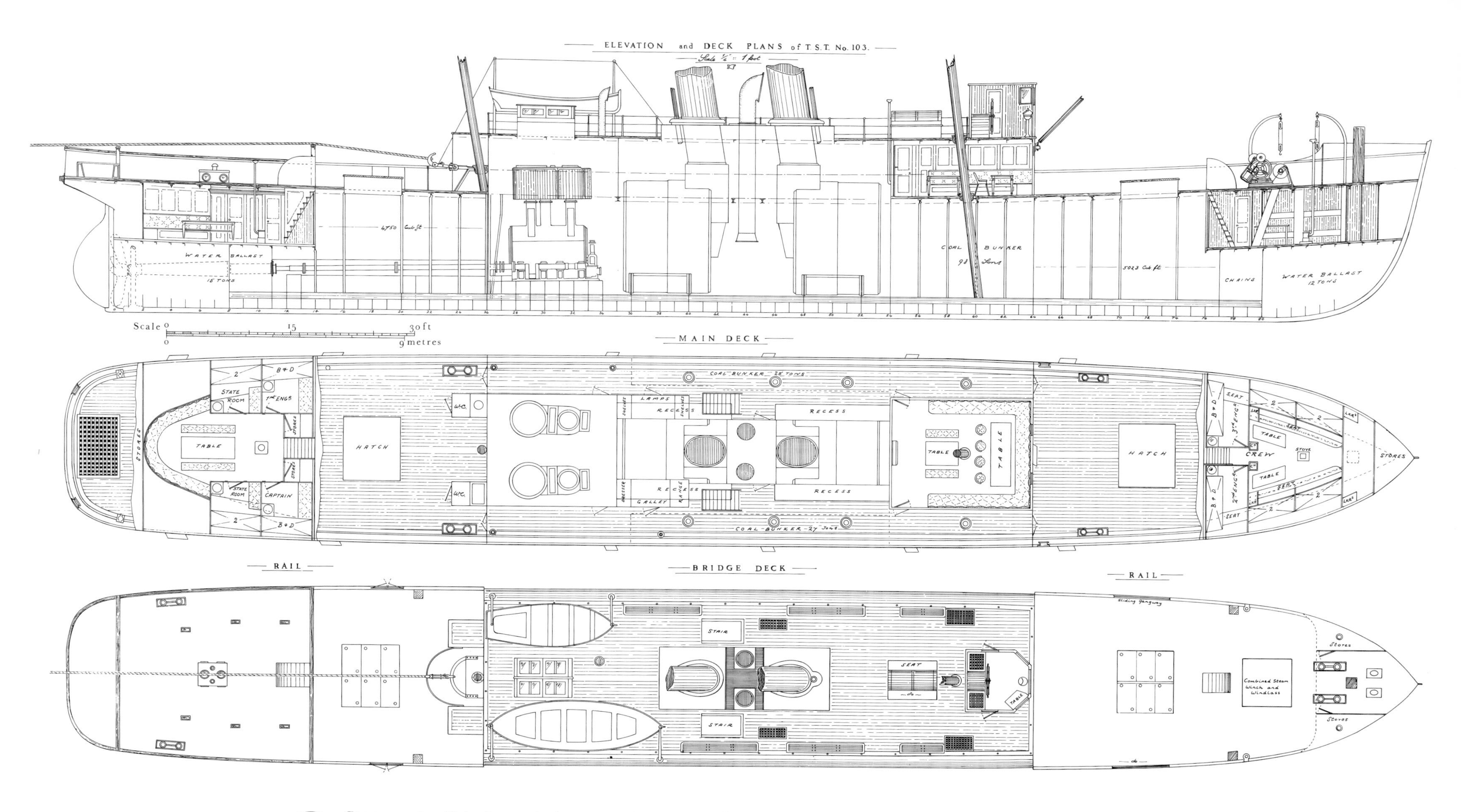

79 **Stormcock.** *This large twin screw tug measuring 161.0 x 24.6 x 12.6 feet was built by H. McIntyre of Paisley for the Liverpool Screw Towing & Lighterage Co. She was purchased by the Admiralty in 1885 and renamed* ***Traveller.*** *She was sold out of service in 1921 and renamed* ***Bullger*** *by the Leith Salvage & Towage Company.*

Here the **Anglia** thankfully handed over her awkward tow to the river tugs. In 1880 the **Anglia** was overhauled and went back into service towing dredging plant from the Hook of Holland to Malaga and from Fiume to Malaga. Some of the lighters were lost in tow being unfit for the passage. By this time William Watkins had added screw tugs to his fleet and in 1885 two of his tugs each towed a dredger to Alexandria; the **Columbia** (1884, 121.0 ft. 214 tons, 120 n.h.p./900 e.h.p.) and the **Hibernia** (1884, 121.0 ft. 219 tons, 120 n.h.p.). In the meantime the Liverpool tugs were still kept busy with their voyages of 'recovery'. In 1889 the Portuguese steamer *Mocambique* broke down on her way from Rio de Janeiro to Lisbon and had to be taken to Ceara in Brazil by the steamer *Maranheuse*. As there were no repair facilities at this port it was necessary that the crippled ship be towed back to Rio. A Liverpool screw tug **Blazer** (1888, 130.0 ft. 283 tons, 130 n.h.p.) was engaged and left Middlesborough on 17th August, calling at Las Palmas and St. Vincent for coal, arriving at Ceara on 5th September, having covered the distance of 5,000 miles at an average speed of 10 knots. The damage to the *Mocambique* was quite serious; her shaft was broken as was the stern tube, the propeller was hanging by chains from the stern, and her after compartment was filled with water. She towed badly but the **Blazer** managed to tow to Rio in 18 days including a call at Bahia for coal. This business of coaling played an important part in selecting what tows a tug could carry out and what route she would have to follow. The wide ranging activity of the deep sea/coastal tug is illustrated by looking at less than five months in the career of the **Blazer** (1888) in 1895. Ship *Godwin* (London to Penarth), ship *Buccleuch* (Penarth to Bremerhaven), ship *Sierra Blanca* (Bremerhaven to Penarth), ship *Lydgate* (Queenstown to La Havre), the barque *Marion Woodside* (Queenstone to Liverpool), ship *Mashona* (off Fairlie to Rotterdam), ship *Lucena* (Liverpool to Penarth). In between times she had towed at least nine other vessels in or out of Liverpool or Barry. During 1889 Watkins directors decided to strengthen their fleet to meet the competition in the long distance towing business and ordered from Gourlay of Dundee the twin screw tug **Oceana** (6). Shortly after the delivery the Dutch tugowners made a determined effort for supremacy in the deep sea towing field and they wrested a lot of work from the British tug owners. One of the **Oceana**'s first jobs was a nasty one. Lying at Milford Haven was a bucket dredger bound for Alexandria. She had already spent seven weeks struggling under her own steam from Greenock to Milford - and the **Oceana** was engaged to tow her the rest of the way. She proved to be amost unwieldy tow and the crew of the tug were vastly relieved when the tow was terminated at Gibraltar.

The **Oceana** had a small forecastle deck for stowing her anchors and to protect the anchor windlass. The deck in way of the boiler and engine was raised to the height of the wooden bulwarks with short ladders fore and aft. This gave her a kind of well-deck forward which was the trademark of the early Dutch deep-sea tugs. The arrangement of the two towing hooks is worthy of note, each with its own bracing system. The 'afterguard', the officers were still housed aft, but in a few years time the new screw tugs would have them forward. The **Great Britain** (76) and the **Stormcock** (79) both had wheelhouses but the **Oceana** had the steering wheel exposed to the elements although the owners did provide a charthouse where the captain could take shelter. The **Oceana** was quite narrow for a tug of her size and the midship section shows a steep rise of floor (83). Illustrations show that the **Oceana** had a very tall funnel and two very tall masts (Plate 6), the mainmast being later reduced in height. Her tonnage was 337 reduced over twenty years to 282 and her two engines totalled 160 n.h.p. (1,000 e.h.p.) In World War I the **Oceana** was taken over by the Admiralty and put on examination duty. With her twin screws she had already sunk one sailing ship and was not suitable for going alongside vessels at sea, and it was not long before she was put on to deep sea work. She met her end at Scapa Flow when she was run down by the **Stobo Castle** while lying at anchor.

One of the Liverpool tug fleets which boasted big, deep-sea tugs was that of William Jolliffe whose tugs carried out a large number of recovery voyages. In 1890 the steamship *Dunedin* broke her shaft in mid-Atlantic and was towed to Fayal in the Azores. The 138 foot **Sarah Jolliffe** (81) left Milford Haven on 12th July and arrived at Fayal 1,500 miles away five days later. She left with the fully laden ship in tow on the 18th and reached Barry Roads on the 27th after a trouble free tow. Tows were not always so simple; the **Sarah Jolliffe** was despatched to Greenock to tow the newly built ship *Tracia* back to Liverpool to take on her first cargo. During the tow, in the Irish Sea, a heavy squall struck the vessels and the tug, to save herself, had to slip the tow. When the squall passed there was no sign of her tow which was in ballast, the ship having capsized and sunk in a matter of minutes. In April 1909 an almost similar mishap occurred. The ship *British Isles* arrived in Queenstown for orders and the **Sarah Jolliffe** was despatched to tow her to Limerick, only 165 miles distant. After a delay of two days waiting for the bad weather to ease, the two captains decided that the tow should commence and the rope was passed, 120 fathoms of steel wire shackled to 15 fathoms of the ship's anchor chain cable. Eight hours later a heavy squall sprang up driving the ship broadside on and causing the towline to part. The ship was now only three miles from a rocky coast and the heavy towline was hanging over the bow. The captain ordered the line to be cut and set some sail in an attempt to claw away from the rocks. When the squall passed the seas were clear and the **Sarah Jolliffe** searched for hours for a trace of wreckage or survivors. Finally she had to give up and made her way to Limerick to report the loss of the *British Isles*. To the amazement of her crew they found the sailing ship already in the harbour. Despite the hurricane force winds the sailing ship had managed to set some sails, some of which blew away, and had sailed parallel to the deadly rocky shore to the safety of Limerick harbour. Despite this mishap the owners of the *British Isles* still used the **Sarah Jolliffe** on numerous occasions between 1905 and 1909 to tow their ship to sea to give her an offing from the land.

81 ***Sarah Jolliffe*** *of Liverpool was built in 1890 by J. Readhead & Sons, South Shields (138.0 x 25.6 x 13.5 feet, 333 tons gross and 126 n.h.p. (900 a.h.p.))*

Though the **Sarah Jolliffe** was built only seven years later she was quite different in appearance to the **Knight of St. John** (78). She resembles the early Dutch deep-sea tug with her raised anchor deck with a breakwater and well deck forward. She had stockless anchors lashed down on the anchor deck and the anchor davits folded down. The side passages were sheltered by the half round plating. The side lights were in little lighthouses exactly like those of the sailing ships which she towed. By the time the photograph was taken she had been fitted with wireless (81).

From time to time the big tugs had opportunities of winning salvage awards. Most of them occurred on the 'doorstep' where their long range was not important. Other salvage jobs took the high engine power into account. In February 1894 the steamer *Loch Maree* ran out of fuel near the Irish coast and she was abandoned by her crew. A passing steamer put a towline aboard but was barely able to prevent her from drifting ashore and her crew were thankful when the tug **William Jolliffe** (1885, 149.0 ft. 332 tons. 164 n.h.p./975 e.h.p.) arrived and took over the tow. The steamer received £1,500 and the tug £7,500, a very substantial sum of money. Every now and again a new record was created for a deep sea tow. In 1898 the **Oceana** towed the ship *Kommandor Svend* loaded with 400 tons of coal from Cardiff to Dakar, a distance of 2,400 miles, averaging 170 miles per day. In 1901 she followed in the footsteps of the **Anglia** when she was sent out to St. Helena to tow the Union Castle liner *Lismore Castle* home to the Thames. The *Lismore Castle* had been used for trooping during the Boer War and as a result of years of constant use without repair or overhaul her machinery was in a bad way.

Looking back over the latter part of the nineteenth century some interesting facts emerge:

(1) Liverpool had operated the largest number of deep sea tugs.
(2) The screw tug had been received with more favour in Liverpool than in London.
(3) By 1900 hardly any of the big paddle tugs were still in service.
(4) In general the size of the deep-sea tugs was beginning to decrease while the engine powers remained more or less the same.

The following is a survey of the big deep-sea tugs in service up to about 1900. The list is by no means complete as far as Liverpool is concerned (it is intended only to give an idea of the scale of operations for that port). Disposal details are given where known and vessels sold to the Admiralty are indicated by a star *.

Liverpool (Paddle tugs)

Liverpool Steam Tug Co.	**Cruizer**	1861	156.4 ft.	364 tons	180 n.h.p.	*Sold 1889*
	Blazer	1856	156.4 ft.	337 tons	180 n.h.p.	*Sold 1884*
	Gladiator	1874	144.7 ft.	228 tons	99 n.h.p.	*Sold 1909*
	Pathfinder	1876	161.4 ft.	326 tons	200 n.h.p./ 1200 i.h.p.	*Sold 1910*
	Wrestler	1876	154.4 ft.	338 tons	900 i.h.p.	*Sold 1903*

The comparison between the **Wrestler** (85) and the **Great Britain** is quite startling. Although a similar size and built in the same year the profiles are very different. The **Wrestler** had a straight stem and the superstructure was piled high between the funnels, while the **Great Britain** had a 'canoe bow' and almost no amidships superstructure (76). The upward curve of the rubbing strake at the bow was seen on many paddle tugs and usually indicated that she had wooden bulwarks. The **Wrestler** was built by W.H. Potter of Liverpool.

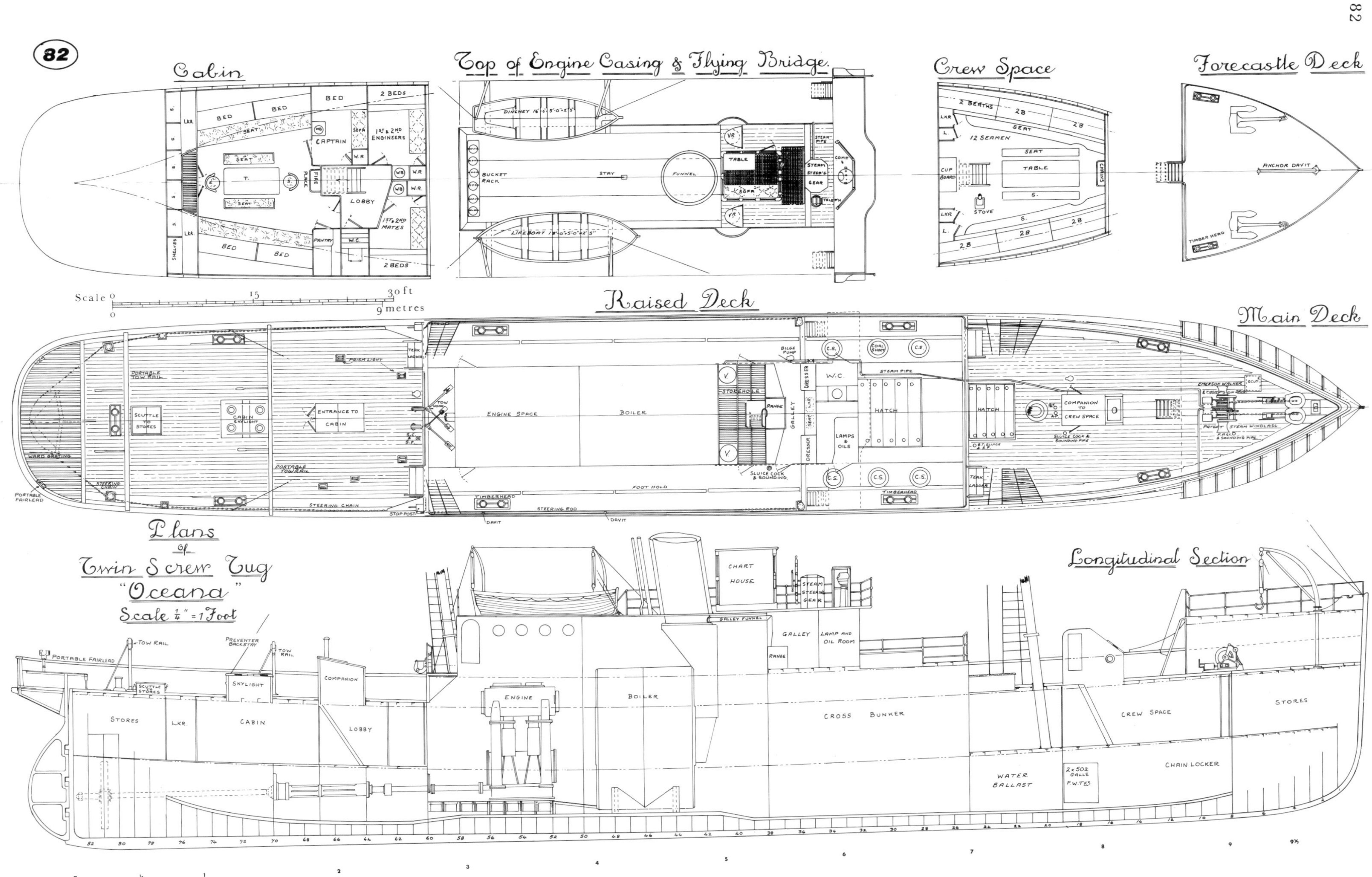
Cabin
2 BEDS
BED
CAPTAIN
1ST & 2ND ENGINEERS
1ST & 2ND MATES
LOBBY
FIRE PLACE
PANTRY
W.C.
SEAT
SHELVES
LKR
Top of Engine Casing & Flying Bridge
DINGHEY
LIFEBOAT
BUCKET RACK
STAY
FUNNEL
TABLE
STEAM STEERING GEAR
Crew Space
2 BERTHS
12 SEAMEN
SEAT
TABLE
CUP BOARD
STOVE
CHAINS
LKR
Forecastle Deck
ANCHOR DAVIT
TIMBER HEAD
Scale
30 ft
9 metres
Raised Deck
Main Deck
PORTABLE TOW RAIL
SCUTTLE TO STORES
CABIN SKYLIGHT
ENTRANCE TO CABIN
STEERING CHAIN
PORTABLE FAIRLEAD
STOP POST
ENGINE SPACE
BOILER
FOOT HOLD
STEERING ROD
DAVIT
TIMBERHEAD
STOKEHOLE
RANGE
GALLEY
DRESSER
BILGE PUMP
SLUICE COCK & SOUNDING
W.C.
LAMPS & OILS
STEAM PIPE
HATCH
TEAK LADDER
COMPANION TO CREW SPACE
SLUICE COCK & SOUNDING PIPE
STEAM WINDLASS
Plans of Twin Screw Tug "Oceana"
Scale 1/4" = 1 Foot
Longitudinal Section
PORTABLE FAIRLEAD
TOW RAIL
PREVENTER BACKSTAY
SKYLIGHT
SCUTTLE TO STORES
COMPANION
STORES
LKR
CABIN
LOBBY
ENGINE
BOILER
CHART HOUSE
STEAM STEERING GEAR
GALLEY FUNNEL
GALLEY
LAMP AND OIL ROOM
RANGE
CROSS BUNKER
WATER BALLAST
2 x 502 GALLS F.W. TKS
CREW SPACE
CHAIN LOCKER
STORES
82

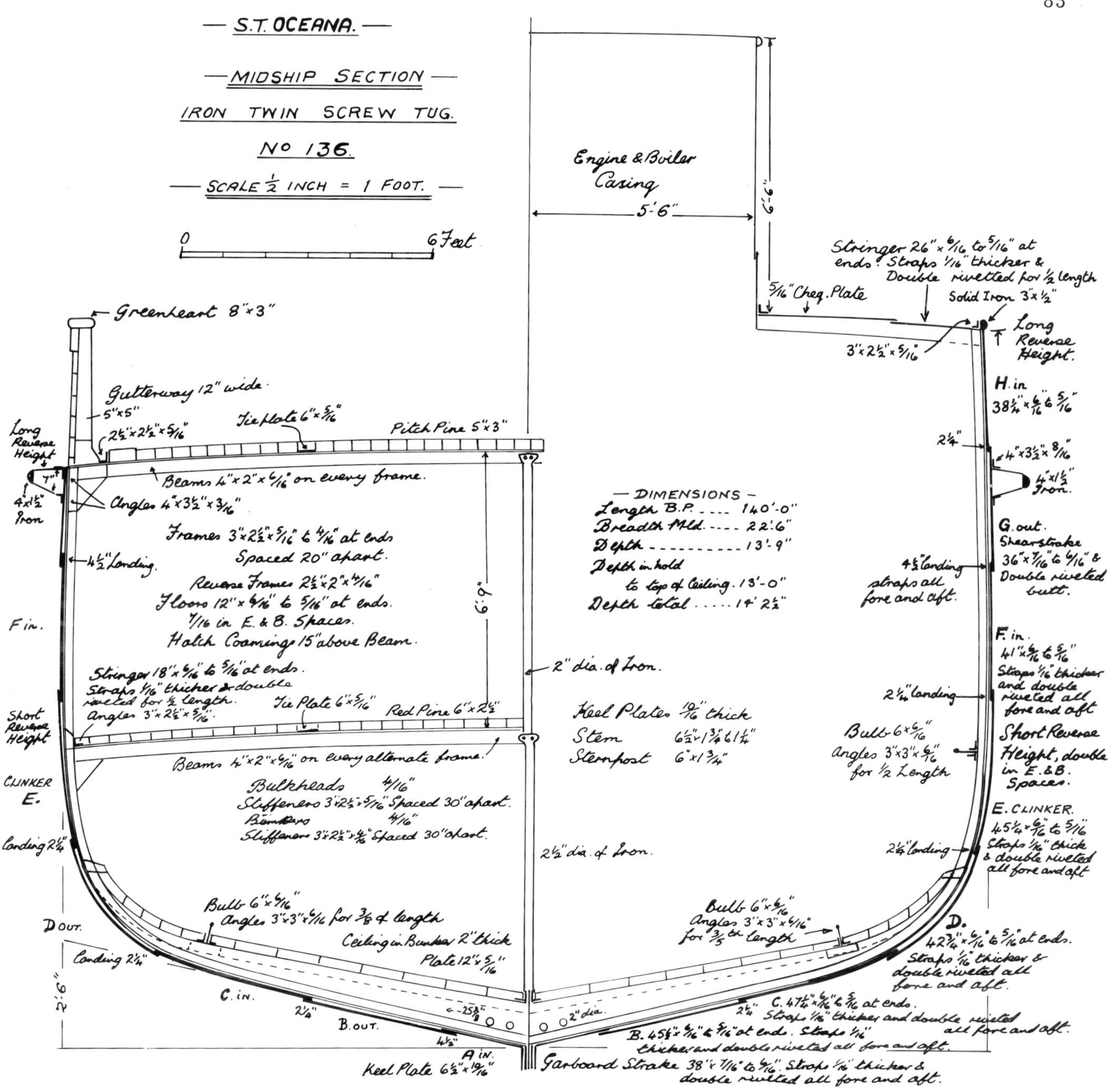

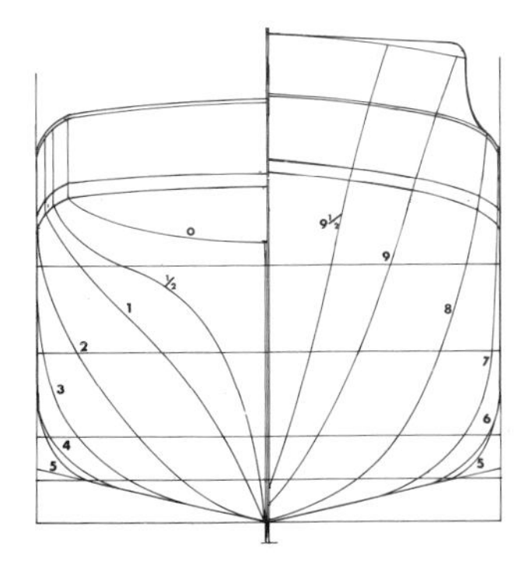

83

Oceana *midship section (above) and body plan (right). The stations for the various sections on the body plan are shown below the longitudinal section (opposite).*

Owner	Tug	Built	Length	Tonnage	Power	Fate
New Steam Tug Co.	**Resolute**	1857	161.4 ft.	375 tons	200 n.h.p.	*Sold 1863*
	Reliance	1857	158.9 ft.	301 tons	140 n.h.p.	
	Retriever	1857	158.8 ft.	300 tons	140 n.h.p. 700 i.h.p.	*Sold 1878*
	Resolute	1863	145.0 ft.	271 tons	120 n.h.p.	*Sold ca. 1905*
J. Prendeville	**Knight Commander**	1868	144.8 ft.	276 tons	160 n.h.p.	*Sold ca. 1900*
United Steam Tug Co.	**United States**	1855	137.1 ft.	235 tons	130 n.h.p.	*Sold 1894*
	Brother Jonathan	1857	140.8 ft.	283 tons	150 n.h.p.	*Sold 1879*
	United Kingdom	1857	154.6 ft.	314 tons	150 n.h.p.	*Sold 1895*
Peter Maddox	**Constitution**	1853	149.4 ft.	263 tons	120 n.h.p.	
	Universe	1855	135.3 ft.	311 tons	120 n.h.p./ 400 i.h.p.	*Sold 1891*
	Enterprise	1855	136.0 ft.	319 tons	120 n.h.p.	
Strong Steam Tug Co.	**Brilliant Star**	1876	158.4 ft.	330 tons	180 n.h.p.	*Sold 1905*
H.J. Ward	**Storm King**	1857	137.0 ft.	199 tons	100 n.h.p.	*Sold 1892*
E. Griffiths	**Hotspur**	1876	143.2 ft.	224 tons	99 n.h.p. / 700 i.h.p.	*Sold 1910*
A. Muir	**Fiery Cross**	1870	137.1 ft.	239 tons	100 n.h.p.	*Sold 1888*
W. & T. Jolliffe	**Great Britain**	1876	154.1 ft.	300 tons	130 n.h.p.	*Sold 1898*
	Great Western	1876	154.2 ft.	300 tons	130 n.h.p.	*Sold 1898*
London (Paddle tugs)						
Wm. Watkins	**Victor**	1857	136.3 ft.	219 tons	100 n.h.p.	
	Anglia	1866	144.4 ft.	274 tons	140 n.h.p./ 700 i.h.p.	*Sold 1894*
	Friend to All Nations (purchased 1867)	1851	129.7 ft.	168 tons	60 n.h.p.	*Sold 1869*
	Cambria	1870	138.8 ft.	209 tons	100 n.h.p.	*Sold 1913*
	Robert Bruce (purchased 1872)	1865	121.3 ft.	192 tons	120 n.h.p.	*Sold 1892*
	Scotia	1874	139.2 ft.	263 tons	130 n.h.p.	*Sold 1901*
	Hibernia	1874	139.2 ft.	238 tons	130 n.h.p.	*Sold 1883*
	India	1876	138.9 ft.	218 tons	90 n.h.p.	*Sold 1894*
Liverpool (Screw tugs)						
J. Prendeville	**Knight of St. John**	1884	147.2 ft.	275 tons	106 n.h.p.	*Sold 1890*
	Knight of St. Patrick	1886	147.2 ft.	274 tons	98 n.h.p.	
	Knight of the Cross	1883	135.7 ft.	245 tons	99 n.h.p.	*Sold 1883**
William Jolliffe	**William Jolliffe**	1885	149.0 ft.	362 tons	250 n.h.p.	*Sold 1885**
	William Jolliffe	1885	149.0 ft.	332 tona	164 n.h.p./ 975 i.h.p.	*Sold 1907*
	Sarah Jolliffe	1890	138.0 ft.	333 tons	126 n.h.p. 900 i.h.p.	
W.B. Hill (Liverpool Screw Towage and Lighterage Co.)	**Stormcock**	1877	155.5 ft.	325 tons	220 n.h.p./ 1000 i.h.p.	*Sold 1882**
	Stormcock	1883	161.0 ft.	364 tons	193 n.h.p.	*Sold 1885**
	Stormcock	1885	160.0 ft.	373 tons	300 n.h.p.	*Sold 1899*
	Blackcock	1886	146.2 ft.	254 tons	200 n.h.p.	*Sold 1915*

Stormcock (79) exhibits the same 'canoe bow' as **Great Britain** (76) and also the comparatively empty deck. She had a round-down along either side of the boat deck with bulkheads fore and aft which kept the side passages dry. She had a small whaleback at the bow which helped to keep some of the water off the foredeck. Despite the size of this tug she had little accommodation as most of the space was taken up with engine, boilers and holds. With the extent of the superstructure it is surprising to find the two W.C.'s stuck in little houses on either side of the towing hook. A number of seats were provided on the boat deck for passengers when she was acting as a tender. The whole appearance of the vessel was spoiled by the close spacing of the two funnels. She was built on the banks of the River Cart in Paisley by H. McIntyre in 1883. It is interesting to note that the **Flying Eagle** of 1928 was broader in the beam and had the same moulded depth although her length was only 105 ft.

Owner	Tug	Built	Length	Tonnage	Power	Fate
Liverpool Screw Tug Co.	**Cruizer** (ex-**Flying Buzzard** -oo)	1895	150.0 ft.	380 tons	127 n.h.p.	*Sold 1907*
London (Screw tugs)						
William Watkins	**Hibernia**	1884	121.0 ft. (shortened to 107 ft. 1922)	291 tons	120 n.h.p./ 600 i.h.p.	*Sold 1961*
	Oceana	1889	140.0 ft.	337 tons	160 n.h.p./	*Sunk 1918*

Ships were still breaking down but the requirement for 'recovery' towages was becoming less necessary. More ships were twin screw and could limp to port on one. Ports previously without proper repair facilities were now being equipped with dry docks or floating docks and repairs could now be carried out on ships suffering from straightforward breakdowns or damage. It was however the Dutch towing companies of L. Smit and the International Tug Co. who obtained most of the contracts for towing floating docks to their destinations. One of the few such contracts awarded to a British firm was the tow of the graving dock *Sir Alfred* to Nigeria, the **Cruizer** and the **Blazer** undertaking the 4,500 mile tow. The **Cruizer** had been in the news five years previously when she towed the *Indra* back to the U.K. from the Gulf of Aden in company with the **Pathfinder:** 20.8.1900; *Indra* ashore near Guardafui, Gulf of Aden, on voyage Java to United States, probably total wreck. 8.11.1900; *Indra* refloated. 19.11.1900; *Indra* towed to Aden. 17.12.1900; Liverpool Steam Tug Co. screw tug **Cruizer** left the Mersey. 9.1.1901; *Indra* left Aden in tow of the tug **Cruizer.** 22.1.1901; *Indra* and tug reported at Suez. 11.3.1901; *Indra* left Vigo in tow of tugs **Pathfinder** and **Cruizer.** 17.3.1901; *Indra* arrived Mersey and entered Alfred Dock, Birkenhead.

The *Indra* had been badly damaged by her grounding and as she lay there natives in Arab dhows had visited her in large numbers and had taken every nut, screw and bolt from the machinery, the planks off the deck and all the stores and cabin fittings. Temporary repairs were effected in Aden.

In 1905 Watkins contracted to tow an oil hulk called the *Tancarville* from Newcastle to Sumatra, a total distance of 8,200 miles. The hulk was towed by the **Columbia** from the Tyne to Portland where the **Oceana** took over. The tow took 45 steaming days and was the longest tow attempted up to that date. In 1908 the **Oceana** was sent to the Tyne for re-boilering and for alterations to her bridge and when she returned to service she towed the big French liner *Esmeralda* from Bordeaux to La Spezia. Later in the year two paddle steamers were to be towed to the Persian Gulf. Watkins obtained the contract to tow one vessel, the Dutch the other. The passage in tow of the **Hibernia** took 42 days, but the Dutch tug took 53 days; quite a feather in the Watkins' cap. In 1908 five river tugs towed a floating dock for Brazil to the mouth of the Tyne where the dock was handed over to Dutch ocean going tugs!

The First World War broke out in 1914 and such big tugs as were still in service were requisitioned for naval use and their activities are dealt with in the appropriate chapter. Suffice to say that the **Oceana** was lost in collision with the tug **Stobo Castle** in Scapa Flow in 1918. During the war John Watkins went across to Holland and purchased a big deep sea tug the **Oceaan** (1894, 149.2 ft. 424 tons. 165 n.h.p.) which he renamed **Racia** (86), a typical two-funnelled Dutch ocean tug. In 1919 the Admiralty, desperate for large quantities of timber, decided to repeat an experiment tried out years before on the east coast of Canada. A raft of timber was constructed roughly in the shape of a ship and was christened the *Merakerbrug*. She was 360 feet in length and had a beam of 42 feet with a draught of 10'6", and she contained 4,200 tons of timber. The **Racia** carried out the tow at a speed of 2 ½ knots, without incident, but fortunately the weather had been very calm.

Although successful, the experiment was not repeated. The **Racia** was similar to the **Sarah Jolliffe** but with two funnels. Her superstructure was shorter than **Sarah Jolliffe** making the after deck longer and bringing the hook closer to the midships of the tug.

When the war ended there were only one or two of the deep-sea tugs remaining to be returned to civilian service. There were indeed large naval tugs which had been bought before the war or had been built during the war, but those which were sold went abroad. As well as the **Racia** the firm of William Watkins purchased the tug **Dreadful** from the Admiralty (1912, 118.5 ft. 253 tons. 74 n.h.p.) and renamed her **Rumania.** She was a typical north American style tug with a long deck-house. The Navy had brought her over from Canada and despite her small size she was a good sea boat and quite a useful addition to the fleet. There was however, not enough ocean towing to justify keeping the large tugs and the **Racia** was sold in 1920 and the **Rumania** in 1923, the latter fetching £10,500. Some small firms were set up proclaiming their intention to undertake deep-sea work, firms such as Ocean Salvage Co. of London with the tug **Frank Dixon** (1920, 88.5 ft. 133 tons. 42 n.h.p.). It may seem ridiculous but they advertised her as a 'deep-sea tug' and she was fitted out with wireless telegraph-W/T.

(85)

I.P.T. ***Wrestler*** *(1876, 154.4 x 24.1 x 12.9 feet) of the Liverpool Steam Tug Co. Sold for £600 for breaking up 1903.*

By the early 1920s the Dutch tug companies seemed to have the monopoly of the deep-sea towing work, but despite the strength of the opposition the United Towing Company of Hull decided to enter the lists, albeit in a small way. Their first really long tow was in 1922 when the tug **Hullman** (1914, 101.2 ft. 171 tons. 90 n.h.p.) towed a trawler from Murmansk to Hull, a modest beginning but quite a distance for a medium sized tug, around 2,000 miles. In 1924 they put into service a new tug (87), **Seaman** (125 ft. 369 tons. 150 n.h.p.). By previous standards she was not a large tug but she represented the British deep-sea tug of the era between the wars. In 1926 she towed two ex-naval tunnel minesweepers *Stepdance* and *Quadrille* from Boston in Lincolnshire to Buenos Aires. One of the ships was lost in heavy weather in the Bay of Biscay, which is hardly surprising as the two boats were built originally for river use, but the other was delivered safely. Despite the loss the company was paid £3,400 for the tow. Ten years later the **Seaman** was back in South America to tow the cruiser *Garibaldi* from Bahia Blanca to a breakers' yard in Copenhagen. En route the cruiser was resold to British shipbreakers and was taken to Blyth for demolition. The speed of the tow ranged from 64 to 129 miles per day.

In outward appearance the **Seaman** was little different from the coastal tugs of the period as she did not have a raised forecastle. At first glance she looks rather long and narrow, but in fact she had a length to beam ratio of 1:4.45 which compares with the **Ascupart** (206) 1:4.38. The old **Stormcock** of 1883 really was narrow; she had a ratio of 1:6.5 and although she was 36 ft. longer she had 1 ft. less moulded depth. The rise of keel forward of frame 59 is reminiscent of the Dutch tugs. To give her a good operating range she was provided with extensive bunker space holding 214 tons of coal in total, which she burnt at the rate of 16 tons a day at a speed of 12 ½ knots running free without a tow, giving her a radius of action of 4,000 miles. The coal bunkers were serviced by no less than four hatches and four coaling scuttles. She had side passages which were made rather narrow by the inclusion of W.C.s, oil and paint stores, etc. The drawing shows her with a freeboard of 18" and in heavy seas she must have shipped a fair amount of water over the bow and it must have been unpleasant to have tons of water sluicing through those narrow corridors.

As an ocean going tug the **Seaman** was equipped with W/T (wireless telegraphy) which required tall masts spaced well apart to support the long aerials. To keep the towing deck clear of stays the builders provided a spreader plate at each corner at the after end of the engine casing which also served as a rope stop should the tug swing across the rope (this was known as being 'girted'). The tug was fitted with a flying bridge complete with wheelhouse, not too common at that time. On her after deck she had a very large rope cradle to take the large diameter ropes which would be needed for deep sea work.

(86) *Dutch tug **Oceaan** purchased by Watkins and renamed **Racia**, note the funnels have not yet been repainted.*

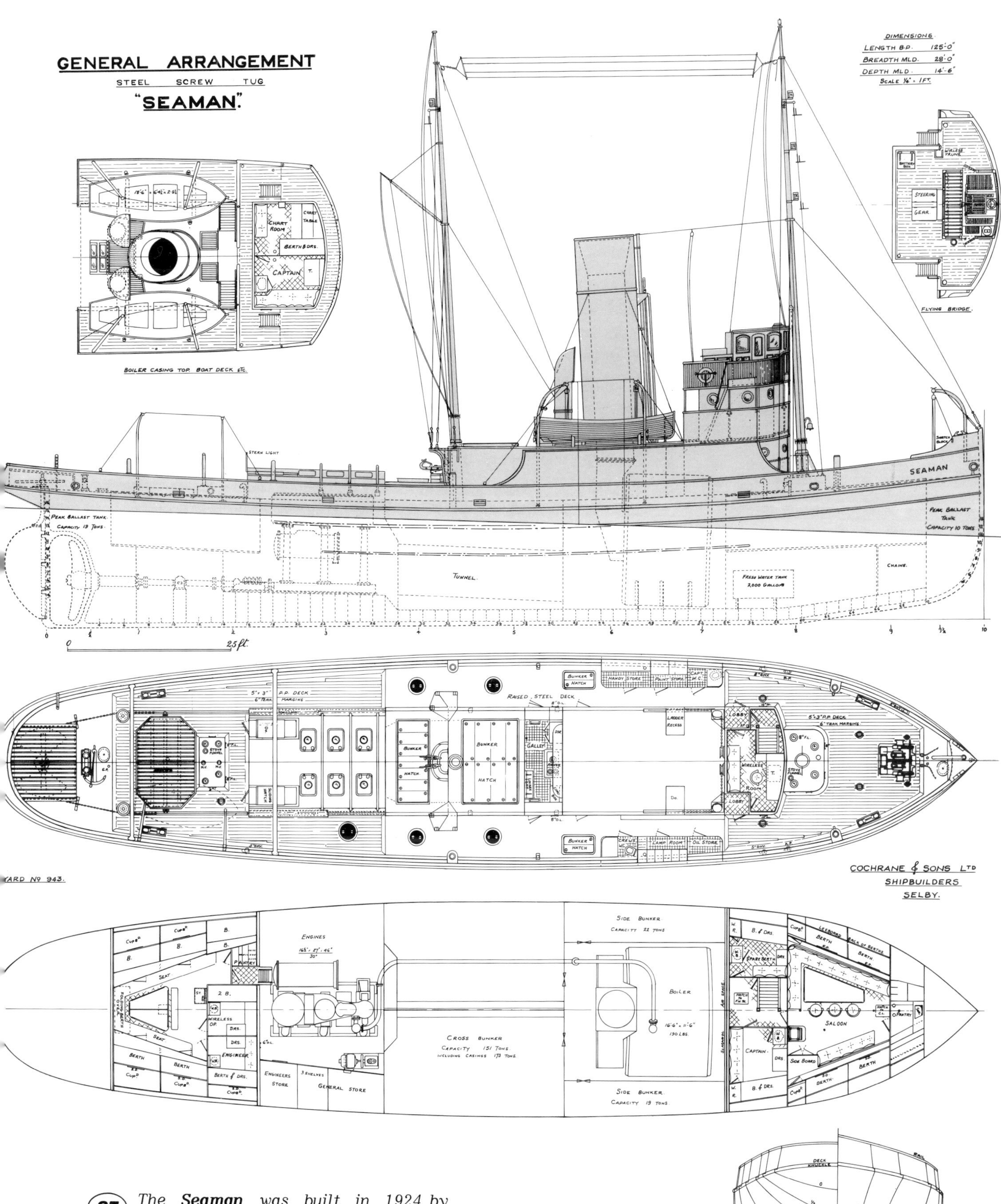

87 *The **Seaman** was built in 1924 by Cochrane's of Selby at a cost of £16,300 for the United Towing Co. of Hull and was their first purpose built deep sea tug.*
Courtesy: National Maritime Museum

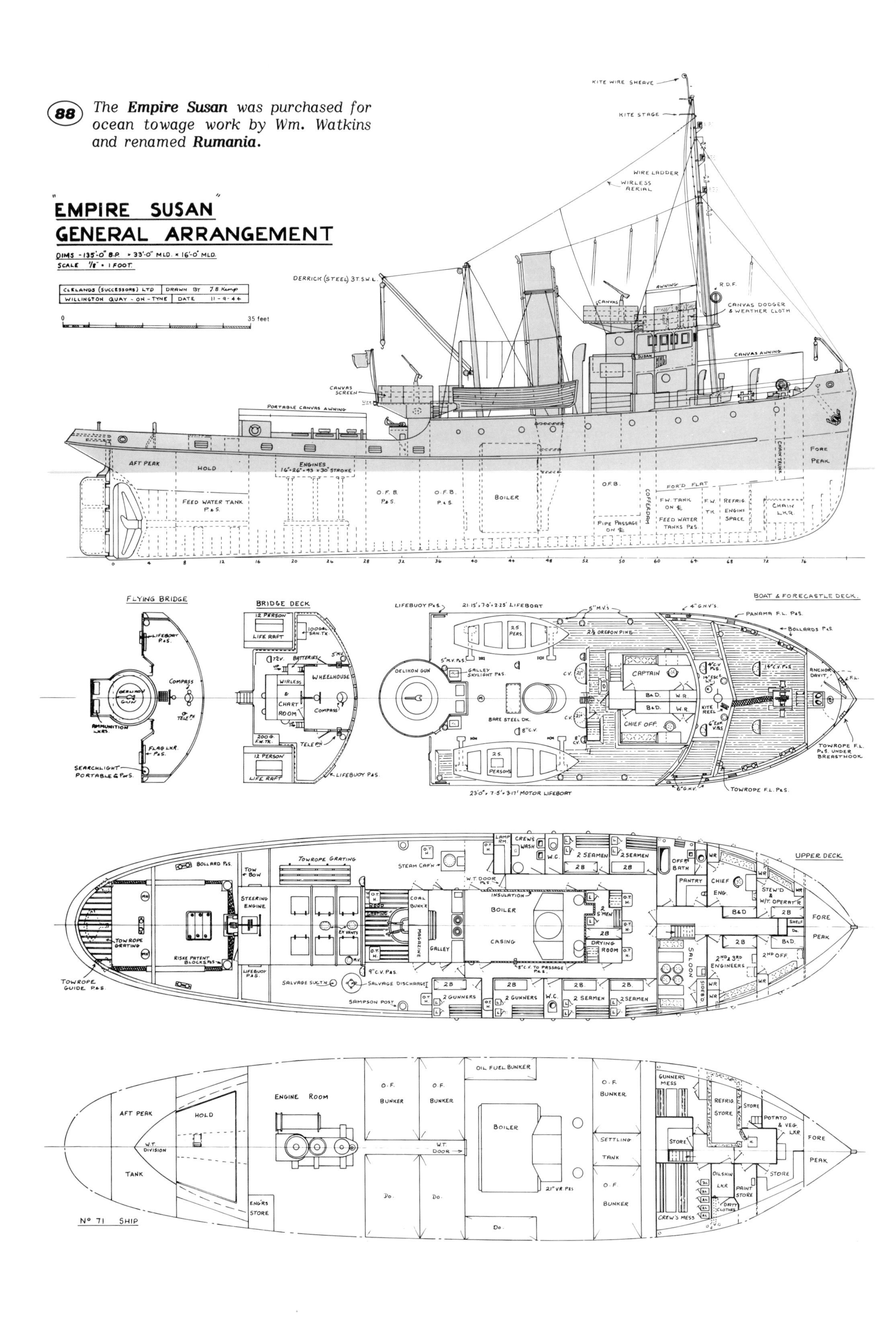

88 *The **Empire Susan** was purchased for ocean towage work by Wm. Watkins and renamed **Rumania**.*

In 1927 there was a bitter complaint in the marine press that the insurance underwriters were weighing their premiums in favour of the Dutch towing companies who already led in the field of ocean towing. Immediately there were two replies, one pointing out that Britain had no big tugs in any number, which was true enough, the second that the German tugowners Bugsier Reederei of Hamburg had bigger and better tugs than the Dutch, 36 tugs totalling 34,724 i.h.p., ranging from 4,000 i.h.p. downwards. In a way one cannot blame the underwriters whose job it was to make money by ensuring that the least risk was taken with ocean towing, and they naturally preferred those firms with a proven record. The crowning blow came when the Dutch and German owners placed tugs on salvage stations at Falmouth and Queenstown to give immediate assistance to ships in distress in the Western Approaches.

United Towing Co. strengthened their fleet with the **Superman** (1933, 120.2 ft. 359 tons. 124 n.h.p.) and the **Englishman** (1937, 135.1 ft. 487 tons. 190 n.h.p.), the latter having a raised forecastle, a style which the British had not used since the war when the **Saint** class were built (5). The **Englishman** was lost in 1941 when she was sunk during an aerial attack. In 1938 another British company took up the challenge and the nautical press, which seemed to have forgotten about the United Towing Company, wrote, "The modern deep-sea tug is a piece of floating plant very much to be admired. For some mysterious reason we as a nation had, until recently, fallen far behind the Dutch in ocean towing. It is pleasing to note that the Overseas Towage & Salvage Company has built some really good deep sea tugs which are a great advance on anything previously owned in this county." Their **Neptunia** was built in 1938 with a gross tonnage of 798, with engines of 2,000 indicated h.p. specially designed for long distance ocean towage. She carried 440 tons of fuel oil and had a towing radius of 9,000 miles at full power without refuelling (91). The **Salvonia** (143.6 ft. 571 tons) built in 1939 had engines of 1450 i.h.p.

To illustrate that in fact Great Britain had not "fallen far behind the Dutch" the following summary shows that the activities of the United Towing Company could bear comparison with those of L. Smit of Rotterdam who before the war were considered to be the leading deep sea towing specialists:

Tows carried out:	Steamers	Obsolete	Sail	Harbour Craft	Sundry	Total	Losses
United Towing Co. 1921-1939	255	137		1542	130	2064	17
L. Smit 1924-1939	346	165	45	2976	22	3554	19

(Under the heading "harbour craft" come dredgers, barges, lighters, floating cranes and floating docks).

After the war the two British companies re-equipped with war-built tugs:

United Towing Company

Masterman ex **Empire Larch**	1941	142'6"	482 tons	1350 i.h.p.	sold 1962
Merchantman ex **Empire Bess**	1945	143'2"	593 tons	1350 i.h.p.	sold 1962
Serviceman ex **Empire Stella**	1945	123'6"	325 tons	750 i.h.p.	sold 1969
			(converted to diesel 1961)		
Tradesman ex **Empire Julia**	1944	143'2"	592 tons	1350 i.h.p.	sold 1963
Airman ex **Empire Clara**	1945	123'6"	333 tons	750 i.h.p.	sold 1967
Guardsman ex **Empire Nina**	1946	123'6"	329 tons	750 i.h.p.	sold 1967
Rifleman ex **Empire Vera**	1945	123'6"	333 tons	750 i.h.p.	sold 1967
Englishman ex **Enchanter**	1944	174'4"	762 tons	1850 i.h.p.	sold 1962

The photograph (91) shows the United Towing Company's tug **Masterman** lying in the Clyde preparing to take in tow two ferries for Turkey. The two sets of heavy towing hawsers are coiled down on the rope cradles with the wires shackled on to the massive eyes.

Overseas Towage and Salvage Company

Dexterous	1942	156'8"	600 tons	1350 i.h.p.	
Turmoil	1944	205'	1136 tons	4000 b.h.p.	
Marinia ex **Empire Mary**	1945	143'2"	593 tons	1350 i.h.p.	sold 1950

Replaced in 1952 with **Marinia** ex-**Empire Aid** a sister ship.

William Watkins made a surprise comeback into the world of deep-sea towage and salvage when they purchased the **Empire Susan** (88) and renamed her **Rumania** (1944, 143'2", 592 tons, 1300 i.h.p.) reviving the name borne by two of their previous tugs built 1912 and 1919. They also put into service the **Zealandia** ex-**Empire Winnie.** Even more of a surprise was the appearance of the tug **Metinda III** ex **Empire Jane** (1945, 143'2", 593 tons, 1350 i.h.p.) owned by Metal Industries (Salvage) Ltd., a subsidiary of Metal Industries Ltd., who were well known in the ship-breaking industry. Salvage tugs had been traditionally placed on station in Falmouth, the French Atlantic ports and the Azores, but Metal Industries saw a gap in the North of Scotland where ships going 'north about' frequently came to grief through there being no salvage tug to give immediate assistance. By stationing their tug **Metinda III** at Scapa Flow they hoped to fill that gap (at a profit of course), and

*The **Seaway** (top) was built as the **Empire Palm** in 1942 by Scott of Bowling (114'6" o.a., 260 tons, 1000 i.h.p.). She worked on the Clyde during the war and was bought in 1946 by the Ardrossan Harbour Board to replace their ageing **Cockspur**. Her captain always kept a full load of fuel aboard as he believed in using the sheer weight of his tug as brake. She was very quiet in operation and there was no vibration.*

*The **Sir John** (bottom) appears to be a steam tug but the funnel hides a diesel exhaust. She was built by Humphrey & Grey for their own use on the River Thames and was 76.2 ft., 83 tons, 500 b.h.p. In this picture she is towing her barges close up to the stern on the after towing hook.*

Neptunia *(1938) was built by Cochranes of Selby. She was 183'9" overall. Unfortunately she did not last long and was sunk on 13 Sept. 1939 by a U-boat's torpedo and gunfire, off the south west of Ireland. To replace her* ***Hesperia*** *was loaned to them by the Admiralty.*

PHOTO: Nautical Photo Agency.

this they did successfully for many years. She belonged to the same group of tugs as the **Empire Susan** (88).

The company survived on the salvage of fishing craft and coasters until 1961 when they were forced to close down their operations for economic reasons. Typical of their work was the rescue of the German ship *Charlotte* which broke down in the North Sea 100 miles east of Aberdeen in gale force winds. By the time the **Metinda III** reached the casualty it had drifted a further 50 miles to the eastwards and in total the tug spent six days at sea. On another occasion she went to the assistance of a Swedish vessel ashore near Duncansby Head. She stood by, returned to base for salvage equipment, stood by again in atrocious weather unable to commence salvage and eventually had to abandon the wreck - "No Cure, No Pay!"

The **Metinda III** shown in the drawing (140) represents the ex-**Empire** tugs with which Great Britain re-entered the ocean towing business after the war. Except for slight differences, especially in the size and shape of the funnel, the **Rumania** and **Zealandia** of Watkins, the **Tradesman** and **Merchantmen**, and the two **Marinia**'s of Overseas Towage were all built to the same plan. The raised forecastle was by now standard for deep-sea tugs, the vessels were provided with a spacious bridge and chartroom with the captain and mate in cabins immediately below. The crew were accommodated in the forecastle below that again as had been the arrangement in earlier days.

After the war many ships were delivered from the European theatre to all parts of the world and it became so commonplace that only record tows or disasters hit the headlines. Unfortunately it was the disasters for which British tugs received the most publicity. In 1951 the British Iron and Steel Corporation (Salvage) Ltd. of London made an offer for the obsolete battleship *San Paulo* as scrap but she still had to be brought back to this country from where she lay in Rio de Janiero. While the *San Paulo* was prepared for the tow, all the openings in her hull being sealed to keep out the heavy seas through which she would have to pass, the **Bustler** and the **Dexterous** of the Overseas Towage and Salvage Co. proceeded to South America. On 20th September 1951 the tow commenced, the **Bustler** with 100 fathoms of 22" manila attached to 350 fathoms of 5" wire secured to a length of the ship's chain cable. The **Dexterous** had 70 fathoms of 10" nylon attached to 230 fathoms of 5" wire. After a slow tow of 45 days the **Dexterous** had to leave her tow and proceed to Dakar to replenish her bunkers. On 4th November a gale forced the tugs to heave to; the runners on board the battleship reported everything O.K. apart from a few minor leaks. At dusk a squall hit the area and the *San Paulo* took a sheer which almost caused the tugs to collide. The tug masters

Masterman *(ex-Empire Larch), lying in the Clyde preparing to tow two ferries to Turkey.*

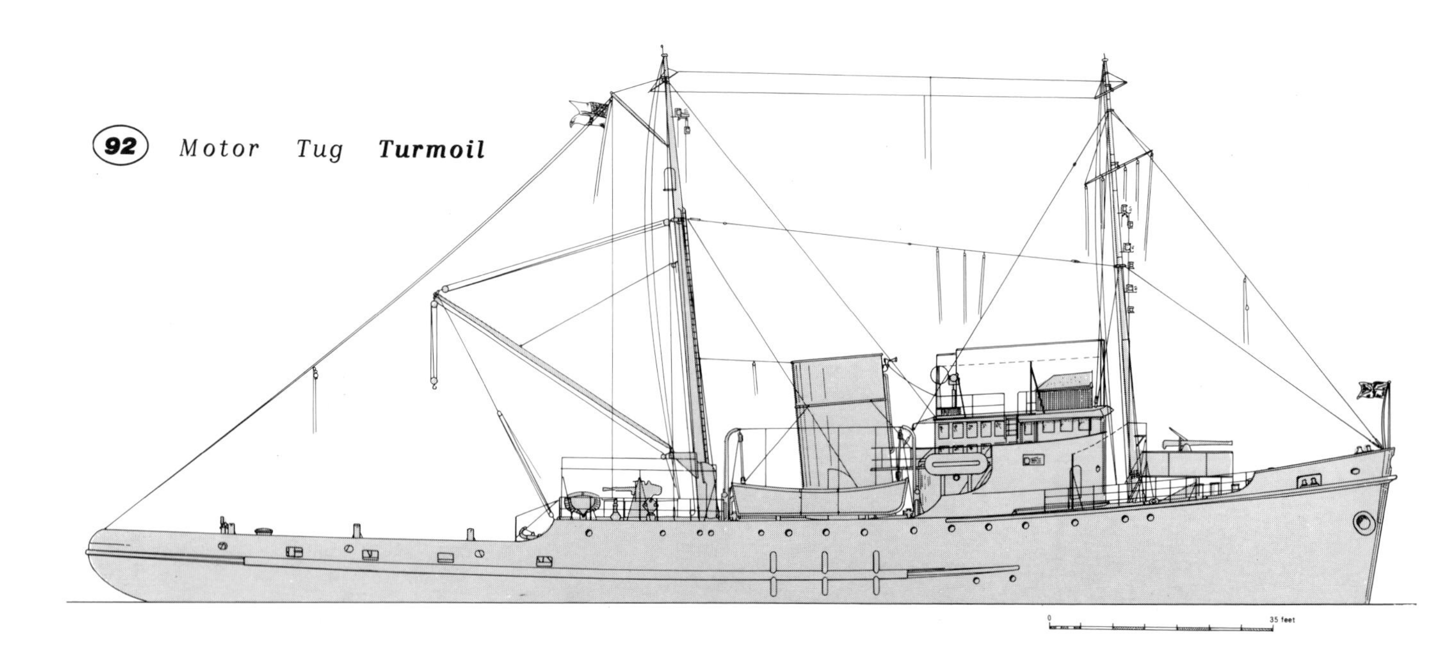

92 *Motor Tug* **Turmoil**

agreed that the **Dexterous** should slip her tow, but in doing so the towline touched the propeller and was cut. Almost simultaneously the **Bustler**'s towline parted, and nothing was ever seen or heard again of the *San Paulo.* While the **Bustler** remained searching the area, the **Dexterous**, badly damaged by the storm put into Ponta Delgada for repairs.

Although this book is about steam tugs it is not possible to write about ocean salvage without mentioning the case of the motor tug **Turmoil** and the *Flying Enterprise.* On Christmas Day 1951 the American freighter *Flying Enterprise* sent out a distress call. L. Smit's **Oceaan** was ordered to her aid but as she set out the **Zwarte Zee** sent a call for assistance as she was on a lee shore with a tow in the Bay of Biscay and in difficulties. The **Oceaan** was therefore diverted to give her help. The **Turmoil** was committed to assist the tanker **Mactra** which had lost her screw off Fastnet. The U.S. transport *General Greenly* and the *U.S.S. Southland* arrived to stand by and rescued the crew and the passengers of the *Flying Enterprise.* The *John W. Weeks*, a destroyer arrived and stood by passing food to Captain Carlsen who had remained behind aboard his ship. On 2nd January 1952 the **Turmoil**, having satisfactorily completed her salvage of the *Mactra* set out from Falmouth to contact the *Flying Enterprise*, arriving on 4th January. First efforts to pass a line showed that it was not possible with only a single man on the casualty so the mate of the **Turmoil**, Dancy by name, leapt aboard the *Flying Enterprise* to assist Captain Carlsen. The tow was passed and made fast and the tow commenced. Since the coast of France was a lee shore and the weather was deteriorating, it was decided to tow the *Flying Enterprise* to Falmouth. Although other tugs were standing by, the *Flying Enterprise* had developed a split in her hull and could not be towed any faster than the **Turmoil** was doing, and their assistance was not used.

At 1.30 pm. on 9th January the tow parted at a position 60 miles from Falmouth and the weather was too bad to allow the towrope to be passed. On 10th January, it was obvious that the *Flying Enterprise* was going down and at 3.22 pm. Carlsen and Dancy jumped overboard and were picked up, and the **Turmoil** set course for Falmouth. The *Flying Enterprise* sank at 4.30 pm. The **Turmoil** had 'steamed' 676 miles for 139 hours at an average of 4.08 knots. For the tow she had used 150 fathoms of 5" wire, 350 fathoms of 5½" wire, putting an average strain on her gear of 20 to 22 tons. After all that there was no reward -'NO CURE, NO PAY' is the condition under which most ocean salvage attempts are made and it means exactly what it says. Some salvage companies agree to work on a daily hire basis and get paid whatever happens, they therefore do not take the risks and do not have to hurry. Under the Lloyds Open Form (No cure, no pay) the salvager will make every effort to ensure success. Not long afterwards the **Turmoil** received another distress call, from the *Robert H. Harrison* which had lost her propeller 420 miles off Land's End in a gale and was drifting at the rate of about 4 knots. The **Turmoil** finally located her 100 miles north of her original position and, as morning broke, passed the tow. Fierce squalls struck the tug and her tow and the line parted. The connection was re-established and the captain of the **Turmoil** decided that he would have to run before the storm up the Irish Sea. Again the tow parted and again it was reconnected, and after a week of constant struggle against the elements the *Robert H. Harrison* was handed over to the local tugs at the Liverpool Bar.

In 1953 one of the worst storms on record swept the seas around the British Isles and caught In its fury was the tug **Englishman** (93) with a tanker in tow which she had brought over 8,000 miles from Singapore. A mountainous wave struck the tug and her tow and the cable parted; 400 yards of chain cable, 20" manila and thick wire rope; which all had to be heaved aboard while the tug was searching for the tanker. Dry, the towing gear had weighed about 80 cwt. but wet, its weight was almost doubled, and it had to be manhandled along the deck as the capstan recovered it. The weather proved too much and two men were injured, so the captain of the tug had to head for the Humber with the towrope trailing behind the vessel. Once in the sheltered waters of the estuary the line was recovered and the injured men sent ashore. The tug then went back to sea and followed

*The **Englishman** was built in 1944 by Cochranes of Selby as the **Enchanter** She was sold in 1967. PHOTO: Graham Farr.*

the track which the derelict tanker would have drifted along. She was finally located ashore near Yarmouth, seventy miles from the point where they had parted company. It took two months to refloat the tanker and it was mid-April before the **Englishman** could complete her task of delivering the tanker to the breakers' yard at Blyth.

The **Englishman** represents the ultimate in the British-owned, deep-sea steam tug, yet her outline was followed by most of the big motor powered tugs. The deck is continuous from bow to the end of the boatdeck, the provision of generous accommodation above the forecastle deck, the tall masts for the W/T aerials. On the modern, ocean going tug, every effort has been made to keep access between various parts of the vessel below deck so that the crew has no need to expose themselves to the dangers of moving about in heavy seas.

As far as deep sea towing was concerned, the steam tug was now on its way out. For years the experts had been discussing the economies of the diesel engined tugs for ocean towing work, the basic points being cheaper running costs, increased range with smaller bunker space, ability to go into action without the delay occasioned by the need to raise steam first. In 1961 the United Towing Company converted some of its tugs to diesel and the following year disposed of the big steam tugs. The Overseas Towing Company was linked with the Dutch firm of L. Smit of Rotterdam, and Metal Industries closed down. Today the diesel tug rules the roost and the size of the tugs has risen to dimensions and powers never dreamt of in the days of steam.

No reference to ocean towing would be complete without mention of the runners, the men who sail aboard the tow itself. Not every tow carries runners, but it is common practice to have them aboard: (1) To carry out a regular inspection of the vessel in tow. (2) To assist in the steering of the tow. (3) To attend to the towing connection to ensure that the hawsers do not fray. (4) Should the tow rope part the presence of the runners may simplify the problem of reconnecting. (5) If the tow rope breaks and reconnection is not possible, the runners are in a position to anchor the tow until better weather arrives, if close to shore. (6) They keep an eye on the machinery on board the tow and maintain it in good condition. (7) Parts of the tow are often dismantled and lashed on its deck during the delivery voyage. The runners keep these lashing in good shape. (8) The runners attend to the navigation lights aboard the tow.

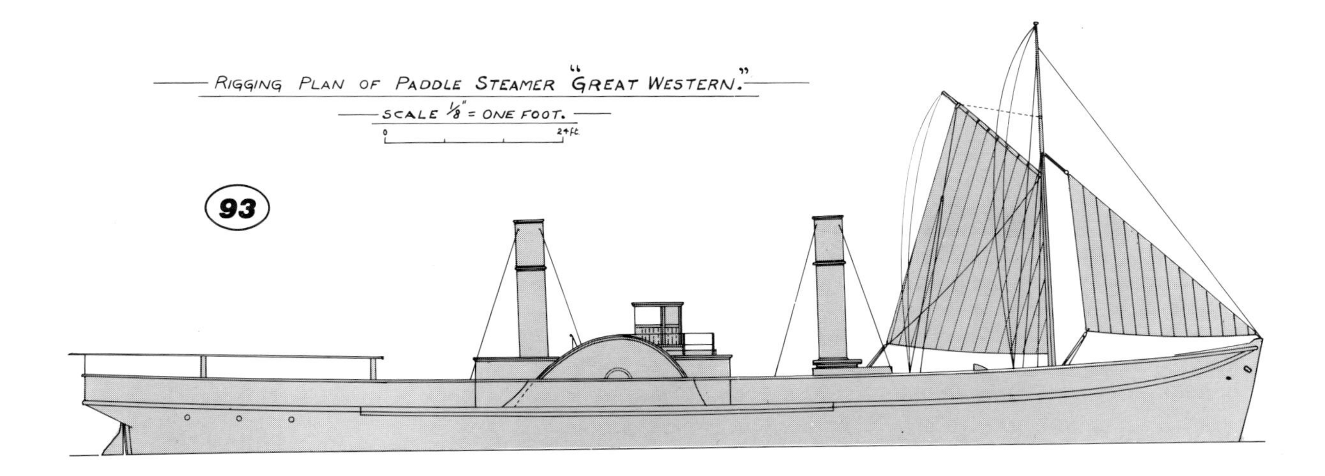

6.

Thames Craft Tugs

(94) *Thames Craft Tug **Hero** built in Hull in 1888 was bought by Chas. Gaselee of London and renamed **Gnat.***

Ship towage on the Thames was introduced when William Watkins put the paddle tug **Monarch** into service in 1833. In the docks, the ships' cargoes were transferred into sailing barges which distributed them down river or into lighters which carried the goods up the river. The lighters had no means of propulsion but, riding on the flow of the tidal currents, they were rowed by the lightermen with a huge sweep or oar. 'Driving' was an art which has been passed on through an apprenticeship system. The art lies, not only in the lighterman's ability to 'drive', but also in his intimate knowledge of the river and its tidal forces, for he relies on its assistance to cover long distances from the lower reaches of the river to the wharves upstream and back. Further upriver beyond the reach of the tidal flow, horses were used to tow the lighters up the river to villages where their contents were unloaded. Encouragement to the "mechanisation" of the trade was given by the Prince Consort who found the clip-clopping of the horses hooves as they passed Windsor Castle somewhat disturbing. Being a progressively minded individual he instructed his agent to consult a Mr. Allen regarding the possibility of towing by steam tugs. Mr. Allen came to the conclusion that the best thing for the Thames was the paddle tug having paddle wheels with feathering floats immersed three feet below the surface. He had an experimental tug built with engines of 30 n.h.p. working as 40 p.s.i. and with that vessel he towed as many as ten barges at one time from London to Richmond and Teddington, where four were left and the remaining six were towed as far as Oxford. The paddle tugs which were used were somewhat fragile and suffered from damage to their paddle boxes sustained during the course of their normal work. No drawings have survived but a few old indistinct photographs show small paddle tugs with no sheer at all, a sharply raked stem and little other than the funnel projecting above the deck. The presence of a figure amidships and none at the stern suggests that the wheel was between the paddle boxes and that tiller steering had been abandoned.

Although Captain John Ericsson built the screw tug **Francis B, Ogden** at Wapping in 1837 and with her proved the effectiveness of the screw propeller for towing, the tugowners of London ignored him. Ericsson was not put out and made a second attempt with his **Robert F. Stockton**, this time towing coal lighters, but again he met with the same lack of interest from British owners. The first operational screw tug on the Thames seems to have been the **Magnet** (1854, 32'7" long, 10 tons, 12 n.h.p.) owned first by Wm. Hughes and then by James Thomas who followed with the **Jackall** (1856, 54.6 ft. 22 tons. 15 n.h.p.). The first well known company whose name appears as owning a screw tug was the Thames Screw Tug and Lighterage Co. who bought the **Victoria** in 1857 (1856, 92.3 ft. 86 tons. 24 n.h.p.). R. Cory built the **Cockerell** in 1859 (59.8 ft. 28 tons.12 n.h.p.) Other firms followed suit until by 1867 at least 20 screw propelled tugs were working on the River Thames, most of them less than 71 ft. long. An early specification gives details of the **Swan** built for R. Cory in 1861. She was 61'0" overall x 9'6" beam and had a maximum draught of 6'0". Her hull was iron, sheathed with wood and she had a wooden deck. She had a single cylinder engine 15" dia. x 12" stroke operating at 60 p.s.i. driving a 4'8" dia. propeller with a pitch of 7'6". They soon became known on the Thames as 'toshers'.

The first drawing shows a craft tug built in 1879 by McIntyre of Paisley which has been identified by elimination as the **Scotia** (95). Although beamier than the **Swan** she still looked very slender with her 13.0 ft. beam and her length of 59.6 ft. The bulwarks sloped in at the stern but not to the same extent as on later tugs. The arrangement of the towing hook was quite common, a small circular table of iron supported on a tripod of iron bars above the engine casing with the hook pivotted on it. The completely open steering wheel was also a common feature of the early boats. There are no towing bows and there is no indication that the funnel could be folded down though the mast may have done so. She has the same single cylinder engine as the **Swan.**

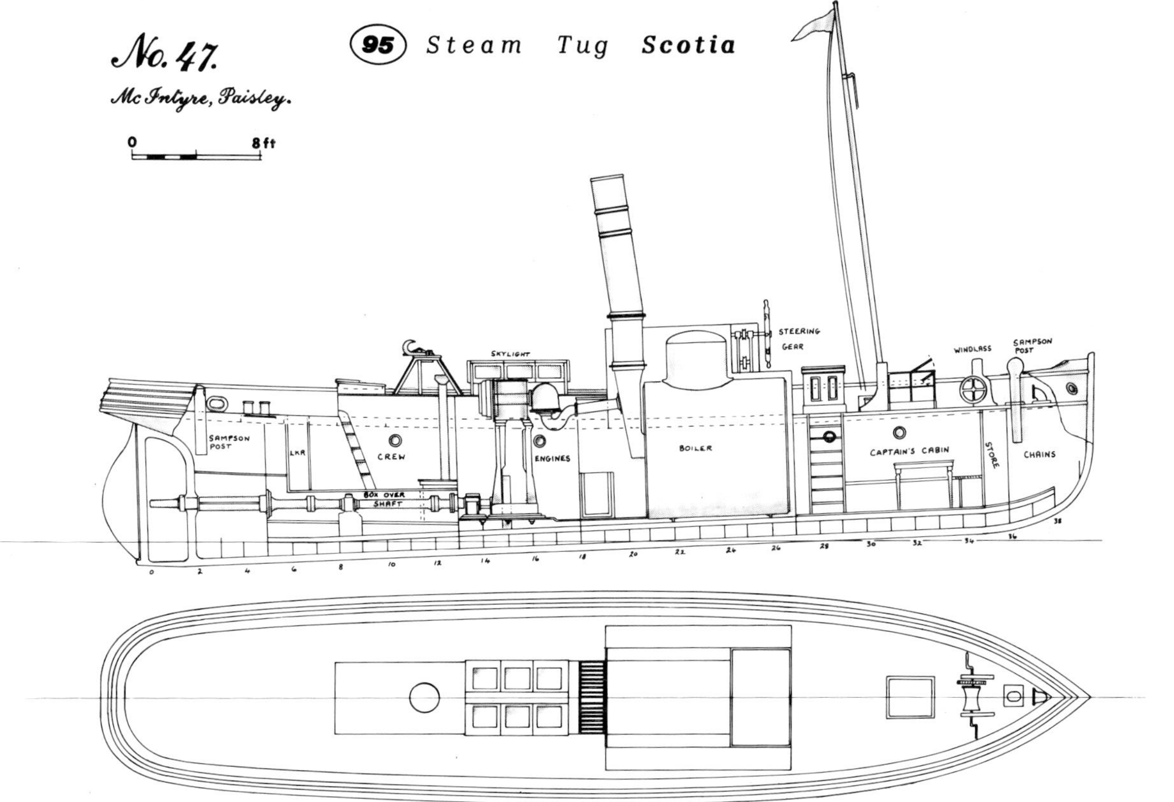

(95) *Steam Tug* ***Scotia***

These early tugs did not have condensers as they were working in the fresh water of the Thames, but the rather muddy river deposited a lot of silt on the boiler tubes giving the poor engineer a lot of extra work in keeping the boiler in a safe condition. Boiler explosions were as common on the Thames as in other areas. The **Prince of Wales** was an unusual tug having started life as a sailing lugger built at some time unknown and converted in 1868 into a screw tug fitted with a single cylinder engine of 12 n.h.p. working at the high pressure of 50 p.s.i. Unfortunately the boiler did not match up to the duty and in 1876 it exploded destroying the whole vessel and killing two of the three crew members. The introduction of the water cooled condenser alleviated the silting problem in the boiler but transferred it to the tubes of the condenser.

The **Hero** in the drawing shows how spartan these old craft tugs were. Built in 1888 she was 59.8 ft. long, 38 tons. The captain had no shelter at all and the big engine room telegraph looked incongruous sticking up beside the steering wheel (94). This was a refinement not usually found on the old craft tugs as signals to the engineroom were generally passed by a gong operated by a wire from the 'bridge'. She has no lightboards but the brackets are there swung inboard out of the way and tied with rope.

The Thames lighter has a "swim bow", i.e. the bow rakes heavily forward and the craft tug usually tows its lighters on a very short line with the stem of the lighter hard up against and overhanging her stern (7). This calls for considerable tumblehome aft to avoid damage, but despite this the **Coborn** (1893, 61.8 ft. 36 tons, ? n.h.p.) showed evidence of frequent knocks on her bulwarks all around the stern. To reduce damage it was quite usual to sheath the stern bulwarks with oak to protect the iron sheeting. The same tumblehome is required all round the tug as she often had to force her way into a tier of lighters to pick out the one which she has to tow. In view of this it was surprising that the **Coborn** did not have the extra protection of a heavy rubbing strake. Just after 1860 the towage of lighters really got under way and for economy's sake they were formed into 'trains'. This was not over-popular with the other users of the river who saw the 'trains' as an obstruction to the free passage of other vessels. The lighters were towed in groups up to a limit of six, and these were arranged in pairs or three abreast in the case of the narrower beamed lighters which were used upstream and which had provision for a rudder. The overall length of the tow from the stern of the tug to the stern of the aftermost lighter was restricted to 320 ft. or 400 ft. depending whereabouts on the river the tow was working. It was apparent from early accident reports that the tugs did not always tow with the lighters hard up against the stern and that many collisions were caused by lighters on a long towline veering about the river if the tug was forced to make a sudden alteration of course because of other traffic. Things were at their trickiest when a tug towing lighters met a tug towing a sailing ship, as in each case, the tow was helpless.

At its largest the Thames lighter was around 87'6" long with a beam of 22'6", carrying 250 tons when loaded. Thus, with the six lighters in tow the small craft tug was shifting as much as 1500 tons of goods. Lighters were used to carry "rough goods", a term used to cover coal, mud and rubbish, or "legal quay goods" which was general cargo for import or export. Before the Second World War tugs towing "rough goods" were not required to carry a mate but instead carried a deck boy, a practice which ceased after the war. Making up a train of lighters was an art in itself. The lighters were connected bow to stern with short ropes and were held together, side by side, by 'breast ropes' (96). Before setting out, the tug skipper would wriggle the lighter train like a snake, allowing the lightermen to take up any slack in the breast ropes, whereupon the tug would straighten up and proceed on its way. As each destination was reached the lightermen would cast off the breast ropes of the lighters which were being delivered, the tug would stem the tide, the lightermen would cast off the tow ropes and the lighter would swing alongside the wharf guided by the lighterman's sweep. Meanwhile the tug continued its turn and once more with the tide astern, resumed its journey. At night a light was placed on the stern of the rear port lighter or on the stern of the rear lighter if there was only a single one at the tail end of the tow.

The **Margaret** (1898, 70.0 ft. 58 tons, 70 n.h.p.) is shown with her lighters arranged three abreast (96). The conditions on board the tug are again somewhat primitive by modern standards - the bridge is open but has iron awning supports above it so that a roll of tarpaulin can be spread to keep off most of the rain. The cover over the engine room consists of wooden planking like a cargo hatch which could be battened down to make things watertight. The skipper of the Thames craft tug had one of the most exacting jobs in his profession, working in a crowded river, towing trains of loaded lighters through numerous bridges with narrow arches, using, as did the lighterman, the tidal sets of the river to assist him.

The river was teeming with vessels of all types and sizes. Not only were there dozens of other craft tugs with their lighter trains in tow, but there were hundreds of vessels including sailing barges, collier brigs, cross river ferries, and "Penny Steamers" on their way up and down river zig-zagging from bank to bank to call at the landing stages to land and pick up passengers. There were excursion steamers on the lower reaches and cargo carriers in tow of larger tugs, or even small sailing ships in tow of other craft tugs which, finding themselves without lighters, offered their services, "seeking tugs" in miniature. There were accidents in plenty as can be seen from the pages of the maritime press which reported on damage to, and collisions with other vessels. Even the bridges which spanned the river from the famous Tower Bridge to the upper reaches did not escape. In 1897 Wm. Cory and Son were sued for the sum of £12,000 for the damage to Rochester Bridge alleged to have been caused by their negligent navigation. The excuse that the bridge was an old one and the stones would have fallen off anyway was not accepted! In 1901 considerable damage was caused to a new bridge which was being constructed over the river at Vauxhall. The tug **Frank** (1896, 74.5 ft. 76 tons. 65 n.h.p.) had been forced to take avoiding action when impeded by a launch used by the bridge builders and one of her barges had swung across the river and struck one of the dolphins of the new bridge with considerable force. Before the year was out a similar accident occurred at the Battersea Bridge when two tugs each with barges in tow met. The **Indian Chief** overtook the **Margaret** as they approached the bridge and then swung across her bow forcing her to slow down resulting in her losing control of her lighters which swung with the current and hit the bridge. One of the contributory causes of the accident was said to be the excessive length of the tow rope which the **Indian Chief** was using to tow her single barge. Frequently when a single lighter was to be towed in the loaded state or loaded down by the head it was lashed alongside the tug (96) which, on arrival off the creek or dock entrance, steered straight towards the entrance and cast off the lighter at the last moment allowing it to glide into its berth. The lighterman then attended to the mooring of the barge. It was quite exciting to watch this display of ship-handling. It was the custom to station a craft tug beside the Tower Bridge ready to render assist-

Margaret *(left) tows Thames lighters three abreast close up on the stern for Clements Knowling. PHOTO: B.J. Collis. The diagram (below) shows how lighters were arranged for towing.*

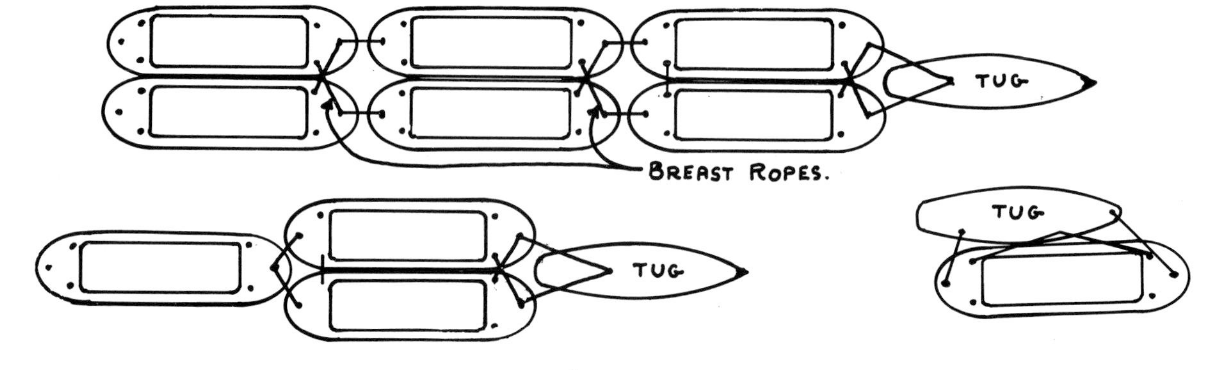

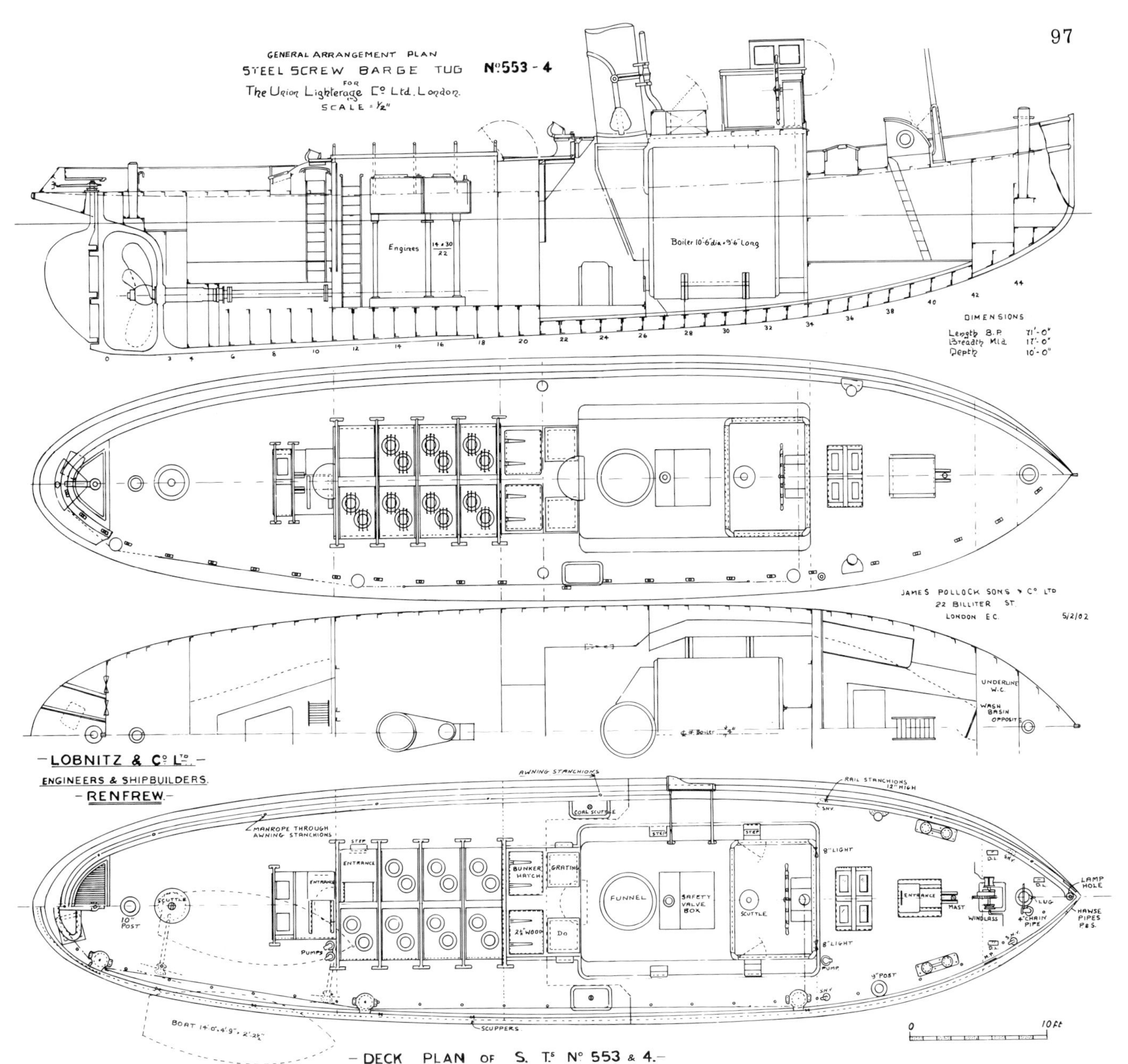

97 ***Dido** and **Juno** of 1902 were designed for the Union Lighterage Co. by Naval Architects, James Pollock. The tender of Lobnitz & Co. was accepted and they then prepared the more detailed (lower) deck plan.*

ance to any vessel requiring it, especially those coming out of the nearby St. Katherine Dock. The tug usually bore upon its superstructure a board with the inscription "TOWER BRIDGE TUG". On one occasion at least the tug failed to do its duty, when the *Oratova* suffered damage to her propeller as she was forced to manoeuvre at slow speed when in heavy barge traffic. The tug **Aid** (1877, 60.6 ft. 32 tons, 250 e.h.p.) which was supposed to come to her aid made no attempt to move and remained at her moorings.

Life on the river had its lighter moments, it was not always doom and gloom! In September 1892 there appeared in the Woolwich Police Court the owner, mate and engineer of the tug **Tiger** (1866, 56.2 ft. 33 tons, 25 n.h.p.). the police had seen the tug come alongside a lighter containing coal and when challenged the skipper had said he was only making fast, but, when the police checked the tug later they found a ton of coal in her bunkers identical to that on board the lighter. The defence stated that it was a custom with masters of tugs, in cases of emergency, when they had not sufficient coal to fulfill a contract, to 'borrow' coal from lighters in the river. The judge's view was not sympathetic, "one might as well call it a 'custom' when a man puts his hand into another's pocket to take money."

In 1902 Lobnitz of Renfrew built two craft tugs, the **Dido** and the **Juno** for the Union Lighterage Co. They were 71'0" long x 17'0" beam, stubbier vessels than the **Scotia.** The tumblehome of the bulwarks was very steep and the superstructure aft was protected by bar type towing bows supported from the deck, leaving a clear passage down either side of the casing (97). The tugs were fitted with two towing hooks, the one placed amidships in the normal position was for towing small ships on a long towline, while the one aft was for towing lighters hard up against the stern. The bridge had a waist high shelter and the windows were arranged to fold down. With the large numbers of boats using the river the reflections from the glass could be very confusing and the skippers

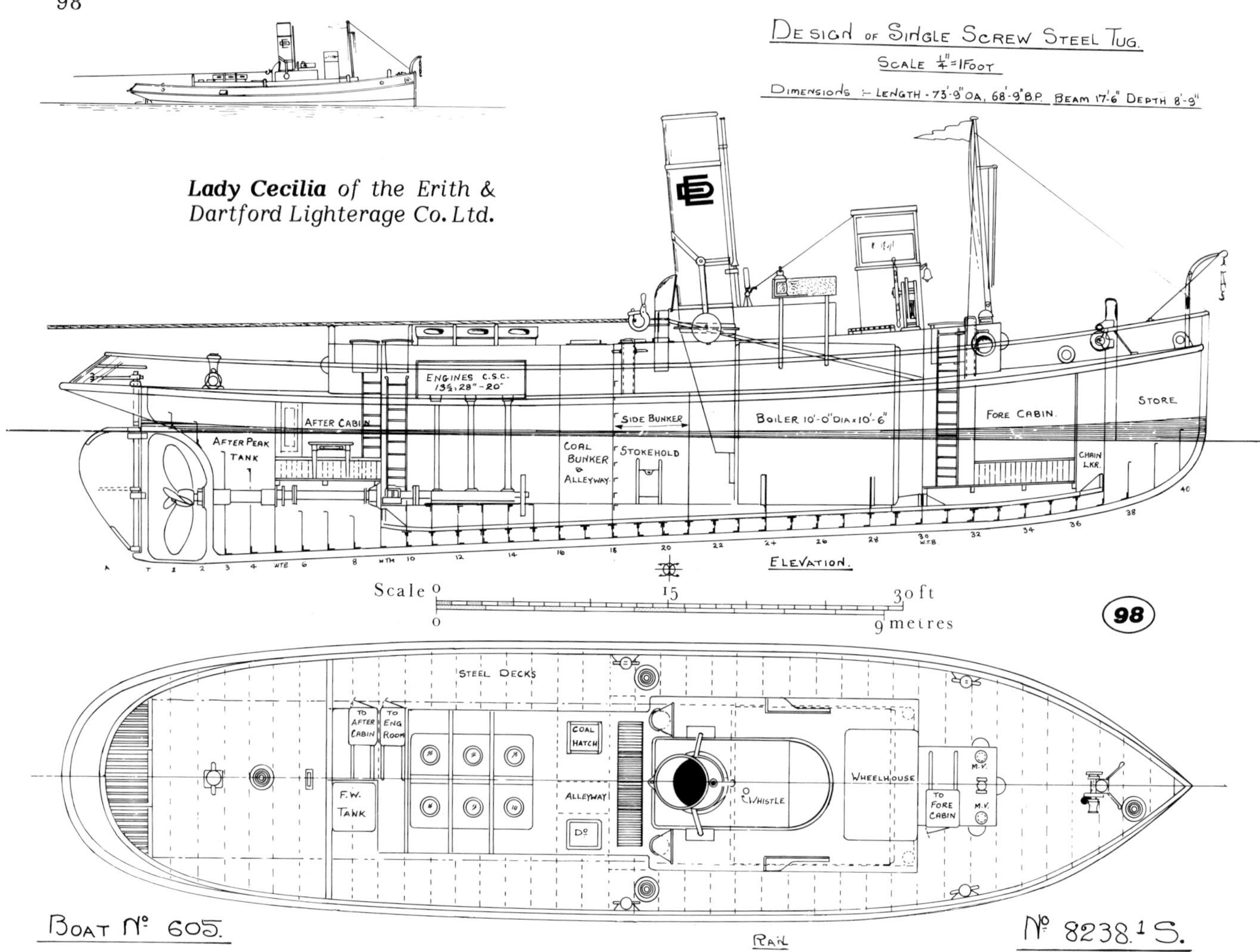

Lady Cecilia of the Erith & Dartford Lighterage Co. Ltd.

preferred to work without the windows at night. The whole impression of these tugs is of a strong, heavy construction. The funnel is arranged to fold down as the craft tugs have to pass below numerous bridges while proceeding up and down the river, where the headroom is limited. The engine was a compound with cylinders of 22" stroke and diameters of 14" and 30". The specification for the **Lion** built in the same year gives some idea of the change since the **Swan** of 1861. Classed 100A1 for towing purposes, with triple expansion engine 24" stroke, cylinder diameters 13", 22" and 35", 70 n.h.p., 550 e.h.p. One single ended boiler 180 p.s.i. Draught 7'6" forward, 10'6" aft. Many of the scantlings were above Lloyd's requirements and she had a steam windlass and steam steering. The propeller was manganese bronze.

The earlier Thames craft tugs for the main part were not built on the banks of the Thames but were built in Newcastle, Hull, Hayle in Cornwall and on the Clyde. Although intended purely for river work they had to be delivered from their builders' yards by coastal voyages. There were some casualties on the way but very few considering the numbers involved. However, one did not even make a start. In 1902 two tugs were built in Greenock, **Tiger** (62 ft.) and **Lion** (75.4 ft. 87 tons, 550 e.h.p.). While the **Tiger** was having her compasses swung at the Tail of the Bank a squall hit her and she sank with the loss of seven lives out of the thirteen on board. The sketch of the **Lion** (7) shows the pair to have been sturdy vessels. Everything was kept well inboard to avoid damage from the overhanging bows of the lighters, even the boiler casing sloped inwards. The towing beams were rather more substantial than usual and spanned from bulwark to bulwark, though the engine casing had the usual round bar protective hoops.

It was possibly with a view to cutting down accidents that the Bye-laws required that every tug should carry a licensed waterman, one of the body of men whose members, among other jobs, manned the passenger ferries. However, the tugowners saw no useful purpose being served by their presence and frequently ignored the Bye-law, an act which could, and did land them in court. One master was fortunate in that the judge agreed with him that the waterman was little better than a passenger boat man and served no useful purpose aboard a tug other than creating a job. (Job creation is apparently not a modern phenomenon.) Mention has been made of the frequent collisions on the river. The masters of the craft tugs were quick to take the opportunity of offering assistance, and equally quick to claim a salvage award. Often the reward was small, £50 or so, which of course was not to be sneezed at, but sometimes they did better. In 1902 a French ship called the *Cordilleras* was involved in a collision and suffered enough damage to render her in danger of sinking. Three tugs came to her assistance and placed her ashore while one of them pumped her out. The damage proved to be so great that the tugs had to stand by again the next day while the hole was patched,

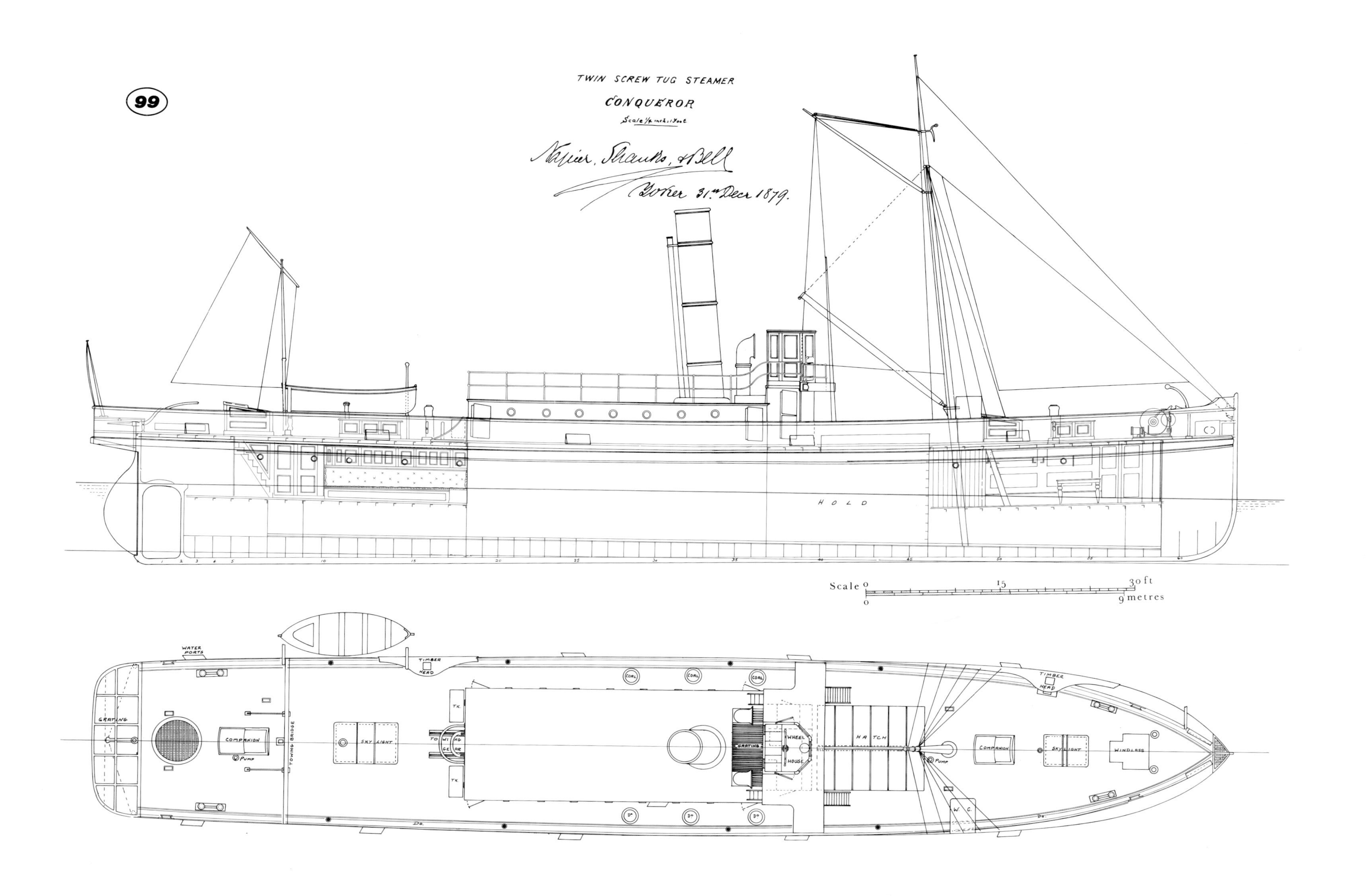
99
TWIN SCREW TUG STEAMER
CONQUEROR
Scale 1/4 inch = 1 foot
Napier, Shanks, & Bell
Yoker 31st Decr 1879.
HOLD
Scale 0 15 30 ft
0 9 metres
WATER PORTS
TIMBER HEAD
COAL
COAL
COAL
TIMBER HEAD
GRATING
COMPANION
PUMP
TOWING BRIDGE
SKY LIGHT
TK
TK
TOWING GEAR
GRATING
WHEEL HOUSE
HATCH
PUMP
COMPANION
SKYLIGHT
WINDLASS
W. C.
Do
Do
Do
Do
Do

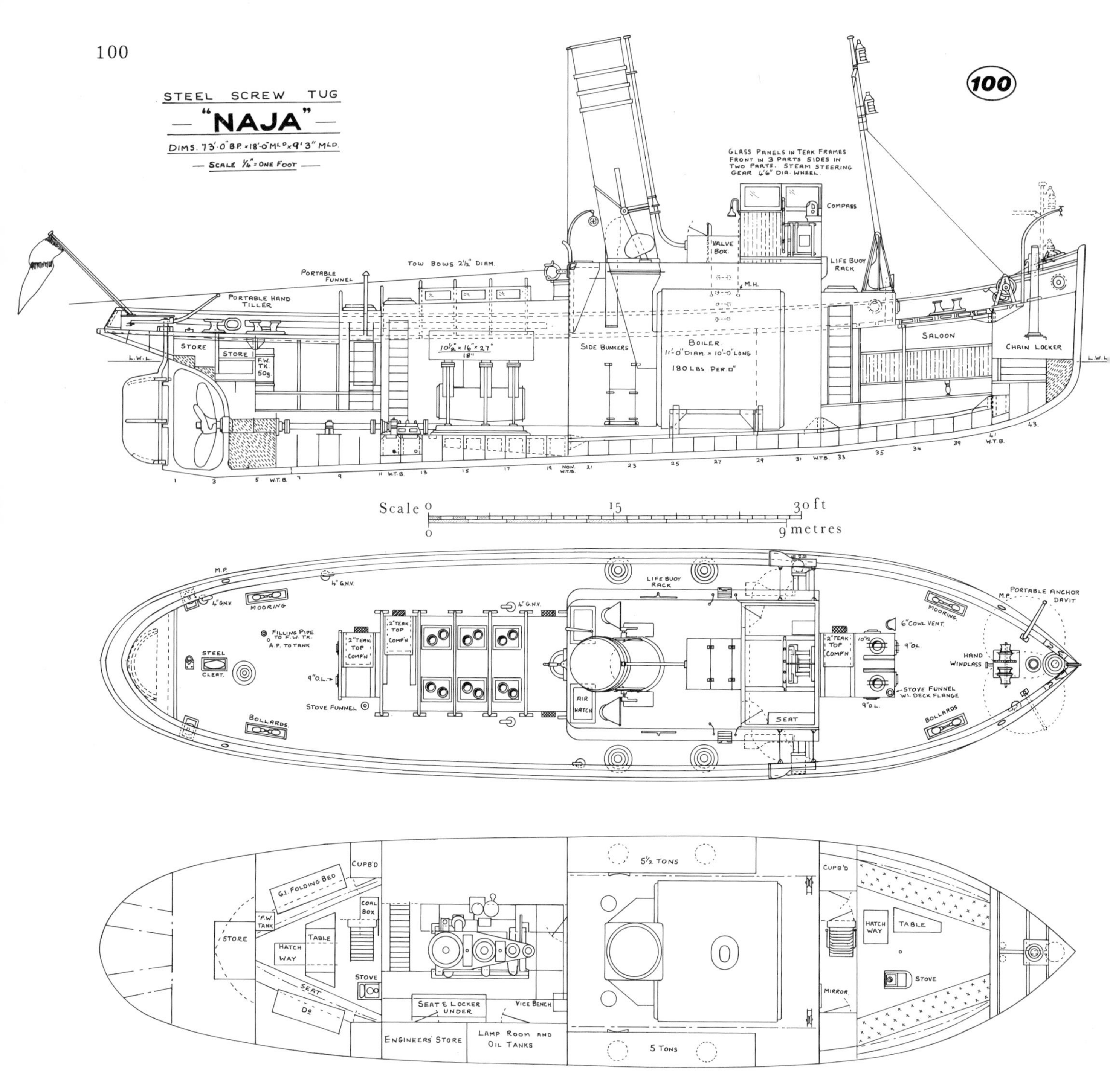

the hull pumped out and the ship towed into dock. The three tugs shared an award of £1,175. The details of the tugs were as follows:

Star in the East	1892	67.5 ft.	55 tons	50 n.h.p.	5 hands	Value £3,500
Success	1890	62.4 ft.	42 tons	35 n.h.p.	5 hands	Value £2,500
White Rose	1893	63.4 ft.	49 tons	49 n.h.p.	7 hands	Value £4,000

It is of interest to note that the **White Rose** was equipped with a salvage/fire pump with a capacity of 450 gallons per minute. This was not an uncommon feature on the craft tugs and meant that they were able to render assistance in case of fire aboard ships in the docks. Ships were not the only floating objects to which the tugs rendered aid. In 1868 there had occurred a most unusual salvage when the tug **Traveller** (1867, 61.0 ft. 30 tons. 30 n.h.p.) had rescued the Waterloo Bridge Pier which had broken adrift from its moorings.

The **Lady Cecilia** of 1921 (98) was built by Philip & Son of Dartmouth (68.7 ft. 66 tons. 300 i.h.p.). Although she is about the same size as the **Naja** (100) she looked much smaller with her low casing and small wheelhouse. The hook was braced by long tie rods to the watertight bulkhead in front of the boiler. Only a primitive anchor windlass was provided, hand-driven gears on a wooden samson post. The navigation lights were set inboard and could not be swung out as could those on the **Naja.** The **Lady Cecilia** was sold to Leith in 1938 and to Grimsby in 1948.

During World War I a number of the craft tugs were requisitioned for service with the armed forces and in addition a large number of small tugs were built for the Department of Inland Water Transport and for various Army units to deal with the towage of barges on the inland waterways of Great Britain and of France. After the war these tugs were sold and several of them were purchased

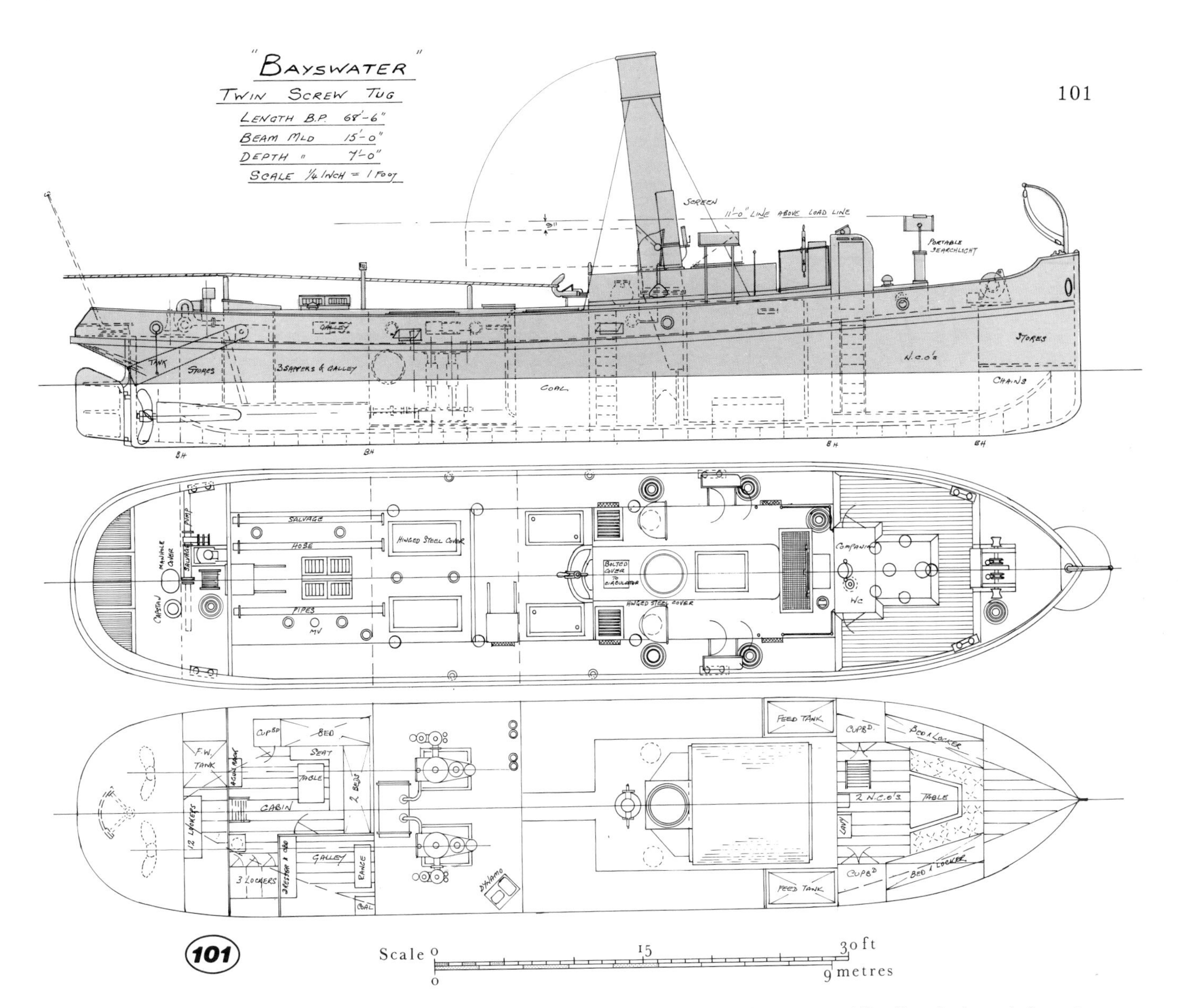

101

Scale 0 15 30 ft
0 9 metres

by firms operating on the River Thames although they had not been specifically designed for the towage of lighters in trains. The **Bayswater** was built in 1915 at Lytham and was 68'6" b.p. with a tonnage of 56 gross and had compound engines of 160 i.h.p. giving her a speed of 9 kts.(101). It is evident at a glance that she was not a traditional craft tug, she had twin screws and no rise of keel, having a constant shallow draught of 4'6". She must have been very handy for some of the more inaccessible creeks and canals. As indicated on the drawing her headroom made her suitable for taking bridges down to 11'0" clearance. The searchlight was for wartime use only and it would be interesting to know if the salvage pump was retained when she took up civilian duty. On either side of the stern was a kind of lee-board to protect the twin screws. She was fitted with a steam anchor windlass and had electric lighting.

The new tugs entering service after the war showed little change from the pre-war vessels. The **Musca** (1922, 72.5 ft. 75 tons, 58 n.h.p.) is shown approaching one of the bridges over the river with her funnel down (103). Another tug of this vintage is the **Naja** (100) shown on the next drawing (1924, 72.2 ft. 72 tons, 39 n.h.p.) and belonging to the same fleet as the **Musca**, H.J.Gaselee. She had all the characteristics previously pointed out, the tumblehome of the bulwarks, the open bridge, the towing bows, the folding funnel and the folding mast. Here an interesting feature is shown, when the mast is folded forward, the top section of the mast pivots to remain upright keeping the navigation lights displayed though at a lower level. The **Naja** had a triple expansion engine with a stroke of 18" and diameter of 10½", 16", and 27". She had steam assisted steering which relieved the helmsman of the physical effort of steering.

When the Second World War broke out, the Thames tugs were soon in the thick of things. Even before the evacuation of Dunkirk started they were called on to help with the organising of the departure and arrival of the small craft. It would be difficult to pick out any specific tug but it should be mentioned that the old **Scorcher** (1878, 62.0 ft. 30 tons, 200 i.h.p.), despite her 62 years was very active towing launches and cabin cruisers to the assembly points (23). The tugs were to be found off the beaches towing barges out to waiting ships and even carrying troops back themselves. One of them, the **Fossa** was lost by stranding on the beaches of Dunkirk and had to be abandoned. When the Blitz started the tugs were exposed to all the dangers of aerial bombardment yet surprisingly few were sunk by German bombs. Mines laid in the river by aircraft claimed several victims, the **Lion** (7) mentioned earlier being one of them. Despite this they never stopped their vital work clearing the cargoes from the East Coast convoys and dispersing them throughout the London area as far as the rivers and the canals would permit. Another rather peculiar

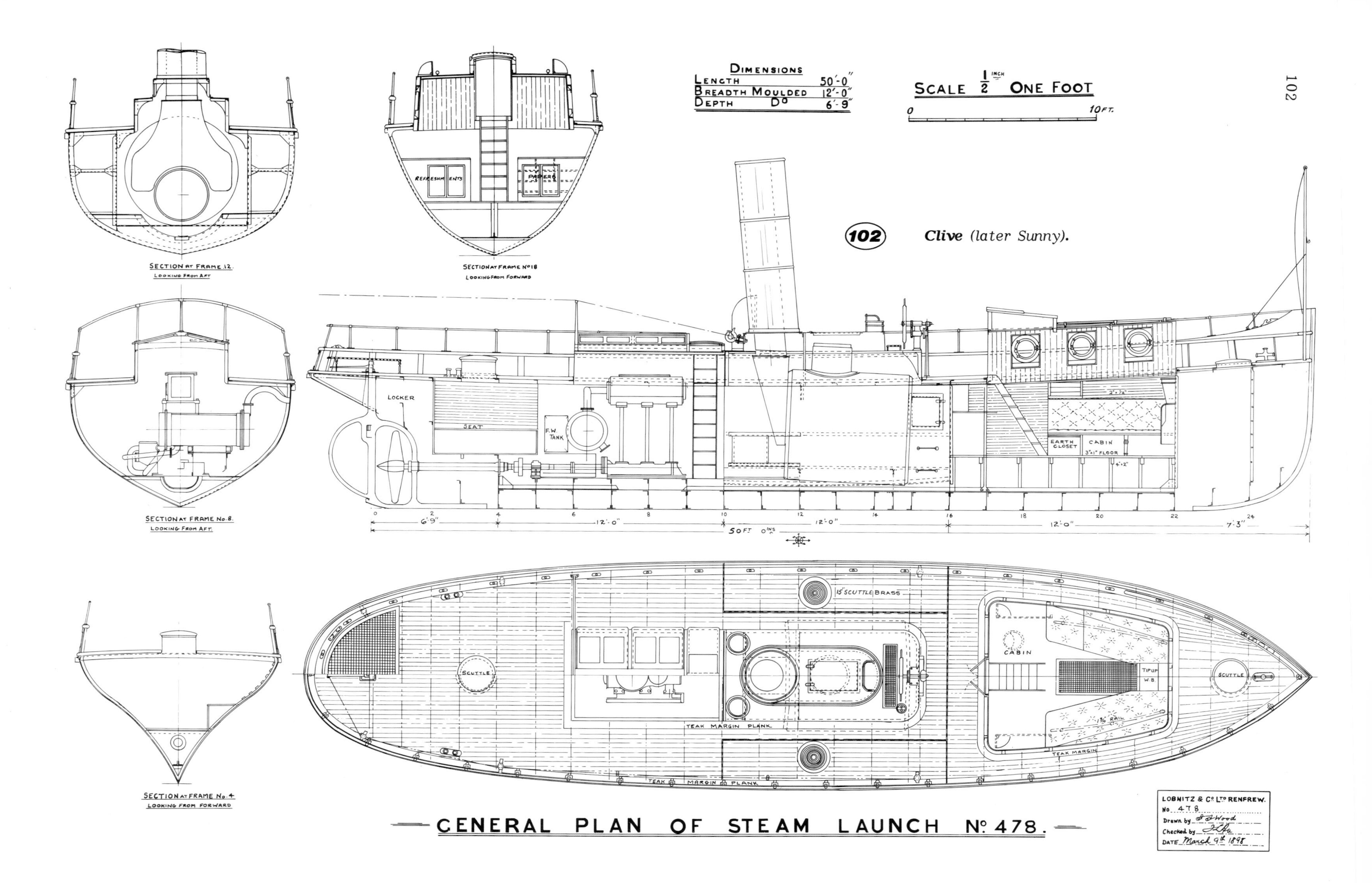

Clive (later Sunny).

***Musca** approaches a bridge with her funnel down. On the side of the boiler casing she carried the placard 'Thames Bridge Tug' mentioned in the text. PHOTO: B.J. Collis.*

contribution to the war effort was started in 1940. Friday, 13th September was chosen for the opening date for the Westminster to Woolwich passenger boat service, organised by the London Passenger Transport Board, in conjunction with the Ministry of Transport, the Port of London Authority and other bodies concerned. Since the London County Council decided thirty years previously to dispose of its fleet of passenger steamers there had been no municipal service on the river. At its start the service was run by a number of Mears steamers, the 40 ft. motor launch *Jeff* and the two motor tugs **Breezy** and **Gnat.** The tugs were not adapted for passenger carrying and their use was entirely an emergency measure. The **Breezy** covered the 6.7 miles from Westminster Pier to Greenwich Pier in 50 minutes, making four calls on the way. The **Gnat** took half an hour to travel from Greenwich to Woolwich, a distance of five miles, with one stop.

Not all the lighterage tugs on the river were in private hands. Some of them belonged to the Port of London Authority who were responsible for five dock systems and seventy miles of tidal waterways, for the movement of vessels and for keeping them serviced for the navigation of ships and lighters. The craft tugs were used to handle the lighters which accumulated at the entrances to the docks at each tide, towing them in through the locks and taking them to berths alongside the ships in the dock. Some of the smaller tugs are utilised for patrol work and for towing duties as required. By the end of the war 12 of the TID tugs were working in the Port of London Authority fleet, but only four were retained to replace obsolete vessels. Seven TID tugs were bought by private companies for use as craft tugs, 5 being converted to motor power over a number of years.

It should be mentioned that a number of small 'launch tugs' have been in use on the river over the years, generally for towing lighters in ones and twos where it was not economical for a larger tug to be used or where the depth of water restricted the use of the bigger craft tugs. These 'launch tugs' were generally quite small, around the forty foot mark, but the one built by Lobnitz of Renfrew in 1898 was somewhat larger than this. The owner of the **Clive** obviously intended her to be an all-purpose vessel as he provided quite comfortable accommodation in the well lit forward saloon (102). It was in the mid-1910s that she entered service on the Thames as the **Sunny** in the fleet of W.H.J. Alexander Ltd., the **Sun** tugs. She is shown 'as-built' but was probably altered before joining the **Sun** fleet to maker her more of a working tug. An appealing feature on the **Clive** was the little seat for the helmsman with the brass rail for his back. Steam launch tugs were not all that common but as mentioned later launch tugs appeared in great numbers once the internal combustion engine had been invented.

The demise of the steam craft tug was rapid; one of the last to be built was the **Ruler** completed by Chas. Hill of Bristol in 1937 for the Wm. Cory fleet, 79'0" o.a. x 19'3" beam and a maximum draught of 10'6". She had a triple expansion engine 22" stroke and cylinder diameters of 11½", 19½" and 33½" giving 520 i.h.p. She had steam steering and a salvage pump with an output of 220 gall. per minute. Only two further steam craft tugs were built, the **Meads** in 1940 (68.6 ft. 67 tons, 300 i.h.p.) and the **Pinklake** in 1943 (71.2 ft. 88 tons. 400 i.h.p.). By 1957 only 59 steam tugs were in service on the River Thames and by 1966 the number had dropped to 8 only. Ten years later none remained in regular work. Although this book is devoted to the history of the steam tug, it is impossible to cover the development of the Thames craft tug without mentioning the motor tugs, as it was on the Thames that the internal combustion engine came into its own in the field of towing. Without going into technical details the following is a very brief history. In

*Motor Tug **Culex** built 1958 in Germany for Gaselee's lighterage fleet.*

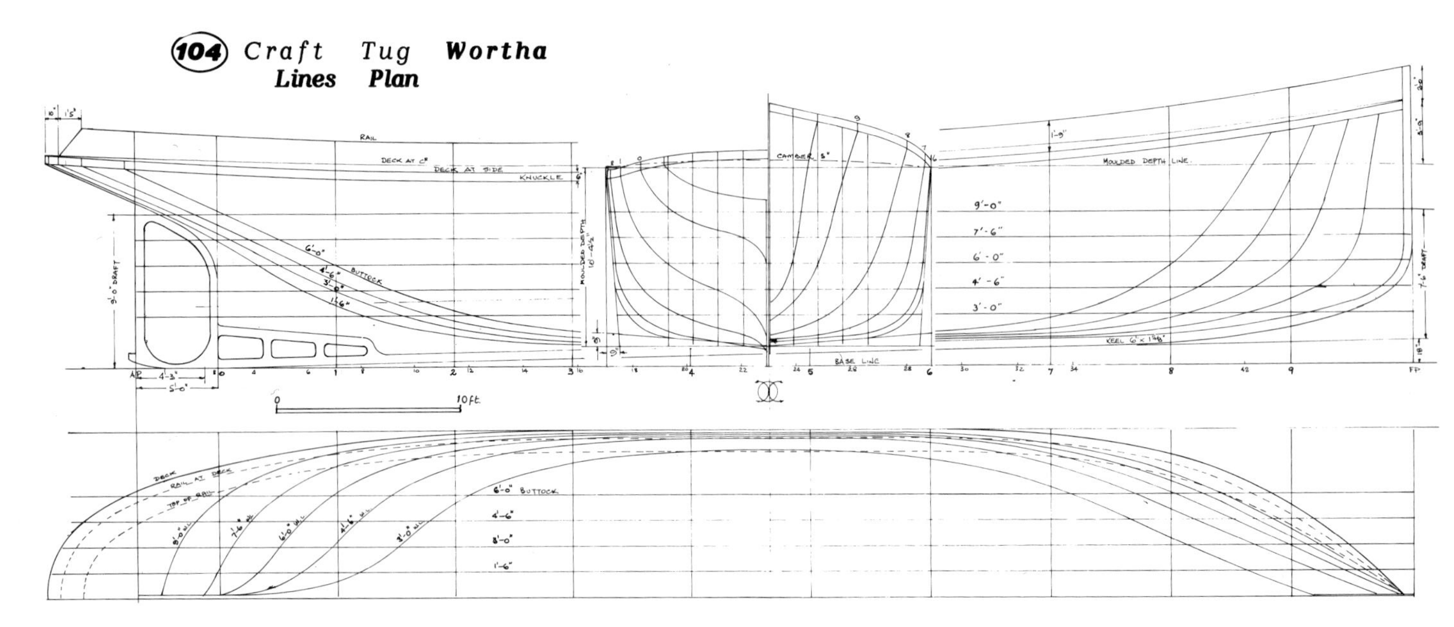

the early 1900s petrol or paraffin engined launches, little more than motor boats came into service towing single lighters. As the years passed the diesel engine was introduced on to the river, the 'hot-bulb' diesel in which a combustion chamber had to be heated with a blow-lamp before the engine could be started (this type of engine had actually been invented as far back as 1890). With this engine the motor driven craft tug could be built to similar dimensions and power as the existing steam tugs. In outward appearance they were very similar to the steam tugs as a large funnel was usually retained unnecessarily. Although more economical to run, the oil engine was still not capable of the rapid reversals required as the tug manoeuvred to pick up its lighters. By the early 1930s cold starting diesels of suitable horsepower had been perfected and the number of motor tugs in service began to increase. The photograph shows the **Culex** (1958, 80.4 ft. 98 tons, 660 b.h.p.) which looks at a glance to be a steam tug. She shows all the usual features and even her deck casings would appear to cover a boiler and an engine (103). Her large funnel is folded down to shoot a bridge and her mast has been lowered to one side of the wheelhouse to reduce the headroom.

The lines plan shows a typical Thames craft tug, the **Wortha** built in 1929 (77.5 ft. 96 tons gross, 360 b.h.p.). she had a fine entry, while aft the hull was very hollow giving a good flow of water to the screw (104). This can be seen both from the shape of the waterlines and the way in which the buttock line sweeps up from Station 3 - compare this with, say, the lines of the M.S.C. **Arrow.** Another feature is the way that the bulwarks are set back from the side of the deck as an added protection against damage. While most British tugs had vertical sides or had some 'tumblehome', the **Wortha**'s hull slopes outwards from the turn of the bilge - a feature found in ice-breakers.

The diesel tug today bears very little resemblance to her forebears. She is very streamlined, the funnel is very short and no longer folds as it is already below the limiting height for the bridges. The whole superstructure rises up from the after end of the engine-room casing until it is level with the bridge. The stern of the tug is very low and she has comparatively little sheer. At one time there was a very large fleet of craft tugs on the Thames and over the period of the high tide it was possible to stand at the Tower Bridge and to watch tug after tug with its lighters passing up and down the river, or running free on their way to take over a new tow. There was nothing impressive about these small tugs and here we might have permitted the words 'bustling little tugs' to be used. Alas these scenes are now less frequent. Over the years the lighter traffic on the Thames had been decreasing and now only small numbers of craft tugs remain. Road transport has been partly to blame, but this has been aided by various developments in cargo handling. The bulk carrier and the container ship have also had their effect. Even the tugs themselves have changed We now have water tractors with Voith Schneider propellers below the hull and the pusher tugs which have been designed to deal with the new idea of "Lighter Aboard Ship" or LASH as it is known. Things are not what they used to be!

Some idea of the decline of the Thames craft tug can be gained from the following table which shows the number of tugs operating on the Thames:

	1956	1965	1975
Steam	67	8	-
Motor-conversion from steam	6	11	19
Motor	98	89	65
Totals	171	108	84
Steam launches	2	-	-
Motor launches	78	93	(no figure available)

The motor tugs which vanished from the Thames did not all go to the breakers' yards, eleven of them at least have survived to operate in various small harbours which have not housed a tug for nearly half a century. One, the **William White** (1915, rebuilt 1951, 51.3 ft. 30 tons. 120 b.h.p.) has been converted for stern trawling and is working in the Firth of Clyde.

(105) Paddle Tender **Satellite**

7. Tenders & Passenger Carrying Tugs

The first vessel to be credited with the title of tug was the **Industry** (Plate 6) built in 1814, but she was a converted passenger carrying steamer and continued to carry passengers for many years. This was the general situation for a long time to come. In 1839 the Nautical Magazine commented that 'in Newcastle all the steamships are registered, most of them combining the two trades of conveying passengers and towing ships.' The number of steamships to which this remark was applied was in the region of 122. Tugs were frequently involved in collisions during their daily round, but changing to passenger carrying did not lessen their chances of catastrophe. In July 1853 the tug **William** of Shields (1842, 71.2 ft. 39 tons, 14 n.h.p.) with about 40 passengers on board was in collision with the collier *Sir John Easthope*. She sank at once, all the passengers being thrown into the water. Fortunately there was plenty of help at hand and it is understood that no lives were lost although the captain died shortly after the accident and several other people were seriously injured. The tug was subsequently raised and found to be badly damaged. The old paddle tug **Jasper** (1870, 78.0 ft. 65 tons. 76 n.h.p.) is shown off-loading her passengers at North Shields (106). There was no shelter for them and probably little seating. The funnel had no outer casing and the bottom was painted with lime to try to cut down the radiated heat. As a gesture towards safety she had at least four lifebelts fixed to the bridge rails.

The early tugs were not equipped for carrying passengers but the people just had to make the best of it. Conversely the passenger steamers were not designed for towing and did not always make a good job of it. However, from time to time, 'tenders' were launched, designed to act in both roles. Such a vessel was the **Satellite** (1848, 108.5 ft. 157 tons. 80 n.h.p.). The **Satellite** was a very basic vessel with no shelter on her open upper deck (105). According to contemporary papers she could carry 600 passengers but it must have been a tight squeeze. She appears to have a small 'promenade deck' aft of the funnel reached by a stair from the after deck. She was sold in 1902 at a price of £410 for breaking up.

In June 1868 the paddle steamer **Walney** (146.5 ft. 200 tons. 100 n.h.p.) built and designed by McNab & Co., Greenock made a satisfactory trial trip with a speed of 14.2 m.p.h. She had been built specially for the Furness Railway Co. and was intended for the passenger traffic at Barrow, and was to be used occasionally for towing; that is the true function of the 'tender'.

In every seaport around the country the local paddle tugs ran trips 'round the bay' or 'round the lighthouse' at so much a head. The Board of Trade had rules governing this traffic but as far as the tug captains were concerned it was a case of 'the more the merrier'. In August 1868 the captain of the wooden paddle tug **Robert Scott** (1863, 87.4 ft. 85 tons. 35 n.h.p.) was summoned to appear in court in Sunderland on a charge of carrying too many people, 320 according to one eye witness, excluding the crew and children carried by their parents, 334 according to another. The tug did have a licence to carry passengers but the limits laid down were 267 when in the river and 112 while at sea. The captain pleaded that the tug had been hired by the local temperance association and that he was to receive expenses only, all profit to go to the organisers who just let people keep coming on board. It was further pleaded that the sea was calm and that the tug was in the hands of a captain of 38 years experience. The court fined the captain £10, but he got off lightly when one considers the casualty rate among tugs in those days. A collision could have been disastrous when one remembers that at best the tug carried only a 10 ft. dinghy. In later years there was much agitation for stricter control over the 'joy-riding' tug owners and their vessels.

When ocean liners became too large for going alongside, it became the practice to station tenders at various ports specifically for the purpose of ferrying passengers from the quay to the liner waiting offshore. Messrs. Steel & McCaskill, (forerunners of Steel & Bennie) ran such a service at

Londonderry and Moville. In 1872 two screw tenders were launched in Glasgow, the **Osprey**, single screw (105.7 ft. 111 tons. 130 n.h.p.) and the **Heron**, twin screw (120.1 ft. 141 tons. 60 n.h.p.). It is strange that two vessels built by the same owner for the same trade in the same year could look so different. The **Osprey** had her machinery placed aft of amidships and her foredeck was long and open, while the **Heron** was more in the style of the conventional tug except that her after deck was somewhat longer than normal. The drawing of the **Heron** is a bit sparse (107) but it shows the after deck clear except for a companionway and a skylight over the spacious saloon. The body plan indicates a hull with a considerable rise of floor as if she had been built for speed (her speed was quoted as 14 m.p.h.) The midships section shows a heavy belting 9" x 7" but placed rather low, it was more usual to set the belting against the ends of the deck beams which could then absorb heavy collision forces. She is pictured with the usual foresail and gaff mainsail, typical of the early tugs. Below the mainsail is a small derrick to work the baggage hold.

The **Heron** was built by one of the lesser known Clyde firms, the London & Glasgow Shipbuilding and Engineering Co., of Govan and worked for Steel & McCaskill until her sale to Hong Kong owners in 1887. The service also employed an old paddle steamer, the **Loch Foyle** and as the years passed other steamers and tugs joined the Moville fleet, the P.S. **Albatross**, I.P.T. **Seagull**, and the I.P.T. **Samson**. At the turn of the century the emigrant steamers docked at Belfast, but the firm, now Steel & Bennie, continued to run pleasure trips until competition forced them to cease operations in 1906.

On the Clyde the ferry work was carried out by the pleasure steamers which abounded on the river, but in 1865/6 the Clyde Shipping Company put into service two tug/tenders, the I.P.T. **Flying Foam** (1865, 96.5 ft. 88 tons. 50 n.h.p.) and the W.P.T. **Flying Scud** (1866, 98.5 ft. 100 tons. 80 n.h.p.). The passenger carrying certificate limits were guided by a line from Dunoon to Gourock, the **Flying Foam** being permitted to carry 330 up river from that line and 171 if sailing beyond it. The **Flying Scud** was certificated for 441 above the line. In 1867 they purchased several second-hand tugs one of which was the I.P.T. **Diamond** (1866, 80.5 ft. 61 tons. 30 n.h.p.) which had second-hand engines from a tug called the **Vixen.** She was renamed **Flying Cloud** and used as a ferry-cum-tug within the harbour of Glasgow. When the emigrants began to leave the south of Ireland, the Clyde Shipping Company built the I.P.T./tender **Flying Sportsman** (1882, 122.0 ft. 187 tons. 98 n.h.p.), 263 passengers in the summer and 188 in the winter, and stationed her at Queenstown. She was joined three years later by the **Flying Fox** (1885, 122.5 ft. 185 tons. 98 n.h.p./400 e.h.p.) and the **Flying Irishman** (1885, 116.0 ft. 162 tons. 90 n.h.p.) these being joined in the following year by the **Flying Fish** (1886, 122.0 ft. 187 tons. 98 n.h.p.). The fact that the vessels were tugs as well as passenger vessels meant that they could be used for salvage work which was always a useful addition to the owners' income. In 1913 the *Haverford* of 11,635 tons ran aground in foggy weather near Cork harbour and a radio message was sent to Queenstown for the tenders to come and take off passengers. Two hours later the tenders **America, Flying Fox** and **Flying Fish** together with the naval tug **Hellespont** arrived and between them transferred 730 passengers to Queenstown. The *Haverford* was later towed off by the combined efforts of the same vessels. For their services the Clyde Shipping Company received £1,200 despite the fact that at no time were their tugs in any danger. At Queenstown the Queenstown Towing Company included in their fleet, tenders which ferried passengers from the harbour to liners which stopped outside the port to pick up their human freight. When the Clyde Shipping Company took over the fleet in 1886 among the boats were the paddle tenders **Mount Etna** (1880, 139.6 ft. 232 tons. 98 n.h.p.) which they renamed **Flying Eagle** and the **Lord Bandon** (1878, 122.2 ft. 154 tons. 95 n.h.p.) which was renamed **Flying Falcon.** The **Mount Etna** held passenger certificates for 572 passengers on the river, 301 within the harbour limits for summer, and 210 for the winter (her engines are on the back endpaper). In addition some of the big tugs which the Clyde Shipping Company kept for the long hauls from the south of Ireland to the Clyde also held certificates and assisted in the tender service when they were in port. In 1888/9 the **Flying Eagle** and the **Flying Falcon** were sold, the first named going to the Admiralty for £5,826, and they were replaced by two new paddle tenders, constructed with the emphasis on passenger comfort, called appropriately **America** and **Ireland** (1891, 131.8 ft. 245 tons. 98 n.h.p.) They looked rather like small Clyde steamers and they remained in service until 1928 when the

Old Paddle Tug ***Jasper*** *acting as a passenger ferry on the Tyne.*

107 Tender **Heron** built 1872.

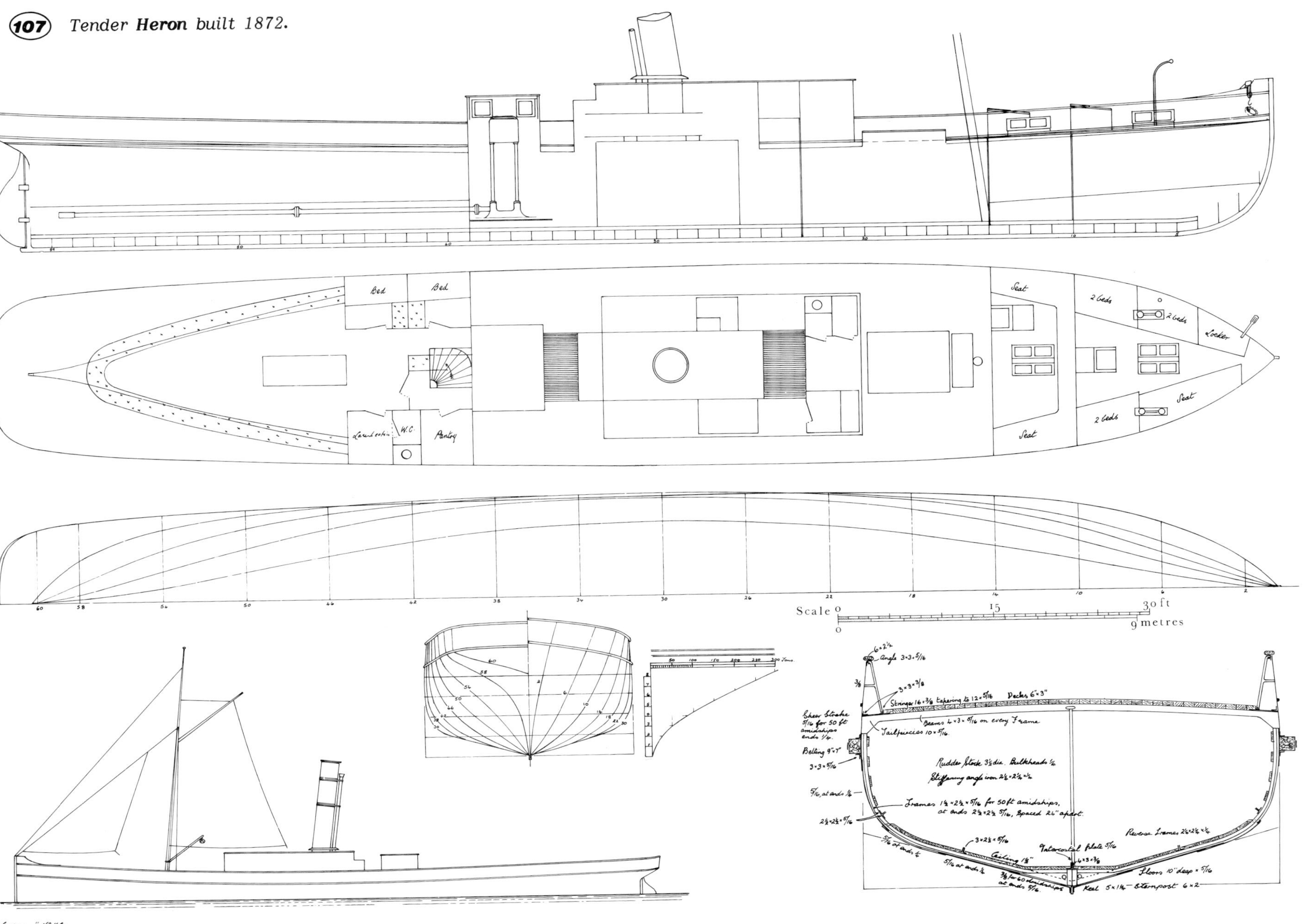

YARD Nº 238
"ROLLCALL"
:::: FOR THE ::::
ADMIRALTY

DIMENSIONS	FT INS
LENGTH BETWEEN PERPENDICULARS	175 · 0
BREADTH MOULDED	34 · 0
DEPTH MOULDED	18 · 6

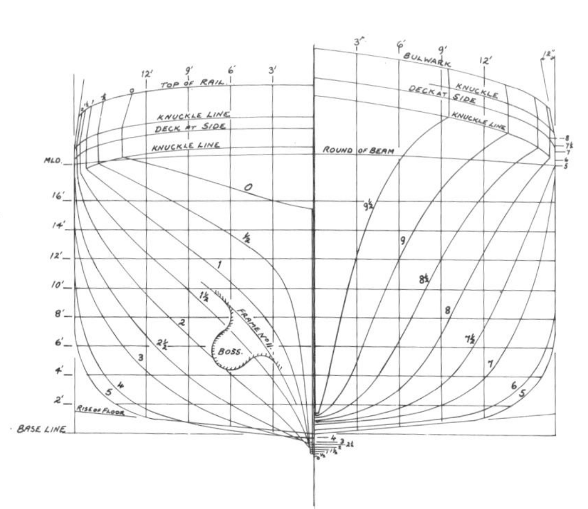

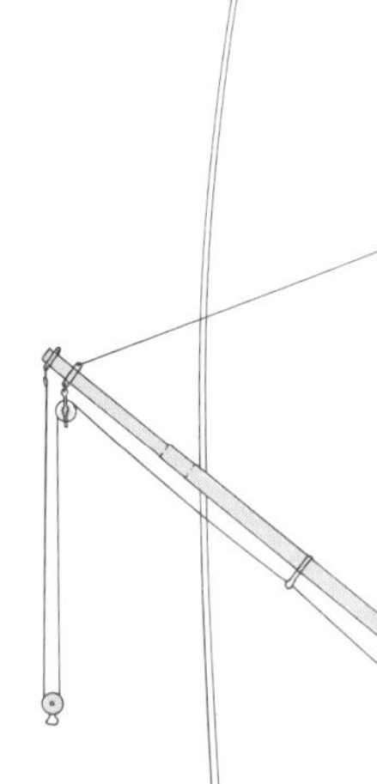

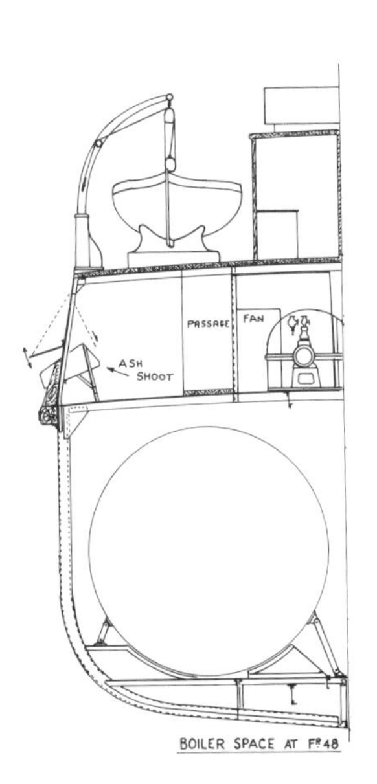

BOILER SPACE AT Fr 48

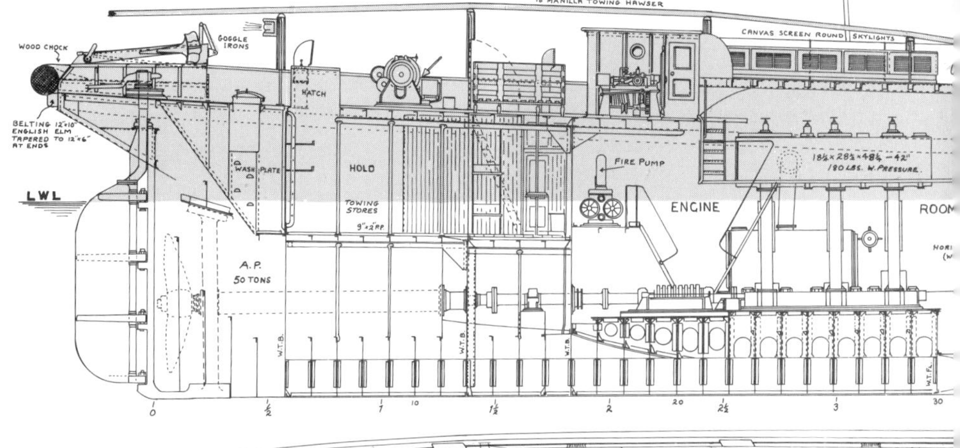

108

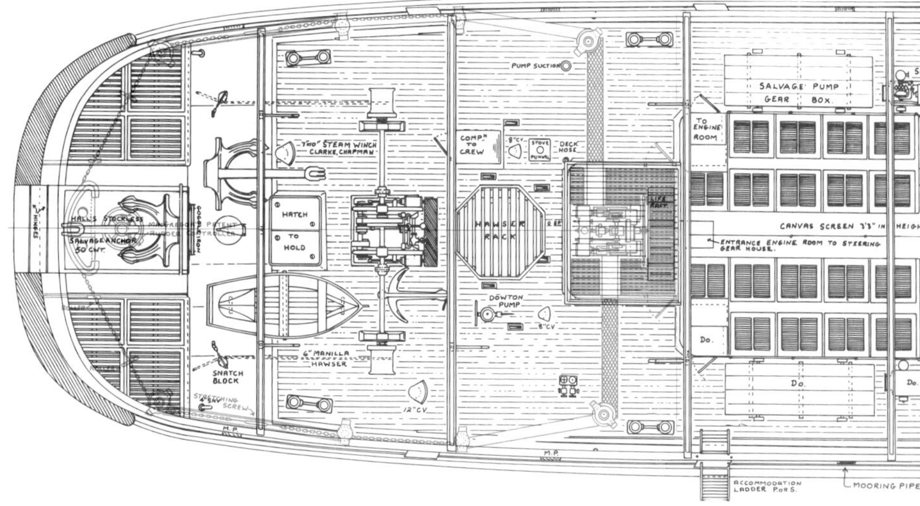

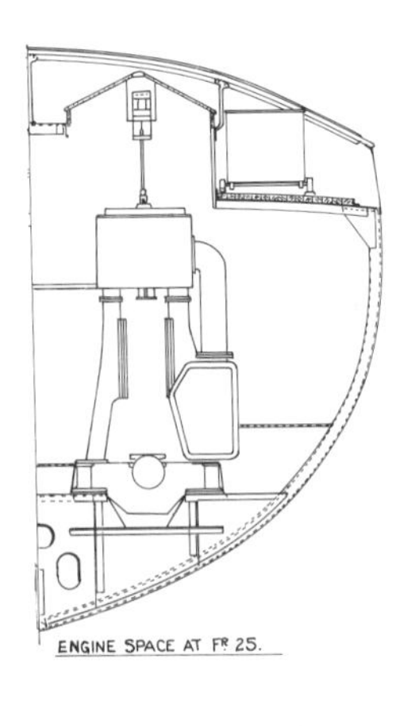

ENGINE SPACE AT Fr 25.

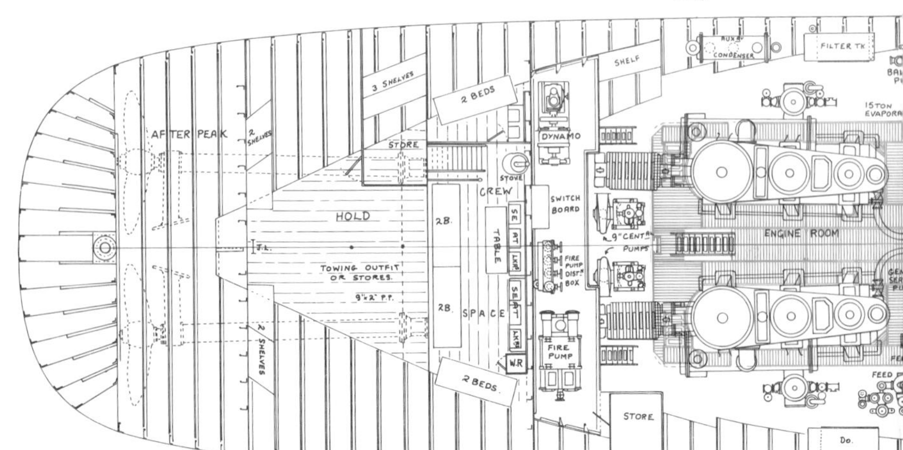

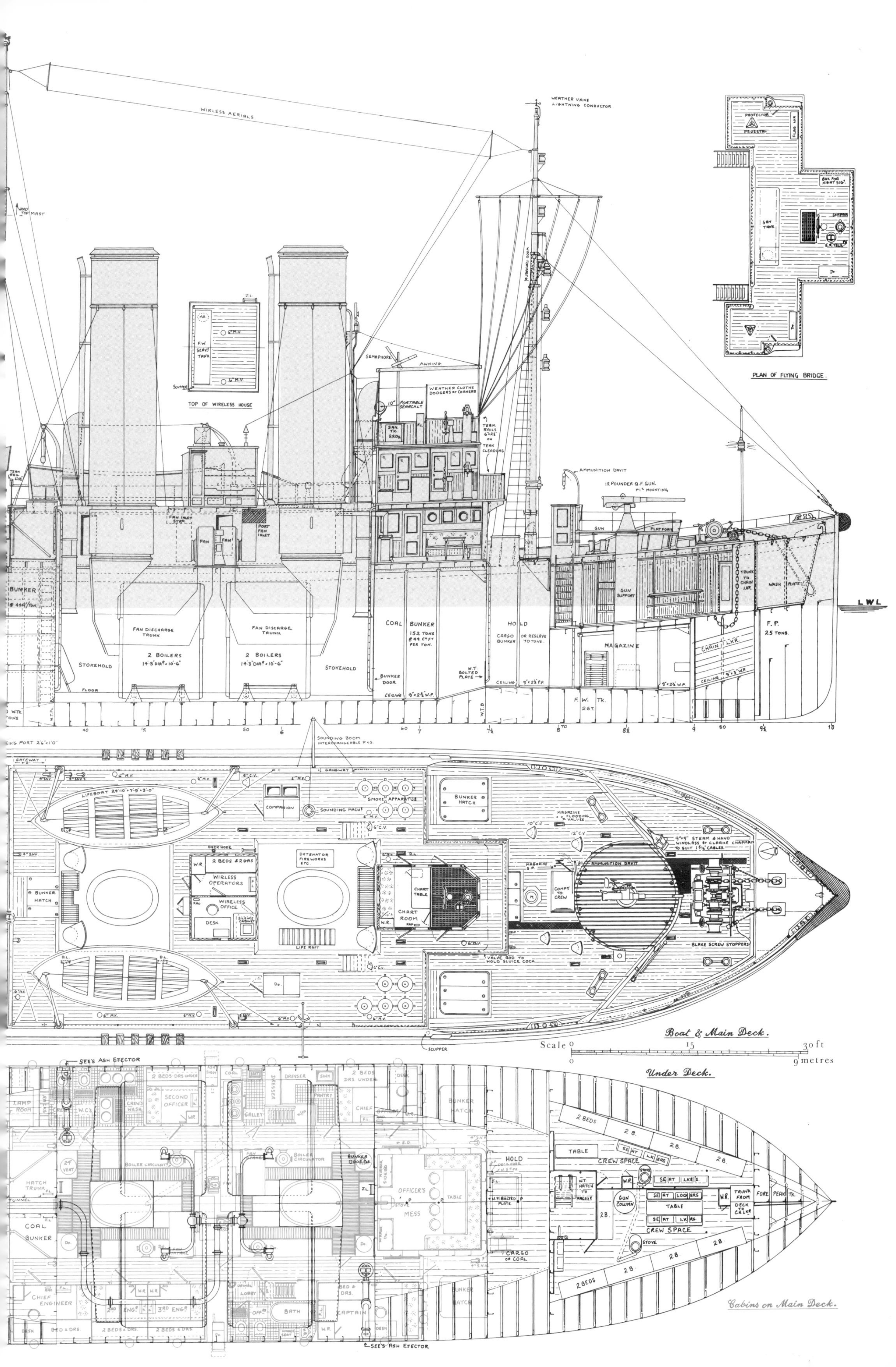
WIRELESS AERIALS
WEATHER VANE
LIGHTNING CONDUCTOR
WOOD TOP MAST
PLAN OF FLYING BRIDGE.
TOP OF WIRELESS HOUSE
F.W. SERVᶜᴱ TANK
SEMAPHORE
AWNING
10" PORTABLE SEARCHᴸᵀ
WEATHER CLOTHS DODGERS AT CORNERS
TEAK RAILS ON TEAK CLEADING
AMMUNITION DAVIT
12 POUNDER Q.F. GUN.
GUN
PLATFORM
GUN SUPPORT
TRUNK TO CHAIN LKR.
WASH PLATE
LWL
BUNKER
FAN INLET
PORT FAN INLET
FAN
FAN DISCHARGE TRUNK
2 BOILERS
14-3" DIAᴿ × 10-6"
STOKEHOLD
FLOOR
COAL BUNKER
152 TONS
BUNKER DOOR
CEILING
HOLD
CARGO BUNKER
OR RESERVE
W.T. BOLTED PLATE
MAGAZINE
F.W. TK.
CHAIN LKR.
F.P. 25 TONS.
SOUNDING BOOM INTERCHANGEABLE P & S.
GATEWAY
LIFEBOAT 24'-10" × 7'-9" × 3'-0"
COMPANION
SOUNDING MACHᴱ
SMOKE APPARATUS
BUNKER HATCH
MAGAZINE FLOODING VALVES
9" × 9" STEAM & HAND WINDLASS BY CLARKE CHAPMAN TO SUIT 1 5/16" CABLES.
AMMUNITION DAVIT
DECK HOSE
2 BEDS & 2 DRS
WIRELESS OPERATORS
WIRELESS OFFICE
DESK
DETONATOR FIREWORKS ETC
LIFE RAFT
CHART TABLE
CHART ROOM
COMPᵀ TO CREW
BLAKE SCREW STOPPERS
VALVE ROD TO HOLD SLUICE COCK
SCUPPER
Boat & Main Deck.
Scale 0 15 30 ft
0 9 metres
Under Deck.
SEE'S ASH EJECTOR
LAMP ROOM
W.C.S
CREW'S WASH
SECOND OFFICER
COAL
DRESSER
GALLEY
PANTRY
CHIEF OFFICER
BUNKER HATCH
2 BEDS
TABLE
CREW SPACE
HOLD
BOILER CIRCULATOR
BUNKER DOOR
OFFICER'S MESS
W.T. BOLTED PLATE
HATCH TRUNK
TUNNEL
COAL BUNKER
GUN COLUMN
STOVE
TRUNK FROM DECK TO CH. LKR
FORE PEAK TK.
CARGO OR COAL
CHIEF ENGINEER
2ND ENGᴿ
3RD ENGᴿ
LOBBY
BATH
CAPTAIN
Cabins on Main Deck.

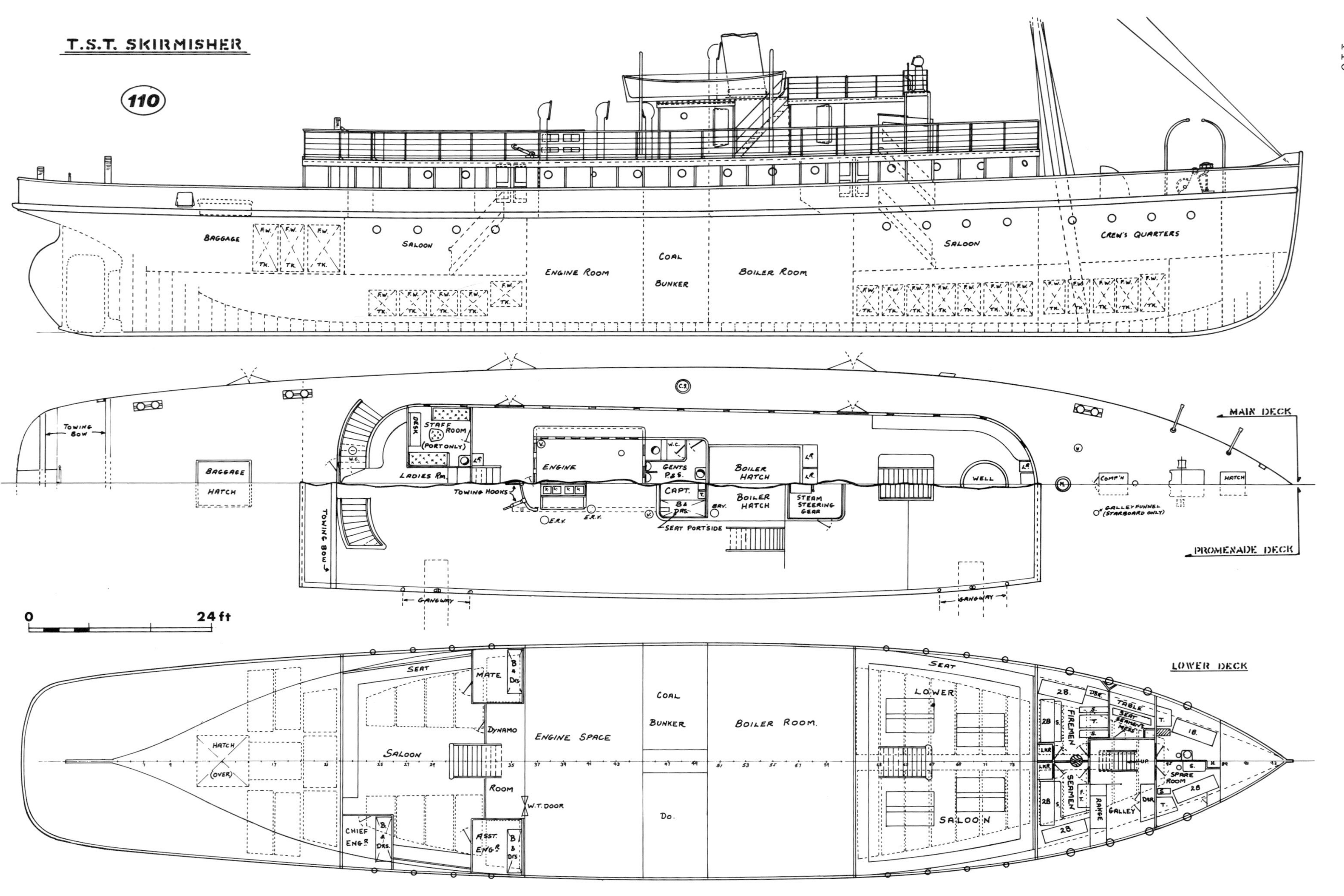
T.S.T. SKIRMISHER
110
BAGGAGE
SALOON
ENGINE ROOM
COAL
BUNKER
BOILER ROOM
SALOON
CREW'S QUARTERS
TOWING BOW
BAGGAGE
HATCH
STAFF ROOM
(PORT ONLY)
DESK
LADIES RM.
ENGINE
GENTS
BOILER HATCH
WELL
TOWING HOOKS
CAPT.
BOILER HATCH
STEAM STEERING GEAR
SEAT PORTSIDE
TOWING BOW
GALLEY FUNNEL (STARBOARD ONLY)
HATCH
MAIN DECK
PROMENADE DECK
GANGWAY
GANGWAY
0
24 ft
LOWER DECK
SEAT
MATE
HATCH
(OVER)
DYNAMO
SALOON
ENGINE SPACE
ROOM
W.T. DOOR
CHIEF ENGR.
ASST. ENGR.
COAL
BUNKER
Do.
BOILER ROOM.
SEAT
LOWER
SALOON
FIREMEN
SEAMEN
TABLE
RANGE
GALLEY
SPARE ROOM

Queenstown operation ceased. When the *Lusitania* was sunk by a U-boat off the south coast of Ireland, the first ship to reach the scene was the screw tug **Warrior** (1895, 106.0 ft. 192 tons. 98 n.h.p./650 e.h.p.) which picked up 74 survivors, followed shortly after by the tender **Flying Fish** from Queenstown which rescued 240 souls and took them to safety at Queenstown.

On the Clyde, tenders were stationed by the operators of the steamship lines. In 1880 the Anchor Line (Paddy Henderson) introduced the **Express** (1880, 150 ft. 306 tons. 170 n.h.p.), a screw steamer which was replaced in turn by the **Paladin** in 1913, (1913, 140.3 ft. 326 tons. 138 n.h.p.) a twin-screw vessel carrying 396 passengers in summer and 279 in winter. At one stage of her career the **Paladin** (116) held a passenger certificate No.5 to carry 697 people. When the *Queen Mary* went on her trials the **Paladin** was assisted by the **Romsey** which had been brought up from Southampton. Although each tender by itself seemed quite a large vessel the photograph shows how they were dwarfed by their huge charge (111). The **Paladin** passed to the Clyde Shipping Company in 1939 and they operated her until 1946 before selling her to Southampton owners. The Anchor Line also used the tender **Skirmisher** from Liverpool for a short time around 1922. Among the tugs in the fleet of the Clyde Shipping Company were a number for which they held passenger certificates. When their last paddle tug the **Flying Scotsman** (43) was built in 1898 (118.0 ft. 177 tons. 90 n.h.p./ 400 e.h.p.), they obtained for her a certificate 'for a ship plying in smooth water in estuaries and lakes, to operate not beyond a line between the Isle of Bute to Skelmorlie in the summer and Gourock to Dunoon in the winter, covering 150 passengers and 7 crew.' The **Flying Scotsman** was equipped with two boats to carry 10 persons each, 4 buoyant appliances to carry 56 persons, 4 lifebuoys, and 157 lifejackets. The tug was fitted out with a saloon and berths at the after end, and when she was sold in 1948 (the last paddle tug in service on the Clyde in Glasgow) she was to be converted to a yacht, a project which unfortunately fell through. When the last three steam tugs were built for the Clyde Shipping Company in 1951 they were given passenger certificates for 150 persons so that they could attend vessels which were running trials, carrying officials and workers between ship and shore. The **Flying Buzzard** and the **Flying Merlin** (114'11". 261 tons. 1150 i.h.p.) each had a small saloon between the bridge and the funnel. This feature was not provided on their near sister the **Flying Petrel** (119'2", 278 tons, 1500 i.h.p.).

In Liverpool several of the early passenger steamers were sold to operate as tugs and many retained the dual role of tug and passenger vessel. One of the first true tenders was the **Satellite** (1848, 108.5 ft. 157 tons. 80 n.h.p.), employed by the Cunard Steamship Co., equipped for carrying 600 passengers. In 1874 the paddle tug **Gladiator** was launched in Birkenhead for the Liverpool Steam Tug Co. (144.7 ft. 228 tons. 100 n.h.p./700 i.h.p.) which was intended to work as a tug during the winter months and as a passenger steamer during the summer. As the trans-Atlantic traffic increased the liner owners decided that it would be to their advantage to own their own tenders and over a period of years a considerable fleet of tenders came into being in the Mersey. In 1884 the Cunard Steamship Co. put into service the **Skirmisher** (1884, 165.0 ft. 612 tons. 147 n.h.p.) to be followed in 1891 by the **Magnetic** of the Oceanic Steam Navigation Co., more commonly known as the White Star Line (1891, 170.5 ft. 619 tons. 175 n.h.p.)

The **Skirmisher** had the appearance of a small ocean liner (Plate 6 and 110) and was typical of the large passenger tender of the period with her promenade deck supported by stanchions and surmounted by a wood topped rail with four-ball stanchions. Regarding passenger comfort the drawing is somewhat sketchy. There were four saloons (one for ladies only) each with seating. Seats may have been provided on the open decks but in Victorian times it would not have been surprising if passengers had had to stand. For the number of passengers carried the toilet facilities seem rather limited, but after all the passengers were aboard for only the short time that it took to sail from the floating landing stage out to the liner waiting in the middle of the river. A peculiar feature of this vessel was the large number of fresh water tanks which are fitted below the floor of the saloon. The towing arrangement looks very awkward as if the rope had to bend sharply over the high towing bow on the promenade deck to drop down to the ones in the stern. However, with the rope attached to the high bow of an ocean liner the rope probably did not even touch the upper towing bow. Another unique feature was the hand capstan head fitted to the anchor windlass; more usual was the Armstrongs Patent lever operated manual gear. The Canadian Pacific Railway Co. owned the tender **Bison** (1906, 125.0 ft. 274 tons. 90 n.h.p.). This vessel saw extensive service in both world

Paladin *(left) and* **Romsey** *(right) acting as tenders to the Queen Mary on her trials.*

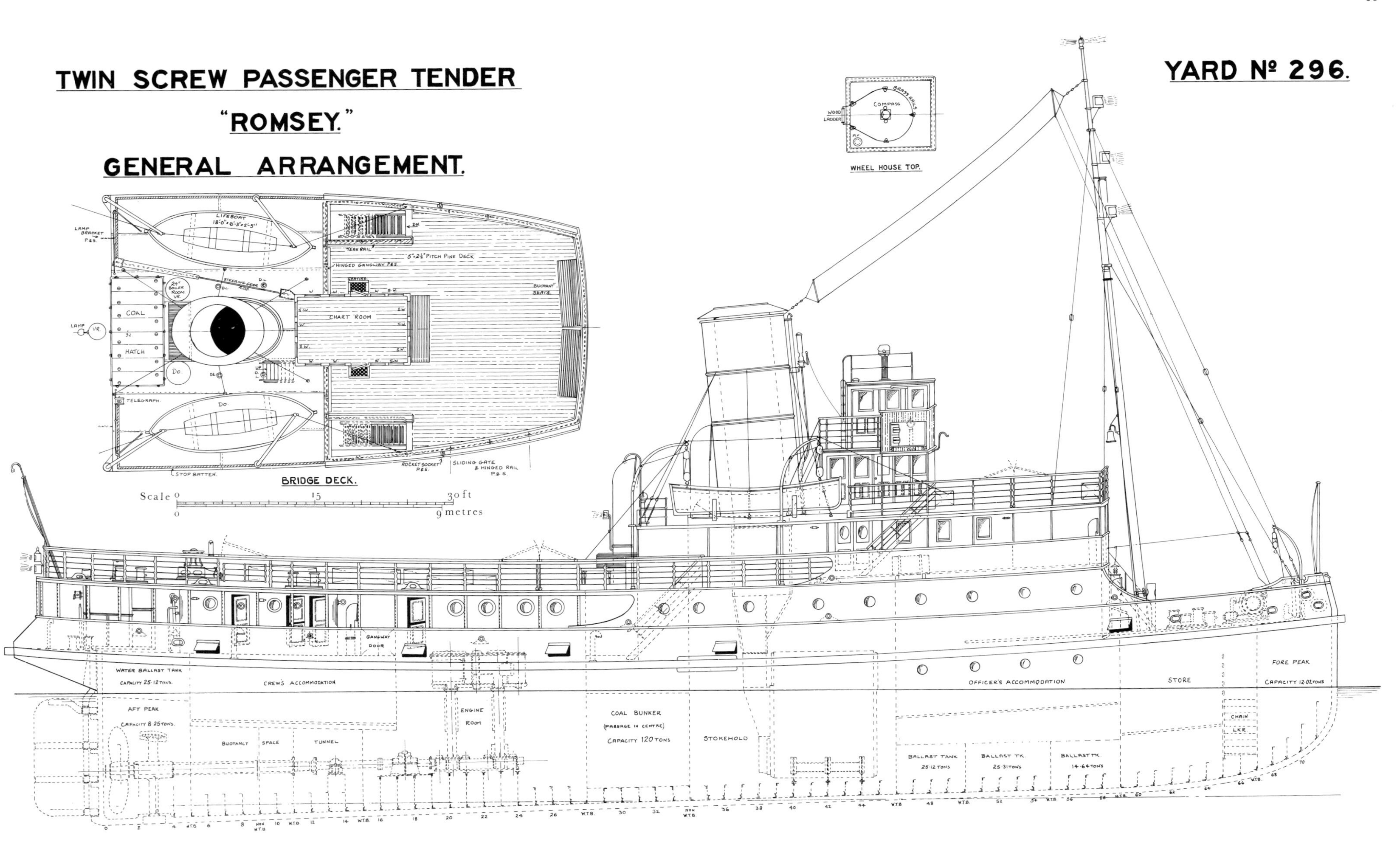

TWIN SCREW PASSENGER TENDER
"ROMSEY."
GENERAL ARRANGEMENT.
YARD Nº 296.
WHEEL HOUSE TOP.
COMPASS
BRASS RAILS
WOOD LADDER
BRIDGE DECK.
LIFEBOAT 18'0"×6'3"×2'5"
CHART ROOM
COAL
HATCH
TELEGRAPH
TEAK RAIL
HINGED GANGWAY P&S
5"×2½" PITCH PINE DECK
BUOYANT SEATS
ROCKET SOCKET P&S.
SLIDING GATE & HINGED RAIL P&S
STOP BATTEN.
Scale 0 15 30 ft
0 9 metres
GANGWAY DOOR
WATER BALLAST TANK
CAPACITY 25·12 TONS
CREW'S ACCOMMODATION
AFT PEAK
CAPACITY 8·25 TONS
BUOYANT SPACE
TUNNEL
ENGINE ROOM
COAL BUNKER
(PASSAGE IN CENTRE)
CAPACITY 120 TONS
STOKEHOLD
OFFICER'S ACCOMMODATION
BALLAST TANK 25·12 TONS
BALLAST TK. 25·31 TONS
BALLAST TK 14·64 TONS
STORE
FORE PEAK
CAPACITY 12·02 TONS
CHAIN LKR

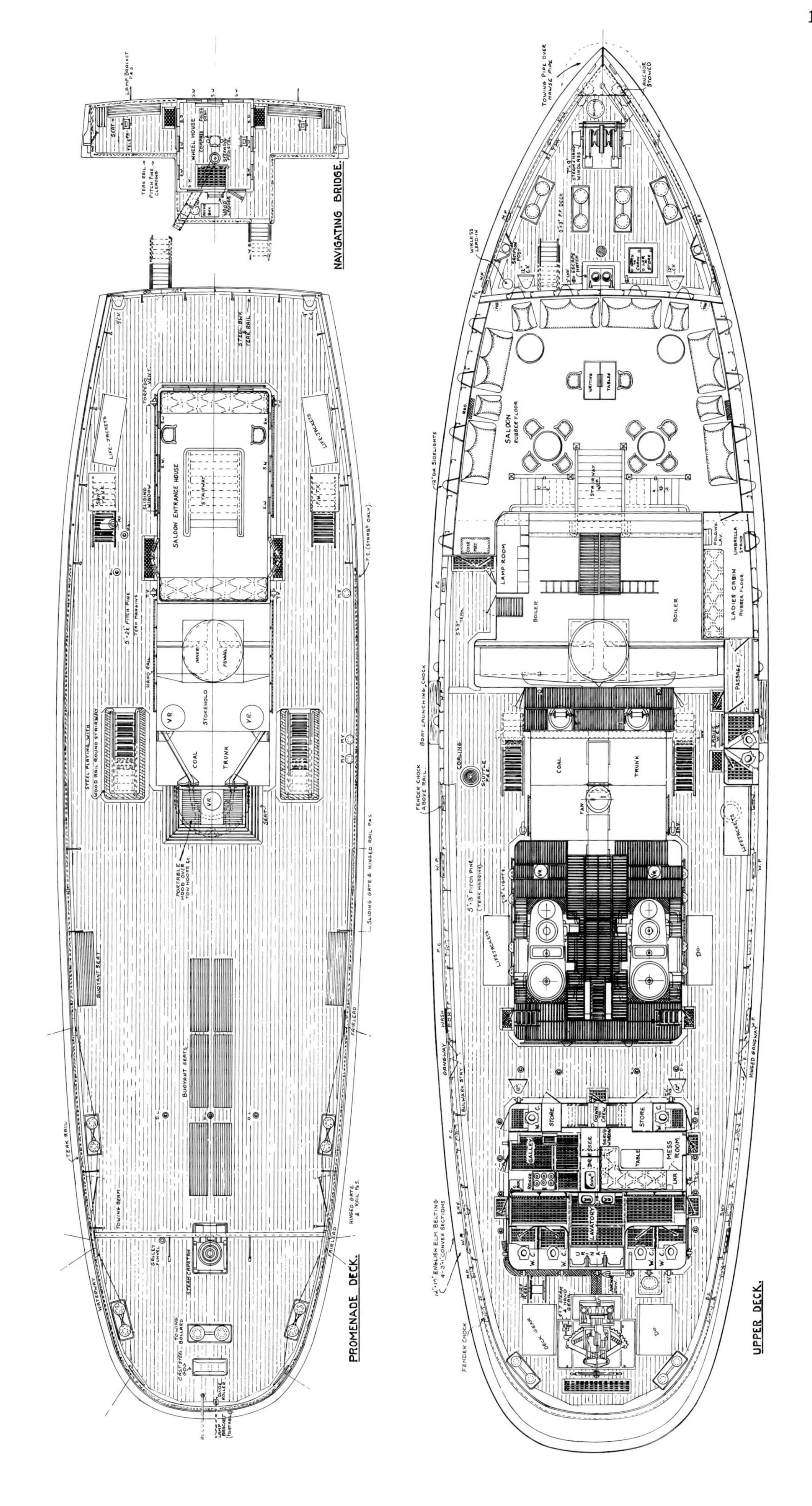
NAVIGATING BRIDGE.
WHEEL HOUSE
PROMENADE DECK.
SALOON ENTRANCE HOUSE
STOKEHOLD
COAL
TRUNK
BUOYANT SEATS
BUOYANT SEAT
STEAM CAPSTAN
UPPER DECK.
SALOON
RUBBER FLOOR
LAMP ROOM
BOILER
BOILER
LADIES CABIN
RUBBER FLOOR
PASSAGE
COAL
TRUNK
FAN
LIFEJACKETS
GALLEY
DRESSER
STORE
STORE
MESS ROOM
TABLE
LAVATORY

wars and was sunk in May 1941 during an air raid on Liverpool. She was salvaged and was still afloat in Greek waters as late as 1964.

In Liverpool, in addition to the Company owned tenders the well-known tug firm of Alexandra Towing Co. established a considerable fleet of tenders to provide service to the various passenger liners which called at Liverpool. The first was the **Herald** (1907, 125.3 ft. 367 tons. 132 n.h.p.), followed by the **Flying Kestrel** (1910, 125.0 ft. 434 tons. 108 n.h.p.), and the smaller **Egerton** (1911, 105.2 ft. 272 tons, 110 n.h.p.). Just before the First World War, first the **Herald** and then the **Flying Kestrel** were sent out to the Mediterranean in the spring cruising season to act as tenders for Cunard cruising liners visiting Monaco. the **Flying Kestrel** was also chartered for several seasons by the Prince of Monaco as a private yacht and she was painted white before she left the U.K., although she retained the Alexandra Towing Co. funnel colours (114). The **Flying Kestrel** had a very high freeboard enclosing considerable accommodation. The promenade deck stretched from bow to stern, and at the after end the towing bows hinged down to leave the deck clear for passengers to walk about. She had an additional deck around the chart house and above was a flying bridge with an open wheel. An emergency steering wheel was fitted right aft.

These tenders performed valuable service for the armed forces during the First World War and even after the war was over two of them were retained for further service at Scapa Flow. the interned German Fleet had become part of the scenery and from time to time the tenders **Flying Kestrel** (1913, 140.2 ft. 700 tons. 166 n.h.p./1750 i.h.p.) and **Flying Breeze** (1913, 125.0 ft. 387 tons. 132 n.h.p./1000 i.h.p.) took visitors along the lines of moored warships. On that fateful morning in June 1919 the two ships were loaded with school children on a sightseeing trip and as the German commander gave the order to scuttle the fleet, the children packed the bulwarks of the tenders and watched millions of pounds worth of shipping sinking to the bottom of the anchorage. In 1919 the Cunard Steamship Co. transferred their express service to Southampton and several Alexandra Towing Co. tugs were sent south, including the tender **Flying Kestrel.** In 1922 she was joined by an unusual vessel, the **Romsey** which had been built in 1918 as the Admiralty tug **Rollcall** (109). The conversion was so complete that there was no resemblance between the new tender and old **Rollicker** class tugs. She was replaced in 1930 by a new **Romsey** (135.0 ft. 509 tons. 254 n.h.p./1700 i.h.p.), a tender very similar in appearance to the vessel which she was replacing. The first impression looking at the drawing of the **Romsey** (112) is one of sturdiness, quite different from the early tenders She had the appearance of a tug first and a passenger vessel second. On her small foredeck were four massive bollards to provide a strong towing connection. The saloon in front of the machinery space was comfortably furnished with settees and easy chairs - a ladies' cabin was provided but it was a very small affair. Aft of the engine casing was a structure containing the crew's mess and toilets, and toilets and washrooms for the passengers. On the promenade deck were a fair number of buoyant seats and lifejacket boxes, not much seating for the number of passengers which she could carry but they were not on board for any length of time. When the towing hook was not in use it could be concealed below a special seat. Only one towing bow was considered necessary as there was little on deck to foul and in any case the lead of the rope would usually be at a steep angle. There was additional deck space in front of the bridge for privileged passengers. The **Romsey** was built by the same yard that had built her predecessor, Ferguson Bros., Port Glasgow and she remained in the Alexandra Towing fleet until 1962 when she was sold to the breakers. She served during the war on the Clyde as an examination vessel. She in turn gave way to another conversion; the **Flying Breeze** (ex **B.P. Protector**) (1938, 120.5 ft. 460 tons. 1000 i.h.p.) the last true steam tender in the United Kingdom. **Flying Breeze** (115) bore some resemblance to the **Romsey** (112) but lacked the stanchions supporting the promenade deck - instead she had solid plating with glazed sections to keep the passengers warm and dry. She had a long promenade deck with only stairways and the engine room skylight on it, and the forward towing bow had removable sections to give a clear deck. Scotts of Bowling built the vessel in 1938 as the **Zurmand** for work in the oil ports in the Middle East. she was renamed B.P. **Protector** in 1955 and early in 1961 she appeared once more at the Bowling yard of her builders. After lying for many months in a partially dismantled state, work was recommenced and in 1962 she appeared in the Alexandra Towing colours as the **Flying Breeze.** Six years later she was sold to Piraeus.

The Alexandra Towing Company's ***Flying Kestrel*** *(1910) on summer charter off Monaco.*

(115) ***Flying Breeze*** *(ex* ***B.P. Protector****) on trials on the Clyde after conversion to a tender in 1962. PHOTO: Alexandra Towing Co. Ltd.*

Also operating was the Southampton, Isle of Wight and South of England Royal Mail Steam Packet Company more simply called 'The Red Funnel Fleet', who had been running a passenger service since 1861. Their first tug was in fact a twin screw tender, the **Albert Edward** (1886, 120 ft. 160 tons. 100 n.h.p.). In 1903 the tender **Hector** joined the fleet (1903, 130 ft. 382 tons. 1400 i.h.p.), a large twin-screw tug which was provided with a small saloon for passengers and a smaller saloon for the ladies, while on deck a number of buoyant seats were set out to give some degree of comfort to the passengers on deck. There was a small hold forward and a heavy derrick on the mast to handle baggage. Their first true tender was the **Calshot** (1930, 147.8 ft. 679 tons. 1500 i.h.p.) with plenty of accommodation and a certificate for 500 passengers. In 1946 she was joined by the **Paladin** which the company bought from the Clyde. At Weymouth Messrs. Cosens and Co. had the **Albert Victor** (1883, 106.0 ft. 128 tons. 350 i.h.p.) which when not acting as a tug had a passenger certificate for 210 passengers winter and 267 passengers summer capacity.

There was on the Thames for a period, a tender the **Ich Dien** which was operated by the Aberdeen & London Steam Navigation Co. for carrying passengers along the Thames to Shadwell from their terminal at Temple Pier where they were landed from the larger vessels (1879, 94.8 ft. 87 tons, 40 n.h.p.). She was little more than a large steam launch with little evidence of her capability to carry passengers (120). She was not unlike the **Heron**, narrow of beam and with the same sharp rise of floor. In her case the cabin was evidently forward of the machinery space. The canoe shaped stem looks rather odd, but this shape does crop up occasionally in early small steamships. The **Ich Dien** came from another little known Clyde yard, that of Cunliffe & Dunlop of Port Glasgow. She remained with the same owners until the Second World War during which she changed hands, being bought by R.G. Odell of London, owners of Thames lighterage tugs who ran a passenger carrying business as a side-line.

All around the country the railway companies owned docks and in many of these the railways owned tenders. At Barrow the Furness Railway Co. stationed the I.P.T. **Walney** (1868, 146.5 ft. 200 tons. 100 n.h.p.) which they replaced in 1904 by another iron paddle tender of the same name (120.0 ft. 185 tons. 66 n.h.p.). At Heysham the Midland Railway Co. had the screw tender **Wyvern** (1905, 110.0 ft. 215 tons. 700 i.h.p.), primarily a tug but provided with a saloon and seating for passengers (115). At Plymouth the Great Western Railway Co. had a series of tenders starting with the iron paddle tender **Sir Francis Drake** (1873, 131.3 ft. 173 tons. 80 n.h.p.) and **Sir Walter Raleigh**

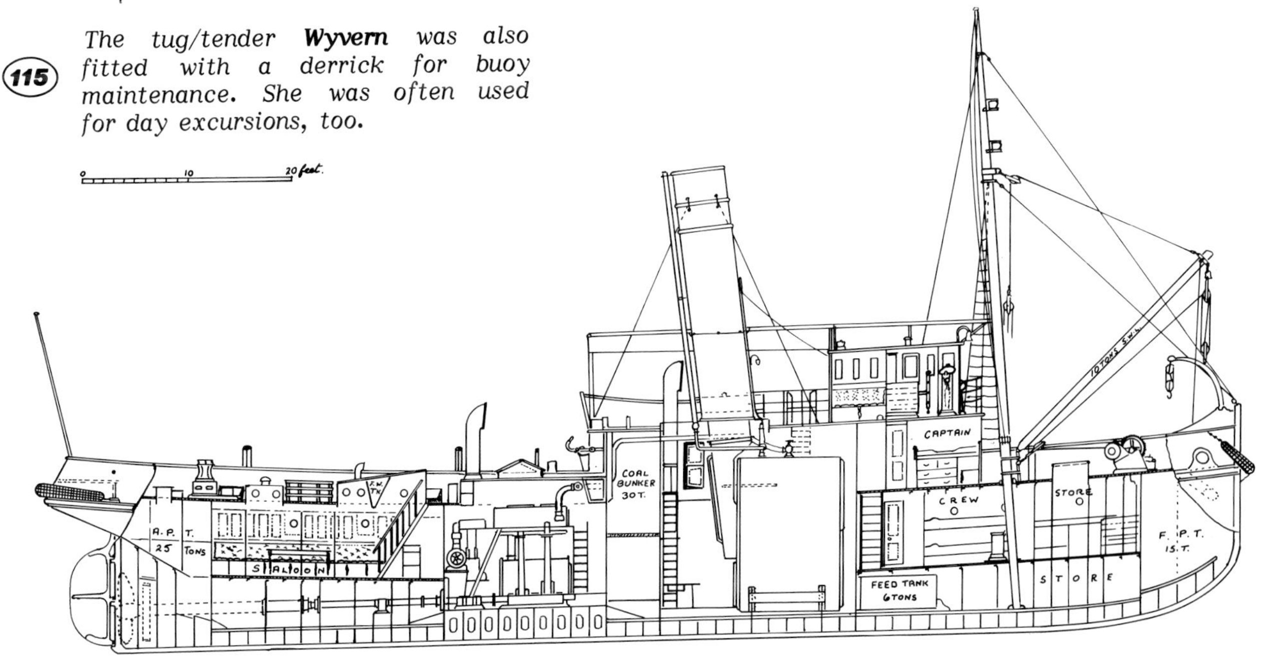

(115) *The tug/tender* ***Wyvern*** *was also fitted with a derrick for buoy maintenance. She was often used for day excursions, too.*

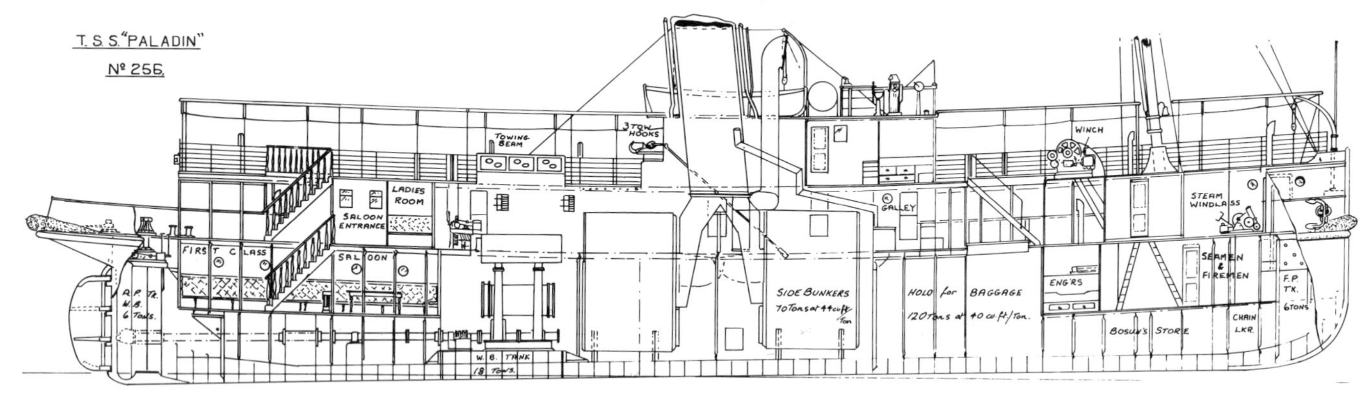

116 *As the* ***Paladin*** *was quite narrow the boilers had to be placed in tandem and this cut down the space below, leaving only room for a first class saloon. On the main deck was a ladies room but all other passengers had to stand or sit in the open, albeit protected by the promenade deck. The engine and boiler casing occupied half of the length of the main deck. She was plated up forward to prevent waves from breaking over the bow and to protect the windlass, W.C.s and the companionway to the crew's quarters. She had a larger baggage hold than the other tenders shown.* (Scale as 117).

(1876, 110.1 ft. 151 tons. 85 n.h.p.). These were followed in due course by other vessels bearing similar historical names; the twin screw tender **Sir Richard Grenville** (1891, 132.0 ft. 379 tons. 118 n.h.p.) with passenger certificates allocated depending on the area in which she operated,No.4, 483 passengers,No.5, 823 passengers. These were tenders in the true sense, passenger carriers first, tug second (see plan, 117). When in service,they customarily wore the flag of the shipping company whose passengers they had on board. Their vessels were replaced at regular intervals until the last of them entered service the **Sir Richard Grenville** (1931, 172.5 ft. 896 tons. 1700 i.h.p.). The company also had tenders at Fishguard, one being the **Pen Cw** (1912, 105.1 ft. 168 tons. 68 n.h.p.), basically a paddle tug which was unusual in that she had her funnel forward of the paddle boxes contrary to common practice. She also had diagonal engines, again not a common feature on the smaller civilian owned paddle tugs. There was no accommodation for the passengers but her decks were fairly spacious and the after saloon was large and comfortable. She ended her days as a tug at Methil, Fife under the name **Elie** (Plate 19). The London North Western Railway Co. had a tender at Fleetwood called the **Lune** (1892, 129.0 ft. 253 tons. 96 n.h.p.), an iron vessel which looked a bit of a hybrid. She was open decked aft like a tug, but was built up forward with a long saloon almost to the bow with a promenade deck above, suitable for buoy laying, towing and passenger carrying.

A number of the navigable rivers in the country were controlled by committees made up of members of the shipowning industry, local traders and the local authority, and these Trusts, Commissions or Authorities often possessed tugs of their own of which at least one was equipped to carry members of the committee on inspection tours and guests on outings. The Clyde Navigation Trust had the twin-screw tug **Clyde** (1912, 104.5 ft. 187 tons. 91 n.h.p.) which had an enlarged bridge deck and a spacious after deck. In Newcastle the River Tyne Commissioners used the **J.C. Stevenson** (1883, 115.2 ft. 183 tons. 60 n.h.p.).

As a River Commissioners' tug the **J.C. Stevenson** was amply provided with accommodation for the officials who travelled aboard her (118). She even had a demountable saloon which could be removed to allow her to undertake the normal work of towing the hopper barges. An unusual departure was to put the officers forward beside the crew so as to leave the after saloon and its 'Ladies Room' private. She had wooden bulwarks and on the bow had the traditional scroll decoration. Note the heavy guards on the paddlebox and the strong bracing of the platform which supported the paddle shaft bearing. This paddle tug was built at the North Shields yard of Hepple & Co. (183 tons gross and 60 n.h.p.). In 1923 she was sold to France Fenwick, Tyne & Wear Co. and was renamed **Dunelm**. Every summer under her new owners she was hired out to the Trinity House who used her to service their buoys off the N.E. coast. If required her mast could be unstepped and a stouter one fitted in its place carrying a derrick.

On the Wear the Tees Conservancy Commissioners had the Iron Paddle Tug/Tender **Sir Hugh Bell** (1913, 115.0 ft. 175 tons. 95 n.h.p.). "The vessel had been generally designed for sea and harbour towage, but especially as a tender and surveying vessel and to the requirements of the Board of Trade regulations for a passenger certificate. Special accommodation was provided for visitors and also a large and thoroughly well-equipped kitchen and steward's store. At the after end there was a large saloon and retiring room for ladies. The propelling machinery was constructed by the ship-builders Messrs. J.P. Rennoldson. The Manchester Ship Canal Company took over some tenders when they bought over the Bridgewater Navigation Co. in 1894 and the Shropshire Union Canal Co. in 1922. Some were tugs with limited passenger accommodation, but the **Earl of Powis** (1882, 105.6 ft. 116 tons. 50 n.h.p.) had an odd profile having a long central superstructure with seating on the upper deck. The **Ralph Brocklebank** (1903, 173 tons. 83 n.h.p.), renamed **Daniel Adamson** in 1936 was a tug-like vessel with very little sheer and in her later years had a very large enclosed "viewing deck" on top of a large saloon with the bridge overlooking them both.

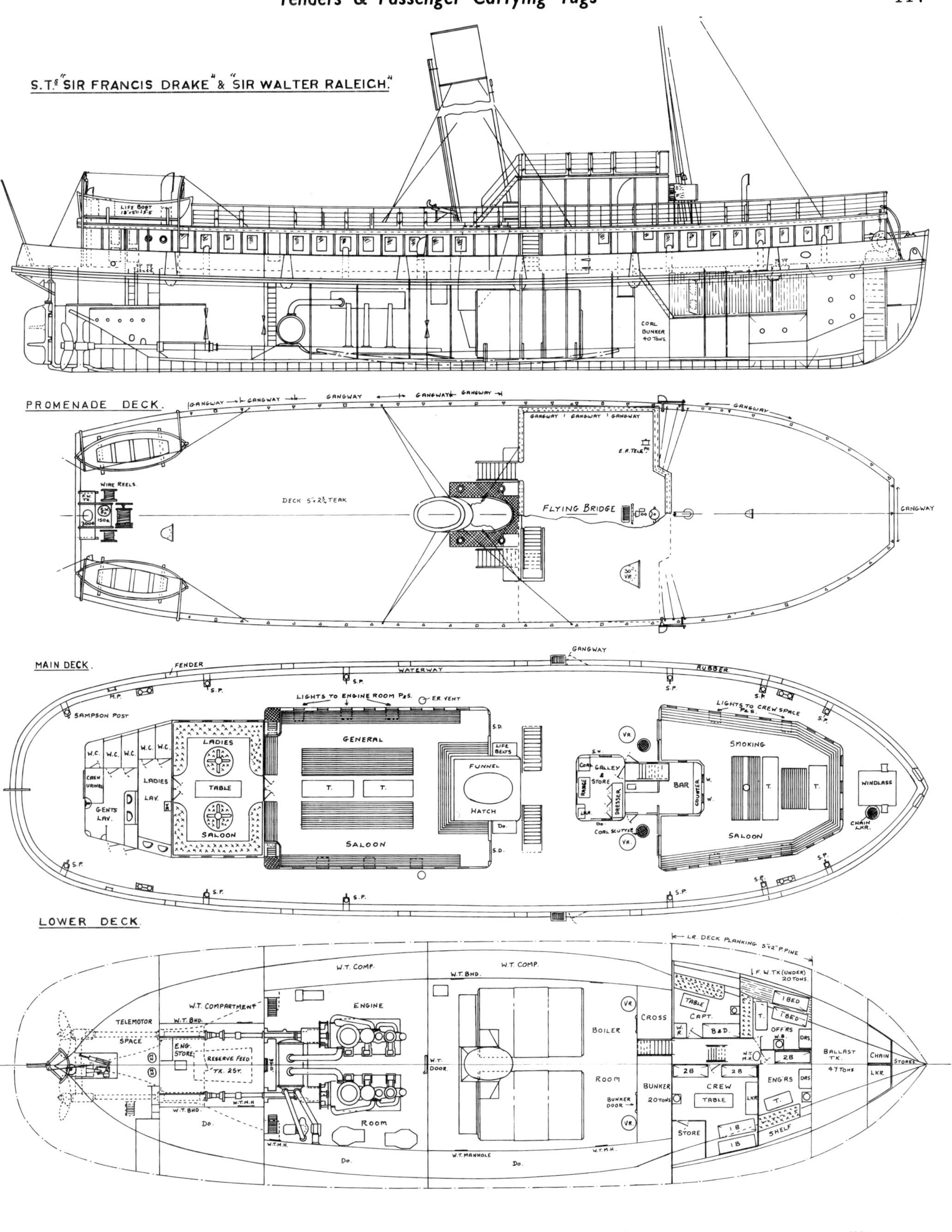

117 *The **Sir Francis Drake** and the **Sir Walter Raleigh** were built in 1908 by Cammell Laird of Liverpool, 145.9 ft., 478 tons, 228 n.h.p. Compared with the **Paladin** (opposite) they were of similar length but were 8 ft. broader so that the boilers could be placed side by side. Despite this there was no accommodation below for passengers but generous provision was made on the main deck which ran most of the length, the engine and boiler rooms being below deck. On these vessels the bridge deck was very extensive as it was used as a boarding platform. These two vessels were used for excursion work during the summer months.*

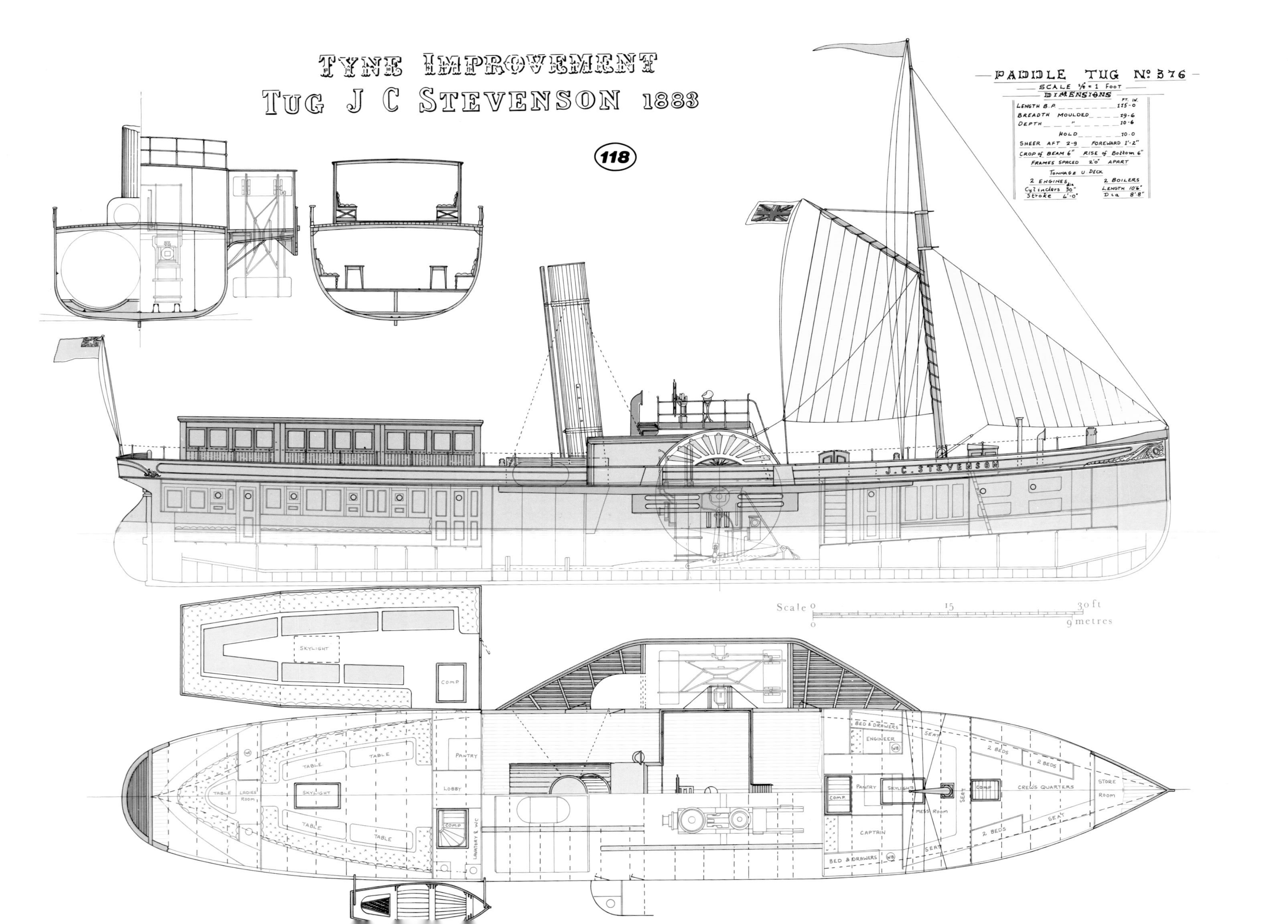

TYNE IMPROVEMENT
TUG J C STEVENSON 1883
118
PADDLE TUG No. 376
SCALE 1/4" = 1 FOOT
DIMENSIONS
FT. IN.
LENGTH B.P. 115-0
BREADTH MOULDED 19-6
DEPTH " 10-6
HOLD 10.0
SHEER AFT 2-9 FOREWARD 1'-2"
CROP of BEAM 6" RISE of Bottom 6"
FRAMES SPACED 2'0" APART
TONNAGE U DECK
2 ENGINES 2 BOILERS
Cylinders dia 30" LENGTH 10'6"
Stroke 4'-0" Dia 8'8"
J. C. STEVENSON
Scale 0 15 30 ft
0 9 metres
SKYLIGHT
COMP
PANTRY
LOBBY
COMP
LAVATORY & WC
TABLE
TABLE
SKYLIGHT
TABLE
TABLE
TABLE
LADIES ROOM
WC
BED & DRAWERS
ENGINEER
WB
SEAT
2 BEDS
2 BEDS
STORE ROOM
COMP
PANTRY
SKYLIGHT
MESS ROOM
SEAT
COMP
CREWS QUARTERS
CAPTAIN
BED & DRAWERS
WB
SEAT
2 BEDS
SEAT

***New Resolute** and **Resolute** (beyond) of Benny & Co, Falmouth mainly operated as ferries but also did some towing.*

A very neat screw tug, the **Violet** (1892, 100.0 ft. 141 tons. 48 n.h.p.) went into service with the Carlingford Lough Commissioners, certificated to carry between 300 and 400 passengers on deck, she was a small version of the big coastal tugs with a long central superstructure, a tall funnel amidships and two masts, very yacht-like in appearance. The Blyth Harbour Commissioners had the **Croft** (1914, 95.5 ft. 149 tons. 620 i.h.p.), above deck an ordinary tug but below deck there was a large saloon with tables and seats, lavatories, galley, steward's pantry and all modern conveniences to give comfort to the 70 passengers which she was allowed to carry. Hidden in the space forward of the saloon was a massive salvage pump; there was not much space wasted on board the **Croft.**

As indicated at the beginning of the chapter there were innumerable passenger carrying tugs in service in almost every port and harbour, sometimes purely tugs engaged in the profitable pastime of carrying passengers for pleasure trips, sometimes tugs designed to accommodate passengers, tugs such as the **Citie of the Tribes** (1872, 99.5 ft. 117 tons. 60 n.h.p.) owned by the Galway Steam Packet Co. The Waterford Steam Shipping Co. owned an iron tug/passenger vessel called **Resolute** (1880, 100.0 ft. 113 tons. 65 n.h.p.). Not all the passenger carrying tugs were paddlers, the iron screw tug **Moss Rose** (1881) was built for D. Guy of Cardiff with two cabins, one forward, one aft, fitted with a lifeboat and life-saving equipment, for passenger work and excursion trips. The port of Falmouth was the home of many small tugs, almost all screw propelled, and there Benny & Co. operated 'passenger vessels used occasionally for towing purposes'. There was the tiny wooden screw tug **Resolute** (1877, 63.6 ft. 32 tons. 15 n.h.p.) and the slightly less tiny **New Resolute** (1882, 71.2 ft. 40 tons. 25 n.h.p.) with 'two powerful engines giving her a speed of 11 kts.' The **Resolute** carried 79 passengers, while the later one carried 240. It is difficult to see from a photograph (119) how so many people could be stowed on such a small vessel, but the problem was helped by folding the towing bows down out of the way. The **New Resolute** had a very low casing over the boiler and engine and had a typical rearward raking wooden wheelhouse set upon it. Seats were fitted all round the bulwarks and a weathercloth attached to small stanchions kept some of the spray off the passengers. The fidded topmast seems superfluous but displays the banner with the tug's name, while the mast has the characteristic jib and loose footed gaff main sail.

The favourite at Littlehampton was the iron paddle tug **Jumna** (1884, 81.5 ft. 51 tons. 24 n.h.p.) which can be seen in many of the picture post cards of that port steaming towards the harbour entrance loaded with holidaymakers. The wooden paddle tug **United Service** (Plate 6) has already been mentioned for her long and very active career as a tug at Great Yarmouth, but she was equally well known to summer visitors as were her fellow paddle tugs. At Bridlington the iron paddle tug **Frenchman** (1892 - rebuilt 1906, 100.4 ft. 137 tons. 350 i.h.p.), owned by the United Towing Company of Hull plied as passenger vessel during the holiday months, with a No. 4 passenger certificate entitling her to carry 246 passengers. She was taken out of service in 1928 and after one season on the Humber was stripped for use as a barge. She was replaced at Bridlington by the twin screw tug **Yorkshireman** (1928, 120.0 ft. 251 tons. 800 i.h.p.) which remained in service carrying passengers until 1965, long after any other tug was used for that purpose (119). The **Yorkshireman** was primarily

*The **Yorkshireman** (1928) packed with passengers off Bridlington. In later years the fore end of the boat deck was glazed to provide protection from the elements. The charge for a trip before the war was 2/- (10p.).*

a tug which packed passengers on her deck from bow to stern and on the boat deck as well. The captain remained aloof on the flying bridge. Just next door Scarborough had a succession of excursion steamers, many of them paddle tugs including the **Clyde** (1882, 116 ft. 164 tons. 60 n.h.p.) which was the first of a fleet of paddle trawlers fishing the Dogger Bank, but carried passengers in summer.

The big iron paddle tug **Conqueror**, owned by W. Sandford of Gravesend, mentioned earlier for her salvage exploits, was very active as an excursion steamer (3). In her first year in service in 1897 she carried 22,000 passengers to review the fleet at Spithead. She continued in her dual role until the First World War when she was requisitioned. In 1921 she appeared under the name of **Hurworth** in the Firth of Forth where the excursion trade was battling against the motor bus, but only three years later she was sold to the Tees where she reverted to towing. Among her rivals on the Forth were the paddle tugs **Forth** (1883, 108.0 ft. 129 tons. 80 n.h.p.) and the **Runner** (1886, 108.0 ft. 146 tons. 80 n.h.p.) operated by the Grangemouth and Forth Towing Company and the **Flying Fish** (1882, 116.0 ft. 169 tons. 76 n.h.p.) owned by D. Wilson of Bo'ness and later the Leith Salvage and Towing Company. One of the more unusual excursions on the River Forth was organised in 1884 when the Army built fortifications on the island of Inchkeith and the Royal Navy carried out a "live" bombardment to see how effective these fortifications were. The tugs **Blue Bonnet** (1866, 83.4 ft. 72 tons. 35 n.h.p.) and the **Robert Stephenson** (1860, 84.0 ft. 74 tons. 40 n.h.p.) were chartered to carry military observers, while among the other vessels which carried civilian sightseers was the wooden paddle tug **Fiery Cross** (1867, 87.3 ft. 87 tons. 35 n.h.p.) with officials from Edinburgh Corporation aboard.

Bo'ness and the surrounding area were very highly industrialised and the workers were inclined to use D. Wilson's rather elderly local tugs for their outings rather than the more elegant paddle steamers which plied on the river.

In the Bristol Channel there was a flourishing excursion trade and until the end of the nineteenth century the local tugs took a large share of the traffic. The passengers on the Cardiff paddle tug **Storm King** (1857, 92.0 ft. 74 tons. 55 n.h.p.) had an alarming experience when they were fired on (with blank shot) by a naval vessel and boarded by its crew who tore down a flag. It transpired that in their enthusiasm to deck their tug overall, the owners had included a naval flag among the bunting and this had not been dipped as protocol demanded in salute to the warship! C.J. King of Bristol owned a small screw tug called the **Sea Queen** (1880, 73.1 ft. 53 tons. 25 n.h.p.) which was billed as a fast passenger steamer. King's paddle tug **Merrimac** (1883, 91.0 ft. 96 tons. 40 n.h.p.) was popular with day trippers and was the last paddle tug to be used on the River Avon.

Frequently in this chapter mention is made of the dual role of tug and passenger steamer. However one owner hedged his bets even wider: "On 2.8.1882 the **Advance** was launched from the Commercial Graving Dock, Cardiff. An iron screw steamer of 85 tons, 90' x 18' x 9' with a B.o.T. certificate for carrying passengers. She is intended for towing and trawling and has cabin accommodation for passengers. Built and engined by the Tyneside Engine Works Ltd., Jute Docks, Cardiff to the order of W. and H.R. Strong. She is the second vessel for the company and the first screw tug in the port."

Tugs were sometimes used for carrying passengers for unusual reasons. When the Merchant Navy Officers Federation wished to deliver a protest about wages and conditions in 1933 they hired the Thames craft tug **Britannia** of only 76 tons and paraded her on the river Thames opposite the Houses of Parliament carrying a huge banner bearing the words "12,000 Merchant Navy Officers Petition Parliament". Tug owners were quick to take advantage of public events. When Queen Victoria visited the Clyde in 1847 the Clyde Shipping Co. sold tickets at 10/- each to sail aboard their tug **Sampson** (1818, 53 tons, 45 n.h.p). When the then Prime Minister Mr.Gladstone visited Newcastle in 1862 numerous paddle tugs carrying hundreds of passengers followed the official barges as they made their way down the Tyne. Now that the excursion steamers and pleasure trip tugs have gone, the trip around the lighthouse is taken in a motor boat or something only slightly larger.

(120) ***Ich Dien.***

8.

Brigand *Class tug. PHOTO: W. Lind.*

Naval and Wartime Tugs

The Royal Navy have always known about towing. After all, following every sea battle there were disabled ships which had to be taken to safety and when they were unable to set up a jury rig they had to be taken in tow by one of their less badly damaged fellows. When the wind died away a sailing warship would hoist out her boats and tow the ship - this they could do because of the large crew which the warship carried. This form of manual towing would also be carried out in harbour when the vessel had to be shifted from one berth to another, although there was apparently a special towing vessel in Sheerness in 1724 which was called the **Sheerness Longboat**, 42 ft. long and 12'6" beam. The *Comet* made her debut in 1812, but, while the steamboat caught on for passenger carrying it was not until June 1819 that John Rennie, in an endeavour to persuade the Lords of the Admiralty of the value of steam power, arranged a trial by hiring the river steamer *Eclipse* for towing the warship *Hastings* from Woolwich to two miles beyond Gravesend against a rising tide. The experiment was successful enough to influence the Admiralty to authorise a steam boat to be built for a similar service. The *Hastings* was a big East Indiaman while the *Eclipse* was a small river steamer about 104 ft. long with a 70 n.h.p. engine. Some sources suggest that the experiment was in fact a failure, but, be that as it may, in 1822 the Admiralty did buy a vessel for towing called the **Royal Sovereign** and renamed her **Monkey.** She was 106'6" long and had been built by Evans of Rotherhithe in 1821 with 100 n.h.p. engines. Later in the year the **Comet** was built for the Navy by Oliver Lang of Deptford. She was 115 ft. long and had 80 n.h.p. engines.

In 1823 a brig called the **Falcon** was fitted with paddles and two 50 n.h.p. engines and a single boiler and trials were carried out. She proved useless as a tug and was sold off. 1823 saw the launch of the **Sprightly** at Blackwall from Wigram and Green's yard and in 1824 the **Meteor** followed, this time from Oliver Lang. Information about these early vessels is sparse, but in 1830 one nautical publication claimed that 'although no official lists existed the Admiralty were now employing 30 steam tugs'. These ships were no larger than their civilian counterparts but their engines seem to have been more powerful.

The Royal Navy is well named 'The Silent Service' as there is very little on paper about the activities of their tugs apart from lists which record the location of each tug in the naval dockyards throughout the world. During the Crimean War when tugs were in such great demand at home, no mention is made of tugs being present in the Black Sea. Towing certainly took place as steam warships towed sailing vessels into position for bombarding shore positions and then removed them from danger when things got too hot or when they had received too much punishment. One of the steam vessels was the paddle steamer **Lightning** which was used to survey and buoy a safe channel for the sailing ships. The **Lightning** (1823, 123 ft.) was described as a wooden paddle gunboat in this case but as a tug elsewhere at a later date. That tugs could have been usefully employed is evident when one reads that 'the British fleet at Baltsch consisted of 100 sailing transports towed by 50 steam vessels each filled with troops, each towing two vessels.'

Homer *armed during the First World War.*

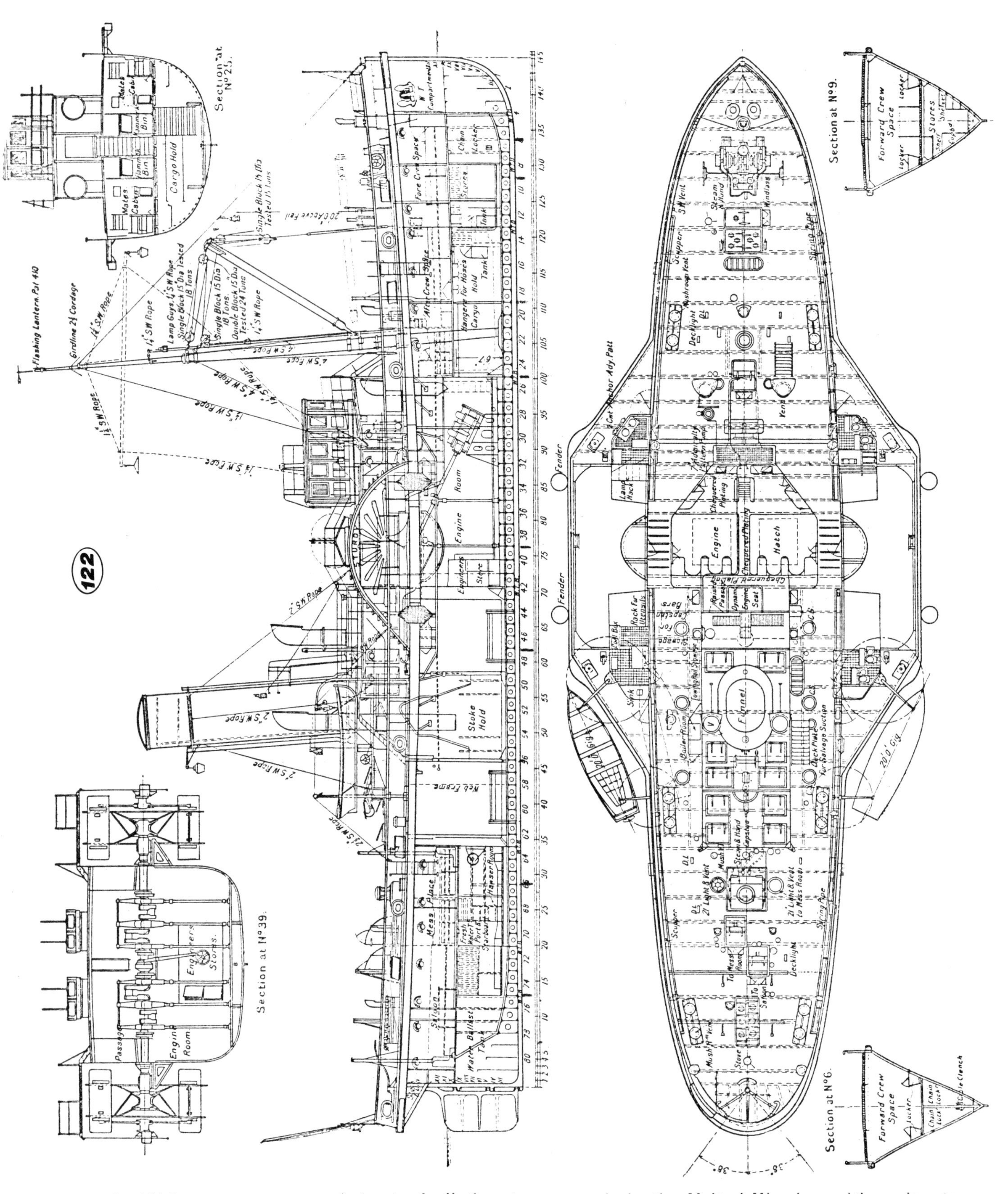

In 1845 a survey was carried out of all the steam vessels in the United Kingdom with a view to determining what armament they were capable of carrying. For example, the Caledonian Steam Towing Company's **Robert Bruce** (1844, 95'8" long, 49 tons) was rated to carry 12-6 pdr. guns. Watkin's little **Monarch** (1833, 64'10", 26 tons, 25 n.h.p.) was not classed to carry any guns at all, hardly surprising in view of her size (14). Yet the Thames Steam Towing Company's **Wear** (1825, 67'7", 33 tons, 34 n.h.p.) could carry 2 to 4 6-pdrs.

In 1859 there was an exchange of correspondence between patriotic gentlemen in Liverpool and the Admiralty on the desirability of having available in Liverpool, vessels adapted for carrying guns which could readily be equipped and placed on defensive patrol off the mouth of the River Mersey. Who the enemy might be is not disclosed but their concern can be appreciated as there

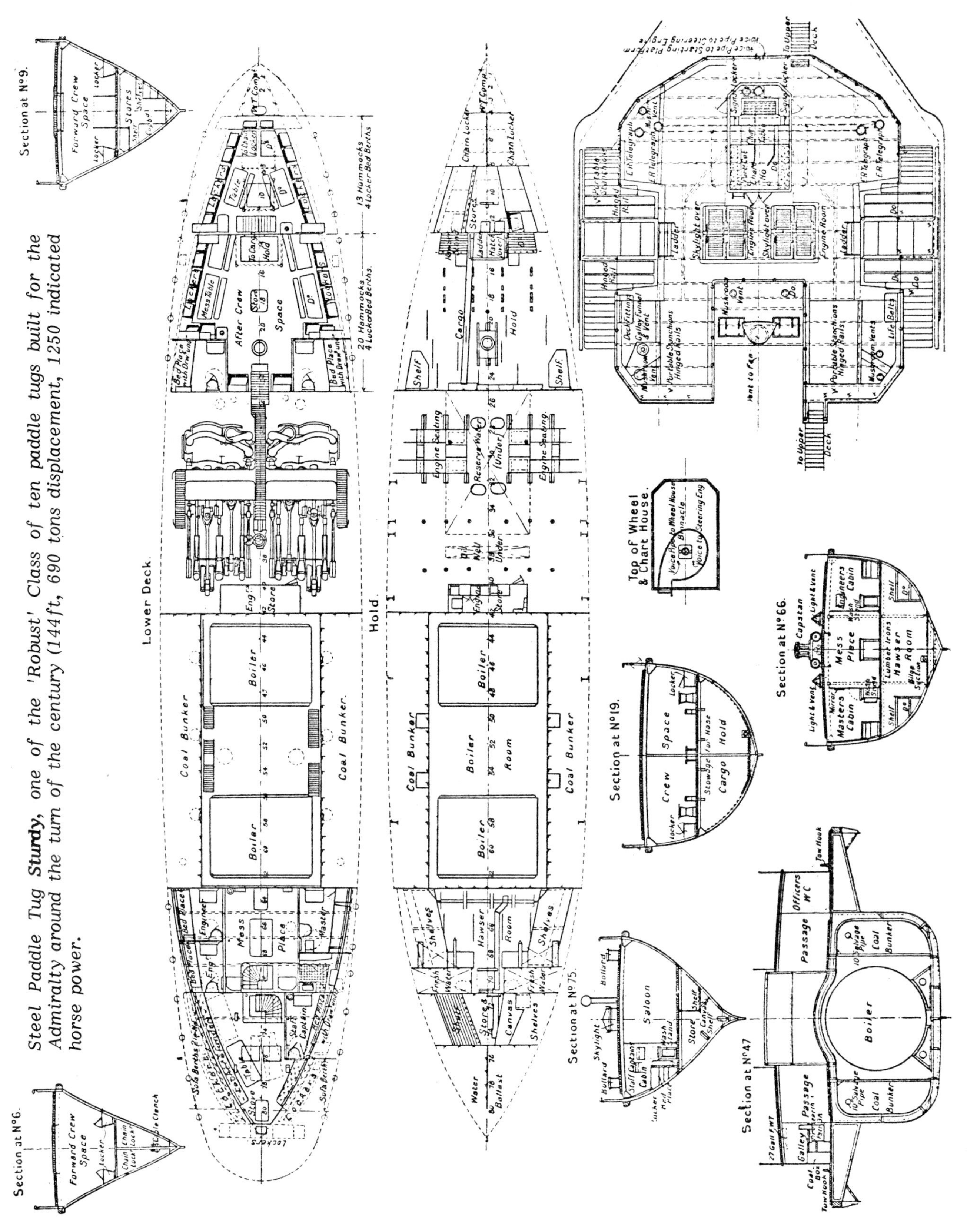

Steel Paddle Tug **Sturdy**, one of the 'Robust' Class of ten paddle tugs built for the Admiralty around the turn of the century (144ft, 690 tons displacement, 1250 indicated horse power.

was no naval base in the Liverpool area and a token show of force might be better than none at all. Among the vessels proposed were some of the big paddle tugs of the Liverpool Steam Tug Company and the St. George Steam Tug Company. The former would provide the **Despatch** (1856, 129.0 ft. 181 tons. 80 n.h.p.) and the **Prowler** (1856, 124.0 ft. 179 tons. 80 n.h.p.) to be fitted with a 32 pdr. or a 45 cwt. gun at both bow and stern. For this service they would receive £6.6.0. and £5.5.0. per day respectively while fitting out and £14 per day while on exercises. The values of the tugs were £7,000 for the **Despatch** and £6,000 for the **Prowler**. The St. George Steam Tug Company would provide the **Storm King** (1857, 137.0 ft. 199 tons, 100 n.h.p.) and the **Fire King** (1856, 105 ft. 120 tons. 60 n.h.p.). These vessels 'were not so substantial in their build as the two previously named' but each could carry two 32 pdr. guns or two 39 cwt. guns in the case of the **Storm King** and two 25 cwt. guns in the case of the **Fire King**. The hire terms were £7 and £5 respectively during alteration and £10.0.0. and £8.0.0. during exercises. The officers appointed to investigate the proposals were full of enthusiasm for the modifications to be carried out, but the correspondence stops without stating if any action was taken. In 1862 twenty vessels were listed in government papers as being tugs in naval service:

Name	Built	Purchased	Length B.P.	Tonnage Builder's	N.H.P.	Iron or Wood	Station
ex-G.P.O. despatch vessels							
Kite		1837	125	300		W	Deptford
Otter (ex **Wizard**)		1837	120	237	120	W	Sheerness
Myrtle (ex **Firefly**)		1837	116	116		W	Portsmouth
Zephyr		1837	116	237	100	W	Devonport
Prospero (ex **Belfast**)		1837	129	249	144	W	Devonport
ex-gunboats							
Locust	1840		120	234		W	Sheerness
Comet				238	80	W	Portsmouth
Spitfire	1845		147	432		W	Bermuda
ex-sloop							
African	1825		112	263	90	W	Sheerness
Echo	1827		112	298	140	W	Portsmouth
Confiance	1827		112	295	100	W	Devonport
ex-passenger vessel							
Monkey (ex **Royal Sovereign**)	1821	1822	106	211	100	W	Deptford
Tugs							
Bustler (ex **Merry Andrew**)	1852	1855	112	217	100	W	Deptford
Sheerness		1863	123	233		W	Sheerness
Scotia (ex civilian)	1862	1862	132	268		W	Devonport
Redpole (ex **Racehorse**)	1855			360		W	Gibraltar
Hearty (ex **Merry Monarch**)	1854	1855	112	221		W	Malta
Wallace (ex **Lyons**)		1855	112	208	100	I	Royal Clarence
Thais	1856		118	302		I	Royal William

This list casts doubts on the statement made in the nautical press in 1830. Of the above nineteen vessels only seven are tugs, the remainder are conversions. The writer in 1830 would have been better saying that '30 vessels capable of towing' were in service. The Admiralty seems to have been rather doubtful about the usefulness of tugs since they employed so few and most were conversions. In 1869 when they wanted to shift a floating dock to Bermuda they employed one of their warships rather than hire civilian tugs.

Four tugs are mentioned in a list dated 1859 as having large sums of money spent on their overhaul and they had not been sold by 1862:

Name	Built	Purchased	Length	Tonnage	N.H.P.	Iron or Wood
ex G.P.O. despatch vessels						
Fearless		1837	112	165	76	W
Widgeon		1837	108	164	90	W
Wildfire (ex **Watersprite**)		1838	116	186	76	W
tug						
Dragon (ex civilian)	1855	1859	85	113		W

It will be noted that all these tugs were comparable in size with the average civilian paddle tug and that at that time the Navy had not shown any inclination to employ big paddle tugs of the type by this time common in London and Liverpool. In 1868 the wooden paddle tug **Grinder** went into service 120 ft. long 505 tons disp. 500 i.h.p. capable of 10.83 kts. It was 1874 before the iron paddle tug came into service, the **Malta** 128 ft. 491 tons. disp. 860 i.h.p. followed in 1875 by the **Perseverance** 130 ft. 505 tons. disp. 860 i.h.p.

In 1881 war broke out in Egypt and the Liverpool tug **Stormcock,** a twin-screw, ocean going tug (1877, 155.5 ft. 325 tons. 1000 i.h.p.) was hired by the Government to assist in conveying troops along the Suez Canal. The performance of the tug impressed the Admiralty who purchased her for naval service. The **Stormcock** (79) was replaced by her owners the Liverpool Screw Towing and Lighterage Company with a larger tug of the same name (1883, 161.0 ft. 364 tons. 193 n.h.p.), but once more the Admiralty, who were building up a fleet of special service vessels in the event of war with Russia, purchased her in 1885 and renamed her **Traveller.** One of the duties assigned to her was the destruction of derelict ships, a very real menace in the days of sail. Once more, in 1885, a third **Stormcock** was built (160.0 ft. 373 tons. 300 n.h.p.) and once again the Admiralty stepped in and bought her in 1896, renaming her **Alligator**. By this time the Navy had a good sized fleet of big paddle and screw tugs capable of handling the new ironclads, but they also were building up a fleet of smaller tugs for harbour service, many of wooden construction, tugs such as the **Plumper** (purchased 1891, 56 ft. long).

The business of arming tugs as patrol vessels was raised once more in 1892 when the Army announced their intention of 'placing two serviceable steam vessels at the mouth of the River Tees for the protection of the river. The vessels to be armed with quickfiring machine guns.' The Tees Conservancy Commissioners offered the I.P.T. **Universe** (1875, 115.8 ft. 143 tons. 85 n.h.p.) and the I.P.T. **Isaac Wilson** (1889, 101.0 ft. 123 tons. 45 n.h.p.). Once more there is no indication that this proposal was carried out and once more no clue was offered as to the enemy or against what form of attack this puny defence was to be effective.

The Government also used tugs for other purposes. In 1885 Thompsons of Dundee started building the **Indra** (212 ft. 1300 tons. disp. 2100 i.h.p.), but she was bought, renamed **Hearty** and used variously as a survey ship, a fishery protection cruiser and eventually as a salvage vessel. (She had probably been originally meant for India as Thompsons had built a number of tugs of this size for use on the River Hooghly). She cannot have been very successful in her role of fishery protection as she had a very distinctive profile with two massive vertical funnels which must have been recognisable miles away, but she did have a speed of 14 kts. which is more than the average fishing boat could manage.

In about 1895 the Admiralty chartered the big Liverpool paddle tug **Gladiator** (1874, 144.7 ft. 228 tons. 700 i.h.p.) and she was engaged for the next fourteen years carrying out survey work on their behalf. When she was returned to her owners in 1905 there was no work for her and she was sold for scrapping. Around this time the War Department began to build up a considerable fleet of vessels for water transport in connection with their activities, mainly towing barges, screw steamers and sailing vessels but included among their numbers were some screw tugs. These were listed in the Royal Navy Pocket Book (the Blue Book), but names only are supplied with no indication as to the type of vessel. Mine warfare had been well established by now, but the Navy regarded it as a defensive measure and were content to leave it in the hands of the Submarine Section of the Royal Engineers. Exercises were carried out by the volunteer divisions of the above force utilising paddle tugs until the work was taken over by the Navy in 1905 and the army mining unit was disbanded. There was however a little screw tug, the **Miner** (1880, 65.2 ft. 51 tons. 23 n.h.p.) which was attached to the mining unit. A handbook on mining shows a rather hazardous method of laying mines. The tug carried the mines supported from her bulwarks with a length of cable attached between the mines to ensure that they were dropped at the correct intervals. The **Miner** was disposed of in 1907 to the Tyne Pilotage Commission for use as a pilot cutter. Everything aboard her was of the best quality and her propeller was even made of brass.

In 1914 during some trouble in Ireland, Steel & Bennie's tug **Cruiser** (1904, 104.8 ft. 167 tons. 99 n.h.p.) was chartered by the London Times to carry despatches between Ireland and the U.K. The charterers undertook not to use the tug for carrying refugees, contraband, nor to take part in hostilities, but they were not to be held responsible for any action of the crew in this respect unless they had given written instructions to the captain.

By the time that war broke out in 1914 the Admiralty had modernised their tug fleet and now had in service paddle tugs and screw tugs capable of handling the largest warships in the Fleet. The paddle tugs were the favourites because of their ability to turn their tow like a top when lashed alongside, and to 'put on the brakes' by reversing their paddles. As one old navy tugman put it - "when the **Pert**'s paddles revolved, even slowly, they shifted TONS of water." Two classes of paddle tug formed the backbone of the tug fleet. There were nine of the **Dromedary** class (144 ft. 680/700 tons. displacement, 1250 i.h.p.), having two funnels set fore and aft of the paddleboxes, and ten of the **Robust** class (144 ft. 690 tons. displacement, 1250 i.h.p.) with a single funnel set abaft the paddles. The most striking feature on the drawing of the **Sturdy** (122) is that single huge funnel towering above the tug behind the paddleboxes. The hull itself was rather square looking, with very little sheer; as they were harbour tugs sheer was not necessary. Being naval tugs the **Robust** class had a large crew, in this case 40, and as the accommodation was correspondingly large there were skylights, companionways and vents scattered all over the deck giving it a more cluttered appearance than her civilian counterpart. Some minor details which could only be found on a naval tug are polished copper vents to the engineroom (below the bridge) polished brass stanchions under the bridge and polished brass tops on the after bollard of each pair. She was powered by two compound diagonal engines, again a feature seldom found on the civilian paddle tugs. The big derrick forward was capable of lifting 5 tons, the power being provided by the big anchor windlass with its vertically mounted cylinders. The **Sturdy** was built in 1912 by Messrs. Thornycroft of Woolston, Southampton, her name was changed in 1919 to **Swarthy**, and she remained in service with the Navy until she was scrapped in 1961.

The **Volcano** was built in 1899 at a time when the last of the big civilian paddle tugs with twin funnels were being broken up. Her funnels were very widely spaced and being so tall they made the vessel look shorter than she was - 144 ft. x 27.2 ft. A noticeable fitting was the huge casting round each anchor hawsehole at the bow, matched by a similar pair at the stern (127). There was one other paddle tug, the massive **Pert** which was built in 1916 (170.0 ft. 1023 tons displacement, 2000 i.h.p.).

In addition a number of large screw tugs had been purchased from civilian owners as had the various **Stormcocks**. Apart from these about twenty or so smaller tugs were used for harbour work with lesser naval craft.

When the war started there was a tremendous demand for transports to ferry troops to France and for cargo vessels to carry their munitions and supplies. All this intense military traffic called for the services of tugs and the government departments in Whitehall, both Army and Naval requisitioned civilian tugs from all over the country leaving the ports and harbours with only a few tugs to carry on their normal business. This lack of tugs threatened to bring some of the ports to a halt and Mr. John Watkins went along to Whitehall personally to explain the consequences of the wholesale takeover of the country's tugs. Fortunately his advice was heeded and many of the tugs were released to return to their normal duties, but the fact remains that during the war some 426 civilian tugs were taken over for service with the armed forces, sometimes for just one or two weeks but in a great many instances the tugs remained under government orders for the duration of the hostilities. Of the British tugs 319 served with the Royal Navy, 28 served with the Army and the Navy at different times and 30 with the Army alone. The remaining 49 tugs were hired from overseas, from Belgium, Canada, Australia, South Africa and even from the United States. These ex-civilian tugs were to be found at the approaches to the major ports in the country operating as boarding vessels putting examining officers aboard all ships entering, searching for contraband or German nationals attempting to return to Germany for military service. They worked at the various locations where convoys were made up before sailing, places such as Loch Ewe in Scotland. The German mining offensive resulted in many casualties and the tugs were needed to tow in crippled ships and to salvage where possible ships which had been sunk or had been run aground in an attempt to save them. The Watkin's tug **Hibernia** (1884, 121.0 ft. 219 tons. 600 e.h.p.) served as the **Carcass** in the campaign in Gallipoli where her long operating range came in useful, while another tug the iron paddle tug **Marsden** (1906, 95.0 ft. 131 tons. 70 n.h.p.) belonging to France Fenwick of Newcastle was wrecked at Sulva Bay in the Dardanelles. Another Watkins tug, the **Racia** (see Ocean tugs 86) was sent seven times to the White Sea, on one occasion bringing back the armed merchant cruiser *Arlanza* which had been damaged by a mine. The Liverpool tug **Blackcock** (1886, 146.2 ft. 254 tons. 200 n.h.p.) was also working in the White Sea in 1918 when she was caught in the ice and crushed.

The **Blackcock** had already featured in the operation which had been mounted against the German Commerce raider *Koenigsberg* which had gone to ground on the East coast of Africa in the Rufiji Delta. The only way to winkle her out was by the use of monitors, so, while smaller warships set up a blockade to keep the German warship locked in her hideout, the monitors *Mersey*, *Severn* and *Humber* were sent out in tow of the tugs **Blackcock, T.A. Jolliffe** (1901, 113.0 ft. 199 tons. 650 i.h.p.) **Sarah Jolliffe** (81) (1890, 138 ft. 333 tons. 900 a.h.p.) and **Revenger** ex Dutch **Maas** (1905, 123.0 ft. 243 tons. 106 n.h.p.). Part of the tow through the Mediterranean was undertaken by the smaller tugs **Danube II** (1910, 100.2 ft. 227 tons. 97 n.h.p.) and the **Hampden** ex-civilian **Southampton** (1910, 100.2 ft. 227 tons. 63 n.h.p.) between Malta and Lemnos. After the successful completion of the operation the tugs returned with the monitors to the Mediterranean where the **Sarah Jolliffe** and the **Blackcock** remained until sent with barges in tow to Archangel in the north of Russia, a very long tow indeed.

Being on charter to, or being requisitioned by, the Admiralty had its disadvantages apart from being subject to naval discipline. Should the tug be involved in a salvage operation there was a likelihood that no award could be claimed. The crew of the Watkin's tug **Simla** (49) (1898, 100.4 ft. 144 tons. 99 n.h.p.) in April 1915 rendered assistance to the ship *Sarpen* ashore in the Orkney Islands and despite the fact that they had saved a ship and cargo worth £30,000 and £19,693 respectively, no salvage award was granted, as the **Simla** was a requisitioned tug. The case was taken to a higher court and an award of £800 was granted; a rather poor reward for the risk which the tug took. The owners of the tug **Warrior** (1895, 106.0 ft. 192 tons. 700 i.h.p.) had shown some foresight and in their terms of charter they had insisted that 'she should be at liberty to assist vessels in distress

H.S. 28 was one of the 'H.S.' tugs with a steam automatic towing winch built in 1917.

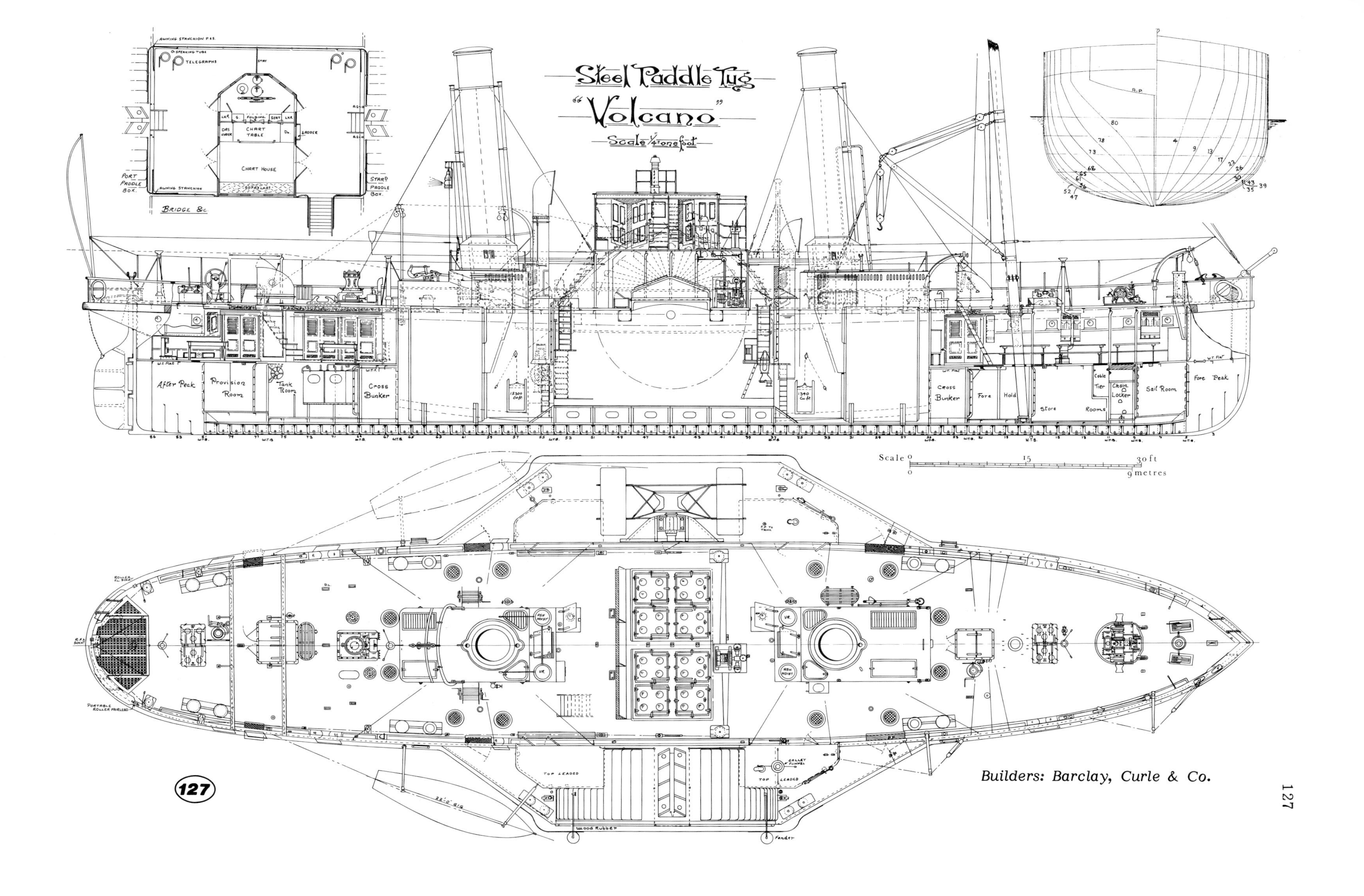
Steel Paddle Tug
"Volcano"
Scale 1/4 one foot
Chart House
Chart Table
Bridge &c.
Port Paddle Box
Starb Paddle Box
After Peak
Provision Room
Tank Room
Cross Bunker
Cross Bunker
Fore Hold
Store
Rooms
Cable Tier
Chain Locker
Sail Room
Fore Peak
Scale 0 15 30 ft
0 9 metres
Top Leaded
Top Leaded
Galley Funnel
Wood Rubber
Fender
22'-0" Gig
127
Builders: Barclay, Curle & Co.

and to deviate for the purpose of saving life and that all salvage cases were to be for the owner's benefit, but during such an action all costs were to be borne by the owner'. When she went to the assistance of the *Miefield* in October 1915 she took little risk but she received £200 for her services without any legal wrangling. Risks were taken when the **Lady Brassey** (1913, 130.1 ft. 362 tons. 1600 i.h.p.) and the **Lady Crundall** (1906, 130.0 ft. 366 tons. 1500 i.h.p.), both belonging to the Dover Harbour Board went to the aid of the *Surrey* which had been mined in February 1915. The tugs had to go through the very minefield which had caused the casualty, to render assistance, at no small danger to themselves considering the draught of the tugs which was about 13'6". Similar services were rendered all round the coasts of the country by the requisitioned tugs and also by tugs from the Navy:

April 1916	**Warrior**) **Framfield**)	*Wayfarer* (cargo - horses)	Mined off Queenstown. Towed to safety. Award £3,200.
February 1916	**Fastnet**) **United Service**) **Athlete**)	*Elswick Manor* (cargo - grain)	Mined off Norfolk coast. Beached. Award £3,390.
August 1915	**Vanquisher**) **Premier**)	*Bretwalda* (cargo - coal)	Mined in Thames, beached. Award £1,500.
November 1917	**Victor**) **Triton**) H.M. tug **Zaree**)	*Ango*	Torpedoed off Lizard. Towed to Falmouth. Award £7,000.
July 1918	**T.A. Jolliffe**) H.M. tug **Deluge**)	*Ango*	Torpedoed off Whitby while being towed to W.Hartlepool for repairs. Towed to W. Hartlepool. Award £1,410.

(The *Ango* seems to have been an unlucky ship).

The tugs were vulnerable when operating off the coast and a number were destroyed by German submarines which sank them by gunfire or stopped them and sank them with a bomb placed in the bilges. It was not usually worth while wasting a torpedo on small vessels like tugs. Some were mined, some were stranded and became total losses, some were sunk in collisions. Several were attacked by submarines but succeeded in escaping. The tug **Englishman** (1913, 71.0 ft. 62 tons. 28 n.h.p.) escaped due to her speed. (The submarine must have been a very old one!) One of the most exciting episodes was the battle fought by the **Homer** (1915, 95.3 ft. 157 tons. 95 n.h.p.) belonging to the Batey fleet of Newcastle which is worth reporting in full:

"A gallant attempt by the master of a British tug to sink a German submarine is reported from St. Helens, Isle of Wight. When about fifteen miles off St. Catherine's Point, on April 8th, 1915, the steam tug **Homer** (121) of South Shields, Captain H. Gibson, towing the French barque *General de Sonis*, laden with grain and bound for Sunderland, sighted a submarine. The commander of the submarine ordered the captain of the **Homer** to abandon his ship. Upon his refusing to do so, the hostile craft changed her course and came up on the other side of the tug, and a warning shot was fired over the bridge. Captain Gibson waited until the submarine came abeam of his vessel, and then, casting off the hawser, steamed at full speed of $11\frac{1}{2}$ knots straight for the submarine. There was a rough sea running at the time and unfortunately he missed the vessel by about 3 feet. feet.

During this time a perfect hail of bullets fell about the wheelhouse and bridge of the tug, doing considerable damage to the woodwork and the windows. The captain escaped injury. The submarine steered away and fired a torpedo which missed. After chasing the tug for about ten minutes the submarine gave up the pursuit. The **Homer** put into St. Helens Roads. The *General de Sonis* was afterwards picked up by the Dover tug **Lady Crundall** and towed into the Downs." The **Homer** had been fitted with W/T in her role as a coastal tug in government service with the addition of topmasts on the after side of the two masts. In the account of her skirmish no mention is made of the gun with which she was armed which is hardly surprising when you see how exposed it was on the fore-deck - with a machine gun firing on her it would have been suicide to try to man it.

As the scale of the war stepped up it became apparent that more tugs were going to be required and so the Government placed orders for new tugs of a wide variety of sizes. There was a large cross-channel traffic in barges carrying coal, munitions and supplies to the French channel ports and for towing these barges two types of tug were required by the Director of Inland Waterways. They were not named but were given numbers with the prefix "H.S." (presumably Harbour Service). The first was a single-screw tug for the cross-channel tow: 86.1 ft. x 21.0 ft. beam, 9'3" draught, 144 tons, 400 i.h.p. - and the second, for the work in the ports and for towing in the canals leading to the Front, a twin-screw shallow draught tug 85.5 ft. x 22.1 ft. (draught 7'6") 144 tons, 400 i.h.p. The **HS 21/22** belonged to the twin-screw class which had no rise of keel being of constant draught (129). As befitted a wartime built tug she was very simply equipped. She was not fitted with an automatic towing winch but was provided with two warping drums, one on each side of the engine casing with the steam engine mounted internally. Note that the accommodation is for N.C.O.s and Sappers (Royal Engineers) showing that she was manned by army personnel. The twin-screw H.S. tugs were built by the Lytham Shipbuilding Co., the Ardrossan Dry Dock & Shipbuilding Co. Ltd. and Philip & Son of Dartmouth in 1916/17.

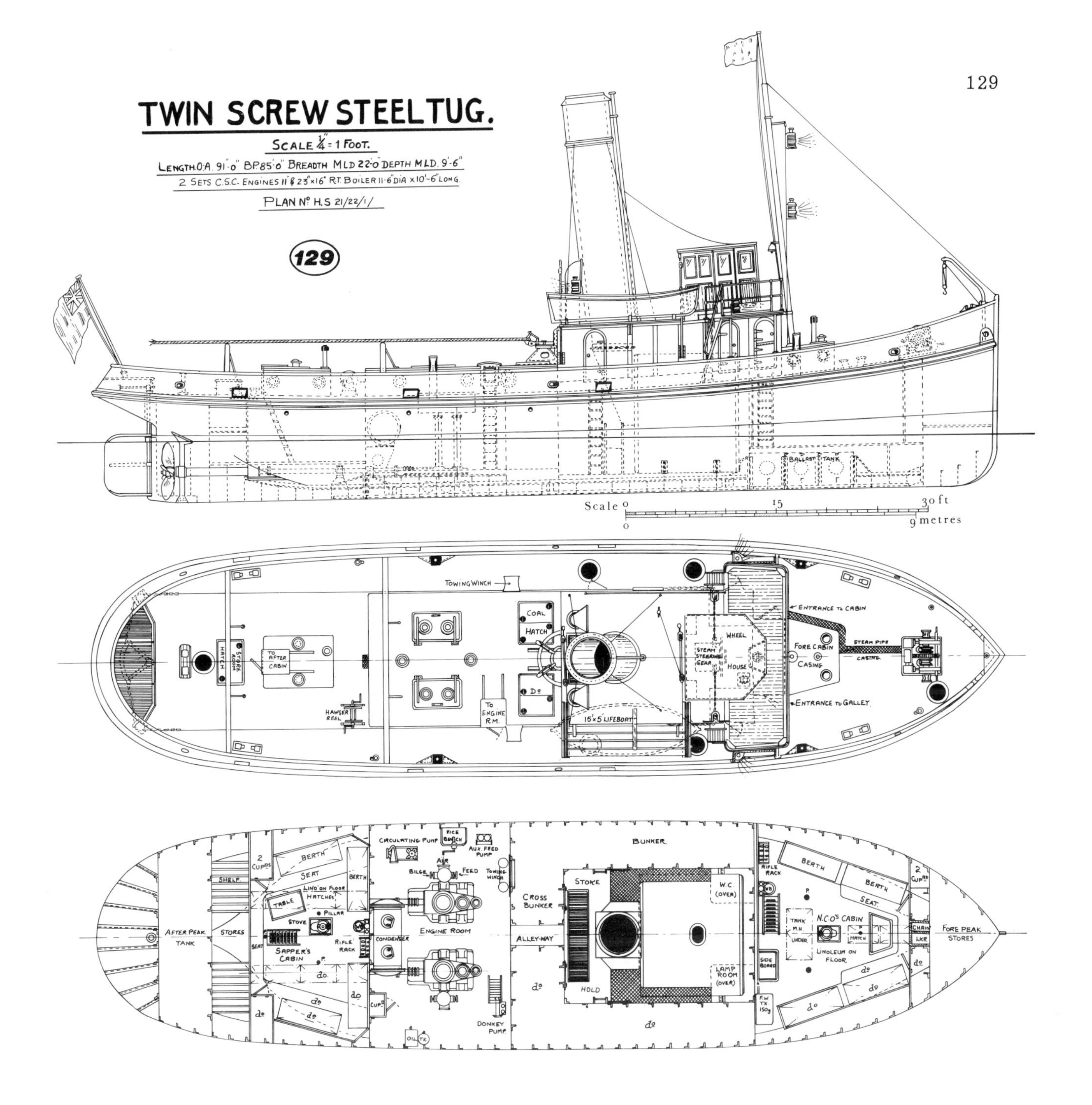

The **H.S. 28** was one of the single-screw tugs built in 1917 and is shown fitted with an automatic towing winch (126). This was designed to maintain a constant tension on the towline and had been invented around 1900. Although adopted widely in America it had been little used in Great Britain and it was therefore somewhat surprising to find towing winches fitted on some of the **H.S.** and **West** classes of tug. Where towing winches were used they were usually fitted on ocean-going tugs, not on 'small fry'. The winch was mounted on the engine casing and because of its height the first towing bows are set high. At a time when most tugs still had simple radial davits the **H.S. 28** has a type which pivotted on the side of the boiler casing simplifying the launching of the lifeboat.

To upset the researcher not only are no official lists available but in addition many existing tugs were requisitioned and given the **H.S.** nomenclature. **H.S. 45** was built in 1909 for Canadian owners as the **J.O. Gravel** (94.5 ft. 197 tons), while the **H.S. 44** had been the American **Julia C.Moran** ex **Harry G. Runkle** (91.0 ft. 164 tons). The highest number traced is **H.S. 102.** The barges which were built for this traffic were 180 ft. overall x 31 ft. beam and were capable of carrying 1000 tons, crewed by 2 officers and 4 seamen. Another group of hired tugs were prefixed **H.T.** the highest number being **H.T. 14.** Slightly larger than the **H.S.** tugs were the **West** class built in 1919, 13 in all, with names such as **West Acre** and **West Hyde** (88.5 ft. 154 tons. 77 n.h.p.). Between 1915 and 1919 at least 36 small tugs, some wood, some steel from 48.5 ft. x 12.5 ft., 25 tons up to 75.2 ft. x 15.1 ft., 67 tons were built for various Government departments, some named, but some bearing numbers only, with prefixes **A.S.**, **A.T.T.**, or **T.T.** Unfortunately no authority has revealed the significance of these letters and so one is left to guess if **A.S.** was *Auxiliary Service* or **A.T.T.** was *Army Transport Tug.* A further group was ordered but was delivered too late to see active service, the **Poultry** class, 75.5 ft. x 15 ft. 65 tons, 185 b.h.p., all called after types of poultry like **Bantam** and **Wyandotte.**

Part of the fleet of hired tugs had been allocated to assist damaged ships into port and was controlled by a special Tug Committee. In May 1917 the disposal of these tugs was 5 at Portland, 2 at Plymouth, 5 at Falmouth, 5 in the Scillies, 2 at Milford, 4 at Stornaway, 5 at Lough Swilly, 5 at Berehaven and 5 at Queenstown. To strengthen their ranks several larger tugs were built between 1916 and 1919. There were five tugs of the **Stoic** class, ugly looking tugs with two funnels placed close together amidships - 141.8 ft. x 29 ft. 885 tons. displacement, 1200 i.h.p. The three **Frisky** class tugs: 155.3 ft. x 31 ft. 612 tons displacement, 1200 i.h.p. were really handsome vessels with two absolutely vertical funnels nicely spaced on a raised boatdeck. They were sometimes called the **Racia** class having reputedly been based on Watkins tug of that name. The **Resolve** class were an enlarged version of the **Frisky** class: 175 ft. x 34 ft. 1400 tons displacement, 2400 i.h.p., the most powerful tugs in the fleet and six of these were built. They too looked very smart and were classed for harbour work and for coastal salvage. Of this class, three had a low open foredeck (**Rollcall** etc. plan 108) while the other three had a slightly raised forecastle and a well deck which somewhat spoiled their appearance. The hull had a pronounced flare and a very sharp bow with a right angled forefoot to permit the fitting of a paravane as a protection against underwater mines. Because of the low deck forward a breakwater was fitted and on the companionway aft of it there was a shield to deflect the seas and allow the door to be opened even in bad weather. Spare salvage and bower anchors were lashed to the breakwater. The bridge was all panelled as was the flying bridge, a very spacious affair complete with chartboard and signalling posts. Between the funnels was the radio cabin. On the hull below the two lifeboats there were a series of chocks to deflect the lifeboat over the broad fender. The engineroom casing was an immense affair liberally provided with wood framed skylights (protected by numerous bars), with a house covering the steam steering engine. On the after towing deck instead of the more usual capstan there was a steam winch with the warping drums at the end of extended shafts. On a platform in the stern was a salvage anchor in position ready for immediate use with a spare anchor on the deck near it. Four high towing bows were needed to give protection to all the structures on the towing deck. The form taken by the rope stops is interesting - a thumb cleat on a metal band at the top of the wooden samson post.

The last class of rescue tugs was the most numerous as 46 of the **Saint** class of tug were built: 135 ft. x 29 ft., 440 tons, 1250 i.h.p. (single screw). These had a raised forecastle which was carried back without a break to the after end of the boat deck (5). They were one of the first tugs to have this feature which has been perpetuated by most ocean-going tugs from that time onwards. On the **Saint** class however, the hull plating stopped below the bridge leaving an open side passage with stanchions supporting the boat deck. The placing of the steam steering engine at the after end of the engine casing shortened the length of the steering chains, a desirable design point on long tugs, as steering chains could stretch or be jammed by debris washing around on the deck.

They were fitted with forced draught fans in the boiler room and as a result the funnel looked rather dumpy. Most of the rescue tugs were equipped with a heavy derrick for salvage work, portable pumps for placing aboard the casualty, and heavy salvage anchors on a platform at the stern to be laid out as kedge anchors. Many were armed with a 12 pdr. gun on the forecastle so that they could defend themselves against enemy attack when they were on convoy escort duty or undertaking coastal tows with a damaged ship. The snag was that their field of fire was limited and the tug had to face up to its attacker if the captain decided to fight (5). The Rescue Tugs were credited with the salvage of 140 vessels and with giving assistance to 500 others before the war ended. The **St. Fergus** and **St. Finbarr** were intended to have guns but were completed for peace time service (131).

Occasionally the Rescue Service had its lighter side. The big tug **Seahorse** (1880, 160 ft. 164 tons), somewhat like the **Stormcock** in appearance, was called to take in tow a tanker which was on fire in the English Channel. A line and grapnel were thrown on to the tanker and two men climbed up it and passed the towrope. The tanker was towed into a small bay and scuttled. Unfortunately the bay was shallow so the tanker did not sink far and continued to burn spreading black soot all over the beautiful whitewashed cottages in the bay. There is a story that when the crew of the tug went aboard to 'salvage' articles of value e.g. food and drink, that they found a member of the tanker's crew still asleep in his bunk?

One more class of wartime tug deserves mention because of its unusual construction. With a shortage of steel the authorities looked for alternative material for the hulls and the answer was to use reinforced concrete. Twelve tugs were built between 1919 and 1920 (125 ft.267 tons,750 i.h.p.) and complimentary to the tugs were 50 or so ferroconcrete barges with a carrying capacity of 1000 tons. All these craft were given names beginning **Crete**, names such as **Creteboom** and **Cretehawser**. The intention had been to use them on coastal tows supplying coal to ports on the east and west coasts of Ireland and to French ports, but they were completed too late to play an active part in the war. However, they continued in service until 1923 towing the coal laden barges to the German North Sea ports, to the Baltic, and to Norway. Right through the winter of 1922/23 they worked in heavy ice in the Baltic towing ships without suffering any damage to their hulls. One such tow was undertaken in 1922 when the **Cretegaff** towed the *S.S. Fluor* from Petrograd to Bremen.

When the hostilities ceased the disposal of wartime tonnage commenced and over the next four or five years almost all the tugs built during the war were sold to buyers in the U.K. and abroad. The small tugs found ready sale to London and many of the lesser ports in this country, while the

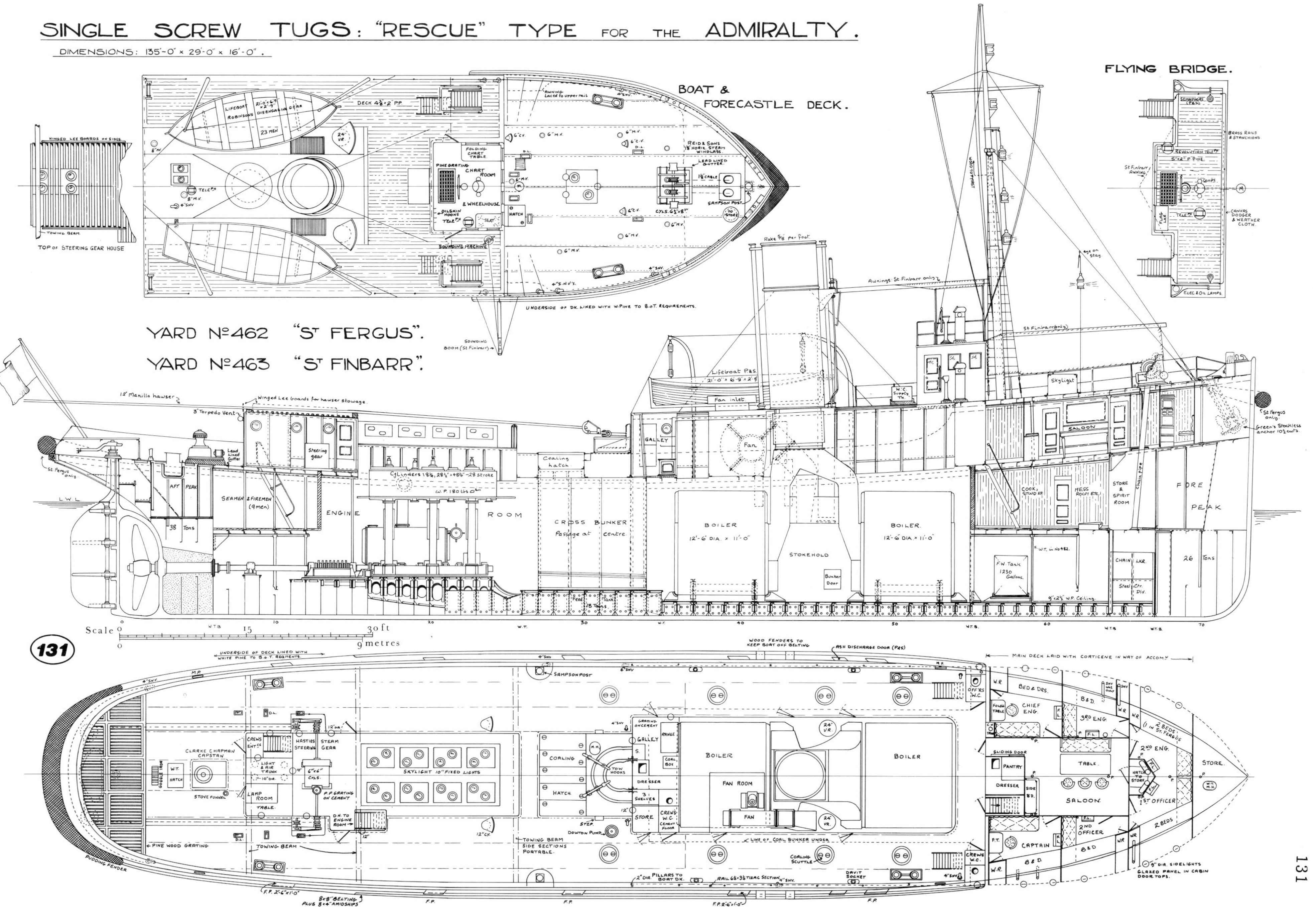

SINGLE SCREW TUGS: "RESCUE" TYPE FOR THE ADMIRALTY.
DIMENSIONS: 135'-0" × 29'-0" × 16'-0".
BOAT & FORECASTLE DECK.
FLYING BRIDGE.
TOP OF STEERING GEAR HOUSE
YARD No 462 "St FERGUS".
YARD No 463 "St FINBARR".
LIFEBOAT
23 MEN
CHART ROOM
& WHEELHOUSE
SOUNDING MACHINE
UNDERSIDE OF DK. LINED WITH W.PINE TO B.O.T. REQUIREMENTS.
12" Manilla hawser
Winged Lee boards for hawser stowage
3" Torpedo Vent
Steering gear
Cylinders 18½, 28½ + 48½ - 28 stroke
AFT PEAK
38 Tons
SEAMEN & FIREMEN (9 men)
ENGINE ROOM
Coaling hatch
CROSS BUNKER
Passage at centre
GALLEY
Lifeboat P&S. 21'-0" × 6'-9" × 2'-5"
Fan inlet
Fan
BOILER
12'-6" DIA × 11'-0"
STOKEHOLD
Bunker Door
F.W. Tank 1230 Gallons
Skylight
SALOON
COOK, STWD &c.
MESS ROOM &c.
STORE & SPIRIT ROOM
CHAIN LKR.
FORE PEAK
26 Tons
L.W.L.
Scale
30 ft
9 metres
131
MAIN DECK LAID WITH CORTICENE IN WAY OF ACCOMy
WOOD FENDERS TO KEEP BOAT OFF BELTING
ASH DISCHARGE DOOR (P&S)
SAMPSON POST
CLARKE CHAPMAN CAPSTAN
STOVE FUNNEL
LAMP ROOM
HASTIES STEERING
STEAM GEAR
SKYLIGHT 10" FIXED LIGHTS
CORLING
HATCH
TOW HOOKS
DRESSER
STORE
FAN ROOM
FAN
CHIEF ENG.
3RD ENG.
2ND ENG.
1ST OFFICER
2ND OFFICER
CAPTAIN
PANTRY
TABLE
SALOON
STORE.
TOWING BEAM
PINE WOOD GRATING
PUDDING FENDER

H.S. tugs went roughly half abroad and half to owners at home. The Manchester Ship Canal Company bought six, two single-screw tugs and four of the twin-screw tugs, which, with their shallow draught and two propellers made them very useful units. the **H.S. 58** was bought by the Port of London Authority and was never renamed, operating under her original designation. Six of the **West** class tugs and fifteen of the **Saint** class were retained for naval use. The **Saint**'s found buyers abroad despite the fact that their towing arrangements had come in for some criticism. "The deck erections abaft the hook caused the tow rope to take a sharp upward lead and the ropes frequently broke. A $4\frac{1}{2}$ " wire was the largest wire which it was possible to use, the fairleads were too small, the tugs pitched heavily, steered badly and had too much top hamper". The fact that the **Saint**s remained so long in service with the Royal Navy and with their new owners leads one to think that these comments were a little harsh.

The **Frisky** trio were sold abroad, the **Frisky** herself becoming the **Foundation Franklin** which has been made immortal in the book 'Grey Seas Under' by Farley Mowat, the story of her achievements in deep sea salvage and towage. The **Saucy** went to Shanghai and features in the early advertisements of the Shanghai Tug and Lighterage Company as a salvage tug. Of the **Resolve** class only the **Rollcall** was disposed of, to be converted to a passenger tender working in Southampton.

Both during and after the First World War the Ministry of Shipping placed rescue tugs under the management of civilian firms, among them the Alexandra Towing Company of Liverpool and Lawson-Batey Tugs Ltd. of Newcastle. The **Saint Florence** which was being managed by the Lawson-Batey company carried out a 6879 mile ocean tow from Bahia Blanca in the Argentine to Cuxhaven in Germany with a call at the coaling station on the little island of Fernado Noronha off the coast of Brazil. In all six of the Saint class tugs were managed by this firm and the tugs were employed towing disabled German vessels from the South American seaboard through the Panama Canal to ports in the U.K. and the Continent.

The period just after the First World War is a difficult one for researchers. During the early 1920s tugs appear in the registers with dates of build anything up to ten years old with no clue as to their original name. The name which is entered has not been entered before and the date of registration is no help. Some of the small tugs were those which were in service with the army units dealing with canal transport, but as these tended to be built in groups it is not possible to sort out which one was which. Some may have been foreign tugs bought up, as many were, to undertake salvage work for a newly formed company, a situation which is made worse when the tug was built in the U.K. in the first place. Such a tug was the **King Tut** which had been built as the **T.T.2;** but there were two other tugs with identical dimensions, all built in 1918. The **King Tut** was first registered in 1924, the **Annie Ritchie** in 1922 and the **Bricklesey** in 1921, but no previous names (or numbers) have turned up for the latter pair.

With the shortage of steel which was general during a war, some tugbuilders were encouraged to use wood and several firms more accustomed to building fishing boats launched tugs. The **King Tut** was one of the small tugs which went into service in 1918 to work in docks where there was lighter traffic. The long casing left little room on the deck and lack of space below resulted in the placing of the W.C. and galley at the forward end of the casing with the steering position just behind it. The funnel folded back but it looks as though the mast would have been unstepped except when required at night for showing the correct lights. Although built of wood there was still quite a bit of steel in the **T.T.2**, as she was then called, in the way of brackets and stiffeners around the engine and boiler casings (133). She was built at Lowestoft, gross tonnage 39 and engine 25 n.h.p. and she served in Hull, Bristol and finally in Milford Docks.

In 1923 an Admiralty floating dock had to be towed from the Tyne to Southampton by five Admiralty tugs and in the photograph of her departure from the Tyne it is possible to pick out the **Creteboom**, one of the **Resolve** class and one of the **Saint**s among the lead tugs. In 1925 a large ex-German floating dock which had been surrendered to Great Britain under the Versailles Treaty was to be transferred to Malta. The contract was offered to private firms who turned it down. The Admiralty decided therefore to do the job themselves, and the **Roysterer** in company with other navy tugs accomplished the 2,000 mile tow without a hitch.

The naval building programme between the wars was restricted but the Admiralty succeeded in adding some tugs to their depleted fleet when a new class of target towing tugs was built in Paisley. The **Brigand** class tugs were 165 ft. long, 840 tons displacement, and with two engines totalling 3000 i.h.p. were capable of $15\frac{1}{2}$ kts. Their appearance was somewhat marred by the short well deck between the forecastle and the bridge but at full speed they were certainly a sight to behold (121). The short funnel also spoiled her looks but with a forced draught fan a larger one was not needed. The decks of the tug were cluttered with casings, companionways and fittings and the towropes were kept clear of these by High arching towing bows. For handling targets and salvage equipment she had two samson posts and derricks at the after end of the boat deck as can be seen on the plan (172).

In 1939 war broke out once more with the Navy having on its strength sixteen of the old paddle tugs, four pre-1914 screw tugs, and twenty-six of the big W.W.I screw tugs. The Admiralty immediately requisitioned a number of civilian tugs, about 60 for dockyard use and for rescue work, and a motley collection totalling 35 which were allocated to various duties; barrage balloon vessels, armed patrol vessels and even auxiliary minesweepers; a small number compared to the total

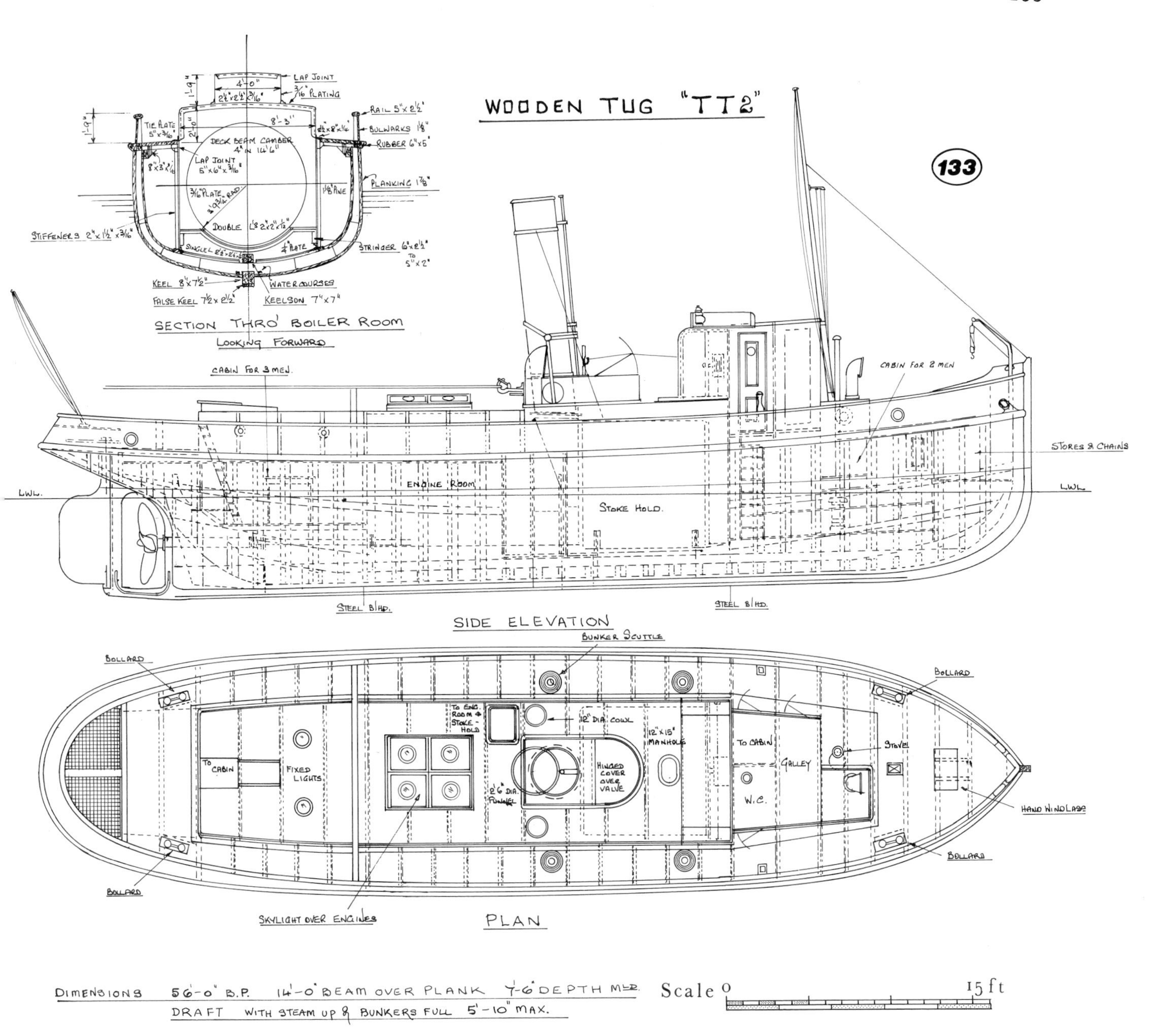

number available. The German attacks on British shipping started at once and the tugs were kept busy assisting crippled ships. When the convoy system was inaugurated tugs were transferred from the South to the Clyde and other assembly points. At the end of May 1940 the tugs of London were asked to play a part in the evacuation from Dunkirk and they responded nobly. The tugs **Simla** (49) and **Gondia** from London and the Hull tug **Roman** were already working in Dover, but as the day of decision approached to start the evacuation proper, other tugs began to arrive in Dover including several Belgian tugs. The Dover Harbour Board tug **Lady Brassey** (48) had already been over at Dunkirk on the 20th May and had been attacked by enemy aircraft. By 30th May only one ship-handling tug was left in the Port of London. Watkin's **Java** crossed to Dunkirk and ferried troops from the shore and the harbour to the waiting deeper draughted ships. The naval tug **St. Clears** and the other **Saint** class tugs were active in towing small craft along the evacuation routes. In the harbours of Dover and Ramsgate the tugs were kept hard at work clearing damaged ships and taking them to other ports for repair. When the *Prague* went aground off the beaches it took the combined efforts (2600 i.h.p.) of the **Lady Brassey** and the **Foremost 87** to refloat her under heavy fire from the German shore batteries. The Royal Navy Saint Class tug **St. Abbs** picked up survivors from the destroyer *Keith, Keith* in turn was then hit by a dive bomber and was also sunk, the survivors of both disasters being picked up by a lighter which was towed in by the **Sun XI.** Some idea of the immensity of the task is given by the fact that the tug **Simla** alone assisted nearly 140 ships in and around Dover Harbour during the two weeks.

As in World War I the government realised that there would be an increasing demand for tugs and they selected three prototypes on which to base their programme of new construction. For coastal work and for short ocean voyages the United Towing Company's **Englishman** was selected and eight tugs were built; 135 ft. x 30 ft. 987 tons displacement, 1175 i.h.p. With a requirement for longer range and greater stability to counteract the effects of the tophamper of additional armament the design of the next five was altered to 135 ft. x 33 ft. and the engine power was stepped up to 1275 i.h.p. For river work and short coastal voyages the basis for the design was Steel & Bennie's **Warrior** of 1935; 107 ft. x 26 ft. 430 tons displacement, 1000 i.h.p. During the war there were several modifications to the design, slight changes in length and beam, conversion from coal to oil fuel, fitting of salvage pumps and firefighting equipment. One of the modified designs was the **Empire Denis**, 1943, 105.0 ft. B.P. x 26.5 ft. beam. Being wartime built the usual wooden sheathing over the accommodation was omitted. This tug had two gun positions fitted for a 20 mm. Oerlikon and a twin .303 in. machine gun. The use of a tripod mast cuts down the rigging and as little exposed glass as possible is fitted, the engine room skylights are hinged metal plates. The Plan shows the similar **Empire Bracken, Empire Ivy** and **Empire Pixie** three of a class of 10 tugs built by yards to the nominal dimensions 108.0' x 26.0'. These three, built at Goole, were purchased by the Clyde Shipping Co, becoming **Flying Spitfire, Flying Tempest** and **Flying Swordfish**(135).

A larger version was introduced later in the war - 116 ft. x 28 ft. but as they were intended for long voyages with light tows the engines were only 600 to 800 i.h.p. These were known as the **Stella** class. Finally there was a smaller tug for harbour work, the **Maple** class, 92 ft. x 20.5 ft., 283 tons displacement, 500 i.h.p. These tugs were somewhat narrow in the beam but this was because the builders' yard was situated on a canal with a narrow lock between the shipyard and the sea. All these tugs bore names beginning **Empire.....** Many of the **Empire** tugs were allocated to the major ports in the U.K. and were managed by the local towing companies as part of their own fleets.

Almost identical to the **Empire Denis** is the **Dunhawk** (134) of the Newport Screw Towing Co., built in 1943 as the **Empire Maisie**, 107.0 ft. x 27.0 ft. beam. She is typical of the steam tug during the last years of their existence with a high bow and a low stern, large boiler casing, and wheelhouse with a flying bridge above. She does not have washports with hinged lids but merely slots cut out in the bulwarks at deck level.

As the submarine attacks on convoys grew in intensity it was evident that ships were being lost because it was not possible to render immediate assistance. The Admiralty therefore planned a series of Rescue Tugs which would accompany the convoys across the Atlantic, able to tow a casualty to safety or to carry out on the spot 'first aid' repairs. Their naval architects came up with a design based on the pre-war salvage and deep-sea tugs and their construction was entrusted to the firm of Henry Robb of Leith. Although the new tugs were diesel powered they are included in this book because of the valuable part they played both during and after the war. The **Bustler** class of tug was 190 ft. x 38'6", with a displacement of 1120 tons and engines giving 4000 b.h.p. with a speed of 16 kts. Eight in all were built and did sterling work. In 1943 the **Bustler** brought the 14,000 ton *Durham* back from Gibraltar with a hole in her bow and most of her stern missing. The 1,500 mile tow was carried out in company with a trawler and a corvette in the face of constant submarine attack. The **Samsonia** was despatched into the Atlantic to recover a Lockheed bomber which was drifting on a raft. The only one of the group which was lost was the **Hesperia** which had been responsible for saving 15 damaged ships. In her first 203 days at sea she had covered 38,237 miles. Early in 1945, she and another smaller tug were towing a floating dock in the Mediterranean when a gale sprang up. The towline of the smaller tug snapped and under the added strain the **Hesperia**'s towrope parted as well. The **Hesperia** placed herself on the lee side of the dock in an effort to push her away from the nearby rocks. The windage on the huge dock was too much for the tug and both tug and dock were driven ashore and lost. Three more classes of tug were built

Dunhawk** of the Newport Screw Towing Company, built 1943 as **Empire Maisie.

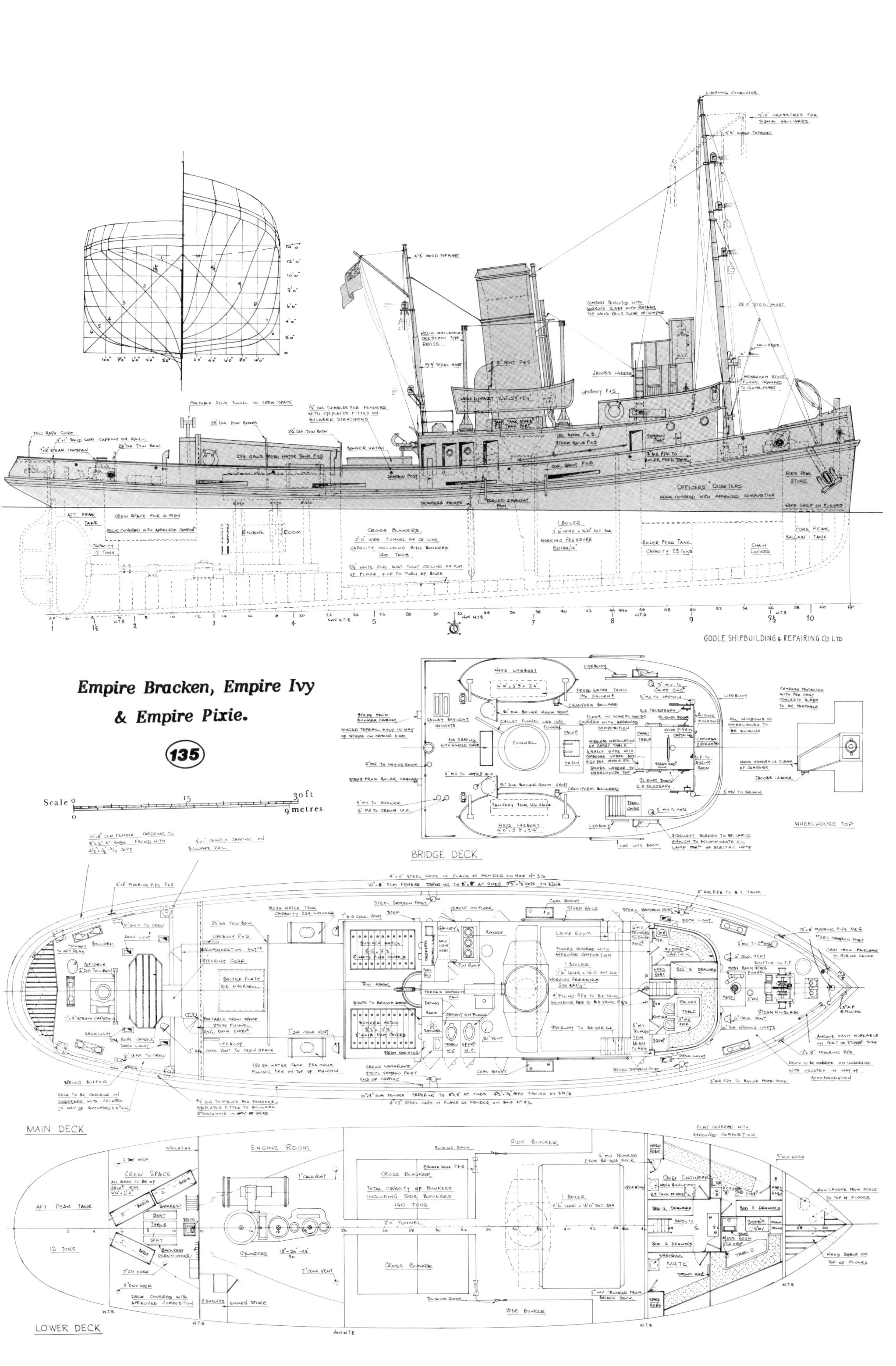
Empire Bracken, Empire Ivy
& Empire Pixie.
135
Scale 0 15 30 ft
0 9 metres
GOOLE SHIPBUILDING & REPAIRING Co LTD
LIGHTNING CONDUCTOR
12'0" CROSSTREE FOR SIGNAL HALLIARDS
15'3" WOOD TOPMAST
4'3" WOOD TOPMAST
28'0" STEEL MAST
19'9" STEEL MAST
JACOBS LADDER
LIFEBUOY P & S
WOOD LIFEBOAT 16'0" x 5'9" x 2'4"
PORTABLE STOVE FUNNEL TO CREW SPACE
TOW ROPE GUIDE
7" x 8" STEAM CAPSTAN
2⅝" DIA TOW BOW
BUNKER HATCH
SAMSON POST
STORM RAILS P & S
COAL SHOOT P & S
OFFICERS' QUARTERS
DECK COVERED WITH APPROVED COMPOSITION
FORE PEAK STORE
WOOD SHELF ON FLOORS
TRIMMERS ESCAPE
FORCED DRAUGHT FAN
AFT PEAK TANK
CAPACITY 12 TONS
CREW SPACE FOR 6 MEN
ENGINE ROOM
CROSS BUNKERS
2'0" WIDE TUNNEL ON CR. LINE
CAPACITY INCLUDING SIDE BUNKERS 140 TONS
1 BOILER
11'6" LONG x 16'0" EXT DIA
WORKING PRESSURE 210 lbs/□"
BOILER FEED TANK
CAPACITY 25 TONS
CHAIN LOCKER
FORE PEAK BALLAST TANK
BRIDGE DECK
WOOD LIFEBOAT
FUNNEL
CHART TABLE
WHEELHOUSE TOP
JACOBS LADDER
MAIN DECK
STEERING GEAR
BOLTED PLATE FOR OVERHAUL
BUNKER HATCH
LAMP ROOM
RANGE
GALLEY
1 BOILER
MESS ROOM STOVE FUNNEL
STEAM WINDLASS
SALOON TABLE
CAPTAIN
BED & DRAWERS
STEAM RADIATOR
CREWS W.C.
OFFRS W.C.
LOWER DECK
CREW SPACE
ENGINE ROOM
AFT PEAK TANK
12 TONS
TABLE
SEAT
CYLINDERS 18"-26"-43" / 30
CROSS BUNKER
TOTAL CAPACITY OF BUNKERS INCLUDING SIDE BUNKERS 140 TONS
2'0" TUNNEL
SIDE BUNKER
CHIEF ENGINEER
MATE
MESS ROOM
TABLE
ENGRS STORE
W.T.B.

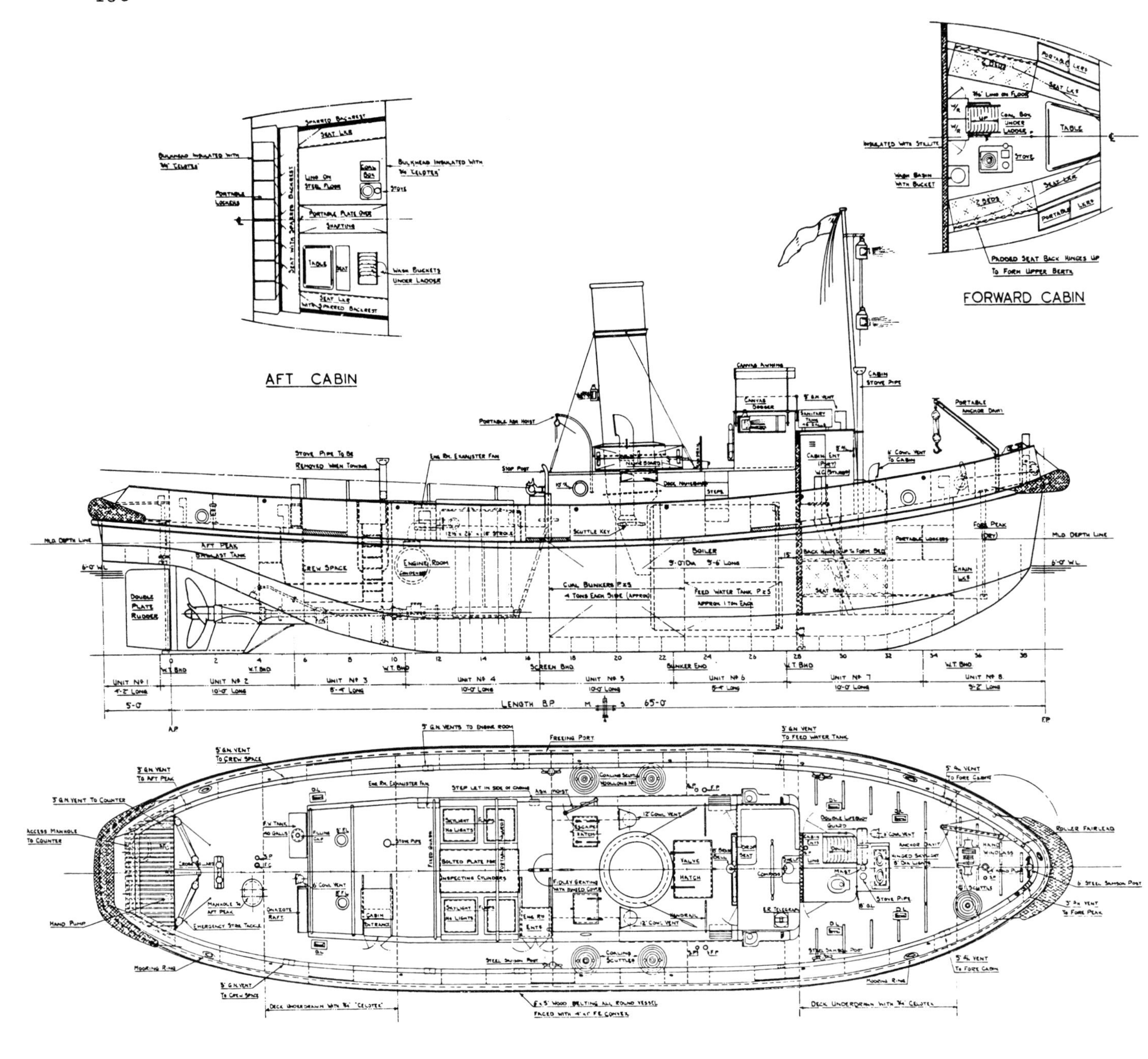

136 ***'TID' Class Tug.***

for deep-sea towing - the **Nimble**, 165 ft. 890 tons displacement, 3500 i.h.p. (steam), the **Assurance**, 142'6" x 33'3", 700 tons displacement, 1350 i.h.p. (steam), and the **Envoy**, 160 ft. x 36 ft. 868 tons displacement, 1700 i.h.p. (steam). All were of a similar style with the now familiar raised forecastle continuous to the after end of the boatdeck. In addition to the above, the U.S.A. made some big tugs available under Lease-Lend, one group with diesel-electric drive, 135 ft. 783 tons displacement, 1875 b.h.p., and the other group steam tugs 147 ft. 1360 tons displacement, 1875 i.h.p. with wooden hulls.

In 1943 the Ministry of Transport decided to introduce a new class of tug, a small one, for general lighterage and dock work. The requirement was for a tug 65 ft. long with a 200 i.h.p. steam engine capable of 7 to 8 kts., and the construction had to be of a prefabricated design. The result was the **TID** tug with a hull made in eight units with a maximum length of 10 ft. and a maximum weight of 10 tons. The sections were fabricated by thirteen structural contractors and were transported by road to suitable riverside sites where temporary slips had been set up, where they were put together and launched. The hull was designed on the 'hard chine' principle so that flat plates could be used and the complicated double curves of the conventional hull were not required. Over 180 of the **TID** tugs were built. The **TID** tug was a very utilitarian vessel and could usually be recognised by her square stern and the "soft" bow (136). Another feature was the bridge (sometimes a wheelhouse) perched on the forward end of the casing, overlooking the W.C. and companionway to the cabin. She had an all steel deck with anti skid bars welded on at the forward part where the deck had considerable sheer. The towing bows were iron bars spanning the casing only.

Planning for the invasion of Europe began soon after Dunkirk and among the ideas put forward was PLUTO (Pipeline Under The Ocean), to supply oil fuel to the invasion forces without risking surface oil tankers. It was evident right from the start that the tugs required for this work would have to be very powerful. The tugs selected were the target towing tug **Marauder** and the deep sea tug **Bustler**, both with tow rope pulls of 24/25 tons. Over 60 miles of 3" external diameter pipe was wound on to the CONUN, a huge floating drum 90 ft. long x 50 ft. diameter which weighed 1650 tons when full and the tugs were able to maintain a speed of 5 to 7½ kts. Sometimes the tugs towed as a pair, but even when they towed singly similar speeds could be maintained.

The civilian tugs suffered losses due to enemy action. The **Neptunia** (91) of Overseas Towage and Salvage Co. was sunk in September 1939 by gunfire and torpedo by a U-boat. The **Sir Bevois** of Southampton was sunk by aircraft in March 1941. The **Bullger** of Leith sank after she struck a mine north of the River Tyne. The United Towing Co.'s **Englishman**, the prototype of one of the **Empire** classes was sunk by aircraft in January 1941. The tender **Romsey** was transferred from Southampton to the Clyde where she ferried troops out to the waiting transports at the Tail of the Bank. She was run down in September 1942 but she was salvaged and put back into service. The tug **Flying Kite** belonging to the Clyde Shipping Co. was completely destroyed when a mine exploded beneath her in the dock where she was working. The London tug **Atlantic Cock** which was with her was badly damaged in the same explosion. One of the oddities of the war was the **Energy** which Lamey's of Liverpool took over and refitted. Finding difficulty in getting plates rolled for a new funnel a square funnel was fabricated out of flat sheet, a freak at the time but today a square funnel would not fetch a second glance.

As new types of mine were sown, new methods of sweeping had to be devised. The pressure mine proved to be a bit of a problem and one of the methods used was to tow over the suspected minefield a huge dumb barge about 360 ft. long x 65 ft. beam with a draught of 25 ft. to simulate the passage of an average merchant ship. For the first trial tows the biggest naval tugs were used to ensure that the proper speeds could be maintained and the **Bustler** and the **Assurance** classes were the ones selected. However, the 'pressure signature' from the tugs was sufficient to detonate the mines, exposing them to the possibility of damage. The trials with these 'Stirling Craft' were abandoned after the vessels had been damaged. Nevertheless following the invasion of France one of these sweeps was resurrected to clear the approaches to Le Havre and it was towed by the **Griper** and the **Jaunty** (both **Assurance** class tugs). The tugs had great difficulty with the awkward tow and the rope broke on more than one occasion. After several sweeps the barge finally broke adrift and went ashore and broke up. As D-Day approached the work involving tugs stepped up to a pitch where hundreds of tugs would have to be allocated various duties in connection with the artificial harbours which had been planned. Five breakwaters were to be created by scuttling old merchant ships and obsolete warships. The fleet which assembled two weeks before D-Day comprised 56 block ships with 10 tugs and 6 corvettes in attendance. On the 7th June the makeshift breakwaters were in position resting on the bottom off the Normandy coast. One of the block ships was the old French battleship *Courbet* and it took the big **Bustler** class tugs **Samsonia** and **Growler** to handle her. An even bigger concept was the creation of artificial harbours constructed basically of Bombardons (floating breakwaters), Phoenixes (hollow concrete structures resting on the seabed), and Whales (floating pierheads). Early the planners had realised that at least 130 tugs would be required to deal with the floating masses of concrete and the minimum acceptable power would be 450 i.h.p. There were 420 tugs in the U.K. at the time which fulfilled the requirements but most were already busy on other duties. The calculations regarding the number of tugs rose to 200 but by D-Day only 132 were available, 108 of which were required for towing the units of the Mulberry Harbours. The unwieldy tows caused a great deal of trouble for the tugs, but not as much trouble as the great storm which left the Normandy beaches strewn with wrecks which had to be salvaged. During the tailend of the storm one of the civilian tugs, the **Dundas** (an ex-Dutch sea-going tug belonging to Grangemouth) was damaged when another tug collided with her and she had to be beached. Although salvaged, she overturned and sank as she commenced her homeward voyage.

When the war ended the disposal of the government owned tugs commenced. Most of the requisitioned civilian tugs were elderly and having been worked hard for six years without much in the way of overhaul were very much in need of repair. The **Plato** (23) for example had been under requisition for a period of five years and when she was handed back to her owners she was surveyed for damage. The survey resulted in a report listing 293 defects which took nearly seven months to repair. The damage to the hull alone in bent plates, broken belting and dented bulwarks covered 100 entries. No wonder some companies did not bother to repair their tugs when they were returned to them. A number of the Empire tugs had been managed by the big towing companies and many of the firms bought their charges as replacements for their old vessels. The remainder found ready sale both at home and overseas as did the little **TID** tugs which had proved most useful for river and dock work (Plate 6).

The Navy too began to up-date their fleet of tugs commencing with the steam tugs **Samson** -1953, **Sea Giant** -1954 and **Superman** - 1955 (165 ft. 850 tons, 3000 i.h.p.) From then onwards their new tugs were to be diesel engined. The one big surprise was the appearance in 1956 of seven diesel electric paddle tugs for working with aircraft carriers, a final tribute to the acknowledged manoeuvrability of the paddle tug.

9. Tug Owners

(138) ***Premier,*** *Ridley Steam Tug Company, Newcastle.*

During the lifetime of the tug there have been many thousands of tugs in Great Britain. Their owners number many hundreds and may have been one man who was also the skipper, a group of merchants and tradesmen with 1/64th shares, or a company with a dozen tugs at their command. Of these owners it is possible to mention but a few.

In the London area the firm of Wm. Watkins is synonymous with tugs. Starting with the little wooden tug **Monarch** (14), about the sixth or seventh tug to arrive on the Thames from the Tyne, the company has been in existence since 1833 until in 1950 it combined with other London fleets. In 1840 Watkins began to order tugs from local builders and kept their fleet in the forefront growing all the time in numbers and in size. They were pioneers in long distance towing maintaining their position until the First World War against strong competition from the Dutch. Their **Oceana** (1889) was in the news in 1905 when she towed a vessel from Portland to Sumatra, a distance of 8,200 miles, spending 45 days at sea (82). The firm made a come-back after World War II, but the loss of their deep sea tug **Rumania** (1944) on the Goodwin Sands while attempting to assist the *Loide Honduras*, brought this side of their business to a close (88). The operations of their smaller tugs were not limited to the Thames and the Watkins tugs, all with names ending with 'A' such as **Iona** (1876) (31) and **Cambria** (1870), were to be found seeking and salvaging as far afield as Harwich, Cuxhaven, Ijmuiden, the Humber, Leith, Cherbourg and Cork. The Watkins family made shortlived attempts to establish fleets on the Mersey 1853 to 1859, and in Middlesbrough as Watkins-Petrie 1911 to 1917.

There was plenty of competition on the Thames and among the bigger fleet owners in the 1850s there was Daniel Barker [19] with his **Caledonia** (1838) and **Highland Maid** (1846). The Caledonian Steam Towing Company [17] operated tugs with appropriately Scottish names such as **Rob Roy** (1848), **Robert Burns** (1837) and **Sir William Wallace** (1841). Thomas Petley's tugs had romantic names like **Friend to all Nations** (1851) and **Grey Mare Meg** (1842).

Tug owners kept finding themselves in court for one reason or another, sometimes to make a claim for services rendered, sometimes for what would be to them a trivial offence. In the 1860s the authorities in London waged a campaign against the tugs because of what they called 'smoke nuisance'. In May of that year the Steam Towing Company were charged on account of their tugs **Victory** and **Tam O'Shanter**. In November Watkins were in court defending complaints against their tug **John Lee**. In May 1861 there was another campaign and seven tugowners were in court.

		Master	Owner
Monarch	1833	C. Cruttenden	Wm. Watkins
Punch	1854	Alf. Soames	Wm. Watkins
Challenge	1856	Thos. Lilley	Jas. Deane
Prince	1859	Fred Spicer	Dan Barker
Dougal **Grey Mare Meg**	1842	Francis Gill Pendrill	Thos. Petley
Alliance	1856	Elliott	T.W. Elliott

The master of the tug **Harold** (49), belonging to S. Pearson and Sons Ltd. of London was even more unfortunate. One day at Dover in June 1902 he blew the whistle of the tug, some horses on the quayside bolted and the carter was injured! The tugmaster finished up in court and all he had been doing was signalling to the lock-keeper to open the lock gates.

Another of the 'big names' in towing was the Elliott Steam Tug Company which started at the height of the seeking era in the 1860s with the Dick and Page tugs. They were notable competitors in the salvage and passenger carrying fields. The **Victor** (1895), **Champion** (1892) and **Warrior** (1895) featured regularly in court cases for salvage claims. To the fleet was added another famous tug, the **Conqueror** (1897) which had previously belonged to W. Sandford of Gravesend (3). She had a formidable list of successful salvage jobs to her credit during the 22 years that she was stationed in the Thames area. The **Revenger** (1880) of the Elliott fleet was actively engaged in World War I when she assisted in the towage of the monitors *Roberts* and *Severn* which were sent to East Africa to destroy the German commerce raider *Konigsberg*. The **Revenger** had been in the news earlier in 1900; the crew had found a naval shell one mile west of Dungeness and while they were hauling it aboard, it exploded killing three of the crew. Elliott's tug **Warrior** hit the headlines on two occasions, once during the First World War when she was one of the first tugs to reach the *Lusitania* after she had been torpedoed, being instrumental in saving 74 lives, and again when she was 'hijacked'. In 1922 she was seized by members of the Sinn Fein who ordered the crew below and with over 20 armed men aboard she was used to intercept a vessel carrying arms. The tug and crew were later released unharmed. Elliott's tug **Vanquisher** (1955) was one of the first diesel ship tugs on the Thames and was unusual with her high built bridge in an area where open bridges were a regular feature.

In about 1880 some river pilots formed their own towing fleet calling it the Gamecock Steam Towing Company, later Gamecock Tugs Ltd. Most of the tugs bore such names as **Storm Cock** (1881) and **Watercock** (1923). W.H.J. Alexander entered the craft towing business in 1884 with the **Little England** (1884), but as time went on the fleet grew and branched into the ship towing side. Known locally as 'Sun Tugs' the majority of their vessels were either prefixed **Sun**, e.g. **Sunrise** and **Sunshine** (1899), or bore a Roman numeral like **Sun IV** (1915) (52).

In 1950 Ship Towage (London) Ltd. was created by the amalgamation of the fleets of Wm. Watkins Ltd., the Elliott Tug Company Ltd., and Gamecock Tugs Ltd. totalling 19 tugs. This fleet later absorbed some of the larger units of the Gaselee fleet and in 1969 became London Tugs Ltd. with the addition of the Sun tugs making a fleet numbering 37. In 1975 the Alexandra Towing Company of Liverpool took over London Tugs Ltd. adding the remaining 22 tugs to their already vast fleet, a third of the tugs having been sold off in the intervening years.

The fleets of craft tugs (lighter towing tugs) built up over the years and about 1965 there were still over 200 small craft tugs on the river. The fall in lighter traffic over recent years has seen a dramatic reduction in this number as take-overs have cut down the number of lighter firms still in business. The name of Clements Knowling was well known on the river as was their old tug **Scorcher** (1878) which was 80 years old when she went to the breakers yard (Plate 23). J.W. Cook's tugs could be recognised by their names **Gusty** (1913), **Misty** (1951) and **Cloudy** (1948). These tugs were bought by one of the most prolific fleets on the river in 1958. The fleet of Wm. Cory of London has owned nearly 80 tugs during its one hundred odd years of existence. In 1883 the company began to christen its tugs with names beginning with an 'R' with the **Rotifer** and **Romulus** right up to the **Regard** (1958). The firm has offshoots, Cory Tank Lighterage Ltd. with **Crowstone** (1932) and others, and The Mercantile Lighterage Ltd. with **Mercedes** (1935), etc. Some of their tugs bore names starting **Cor---**, **Corlea** (1953). Another familiar sight on the river Thames is the Yellow funnel with three red bands belonging to Gaselee & Son Ltd. For a long time it has been the custom to station a tug beside the Tower Bridge to assist ships as they pass through the narrow gap and, more often than not, it was a Gaselee tug which lay moored there displaying a big board bearing the words "Tower Bridge Tug" (103). J.P. Knight of Rochester (black funnel with two white bands and a "K") have operated a fleet of tugs with names beginning "K" from the **Kenley** (1878) through the **Keverne** (1960), growing from craft tugs to the big tanker handling tugs **Kinloch** (1974) and **Kessock** (1975). The big cement company Associated Portland Cement Manufacturers Ltd. have used over 20 tugs in their lighter towing fleet with appropriate names like **Portland** (1936) and **Blue Circle** (1927). Thames Steam Tug and Lighterage Co. Ltd. have owned about 40 tugs over the years (including many diesel tugs). This was one of the first firms in the U.K. to put into service a diesel electric tug, the **Framfield** (1935). The tugs **Danube II** (1910), etc. have been operated by the Tilbury Contracting & Dredging Co. Ltd. and these shiphandling tugs have been backed up by sundry small craft tugs. At one time the docks in London were privately owned and each dock system had its own fleet of paddle tugs and twin-screw tugs. In 1908 the Port of London Authority was formed to unify the dock system and the new authority took over a mixed bunch of iron paddle tugs of about 160 tons and some of the pioneer twin-screw dock tugs. Within a few years these had been replaced with new steel, twin-screw tugs of about 1000 hp. The P.L.A. tugs take over at the dock entrances when the river tugs hand over their tow. Over the last 70 years over 90 sundry tugs have operated under the P.L.A. colours including many small tonnage tugs which are used for towing dredging plant and the hoppers of the dredging fleet. Some of the tugs were fitted with a form of 'rake' for clearing the river and dock bottom. Union Lighterage Co. Ltd. have been on the Thames for a long time having operated 25 tugs mostly with names ending "O" - **Hero** (1898), **Hembo** (1953).

ROLLCALL *of* 1918.

FLYING EAGLE *of* 1928.

0 8ft

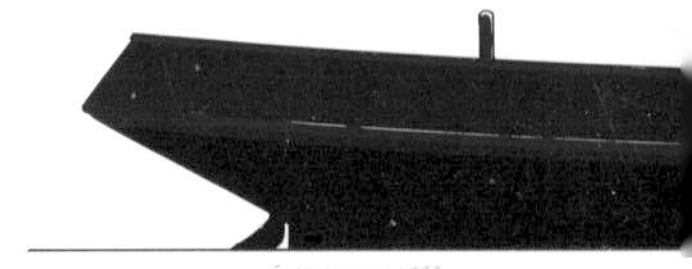

METINDA III *of* 1945

Plate 140

ROLLCALL was built for the Admiralty and was one of the largest coal fired tugs with engines of 2400 i.h.p driving twin screws. At the end of the war she was sold and rebuilt as a tender.
METINDA III was completed in 1945 by Clelands as EMPIRE JEAN for the Ministry of War Transport and sold in 1946 to Metal Industries Ltd for salvage and rescue work off the north of Scotland.
FLYING EAGLE was built for the Clyde Shipping Company with coastal tows in mind, but she was also regularly employed on the Clyde.

The **Hotspur** was built for operation within the confines of the London docks and had twin screws for manoeuvrability, well guarded to prevent ropes from fouling the propellers (143,208). The raised deck along the side of the boiler casing was seen on a number of P.L.A. tugs and in one or two harbour authority tugs elsewhere. The single casing covering both boiler and engine at one height was reminiscent of some of the older coastal tugs, but no use was made of the deck area created. In such a large tug it seems unnecessary to put side houses for W.C.s; it would have been easier to put them below the bridge instead of perching the bridge up on 'stilts'. The lead of the steering chains was different from other tugs, being supported above the casing on pulleys which got lower as they were placed further aft, and they were completely unguarded. They then ran across the deck (not along the waterway) again unguarded. The **Hotspur** came from the Renfrew yard of Wm. Simons & Co. in 1897 who were better known as dredger builders. She was 192 tons and 175 n.h.p. (830 i.h.p.). She worked in the London & East India Docks, passing into the fleet of the Port of London Authority until sold in 1915 to the Whitstable Salvage Company.

The busy River Thames gave plenty of opportunity for salvage as vessels collided and suffered damage. Even little tugs of 35 tons and 57ft. long had their chance to file claims for awards. The dense traffic also led to considerable damage to the tugs themselves and some tugs seemed accident prone:-

Iron screw tug **Australia** (1882) in Holland. 90.4' x 20.6' x 11.3'. 127 tons. (William Watkins).

23. 9.1893	Damaged by fire. Upset paraffin lamp.
30. 8.1894	Damaged in collision with **Lord Churchill** - Blackwall Reach.
6. 6.1895	In collision with tug **Dorunda** off Royal Albert Dock, bow and stem damaged. **Dorunda** sank.
30. 7.1898	Damaged in collision with tug **Mystery** off Gravesend.
17. 9.1899	Damaged in collision with S.S. *Boldern* and *Greyfriars* at Gravesend.
30.11.1899	Damaged in collision with S.S. *Turret Cape* off Gravesend.

A rival for the casualty award was the **Dorunda** (1890) of the Gravesend United Towing Company which was in collision at least seven times in ten years.

Iron screw tug **Dorunda** built Steward & Latham, London (1890, 85.2' x 19.1' x 10.2', 102 tons)

27.12.1891	Damaged in collision with S.S. *Manora* at Gravesend.
6. 6.1895	Beached off Royal Albert Dock after collision with tug **Australia**.
21. 6.1896	Stem damaged in collision with **Lord of the Isles** off Gravesend.
5.11.1896	Stem damaged in collision with S.S. *Massachusetts*, Gravesend Reach.
9. 2.1900	In collision with S.S. *Hurona* at Long Reach.
21. 5.1900	In collision with tug **W.R. Cunis** at Gravesend. Both damaged.
19. 6.1901	Bow damaged in collision with S.S. *Artois* off Gravesend.

Some tugs stayed in the hands of one owner, while others changed hands continually. The **Rescue** (1869) had 5 owners in London before 1891 when she was sold to the North-East Coast where another 6 owners bought and sold her. The **Romulus** (1883) passed through 7 owners' hands before 1916 when she went to Hull to 3 further owners. The **Bulldog** (1867) had 11 owners in London and Newcastle.

The **Geo. Peabody** (front end paper) was another tug which did the rounds. She was a typical paddle tug with two funnels abreast. The davits on the after deck would be 'struck down' before she took a ship in tow. She was used for seeking down the Channel but no protection was provided around the wheel. On her bow she bore rather a fancy bit of scrollwork, and was owned: 1867, Wm. Homewood, Gravesend; 1872, Joseph Martin, Gravesend; T. Banks, Gravesend; 1881, Captain Newman; 1885, F. Pattison, Gravesend; Wm. Cowan, Llanelly; George Dinsdale, Blyth; Blyth Steam Tug Co.; 1907, Wm. Slater, Middlesbrough; Robinson Tug Co., Middlesbrough; Tees Towing Co., Middlesbrough. Broken up 1924.

At Ramsgate, adjacent to the Goodwin Sands, the Board of Trade stationed a tug for many years. The most famous was the **Aid** of 1889, an unusual double-ended paddle tug. Her name crops up again and again in salvage operations on that treacherous coast. She was generally valued at £13,000 and the awards ranged from a mere £75 to a substantial (for 1909) £1,000. She was fitted with duplicate navigation lights which could be altered by raising or lowering shutters over the lights (36) so that she could steam astern correctly lit. She had towing hooks fore and aft, and a bow rudder. She had a predecessor of the same name which had a similar reputation for rendering assistance. A Spanish brig, the *Samaratino* had gone aground on the Margate sands and the Margate lifeboat had failed to reach her. The **Aid** towed the Ramsgate lifeboat to the wreck in appalling weather and enabled the lifeboat to save the crew of the brig.

There had been a tug at Dover from about 1850. In 1866 a London tug called the **Nelly** of 1859 was engaged by Messrs. Brunel and Hawkshaw and was stationed at Dover while they surveyed between Dover and Calais in connection with the projected tunnel. The vessel was specially fitted with scientific instruments for this purpose. In 1864 the Dover Harbour Board began to build up a fleet of tugs as the traffic into the harbour increased. They later adopted names beginning **Lady** starting with the paddle tug **Lady Vita** in 1882. Over the years the size of their tugs increased until the **Lady Brassey** of 1913, an impressive two funnelled vessel (48) which was finally sold in 1958 to be replaced by modern diesels. The Dover tugs were well placed for salvage work and

143

Hotspur. *A twin screw dock tug fitted with propellor guards (right). For the midship section see page 208 and for towing bows, see page 213.*

by their efforts the Board had a steady income. On one occasion their **Lady Crundall** was awarded £2,000, and on another she shared £3,450 with three London tugs. It was quite surprising at times how many tugs might be involved in a single salvage operation, for example in 1910 when the *Salatis* was in trouble no less than 14 tugs took part:

Name	Built	Tonnage	Horsepower	Value	Owner
Lady Crundall	1906	366	1600 i.h.p.	£20,000	Dover Harbour Board
Lady Curzon	1904	253	1000 i.h.p.	£13,000	Dover Harbour Board
Oceana (6)	1889	337	900 e.h.p.	£ 9,000	W. Watkins, London
Columbia	1884	213	700 e.h.p.	£ 7,000	W. Watkins, London
Doria	1909	150	500 e.h.p.	£ 7,000	W. Watkins, London
Expert	1892	100	450 e.h.p.	£ 3,000	Michael M. Mitchell, London
Victor	1895	133	650 e.h.p.	£ 7,500	J. Page, London
Warrior	1895	192	750 a.h.p.	£ 7,500	J. Page, London
Sun II	1909	199	1250 i.h.p.	£10,500	W.H.J. Alexander, London
Sun III	1909	197	1250 i.h.p.	£10,500	W.H.J. Alexander, London
Zwarte Zee		558	1500 i.h.p.	£20,000	Dutch
Noorde Zee		298	800 i.h.p.	£16,150	Dutch
Zuider Zee		189	500 i.h.p.	£ 7,000	Dutch
Simson		213	550 e.h.p.	£ 600	Dutch

The value of the *Salatis* and her cargo was £118,872 and the total award was £ 15,832. It is interesting to note the way in which the horsepowers are quoted:- a - actual, e - effective, i - indicated. Messrs. Watkins only three months previously had admitted that they generally exaggerated the power of their tugs when presenting claims for salvage awards. They had quoted their **Guiana** as 1100 e.h.p. while she was in fact only 600 i.h.p.

Many small ports had a tug available to assist sailing ships. Shoreham had the small iron paddle tug **Stella** of 1879, 76 tons, and now operates the motor tug **Kingston Buci**, 1960, still only 76 tons. Littlehampton has only had one tug, the iron paddle tug **Jumna**, but she was well known with the holidaymakers whom she carried on trips out of the harbour and round the bay. **Jumna** (81.5ft. 51 tons, 24 n.h.p.) (145) was built in 1884 for C.H. Campbell of Littlehampton who were involved in dredging and construction work. Her boiler bulged above the deck and was insulated but not cased. Her timberheads curved aft to form rope stops, a unique arrangement. She had a very tall fidded topmast, the only function of which seems to be to flaunt her owner's house flag.

Apart from the naval tugs at Portsmouth, Harry Crampton owned a number of small tugs over the years. Across the water in Cowes was the Cowes Steam Tug Company providing towage and fresh water as required with their screw tug **Malta** of 1883 (ex. Watkins, London). Although the **Malta** was small, 73' long and 59 tons she features in several salvage jobs, though her awards seldom exceeded £50. However it was money! Built by E. Wales of Hull in 1883 the **Malta** was rather old fashioned looking with her bell topped funnel and gaff rigged mast (front endpaper). Her wheel was open between a little saloon and the engine casing. Her hook was not fixed to the casing but pivotted about a vertical stanchion which was braced back down to the deck. She had "Cowes Steam Tug Co. Water Tank" emblazoned along her side in a style which one associates with today's freighters and liners.

Towage in Southampton grew from small beginnings with the New Southampton Steam Towing Company operating four tugs between 71 and 129 tons. In 1901 Edward Agius started up a new fleet with the **Ada** of 1885. About the same time Hemsley Bell also 'launched' a towing business. The Southampton, Isle of Wight and South of England Royal Mail Steam Packet Company, affectionately (and for handiness) called the 'Red Funnel Fleet' operated passenger services to the Isle of Wight and also a fleet of tugs to assist with the docking of the large liners which began to use Southampton as their terminus. Many tugs doubled as tenders for carrying out passengers and mail to vessels which were calling but not docking. The tugs were large e.g. **Hector** of 1903 was 130' long and 316 tons, a size well suited for coastal salvage for which her owners received handsome awards. For one job the **Hector**, valued at £16,000 received £2,500. The Alexandra Towing Company of Liverpool began to station tugs at Southampton in 1919 and rapidly expanded their fleet in that port. Probably their best known vessel was the tender **Romsey** of 1930 (42), a tender which appears in almost every photograph of the docking of the two **Queens** (111). She was even sent up to the Clyde to assist in their launching and in the tow down the winding River Clyde to the Tail of the Bank.

Salvage does not need to take place in gales on the high seas or on rocky coastlines, but when assistance has been given there is the inevitable argument of 'who gets what?'

On 14th April, 1947 the liner *Queen Elizabeth* went aground on the Brambles in Southampton Water and no less than eighteen tugs were engaged in the effort to tow her off. The owners claimed that the liner had not been in any danger of loss and that in fact she had had to use her own engines to assist the tugs to refloat her. The salvors for their part made the point that delay cost money and that the liner had suffered some damage which would have undoubtedly have become more extensive had she lain aground longer. It was their contention that because they had saved delay and damage that they were entitled to monetary reward.

The assessor agreed with the salvors that the hull of the liner had not been built for grounding and that it would have been strained if subjected to the rise and fall of the tides. Although the conditions had been calm, the fact that 16 tugs were involved made the risk of collision possible with resultant damage and that risks had in fact been taken. It only remained for him to determine the amount and distribution of the award. Two of the tugs were salvage tugs and as they were professionals they were entitled to a proportionately greater award than the others. These were the **Bustler** and the **Metinda III.** By engaging themselves to salvage the *Queen Elizabeth* they were prevented from taking on any other salvage operations which might have cropped up. At one time the crews of Admiralty tugs would have been precluded from receiving awards for salvage services rendered, but in 1940 legislation had been passed which put them on the same conditions as any other salvors. The value of the tugs involved and the size of the awards were as follows:

Name	Value	Award
Bustler	£110,000	Shared £15,000
Metinda III	£ 55,000	
H.M. Tug **Volcano**		£2,500
H.M. Tug **Swarthy**		£2,500
H.M. Tug **St. Mellons**		£2,500
H.M. Tug **Resolve**		£3,500
H.M. Tug **Saucy**	£ 70,500	£2,750
H.M. Tug **Antic**	£ 70,500	£2,750
Clausentum	£ 60,000	Shared £12,000
Canute	£ 50,000	
Neptune	£ 40,000	
Vulcan	£ 40,000	

The six other tugs which took part but which made no claim were the **Romsey**, **Hornby**, **William Poulsom**, **Selsea**, **Empire Raymond** and **Sloyne**.

Two other companies which must be mentioned are Risdon Beazley who today go in for salvage work, and the James Dredging and Towing company. The latter name has had a variety of forms over the years and in their lifetime they have bought and sold over 60 tugs, many of them bearing the name **Foremost** (154) followed by a number. Small tugs are still based in Poole harbour and tugs were at one time stationed further down the coast at Teignmouth, Dartmouth and Exeter. The little 42 ton **Verne** (1896) of Dartmouth regularly took on salvage in bad weather and along with the 55 ton **Petrel** (1892) and two tugs from Weymouth on one occasion shared £10,000 - the total assessed value of the tugs being only £20,500, quite a return on investment!

In Plymouth the fleet of W.J. Reynolds was established nearly 100 years ago from a very humble beginning towing lighters loaded with ashes from the naval dockyard to dumping grounds. The firm has owned about 30 small tugs throughout their existence (170) and apart from providing towage they have been used often before the war to take the relief keepers out to the Eddystone Lighthouse. Falmouth was the port of call of sailing ships putting in for orders. Falmouth as a result, has always had tugs based in the harbour, and over the years nearly 70 tugs have served 10 owners, among them J. & G. Cox, P. Thomas, Thos. Fox, Falmouth Docks and Engineering Co., and Falmouth Towage Company. Times without number sailing ships were driven by stress of weather to run for shelter into Falmouth Bay and its vicinity. The Falmouth tugs were always willing to assist; at a price, of course. Although the tugs were small they were found as far afield as Newquay in pursuit of salvage opportunities. For helping the *Caucasan* off Cape Cornwall, the tugs **Triton**, **Dragon**, **Victor** and **Marion** received £1,800. Just around the corner in Fowey the Fowey Tug Co., and the Fowey Harbour Co. maintained two or three smallish tugs.

Paddle Tug ***Jumna*** *entering the harbour at Littlehampton. She often carried holidaymakers on trips.*

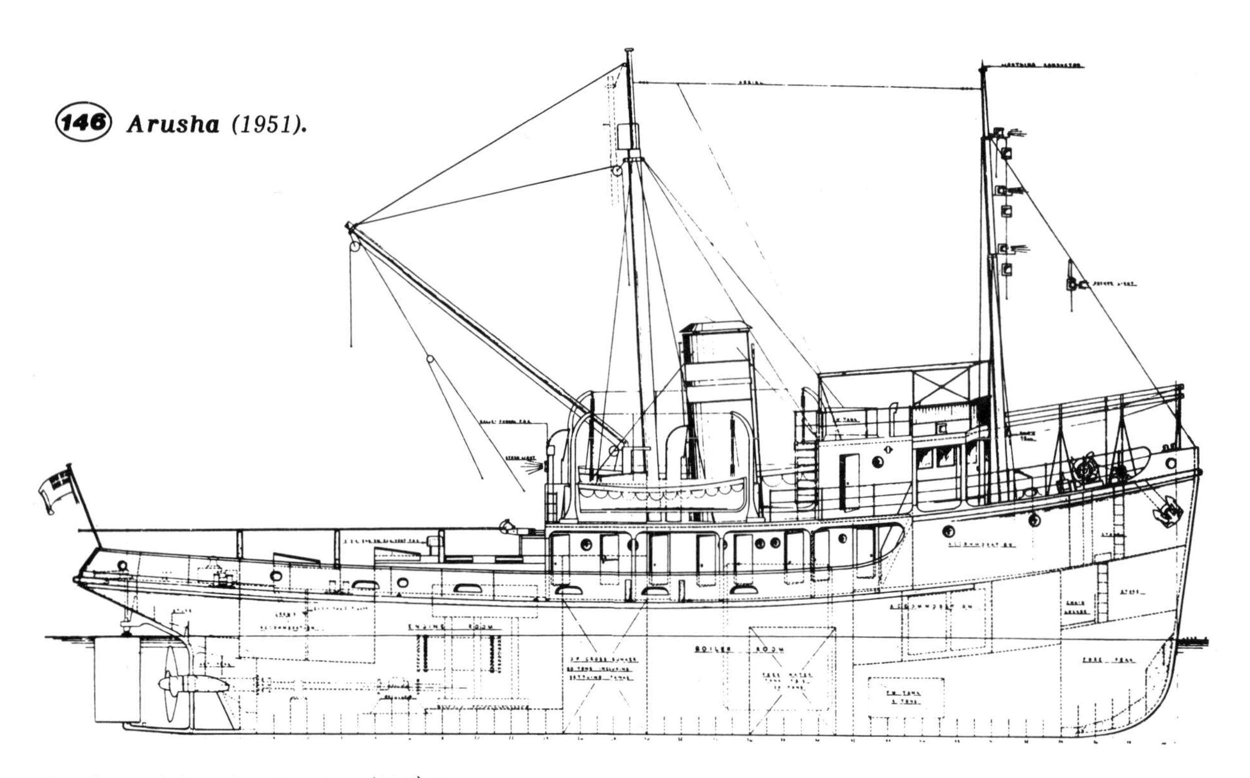

146 ***Arusha** (1951).*

At first sight the **Arusha** (146) looks like a smaller version of the **Saint** class of Admiralty tug, with her raised forecastle and the open side passageway, but in plan view her hull shape is stubbier and more rounded. She had no rise of keel, a feature usually associated with dock and canal tugs. She was built in 1951 by H. Robb of Leith for the British India Steam Navigation Co. for service in the Far Eastern ports and could accommodate a large crew (4 officers and 11 men) there was a separate galley for each group as the crew would be Asian with English officers. She was fitted with a towing winch which, even as late as 1951 had still not been adopted on British tugs of coastal size. She was bought in 1955 by the Falmouth Towage Co. and in 1959 her name was changed to **St. Mawes.**

On the North coast of Cornwall, at Padstow was an unusual tug. In 1901 the Royal National Lifeboat Institution finding that the sailing and pulling lifeboats were having a very hard time, had built the **Helen Peele** of 133 tons specially commissioned from the yacht designers G.L. Watson to assist these unpowered lifeboats to reach their casualties. This rather unusual tug, which bore the style of the American tug with her long superstructure, remained in service until 1929.

The **Helen Peele** had a very yachtlike appearance (Plate 6) as well she might, considering who designed her and who built her; Ramage & Ferguson of Leith who built quite a number of steam yachts in their time (147,148,149). The association with the steam yacht was carried through in the interior finish of the vessel with the wood panelling and fancy stair handrails. The unusually long superstructure is obvious in the profile, but not obvious is that the fore deck had been raised to the level of the bulwark rail. This was a rare feature in a British tug but can also be seen on the **Southern Cross** of Hull (74). This, together with the breakwater would help her in the rough seas in which she was expected to work. Note too that a second steering position had been provided within the superstructure, completely protecting the helmsman from the elements, a feature seldom if ever seen in British steam tugs. A finishing touch was the brass-bound wooden harness cask (meat store) on the forecastle. The **Helen Peele** had what seems a rather low engine power of 331 i.h.p., considering that she had twin screws.

The **Helen Peele** was put into service in 1901 after the loss of the steam lifeboat *James Stevens No.4.* She had a distinguished record having rescued 78 lives while working with a lifeboat and 11 while working on her own. Less than a year before she was sold she went on her own to the rescue of the crew of a fishing boat and had to go right inshore until she was nearly taking the ground; only the captain's skilful handling avoided disaster. During the war she was requisitioned and saw service as a rescue tug with the Grand Fleet during which time she added another 11 lives to the number already to her credit. She was sold in 1929 and went to the Clyde where she was used as a yacht tender and was still afloat as late as 1953 apparently as a privately owned steam yacht.

The Bristol Channel was a busy approach to the important ports of Bristol, Newport, Cardiff, Barry, Swansea and Port Talbot. The Bristol Steam Navigation Co. had quite a considerable fleet of tugs with names like **Hercules** (1838); **Lion** (1836); **Sampson** (1841); **Panther** (1847). Most of the tugs on the River Avon were small and were spread amongst owners such as J. Payne, T.R. Brown, F.A. Ashmead, Gamecock Tug Co., S.C. Roberts and Fairplay Towage and Shipping Co. and C.J. King (Alarm Steam Tug Co., Bristolian Steam Tug Co.). The latter company were registered owners of the **Merrimac** (150) which came from the yard of J.P. Rennoldson of South Shields in 1918 and she went straight into service with the Royal Navy, hence the gun on her foredeck for defensive

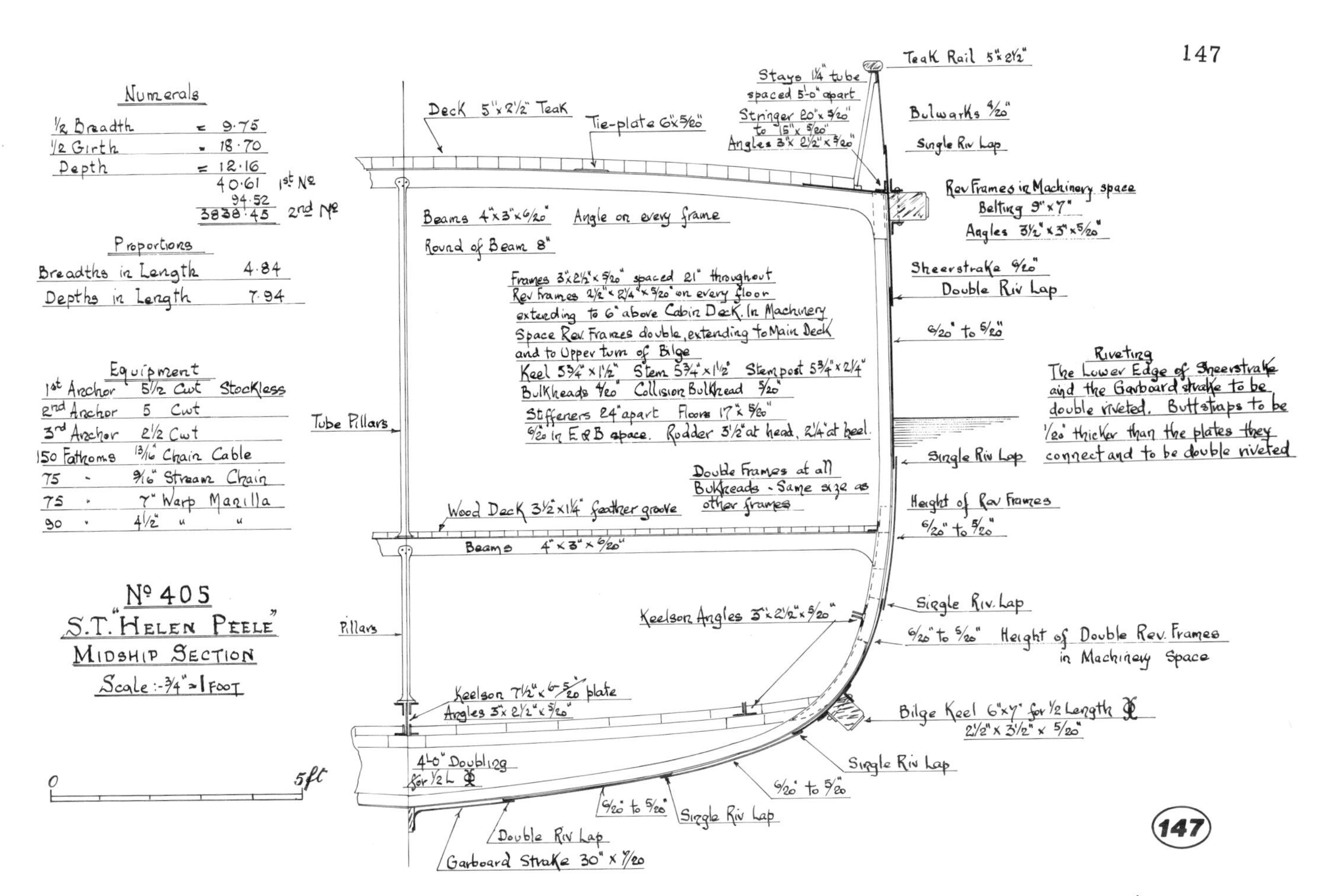

purposes. Her crew was made up of a lieutenant, towing master, engineer, two gunners, six crew members and a wireless operator. She was 226 tons gross and her 750 i.h.p. engine gave her a speed of $11\frac{1}{2}$ knots. She was obviously intended for coastal use with her W/T aerials and the two big rope cradles aft. Although her bunkers do not look large they could hold 100 tons of coal. The shape of the engine casing, sloping upwards towards the stern was quite common on tugs even as late as the **Empire** tugs of World War II. Note the heavy angles which brace the towing hook.

In 1904 there was a bit of unpleasantness when the local tug companies were accused of operating a 'ring' to keep up towage charges, an accusation which was made in many other areas from time to time. Operating as they did in the confines of the narrow Avon Gorge, collisions were frequent. The **Peri**, 1874 51 tons, was damaged no less than six times in eight years. The **Sea King**, 1875 45 tons, was actually in the Bristol Channel 'seeking' when she was sunk in a collision (56). She had on a previous occasion collided with a lightship. Sometimes the Bristol tugs queued up at the mouth of the River Avon taking their turn for a tow, one tug if the ship was small, two if the ship was big. Complaints against the Bristol tugowners were common. On one occasion a ship's captain paid £14 for two tugs for a tow inwards from Kingroad to Bristol and £5 for a single tug outwards. He later found that there was a standard scale of charges in force which was a great deal cheaper. He took the Bristol Screw Towing Company to court but received little sympathy as he had entered into a contract!

At Newport in the mid-1860s John Sully owned four tugs; another firm G.B. Sully had five tugs at Bridgwater, several miles up the River Parrett. Also in Newport Mordey, Carney the shipbuilders also owned tugs, the **Belle of the Usk**, **Pride of the Usk** and the **Queen of the Usk**. Wm. Williams owned several tugs including the **Bob Chambers** 1864. This was a popular name throughout the country and at least four tugs bore the title. There was nothing common about them except that they were all built on the Tyne. The 1862 tug was built for Montrose, the 1863 for Shields, the 1864 for Gibbs of Cardiff and the 1865 for Greenock. The surviving local company was the Newport Screw Towing Co. and were relative newcomers. All their tugs bore names beginning **Dun** e.g. **Dunsnipe** and **Dunhawk** (134).

Cardiff was a prosperous port and as such a large number of tug companies have been registered there over the years. Over 20 fleets of varying sizes have towed ships in and out of Cardiff and over 200 tugs have passed through the port. As might be expected there was a Cardiff Steam Tug Co. at the start. Nicholas Strong followed with patriotically named tugs **Victoria** (1867); **Royal Sailor** (1866); **Prince Consort** (1874). C.O. Young's tugs were called after lighthouses - **Lizard** (1868); **Hartland** (1870); **Galloper** (1882). W.H. Martin's tug names were prefixed **Earl of --**, e.g. **Earl of Glamorgan** (1869); **Earl of Bute** (1886). Charles Christie took over the Young tugs and carried on with the **Fastnet** (1890). Elliott & Jeffrey built ships and owned tugs as well. Other owners were W.H. Tucker, R. Lee and S.C. Roberts. Four of the companies have survived until recent years among them the Bristol Channel Towage Co., with their tugs **Loyal Briton** (1903) and **Loyal Celt** (1928), and J. Davies Towage & Salvage Ltd, who have owned at least 20 tugs.

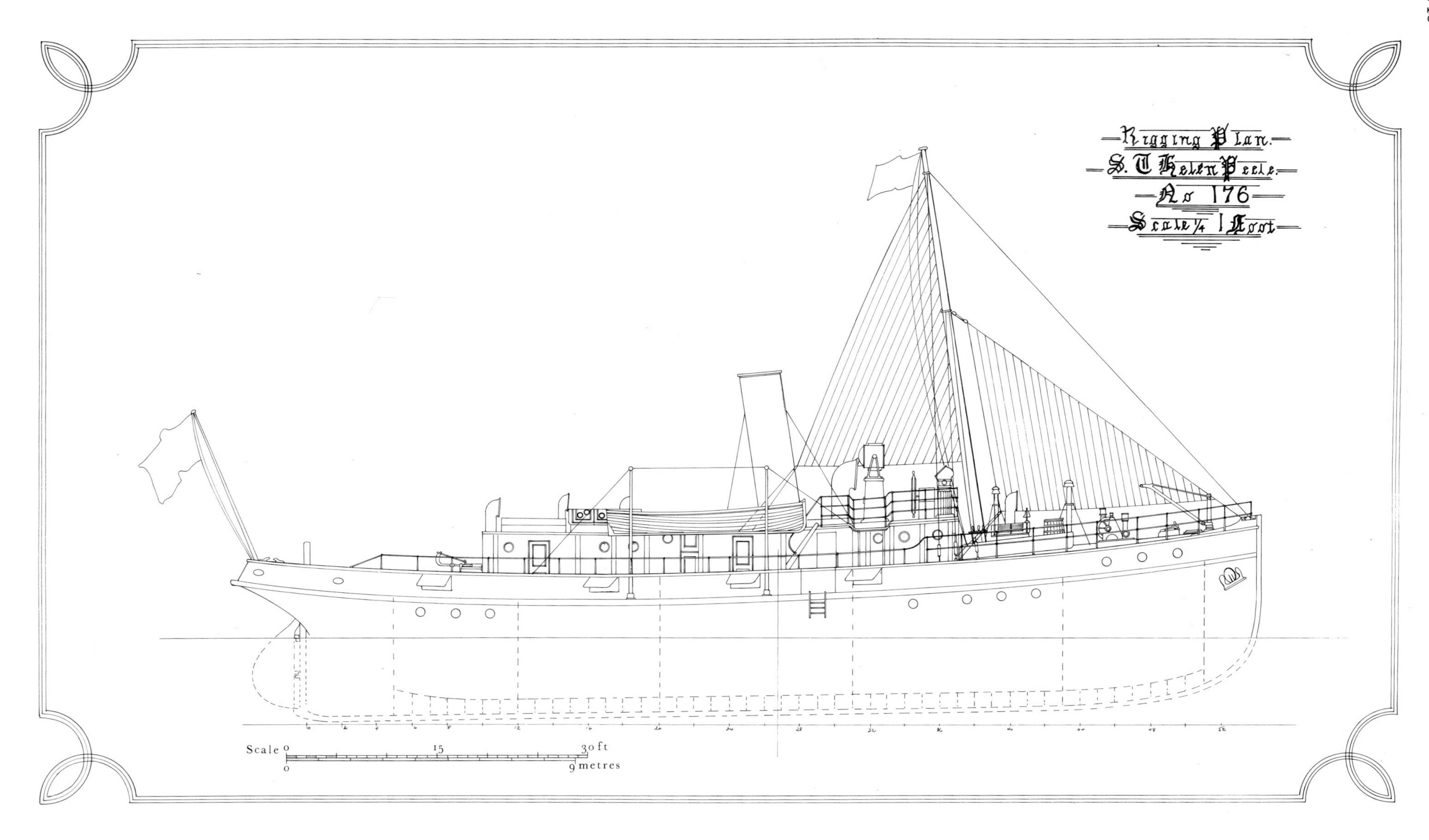
Rigging Plan.
S.T. Helen Peele.
No 176
Scale 1/4 1 Foot
Scale 0 15 30ft
0 9 metres

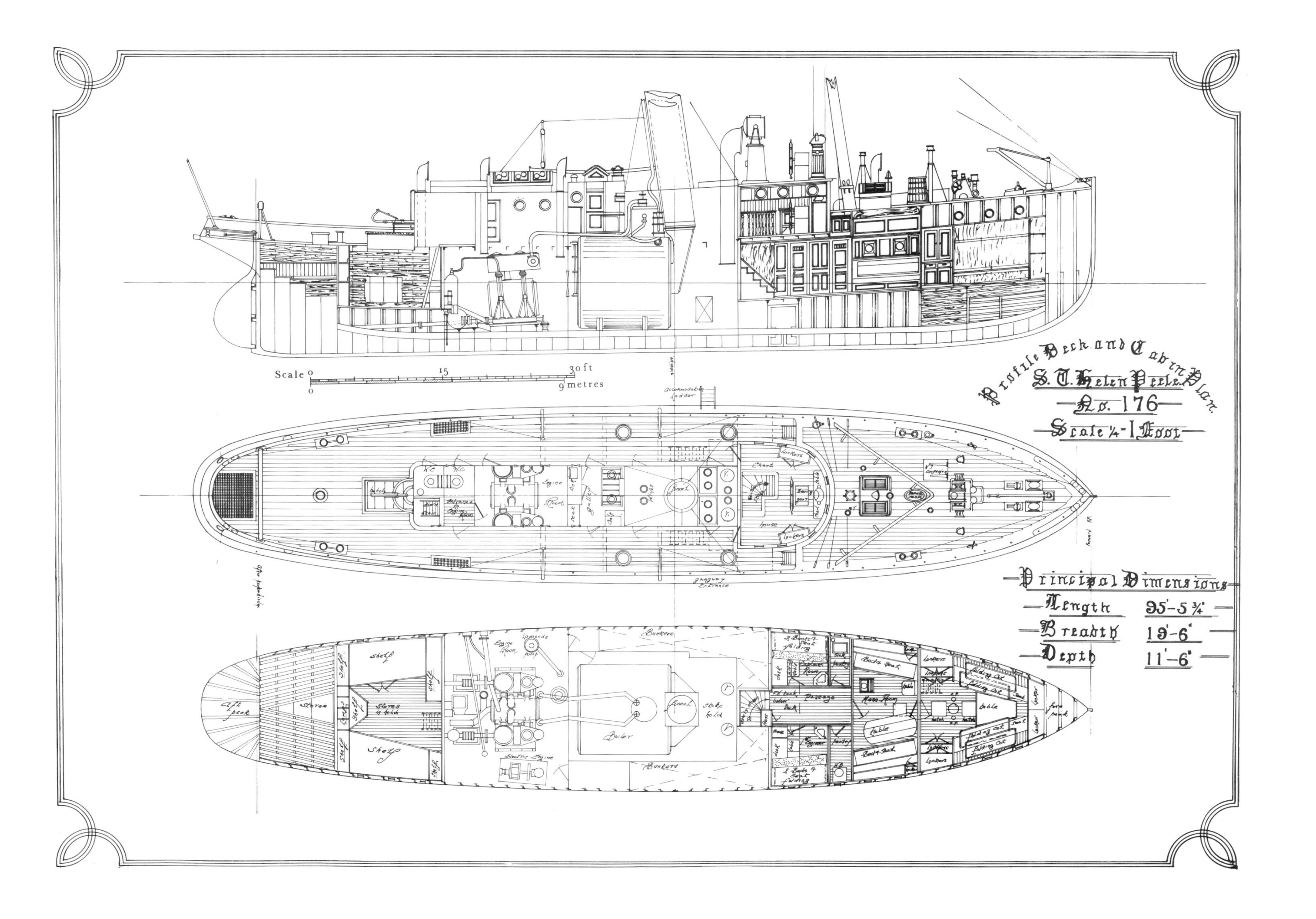
Profile Deck and Cabin Plan.
S. T. Helen Peele.
No. 176
Scale ¼ - 1 Foot
Principal Dimensions
Length 95'-5 ¾"
Breadth 19'-6"
Depth 11'-6"
Scale 0 15 30 ft
0 9 metres
Accommodation Ladder
Gangway Entrance
Chart
Lockers
House
Funnel
Galley
Engine Room
Bunkers
Boiler
Stoke hold
Passage
Mess Room
Table
Lockers
Folding Cot
Stores
Aft peak
Shelf
Fore peak

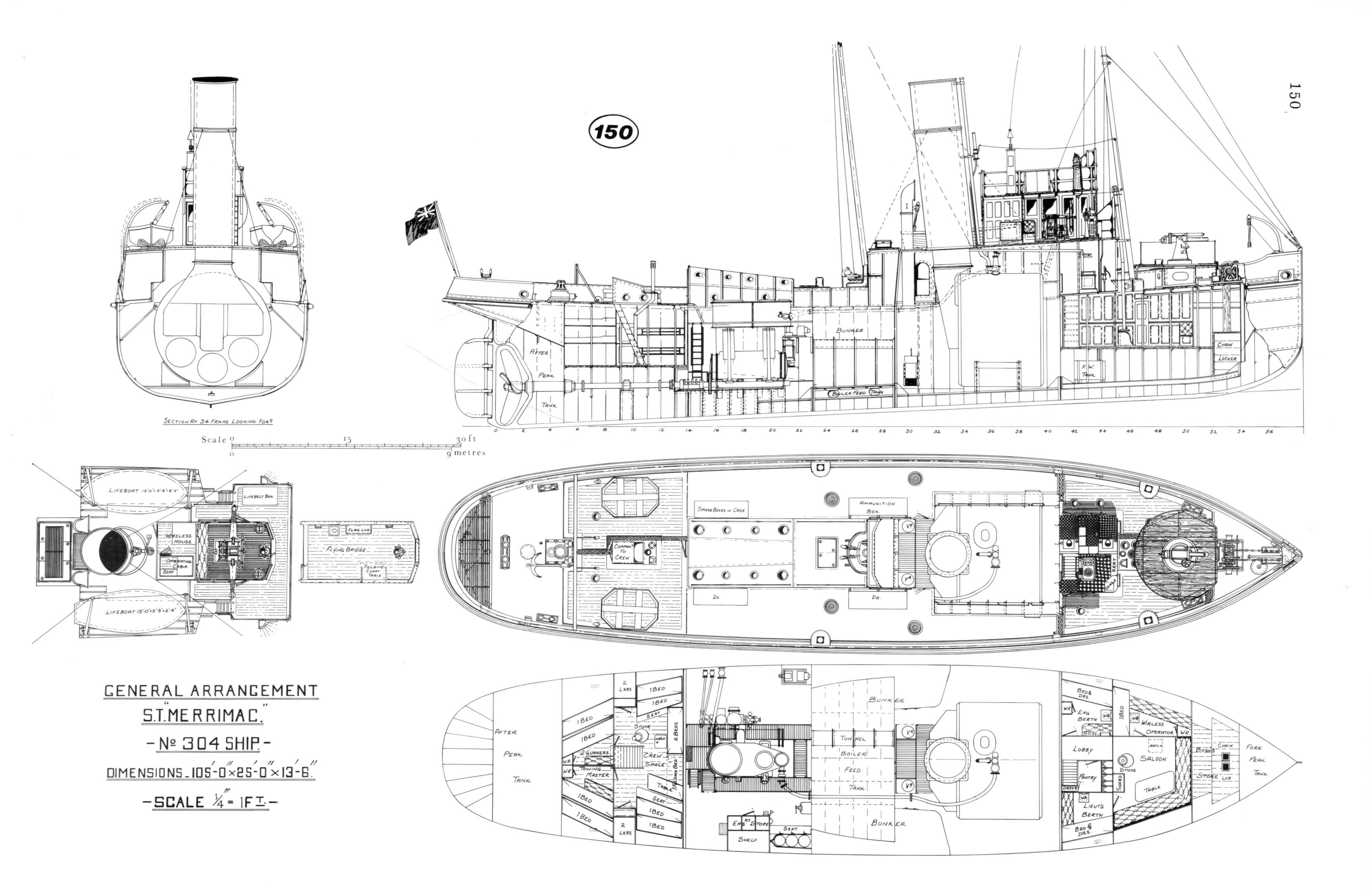

150
SECTION AT 34 FRAME LOOKING FORD
Scale
0
15
30 ft
9 metres
AFTER PEAK TANK
BUNKER
BOILER FEED TANK
F.W. TANK
CHAIN LOCKER
LIFEBOAT 15'-0" × 5'-9" × 2'-4"
LIFEBELT BOX
WIRELESS HOUSE
OPERATING CABIN
SEAT
FLAG LKR
FLYING BRIDGE
FOLDING CHART TABLE
SMOKE BOXES IN CASE
AMMUNITION BOX
COMPANION TO CREW
DO.
1 BED
2 LKRS
2 BEDS
SEAT
STOVE
2 GUNNERS
CREW SPACE
TOWING MASTER
FOLDING BED
TABLE
ENG STORE
SHELF
TUNNEL
BOILER FEED TANK
BED & DRS.
ENG BERTH
WIRELESS OPERATOR
LOBBY
SALOON
PANTRY
LIEUT'S BERTH
BOSNS
STORE LKR
FORE PEAK TANK
GENERAL ARRANGEMENT
"ST. MERRIMAC."
– No 304 SHIP –
DIMENSIONS. 105'-0" × 25'-0" × 13'-6"
– SCALE 1/4" = 1 FT. –

The two most obvious features of the **Loyal Celt** are her tall funnel and the steep rise of keel with the extra 'kick-up' about 12ft. from the bow. She was built in 1928 by A. Hall of Aberdeen as the **Foremost 43** and the outline of her hull in plan view was typical of many of the other **Foremost** tugs, so too was the round fronted saloon at the foreward end of the superstructure (154). The officers and crew were all accommodated forward, an arrangement which became the norm when diesel tugs were built. As with most of the other **Foremost** tugs she was bought by the James Dredging and Towing Co. registered London, and sold soon after to Canadian owners. She came back to the U.K. in 1949 when Steel & Bennie of Glasgow bought her and renamed her **Battleaxe**. She was sold again in 1957 to the Bristol Channel Towage Co. and renamed **Loyal Celt**. With 90 tons of bunkers and a speed of $12\frac{1}{2}$ knots, she was a useful tug for coastal work. W.J. Guy have had about 30 tugs many of which had **Rose** names - **The Rose** (1909), **Welsh Rose** (1927), **Royal Rose** (1904) and so on. Edmund Handcock (1929) Ltd., was the other survivor. The name of Wm. Cory was familiar in Cardiff for many years although they owned only a few tugs at a time until recent years, when they have taken over the local fleets.

The **G.W.R. 127** was built in 1887 for the Great Western Railway Company docks in Cardiff (90.2ft. 101 tons. 70 n.h.p.). She was no beauty, she had none of the handsome sheer associated with the steam tug and the absence of a mast made her look bare (151). Indeed many of the dock tugs were made worse looking by a system of 'jumper wire' bars which curved up over the funnel from the bow. These guards prevented damage to the tug should she swing below the tow rope. A guard such as this might have helped the **Forager** in 1962 when she was capsized by the tow rope which caught her funnel and forced her over in the River Clyde. The way her ribs are showing make her look like a starved workhorse. The strange looking object on her fore deck was a large centrifugal pump for firefighting.

Swansea has seen the fleets of Thomas Milward with the **Antelope** (1893) and **Gazelle** (1892) and Rosser Rosser with the paddle tugs **Pero Gomez** (1869) and **Digby Grand** (1871). Still to the fore until 1962 was the Britannia Steam Towing Co. with their **Forth** tugs, **Brynforth** (1942) etc., but now the Alexandra Towing Co. from Liverpool have acquired their tugs to add to the fleet which they already owned in Swansea. The little **Criccieth** which was familiar on the Tyne, started life as the **Conqueror** (57) in Swansea.

The Swansea tugowners also had many complaints levelled against them. In the late nineteenth century there was one 'restrictive practice' which particularly irritated the shipowners at a time when the local tugs were too small to handle a ship on their own. When a large ship arrived off the port two tugs had to be used and the charge was £3.10.0. for each tug. the first tug to 'speak' an incoming ship had the right to claim all the handling of the ship in that port at any time during her stay. If a ship arrived at the harbour entrance in tow of a non-Swansea tug then all towing within the port was charged at twice the normal tariff! Just around the corner in the port of Llanelly there was enough activity to warrant the presence of small tugs until 1925 when the 65 ton **Orpington** (1920) was sold by the Harbour Trustees. Milford Haven was an unimportant harbour with but one tug until the Overseas Towage and Salvage Company moved there in 1937 and established a base for their ocean towing operations. The O.T.S. were active during the war, but somewhat unfortunate! They lost their **Neptunia** in September 1939 and the Admiralty loaned them the **Hesperia** in her place. The **Hesperia** was in turn lost in North Africa in 1945 and the O.T.S. received the **Turmoil** (92). This tug was their most well known. While on charter from the Admiralty she made the unsuccessful but gallant attempt to salvage the *Flying Enterprise*. No cure, No pay!! They were in part responsible for Britain's re-entry into the deep sea towing field. When Milford Haven became an oil terminal the Rea Towing Company, part of the Cory Group introduced special motor tugs into the port, designed for handling oil tankers and equipped for dealing with fires aboard them.

Most of the ports in North Wales were small and had at one time single tugs in service, mostly small in size and low in power. Portmadoc had the **Wave of Life** (1860) and the **Snowdon** (1885) which have been described in the book 'Immortal Sails'. Almwch, Conway, Point of Ayr Colliery, and Connah's Quay each had a tug at some time, at the latter under the ownership of the well-known ship owner John Coppack. Holyhead seems to have relied on tugs from Liverpool which

G.W.R. 127 of 1887.

hung about waiting to pick up a tow back into that port. In 1866 shipowners were writing letters in the shipping papers complaining about the exorbitant charges demanded by these tugs. Whenever a ship was in difficulties near Holyhead the tug which appeared on the scene was inevitably from Liverpool. Recently, however, a new tug fleet has been established in the port, the Holyhead Towing Company which operated the steam tugs **Afon Cefni** and **Afon Wen** for a short time (170) before replacing them with diesel tugs.

Liverpool has always been a key centre for tug activity as the river has been for so long a busy outlet for the goods to and from the Midlands. There have been over 40 fleet owners in the Mersey, not counting single tugs. The early companies adopted resounding names; The Mersey Original Steam Tug Company (John Prendeville, mgr.), The Old Steam Tug Company, The New Steam Tug Company with their **Reliance** (1857), **Retriever** (1857) and the **Resolute** (1857) which spent nine days in appalling conditions in the Atlantic searching for a ship in trouble. There were two Mersey Steam Tug Company's 1850 and 1857, each changing its name after a few years. There was The United Steam Tug Company and Ward and Son's 'King Line' with the **Iron King** (1854) and **Sailor King** (1857), R. Strong, Jas. Tyrer, Gottschalk & Co.'s 'Sunshine Tug Co.' All these fleets included big sea-going tugs which crop up from time to time in salvage claims and in reports of long distance tows all over the Atlantic. Thus we find the **Pathfinder** (1876) in Ballycastle Bay in 1900 and Falmouth in 1901, the **Knight Templar** in the River Loire and the **Jane Jolliffe** in Cuxhaven. In wild weather the difficult entry to the River Mersey produced a harvest of casualties which the local tugmen were only too willing to reap. Money did not always count, the Mersey tug men also had a sense of honour. There was real competition between the tug companies for the opportunity to assist the pulling and sailing lifeboats based at New Brighton and Liverpool. When the lifeboats were called out and the ship was beyond help but the crew might be saved the tug men risked all to tow the lifeboat to the windward of the wreck, to wait until the errand of mercy was complete, and then to tow the lifeboat back into the safety of the river. Some of the companies were shortlived, while others lasted many years. The Liverpool Steam Tug Company was formed in 1836 and ceased business in 1910 having owned over 40 tugs including the famous **Pathfinder** (1876) and the **Blazer** (1888), both much used for long sea tows. Their **Cruizer** (1895) towed a floating dock 4,500 miles to Nigeria in 1905. Prendeville & Sons were very active with their **Knight** tugs. For some time they registered each tug under its own name, eg. Knight of St. John (78) Tug company; presumably to limit financial liability. A number of smaller fleets had shortlived careers on the river - Stephenson Chisholm, W. Downham, Ed. Forster, D.L. Griffiths, to name but a few.

Another household name in Liverpool was W. and T. Jolliffe, owners of over 40 tugs, established in 1852. At first their names varied, **Lion** (1847), **Great Conquest** (1857), but about 1879 the firm adopted family names with **Thomas Jolliffe**, **Jane Jolliffe** (1888) and so on. Jolliffe tugs were registered in other ports such as Cardiff, Leith and London, indicating that their tugs operated from these ports at some time. In 1901 the fleet was absorbed into that of the Alexandra Towing Company which today operates a large fleet in Liverpool and has extended its sphere of influence into the London area, South Wales and Southampton. Today there are 30 tugs in the fleet and the numbers are being increased. Usually they are named after local areas such as **Waterloo** (1954), **Nelson** (1966), **Mumbles** (1969). W.B. Hill started the Liverpool Screw Towing and Lighterage Company in 1877 and later the tugs appear under the ownership of G.R. Nicholson and Harold Edwards. The company was one of the first to order screw tugs for deep sea work, but their early screw tugs were purchased almost at once by the Admiralty. The **Stormcock** (1883) became the H.M.S. **Traveller** in 1885 (79). The suffix **Cock** only disappeared in 1970 when the company was taken over by Alexandra Towing, and familiar names like **Flying Cock** (1960) and **Weather Cock** (1958) ceased to exist.

Wm. Cory & Son Ltd. were represented on the river by the Rea Towing Co. Ltd. bearing on the funnels of their tugs latterly the Cory black diamond. This fleet, one of the later arrivals, has always been large and apart from the distinctive funnel markings can be identified by the names which all end in **Garth** e.g. **Brackengarth** (1969). The **Rosegarth** was another tug from the Aberdeen builders A. Hall & Co. The drawing shows clearly how the Rea tugs were built with an enclosed side passage, plated in along the side with accommodation forward with a bulkhead at the after end (153). The only snag was that to reach the anchor deck the crew members had to go up to the boat deck and climb down a ladder. This tug had all her accommodation forward as had

Florida (1902) seen in the colours of Jas. Lamey of Liverpool.

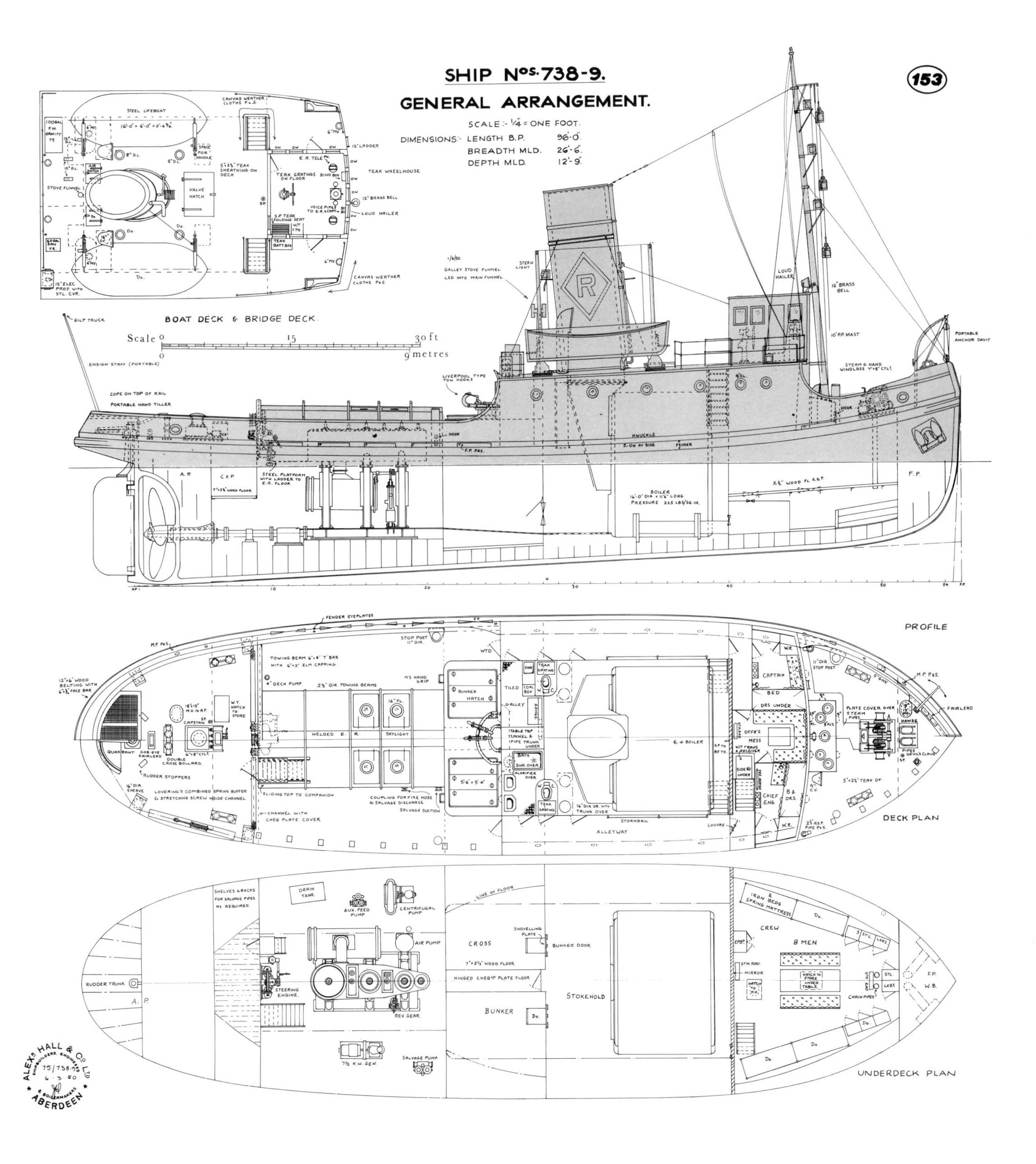

the **Loyal Celt**, another Hall built tug. This plan also illustrates the arrangement of the towing lights with three fixed electric lights and a system of guide ropes, halliards and cradles for the emergency oil lamps. She was built in 1954 for Rea Tugs Ltd. of Liverpool (96.0ft. 231 tons. 1120 i.h.p.) and was sold by them to the Holyhead Towing Co. in 1970 being renamed **Afon Wen** (170).

Another late comer was Alfred Lamey who started his fleet in 1916 with the little **Hero** (1896) and the converted steam yacht **Iris** (1892). He built up a small but useful fleet which earned quite a reputation on the river for unorthodox behaviour; legend has it that the opposition presented a pirate flag to the Lameys, which they flew as if they were proud of it. On the credit side the Lamey family were progressive and used motor tugs, radar and exhaust/mast combinations before their more conservative competitors. Jas. Lamey's **Florida** was built for London owners in 1902 and brought to Liverpool in 1933. After some modernisation she went into service in the Mersey. The picture shows how jaunty a good screw tug design looked with a nice sheer from bow to stern (152). She was given a roomy wheelhouse and a single arm davit which made boat handling easier; another example of her owners progressive attitude. The funnel colours were striking and are easily recognised; black over white over red with a black "L" on the white band.

S.T. "BATTLEAXE".
GENERAL ARRANGEMENT.

105'-0" B.P. x 27'-0" B'DTH M'L'D x 12'-6" DEPTH M'L'D.

SCALE :- ¼" = 1 FOOT.

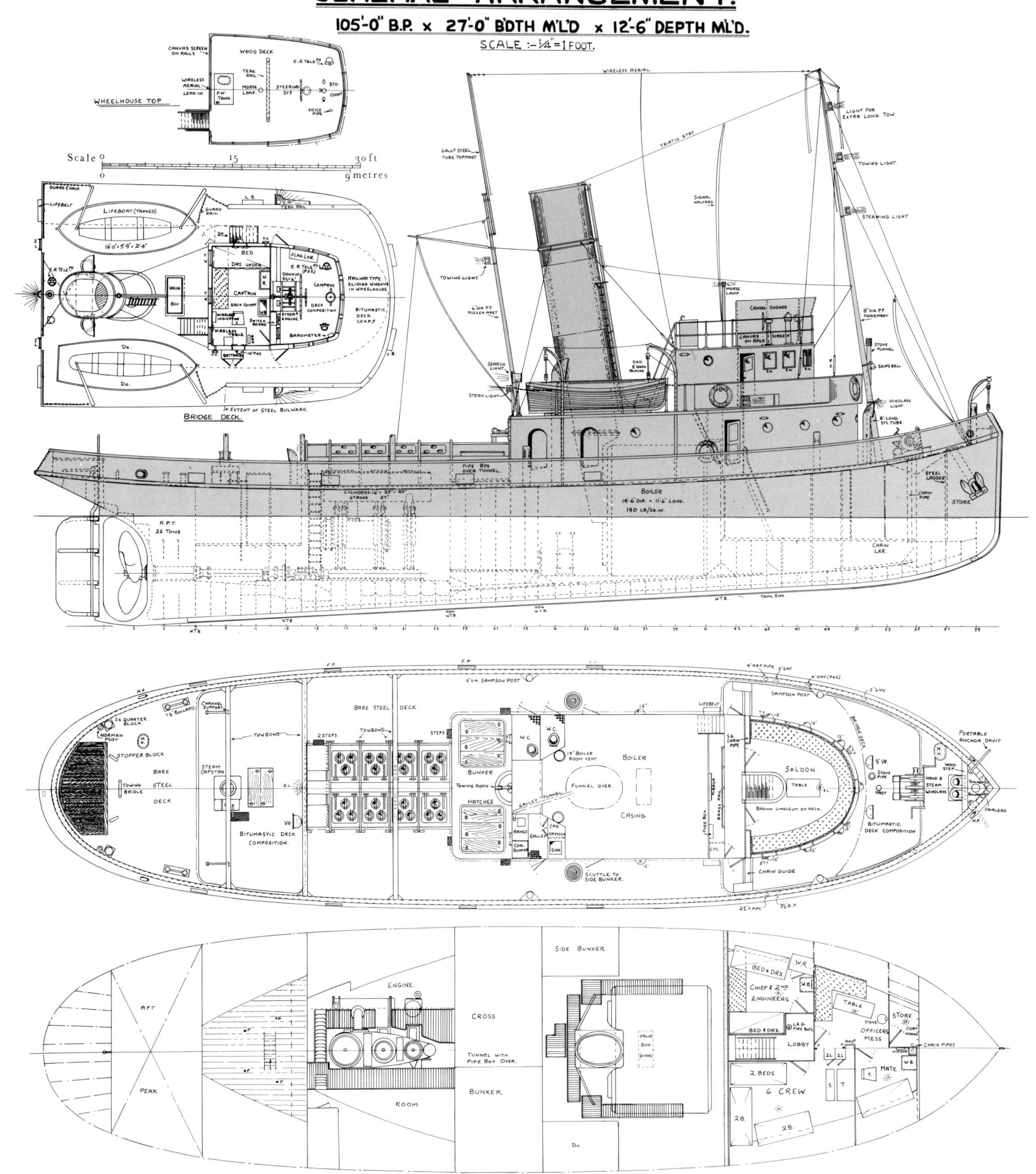

As mentioned so often, tug work is dangerous and Liverpool has had its share of accidents and fatalities. However, there was one incident which nearly cost the "Cock" fleet three tugs and they were not even involved in towing at the time. In 1956 the three tugs were waiting to lock out into the river when the dock gates burst and the tugs were swept out of control into the Mersey and all but capsized in the process.

Two other aspects of the port deserve mention. Many liner services were based on Liverpool and passenger tenders cum tugs were maintained by several of the shipping companies. The Canadian

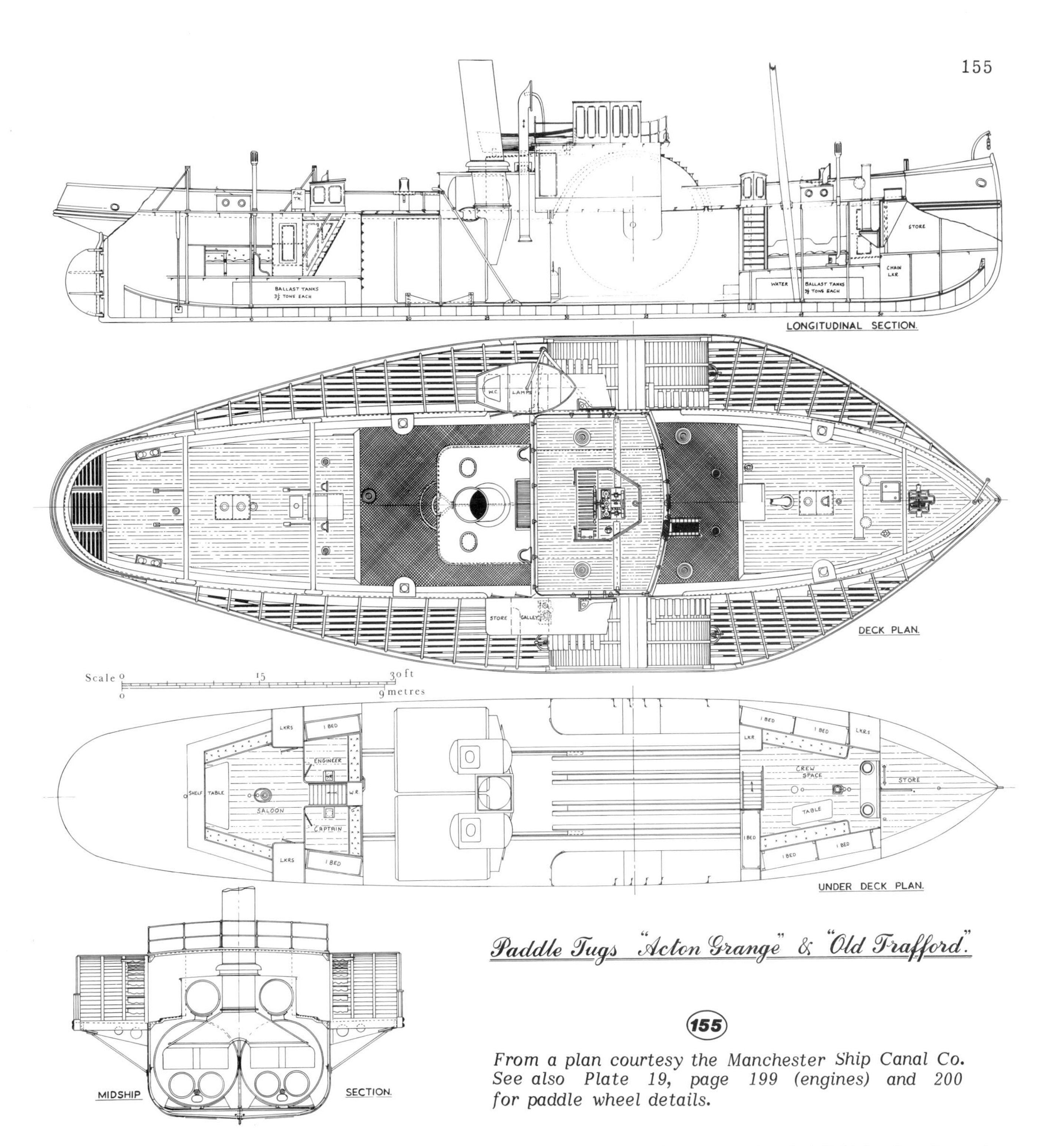

From a plan courtesy the Manchester Ship Canal Co. See also Plate 19, page 199 (engines) and 200 for paddle wheel details.

Pacific Railway Co. had tenders with names of animals, **Moose** (1915) and **Wapiti** (1915). The Cunard Steamship Co. ran the **Skirmisher** (1884) which resembled a miniature liner herself (6). Being the terminus of several canal systems there has always been a fair amount of barge traffic and there have been several companies such as Richard Abel and Liverpool Lighterage Co. operating tugs of a size comparable with the London craft tugs, tugs such as Abel's **Water Fly** (1901) of 49 tons.

A ship canal must have tugs, as a big ship moving slowly, lacks control. Thus the Manchester Ship Canal Co. have always maintained a fleet of tugs, assisting vessels as they made their way up the narrow confines of the canal. When the canal was opened in 1894 the basis of the fleet was a group of old paddle tugs which had been in use on the Bridgewater canal system, odd double-ended paddle tugs, built between 1857 and 1877, including the **Earl of Ellesmere** (1857) and **Dagmar** (1863). The new Manchester Ship Canal Company began to purchase new tugs, some screw, some paddle, their last paddle tug being the **Reliant** of 1907 which has been preserved in the National Maritime Museum. In 1922 they introduced twin screw boats to the canal as these gave better control of the tows. In 1927 they began a new nomenclature where all the names were prefixed **MSC,** such as **MSC. Firefly.** Later they started to work through in alphabetical order.

The drawing (155) represents the **Eccles** and **Rixton** (1905), **Acton Grange** and **Old Trafford** (1907), all of which were built for the Manchester Ship Canal Co. These paddle tugs had the distinctive feature of sponsons which were carried right from the bow to the stern in one sweep to give maximum protection against damage. The big double cruciform bollard on the foredeck was common

At Barrow the thriving shipbuilding industry launched large battle ships and liners and powerful tugs had to be in attendance. After a series of paddle tugs the first screw tug was the **Furness** *(1898, 128.8', 225 tons, 900 i.h.p.). She evidently had a towing point forward as she has a towing bow on her bows. Tyres were not yet in use, but she has four points along the bulwarks faced with heavy timber where plaited rope fenders were hung. Here she tows the Caronia out of Barrow on the 5th of April 1924.*

M.S.C. practice as their tugs connected bow-on when working as the stern tug. The way it was mounted on a shelf in the crew space is rather peculiar. She had steam assisted steering which must have made things easier for the helmsman but there was no shelter for him. The hook assembly was braced to the keelson by a big steel bar. Although she had disconnecting engines, cant hooks are fitted on the sponsons. (The use of cant hooks is explained in 'Fittings', page 215). These tugs were 100.0 ft. x 20.2 ft. x 9.8 ft., with a gross tonnage of 156 and engines of 80 n.h.p. Built by J.T. Eltringham & Co. of South Shields they remained in the Manchester Ship Canal fleet until the early 1950s except for the **Old Trafford** which went first to the Tyne in 1950 where she became the **Reliant**, then to Seaham Harbour and finally to the National Maritime Museum for preservation.

Further up the coast lies Preston where Wm. Allsup, the shipbuilder, owned tugs, and Preston Corporation kept a fleet of tugs to assist ship on the River Ribble and in the docks. The Ribble does not seem a likely place for salvage but in 1901 the tugs **Energy** (1899) (61), **Perseverance** (1896) and **Enterprise** (1894) shared an award of £10,000, no mean sum in those days. In Fleetwood Docks the Railway Company have always had tugs and tenders available, two being called **Fylde** (1881 and 1904). At Barrow there were tugs belonging to James Ramsden who also served Lancaster, at one time quite a busy port. The Furness Railway Company had magnificent two funnelled twin screw tugs (156), the **Furness** (1898), and the **Cartmel** (1907) which later became the **Bullger** at Leith. The shipowners at Barrow, James Fisher had tugs until recently when they disposed of their ex-'Empire' tugs **Fisherhill** and **Fishertown** which were often to be seen at Heysham. On the Cumberland coast there are several little ports which had tugs at one time, Whitehaven, Maryport and Workington, the last named having had until 1975 another ex-Empire tug, the **Solway** (90). For many years the Clyde Shipping Company of Glasgow sent one of their tugs down from the Clyde to assist the **Solway** at Workington when the need arose.

In the Firth of Clyde there are a number of seaports which had a fair amount of shipping activity which necessitated the presence of a tug. The Ayr Harbour Company's fleet had been reduced to the one tug **Ayr** (1896), the third to bear the name, when they handed over to the Glasgow and South-Western Railway Co. in 1920. At Troon the Duke of Portland's **Titchfield** (1879) and **Portland** (1876) passed to the same owners. Irvine Harbour Company had operated small wooden paddle tugs until the iron hulled **George Brown** (2,44) arrived in 1887, to be replaced in turn by a motor tug **Garnock** in 1956; built as it happened by Geo. Brown of Greenock. An old newspaper report gave an account of an interesting local "disaster". In September 1872 a serious disaster took place in Irvine Harbour. The river was swollen due to recent rains and a current of seven knots was running. The *Mary Wilson* loaded with deals had arrived earlier and had grounded at the upper wharf. During the night her moorings broke and she was swept broadside on down the river, coming in contact with vessels lying in tiers against the wharf. These vessels were torn from their moorings and rushed with the current sweeping all before them. The tug **Scottish Maid** shared the fate of the other vessels. The stoker was still aboard and, as soon as he saw that they were bound for the sea, he went below to give her a fire, there being only 10 lbs. in the boiler at the time. She struck near the bar, so he started one of the engines and backed her out to sea. He went below to give her another fire, but the tug shipped a heavy sea much of which entered the stokehole. The steam began to rise, so he went on deck, started the engines at a slow pace, and went to the wheel so as to knock about the bay until daylight. To his surprise the wheel chains had parted. He went aft to try to ship the tiller, but owing to its not being in use since the boat came to the harbour it would not work. He then resolved to steer by the engines which were double. Finding that things were going more smoothly he went to examine the rudder chains and discovered the broken link. Securing a piece of rope he spliced the chains and was thus enabled to steer the boat. Between firing the boiler, working the engines and steering the tug it was not an easy job (an understatement). However, after dodging about the bay all morning he made for the harbour. During the night he had exhibited lights and sounded the steam whistle for assistance but none came. It blew hard and a heavy sea was running all night! In all nineteen other small ships were either lost or severely damaged during the night, and two rafts of timber were washed out to sea.

The Earl of Eglinton owned the busy harbour of Ardrossan with the **Terrier** (1864) and **Northumberland** (1852), until the Harbour Company was formed in 1886. Nine tugs have worked there, one, the **Cockspur**, had been the naval tug **Peter Pan** (1919) which had worked at Zeebrugge assisting the salvage teams to remove the blockships sunk there during the famous naval action. The last vessel was the **Ardneil**, at one time the pride of the Steel & Bennie fleet under the name of **Crusier** (162) (1953), already converted to diesel power. For a short time the Ardrossan Salvage Co. worked out of the port using old secondhand tugs. The **Greville Vernon** (158) was the first screw tug built for the Ardrossan Harbour Company and they chose the twin-screw arrangement. The hull was slender with a fine entry and it had quite a shallow draught with only a little rise of keel. The towing hook on the fore deck was characteristic of the North East Coast tugs, the Scottish tugs usually having a 'timberhead' at the bow (i.e. a samson post); to have it incorporated into the anchor windlass was even more unusual. The arrangement of the bridge was very cramped indeed considering the size of the vessel and the two sets of steps leading up to it at the front were again peculiar to this vessel. She was built by A. Rodger of Port Glasgow in 1898. (105.0 ft. 170 tons. 75 n.h.p.). In 1915 she was sold to Liverpool owners and renamed **Egad**, serving with the Star Steam Tugs Ltd., Egad Tug Co., and Ashbrooke Shipping Co. in turn. In 1922 the Aberdeen Steam Tug Co. bought her and renamed her **St. Machar**, giving her a heavier funnel and improving her appearance thereby.

Being the cradle of the steamship, and a busy trade outlet for Scotland, the Clyde saw a rush to form tug companies when the principle of ship towage had been shown to work. As was customary high sounding names were adopted; New Clyde Towing Company, New Clyde Shipping Company, United Steam Towing Company, United Steam Towing & Navigation Company, Greenock and Bowling Towing Company. The tugs did not receive local names but were called **Samson** (1840), **Defiance** (1850), **Powerful** (1848), or more modest names like **Helen McGregor** (1848) or **Maid of Orleans** (1855). Later these fleets reverted to bearing the name of the owner, John Duncan, Archibald Hendry, Wm. Liddell, Archibald McKinnon, Wm. Park, all registered in Greenock. Also registered in Greenock were a number of small independently owned tugs, often converted steam yachts whose sole purpose in life was to tow lumber rafts from the seasoning ponds up-river down to Port Glasgow. Andrew Inglis was one such owner and his **S.T. Cress** (1919) of 13 tons finished up on the Thames as a craft tug. But going back in time; when the arrival of the new paddle tug **Flying Dutchman** was announced on 30th April, 1861, the newspapers listed the tugs in service on the river: Clyde Shipping Company (6 tugs); River Towing Company (4 tugs plus one building); Glasgow and Greenock Shipping Company (3 tugs); New Clyde Towing Company (3 tugs); Greenock Towing Company (3 tugs); River Clyde Towing Company (2 tugs); Greenock and Bowling Towing Company (2 tugs). There were also four tugs used for punts and timber rafts. The total number of tugs was 28 with an aggregate power of 1,356 horses. All but 4 were built on the Tyne." That last statement is somewhat surprising, as by this time the Clyde was a major shipbuilding centre. In 1875 the Screw Tug Company of Glasgow started up in opposition to the paddle tugs with a unique design of screw tug with a propeller at each end of the hull (62). Their tugs lasted only a short time on the river, being sold first to the Clyde Shipping Co. and then in 1886 to the Alexandra Towing Co. of Liverpool where the **Flying Tempest** ex **Tay** and **Flying Whirlwind** ex **Forth** were the basis of their new fleet.

The best known names on the River Clyde were the Clyde Shipping Company and Steel & Bennie, now Cory Ship Towage (Clyde) Ltd. The Clyde Shipping Company started in 1815 with the luggage steamer **Industry** (below) and built up quite a fleet of steamers, lighters and towing vessels. In

Industry *(1814) from an old photo taken in her later years.*

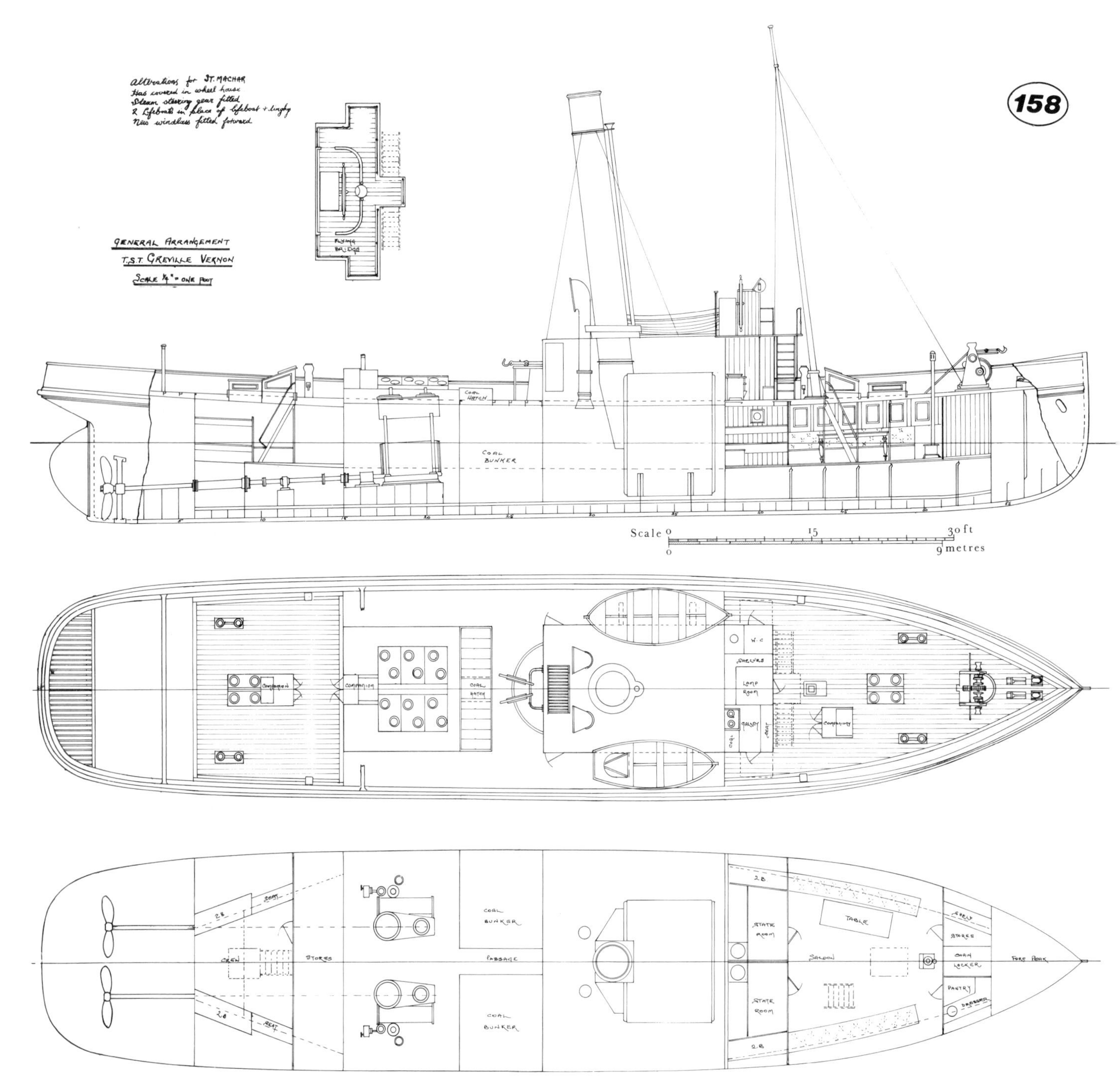

1856 the company was re-formed under the same name and sold off its cargo craft to a former employee, James Steel. The first new tug built for the company was called the **Flying Childers** (1856) after a famous racehorse, and apart from five **Conqueror**s (1863, 1864, 1865, 1871, and 1880) and 10 other tugs, all the 130 or so tugs owned by the company have had names prefixed **Flying.....** The **Flying Foam** was the first screw tug in the fleet and was unusual in that the wheel was aft of the funnel (66). The company ran two 'separate' fleets, one consisting of large screw and paddle tugs which were engaged in towing sailing vessels to and from the south of Ireland under contract to the shipowners, and the other with small paddle tugs which operated within the confines of the Firth of Clyde. One feature of these paddle tugs was that every one of those built new for the company had only a single side-lever engine, even the last one which was built in 1898, the **Flying Scotsman** (43). In view of the superior manoeuvrability of a paddle tug with the independent engines, this is rather surprising. In 1915 when the *Lusitania* was torpedoed off the south coast of Ireland, the Clyde Shipping Co. **Flying Fish** (1886) was one of the first vessels to arrive on the scene, rescuing some 240 people. A report from an old newspaper gives a graphic account of the adventures of one of the Clyde Shipping Company's tugs on one of her voyages away from home. The scene is set in Ramsey, Isle of Man and the date is 25th July, 1860.

"Extraordinary Riot and Capture of a Steamer's Crew."

"The tug **Flying Childers**, towing the ship *William Kidson*, McGregor, from Liverpool to Troon where the ship is to take coal for China, put into Ramsey on Friday night, being short of coals for the passage. The tug having received a supply of coals, was preparing for sea, when it was discovered that both the Captain and the Crew had also taken in a good supply of something stronger than water, which rendered them quite unfit for duty. The steamer's paddle wheels revolved, only

Screw Tug CONTEST

CONTEST was built in 1933 for the Elliott Steam Tug Co. She was employed on the Thames until 1972 and is shown in her final colours, those of London Tugs Ltd.

Screw Tug ROSEGARTH

ROSEGARTH was built in 1954 for Rea Towing Co. Ltd., of Liverpool. She was sold to the Holyhead Towing Co. Ltd., in 1970 and then to Italian owners shortly afterwards.

to cause some damage to a fishing lugger and send a smack adrift. This caused some angry words to pass between the crew of the lugger and the Captain of the tugboat, and it became evident that the conduct of the Captain would get him in a mess. After turning ahead and backing for a considerable time, he brought the tug alongside a windbound schooner, made fast, and came ashore,the Crew followed on board the schooner and commenced a fierce and bloody fight among themselves, which was continued until the belligerents were separated by the townsmen who rushed to the rescue and dragged them on shore.

While this was going on, the firemen on board the tug were equally jolly; they threw off the ropes and steamed up the harbour and then down again, one of the firemen mounting the gangway and issuing orders. The tug steamer had gone up with the tide toward the shipyard, and in coming down again ran into a cluster of small boats, breaking one with her floats. By this time a very large crowd had gathered on the quay opposite, and the utmost excitement prevailed. The Harbour Master felt it to be his duty to send off a number of men aboard and take charge of the steamer. This was accomplished in grand style, after a hard fight wherein the men in the steamer were completely mastered. Hawsers were then passed on shore, and the steamer hauled alongside the shipping. The Captain of the steamer and part of the Crew, who had been fighting on the shore, then rushed on board, and the fiercest and most bloody contest which Ramsey had witnessed for many a long year ensued. We could see the Crew and Firemen strike and get knocked down in turn. Scores of the townspeople rushed on board from the quay. One of the crew drew a knife, open, and was about to use it, when he was knocked down, the knife taken from him, and he was handed to a policeman. Another was striking with an engineer's turnkey when he was served in a similar manner, and soon the whole gang (Captain and all, with the exception of the Chief Engineer) were captured, handcuffed, and in the most frightful looking state, covered with their own blood, and full of wounds, marched off to prison.

Captain Teare, the Harbour Master with his deputy, Mr. Bryden, being now solely in command, mounted the paddlebox, and took the steamer to the Custom House Quay. All the time the most intense excitement prevailed and it was feared that fatal wounds had been received. As it turned out, however, bloody wounds, black eyes, broken jaws and cheek bones, etc., were the only personal results. His Worship, the Bailiff, after the crew had had a few hours confinement, fined each one of them 1/- and agreed costs of all the damages, making in the aggregate about £7. Seeing they had suffered so severely in the melee, they were liberated on payment by the Captain of the ship, who guaranteed to take them off without any more trouble, and thus ended the affair."

After James Steel bought the Clyde Shipping Company's cargo fleet he went on to build up another towing fleet in opposition, and competition was very keen, especially on the 'seeking' side. Their three tugs built by Stephens of Linthouse were built with speed in mind, the **Cruiser** (1904), **Victor** (1906) and **Campaigner** (1911). Although not of any great size these tugs carried out a number of coastal tows. Two of these tugs had a chance to demonstrate the quality of Clyde shipbuilding. In December 1907 the ship *Dartmoor* went aground on the Isle of Arran and the Steel & Bennie tugs were chartered to pull her off. The weather was bad at the time and the **Victor** and **Cruiser** were driven aground being damaged on the rocks in the process. The **Cruiser** lay aground for four months before she was refloated. In their 120 years the firm of Steel & Bennie have owned some 50 tugs. Another **Cruiser** was launched in 1953 by A. Hall of Aberdeen, a tug which was regarded by Clyde tugmen as the peak of coastal tug development; indeed she was one of the last steam powered coastal tugs to be built (162). Her dimensions were somewhat similar to those of the **Joffre** (70) but somehow she managed to look bigger and more powerful. One of her most noticeable features was the tremendous sheer which carried her bow high above the waterline while leaving the usual low freeboard amidships. Her masts were stepped in sockets on the boat deck and had to be strongly stayed. There were no cowl vents: instead the stokehole fans drew their air through special low profile vents with hinged lids, vents which did not interfere with the view

***Scot** built in 1876 for the Caledonian Canal.*

aft from the bridge. By this time the use of wood for deadening over accommodation had almost ceased and a bitumastic compound was used instead. The lines plan shows a very full hull with little rise of floor, yet at the same time the entry is fine. A peculiarity of the plan is the way the draughtsman has set out the waterlines working down from the load waterline of 13ft. 7 $\frac{1}{2}$ ins. instead of working up from the baseline as did most other shipyards. The **Cruiser**, having been converted to motor power in 1963, remained in the service of Steel & Bennie until 1969, when she was sold to the Ardrossan Harbour Co. who renamed her **Ardneil**. Under steam she had engines of 1200 i.h.p., with her diesels she was rated at 1350 b.h.p. She made a name for herself with coastal tows, tows to the Continent and with numerous short sea rescue missions.

The Anchor Line (Henderson Bros.) had a tender stationed in the Clyde to serve their passenger liners, the last being the **Paladin** (1913) which was sold first to the Clyde Shipping Co. and then to the Red Funnel fleet at Southampton (46). The Clyde Shipping Co. operated tenders both on the Clyde and at Cork, one of them, the **Ireland** was like a small Clyde steamer. They also had passenger certificates for many of their tugs so that they could carry workmen and visitors to ships running trials in the Firth of Clyde while Steel & Bennie had a service for passengers at Londonderry.

In 1936 Metal Industries Ltd. bought tugs to assist at their shipbreaking yards and to tow ships in for scrapping. In the years after the war they stationed a tug the **Metinda III** (Plate 140) on the north coast of Scotland where she made a number of rescues of ships in distress. The Clyde Navigation Trust kept a tug to stand by their dredging craft and to tow dumb lighters, the second one was the iron paddle tug **Clyde** of 1851 (32) whose engines may still be found on the riverside at Renfrew and one of the few examples of the old side-lever engine which has been preserved. Her successor, a twin-screw tug again called the **Clyde** (1912) has in turn been replaced, but by a small passenger launch.

In the north of Scotland one or two small paddlers were to be found but little is known about them. On the Caledonian Canal there was a tug called the **Scot** which helped with the maintenance, a little iron screw vessel. There is no information in the registers about the **Scot** but it is known that she was built in 1876 by Cunliffe & Dunlop, 70.0ft. long. She was narrow and sharp forward and had a very cluttered deck, having a saloon aft of the funnel (160) pushing her hook very far aft. Her bow is reminiscent of the **Ich Dien** which came from the same yard a year later (120). She was replaced in 1931 by a screw tug which was converted to motor in 1961 and now runs pleasure trips on the canal.

There were a couple of tugs in Peterhead, Wm. McKinnon's **Pride of Scotland** (1871) and Wm. Leask's **Flying Scud** (1877); probably the latter was used more as a paddle trawler. Mitchell & Rae at Newburgh, north of Aberdeen had a strange little paddle tug called the **Despatch** on the River Ythan, little more than a barge with paddles. In Aberdeen itself there have been a large number of tugs and paddle trawlers. There was Mrs. Helen Taylor in the 1850s with the **Heather Bell** (1857); the name disappears in 1883 but in 1917 the name occurs once more as R. Taylor with the **John McConnachie** (1879). W.A. Adam had tugs from 1857 to 1880, one being the **Bon Accord** (1862) a local name. Most others were owners of paddle trawlers which towed as well. J. Newton owned paddlers from 1878 starting with the wooden **Fairweather** (1871) and ending in 1917 with the **William Findlay** (1884). The Aberdeen Steam Company started in 1921 with the purchase of the **Chester** (1900) from Hull, and was taken over in 1959 by the Aberdeen Harbour Co. who straightaway replaced the old steam tugs with two new diesel tugs the **Sea Griffon** and **Sea Trojan**, both built in 1962. The Aberdeen Steam Tug Co. tugs had all been fairly small vessels being intended for use within the confines of the docks. When trawlers are in harbour the crews do not stay aboard and the tugs are kept busy shifting their berths. However from 1922 to 1928 the company owned an ocean going tug called the **Audax II** (1918) formerly the Dutch **Gelderland.**

The **Audax II** was used mostly for making wireless corrections for signal stations around the coast of Great Britain, being fitted with W/T aerials, besides towing many of the salvaged vessels of the German fleet scuttled at Scapa Flow. She towed many surplus warships round the coast to the scrapyards. The owner of the tug was so beset by requests for her services that he sold her in 1928, not the usual reason for such a move, normally lack of work was the cause. The **Danny** was another very handsome tug with a fine sheer and a high bow. She began life as the **Mary Tavy**, a naval tug (1918, 93.5ft. 182 tons. 800 i.h.p.), being bought in 1948 by the Aberdeen Steam Company. The battered state of her bulwarks shows how hard she was worked (165).

Montrose was only a small port but had its own tug, the **Bob Chambers** (1862) up until 1893. There was a large seasonal grain trade between the Baltic ports and Montrose and the Newcastle tug **John Batey** regularly came up the coast to assist the local tug, indeed from 1893 to 1906, Francis Batey stationed a small wooden paddle tug **Rapid** (1868) in Montrose and registered her in that port. The **John Batey** (89.0ft. 90 tons. 40 n.h.p.) nearly did not make it back to Newcastle in 1909 as she went ashore on her way back to the Tyne. However she was got off safely and went back into service.

The **Rapid** was built for G.G. McKay of Grangemouth. She went to Montrose in 1884 and was taken over by Francis Batey of Newcastle in 1893, being retained at Montrose to handle the grain ships which called at that port. She finally went south in 1906. She was a very trim looking tug and considering that in the photograph she must have been at least 25 years old, she had obviously been maintained in very good condition (165). Her anchors were balanced on the bulwarks which would indicate that they were used quite often. She had the slight rake of bow of the latter day

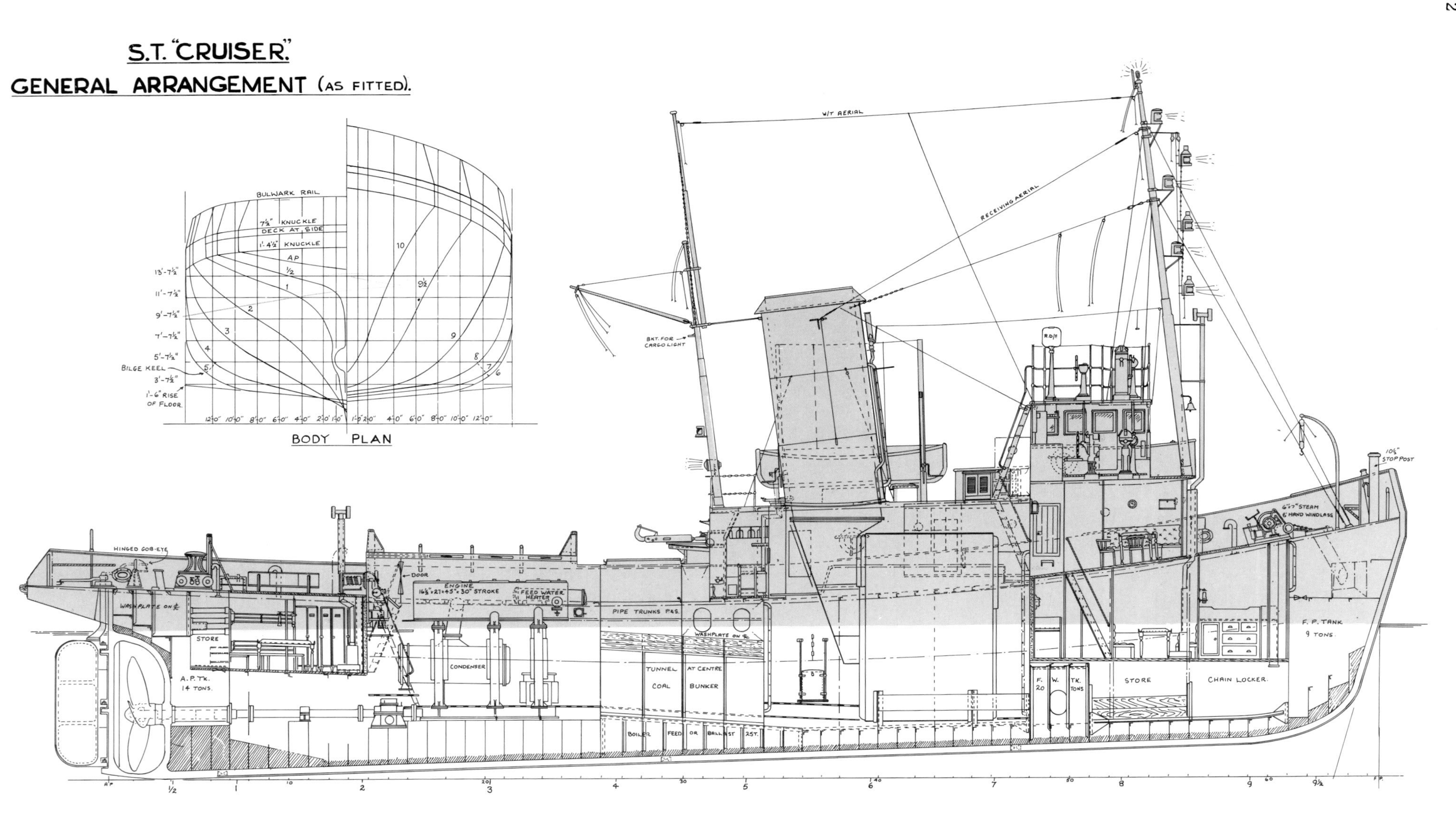

S.T. "CRUISER."
GENERAL ARRANGEMENT (AS FITTED).
BODY PLAN
BULWARK RAIL
7½" KNUCKLE
DECK AT SIDE
1'-4½" KNUCKLE
AP
½
1
2
3
4
5
10
9½
9
8
7
6
13'-7½"
11'-7½"
9'-7½"
7'-7½"
5'-7½"
BILGE KEEL
3'-7½"
1'-6" RISE OF FLOOR
12'0" 10'0" 8'0" 6'0" 4'0" 2'0" 1'0" 1'0" 2'0" 4'0" 6'0" 8'0" 10'0" 12'0"
W/T AERIAL
RECEIVING AERIAL
BKT. FOR CARGO LIGHT
RD/F
10½" STOP POST
6"×7" STEAM & HAND WINDLASS
HINGED GOB-EYE
WASHPLATE ON ℄
DOOR
ENGINE
16½"+27"+45"×30" STROKE
FEED WATER HEATER
PIPE TRUNKS P&S.
WASHPLATE ON ℄
STORE
A. P. TK. 14 TONS.
CONDENSER
TUNNEL
AT CENTRE
COAL
BUNKER
BOILER
FEED
OR
BALLAST
25T.
F. W. TK. 20 TONS
STORE
CHAIN LOCKER.
F. P. TANK 9 TONS.
AP
½
1
10
2
20
3
4
30
5
40
6
7
50
8
9
60
9½
FP

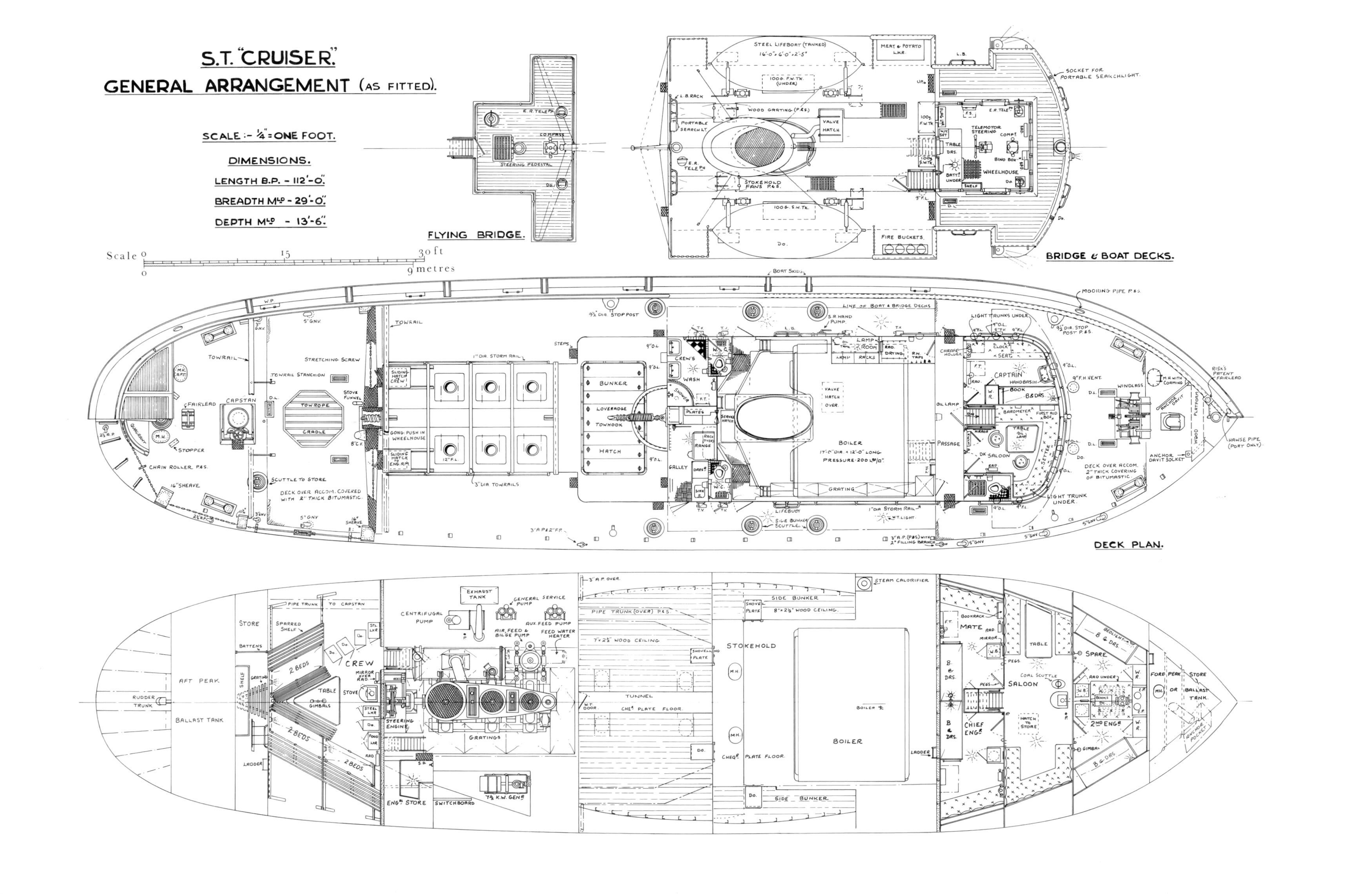

S.T. "CRUISER."
GENERAL ARRANGEMENT (AS FITTED).
SCALE :- 1/4" = ONE FOOT.
DIMENSIONS.
LENGTH B.P. - 112'-0".
BREADTH MLD - 29'-0".
DEPTH MLD - 13'-6".
Scale 0 15 30 ft
0 9 metres
FLYING BRIDGE.
BRIDGE & BOAT DECKS.
DECK PLAN.
STEEL LIFEBOAT (TANKED) 16'-0" × 6'-0" × 2'-5"
MEAT & POTATO LKR.
SOCKET FOR PORTABLE SEARCHLIGHT.
WHEELHOUSE
FIRE BUCKETS.
STOKEHOLD FANS P&S.
VALVE HATCH
CAPSTAN
TOWROPE
CRADLE
BUNKER
LOVERAGE TOWHOOK
HATCH
BOILER 17'-0" DIA. × 12'-0" LONG PRESSURE 200 LB/□"
CAPTAIN
SALOON
WINDLASS
STOKEHOLD
BOILER
TUNNEL
CREW
MATE
CHIEF ENGR
2ND ENGR
SPARE
AFT PEAK.
BALLAST TANK
STEERING ENGINE
ENGR STORE
SWITCHBOARD

wooden tugs, and a nicely rounded stern. The 'B' on the paddle box indicated her ownership; Francis Batey. Arbroath is best known as a fishing harbour, but Wm.K. McDonald had three small tugs there until 1911.

Dundee and the Tay were busy with tugs at one time. The Dundee, Perth & London Shipping Co. started with the **Sir William Wallace** (1830) and **Samson** (1840) in 1840, and finished with the screw tugs **Benvie** (1915) and **Buddon** (1908) in 1953. The Dundee Harbour Trust have had tugs since the **P.T. Fairweather** of 1871 and only in 1976 did they dispose of their last steam tug the **Harecraig II** (1951). Y.A. Cappon disappeared from the Tay in 1946 after about 30 years in business. For three years he owned the two funnelled paddle tug **Conqueror** (1884) which was one of the last of its design when owned in North Shields until 1956. Another Dundee owner Wm.Cowperthwaite made a mistake when in 1909 he bought the P.T. **Anglia** (1885); she must have had a jinx on her as she had already been in collision four times and beached once. In 1913 she went ashore and became a total loss. During the building of the second Tay railway bridge F.Warren of Newcastle maintained a number of tugs at Dundee. The new bridge was built in sections by the quayside on pontoons, and half a dozen tugs were required to tow the pontoon out into the river and to hold it in position while it was jacked into place. One of the tugs, the **Iron King** (1880) featured in the 'Dundee Whale' episode (164). The Scotsman 2nd January 1884: Extraordinary Adventure With a Whale (condensed):

The steam tug **Iron King** returned to Broughty Ferry at midday yesterday after having engaged with the large whale which was harpooned in the Tay on Monday morning and the account of the hunt as given by those on board shows that they have had a most extraordinary adventure.

When it was learned that local boats had harpooned a whale in the Firth it was deemed advisable to send a steam tug to render assistance. Accordingly the **Iron King** proceeded down the river with an experienced whaler on board. The line of one of the boats was transferred to the tug and steam was shut off to the engines. The whale swam wildly about despite the drag of the tug and the two whale boats. The men in the boats thrust lances deep into the whale which continued up and down the river, in the course of which it overturned one of the boats. As darkness fell there was no sign of the fish weakening despite the loss of blood and in the course of the night two ropes broke leaving the whale towing the tug, first out towards the Bell Rock and then towards Montrose. It then turned south until it reached the Firth of Forth, when it once again turned north. When daylight approached, one of the whaleboats, having no harpoon, discharged from its harpoon gun two marlin spikes, followed by a bar of iron, and then sundry nuts and bolts until all available projectiles were finished. Although this slowed the whale down, it later seemed to revive and set off again until the last rope broke. The tug then put steam on her engines and followed the whale in the hope of picking up the broken line but on the seas becoming rough the chase was abandoned. and the tug returned to Dundee. The whale was of "hunchback" type about 70' long with fins 10' long and a tail about 15' across which gave the fish a tremendous pulling power.

On the south side of Fife are a number of harbours associated with the fishing industry, but even here tugs have seen service. Peter McLeod of Alloa had a small shipyard and he also ran a fleet of tugs which often doubled as passenger vessels on the ferry services which he provided across the Forth. On the other side of the Firth lies Grangemouth and it has seen a tidy number of tugs starting with the **W.P.T. Venus** (1857) owned by John Strong (later George). A. McKay started in 1868 with the new **W.P.T. Rapid** (165) followed by the **I.P.T. Jupiter** (1876) which worked also as a pleasure boat. Wm. Taylor launched his fleet in 1890 with the **Samson** (1878) which was one of the tugs employed by Sir Wm. Arroll during the building of the Forth Bridge. The Forth Towing

164

__Iron King__ is seen towing out one of the spans for the new Tay railway bridge; the other tug can just be seen on the right. There is no one at the wheel which is surprising for a single engined tug which could not be steered with her engines. The man on the paddle box is probably relaying instructions from the bowler hatted official on the pontoon through the open back of the engine house to the engineer at the controls.

Danny *(above) of the Aberdeen Steam Tug Company was originally a Naval tug built in 1918 as* ***Mary Tavy.***
PHOTO: Don Smith.

Rapid *(below) is seen here at Montrose and was retained there to assist with the seasonal grain ships loading at Montrose by her Newcastle owner, Francis Batey. Note the 'B' for Batey on the paddle box. She was built on the banks of the Tyne at Hepples yard in 1868.*

Company came into existence in 1892 and in 1895 they amalgamated with A. McKay to form the Grangemouth and Forth Towing Company which survives today having owned about 25 tugs. They provided passenger and excursion services and also stationed a paddle tug at Methil until a few years ago, the last being the **Roker** (1904) which was scrapped in 1966. Her predecessor the **Elie** had the unusual feature of having her funnel before the paddle boxes (Plate 19). The fleet made extensive use of paddle tugs up to the war. They had an ex-Dutch ocean going tug, the **Dundas** (ex **Atlantic**), a typical Dutchman with two funnels, and she was lost during the D-Day invasion. Almost next door is Bo'ness (now unused). Here J. Wilson ruled the roost from 1876 when he bought the **W.P.T. Boreas** (1872) and owned 17 assorted paddle tugs, screw tugs and ferry steamers, until taken over by the Leith Salvage and Towage Company in 1919. There were some fancy names among them - **Pero Gomez** (1869), **Royal Norman** (1881) and **Betefdoe** (1877). Taken over or amalgamated at the same time was the Nicholson Steam Tug and Salvage Company which had begun as Wm. Nicholson in about 1880. Through their hands had passed the **Conqueror** (1884), mentioned earlier. Altogether 19 tugs were owned from the **W.P.T. Earl of Windsor** (1867), 79 tons to the **R. Nicholson** (1914), 200 tons. The latter's half model showed a very sharp rise of floor and she was reported to have been very 'tender', rolling over frighteningly if she was 'girted', i.e. across the tow rope. Also into the new fleet went Archibald McKinnon's tugs which Nicholson had taken over in 1911. McKinnon had owned over 11 tugs from 1897 including the odd looking **Earl of Powis** (1882) which had a long superstructure reminiscent of the American tug. She had originally been a tender owned by the Shropshire Union Railway. Two of the steam tugs which were transferred were the **Emperor of India** (1877), an iron paddle tug, and the **Renown**, a small screw tug built in Holland in 1879. Quite an important fleet, the Leith Salvage and Towage owned 28 tugs of varying sizes. They ranged from the **Lady Cecilia** (1921) 66 tons, a craft tug (98) from London, to the **Bullger** (1883) 364 tons (named after the then chairman's dog); she was a big two funnelled salvage tug which had been built as the **Stormcock** (29) for Liverpool and had been sold to the Admiralty and renamed **Traveller**. When she was wrecked in 1934 she was replaced by another **Bullger** (1907) ex. **Cartmel** of Barrow, another two funnelled tug. As a heavy lift vessel for salvage work they employed the **Storeton** (1910) which had been a Mersey ferry, extensively altered. In 1953 the Leith Harbour Commission took over and shortly after introduced the first motor tug, the **Martello** (1957). Towage on the Forth goes right back to 1817 when the **Tug** was launched. The early tug owners in Leith were Helen Stoker, Jas. McGregor, Geo. Jamieson, Jas. Minto and Alex Bridges, predecessor to A. McKinnon. One of the Jamieson tugs, the **Fiery Cross** (1867) which he had used extensively for passenger carrying was burned on the shore to celebrate one of Queen Victoria's birthdays.

There was in Berwick a tug called after the town, built in 1859, and further down the coast at Warkworth, Hugh Andrews owned three tugs from 1876, the third tug being appropriately named **Coquet** (1892) after the river on which the town stands. Blyth has always been a busy coal exporting town and George Dinsdale was the best known owner of tugs there. His company was later restyled the Blyth Steam Tug Company. There had been a couple of smaller fleets at one time, J. Dent and Octavious Jewels but after Geo. Dinsdale started in 1890 they faded out. The Blyth Tug Co. as it is known today is maintained by the Tyne Tug Co. of Newcastle. The fleet included some of the last paddle tugs on the North-East Coast, the **Steel** (1890), **Greatham** (1893) and the **Earl of Beaconsfield** (1889), finally scrapped in 1958. For many years the Harbour Commission has stationed a tug in the harbour, one of the last being the **Chipchase**.

Towing has its roots on the Tyne; by 1821 there were 14 steamboats operating as tugs, among them the **Perseverance, Swift, Eagle, Enterprise, Speedwell, Hope, Swift, Tyne, Two Brothers, Indefatigable, Duchess of Northumberland, Navigator, Safety** and **Union**. On the Tyne the list of tug owners runs into hundreds, so only the owners of the larger fleets with the approximate number of tugs owned can be listed. The big difficulty for anyone not steeped in local history is to know when a common surname relates to a family concern or to rival owners. Then too, the tradition of dividing the ownership of vessels into 64 shares was very strong on the Tyne and many owners had shares in tugs, other than those registered in their own name. The initials in front of the surname are all the different names in the registers. Although so many tugs were employed on the Tyne, most of them were small, old and secondhand, and many of them got themselves into trouble or just sank, but bear in mind they put to sea in all manner of weather. One of H. Anderson's tugs had been involved in a rather peculiar incident; in December 1867 he sent his wooden paddle tug **Renown** (1863, 85.6ft. 88 tons. 45 n.h.p.) 275 miles northwards to Inverness to pick up the sailing ship *Tornado* and to tow her to Sunderland. For some reason not specified the barque kept her fore and aft sails set while being towed and 'the agreement was that the *Tornado* would keep the course and that the tug should keep right ahead of her!' A few miles past Fraserburgh the tug ran aground and although a warning was called to the crew of the *Tornado* she came on and struck the rocks alongside the tug, being badly holed. The tug got herself off with little damage. The Cairnbulg Reef where the incident occurred was a dangerous reef, well known locally, but the report does not comment on carelessness or lack of local knowledge on the part of either crew.

(H)(J) Anderson	8	(Andrew)(Allen)(Geo.)(Leonard)(Wm.) Brown	48
Armstrong & Co.	9	(J),(C),(M),(T) Charlton	15
Andrew Bain	9	(J),(R),(S),(W) Chisholm	30
(J),(Wm),(D),(S) Bests	9		
(J),(R),(C) Boag	10		

R.Chisholm's wooden paddle tug **Guide** (1866, 75.8ft. 58 tons. 24 n.h.p.) was in collision in February

1867 when she was struck abaft the paddle box by the S.S. *Euclid* 4 miles from Tynemouth. As a result of the collision the boiler burst and the tug sank.

Coulson Tug Co.	12	Joseph Crosthwaite	9

In 1901 J. Crosthwaite's wooden paddle tug **Selina** (1877, 85.6ft. 78 tons, 35 n.h.p.) was seeking and fell in with the *Wineland*. The tug asked £5, the ship refused and offered £2. As the bargaining proceeded the ship ran aground, the **Selina** assisted her and demanded salvage. The court, however, refused to grant the claim saying that the tug should have prevented the grounding!

(J),(O),(P) Cunningham	10	(P),(R),(M),(W) Dixon	11

In 1859 R. Dixon's wooden paddle tug **William and Mary** (1855, 71.2ft. 54 tons. 20 n.h.p.) was badly damaged when one of her boilers exploded killing one of the crew. Her normal speed was 6 to 7 knots while the speed of the ship she was attending was 11 to 12 knots. To gain the extra speed the engineer had loaded chains and weights on the safety valve. She was repaired and put back into service but she only lasted until 1865 when she was wrecked.

John Dry's Steam Tugs [13]. One of John Dry's tugs, the **Great Emperor** (1909) towed a dock gate from Wallsend to Portsmouth in 1913.

(J),(M),(W) Dodds	19	(J),(W) Hall	31
(A),(J),(R) Forster	24	(J),(W) Heads	14
(J),(H),(T),(R) Gibson	19	(J),(G),(R),(W) Hunter	10
(J),(G).(R),(W) Gray	23		

R. Hedley: "In 1902 the **Great Emperor** (1876) owned by J. Hedley left the Tyne for Port Mulgrave. The bottom crosshead of the engine broke and the guide rod went through the vessel's bottom causing her to sink off Port May. Wind SW.4."

(J),(R) Kerr	8	(F),(L),(T) Newton	13
(G),(W) Lamb	9	(E),(S) Oliver	8
Lambton,Hetton & Joicey Collieries	11	(J),(W) Ostens	18
J. Minto	10	Palmers S.B.& Ironworks	8
(J),(E),(R),(W) Moore	10	(B),(E),(M) Pearson	20
(T),(W) Nelson	13	(M),(R) Redhead	39

J. Redhead: In 1901 the **Sensation** of 1877 wood, owned by R. Redhead on a voyage from Tyne to Middlesbrough. Breakdown in engineroom caused the vessel to leak and founder 10 miles N.E. of Hartlepool. Wind W.S.W.5."

(W),(G),(J) Reid	12	(C),(J),(R),(T),(W) Robson	39

One of W. Robson's tugs was involved in a legal wrangle in 1868 when the wooden paddle tug **Harkaway** (1859, 83.0ft. 71 tons. 30 n.h.p.) asked another paddle tug to assist her while towing the ship *Bosphorous*, the **Renown** belonging to H. Anderson (mentioned earlier). At this time an agreement was in force that, when the assistance of a second tug was requested £1 was added to the original towing 'foy' (fee) and the total 'foy' was then divided 2/3 to the first tug to be engaged, 1/3 to the second tug. In this case the **Renown** had agreed to help for £1 and had been granted the privilege of towing the ship about in the river and the docks, which Mr. Robson considered cancelled normal arrangements. The court agreed with him.

(A),(R),(G),(J),(W) Scott (10). The **Robert Scott** (1862, 82.3ft. 77 tons. 33 n.h.p.) was sold to Russia in 1864 but was wrecked soon after setting out on her delivery voyage; one account states that she went ashore at Anstruther, another gives the location as 6 miles south of Peterhead, nearly 120 miles away!

T. Simpson	8	(R),(G),(W) Stephenson	31
Mr. Smart	12	H. Stobbs	10
(G),(R),(W) Smith	18	(J),(M),(T) Stoker	16

The wooden paddle tugs in use on the Tyne were quite small but this did not stop John Stoker of North Shields from sending his 86' **Electric** (1883) 100 miles out into the North Sea in 1912 on a rescue mission.

(W),(M) Storey	11	(G),(J),(R),(W) Todd	16
A. Strong	22	F. Warren	10
(J),(R),(T),(W) Thompson	14	(J),(T),(R),(W) Watson	15

When in 1862 Mr. Gladstone visited Newcastle, 29 tugboats and ferries accompanied the eight-oared Commissioners Barge up the river followed by numerous small craft. Part exchange was not uncommon and builders sometimes took an old tug in part payment. In 1893 the Tyne Steam Shipping Co. bought the **W.D.S.**. a screw tug, and Schlesinger Davis & Co., Wallsend, the builders accepted the wooden paddle tug **Iona** of 1866 in part exchange.

An entry in an old notebook belonging to the tugowner Thomas Appleby relating to the running of his wooden paddle tug **Helen Macgregor** gives an insight into the economics of tug owning in 1891: Aug. 24 Schooner to Hebburn by sea (£1.13.0); Aug. 25 Nil; Aug. 26 Nil; Aug. 27 Schooner to Stockton from sea (£5.0.0.); Aug. 28 Schooner to Hebburn from sea (£2.10.0). Wages £5.13.0; Overtime 10s.0.; 12 tons of coal (at 6/5d.) £3.17.0. He thus made a loss of 17 shillings!

The American river steamer and tug races are often mentioned but the Tyne also held races. In 1847 Mr. A. Strong with his **Scottish Maid** (1846) made a challenge to Mr. Joseph Hall who owned the **Harvest Home** (1847). The tugs had similar engines and boilers, but were made by different builders. The race was 12 miles from the Tyne to Sunderland and back, the time of the winner was 1hr. 12 min. Other more powerful tugs joined in but were easily out distanced.

Soon after World War II, only three tug fleets were left active on the Tyne but the work dwindled still further, and these have combined into a single unit, Tyne Tugs Ltd. The first, John Batey started in about 1840 with a little wooden paddler of 42 tons followed by the **Montrose** in 1862, 51 tons. As mentioned earlier he sent tugs to Montrose each year to assist the handling of grain ships, a service which he provided from 1857 to 1904. The paddle tug **John Batey** (1884) was sent to Ramsgate to stand by while the Board of Trade tug **Aid** was on the slip for overhaul.

Although at 96.3ft. long the **John Batey** might be regarded as a river tug, she actually went as far afield as Cuxhaven in Germany to pick up a tow. She took in tow a full rigged ship the *Jupiter*, though only after she had been arrested for hoisting the pilot jack before the pilot had actually boarded her. A minor breach of sea etiquette but it cost her owners 150 marks.

The Tyne was a busy river and collisions were frequent. One of Batey's tugs the **Titan** (ex **Atlas** (1865) Watkins, London) was damaged four times and sank once within a period of ten years. The Batey tugs had a yellow funnel with a blue Maltese cross. J.R. Lawson started ownership about the same time, commencing with small single-engined wooden paddle tugs, such as the **Expert** (1856, 75ft. 52 tons). His **William** (1865) appears in a painting and is shown towing a collier brig in 1873 in a rough sea. This is not necessarily artist's licence as Tyne tugs were to be found at sea in all conditions. The **Ulysses** (1874) is remembered for one of her exploits when, in 1880, she went out in seemingly impossible conditions and, continually swamped by heavy seas, succeeded in bringing in to safety a steamer in distress, the *Isaac Rennock*. In 1895 she performed a similar rescue with the **Endeavour**. Both vessels were waterlogged by the time they reached safety (164). The Lawson funnel was light ochre with a black top, bearing a black diamond. In 1920 the two companies amalgamated under the title of Lawson-Batey Tugs Ltd.

The next firm was the Ridley Steam Tug Company, also of long standing, one of the earliest tugs being the **Wonder** of 1848. The funnel colours of this company changed to match their most important contract, and the last was the Bergen Shipping Co., a black funnel with three white bands, and these were the colours of the **Reliant** before she went to Seaham Harbour. The Ridley tugs seem to keep out of trouble and out of the news. However in 1930 their **William Fallows** (1888), in company with the **Rescue** (1869) belonging to France Fenwick Tyne & Wear salvaged the steamer *Olavus* after a collision in the Tyne and received an award of £450 for their efforts. Their screw tug **Wonder** (1921), built as the French **Bacalan** was in service at Seaham Harbour until recently. The firm bought a number of foreign built tugs including the **Trover** (1920) ex-**Koenigstein**, and the newly built motor tug **Impetus** (1954), one of the first diesel tugs on the river. The **Trover** was an unusual tug for the Tyne having an icebreaker bow and being fully fitted out with salvage pumps.

With her upright bulwarks and lack of sheer the **Premier** was not a very pretty vessel, but many of the old tugs suffered from the same complaint; she did have some scrollwork on her bow but it has been painted over. The bridge was fully enclosed by a waist high wooden screen which surrounded the whole area forward of the funnel with access via a ladder up the front (138). Even in the 1920s she retained the fidded topmast and gaff. Her funnel had the same colours as her tow, the Thule of the Svenska Lloyd. The **Premier** (1894, 79.4 ft. 83 tons. 350 i.h.p.) saw service on the Thames in Grimsby, on the Tyne and on the Forth.

The last owner was France Fenwick Tyne & Wear Co. Ltd. with the most colourful funnel on the river, white with black top, and a black anchor on a broad band of blue and white stripes. The colours of the France Fenwick funnel are said to originate from the sleeve band worn by the police in Sunderland which the company adopted as meaning - "Safety and Security". This was a relatively new fleet started in 1918 by an amalgamation of Sunderland Towage Co., Anchor Steam Tug Co. and J. Dawson. In turn the Coulson Tug Co. (1925), Redhead and Dry (1944), Lambton, Hetton & Joicey Collieries (1945) and R.L. Cook (1947) were absorbed to make this the largest fleet on the North East Coast. They kept tugs in Newcastle and in Sunderland, where they had paddle tugs up until 1967 when the **Eppleton Hall** (1914) was sold to Seaham Harbour. They were one of the last companies to use paddle tugs and their tug **Conqueror** (1884) was the last twin-funnelled

168

***Ulysses** tows the S.S. Pear Branch out of the Tyne. She is a typical iron paddler with twin funnels. Note the galley funnel is also buff with a black top, lacking only the black diamond. Built in 1874 for London owners she went to the Tyne in 1895 (100.6', 115 tons gross, 70 n.h.p.).*

tug to operate on a U.K.river. In 1955 they carried out a very successful motor conversion to the screw tug **George V** which had been built in 1915 for Redhead and Dry's Tugs (69). The streamlining of the funnel and superstructure gave her a most modern appearance (175). Among the tugs which they have in Sunderland are some of American origin, ex-wartime tugs with the typical long superstructure, the only ones of their kind in Britain. Now as Tyne Tugs Ltd. there are only twelve tugs left on the Tyne for shiphandling.

In 1923 France Fenwick of Sunderland ordered the **Marsden** and **Hendon** (171) from J.P. Rennoldson of South Shields (105.0ft, 241 tons. 950 i.h.p.) to be suitable for coastal towing work; powerful tugs with a large bunker capacity of 128 tons. On the fore deck there was a big double cruciform bollard in place of the more usual North-East coast towing hook. Aft they had two sets of towing hooks, a spring-loaded hook amidships attached to the boiler casing which was strengthened with steel plate knees, and right in the stern a plain hook for towing lighters and barges close up to the stern on a short tow rope. These tugs had a large wheelhouse but most of the space was taken up by the steam steering engine; when a lot of manoeuvring was required the noise in the wheelhouse rendered speech nearly impossible. The short plated-in section below the bridge wings was a common feature of the N.E. coast tugs. Around the top of the rudder post the drawing shows a band brake. Out of about 400 drawings examined during the preparation of this book only these tugs and the **Rollcall** had this feature. Not uncommon on coasters, the idea was to relieve the sudden strains on the steering chains (and helmsman's arms) as the vessel's rudder was hammered by rough seas. Two of the older generations of tug skippers, when questioned, had never heard of this device on a tug and would not have used it under any circumstances anyway.

The **Marsden** was sold in 1926 to owners in Argentina, but the **Hendon** continued in service until 1966. During the Second World War she had a very exciting career and on numerous occasions she rendered assistance to vessels in distress, either through enemy action or from damage due to grounding. On one occasion the ship *Eskdene* had been torpedoed off the north-east coast but was being kept afloat by her cargo of timber. She was taken in tow and in worsening weather conditions she was towed to the Tyne, but as she entered the river an explosion aboard the **Eskdene** caused further damage and she began to sink. The **Hendon** and her companion of this adventure, the **George V**, immediately went full speed ahead and managed to beach the casualty clear of the main channel.

The River Tyne Improvement Commissioners have had a long association with towing on the Tyne. In 1880 they had a fleet of 6 tugs in commission:

No.2 steam tug	**Cowen**	25 hp.	Commenced work 1859
No.3	**Usher**	32 hp.	1860
No.4	**Northern Light**	38 hp.	1861
No.5	**Moselle**	38 hp.	1861
No.6	**Commissioner**	45 hp.	1862
No.7	**Progress**	38 hp.	1863

They always maintained a tender which they would use for transporting visitors or the members of the Commission on tours of Inspection. The last was the **J.C. Stevenson** (1883) (118) which was fitted with a removable saloon so that she could be used as a tug between trips. She was later bought by France Fenwick and renamed **Dunelm**, remaining in their hands from 1923 to 1956. In contrast to the shiphandling tugs, Smith's Dock Co. Ltd. had a number of small tugs for general use, ranging from 27 to 39 tons. These had no name but were usually marked with the owners' name and a number, eg. **Smiths Dock No.1.**

Sunderland was another busy port where the tug fraternity thrived. R. Lister was early in the scene in 1847 with his **Jack Tar** of 1829, a wooden paddler of 20 tons. Michael Thurlbeck was another early starter in 1857 with the **Queen** (1837), 50 tons, and the **Prince Albert** of 1840. The **Gleaner** (1856) was lost in 1859 when her boilers burst off Blyth. The tug drifted ashore, was got off, but sank off Tynemouth as she was being towed back to Sunderland. She was owned by Matthew Ross. Also on the river in the 1840s was Charles Taylor with the **Pilot** (1831) and **Haswell** (1844). W. Nicholson and T.M. Scott started in the 1850/60s and then some well known names appeared in the 1880s, J. Irwing, R.L. Baister and R.L. Cook Towage. One familiar sight was the **King Edward VII** (1901) with a funnel which sported a 'strange device' (41). Cook's tugs included the **Stag** (1885), an attractive wooden paddler of 123 tons. (Just to confuse matters Irwing had a **Stag** at the same time, a wooden paddle tug of 86 tons, 1884). The North East Coast is a dangerous lee shore and many sailing ships needed the help of tugs to tow them out of trouble. In 1897 the *Barbara* called for assistance and four tugs from Sunderland were involved:

Cruiser	W.P.T. 1880	84 tons.	4 hands.	35 nhp.	value £2000	Award shared £700.
Earl of Glamorgan	W.P.T. 1869	82 tons.	4 hands.	45 nhp.	£1500	
Electric	W.P.T. 1884	62 tons.	4 hands	30 nhp.	£2200	
Pactolus	W.P.T. 1870	93 tons.	4 hands.	38 nhp.	£1600	

Cruiser and **Earl of Glamorgan** belonged to R.L. Cook, the **Electric** to T. Hutchison, and the **Pactolus** to J. Irwing. Salvage did not always produce the hoped for rewards. In 1904 the wooden paddle tug **Rescue**, belonging to R.L. Cook of Sunderland, (1883, 92.0ft. 96 tons. 400 e.h.p.) rendered assistance to the *Diana* in the North Sea for an agreed sum of £200. When the case came to court the owners of the *Diana* contested the agreement and luckily for them it was put aside and the owners of the tug received only £25 for their services. (Incidentally the year before R.L. Cook had claimed only 190 e.h.p. as the power of their tug.)

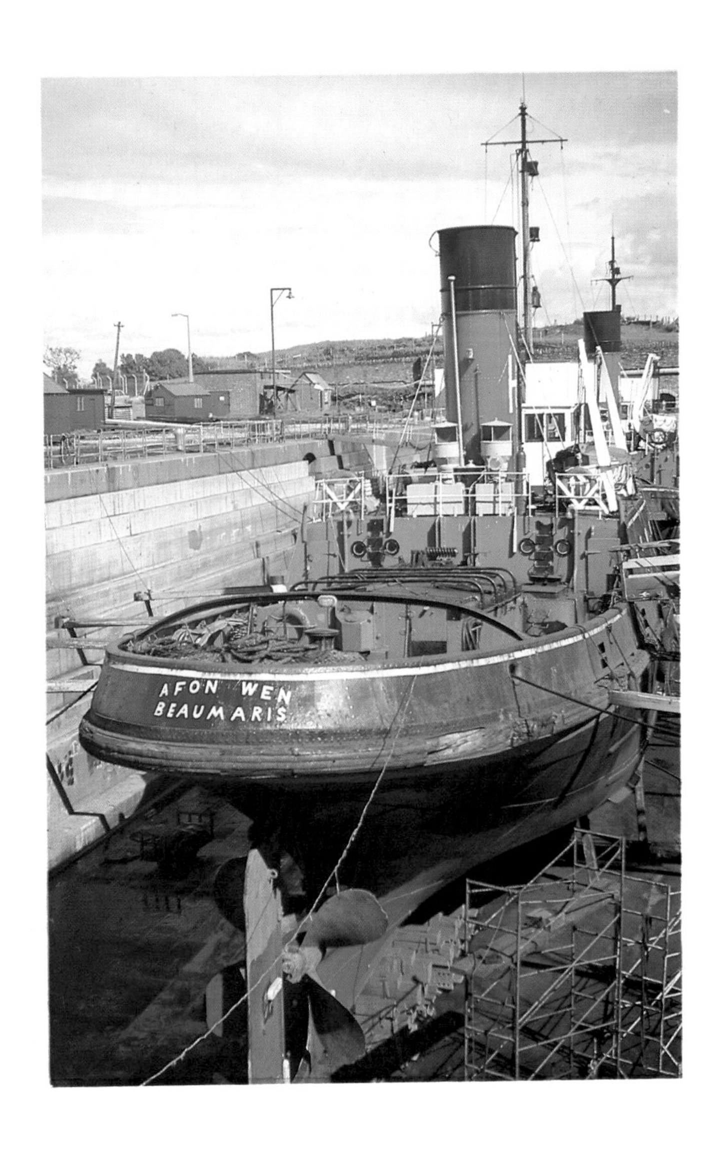

Afon Wen *was built in 1951 by A. Hall as* ***Rosegarth*** *for Rea Towing Co. Ltd., Liverpool and was sold with* ***Applegarth*** *(which became* ***Afon Cefni****) to Holyhead Towing in 1970. Here they are both seen in the large drydock at Holyhead.*

Antony *and* ***Trevol*** *(below) are twin tugs built in 1921 by Cox of Falmouth for R. & J.H. Rea of Liverpool for service in their Bristol fleet (85.2 ft,137 tons and 650 i.h.p.) they were bought by W.J. Reynolds of Plymouth in 1960 and 1963 respectively and are seen here in his colours. At first glance they look like the single screw H.S. tug and in fact the dimensions are almost identical. The 'timberheads' forward are in fact wooden and the pair on the quarter are shaped to lean inboard. Reynolds had in fact already owned two 'H.S.' tugs (29 and 28) which had been given the names* ***Antony*** *and* ***Trevol****.*

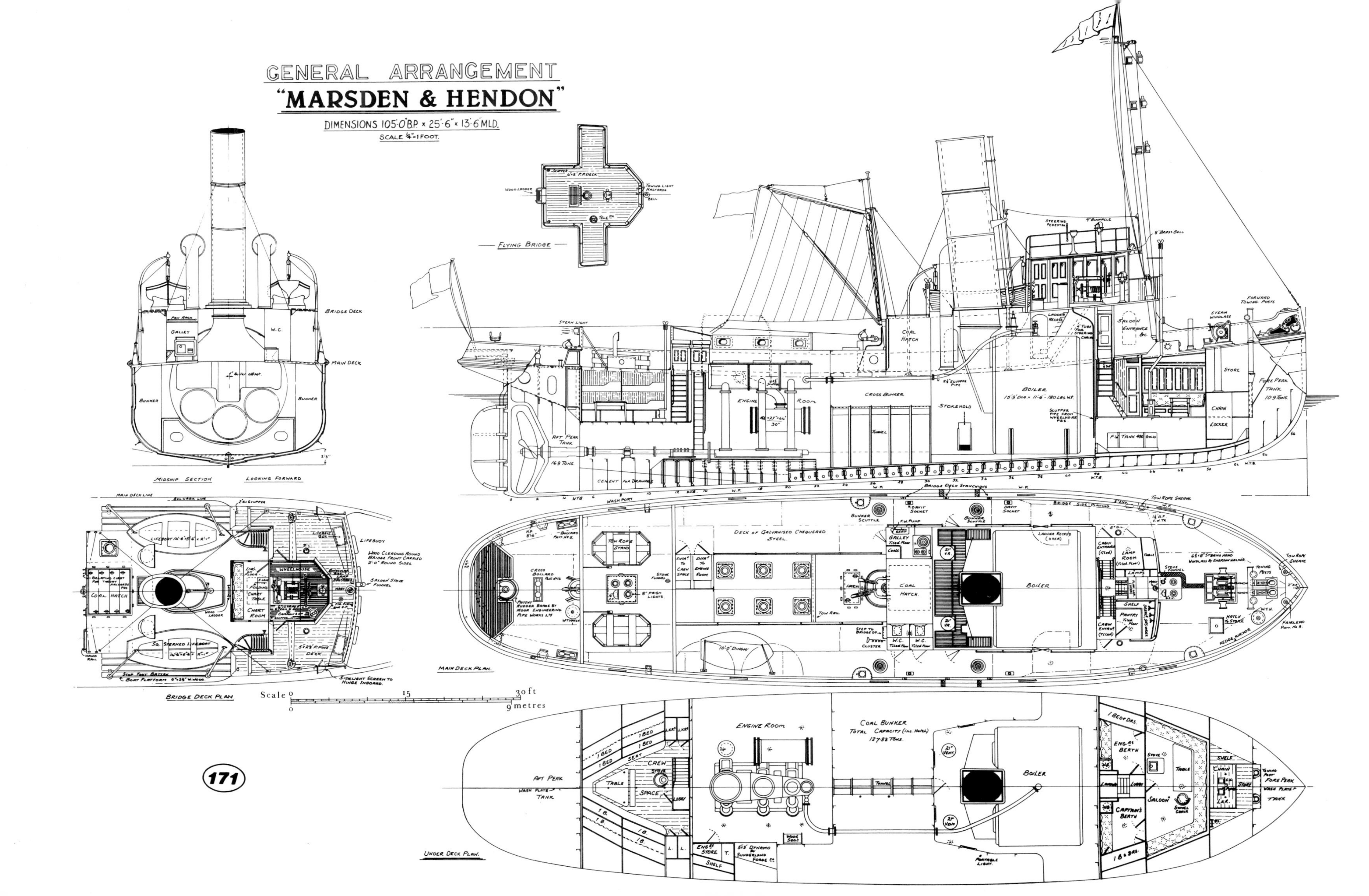
GENERAL ARRANGEMENT
"MARSDEN & HENDON"
DIMENSIONS 105'0"B.P. × 25'6" × 13'6" MLD.
SCALE ¼"=1 FOOT.
FLYING BRIDGE
MIDSHIP SECTION
LOOKING FORWARD
BRIDGE DECK
MAIN DECK
GALLEY
W.C.
BUNKER
BRIDGE DECK PLAN
MAIN DECK PLAN
UNDER DECK PLAN
WHEELHOUSE
CHART ROOM
CHART TABLE
COAL HATCH
LIFEBUOY
WOOD LADDER
TOWING LIGHT HALYARDS
BELL
STERN LIGHT
STEERING PEDESTAL
9" BINNACLE
8" BRASS BELL
FORWARD TOWING POSTS
STEAM WINDLASS
SALOON ENTRANCE &c
STORE
FORE PEAK TANK 10.9 TONS.
CHAIN LOCKER
BOILER
15'9" DIA × 11'6" - 180 LBS W.P.
STOKEHOLD
CROSS BUNKER
TUNNEL
ENGINE ROOM
AFT PEAK TANK 16.9 TONS.
CEMENT FOR DRAINAGE
WASH PORT
BRIDGE DECK STANCHIONS
TOW ROPE SHEAVE
DECK OF GALVANISED CHEQUERED STEEL.
TOW ROPE STAND
CROSS BOLLARD
TOW RAIL
10'0" DINGHY
BUNKER SCUTTLE
DAVIT SOCKET
LADDER RECESS (OVER)
LAMP ROOM
LAMPS
PANTRY
SHELF
CABIN ENTRANCE
TOWING POSTS
KEDGE ANCHOR
W.T.H.
HATCH TO STORE
FAIRLEAD
COAL BUNKER
TOTAL CAPACITY (inc. Hatch) 127.83 TONS.
ENGINE ROOM
ENG^RS BERTH
CAPTAIN'S BERTH
SALOON
TABLE
STOVE
1 BED or DRS.
1 B & DRS.
CREW SPACE
SEAT
1 BED
1 B.
AFT PEAK
WASH PLATE
TANK
ENG^RS STORE
SHELF
5½ DYNAMO by SUNDERLAND FORGE Co.
PORTABLE LIGHT.
Scale 0 15 30 ft
0 9 metres
171

H.M.S. BRIGAND, BUCCANEER.

Scale 0 — 15 — 30 ft
0 — 9 metres

SCALE : ¼" = 1 Foot.

AS FITTED.

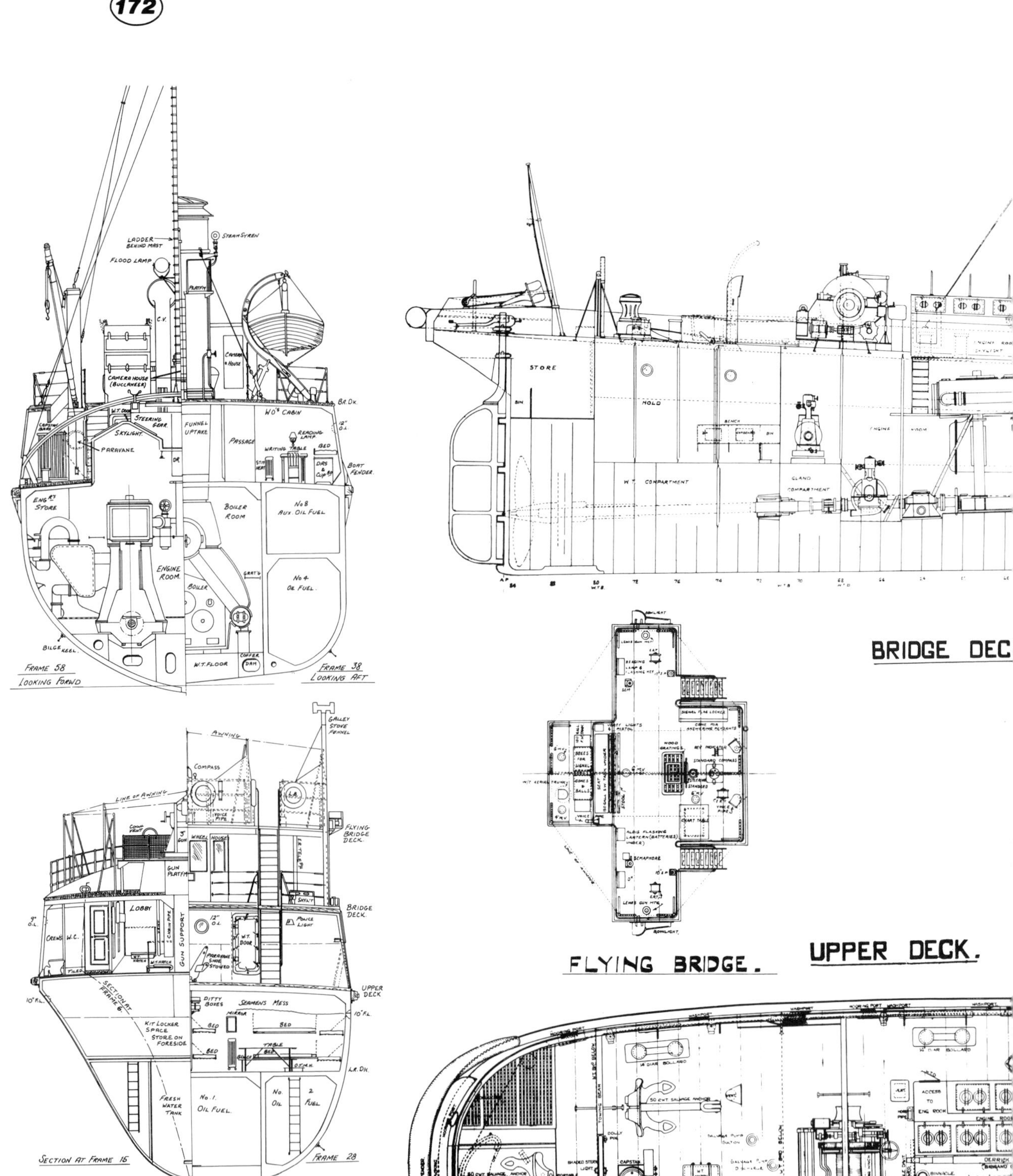

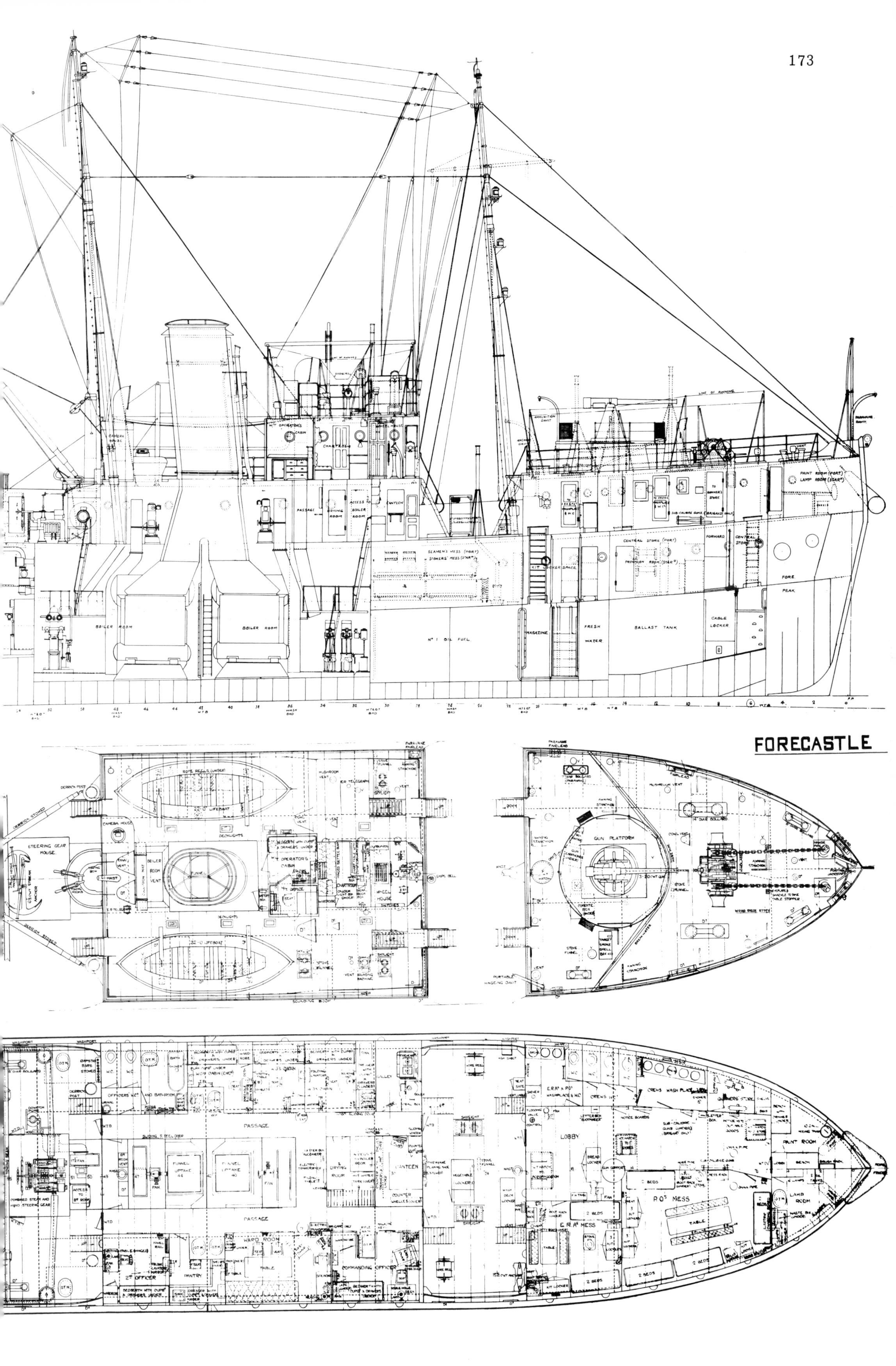
FORECASTLE
BOILER ROOM
BOILER ROOM
Nº 1 OIL FUEL
MAGAZINE
FRESH WATER
BALLAST TANK
CABLE LOCKER
FORE PEAK
CHART ROOM
WHEEL HOUSE
CANTEEN
PASSAGE
DRYING ROOM
ACCESS TO BOILER ROOM
KIT LOCKER SPACE
CENTRAL STORE (PORT)
PROVISION ROOM (STARᴰ)
PAINT ROOM (PORT)
LAMP ROOM (STARᴰ)
STEERING GEAR HOUSE
FUNNEL
GUN PLATFORM
PASSAGE
LOBBY
PAINT ROOM
LAMP ROOM
TABLE
2 BEDS
WARD ROOM
PANTRY
2ND OFFICER
COMMANDING OFFICER
CANTEEN
DRYING ROOM
COMBINED STEAM AND HAND STEERING GEAR

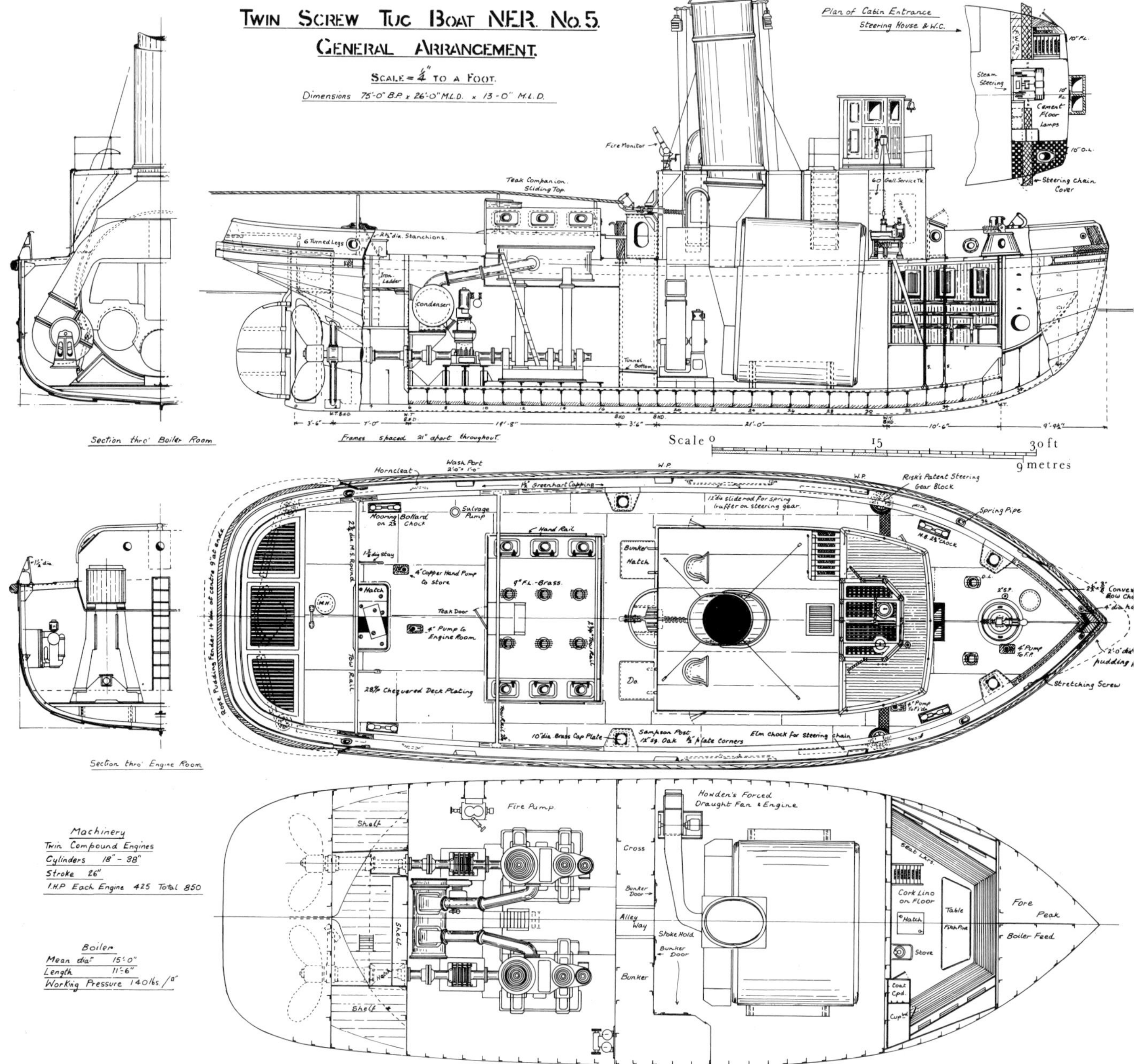

(174) ***N.E.R. No. 5** was built by Cook, Welton & Gemmell. After 15 years at West Hartlepool she became **T.I.C. Tug No. 2.** of Newcastle until 1954 when she was sold to the Newport Screw Towing Company who renamed her **Monnow.***

The River Wear Commissioners kept several small tugs to tow their dredgers and hoppers. There was the **Cinema Star** of 1884 and a couple of ex-**Tid** tugs, the **Pallion** and the **Biddick**, built 1944 and 1943 respectively. Sunderland Towage, which was taken over by France Fenwick Tyne & Wear Co. had a tug called the **Marsden** (1906) which was taken out to Gallipoli and was wrecked during the campaign there.

Seaham Harbour is a 'hole in the wall' port, surrounded by high cliffs, and since 1888 there has been at least one tug there. The **Eppleton Hall** (Plate 19) was there before going off to America, and the **Reliant** spent several years in operation at Seaham before being rescued for preservation in the Maritime Museum. Now the paddle tugs have gone and the screw tugs have taken over, first the **Wonder** from Newcastle, then the **Conservator** (1925) from Kings Lynn, followed by the **Chipchase** (1953) from Blyth.

At Hartlepool we find British Transport Docks Co. tugs, descended from a fleet of tugs owned by the North Eastern Railway, stationed at Shields, Hartlepool, Middlesbrough and Hull, and later ones being unimaginatively named **N.E.R.No.1, N.E.R.No.2,** etc. An unusual tug which served on the North East coast was the **N.E.R.No.5.** (1922, 75.0ft. 161 tons. 850 i.h.p.), designed for service in West Hartlepool. To ensure that she occupied as little space as possible when she entered the lock with her tow she was built with a length to breadth ratio of 3:1 instead of the more normal 4:1. She had twin screws to make her more manoeuvrable and her square stern served to protect her screws from damage (174), and incidentally to save the tow from damage. Twin-screw tugs have been known to hole their tow in what might otherwise have been a minor collision.

The twin-screw tug **N.E.R.No.5.** was an 'ugly duckling' by any standards with her squat square hull. The hook forward was typical north-east coast practice and it is interesting to note the conical support which carried the circular table on which the hook swivels. The after hook had a most

The attractive colour scheme of the France Fenwick, Tyne & Wear tugs is shown off by the ***President*** *(top), 80 years old when the picture was taken. Built by Readhead's of South Shields in 1876. She was 100.0 ft., 130 tons and 70 n.h.p. (420 i.h.p.) and the design on her paddle box was of the 'fan' type. Built for Limerick she came to the north-east coast in 1891 and was scrapped in 1959.*

The ***George V*** *(bottom) started life in 1915 as a steam tug and she was completely rebuilt as a motor tug in 1954. Here she is seen turning the collier* ***Arundel*** *in 1972.*

unusual shock absorbing system inside the boiler casing emerging through what appears to be a heavy casting.She had a forced draught fan to increase boiler efficiency and as befitted a dock tug her bunker capacity was very small. The check post arrangement of a hook on the metal band on the samson post is reminiscent of that on the naval tug **Rollcall**, as are the rope pudding fenders fore and aft. Her accommodation was minimal, just some benches and a table forward. The steam steering gear was placed in a separate compartment below the bridge.

The Tees was another busy river. George Alder started around 1859 with the **Rapid** (1859) and was in business until about 1929. F.J. Leach began in 1858 with the **Caledonia** of 1846, one of his later tugs was the **Friend to All Nations** of 1863. Graham and Lister ran tugs on the river until 1911 and the fleet included the **Challenger** of 1873 and the **Glen Rosa** of 1895. The Robinson Tug Company was a well known firm which owned about 17 tugs from 1920, one with the name **Samphire Batts** (1893). Another was a very elegant wooden paddle tug the **Sir Geo. Elliott** (1875) (29). Charles Duncan owned about 42 tugs in all, starting in 1857 with the **War Eagle** of 1847, 56 tons and finishing in about 1950 with the **Flying Fish** of 1882, an iron paddle tug bought from Leith. In 1903 they purchased from Irish owners an iron paddle tug called the **Citie of the Tribes** of 1872, a resounding name indeed. Many of the tugs bore a family name: **Dora Duncan** (1891), **Beattie Duncan** (1893) and so on. The London based firm of William Watkins made a short-lived venture on to the Tees in 1911 as Watkins Petrie, when they introduced six tugs including the **Hibernia** (1874), **Liberia** (1900) and **Scotia** (1874). They departed in 1914; apparently giving up against local competition. In 1911 the Tees Tug Company was formed with the Lister tugs as a nucleus and it in turn became the Tees Towing Company in 1920, combining tugs from the Robinson fleet. Among the Tees Tug Company vessels was the **Lingdale** (ex **Lady Vita**) (39) of 1882 originally from Dover, easily recognisable by her twin upright funnels. The new company began to name their tugs with names ending in **Cross**, e.g. **Hutton Cross** (1897), **Ingleby Cross** (1912), which nomenclature they still use today. The company was one of the first to use diesel electric power for a shiphandling tug; the **Acklam Cross** of 1933, and the first to use Voith Schneider propulsion units for ship towage; the **Hutton Cross** of 1958.

The Tees Conservancy Commissioners have owned tugs since 1880, each vessel being named after a member of the board, e.g. **Sir Joseph Pease** of 1896. There was a bit of excitement in 1892 when the military authorities planned to fit machine guns on the paddle tugs **Universe** of 1875 and the **Isaac Wilson** of 1889 and to use them as gunboats to patrol the approaches to the river. As with most river authorities they always had a tender, their last being the **Sir Hugh Bell** of 1913. The tugs varied greatly in size according to the work which they did, and I remember seeing the **Lackenby** (Plate 6) ex-**T.I.D. 182** of 1946 running up the river with the pay clerk aboard calling at each of the Commissioners' vessels and shore establishments.

The **John H. Amos** was the last paddle tug built in Great Britain for civilian owners. She was a river commissioners' tug but she was not provided with the usual big saloon to accommodate the dignitaries who used to inspect the river installations. However she did obviously carry passengers as is shown by the number of lifebelts which were stowed in the boxes on the foredeck and the bridge deck (178). Like the screw tugs of her time she had wood sheathing only over the living quarters to reduce the noise of feet tramping over the deck. Like them also, she had a close stowing anchor in a hawse pipe. The compound diagonal engines were almost unique and, as can be seen, they took up a lot of space below deck, and as a result the mast had to be stepped in a fabricated socket on the deck. She was beamier than the average paddle tug and her lines show a resemblance to those of the **Flying Eagle** of 1928, which was built in the same yard. She was broad for a paddle tug being 110.0ft. x 22.6ft. x 10.7ft. 202 tons gross and 127 n.h.p., a considerable horsepower for a paddler.

The following comments regarding the **John H. Amos** were made by an old tug skipper:

"This tug was the last paddle tug that the Tees Commission built, she was intended for official guests of the Commission. I believe her estimated cost was £6,000 delivered complete.

However, the firm building went bankrupt before she was completed but the liquidators decided to finish the job with what was in the yard, hence she never got the boilers she was designed for, they were made up jobs on the small side, so her best speed was 11 knots instead of the intended 13 knots.

She lost out on the boilers but gained on the fittings she was equipped with which were used up on the tug but never intended for her. The tug being intended mainly for passengers was fitted with a DIAGONAL ENGINE not really suitable for towing.

The commission was very disappointed with her but she had a beautiful hull and engine with superlative fittings so it was decided to make the best of it; she cost less than the estimated price.

Her towing duties were confined to an occasional hopper from the numerous dredgers of the commission; they were bucket dredgers with no propulsion of their own.

The main duties of the **Amos** was taking out the crews of the dredgers to relieve those that had worked their shift, these were taken ashore for their rest period by the tug.

She was also used to take out V.I.P.s to view the work being done, and her fittings were greatly admired; one other activity was taking all the workers to sea for their annual treat.

P.S. She was by no means regarded as an utter failure."

There were several small tugs at Whitby - the **Goliath** (1854) owned by the Whitby and Robin Hoods Bay Steam Packet Co., the **Samson** (1839) belonging to Jas. Swallow and the **Emu** (1871) of the Whitby Steam Boat Co. Most of the tugs were underpowered and there were a number of occasions when the tug had to slip the towrope and leave the sailing ship to look after herself, often with disastrous results.

In 1874 the tugboat **Emu** (1871, 82.1ft. 73 tons. 30 n.h.p.) owned by the Whitby Steamboat Company was cruising for vessels off Whitby High Lights when the captain saw a schooner in tow of a smack. On being asked if any assistance was required the master of the smack who was on board the schooner said that the vessel was sinking and that there was no use trying to save her. Suddenly the mate began to chop holes in the deck to release the air that was trapped inside her, supporting the schooner. The **Emu** took the schooner in tow and ran her ashore on the sands near Whitby West Pier. It was found that the schooner, the *Johannes*, had holes knocked in her hull and the foremast had been chopped away with an axe in an attempt to sink her! The tugs in Whitby frequently operated passenger excursions at the height of the season.

There was no real tug service in Bridlington and Scarborough, but at one time the harbours were thronged with paddle trawlers. In addition, during the summer the paddle tugs came up from Hull to provide trips round the bay. A familiar sight at Bridlington was the Hull tug **Frenchman** (1892), an iron paddle tug belonging to T. Gray and later the United Towing Company. She was superseded by a screw tug, the **Yorkshireman** of 1928, also United Towing (119).

Hull has been an active port for centuries and during the years a large number of tugs has passed through the port and through the hands of innumerable owners. Among the early owners were Henry Booker from the 1860s whose tugs bore some odd names - **Peep O' Day Boy** (1848), **Fletcher's Despatch** (1839) and the **Willing Mind** of 1855 which was lost in 1882 when the boiler blew up while she was towing. There was Joseph Maycock in the 1870s with his **Telegraph** of 1857. (At least 5 tugs bore that name.) Geo. F. Precious started as part owner of the **Lady Bute** of 1857 and the **True Briton** of 1852 but in the 1890s began to register tugs in his own name. T.W. Thompson started in the 1880s with the **Caledonia** of 1846, but he did not have her long; in 1883, off Hull, the funnel fell and the vessel was abandoned. In 1921 the firm became Thompson Towage Co.

One of the earliest tug owners in Hull was Stephen Gray who started about 1836 a fleet which owned over 50 tugs during an existence which ended in 1921. The early tugs were small wooden paddlers such as the **True Briton** of 1852, bought secondhand in 1876, but in 1881 came the first screw tug **Lady Bute** of 1857 bought from Falmouth. In 1889 the **Welshman** joined the fleet setting the pattern for the naming of the Gray tugs, where all the names ended **.....man**. Many of the tugs were only in the fleet for a few years as T. Gray bought and sold with great regularity, mostly to foreign buyers. In 1902 he had built the **Huntsman** and sold her in 1904 to Italy. During those two years she had been on three salvage jobs, for one of them receiving no award. It was a case of "No Cure, No Pay!" - the court did not judge that the service should be counted as salvage and the would-be salvor received the standard towing fee. The Gray tugs I.P.T. **Frenchman** (1892,118 tons, 350 i.h.p. 7 hands, value £5,750) and the S.T. **Norseman** (1898, 52 tons, 300 i.h.p. 4 hands, value £4,000) had better luck in 1902 when they rendered assistance to the *Oranasia* and were awarded £1,150. The **Frenchman** was better known as the excursion steamer at Bridlington. The tugs in the Humber were mainly small but could be found seeking off the coast; the **Southern Cross** of 1896 was only 82ft. b.p. and 78 tons, but she had a forecastle flush with the bulwarks like a deep sea tug (74). She belonged to R.W. Wheeldon, a late arrival in Hull. In 1913 "in consequence of continued complaints from the shipping and coal trades of Hull as to the high charges of towage at the port, a new association was formed called the Hull Associated Tugowners. The new association owned 25 tugs and comprised T. Gray, City Steam Towing Co. (R.W. Wheeldon), Humber Steam Towing Co., S. Harrison and T.C. Spink. The new association then drew up a much reduced tariff for towing charges to come into operation in January 1914 and to remain in force for a period of two years. Those charges, however, depended on shipowners contracting towage to the association for a period of years!

In 1921 the association formed the United Towing Company, being joined by the Premier Towing Company with 7 tugs, bringing the total number of tugs in the U.T.C. up to 38 vessels. The older boats were sold off and replacement began in 1923, still keeping the **.....man** suffix, when the **Superman** was built by Cochrane who have since built many tugs for the company.With an eye to the coastal and deep sea towing business the company began to order larger more powerful tugs and the **Seaman** (87) joined the tug fleet in 1924. The fleet of the United Towing Company has always been large and has ranged from craft tugs to big ocean-going tugs. In 1957 they owned 33 tugs between 40 tons (**Waterman** of 1930) and 716 tons (**Englishman** of 1945) (93) and in addition had on charter from the Admiralty, the **Welshman** ex **Turmoil** of 1942, 1100 tons. The oldest unit in the fleet was the **Roman** built in 1906. They had by this time carried out 4,228 tows and their vessels had covered 1,803,204 miles. During this time only 26 tows were lost, but many of them were old ships or unseaworthy craft. The United Towing have continued to expand in this field with motor tugs. The smaller tugs are now registered under the name of Humber Tugs Ltd., operating in the docks at Hull, Grimsby and Immingham, having recently taken over the tugs formerly belonging to J.H. Pigott & Son Ltd. of Grimsby.

Other owners who have had tugs working in and around Hull in recent years have included John Deheer, generally small tugs such as the **Ian** of 1907, 67 tons, Ellerman Wilson Line Ltd. whose

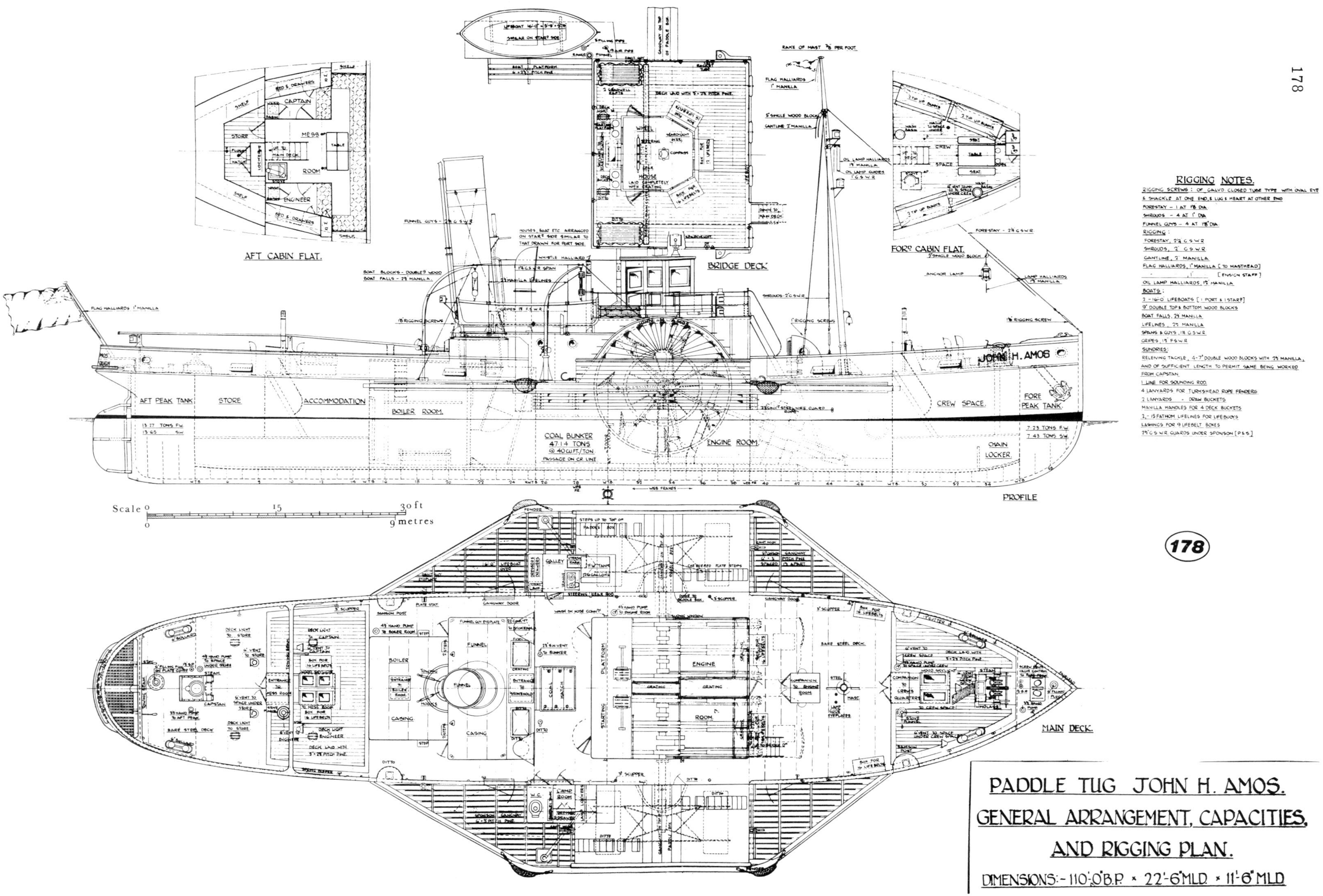
PADDLE TUG JOHN H. AMOS.
GENERAL ARRANGEMENT, CAPACITIES, AND RIGGING PLAN.
DIMENSIONS:- 110'-0" B.P. × 22'-6" MLD. × 11'-6" MLD.
178
AFT CABIN FLAT.
BRIDGE DECK
FOR^D CABIN FLAT.
PROFILE
MAIN DECK.
Scale 0 15 30 ft
0 9 metres
AFT PEAK TANK
STORE
ACCOMMODATION
BOILER ROOM.
COAL BUNKER
47.14 TONS
@ 40 CU.FT./TON
PASSAGE ON C.L. LINE
ENGINE ROOM.
CREW SPACE.
FORE PEAK TANK.
CHAIN LOCKER.
JOHN H. AMOS
RIGGING NOTES.
RIGGING SCREWS: OF GALVD. CLOSED TUBE TYPE WITH OVAL EYE
& SHACKLE AT ONE END, & LUG & HEART AT OTHER END
FORESTAY - 1 AT 1⅛" DIA.
SHROUDS - 4 AT 1" DIA.
FUNNEL GUYS - 4 AT 1⅛" DIA.
RIGGING:
FORESTAY, 2¾" G.S.W.R.
SHROUDS, 2" G.S.W.R.
GANTLINE, 2" MANILLA
FLAG HALLIARDS, 1" MANILLA [TO MASTHEAD]
" " , 1" [ENSIGN STAFF]
OIL LAMP HALLIARDS, 1½" MANILLA
BOATS:
2 - 16'-0" LIFEBOATS [1 PORT & 1 STAR^D]
9" DOUBLE TOP & BOTTOM WOOD BLOCKS
BOAT FALLS, 2½" MANILLA
LIFELINES, 2½" MANILLA
SPANS & GUYS, 1¾" G.S.W.R.
GRIPES, 1½" F.S.W.R.
SUNDRIES:
RELIEVING TACKLE, 4-7" DOUBLE WOOD BLOCKS WITH 2½" MANILLA,
AND OF SUFFICIENT LENGTH TO PERMIT SAME BEING WORKED
FROM CAPSTAN
1 LINE FOR SOUNDING ROD.
4 LANYARDS FOR TURKSHEAD ROPE FENDERS
2 LANYARDS - DRAW BUCKETS
MANILLA HANDLES FOR 4 DECK BUCKETS
2, - 15 FATHOM LIFELINES FOR LIFEBUOYS
LASHINGS FOR 9 LIFEBELT BOXES
2½" G.S.W.R. GUARDS UNDER SPONSON [P & S]

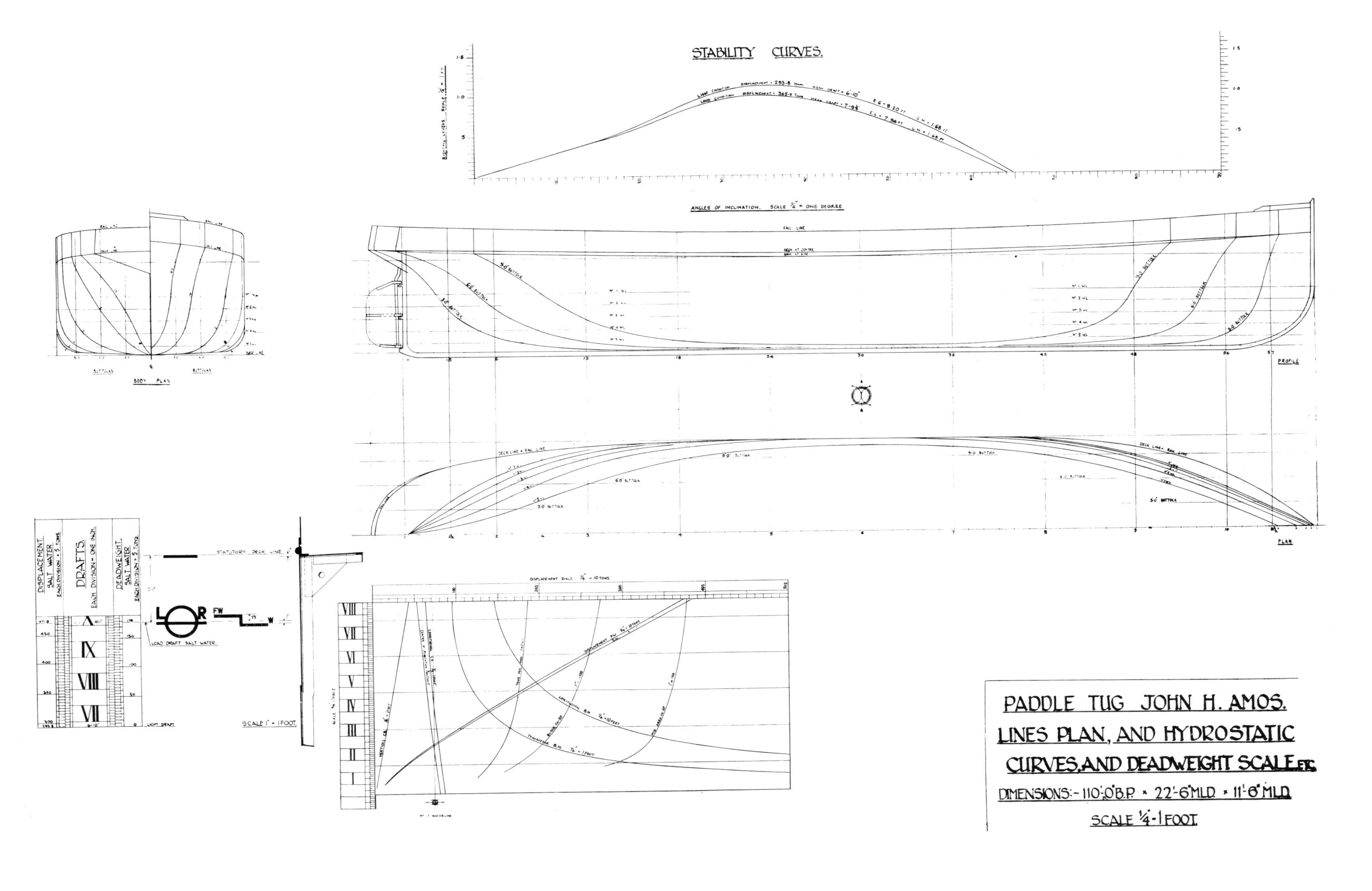

STABILITY CURVES.
ANGLES OF INCLINATION. SCALE 1/4" = ONE DEGREE
RAIL LINE
PROFILE
PLAN
BODY PLAN
BUTTOCKS
DISPLACEMENT. SALT WATER EACH DIVISION = 5 TONS
DRAFTS. EACH DIVISION = ONE INCH.
DEADWEIGHT. SALT WATER EACH DIVISION = 5 TONS
STATUTORY DECK LINE
LOAD DRAFT SALT WATER
LIGHT DRAFT
SCALE 1" = 1 FOOT.
DISPLACEMENT SCALE 1/4" = 10 TONS
PADDLE TUG JOHN H. AMOS.
LINES PLAN, AND HYDROSTATIC
CURVES, AND DEADWEIGHT SCALE ETC.
DIMENSIONS:- 110'-0" B.P. × 22'-6" MLD × 11'-6" MLD
SCALE 1/4 - 1 FOOT.

tugs bore names ending in 'O' like the big ships of the fleet, tugs such as the **Presto** ex **Empire Sara** of 1943. An earlier tug in the fleet was **Plato.**

The most obvious feature of the **Plato** was her very tall thin funnel which was required to give her boiler a good natural draught (181). The arrangement of the two towing hooks is worthy of note, the hooks being shackled on to a bar which had four positions for each hook. The lead of the steering chains differed from other tugs as it ran at an angle across the boiler casing before descending at an angle to the deck. Her anchor windlass had a chain gipsy for the anchor chain and a barrel for dealing with ropes. It must have been somewhat dangerous on the boatdeck at night with the stair leading down to the main deck right beside the exit from the steering position. The boats were placed rather far back so that the after davits were stepped clear of the round-down of the deck. She was built by Cook, Welton & Gemmell in Hull in 1901, 90.0ft. x 22.1ft. x 9.5ft., 135 tons, 65 n.h.p. Her first owner was Thos. Wilson of Hull, later the Ellerman Wilson Line of Hull, passing to J.A. White of North Queensferry just before World War II.

Finally, there was Peter Foster who has owned around 24 tugs since the 1920s ranging from the **Ace Tut** of 1886, 51 tons, to the **Cockspur,** an ex-naval tug of 1918, 135 tons. Six of his tugs were called **......Tut;** and the trawler owners of Hull formed their own company, the Hull Steam Trawlers Mutual Insurance and Protecting Company Ltd. and they have owned 14 tugs to date, now being equipped with four Voith Schneider propelled tugs of 50 tons.

Further up the river was the Goole and Hull Steam Towing Company whose tugs dated from 1871 when the **Havelock** and **Colin Campbell,** both of 1858, went into service. These were followed by a variety of names like **Aunt Alice** (1863) and **Queen of the Bay** (1874), but soon the standardised name like **Goole No.1, No.2, No.3** (75), etc. was adopted. Operating as they did so far up the River Ouse the tugs of this fleet do not feature much in the papers. Their paddle tug **Goole No.2** was recorded as "launched by J.T. Eltringham in 11.6.1877, fitted with Archimedian paddle wheels as patented by Mr. J. Simpson of Stockport." The Humber is fed by a network of canals and there have always been lighterage tugs busy towing barges around the docks. John Harker of Knottingley was an owner of such tugs as the **Lion H.** of 1931, 45 tons and **Elsa Partiss** of 1908, 42 tons; this latter tug did the rounds in the area being owned by five different firms before vanishing soon after 1956.

The busy port of Grimsby provided employment for many tugs in the fleet of J.W. Jewitt who started with the tiny wooden paddle tug **Saint Clare** of 1853, only 37 tons. They owned two tugs called **Gipsy King,** one of 53 tons, 1855, the other 58 tons, 1872. Charles Buxton regarded the name **Stag** as a lucky name for a tug and owned one; a screw tug of 38 tons, built 1883, and another built 1904 of 44 tons. James Turner adopted local names such as **Humber** of 1876, 97 tons and of 1895, 131 tons, both paddle tugs, and **Spurn** of 1873, 80 tons - a wooden paddler and 1907, 103 tons, a screw tug. Isaac Richardson started in 1895 with the **Spurn** of 1873 from Turner, and in the following year added the **Southern Cross** 1896 (74) which he sold later to Wheeldon in Hull. Still in existence are the Grimsby Salvage and Towage Co. Ltd. who have owned around 19 vessels. The current fleet are all motor and all small, between 35 and 52 tons. The other fleet, now under the wing of Humber Tugs Ltd. is J.H. Pigott & Son Ltd., who have owned nearly 40 tugs since they began in a small way in the 1920s, with the **John Bruce** of 1886, a screw tug of 36 tons. After the Second World War the fleet was built up with secondhand tugs such as the **Holka** of 1929 and the **Daimler** of 1915. At this time the new naming of tugs began and all vessels now bear the name **Lady......** The **Lady Vera** of 1913 was 48 tons, while the **Lady Elsie** of 1925 was 157 tons. The tugs in the present fleet are mainly ship handling motor tugs.

The tugs from Grimsby competed with those from Hull for all towage and salvage on the Humber, but they did not hesitate to join forces if it were necessary. In 1899 the *Inchmaree* got herself into

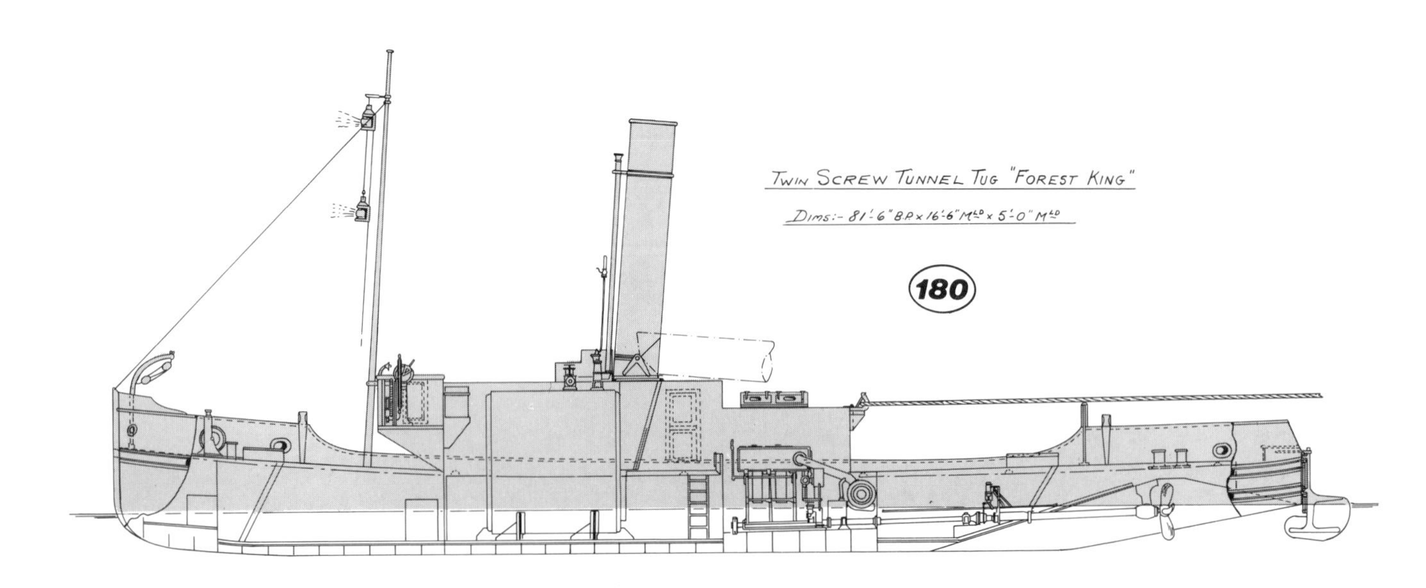

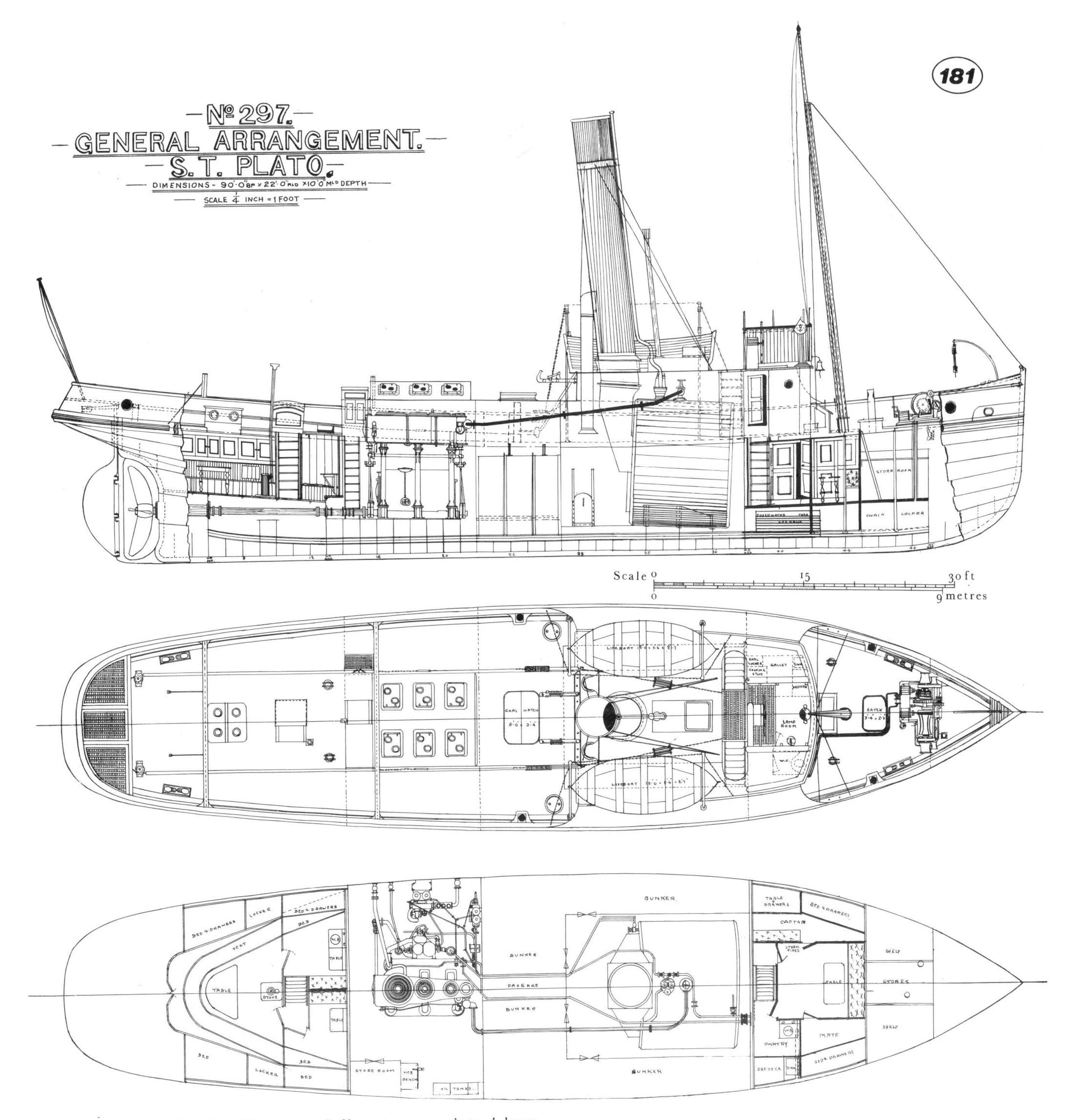

difficulties in the River and five tugs assisted her:

Seagull	1884	66 tons	40 nhp.	value £4000	T. Commander, Hull.
Spurn	1907	15 tons	32 nhp.	£1800	G.F. Precious, Hull.
Janet	1898	99 tons	90 nhp.	£6000	F.T. Munkman, Hull.
Majestic	1898	157 tons			Grimsby Deep Sea Towage & Salvage Co.
Samson					No details given.

Into the River Humber about 15 miles above Hull flows the River Trent which is navigable for quite large vessels for over 100 miles. Beyond that the river shallows, restricting the draught of the vessels which have to reach riverside ports further inland. Even here there are tugs, one of which was the tunnel tug **Forest King** (180). She was built by Warren of New Holland in 1917, presumably for a Government department. She does not appear in the registers until 1924 when she was purchased by Robert Teal of Newark. She was little more than a powered barge (62 tons, 30 n.h.p.) and with her draught of only 3ft. the boiler had to project well above the deck. The bridge looks most precarious perched on brackets at the forward end of the boiler casing. The propellers were in tunnels, for full efficiency the after end of the tunnel had to be kept just below the surface of the water. R. Teal also owned a sister tug called **Allan-a-Dale**.

On the Wash are several minor ports, Boston, Kings Lynn and Spalding. In Boston there were several owners of single tugs, the only fleet of any size being the Boston Steam Tug Co. which consisted at its height of the **Boston**, a wooden paddler built 1875, the **Bulldog**, a screw tug built 1884 and the **Privateer**, an iron paddler built 1883. The two paddle tugs were frequently to be seen loaded with passengers for trips down the river. The **Privateer** was lost in 1918 when she was torpedoed in the Channel while towing a coal barge off the French coast. The Port of Boston Authority employed single tugs. At Kings Lynn, again, there were owners of single tugs until the Kings Lynn Steam tug Co. was formed; they had a wooden paddle tug called the **Spindrift** (1868) which they lost on a coastal voyage to Grangemouth. She was 107 tons and so was big enough to attempt such a trip. The Kings Lynn Conservancy Board owned tugs, three bearing the name **Conservator**, 1902, 1925 and 1963. The Welland River Board at Spalding have owned small tugs among them the **W.D.B. No.1** and **2**. Round the coast at Ipswich the main fleets have been R. & W. Paul, the millers, and the Ipswich Dock Commission. Paul's started with the **Little England** of 1884 purchased from W.H.J. Alexander in London and finished with the **Foam** of 1904 which was their last tug in service when they sold her in 1912. The Dock Commission operated within the docks and locks and had the **Stronghold** of 1931 (183) which went to Grangemouth as the **Dundas.** She was replaced by the **River Orwell**, a motor tug built in Germany in 1943. Although Ipswich is many miles from the sea, tugs of the Paul fleet managed to find salvage work as far away as the River Thames. In 1899 the **Merrimac** (1883) and the **Spray** (1897) shared £800 when they rendered assistance to the *Amiral Aube.*

The fishing port of Great Yarmouth has for a long time required the presence of tugs to assist the sailing fishing boats, and many paddle and screw tugs have worked for the Great Yarmouth Standard Steam Tug Company, the Star Tug Company, Nicholson Towage, and the Great Yarmouth Steam Tug Company, not forgetting the Port and Haven Commissioners, who have spanned 70 years with only three tugs. The Great Yarmouth Standard Steam Tug Company began in 1862 and within the next few years had assisted several ships in distress off that dangerous coastline; in 1863 their **Pioneer** (1861) and **Sailor** (1862) helped the brig *Garibaldi.* The vessels of the Star Tug Company, were aptly named **Star** (1874), **Meteor** (1875), **Comet** (1876) etc. They were a bit unfortunate with their tugs, losing the **Planet** and **Reliance** just before the firm was joined to the Great Yarmouth Steam Tug Company in 1880. This fleet had several paddle tugs, **Comet** (1876), **Andrew Woodhouse** (1856) and **Victoria** (1872) which was lost at Cromer in 1888. Nicholson Towage's fleet were mainly paddle tugs, **Tom Perry** (1879), **Reaper** (1867) and **King Edward VII** (1901) (41) which went to Sunderland. The North Sea kicked up quite rough at times and with the volume of coastal traffic passing the port, casualties were bound to occur and the tug crews from Great Yarmouth were only too ready and willing to take risks for the salvage awards. They were successful too as evidenced by the money which they piled up. In one incident in 1906, nine tugs were involved in the rescue of the *Newburn.* Nicholson's **Cruiser** - £700, **King Edward VII** - £500, **Gleaner** - £300, **Tom Perry** - £200, and the Great Yarmouth Steam Tug Co.'s **Meteor** - £300, **Yare** - £450, **United Service** - £300. The two other tugs were from London, the **Champion** and **Victor** of the Elliott Steam Tug Co. which shared £1,000.

In December 1912 the death was reported of H. Nicholson at the age of 83, tug owner at Great Yarmouth for 62 years. He worked up from fireman and engineer, and had been chief engineer aboard the **P.S. Buccleuch.** He had formed the Standard Steam Tug Company (4 tugs) and had joined the Star Tug Company with J. Jackson.

United Service (6) was a wooden paddle tug built in 1871 which lasted until the 1940s and whose name crops up time and time again in salvage cases. She was also well known as a pleasure steamer. The Great Yarmouth Steam Tug Co. also had three pleasure steamers in addition to the tug fleet. The **George Jewson** of the Port and Haven Commission made the papers in 1913 when she salvaged "a naval waterplane". The **Gleaner** (1885, 89.1ft. 87 tons. 54 n.h.p.) spent most of her career towing fishing boats in and out of the port of Great Yarmouth (182).

The various ports around the country adopted different 'codes' for their local sailing ships to indicate that they required the services of a steam tug. In Yarmouth the ship would hoist her top gallant yard, but it was also common for the ship to haul in her jib-boom, a clear indication that she was ready to take a towrope aboard. In 1866 some confusion was caused when a strange ship approaching the harbour hoisted a 'waif' to her masthead i.e. a flag with two stops on it, that is caught up at two points with spunyarn.

The Wood Paddle Tug ***Gleaner*** *tows a string of fishing boats into Great Yarmouth. The wheel is on the fore deck, just abaft the mast.*

PHOTO: Ken Turrell.

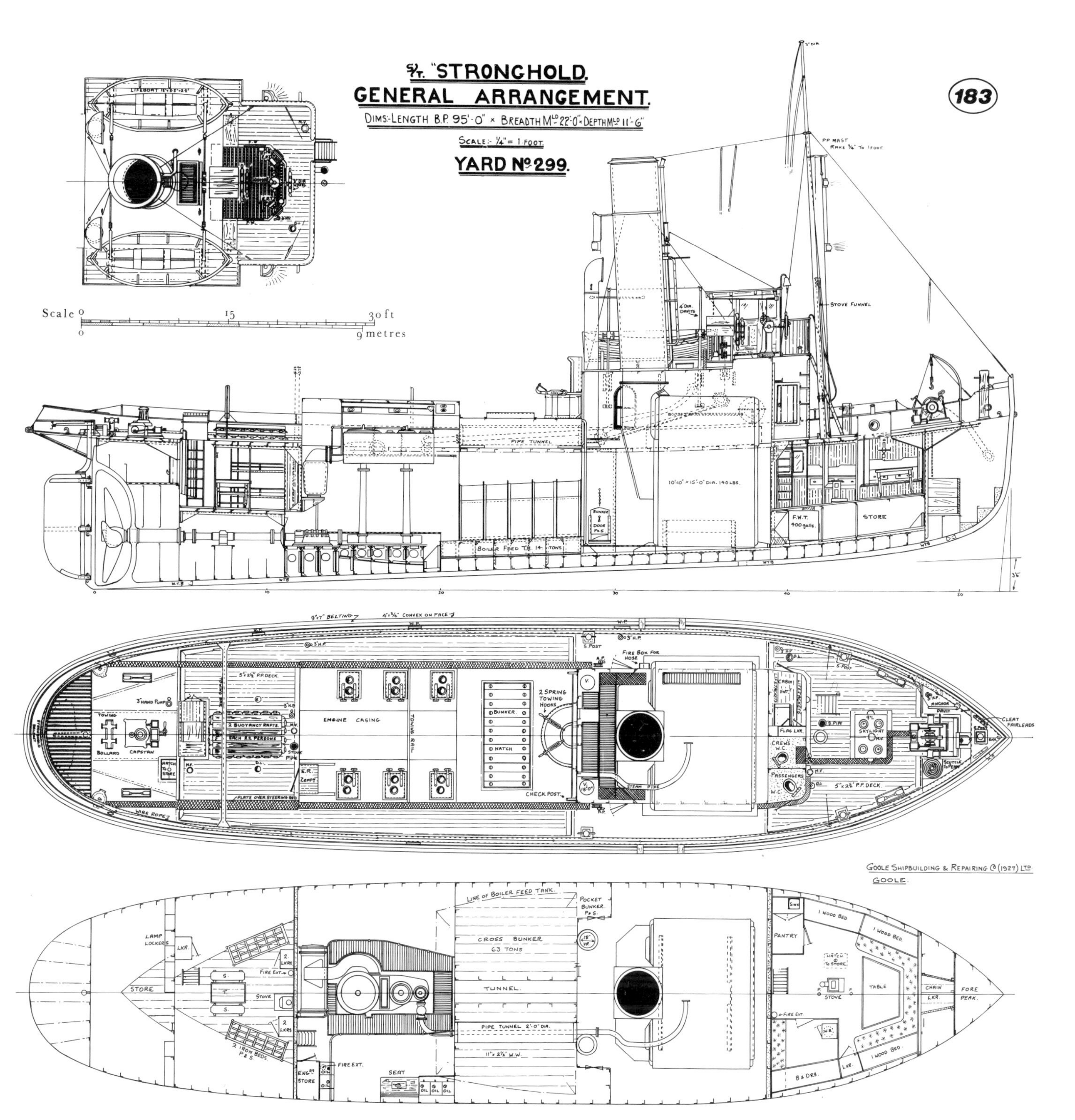

In Northern Ireland, Belfast is the most important port. Hugh Andrews first appeared in Belfast in 1862 with the paddle tug **Wonder** of 1857 and by 1866 had built up the numbers to five. He bought the wooden paddle tug **Pioneer** (1862) in 1863, but sold her in 1866, replacing her with another **Pioneer** (1862). He must have been desperate in the 1870s when he bought the **Souter Johnny** of 1836, an old paddle tug which had been built for the Caledonian Steam Towing Company of London. The next on the scene was James Douglass (there had been an owner of this name in Shields until 1868). James Douglass appears in the 1878 register as owning the **Alderman Ridley** in Coleraine (1861 W.P.T.), and then his tugs are registered in Belfast until about 1906 when the **Hugh Bourne** (1871) was sold to Shields. About the same time (1878) the Belfast Harbour Commissioners bought their first tug the **Lion** of 1859 (35), quite a large iron paddle tug which had already served in Liverpool, Londonderry, and London. She was sold to McKinnon of Leith in 1897. They operated 14 tugs in all including the tenders **Duchess of Abercorn** (1936) and **Musgrave** (1897). A lot of the tugs were small like the **Connswater**, an ex-W.W.I. Army tug 1918 of 62 tons, and the optimistically named **Salvor** (1890) of only 62 tons which they had on charter for a while. The name Jas. Waterson appears in 1857 with the tug **Samson** (1844), disappears in 1862 and re-appears in 1892 with the screw tug **Harbour Light**, a new vessel of 45 tons. In contrast he bought the **Hercules** of 1885, one of Clyde Shipping Company's big coastal tugs. Mrs. Jane E.Strong had a short spell as a tug owner, 1921 to 1934 including the **John Coulson** of 1896.

The **Stronghold** was a sturdy looking tug with no frills (183), characteristic of her type. She became a Commissioners' tug and carried two liferafts as well as the standard two lifeboats. The lead of the steering chains was arranged with the first pulley only half way down the side of the boiler casing. As the chains run down either side of the casings they were protected by a chequer plate cover throughout their entire run along the deck. The towing hooks were spring loaded and the check posts were fabricated from steel plate, both features more commonly found in tugs of later years. It was unusual to carry the wooden sheathing so far forward; normally it was put down only over accommodation. She was built in 1931 by the Goole Shipbuilding & Repairing (1927) Ltd. for J.E. Strong of Belfast but within two years she had been sold to the Ipswich Dock Commission. In 1949 she was purchased by the Grangemouth & Forth Towing Co. and renamed **Dundas.** She had a tonnage of 150 gross and a 111 n.h.p. engine.

Workman Clark, the shipbuilders had two salvage vessels, the **Milewater** (1888) and **Ulsterman** (1885), both converted Clyde Shipping Company coastal tugs. The tugs from Belfast do not seem to have had much opportunity for salvage work. One of the few times that they made the papers was in 1934 when, in a comparison between towage facilities in the U.K. ports, Belfast came in for some hard criticism for the poor quality of their tugs, this being quickly defended by John Cooper. This company had started in 1908 with the **Harbour Light** purchased from Waterson, followed by the **Violet** of 1892, a nice yacht-like tug from Carlingford Lough. They have owned 15 tugs, and now under the wing of Cory Ship Towage (N.I.) Ltd. operate modern motor tugs. Another tugowner of modern times who spent a few years operating in Belfast was H.P. Lenaghan, most of whose tugs began **Lena.....** The smallest tug was the **Lenaship** ex W.D.S. of 1892, but he also had three big ex-foreign vessels - **Lenadil** ex **Goldingen** of 1942, 549 tons; **Lenamill** ex **Arnagast** of 1940, 745 tons; **Lenaship II** ex **Storebror** of 643 tons.

In Northern Ireland is the port of Londonderry where W. Coppin ran a tug fleet from 1853 until the late 1860s with the tugs **Lion** (1863) and **Lioness** (1853). After a long gap the Londonderry Bridge Commissioners put the screw tug **Victoria** of 1887 into service, a very small tug of only 10 tons. At Newry where there was quite a lot of shipping, Moses Hunter had a couple of tugs, the **Flying Childers** of 1859 and the **Dandy** of 1857 which passed into the hands of Carlingford Lough Improvement Commissioners. They also had the **Mourne** of 1887 'specially built to take the ground' and the **Violet** of 1892 which went later to Belfast. Just south of the border is Dundalk, where the Harbour Commissioners put a tug into service as early as 1853, the old **James Watt** of 1835. One of their tugs the **Michael Kelly** was built in 1872 as an iron paddle tug, but in 1890 was converted into a three-masted schooner.

Liberator (185) was another of those tugs whose size was deceptive because of her low profile. She was a typical commissioners' tug with plenty of open deck space and extensive passenger accommodation below, with the usual upholstered settees in the saloon. Being twin screw the draught had been kept shallow. She reminds one of the **Triton** with that gap between the casings and the turned wooden legs which support the towing bows. The position of the wheelhouse looks rather precarious. Built in 1906 the tug was 90.4ft. x 18.0ft. x 8.2ft. and came from the yard of Philip & Son, Dartmouth, being 93 tons gross and 47 n.h.p. She was built for the Dundalk Harbour Commissioners for the use of the pilots of the harbour. She was sold in 1920 to the Alexandra Towing Company of Liverpool who changed her name to **Salthouse**, then to the Port Talbot Pilot Cutter Company who changed her appearance considerably (see lower profile, 185), renaming her **Lady Eveline** with a later change of name to **Lady Howard Stepney**. In 1942 she went to Jos. Crosthwaite of Middlesbrough.

In Dublin David Renwick began in 1857 with the **Voltigeur** of 1851 followed in 1861 with a new tug the **Pilot**, a very popular name borne by nearly 20 tugs. Another of his tugs the **General Havelock** of 1858 is a bit of a mystery; she was sunk in 1865, sunk in 1893 and reported as a total loss, and then lost again in 1903. The Dublin Port & Docks Board owned their first tug in 1867 when they bought the **Number One** of 1866. She was followed in 1899 by the **Energy** of 1884 (61). There have been two **Anna Liffey**'s 1904 and 1917, and two **Ben Eadar**'s 1932 (184) and 1973. On the south

***Coliemore** of 1926 (ex-**Foremost** 42) and **Ben Eadar** of 1932 (ex-**Foremost** 84) of the Dublin Port and Docks Board make a run up the Harbour for the camera.*

PHOTO: Dublin Port & Docks Board.

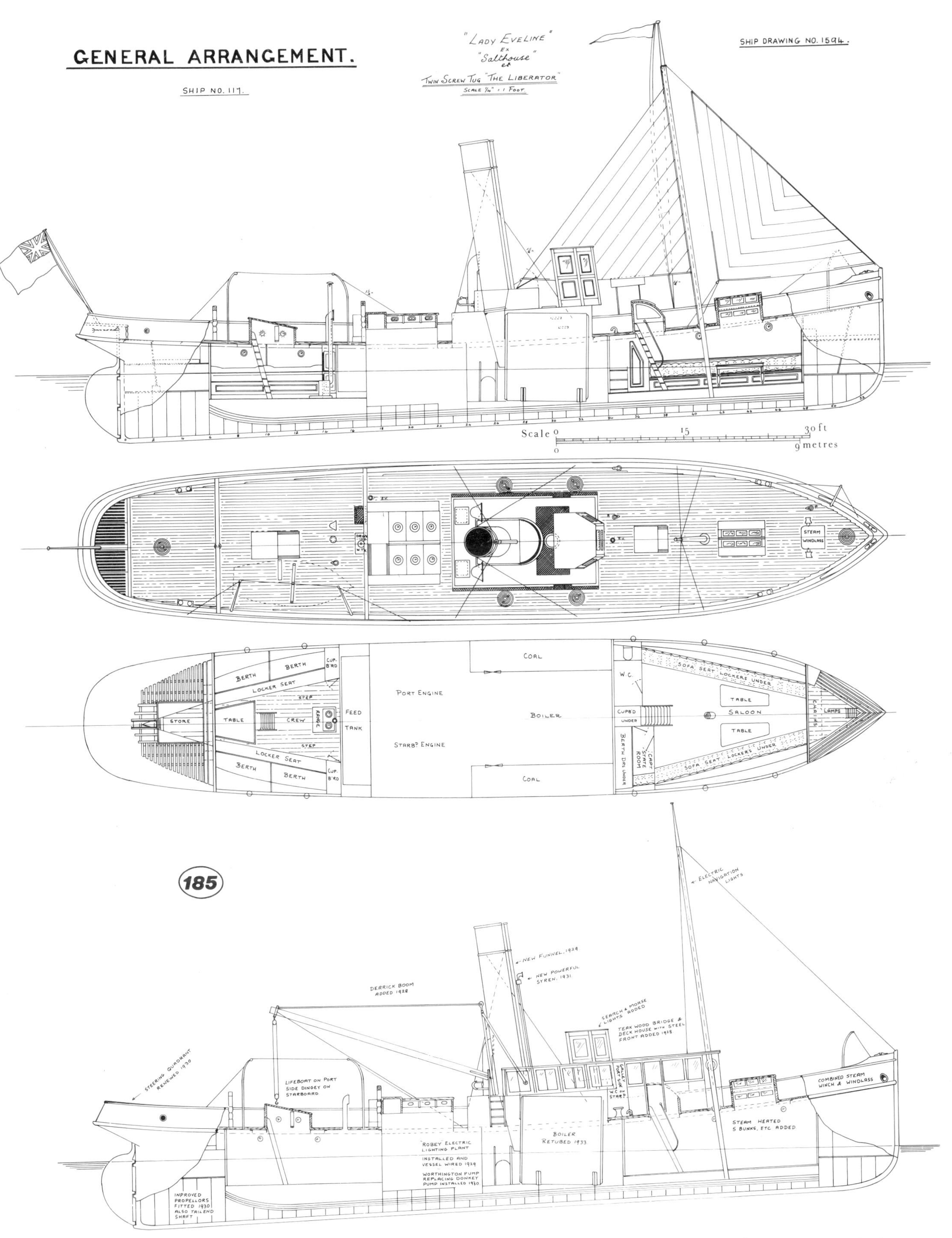

coast lies the harbour of Queenstown, Cork or Cobb. There were a number of single tug owners but the main fleets belonged to the Queenstown Towing Co. who ran a number of big tugs. The **Brother Jonathan** of 1857, 283 tons, the **Commodore** of 1876, 158 tons, the **Mount Etna** of 1880, 232 tons. They lost the first in 1879 after she had been only a year in the fleet, and lost the second in 1885 after only three years. It would seem that this company was the new name for the fleet owned by J. Dawson who had started with the **Black Eagle** (1850) shortly afterwards buying the **Telegraph** of 1852 and **Powerful** of 1854. The Cork Harbour Commission began their fleet in 1863 with the **Commissioner** of 1862.

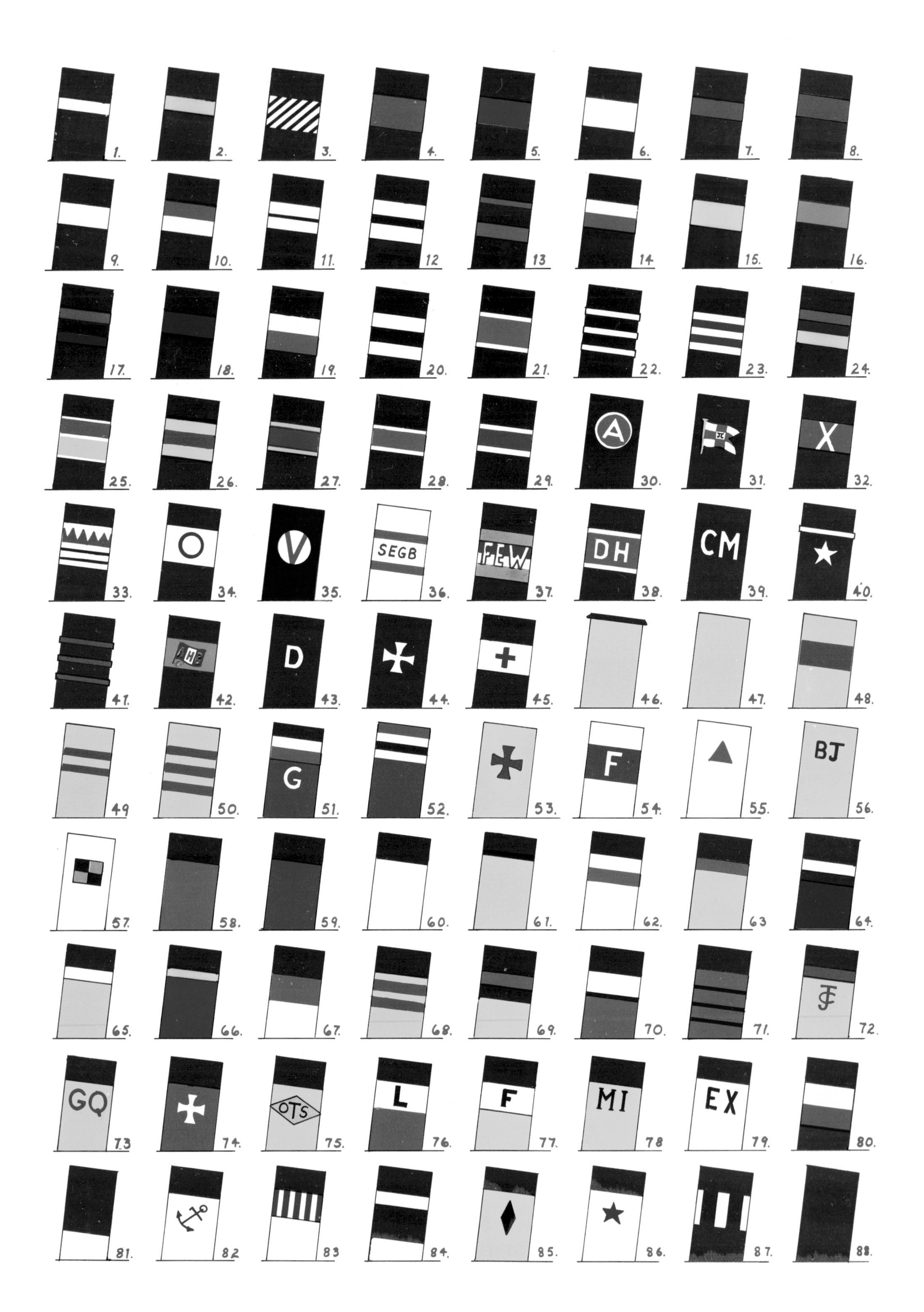
A
X
SEGB
FEW
DH
CM
D
G
F
BJ
GQ
OTS
L
F
MI
EX

FUNNEL COLOURS of TUG COMPANIES (Past and Present).

Company	No.
R.Abel & Sons Ltd, Liverpool	27
Aberdeen Steam Tug Co. Ltd, Aberdeen	21
W.H.J.Alexander (Sun Tugs), London	21
R.S.Allen, Newcastle	81
Alpha Towage, London	30
Anchor Steam Tug Co. Ltd, Newcastle	82
Ardrossan Harbour Co, Ardrossan (to 1960)	42
W. Bate & Co. Ltd, Liverpool	58
Belfast Harbour Commissioners	61
Blyth Tug Co. Ltd. (Before 1958).	43
Blyth Tug Co. Ltd. (After 1958)	44
Bowater Lloyd Pulp & Paper Mills Ltd, Near London	6
Port of Boston Authority	60
Britannia Steam Towing Co. Ltd, Swansea	16
British Railways	61
British Transport Docks	2
British Waterways	15
T.R.Brown & Sons Ltd, Bristol (Silver Bands)	21
J. Carney & Sons Ltd, Sunderland	14
Clements Knowling & Co. Ltd, London	72
Clyde Navigation Trust, Glasgow	88
Clyde Shipping Co. Ltd, Glasgow	88
James W. Cook & Co. Ltd, London	69
John Cooper (Belfast) Ltd, Belfast	58
John Coulson, Newcastle	81
W. R. Cunis Ltd, London	62
J.Davies Towage & Salvage Ltd, Cardiff	70
W. H. Dodds, Newcastle	40
Dover Harbour Board	38
Dublin Port & Dock Board	61
Dundee Harbour Trust	61
John Dry, Newcastle	8
Ellerman's Wilson Line Ltd, Hull	58
Elliott Steam Tug Co. (1949) Ltd, London	31
Falmouth Docks & Eng. Co. Ltd.	58
Falmouth Towage Co. Ltd. (C.L.Fox).	6
James Fisher & Sons Ltd, Barrow	77
Flower & Everett, London	48
P. Foster & Co. Ltd, Hull. (Silver Band).	6
Fowey Tug Co. Ltd, Fowey	61
France, Fenwick, Sunderland (until 1925).	83
Fraser & White Ltd, Portsmouth	65
Gamecock Tugs Ltd, London	59
Gaselee & Son Ltd, London	50
General Lighterage Co. Ltd, London	51
Grain Elevating & Automatic Weighing Co. Ltd, Liverpool	9
Grangemouth & Forth Towing Co. Ltd.	61
Gravesend United Towing Co, London	11
T. Grey, Hull.	19
Great Yarmouth Port & Haven Commissioners	61
Greenhithe Lighterage Co. Ltd.	47
Grimsby Salvage & Towage Co. Ltd.	79
W. J. Guy & Sons, Cardiff.	74
Harrisons (London) Ltd, London	3
Edmund Handcock (1929) Ltd, Cardiff	61
John Hawkins Ltd, London	55
Hercules Steam Tug Co, Liverpool	10
Hull Steam Trawlers Mutual Insurance & Protecting Co Ltd, Hull.	61
Independence Steam Tug Co, Liverpool	88
Ipswich Dock Commission	61
Irvine Harbour Board (after 1956).	58
B. Jacob & Sons, London	56
James Contracting & Shipping Co. Ltd, Southampton	60
Jarrow Tug & Hopper Co, Newcastle	84
Johnston Warren Lines Ltd, Liverpool	13
C. J. King & Sons Ltd, Bristol	67
Kings Lynn Conservancy Board	61
Lambton, Hetton & Joicey Collieries	41
J. H. Lamey Ltd, Liverpool	76
Lawson - Batey Tugs Ltd, Newcastle	53
Lawson Steam Tug Co, Newcastle	85
H.P.Lenaghan & Sons Ltd, Belfast	47
Leith Dock Commissioners	88
Lion Steam Tug Co, Liverpool	62
Lion Wharf Ltd, London	57
Liver Steam Tug Co, Liverpool	71
Liverpool Lighterage Co. Ltd, Liverpool	29
Liverpool Steam Tug Co, Liverpool	80
Liverpool Screw Towage & Lighterage Co. Ltd, Liverpool. (Cowl top).	47
Mc Dougall & Bonthron Ltd, London	32
Manchester Ship Canal Co.	12
Marine Contractors Ltd, Southampton	66
Mersey Docks & Harbour Board	61
Metal Industries (Salvage) Ltd, Glasgow	78
Milford Docks Co, Milford Haven	6
W. S. Murphy, Bristol	6
Charles Murrell, London.	39
Newport Screw Towing Co Ltd, Newport	12
North Thames Gas Board, London	33
R. G. Odell Ltd, London	34
Olympia Oil & Cake Co. Ltd, The Ouse	18
Original Mersey Steam Tug Co, Liverpool	1
Overseas Towage & Salvage Co. Ltd, Milford Haven	75
G.J.Palmer & Sons, London	52
Benjamin Perry & Sons Ltd, Bristol	61
J.H.Piggott & Son Ltd, Grimsby. (Silver Bands)	20
Poole Harbour Commissioners	61
Port of London Authority	61
J. Prendiville & Co., Liverpool	11
J. Redhead, Newcastle	80
Redhead Tugs, Newcastle	61
W.J.Reynolds Ltd, Plymouth.	61
J. Ridley, Newcastle	86
Ridley Steam Tug Co. Ltd, Newcastle	22
River Lighterage Co. Ltd, London. (Stephenson, Clarke Ltd).	63
St. Johns Steam Tug Co, Liverpool.	58
Seaham Harbour Dock Company	8
Shoreham Harbour Trustees	88
Silvertown Services Ltd, London (Silver Bands)	23
Smith's Dock Co. Ltd, Newcastle	45
South Eastern Gas Board, London	36
Southampton, Isle of Wight & South of England Royal Mail S.P. Co. Ltd	58
Steel & Bennie Ltd, Glasgow.	6
Tees Conservancy Commissioners, Middlesbrough	61
Thames Steam Tug & Lighterage Co Ltd, London	24
Tilbury Contracting & Dredging Co. Ltd, London	25
Topham, Jones & Railton Ltd, London	28
Tough & Henderson, London (After 1957).	63
Tyne Hopper Company, Newcastle	81
Tyne Tugs Ltd, Newcastle	58
Union Lighterage Co. Ltd, London	88
United Towing Co. Ltd, Hull	60
Vokins & Co. Ltd, London	35
F. E. Walker & Company, London	37
H.J. Ward, Liverpool	68
William Watkins Ltd, London	4
John White, Newcastle	87
J.A.White & Co. Ltd, North Queensferry	7
W. J. R. Whitehair Ltd, London	73
J.H.Whittaker (Tankers) Ltd, Hull	17
Wiles Lighterage Co. Ltd, London	64
Samuel Williams & Sons Ltd, London	5
W. J. Woodward Fisher, London	54
Workington Harbour & Docks Board	1

To give some idea of how tug ownership and "density" have changed over the years the following is a table showing how many tugs were owned in each port in the U.K. in various years. It must be emphasised once more that due to the difficulty of obtaining information this cannot be guaranteed 100% accurate.

Port	1868	1966	1975	Port	1868	1966	1975
London	116	274	122	Heysham	-	2	-
Faversham	2	-	-	Barrow	-	2	-
Dover	1	2	2	Workington	-	1	1
Newhaven	1	1	1	Clyde area	50	28	20
Southampton	5	24	21	Kirkwall	1	-	-
Shoreham	-	1	1	Aberdeen	4	4	2
Portsmouth	5	2	5	Montrose	2	-	-
Poole	1	2	3	Dundee	3	2	2
Plymouth	4	5	-	Forth area	25	9	8
Dartmouth	2	-	-	Berwick	1	-	-
Clay	2	-	-	Blyth	-	5	2
Falmouth	5	8	5	Tyne area	236	19	12
Exeter	1	-	-	Whitby	2	-	-
Fowey	-	2	2	Sunderland	52	9	6
Penzance	1	-	1	Seaham	-	3	1
Bristol	12	17	10	Tees area	28	24	20
Bridgewater	5	-	-	Hartlepool	4	3	-
Gloucester	-	6	4	Humber area	29	57	54
Cardiff	32	9	)	Lowestoft	3	1	4
Swansea	14	10	) 24	Yarmouth	7	3	1
Newport	5	7	)	Boston	1	1	1
Milford	1	11	)	Kings Lynn	-	1	1
Llanelly	4	-	-	Ipswich	-	1	1
Chester	2	-	-	Belfast	3	13	9
Holyhead	-	-	2	Coleraine	1	-	-
River Mersey	83	60	46	Cork	12	3	3
Manchester	-	39	26	Dublin	9	4	4
Fleetwood	1	2	1	Londonderry	1	-	-
Preston	3	4	3	Sligo	1	-	-
Lancaster	2	-	-	Wexford	2	-	-
Maryport	4	-	-	Newry	2	-	-
				Bantry Bay	-	-	4

Prices charged for the services of tugs were made up in a variety of ways. Old diaries preserved by the Clyde Shipping Co. reveal just how varied they were. In 1842 the tug **Conqueror** (1840, 114.1ft., 120 n.h.p.) was hired to tow a schooner from the Isle of Skye to Liverpool for the sum of £150. In 1843 she was hired to carry out the salvage of the ship **Romeo** which was ashore in Dublin Bay at the rate of £30 for each 24 hours. In 1861 they quoted the owners of the ship **Nugget** a range of prices depending on the distance towed from Greenock to the following destinations: Cumbrae (18 miles) £12, Holy Isle (30.5 miles) £15, Pladda (37.5 miles) £16, Ailsa Craig (47 miles) £19.10.0, Sanda Island (55.5 miles) £22, Rathlin Island (74.75 miles) £30, and Inistrahull (111.25 miles) £40. The rate falling from 13/4d to 7/3d per mile. In 1863 they were quoting standard rates based on draught and tonnage from Greenock to Glasgow ranging from 6d. per ton up to 15ft. draught, to 9d per ton for 15ft. upwards. However, from Greenock to Ailsa Craig the rate was based solely on tonnage and ranged from £13 for vessels up to 200 tons, to £19.10.0 for 1000 tons. In 1870 came the strangest charge scale - the tugs could be hired 'by the tide' at a price depending on the diameter of the tugs engine cylinder: Up to 33" dia.(£4), 36" dia.(£5), and over 36" diameter (£6). For **Conqueror** a special price of £8 was charged as she had two 34" dia. cylinders.

188

*The photograph shows a group of the United Towing Company's tugs waiting for the lock gates at high tide and shows the wide range of tugs which the company owned: **Rifleman** (ex-Empire Vera) (1945 123'6", 333 tons, 750 i.h.p.), **Serviceman** (ex-Empire Stella) (1945, 123'6", 325 tons, 750 i.h.p), **Handyman** (ex-Empire Cedar) (1941, 97'6", 129 tons 500 i.h.p.), **Pinky** (1916, 85.2', 103 tons, 63 n.h.p.), **Pressman** (ex-Tyburn Brook), (1950, 68.0', 68 tons, 545 b.h.p.), and **Bargeman** (ex-Brentonian) (1955, 56.9', 37 tons, 360 b.h.p.).*

It is not possible to make direct comparisons between ports or between different years. It seemed simpler, therefor, to take just one year and select some of the ports of the country giving details of how the charges were made up. The following figures are taken from a table which appeared in 1906 and the tonnages referred to are 'register tons'.

Aberdeen: 2.5d. per ton. Avonmouth 3d. per ton sail, 4d. per ton steamers. Maximum £14. Belfast: By agreement. Cardiff: In dock the scale ranges from 3/9d. for 50 tons to 48/9d. for 1500 tons; 13/9d per 100 tons over 1500 tons. Ships towed in from sea 7d. per ton - towed out free. If towed in by non-Association tug 3.5d. per ton will be charged for towing out. Dublin: 6d. per ton. Glasgow: (In River) Based on draught on a sliding scale, over a range - up to 10 feet, 7d. per ton, increasing to 9d. per ton for ships over 20 feet draught. Clyde to Ailsa Craig from £13 to £19 depending on size. Liverpool: Based on a table ranging from £5 for vessels up to 200 tons to £20 for ships over 3000 tons. The tugowners refused to use wire ropes "in consequence of the risk to life and property." Mersey to Tuskar Rock off south coast of Ireland from £54 for 500 tons up to £125 for a ship of 3400 tons. Middlesbrough: sail 4d per ton, steam 1.75d. per ton. Newcastle 2.125d. per ton loaded. 1.5d per ton light. Sunderland: Sail (inward) 1.5d per ton for first tug, 1d per ton for each additional tug; (outward) 1.25d. per ton for first tug, .625d. per ton for each additional tug. Steam - inward and outward - 1d. per ton. Newport: 8d per ton for tug not belonging to Bristol Channel Tug Owners Association. 4d. per ton for association tug. Plymouth Vessels up to 250 tons £1.10.0, 1000 tons £3.0.0., 2000 tons £5.0.0. Southampton: Charges varied with distance towed and size of vessel between £1.10.0 and £4.0.0. If towed to the Needles the charge was between £8 and £25. The table rates were for vessels in the Home Trade, if foreign going 1d. extra per ton was charged up to 300 tons and 0.5d. extra per ton above 300 tons. Workington: Steamers 0.5d per ton. Sail 1d per ton.

In 1934 there appeared in one of the shipping journals a letter of complaint about the cost of towing in British ports. The writer did not specify the size of his ship but the figures given do indicate how widely these towing charges varied:

Port	Length of tow miles	Number of tugs	Charge
Aberdeen	1	2	£29. 3. 4.
Avonmouth	1	2	£20. 9. 6.
Belfast	-	2	£12. 0. 0.(poor tugs)
Blyth	1 1/2	2	£11.13. 4.
Cardiff	3/4	2	£31.12. 0.
Dublin	-	-	£75.16. 8.(towage not compulsory)
Glasgow	21	2	£20. 3. 9.(second tug from Shieldhall)
Greenock	1/2	2	£18. 1. 0.
Leith	1 1/2	2	£22. 0. 0.
Liverpool	2	2	£22.16. 0.
London (Millwall)	20	2	£30. 5. 0.
Manchester	36	2	£34. 4. 0.
Middlesbrough	6	2	£17. 6. 5.
Newcastle (Trading)	-	2	£17. 6. 2.
(Bunkering)	-	2	£10.15. 0.
Newport	2 3/4	2	£32.12. 0.
Sunderland	-	2	£14. 0. 0.
Swansea	4	2	£16. 9. 2.

(189) *Busy Bee*

10.

(190) *The yard of J. & D. Morris.*

Tug Builders, Engines & Fittings.

Many shipbuilding firms built tugs by the dozen whilst others launched but one or two during their lifetime. Only the more important tug building firms are mentioned. London was not famed for tugs in the nineteenth century but the few which were built on the banks of the Thames were generally large in size. Between the 1840s and the 1860s tugs were launched from the yards of James Ash, J. & W. Dudgeon of Cubitt Town, C. Lungley of Deptford, and C.J. Mare of Blackwall. It was from Mare's slips that Watkins' well known tug **Uncle Sam** came in 1849. This yard built also the **Vulcan** in 1858, a paddle tug which was stationed at Ramsgate specifically for salvage purposes before the famous **Aid** of 1889. When steam tugs came into use as craft tugs towing the lighters on the Thames, most of the small tugs were 'imported', but after the turn of the century more and more came from yards in and around London. J.W. Cook & Co., started constructing tugs for themselves and for other owners. E. Jones of Brentford produced launch type tugs. Jas. Pollock, Sons & Co. Ltd. of Faversham were prolific builders of all sizes from 12 ton launch tugs to shiphandling tugs such as the **Sun XXIV** of 1961, 113 tons. The Rowhedge Ironworks built tugs from time to time from the First World War onwards. The Thames Launch Works made tugs spasmodically from the 1880s. Away inland at Stoney Stratford was the yard of Edward Hayes which made small tugs and river launches.

On the south coast at Shoreham during World War I appeared a tug builder with a difference. J. van Mehr built six reinforced concrete tugs together with concrete barges to match. In Southampton J.G. Fay built six tugs for London and Liverpool in 1898 and 1899 and that was that. J.I. Thornycroft & Co. Ltd. however took it more seriously and from around 1907 until they ceased shipbuilding launched around 30 tugs including several for the Admiralty. Most of the civilian tugs were built for operation in Southampton. At Dartmouth, further along the south coast was the yard of Philip & Son, which launched over 60 tugs for British owners including many of the wartime standard **H.S.** and **West** types. In 1909 the tug **Doria**, a new vessel of 152 tons, 500 i.h.p. assisted the *Colbert* in the English Channel. As she was still in the hands of her builders Philip and Sons, not having undergone her trial trip, they received the award of £100.

There were not many screw tugs which were constructed of wood but the **Venture III** was one of the few (191). She was heavily built with doubled frames, though the deck beams appear to be steel in way of the boiler and engineroom. She had a very long casing which incorporated the skylight and companionway to the after accommodation, but this casing was kept low throughout its length, with the wheelhouse perched on the forward end. She had no anchor windlass but instead had a little yacht style hand wound capstan. Built in 1909 she was 62.0 ft. x 14.6 ft. x 7.8 ft., 42 tons and 50 n.h.p. Built in Dartmouth for Geo. N. Philip of the same port, she was sold to the Mayor, Aldermen and Burgesses of the City of Exeter. At Falmouth, Cox and Co. constructed many ship-towing tugs from the 1880s. On the north coast of Cornwall, on a most unlikely site near St. Ives, Harvey of Hayle built a string of tugs of the smaller sizes many for London owners. Further north the port of Appledore housed tug builders from the early 1900s when R. Cock & Sons built some small tugs. After a long gap P.K. Harris (Shipbuilders) Ltd. began building in 1955.

In Bristol there were few tug builders - C.K. Stothert & Co., from the 1860s, John Payne, (tug owners as well) from the 1870s, and Newall & Co. from the 1880s. The last company to enter the field was Chas. Hill & Sons who closed down a few years ago. In Cardiff J. & M. Gunn were building tugs in the 1870s, while in the 1880s Elliott and Jeffery started launching tugs for their own fleet and other owners.

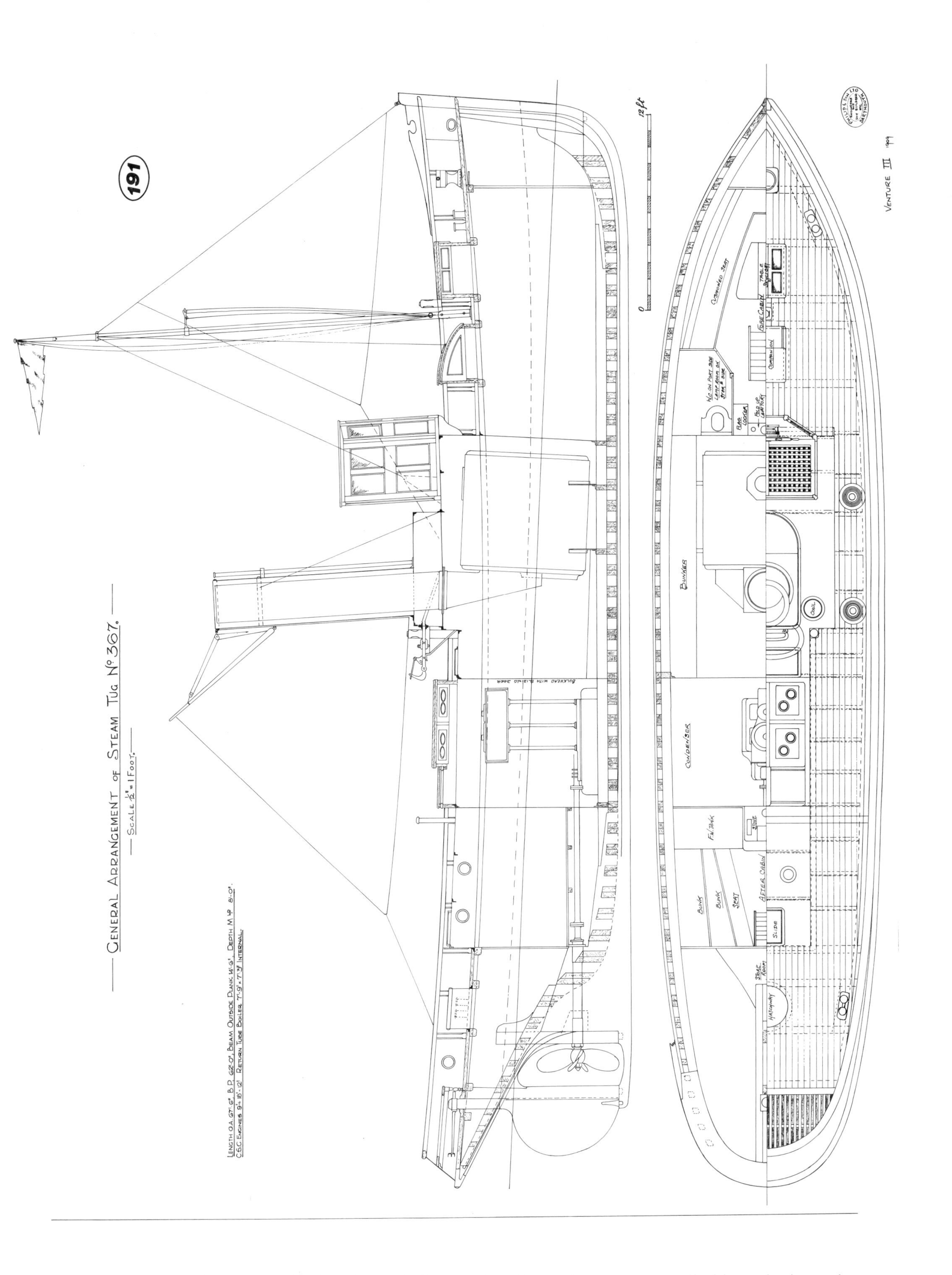

On the River Weaver at Northwich, W.J. Yarwood & Sons Ltd., had a small shipyard where they built barges, launches and tugs. Many of the tugs in the Liverpool fleets came from this yard. Also in Northwich was Isaac Pimblott & Sons who built extensively for overseas owners as well as for U.K. owners. Nearby at Saltney J. Crichton & Co. Ltd. also supplied tugs to Liverpool owners during the 1930s. Nearer the sea at Queensferry I. J. Abdela & Mitchell Ltd. made tugs, mainly small in size, for foreign owners. Isaac J. Abdela also had a yard at Brimscombe near Stroud in

Gloucestershire where the tug in drawing No. 3213 was built (192). The style was fairly standard, a skylight forward, a casing over the boiler and engine and aft, either a hatch with a hold below or another skylight over a small cabin. The steering wheel was open either on the deck forward of the mast or else on the casing abaft the mast. Tugs of this type were sold through advertisements in engineering supplies catalogues.

Despite the fact that in Liverpool were to be found some of the largest tug fleets in the country not many of the early tugs were built on the banks of the Mersey. There were Bowdler, Chaffer & Co. of Seacombe and W.C. Miller in the 1860s and 1870s whose tugs plied on the Mersey, and H. & C. Grayson of Garston building for local owners in the 1910s. Laird Bros., later Cammell, Laird & Co. Ltd. have built nearly 50 tugs, mostly for Liverpool.

On the Clyde south of Glasgow, Samuel McKnight & Co. Ltd. of Ayr, and the Ailsa Shipbuilding Co. Ltd. of Ayr and Troon owned yards from which several tugs came. The Ardrossan Dry Dock & Shipbuilding Co. Ltd. launched about 6 tugs in their early days as shipbuilders. At Dumbarton, Wm. Denny & Bros., one of the oldest shipyards in the country started tug building with the **Samson** of 1818 and have launched numerous towing vessels for British and foreign owners. Still on the north bank, at Bowling, lies the small yard of Scott & Sons who have launched over 40 tugs for use in British ports, though few of them were destined for Clyde owners.

On the south bank a few tugs were built for Clyde owners at yards more accustomed to sailing ships and cargo boats, yards such as Blackwood & Gordon, Murdoch & Murray, and William Hamilton & Co. Ferguson Bros. of Port Glasgow, who started later than the aforenamed, supplied 20 odd tugs for the Clyde Shipping Co. starting with the **Flying Swift** in 1903, and ending with the **Flying Spray** in 1962. The **Flying Cormorant** (194) was a seeking tug on the Clyde and can be compared with the **Simla** (49) of London. She was a sleeker looking vessel in elevation though in plan she was equally narrow and fine lined. The circular skylights with their vents were frequently found on tugs of the period. The big samson post in the bow had not yet arrived and this vessel had a double cruciform bollard arranged fore and aft. On the towing deck aft there was a steam capstan which was a standard feature on Clyde tugs and those of the north-east coast. The coaling hatch was carried up to the level of the boatdeck to give an extra capacity of 79 tons of coal which must have made her just a little 'tender'. She had an engineroom telegraph at the after end of the boat deck with which the captain could pass orders to the engineroom while keeping his tow in full view. The lines of a near sister ship show that she was built for speed with a sharp rise of floor, rounded bilges and a very fine hull forward. The lines belong to the **Flying Foam/Spray** which were a later edition of the **Flying Cormorant.** Built in 1908 she was 203 tons and 99 n.h.p. After serving in the Clyde Shipping Company's fleet until 1945 she was sold to the Dundee, Perth and London Shipping Co. and worked for them as the **Buddon** until broken up in 1953.

In the neighbouring yard owned by Jas. Lamont & Co. Ltd. orders for tugs for British owners were not frequent though they have supplied 8 tugs in the last 20 years. Some of these incorporated completely new ideas in tug design, ideas such as the diesel exhausts positioned at the after end

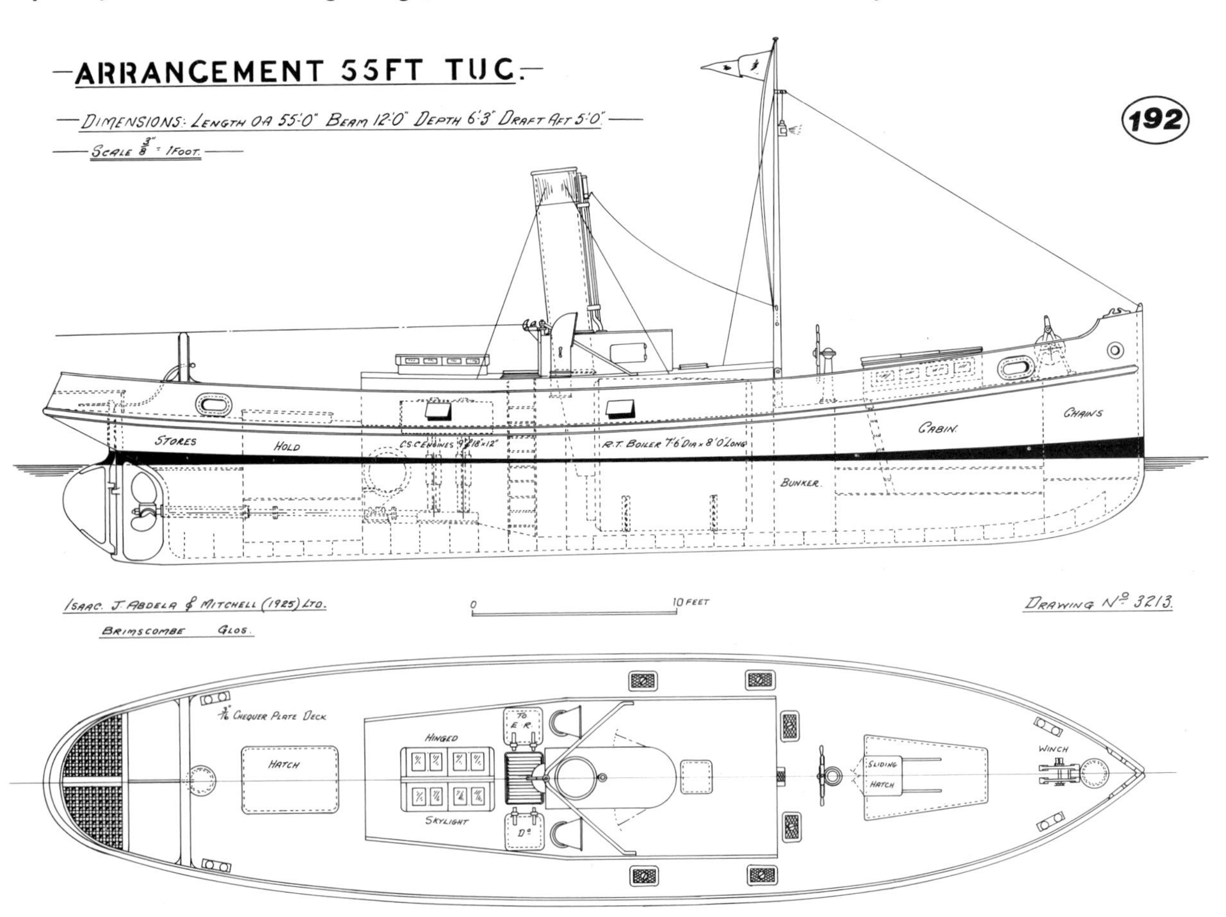

of the boat deck as in the Liverpool tug **B.C. Lamey** of 1966. Rather unexpectedly Paisley, situated some distance up the narrow River Cart, housed a number of thriving shipyards, and not unnaturally many of the craft which were launched were tugs. H. McIntyre & Co. built a few tugs before being taken over by Fleming & Ferguson Ltd. who built about 24 tugs, most of which were destined for the Admiralty or overseas owners. Bow, McLachlan & Co. Ltd. built the last paddle tug to be launched for British civilian owners; the **John H. Amos** of 1931; incidentally this was the last vessel which they built (178). Most of the big shipyards on the banks of the upper Clyde built the occasional tug. Barclay, Curle & Co. Ltd. launched several large tugs for Southampton owners and the Admiralty. Napier, Shanks & Bell of Yoker built some of the big coastal tugs employed by the Clyde Shipping Co. Nearer the heart of the city A. & J. Inglis produced tugs just before they were forced to close in the 1950s. Upriver from the middle of Glasgow was the famous yard of T.B. Seath & Co. of Rutherglen who floated at least 5 tugs down the river at high tide.

On the north-east coast of Scotland, Aberdeen housed three long established yards Alexander Hall & Co. Ltd., Hall, Russell & Co. Ltd., and J. Lewis & Sons Ltd. whence came a large number of tugs. During the 1930s Hall, Russell's were engaged in building tugs for James Dredging & Contracting of Southampton, all with names prefixed **Foremost.......**most of which were quickly resold. Further south Dundee supplied tugs from the yards of Dundee Shipbuilders' Co. Ltd., Gourlay Brothers & Co. (Dundee) Ltd., and W.B. Thompson & Co. Ltd., all of whom built a number of large tugs for coastal and ocean work and also several over 200' long for service on the River Hooghly.

In the Firth of Forth were the ports of Leith and Grangemouth. At Leith from the 1880s the yards of John Cran & Co. Ltd., Hawthorns & Co. Ltd., and S. & H. Morton & Co. built tugs until they had to close during the slump. Out of the ashes rose a new yard Henry Robb Ltd. which has constructed over 40 tugs including the now famous group of tugs for the Admiralty, the **Turmoil** and her sisters. Less spectacular but equally rewarding was a long standing contract with the Manchester Ship Canal Co. which started with the **M.S.C. Firefly** in 1935 and ended with the **M.S.C. Rover** in 1953. From the Grangemouth Dockyard Co. Ltd. came one of the big deep sea tugs for Liverpool; Prendeville's **Knight of St. Patrick** of 1886. More recently they launched two motor tugs to modernise the local fleet, **Dalgrain** 1963 and **Zetland** 1961.

On the North-East Coast the River Tyne was the home of tug building from the very early days of tugs and towing. At first single boats were built on the banks of the river on convenient sites, but over the years proper yards were established. The four outstanding building yards were Jos. T. Eltringham & Co., Hepple & Co., J.P. Rennoldson and Sons and Readhead Softley & Co. From these yards came scores of paddle tugs which were destined for owners all over the country followed later by dozens of screw tugs. The depression of the 1930s saw the demise of these builders whose names were a byword for tug suppliers. Among the less important yards were Brodie of North Shields, C. Mitchell & Co., C.W. Dodgin & Co., Wouldhave and Johnson. A short-lived yard of modern times was T. Mitchison Ltd. of Gateshead. From time to time a tug has gone down the slips of Clelands of Wallsend.

It was not the intention to go into the details of how tugs were constructed as their construction was similar to coasters (See 'Steam Coasters and Short Sea Traders' also in this series). However, since the methods used in the building of a wooden paddle tug were so unusual, it is appropriate to describe them. In the Smith's Dock Journal of May 1933 the author of an article on tugs gives the following account of the construction of an old wooden paddle tug: 'Building these vessels was a craft which needed a high degree of skill, an eye for symmetry, and a thorough knowledge of how the details of the underwater form affected the performance of the finished tug. First of all the keel was laid down, and about three-fifths of its length was rabbeted (i.e. recessed) to receive the edge of the first plank, stroke or strake. Towards the bow and stern where the hull planking was twisted almost vertical, the rabbet was, of course, not necessary, and these parts of the keel forward and aft were called the 'huddings' (193). On each side of the keel twenty-two strakes of planking were laid as a rule. The tug **Zephyr** (27), was an exception and had twenty-four strakes on each side. Two shipwrights would stand one on each side of the keel and each would do his half of the hull. This method usually developed into a race to get done before the other

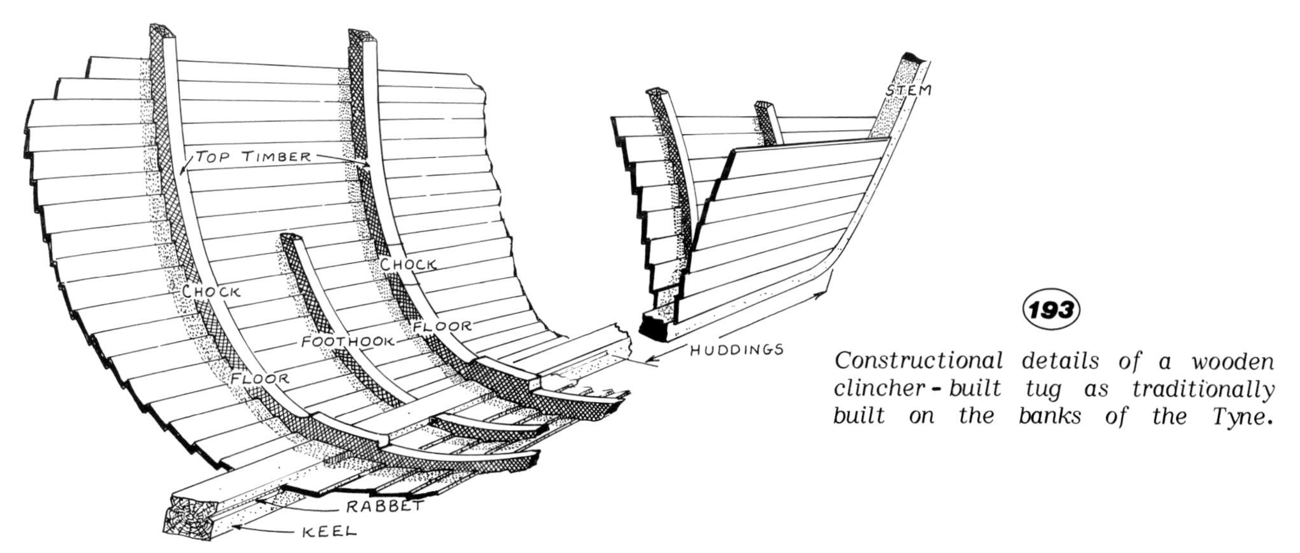

193

Constructional details of a wooden clincher-built tug as traditionally built on the banks of the Tyne.

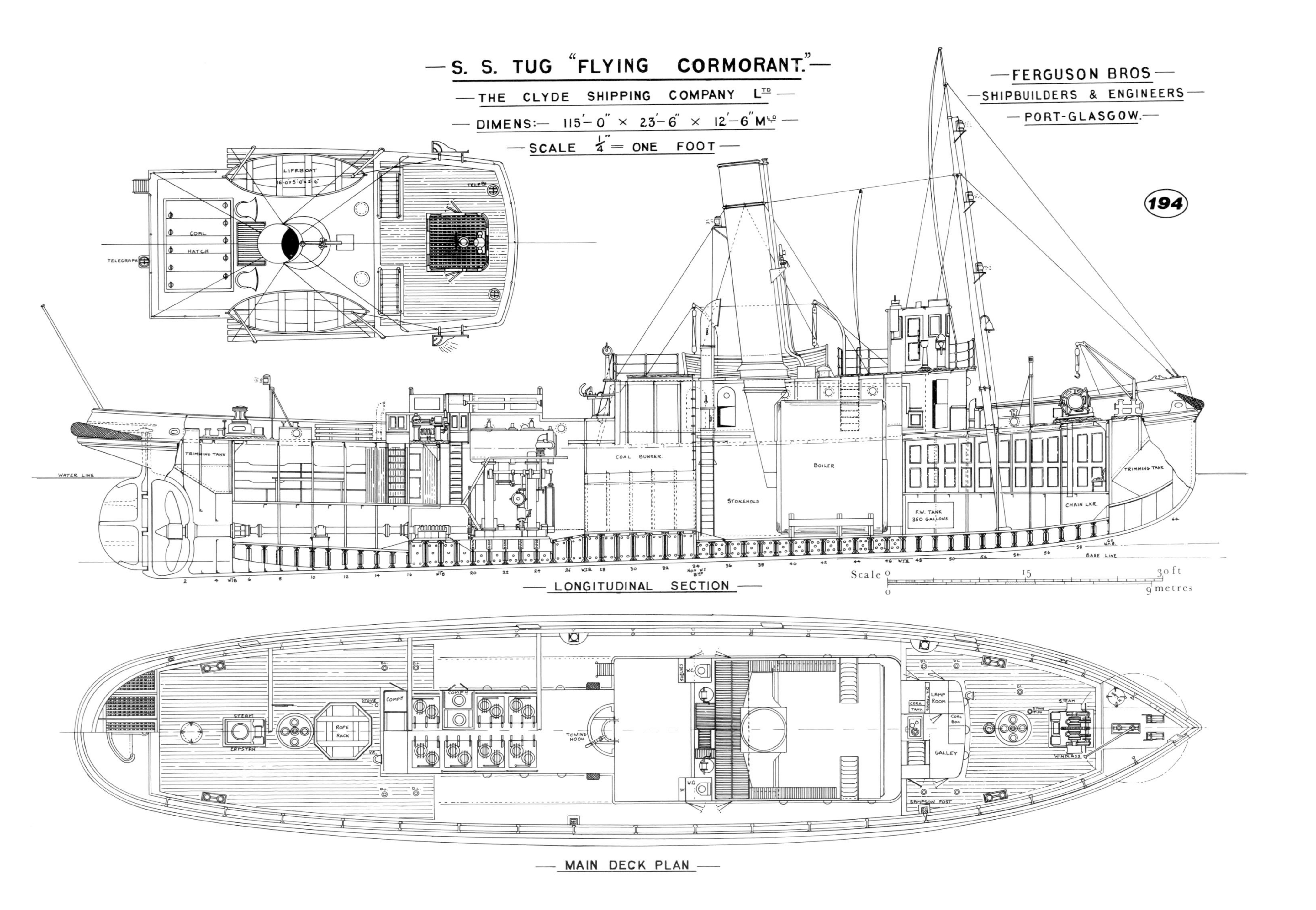

S. S. TUG "FLYING CORMORANT."
THE CLYDE SHIPPING COMPANY L^TD
DIMENS:— 115'–0" × 23'–6" × 12'–6" M^LD
SCALE 1/4" = ONE FOOT
FERGUSON BROS
SHIPBUILDERS & ENGINEERS
PORT-GLASGOW.
194
LIFEBOAT
COAL
HATCH
TELEGRAPH
TRIMMING TANK
WATER LINE
COAL BUNKER
STOKEHOLD
BOILER
F.W. TANK
350 GALLONS
CHAIN LKR.
BASE LINE
LONGITUDINAL SECTION
Scale 0 15 30 ft
0 9 metres
STEAM
CAPSTAN
ROPE
RACK
STOVE
TOWING
HOOK
SHELVES
W.C.
LAMP
ROOM
COAL
BOX
GALLEY
OIL TANKS
WINDLASS
SAMPSON POST
MAIN DECK PLAN

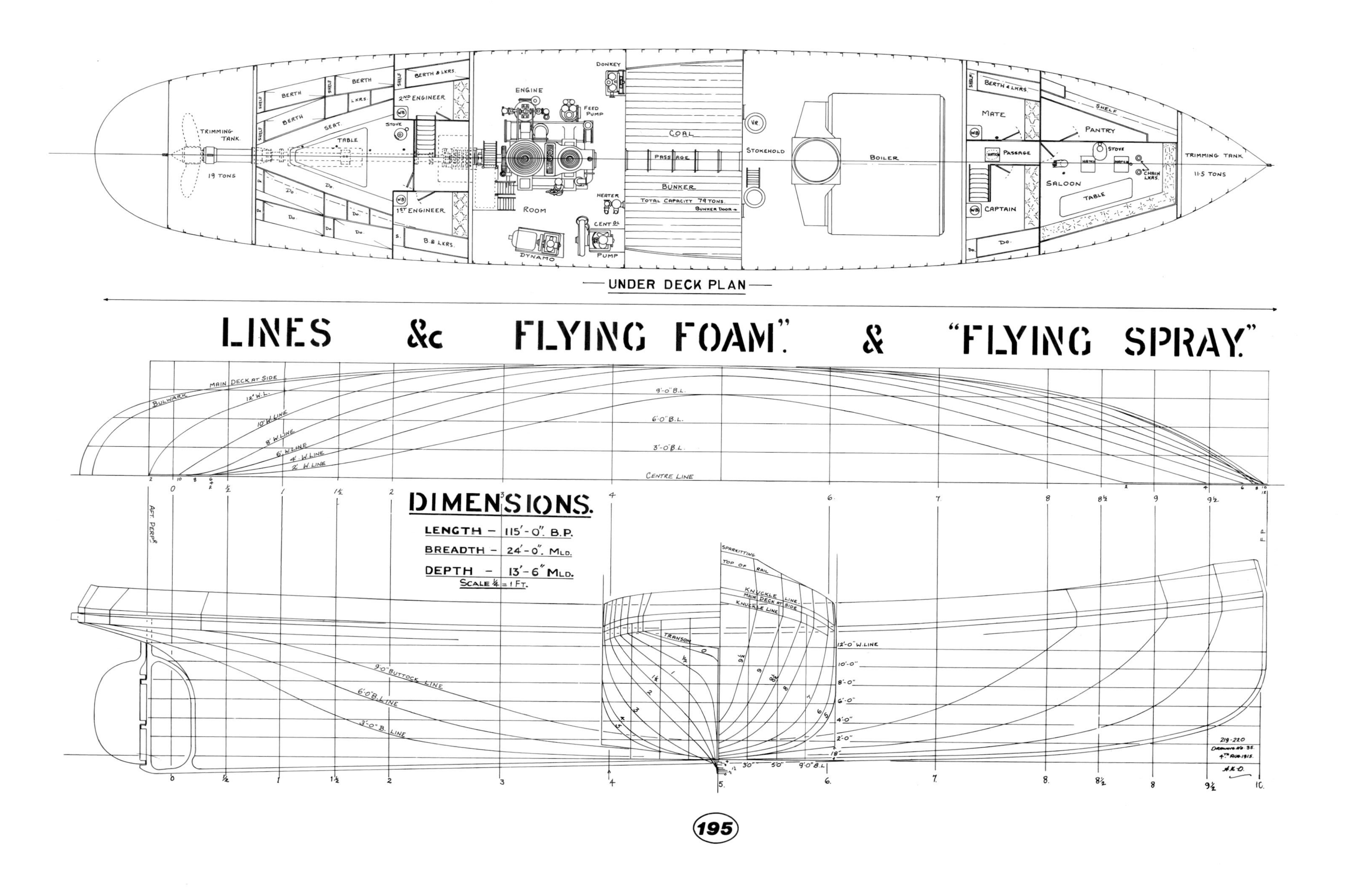
UNDER DECK PLAN
LINES &c "FLYING FOAM". & "FLYING SPRAY."
DIMENSIONS.
LENGTH - 115'-0". B.P.
BREADTH - 24'-0". MLD.
DEPTH - 13'-6" MLD.
SCALE ¼ = 1 FT.
TRIMMING TANK
19 TONS
BERTH
SEAT.
TABLE
STOVE
2ND ENGINEER
1ST ENGINEER
BERTH & LKRS.
B & LKRS.
ENGINE
ROOM
FEED PUMP
DONKEY
HEATER
CENT. PUMP
DYNAMO
COAL
PASSAGE
BUNKER
TOTAL CAPACITY 79 TONS.
BUNKER DOOR
STOKEHOLD
BOILER
MATE
CAPTAIN
PANTRY
SALOON
SHELF
CHAIN LKRS.
TRIMMING TANK
11.5 TONS
MAIN DECK AT SIDE
BULWARK
12' W.L.
10' W.LINE
8' W.LINE
6' W.LINE
4' W.LINE
2' W.LINE
9'-0" B.L.
6'-0" B.L.
3'-0" B.L.
CENTRE LINE
AFT PERPR.
F.P.
SPARKITTING
TOP OF RAIL
KNUCKLE LINE
MAIN DECK AT SIDE
TRANSOM
12'-0" W.LINE
9'-0" BUTTOCK LINE
6'-0" B.LINE
3'-0" B. LINE
219-220
DRAWING No 35.
4TH AUG 1915.

man and also into a competition to see how nearly the top strakes met when the hull was planked. The work was marvellously accurate and was faired entirely by the eye. After the first strake had been fastened into the rabbet the next was clipped on, adjusted according to the shipwright's judgement and then clinched with copper nails. There were no timber frames at intervals to act as a guide. Seven strakes were built up in the fashion described before any support was given to the planking apart from the clinching nails. Then when seven strakes were laid the floors were shaped and put in place, and after another strake or two had been added pieces of shaped wood called foothooks were fixed halfway between each floor. The planking proceeded and when it was complete the top timbers were dropped in. These stopped short of the floors but a continuity was obtained by inserting chocks in the space and securing them to the floors and timbers by copper nails. The bottom strakes were made of American elm $1\frac{3}{4}$" thick. In way of the top timbers American oak was used for the planking. The timbers were placed about 20 inches apart and were about $3\frac{1}{2}$ inches square on the landing.' The picture from an old Smith's Dock Journal shows the yard of J. & D. Morris at Bill Quay on the Tyne with a little paddle tug called **Pioneer** (190) on the slipway. In Middlesborough a few tugs were launched by Leach between 1850 and 1870, and by Richardson, Duck & Co. between 1860 and 1900.

Although Hull never boasted large tug fleets, there were several shipyards in the surrounding countryside from which a continuous stream of tugs, trawlers and drifters were launched, all the yards being miles from the sea up a river or canal. Cochrane and Cooper (later Cochrane & Sons) of Beverley and Selby, Richard Dunston (Hessle) Ltd., J. Scarr & Son, Beverley (later H. Scarr Ltd., Hessle), Cook, Welton & Gemmell Ltd., Hull, Chas. D. Holmes & Co. Ltd., Beverley, all household names amongst tugmen. Further inland the Goole Shipbuilding and Repairing Co. Ltd. and John Harker Ltd. of Knottingley had building yards which produced tugs both large and small. In the early 1900s W.H. Warren built several tugs at New Holland, and more up to date J.S. Watson (Gainsborough) Ltd. launched several of the **Empire** class of tug 50 miles from the sea. A new name in the tugbuilding field is that of J.S. Doig (Grimsby) Ltd. The ports of Norfolk are famous for their fishing fleets, but their yards managed to fit tugs into their building programme. There was Crabtree & Co. Ltd., and Fellows & Co. Ltd. of Great Yarmouth, and Richards (Shipbuilders) Ltd. of Lowestoft most of whose tugs have been built since the last war.

Only a few tugs have come from Irish yards, G. Robinson & Co., having built a few in the 1860s/1870s, while Harland & Wolff Ltd. of Belfast have launched a few in between the large ships for which they are renowned. Readers may know of other yards which have built a few tugs, but those named above are those which built and launched a number during their existence.

To give some idea of the cost of owning a tug the following are the prices extracted from the records of Scott & Son Ltd. of Bowling. As the sizes of the tugs varied, a figure has been given "£/ton gross". It was not uncommon for ship sales brokers to quote this figure when selling ships. It can clearly be seen that after the two world wars prices climbed steeply:

		£/ton gross
1897	**Musgrave** for Belfast Harbour Comm. 115.0 ft. 253 tons. 150 n.h.p. £4840 (hull only)	£19.13
1905	**Tartar** for Millward of Swansea, 90.2 ft. 95 tons £3236	£34.06
1908	**Dencade** for Denaby & Cadeby Collieries. 72.2 ft. 56 tons. 50 n.h.p. £2400	£42.86
1912	**George Dinsdale** for Blyth Steam Tug Co. 90.0 ft. 90 tons. 60 n.h.p. £3670	£40.78
1914	**Wrestler** for Steel & Bennie. 106.4 ft. 192 tons. 99 n.h.p. £7550	£39.32
1935	**Warrior** for Steel & Bennie. 107.1 ft. 249 tons. 112 n.h.p. £23,700	£95.18
1942	**Empire** tugs for Ministry of Transport. 107.1 ft. 260 tons. 123 n.h.p. £40,000 approx.	£153.85
1954	**North Beach** for Alexandra Towing Company. 96.7 ft. 220 tons. £95,000	£431.82

It was not only inflation which was causing the steady increase in the £/gross ton cost, but also the increasing complexity and sophistication of the equipment on board the tugs. Shortly after the **North Beach** was launched the first diesel tugs were built on the Clyde, for the first time passing the £100,000 mark.

It is not so simple to follow the prices of the old paddle tugs as there are no proper records for one builder. However, comparisons can be made from odd scraps of information:

		£/ton gross
1855	**Maid of Orleans**, Wood Paddle Tug built N.Shields for McFarlane,Greenock. 80.6 feet, 64 tons, 32 n.h.p. £1575.	£24,6
1864	**Flying Spray**, Wood Paddle Tug built N. Shields for Clyde Shipping Co. 79 feet, 69 tons, 30 n.h.p. £1550	£29,5
1865	**Conqueror**, Iron Paddle Tug built by Wm.Simons for Clyde Shipping Co. (See page 38) 135 feet, 199 tons, 120 n.h.p. £5200	£26
1864	**Flying Meteor**, Iron Paddle Tug built by Blackwood & Gordon (Clyde) for Clyde Shipping Co. 111.5 feet, 127 tons, 240 i.h.p. £4200	£33,1
1870	**Cambria** for Watkins by London Iron Engineering & Iron Shipbuilding Co. 138.8 feet, 209 tons, 100 n.h.p. £10,000	£47,85
1876	**India** for Watkins by Westwood & Baillie. 138.9 feet, 218 tons, 90 n.h.p. £9245	£42,41

From these figures it certainly looks as though the paddle tug was more expensive than screw tugs. The records available for Watkins tugs show that the Scott prices were about average e.g. Screw Tug **Tasmania** (1883, 80.0, 81 tons, 45 n.h.p), £3168 or £39.11 per gross ton. Denny's tugs look rather expensive e.g. Paddle Tug **Portland** (1876, 95.4, 122 tons, 80 n.h.p.) £10,517 (£86.2 per gross ton) and the screw tug **Snark** (1878, 60 ft., 29 tons). £2168 (£74.26 per gross ton).

The problem of the pioneers of the steam engine was to convert the liner motion of the piston rod into a rotary motion to drive the paddlewheels. Jonathan Hulls proposed to use a ratchet mechanism. Other engineers on land solved the question by using a beam pivotted at its centre mounted above the engine driving a crank on the output shaft. The headroom required was far too great for marine use and so the beam was replaced by a pair of levers placed one either side of the engine, the 'side lever engine'. Depending on the arrangement of the lever pivot the engine could also be called a 'grasshopper' engine, though the term 'side lever' was applied indiscriminately to both forms.

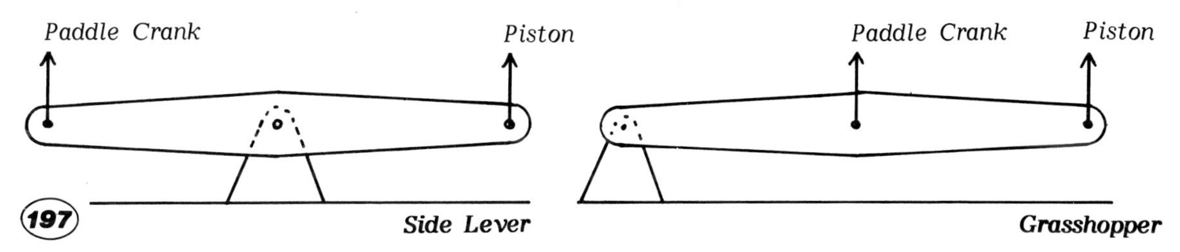

The drawing shows a grasshopper engine with a stroke of 54" and a diameter of 34" (199) built for the tugs **Old Trafford** and **Acton Grange** of the Manchester Ship Canal Co., by Hepple & Co., South Shields in 1907. The cylinder is arranged in a vertical position mounted on the condenser which in turn is mounted on a hollow base containing the 'hotwell' in which the condensed steam is collected for return to the boiler. The piston rod is connected to a crosshead sliding up and down guides above the cylinder. A rod on each side connects the crosshead to the levers at the bottom of the engine on each side. As the lever rocks up and down it drives: (a) The paddle shaft crank; (b) The air pump which maintains the vacuum in the condenser; (c) The water feed pump which returns the water from the hotwell to the boiler; (d) The bilge pump which keeps the bottom of the tug clear of water from leakage or spillage.

The early manufacturing machinery could not work to fine limits and the engines had to be fitted together by hand; hence the practice of calling an engineer a 'fitter'. Joints were made steam tight or vacuum tight with rust, formed by steaming in a mixture of fine metal turnings, sal ammoniac and water; crude but effective. As manufacturing methods improved joints were machined to give a good fit and the old rust jointing was abandoned.

A single loose eccentric on the paddle shaft driven as desired by either end of a fixed segmental metal stopper attached to the paddle shaft worked the main slide valve for both ahead and astern rotation. The valve was operated through a weigh shaft and lever arms, but the connection between the eccentric rod and its arm on the weigh-shaft could be broken at will by lifting the 'gab' (near the end of the rod) off the pin secured in the arm on the weigh-shaft. This disconnection permitted the main slide valve to be moved by hand to start the engine in the desired direction. As the paddle shaft rotated the appropriate end of the stopper came up against the one side of a projection or 'dog' on the eccentric sheave and if the gab was then allowed by the engineman to drop on to the pin on the weigh-shaft arm, the valve continued to be operated by the eccentric so as to continue to run the engine in the desired direction. The lifting of the 'gab' end of the rod out of connection with the weigh-shaft was done by the so-called 'trippet' gear, operated usually by a pedal projecting a little above the engine platform. The long hand levers for manual operation of the main slide valve which moved back and forward above the deck level as the engine ran were a familiar feature to all who have ever been on board a paddle tug with side lever engines(198).

An expansion valve was fitted in the same chest as the main slide valve. The eccentric operating this was in a fixed position on the shaft for use in the headway motion only. This valve was put out of operation by a trippet pedal and gab link, while the main slide valve was being operated by hand, and during astern running, the expansion valves being at such times placed so that the steam ports controlled by it were fully open. A means of varying the travel of the expansion valve while the engine was running, was provided to allow variation of points of cut-off. This saved fuel since not only the steam pressure was used but also the heat energy of the steam which cooled as it expanded converting heat to work moving the piston.

In early engines it was not customary to fit main steam stop valves, a throttle valve in the expansion valve chest being the only means of regulating the steam to the engine, other than the variation of points of cut-off by the expansion valve. When the steam was exhausted from the cylinder it entered the condenser where it was cooled to create a vacuum which was essential to the efficient running of the engine. In the early days a jet condenser was used where raw sea water was sprayed into the condenser to mix with the steam from the exhaust. Part of the diluted sea water was discharged overboard while part was returned to the boiler as feed water. As a result the concentration of salt in the boiler water increased and if ignored could result in a deposition of salt on the fire tubes which produced uneven expansion and uneven heating which could be dangerous. In any case it reduced the rate of heat transfer leading to loss of power. It was necessary for the engineer from time to time to check the boiler water which he did by simply drawing off a bucket of water and dropping a potato into it. If the potato sank there was no danger but if the potato floated it was high time to blow down the boiler. To change the water in the boiler the fire was first banked up, then the blowdown valve was opened allowing the steam pressure to force most of the water out of the boiler. The blowdown cocks were closed and after a minute or so a few buckets of cold sea water were thrown over the boiler, the blowdown cocks were opened and the vacuum in the boiler drew in water from the sea. The fire was then brought to life and within about two hours the tug was ready for service once more. This could be a somewhat chancy business if the tug was at sea in rough weather as she was helpless until the process was complete.

In the later engines the cooling was done in a surface condenser in which the boiler water and the sea water flowed through separate parts of the condenser and the purity of the boiler water was preserved. The vacuum in the condenser played an important part in the efficient running of the engine, and engineers were proud of their ability to maintain a high vacuum, sometimes as high as 28" water gauge, and they could judge the vacuum without a gauge just by the 'liveliness' of the engine. One old engineer was heard to boast that he could shut off steam and keep his tug going for several miles on the vacuum alone! It was said that the jet condenser produced a very 'lively' engine, so much so that even after the surface condenser had become a standard installation some owners had special cocks fitted so that the condenser would become a jet condenser if required.

The boilers were generally made to fit the hull resulting in some rather strange shapes. There were usually two fireboxes and either one or two return flues leading to the uptake and funnel. Because of the cramped space available the fireboxes and flues were seldom circular and must have taken a lot of skill in fabrication. At one time the safety valves were not fitted directly on the boiler but on the steam pipe between the boiler and the engine. For safety a direct loaded and lever loaded safety valve were required and as the tug heaved in heavy seas the valves would lift and blow off steam intermittently. Mention has been made from time to time about the way in which the engineer used to load the safety valve to try to gain an extra knot or so. The result was frequently disastrous and up to the end of the century boiler explosions were regular items in the local press and the maritime newspapers. The old boilers did not have a very long life and the entry 'N.B.' followed by the year fitted was common in the registers. Boilers were patched when necessary with 'one-eyed' patches, a bolt and a nut introduced into a hole in the shell of the boiler and screwed up tight after red lead and tar had been applied. One boiler was reported to have had twelve patches when it was finally condemned.

One of the greatest problems faced by the owners of the paddle tugs was that their furnaces produced a fair amount of smoke when full output was demanded of them for a high speed run for a tow or for towing a heavy ship. Anti-smoke laws were introduced and tugowners received summons after summons. Various modifications were introduced to the boilers so that they might 'consume or burn their own smoke' but they either did not work properly or owners found them too expensive. It was claimed that even Government owned tugs with all the nation's money behind them also produced smoke under working conditions. In 1860 Mr. Wm. Watkins himself appeared in court and stated that it was not possible for a steam tug to generate enough steam for towing without emitting smoke. He had spent £100 on experiments and modifications but in all cases his tugs had suffered unacceptable loss of power. He did say, however, that by using Welsh coal smoke nuisance emission could be avoided, but as this would increase the running costs of the tugs it was not a popular solution with the tugowners, and the smoke nuisance continued and so did the prosecutions and the fines.

The safety standards below deck were almost nil. The engines were not guarded and if, in rough weather the engineer lost his balance while passing between a set of two engines he would almost certainly be badly injured, an event which was quickly reported in the Victorian press which thrived on death and disaster. The machinery itself although apparently very strongly built, sometimes caused trouble when some part came loose and caused damage which would often sink the tug. Today, examples of the 'grasshopper' engine can still be seen, in the **Reliant** in the National Maritime Museum, also on the riverside at Renfrew where the engines from the **Clyde** of 1851 have been preserved (217) and in the Museum of Industry at Newcastle where a single engine from the **Lingdale** of 1882 is on view. The 'engine-driver' was usually a man without qualifications who had graduated from the position of fireman. Government inspectors set the safety valves but when their backs were turned the engineer would sometimes load a chain on the lever. This could hardly be from ignorance as boiler explosions were frequently reported. It was generally done as a simple expedient

*The engineer of the **Elie** stands on the working platform holding the two hand levers. At night the engine room was lit by the two big paraffin lamps.*

PADDLE TUG ENGINE

Scale 1½" To 1Ft.

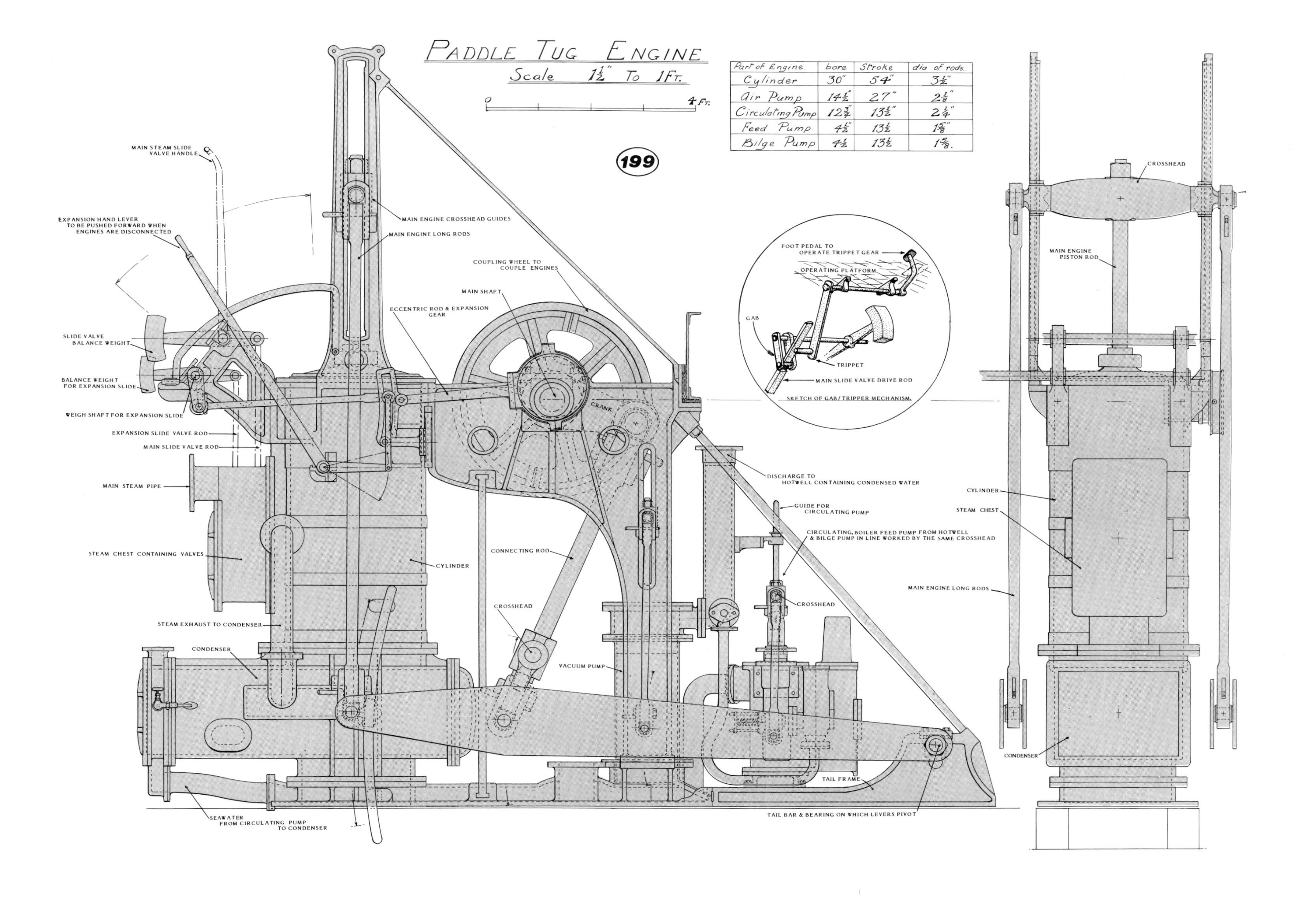

Part of Engine.	bore	Stroke	dia of rods.
Cylinder	30"	54"	3½"
Air Pump	14½"	27"	2⅛"
Circulating Pump	12¾"	13½"	2¼"
Feed Pump.	4½"	13½	1⅝"
Bilge Pump	4½	13½	1⅝.

to gain more power to combat more powerful rivals who were stealing the tows. In 1866 the engineer of the **Jasper** (1863, 103.2ft. 123 tons, 50 n.h.p.) stood in the dock of the court accused of being responsible for the death of his two firemen. The experts asserted that 23 p.s.i. was the correct working pressure of the boiler, but that, due to the chain of the safety valve a pressure of 31 p.s.i. had caused the boiler to explode, not much of a factor of safety! What the **Jasper**'s engineer had done was definitely not done in ignorance as the tug's boilers had burst only three years previously killing one of the firemen.

In the introduction, reference was made to the question of engine horsepower and its measurement. The definition of horsepower is the rate of doing work equal to 33,000 foot pounds per minute and could be calculated from the following formula:

$$\text{(Indicated) Horse Power} = \frac{\text{area of piston x stroke x r.p.m. x mean effective pressure}}{33{,}000}$$

The difficult figure to measure was 'mean effective pressure' and the early pioneers worked on a different formula to obtain what they called "nominal horsepower":

$$\text{N.H.P.} = \frac{(\text{diameter of cylinder in inches})^2 \text{ x } \sqrt[3]{\text{stroke in feet}}}{47}$$

This was reasonably close as long as the steam pressures were very low, but the formula became outdated as working pressures in engines increased. The North East Coast Institution of Engineers proposed a modified formula for paddle engines. Lloyds rule was:

$$\text{N.H.P.} = \frac{1/2(\text{diameter of cylinder in inches x stroke in feet + total width of firegrate in inches})}{630}$$

As will be appreciated the resultant figure was exactly what the name suggests 'nominal horsepower' and as time went on the figure bore less and less relationship to the 'indicated horsepower' which is the power developed in the engine cylinders. In the early days the ratio of I.H.P.: N.H.P. was about 3 or 4, but by the time the steam tug had reached its heyday, just before the First World War the ratio had risen to about 8 to 10. In lawsuits a description of the tug was often given and the power of the tug was described in terms of 'effective horsepower' or 'actual horsepower', terms which have today been replaced by 'shaft horsepower' which is the power delivered by the engine for the paddles or propeller. The reason for quoting the tug's power in lawsuits was to try to impress the judge and jury and convey the importance of the tug's contribution in carrying out the salvage. It was not unusual to exaggerate the figures and even big firms such as Watkins of London were admonished by the judge for this practice.

Engine and boiler makers were always striving to improve the performance of their plant. In 1863 the **Resolute** (1857, 161.0ft. 375 tons. 200 n.h.p.) was sold by her Liverpool owners to India, but before she was handed over her engines and boilers were replaced. Her coal consumption went down from 30 tons per day to 18 tons per day, and her top speed went up by one knot. Wm. Watkins of London had a tug called the **Albion** (1851, 129.7ft. 168 tons. 120 n.h.p.) which was proving a rather expensive vessel to work, so he resolved to fit her with new boilers and machinery. this he did in 1868 with boilers working at 30 p.s.i. and engines of 80 n.h.p. total which gave 400 i.h.p. and a greater speed than before, she could now do nearly 13 knots. Having continually been in trouble for making too much smoke he also had incorporated new anti-smoke modifications. It was said that "In half an hour any engineer who is up in his business ought to be able to understand the parts of the machinery and drive the engines in the **Albion** with confidence." Some larger tugs were fitted with a pair of diagonal engines (122). The later engines of the screw tugs such as the compound of **Stronghold** (201) were closely similar to the compounds and triple expansion engines fitted in coasters. Further details of their workings, auxiliaries and the associated 'Scotch' boilers will be found in 'Steam Coasters and Short Sea Traders', also in this series.

Paddle Wheels: The first paddle wheels were equipped with fixed floats; that is paddle blades fastened to the radial arms of the wheel. They were not very efficient as a lot of power was lost forcing the water down as they entered and lifting water as they emerged. This could be partially offset by using a large number of narrow blades and ensuring that they did not go too deep into the water. On a tug this was not easy as the small size of the wheel restricted the number of blades and the change of draught as coal was consumed meant that at her departure to sea the floats were deeply immersed. Various patents were taken out for 'reefing floats' which altered the area of the float to suit the draught. These were still being fitted in the 1860s despite the existence of 'feathering floats'.

As early as 1813 'feathering floats' were invented being a system whereby the angle of the paddle blade was altered so as to enter and leave the water in a nearly vertical angle. However, it was not until 1835 that the universally applied 'star centre' was introduced. Each paddle float was mounted on a pivot and had an arm fixed to it. Slightly forward of and slightly above the axis of the paddle shaft was mounted a boss on which a star shaped casting revolved (202). Between the arm and the star were links, and the eccentric action of that arrangement produced the required adjustment to the angle of the floats. One of the arms was fixed to the star wheel, all the others were pivotted. This was known as the 'overhung' type of feathering paddle wheel. The basic problem of the design was that the fixed pivot of the star wheel was fastened to the paddle sponson which had to be made rigid and strong to ensure that the correct relative positions of the two centres,

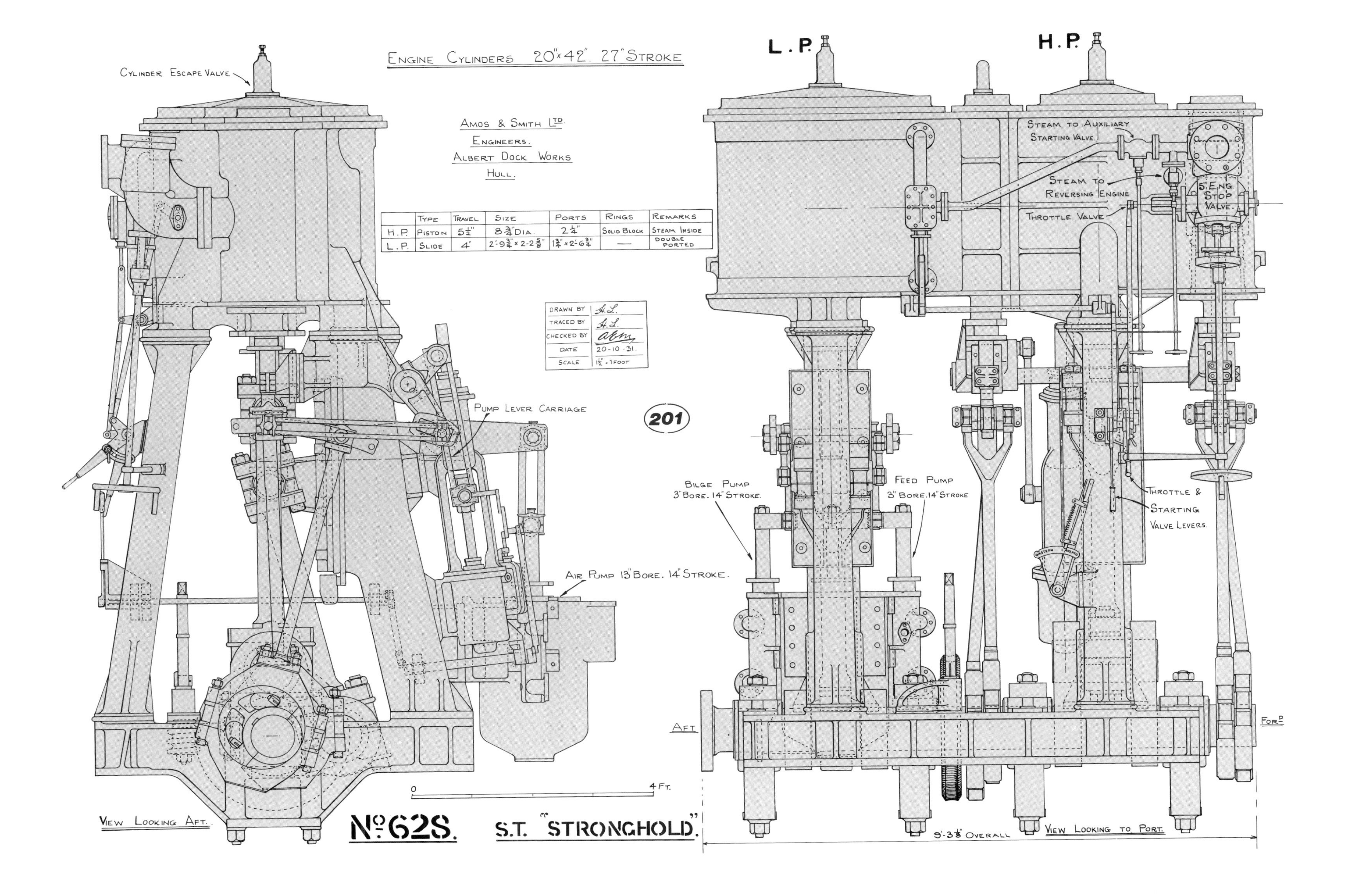

Engine Cylinders 20"x42". 27" Stroke
Cylinder Escape Valve
Amos & Smith Ltd.
Engineers.
Albert Dock Works
Hull.
Type | Travel | Size | Ports | Rings | Remarks
H.P. | Piston | 5½" | 8¾" Dia. | 2¼" | Solid Block | Steam Inside
L.P. | Slide | 4" | 2'-9¾" x 2-2⅝" | 1¾" x 2'-6¾" | — | Double Ported
Drawn by A.L.
Traced by A.L.
Checked by
Date 20-10-31.
Scale 1½" = 1 Foot
Pump Lever Carriage
201
Air Pump 13" Bore. 14" Stroke.
0
4 Ft.
View Looking Aft.
No. 62S.
S.T. "Stronghold".
L.P.
H.P.
Steam to Auxiliary Starting Valve.
Steam to Reversing Engine
Throttle Valve
S. Eng. Stop Valve.
Bilge Pump 3" Bore. 14" Stroke.
Feed Pump 3" Bore. 14" Stroke
Throttle & Starting Valve Levers.
Aft
For'd
9'-3⅜" Overall
View Looking to Port.

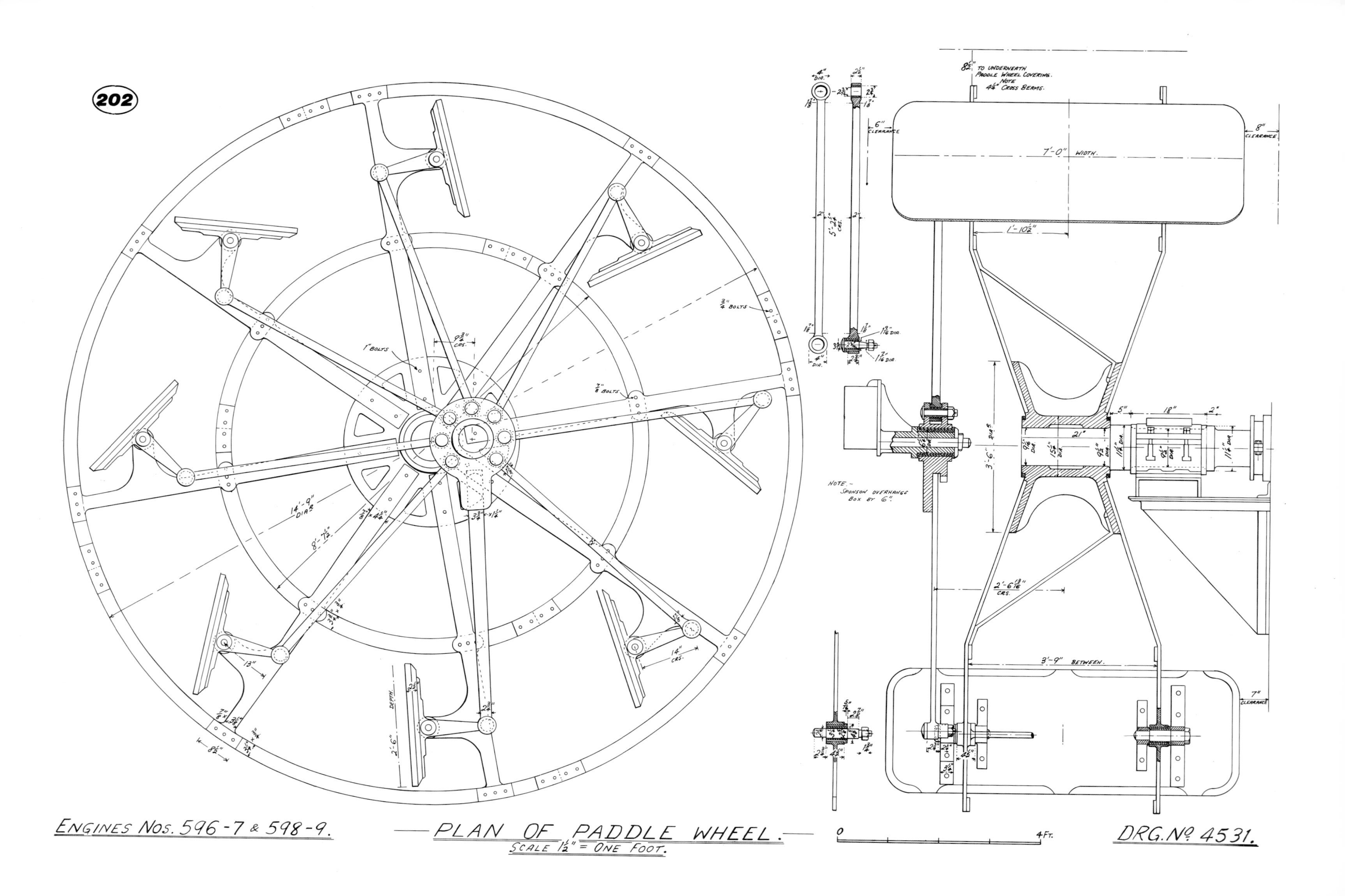

ENGINES NOS. 596-7 & 598-9.

PLAN OF PADDLE WHEEL.

SCALE 1½" = ONE FOOT.

DRG. No. 4531.

Paddle Box Designs.

1. *Irlam.* J.P.Rennoldson & Sons (1903) for Manchester Ship Canal Co.

2. *Daring.* J.Readhead & Co. (1876) for Wm. Sandford, Gravesend.

3. *United Service.* C. W. Dodgin & Co. (1872) for Great Yarmouth Star Steam Tug Co.

4. *Emperor of India.* J. & M. Gunn (1877) for W. Strong, Cardiff.

5. *Warrior.* Readhead, Softley & Co. (1871) for T.W.Elliott, London.

6. *Vanguard.* Robertson & Co. (1868) for J.Steel, Glasgow.

7. *Imperial.* Thames Iron Works (1879) for Great Eastern Railway, Lowestoft.

8. *Milton.* Built at Milton, Kent (1866) for A.R.Fisher, Gravesend.

(203)

of the paddle shaft and feathering gear, remained unchanged. A bad blow coming alongside or collision could render the paddle unserviceable. The answer was to have a large eccentric disc inboard of the paddle where it was protected. It was more difficult to make and fit, but it eliminated damage. It was however, not adopted widely on British paddle tugs.

Despite the satisfactory results obtained by the above feathering system, Victorian inventors persisted with variations and over 100 patents were taken out. One was "Aston's Disc-wheel Propeller" which was tried on one of Watkins' tugs in 1860. Each wheel was 14 feet in diameter, of 5 iron discs with spacers, dipping 2 feet into the water. On trial at 47 r.p.m and steam at 3 p.s.i. (according to the account!) it gave a speed of 6 knots. As it relied solely on the drag between the discs and the water, the starting and stopping was poor but "the patentee was confident that this could easily be overcome."

The paddle boxes were made of wood and on the wooden tugs were supported on wooden beams which spanned the vessel between the extremes of the paddle boxes and usually on wooden tugs there was an additional supporting framework of iron rods. The paddle boxes had vents to prevent the build-up of air and water and it was here that builders were able to include some decorative work. Vents followed four basic patterns: (a) A simple hole, usually oval or diamond shaped. (b) A number of horizontal slots. (c) Slots parallel to the rim of the box. (d) Slots arranged in a fan: this form had the widest variety of patterns (203).

Sometimes the name of the tug was placed on the rim or bottom boards. Investigation has shown that there is no link between design, builder and owner, i.e. they cannot be used for identification. Steps were usual fore and aft on the paddle boxes, even when sidehouses were present, and along the top was a short gangway from the bridge to the edge of the paddlebox.

Screw Propeller: It is not proposed to go into the subject of propeller design, suffice it to say that the propeller of a tug has to be somewhat of a compromise in that it has to provide thrust under two conditions. Firstly when the tug is running free at high speed, secondly when she is moving at slow speed with a ship in tow. The noticeable features of the tug propeller are the large diameter for the size of vessel and the large area of the blades. In recent years the performance of tugs in respect of pulling power and manoeuvrability have been improved by the fitting of the Kort rudder. This is in essence a tube fitted round the propeller having a cross-section almost like that of an aircraft's wing. The result is an increase in the thrust from the screw in the region of 50%. When first introduced the Kort nozzle was fixed and although the thrust was increased the manoeuvrability was affected. When the Kort nozzle was combined with the rudder so that it could be rotated (the Kort rudder) the manoeuvrability was vastly improved, so much so that it is possible to run full speed astern in a straight line, a feat which is extremely difficult in a tug with an open screw.

However before the Kort nozzle, there came the Gill shrouded propellor. It was fitted to Watkins' **Palencia** (1916, 75.5ft. 95 tons. 41 n.h.p.), in 1923. This was a narrow slightly tapered ring fitted to a propellor with flat tips, in effect a rotating Kort nozzle. The aim was to improve propellor efficiency rather than achieve higher bollard pull. From 8.5 knots with 320 i.h.p. at 121 r.p.m., the **Palencia** after conversion gave 9.5 knots, with 305 i.h.p. at 119 r.p.m. The Kort nozzle was first introduced into Great Britain in 1934 when the **John Hamilton** (1918, 75.0ft. 58 tons. 21 n.h.p), of Falmouth had one fitted. On trials the bollard pull was increased from 1.95 tons to 3.1 tons at 140 i.h.p., and when towing a barge the towrope pull increased from 1.3 tons to 1.7 tons at 140 i.h.p.

Ideally a tug propeller should be as large as possible in diameter within the restrictions imposed by draught and should be immersed as deeply as possible. Where draught allows it is preferable to fit a single screw rather than twin screws. If, because of draught restrictions, it is necessary to fit twin screws, the stern of the tug has to be made broad and square to ensure a good flow of water over the propellers (as well as to protect the propellers from damage).

Tug propellers were generally made of cast iron. Working as they did in restricted waterways, frequently in rivers where the banks sloped, they were vulnerable and from time to time a touch would chip a blade and put the screw off balance. It was cheaper to replace a cast iron propeller than a bronze one. Ferguson Bros. (Port Glasgow) had the right idea when they fitted many of their tugs with screws with individual blades which bolted on to a square boss. The list on the original drawing of orders for replacement blades proved the wisdom of their idea. These propellers were fitted on the series of tugs which included the **Flying Cormorant** (194). The second propeller was fitted to the **Empire** class tugs which Ferguson Bros. built in 1941. This time the screw was a one piece casting, still of iron. This drawing also carried a list of orders for replacement propellers. It is worthy of note that the areas of the blades have been increased on the later propeller:

	1908 prop.	1941 prop.
Diameter	9'1"	10'0"
Total blade area	26.6 sq.ft.	40 sq.ft.
Ratio - blade area / total disc area	40.3%	50%
Horsepower	800 i.h.p.	1000 i.h.p.

 *Myer's Patent Propellor design.*

One sometimes comes across an odd type of propeller - the drawing of the **Knight Templar** built by McKie & Thomson shows a propeller in which the centre of each blade appears to have been removed (204). In fact the **Knight Templar** (1893, 95.2ft. 146 tons. 700 e.h.p.) was fitted with a Myer's Patent Propeller, introduced about 1892, a propeller with six narrow blades each with its own 'twist', but with the tips of each pair joined. The designer claimed an improvement in efficiency of 10 to 15 per cent and "a quiet action on the water which was most beneficial for use in canals - the Irwell Steam Passenger Company who operated vessels on the Manchester Ship Canal recorded a considerable increase in speed and greater command of their steamers."

When one considers how vulnerable was the tug's propeller to a tow rope hanging over the stern, either broken or washed overboard by heavy seas, it is surprising how seldom protection was provided to prevent the fouling of the screw. There were many occasions on which a tug skipper must have wished that a guard had been fitted. In September 1917 the tug **Flying Falcon** (1904, 107.0ft. 184 tons 800 i.h.p.) was despatched from Lough Swilly to meet and escort an inbound convoy. Soon after the tug joined the convoy the weather deteriorated and just off Islay a tremendous sea broke over the tug's after deck smashing the rope cradle and sweeping the ropes over the stern, fouling the propeller. The crew stood helpless while the tug was driven towards the island of Islay. They had already tried to launch the lifeboat but three of the crew had been drowned in the attempt and although the anchors were let go, the cables snapped and the vessel was driven up on the sandy beach at Machrie Bay where she literally sank into the sand. Two years later the tug was successfully salvaged and sold back to her owners, the Clyde Shipping Company. One of the few tugs on which rope guards were fitted was the **Hotspur** (143), the sketch shows how the rope guard was constructed. A simpler form of guard can be seen in the drawing of the propeller with bolted blades (205) where a sheet steel shroud covers the gap between the propeller boss and the stern frame.

FITTINGS

All the fittings described in the following paragraphs can be seen on the plans in the book.

The screw tug plan shows the **Ascupart** and **Morglay** (206) (1921, 101.1ft. 171 tons. 75 n.h.p.) which Bow, McLachlan of Paisley built for the 'Red Funnel' fleet of Southampton. In 1920 they

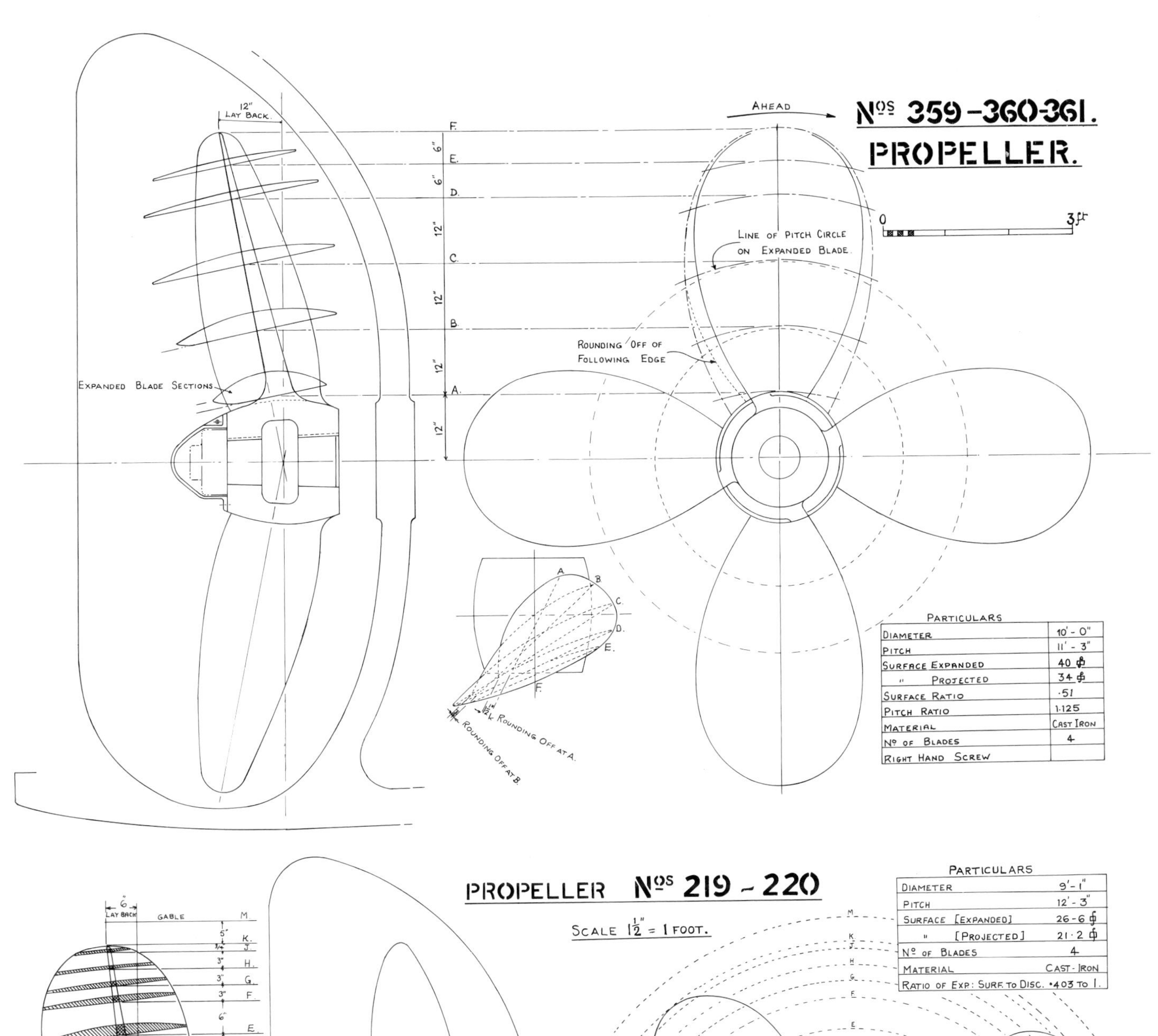

PARTICULARS

DIAMETER	10' - 0"
PITCH	11' - 3"
SURFACE EXPANDED	40 ☐'
" PROJECTED	34 ☐'
SURFACE RATIO	·51
PITCH RATIO	1·125
MATERIAL	CAST IRON
No OF BLADES	4
RIGHT HAND SCREW	

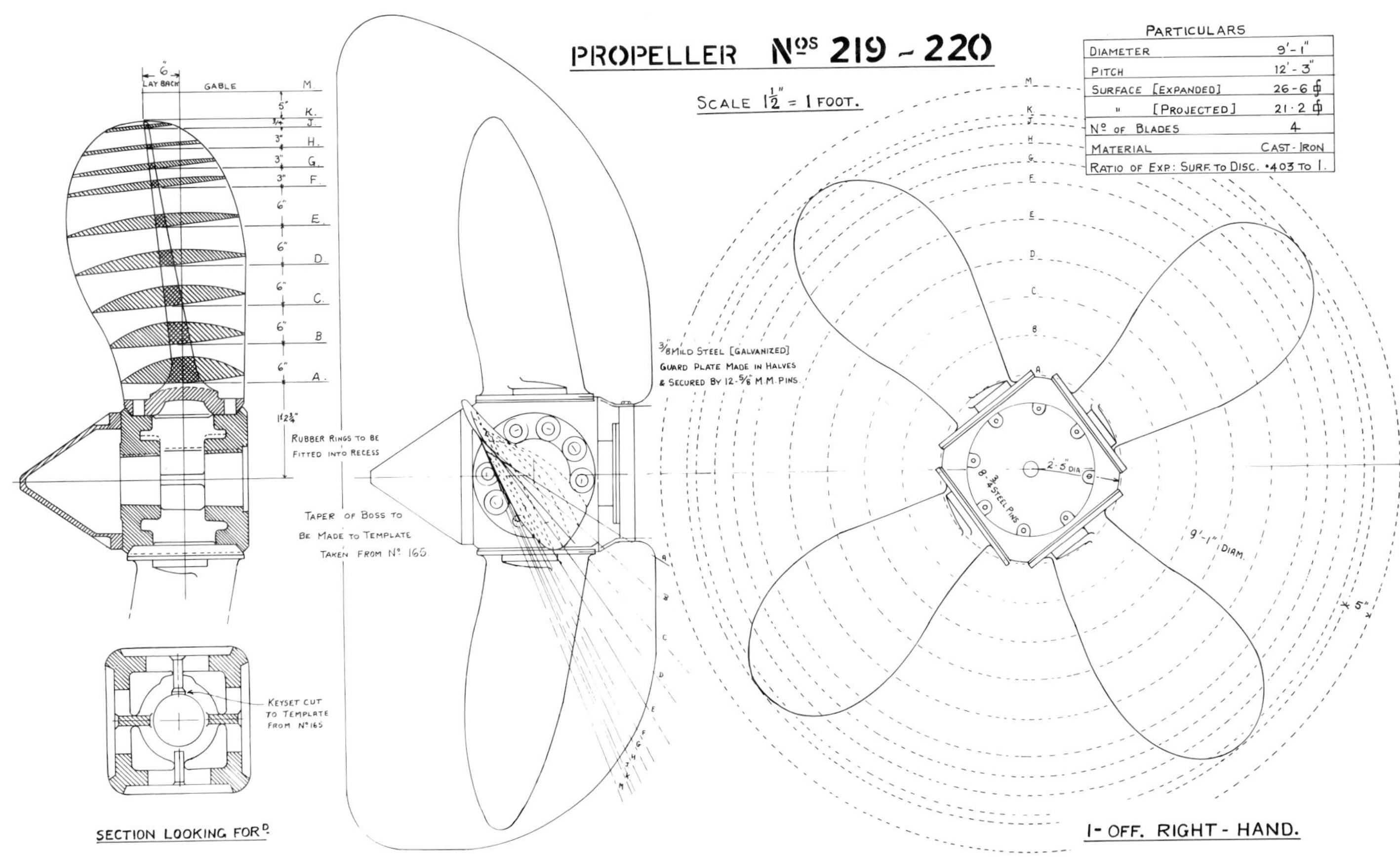

PARTICULARS

DIAMETER	9'-1"
PITCH	12'-3"
SURFACE [EXPANDED]	26-6 ☐'
" [PROJECTED]	21·2 ☐'
No OF BLADES	4
MATERIAL	CAST-IRON
RATIO OF EXP: SURF. TO DISC.	·403 TO 1.

had built the **Vanguard** and the **Thunderer** for Steel & Bennie to almost identical plans. It is interesting to compare these tugs with the **Flying Eagle** (67) which was launched from the same yard seven years later.

Although the records of the 'Red Funnel' fleet were partially lost during the war it is understood that this pair of tugs were fitted with the engines intended for a twin-screw minesweeping sloop, constructed for a vessel which was cancelled at the end of the war. Consequently one tug had a right-handed screw, the other a left-handed screw. Now, for those who are not familiar with tugs this feature is more important than it sounds! When a tug is moving ahead and the engines are suddenly put astern, the stern of the tug 'quarters' or 'throws' to port or starboard depending on the direction of rotation of the propeller. This can be a nuisance, but it can also be used to advantage while manoeuvring in a tight space. Imagine the result if the tug skipper had been used to one tug and he had been transferred to the 'non-standard' vessel. Incidentally the highly unusual names of these tugs had a very significant local meaning. **Morglay** was the name of a mythical local giant, while **Ascupart** was the sword of another, whose name was **Sir Bevois.** (A tug of this name was built in 1916 and another in 1953).

Anchors: Although one tends to think of tugs as tying up alongside quays or mooring to buoys, the anchor has always been an essential item of a tug's equipment. The "seeking" tug caught in a

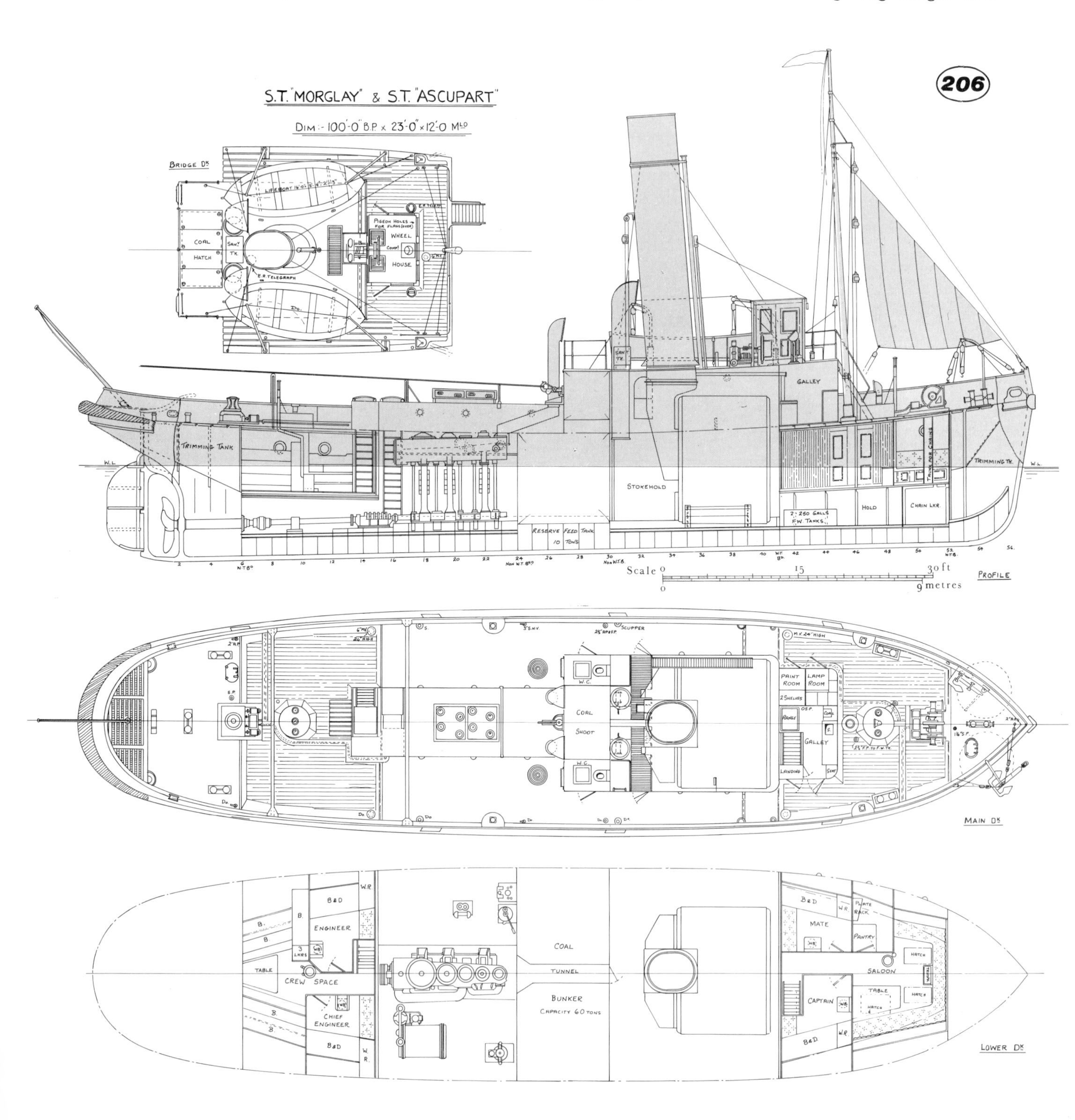

gale would run for shelter and ride out the storm lying at her anchor. The coastal tug with her tow, finding herself in danger of being driven on a lee shore, would have recourse to her anchor. On more than one occasion lives have been saved from vessels aground, by a tug which ventured out in foul weather and after dropping her anchor to windward of the wreck, payed out her anchor cable until she was able to render assistance.

At first stocked anchors were used and kept on the foredeck resting on chocks and clamped to prevent movement or else standing upright against the bulwarks and lashed tightly in position. To lift the anchor overboard an anchor davit was required, usually demountable, and fittings were provided so that it could be used on either bow. The davit was of the radial type, generally of the curved pattern (211) but occasionally it resembled a small crane.

On later tugs the anchor was of the stockless type and stowed in a hawsehole ready for immediate use. It was protected from causing damage by the overhang of the flared bow. On the modern tug there is a recess built into the hull and the anchor fits snugly into this with no part projecting beyond the hull (59). It is not uncommon to find a tug with only one hawsehole and one anchor ready for use, while a second anchor is stored on the foredeck as in years gone by.

Even the harbour tug has a use for an anchor. I have seen a tug drop its anchor in the middle of an undocking operation when the proceedings were unexpectedly held up for half an hour. It was simpler to do this than to have to maintain position by using the engines.

Anchors on board tugs fell into two basic categories:

The Folding Stock Anchor: The shank and arms are in one piece but the stock is round in section and is bent over at one end so that it can slide through a hole in the shank and lie along the shank when stowed on deck. There is a shoulder on the stock half way along to position it when the anchor is set up for use, being secured by a key through the stock.

The Stockless Anchor: There are several designs under this heading and as there is no stock the anchor can be hauled right up into a hawsepipe. The arm is arranged to pivot about the end of the shank so that the flukes lie snugly against the hull of the tug.

It is not unusual to find several different types of anchor on board a tug. The Admiralty tug **Rollcall** carried Byer's stockless anchors at the bow, a 50 cwt. Hall's stockless anchor on a platform at her stern, and a folding stock anchor on the after deck beside the salvage winch (108).

In the specification of a tug or if you examine the drawing of the midship section you will probably find the following terms being used:

Bower Anchors: These anchors are used for the ordinary purpose of mooring and are carried in the bow of the tug.

Stream Anchor: This is a lighter anchor than the bower and is used at the stern. No anchor cable is provided but a wire is shackled on when the anchor is needed.

Kedge Anchor: This is a small anchor which is laid out when the tug is being moved without its engines.

Typical outfits on tugs were as follows:

Twin screw tug **Hotspur** 1897 - dock tug.
Two bower anchors 5cwt., one stream anchor $1\frac{1}{2}$ cwt., one kedge anchor $\frac{3}{4}$ cwt.
135 fathoms anchor cable, 45 fathoms stream cable.
75 fathoms 6" tow rope, 90 fathoms 4" hawser.

Screw tug **Conqueror** 1905 - river tug
One bower anchor $3\frac{1}{2}$ cwt., one stream anchor $1\frac{1}{4}$ cwt.
60 fathoms anchor cable.
60 fathoms 5" manilla, 60 fathoms $3\frac{1}{2}$" warp.

Screw tug **Saint** class salvage tug 1918
Two bower anchors $10\frac{1}{2}$cwt., one kedge anchor $1\frac{3}{4}$ cwt., two salvage anchors 50cwt.
120 fathoms and 60 fathoms chain cable.
115 fathoms 12" manilla, 75 fathoms $7\frac{1}{2}$", manilla 120 fathoms 9" manilla.
260 fathoms 6" manilla, 90 fathoms $5\frac{1}{2}$"' manilla, 260 fathoms $4\frac{1}{2}$" manilla,
100 fathoms 3" manilla, 60 fathoms $3\frac{1}{2}$" steel wire.

The sizes of the anchors and chains was not a haphazard selection: Lloyds Register of Shipping laid down a set of rules which covered these items. The details of the calculation changed over the years but the principle was the same. Based on the length b.p., the moulded breadth and the depth of the tug an 'Equipment Number' was calculated. In the Rules is a table laying down the sizes of the anchors, chains and hawsers against given 'Equipment Numbers'. When the **Helen Peele** was built in 1901 the Equipment Number was based on half breadth, half girth, depth and length (147), while for the **Ascupart** of 1921 the figures used were the length, breadth and depth, with an allowance for superstructure. These calculations together with the details of the anchors, etc. were given on the drawing which showed the midship section and was sent to Lloyds for their approval.

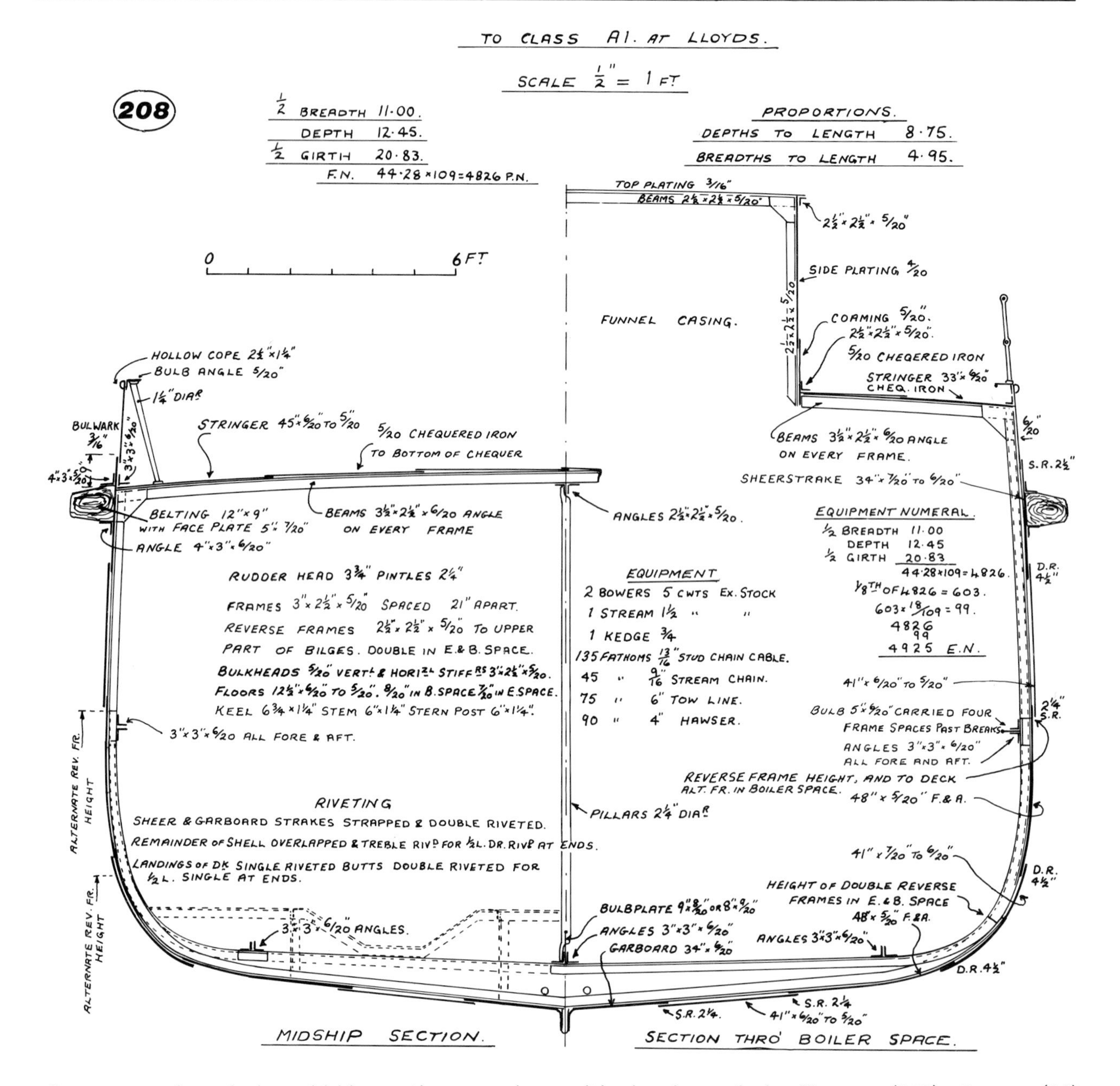

Some examples of the midship section are given with drawings of the **Hotspur** (208), **Oceana** (83), **Simla** (50).

Bridle or Gog-Rope: When the old paddle tug was working as the stern tug it was customary for her to be bow on to the ship she was assisting with the rope made fast to a timberhead in the bow. In most ports in this country the screw tug is placed stern to stern with her tow when working as stern tug. When the tow and her tugs are moving ahead the tow rope on the stern tug is "bowsed down", that is, hauled down by the bridle or gog-rope (209) until it is hard down on the stern rail. By this means the tug maintains control of the tow and does not swing from side to side. As soon as the tow commences to move astern at any point of the docking operation the bridle is eased off and the towrope resumes its normal angle, while on the bow tug the bridle is brought into play. The bridle is made fast to one arm of the double cruciform bollard, passes over the towrope or through a block attached to a broad thimble sliding on the towrope, and then down under the centre bar of the bollard to be lead to the capstan on the after deck. Where the tug is not equipped with a capstan the end of the bridle is made fast to the other arm of the bollard, but in this case the strain must be taken off the towrope each time the bridle has to be hauled down or eased off by hand.

Deck Machinery: The old wooden paddle tugs had a very simple windlass for recovering their anchor cables. Two wooden uprights strongly braced with big wooden knees carried two shafts, one with the winding handles and a small gear which drove a big gear on the other shaft. On the second shaft was the barrel for winding in the rope. As the tugs became larger the windlass became larger and a sampson post was added to carry the pawl for a ratchet on the barrel.

Deep sea tugs often had a steam cargo winch on the foredeck working the lifting tackle on the salvage derrick and the anchor windlass was driven from this by a rope or chain 'messenger'. On smaller tugs steam driven windlasses of a variety of types were introduced and it was some time before any degree of standardisation was achieved. The **Simla** of London had a windlass with the cylinders driving up at an angle to save deck space (49). The **Hardback** of Seaham had a windlass with a chain gipsy on one side and a barrel for a rope on the other.

In conjunction with the anchor windlass some form of 'chain stopper' may be fitted. It is usually a cast guide sitting on the deck equipped with a pivotting bar which sits between the links of the anchor cable. A simple chain stopper is the 'devil's claw' on the end of a chain fastened to the windlass, the 'claw' being hooked over a link on the chain.

The larger the tug the larger the anchor. The larger the anchor the larger the windlass. On the average tug the windlass has only a single reduction gear. On the deep sea tugs the windlass will have a double reduction gear. Very often a hand turned gear wheel is incorporated which can be slid along a shaft to engage the main pinion in the event that the power drive fails. A long job indeed by hand! The warping drums on the ends of the main shaft are used for hauling in ropes, to draw the tug into the quay side or to tighten up ropes lashing a lighter alongside. As mentioned previously the deep sea tugs usually had a cargo winch to deal with the salvage equipment. The principle of operation is basically the same as the anchor windlass except that a wire rope drum is used in place of the chain gipsy.

Most tugs designed for use in docks, harbours and rivers have a capstan on the towing deck for hauling down the bridle against the strain of the towrope and for recovering the towrope itself.

Fenders are fitted to tugs to prevent them from being damaged when they come alongside their tow or alongside the quay. On the paddle tugs it was only necessary to protect the paddle boxes and at the fore and aft end was hung either a Turks Head fender made of rope or more simply a piece of round timber which acted as a buffer-cum-roller. There was also a light rubbing band of wood or half round iron running right round the hull at deck level but this was usually of small proportions. On the Manchester Ship Canal the **Reliant** or rather the **Old Trafford** as she then was, and her sister tugs were unusual in having the paddle sponsons extended right to the bow and stern and these were heavily guarded with an iron band (155).

Screw tugs almost invariably have a continuous heavy rubbing band right round the hull just at deck level consisting of: (1) Pitch pine or elm faced with steel flat bar or half round iron and supported from the hull by angle iron. (2) On Thames tug - a half-round hollow iron section.(3) Square section rubber supported between steel angle. This is a comparatively new idea and apart from giving a good service life it is simple to replace worn sections.

In addition there is the very necessary but unsightly array of old motor car tyres hung round the bulwarks. At the bow the tugs used to carry an extra big tyre, maybe off a tractor, as quite often a tug may push a ship bodily to ease her into a berth. In Grangemouth where there was a narrow 'gate' in way of a sliding bridge, a 'gate tug' was stationed in windy weather and her duty was to maintain a thrust against the side of the ship as she passed through the 'gate' on her way to the inner dock system. In some of the dock systems where space is limited it is not unusual for a tug to ease a ship around a tight corner by pushing with her stern which may be protected by an elegant woven rope "pudding fender" or another collection of tyres.

On the Thames the protection is sometimes limited to the elm sheathing on the stern while at other times the bulwarks are hung with tyres.

Funnels: This is the feature which to the shiplover can make or mar a tug. The pioneering tugs generally had tall thin funnels with no rake, possibly with a bell top or a crown of spikes like the early locomotives. Some of the photographs of the old wooden paddle tugs show these features.

The bridle 'bowsed down' on board ***M.S.C.Badger.*** *Two tow ropes are in use one to either bow of her charge.*

Without forced draught the funnels of these old tugs were of necessity long, and not having a casing round them they appeared ridiculously thin. As the heat of the funnel would have scorched any light coloured paint they were inevitably painted black. However, in most paddle tugs the engine-man's platform was immediately in front of the funnel and it was customary to paint the lower part of the funnel with lime to reduce the radiation of heat on to the poor man's back. It was only after the introduction of casings round the funnels that owners were really able to adopt individual funnel colours (Plate 186) which could be used to identify the fleet to which the tug belonged. The combination of colours was generally simple, black, white, yellow and red being the most popular. Nowadays with the amalgamation of fleets some very complicated colour schemes have emerged as the parent firm has endeavoured to retain the identifying features of each of the individual companies.

When 'seeking' was in full swing designers gave their tug funnels a heavy rake to give them a racy, fast appearance and in Steel and Bennie's **Victor** of 1907 the rake was $11\frac{1}{2}°$. This was extreme and a more usual figure was $6\frac{1}{2}°$. The size of the funnel seems to have had a pyshological effect and sailing ship captains were often tempted to give preference to the 'powerful' tug with the big funnel.

Lifeboats: Ever since the early days the tugs have carried a boat of some kind, to put a pilot aboard a ship or to row the crew ashore when the tug was moored to a buoy. The boat was usually a dinghy and therefore no davits were required as the dinghy could be manhandled when required. It would be towed astern when running free, alongside when a ship was in tow, or, if the river were busy, the dinghy would be hauled up on to the paddle sponson out of the way. It can be seen in this position in many of the photographs of the small wooden paddle tugs. When the paddle tugs increased in size the boat became larger and could no longer be manhandled. Portable davits were carried and these could be stepped in sockets on either side of the after deck when the lifeboat was needed. This was not very handy and a new arrangement was adopted where the davits were stepped on the sponsons and the lifeboat was carried on chocks on the sidehouses. In this position the boat was liable to damage if the tug went under the overhang of a ship's stern but it was the most convenient place.

On the small screw tugs which had no boiler casing as such, and therefore no boatdeck the old arrangement of portable davits and the lifeboat carried on the deck was common. The larger tugs with a proper boiler casing had a boat deck and the lifeboats were carried on either side of the funnel. Where the funnel had no casing the wooden lifeboat was exposed to the full heat from the funnel and the seams were anything but watertight. The introduction of casings round the flue did help the situation somewhat (51). Now that boats are of steel or aluminium this problem no longer exists.

The original davit was of the radial type (211) and these were carried on board tugs until recent years. There have been a number of quick-acting davits invented and these have appeared from time to time on tugs and can be seen in the plans and photographs. On the average tug speed of operation is not essential. If a tug is struck by a ship during a docking operation the tug sinks in seconds as they are single skin construction. The crew do not have time to lower a boat; they have barely time to jump clear. If the tug is limited to working within the port or estuary, owners are permitted to use inflatable dinghies in place of lifeboats.

The big deep sea tugs generally have at least one of their lifeboats equipped with an engine so that it can be readily used as a tender between tug and tow for carrying ropes, pumps and other salvage equipment.

Lights: Tugs are required to carry the standard navigation lights. On the mast one white light at a height above the waterline equal to the beam of the tug; a green light on the starboard side; a red light on the port side and a white light facing aft. In addition she must carry towing lights, one six feet below the navigation light at her masthead and another one six feet below that if the overall length of the tow exceeds 600 feet.

When the lamps were of the old-fashioned oil burning type they were carried in some form of cradle which slid up and down two guide wires. The guide wires were fastened at their upper end to an arm which curved out from a collar on the mast so as to keep the lamps clear of the forestay. The cradle might have been a flat plate with four lugs on the back sliding on the wires, the plate might have had a tray at right angles, or a cage into which the lamp could be placed. Even after the introduction of fixed electric navigation lights it was customary to provide all the necessary fittings for oil lamps for use in the event of a power failure. Sometimes instead of sliding cradles the tug will have fixed platforms on the mast to take the oil lamps. These two variations can be seen on the tugs of the Liverpool Lighterage Company and the Tees Towing Company.

The red and green side lights on the paddle tugs were carried in screens resting on the paddlebox at the after end and supported on struts at the forward end. On the screw tugs the screens were often placed on the boat deck abreast of the wheelhouse or, if no boat deck was available on either side of the wheelhouse on arms which could be swung out at night or swung inboard during the day to keep the lights out of the way. The seeking tug **Sarah Jolliffe** which belonged to the Alexandra Towing Company of Liverpool carried her side lights in little lighthouses at the forward end of her boat deck (81) in just the same way as the sailing ships which she towed.

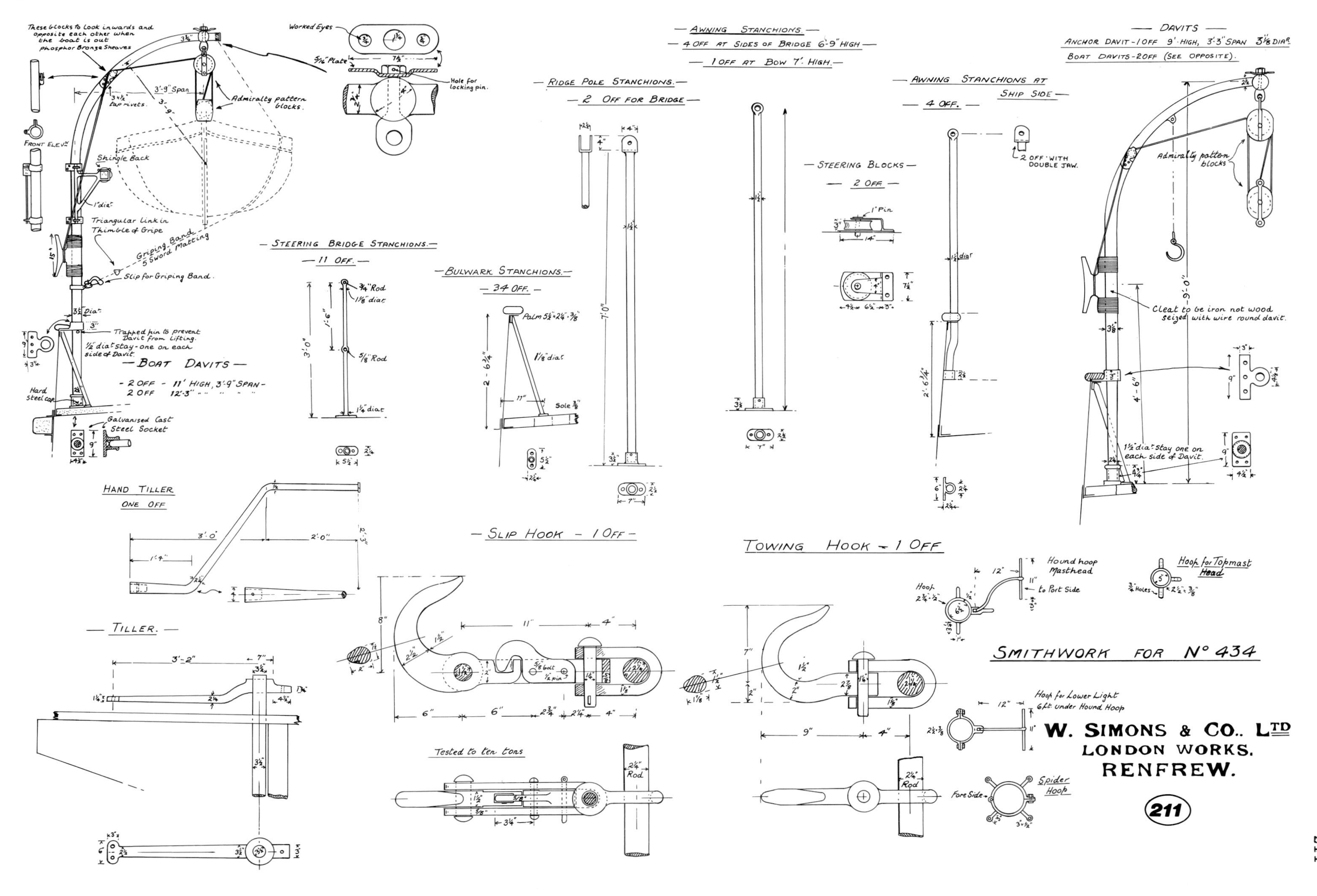
— DAVITS —
ANCHOR DAVIT - 1 OFF 9' HIGH, 3'3" SPAN 3⅛ DIAR
BOAT DAVITS - 2 OFF (SEE OPPOSITE).
Admiralty pattern blocks
Cleat to be iron not wood seized with wire round davit.
1½" diar stay one on each side of Davit.
— AWNING STANCHIONS —
— 4 OFF AT SIDES OF BRIDGE 6'9" HIGH —
— 1 OFF AT BOW 7' HIGH. —
— RIDGE POLE STANCHIONS. —
— 2 OFF FOR BRIDGE —
— AWNING STANCHIONS AT SHIP SIDE —
— 4 OFF. —
2 OFF WITH DOUBLE JAW.
— STEERING BLOCKS —
— 2 OFF —
1" Pin
— STEERING BRIDGE STANCHIONS. —
— 11 OFF. —
¾" Rod
1⅛" diar
⅝" Rod
1¼" diar
— BULWARK STANCHIONS. —
— 34 OFF. —
Palm 5½ × 2¼ × ⅜
1⅛" diar
Sole ⅜"
These blocks to look inwards and opposite each other when the boat is out
phosphor Bronze Sheaves
3'-9" Span
Admiralty pattern blocks
3 × ½ tap rivets.
FRONT ELEVN
Shingle Back
1" diar
Triangular Link in Thimble of Gripe
Griping Band 5 Sword Matting
Slip for Griping Band.
Trapped pin to prevent Davit from Lifting.
½" diar stay - one on each side of Davit.
— BOAT DAVITS —
- 2 OFF - 11' HIGH, 3'-9" SPAN -
2 OFF 12'-3" " " "
Hard Steel cap
Galvanised Cast Steel Socket
Worked Eyes
5/16" Plate
Hole for locking pin.
HAND TILLER
ONE OFF
— TILLER. —
— SLIP HOOK - 1 OFF —
⅝ bolt
½ pin
Tested to ten tons
TOWING HOOK - 1 OFF
Hound hoop Masthead
to Port Side
Hoop
Hoop for Topmast Head
¾ Holes
SMITHWORK FOR N° 434
Hoop for Lower Light 6ft under Hound Hoop
Spider Hoop
Fore Side
W. SIMONS & CO., LTD
LONDON WORKS.
RENFREW.
211

When electric side lights were introduced it was the usual practice to make the light screens deeper and to fit a bracket which could take an emergency oil lamp. On the modern tugs the wings of the bridge often extend to the width of the vessel and the sidelights are recessed into the wings with access from the bridge deck itself.

The white light which faces aft has appeared in many different places on different tugs. The old **Cruiser** on the Clyde had guide wires and halliards fixed to the funnel. When the tug had a mainmast abaft the funnel the light was mounted on it. Sometimes the light was fixed on a bracket mounted on the rail at the rear of the boatdeck. There are also bulkhead lights on the superstructure so that the crew can find their way about at night and above the hook there is often a floodlight which illuminates the after deck at night when the towrope is being connected (51).

On the craft tugs on the Thames the lamps on the mast are placed as high as is feasible and there are only two white lights four feet apart. These are to be mounted in such a way that even when the mast is lowered for shooting a bridge the lights must still show one above the other, though at a lower level. This is usually done by mounting the lights on a short spar which pivots on the mast and remains vertical as the mast is pulled down (100).

Sampson Posts (or Timberheads): In addition to the bollards which are fitted on tugs, sampson posts are also provided, two forward of the superstructure and two just aft of the superstructure. On the old paddle tugs and even on many screw tugs these posts were made of 6" to 12" square timbers with a 'cavil', that is a horizontal bar of square timber set into and bolted to the uprights. Even as late as 1935 this kind of sampson post was fitted aboard Steel and Bennie's tug **Warrior**. These posts were stepped in iron "shoes" and clamped to the bulwarks with iron brackets. The top of the post above the bulwarks was rounded off to prevent chafe on the ropes and sometimes a thumb cleat was bolted on the lower part of the post. These wooden posts have now been superseded by tubular steel posts 9" to 12" diameter with a cap welded on the top slightly larger in diameter. They are fixed to the bulwark rail by a steel plate through which they pass. They too may have a thumb cleat fitted or maybe a steel bar parallel to the rail, fixed through the post.

It is customary to fit a large sampson post right in the bow of the tug braced to the rail by a breasthook and provided with up to three rings of half round iron. When the tug is working bow on to the tow, the towrope is secured by giving it two or three turns round the post, down under the cleat and up again round the post. The rings prevent the rope from riding up the post. On the old paddle tugs this bow post was usually set back from the bow, sometimes forming part of the hand windlass assembly, sometimes acting as a support for a towing hook. Many of the paddle tugs used on the North-East coast were equipped in this fashion. Even today the older tug men still refer to the sampson posts as timberheads!

Steering Gear: The first tugs were steered with tillers as in the small sailing craft from which they were developed. They seem to have towed with ropes fastened to bitts on either quarter. When the hook was introduced we do not know but it is easy to imagine how awkward steering must have been, dodging the towrope and coping with the bad visibility forward. One or two skippers modified the arrangement by fitting lines to the tiller and steering the tug from a position beside the funnel where it was less dangerous, the visibility was better and it was warmer! When the steering wheel was fitted at the beginning it was mounted on the deck between the paddle boxes, again this was safer but the field of view was restricted. An old photograph of a Clyde Shipping Company tug shows the skipper standing on the paddle box directing operations (212). After the engine room casing had raised the deck level to that of the paddle boxes, the wheel was positioned there with an excellent field of vision forward but with the funnel hiding the tow. At least one screw tug was built with the steering wheel aft of the funnel, which cured one complaint but left the view forward obscured (66).

At first the wheel was entirely open but after a while the builders provided a waist high screen which afforded a small degree of protection from the elements. When a wheelhouse was fitted it was often just large enough to contain the wheel and the helmsman. It is quite amusing to see

Flying Tempest; the captain directs operations from the paddle box.

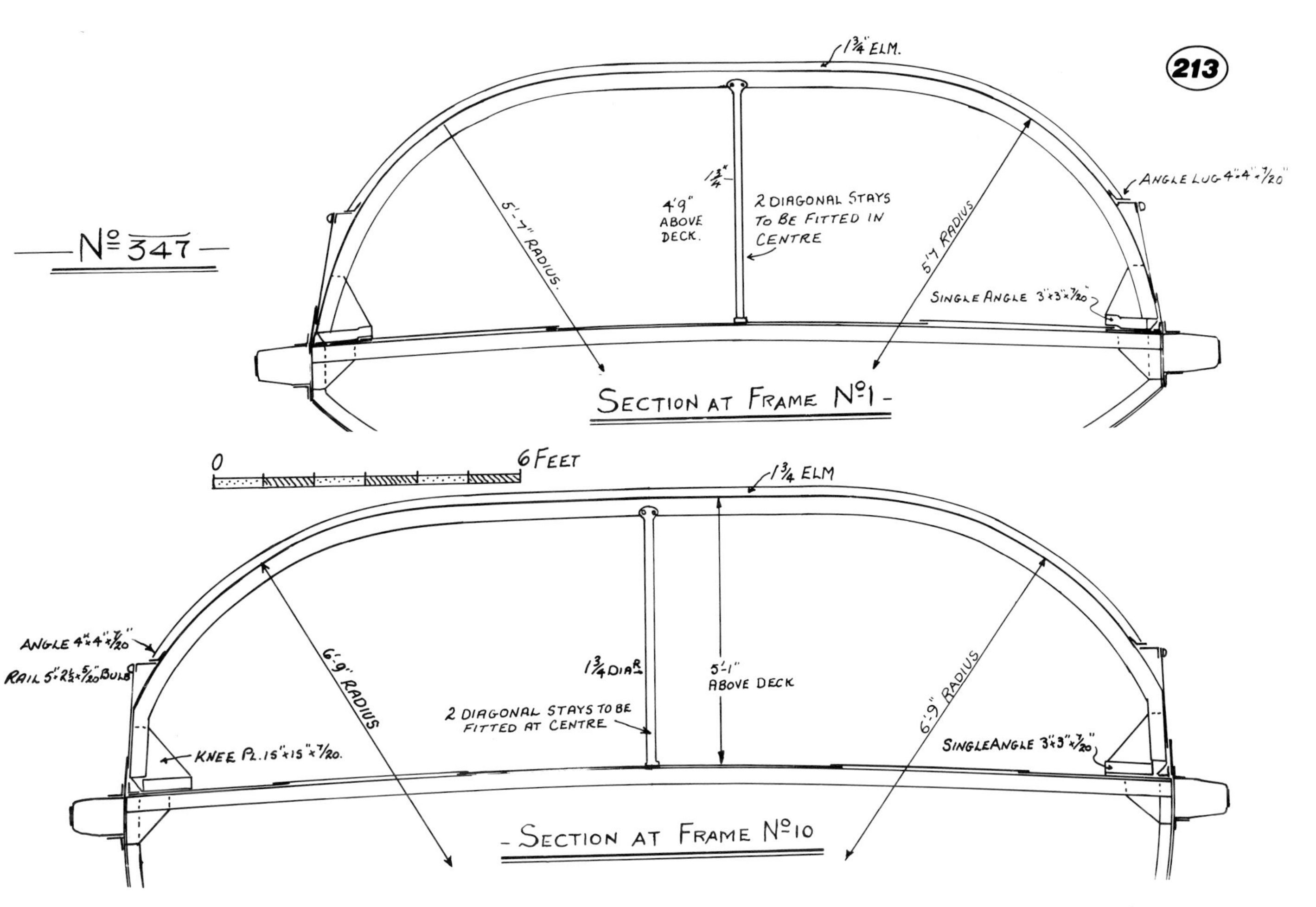

some of the wheelhouses on the early screw tugs; the funnel and the masts raked to give the impression of speed and the wheelhouse raked at the same angle (54). You can almost imagine the helmsman having to lean backwards to fit himself into the wheelhouse. Eventually the size of these wheelhouses was increased to that they could accommodate the compass and the engineroom telegraphs.

When steam power assisted steering was introduced the steering engine was positioned in the after end of the wheelhouse where the noise of its working made conversation impossible. The movements of the wheel were conveyed to the rudder by lengths of chain and rod which ran through guides on the deck along the bulwarks where they were liable to be jammed by flotsam washing around the deck. The steering engine was later placed at the after end of the engine casing, a move which shortened the length of the rods and chains. This was an advantage as the steering rods and chains were liable to stretch in use and the shorter they were the better. Where they crossed the deck they were usually protected by a chequer plate cover.

Open wheels are by no means a thing of the past as in many ports it is customary to have a 'docking bridge' above the wheelhouse, and indeed when tugs are bought second-hand for these ports, the first thing the new owners do is to fit the docking bridge.

Towing Beams, Bows or Rails: This curved bar on the after deck of the tug is the feature which identifies her for what she is. The wooden tug had of course wooden towing rails, generally supported on either side of a companion or a skylight by pillars. These pillars were often plain square posts but sometimes they were quite fancy being turned like chair legs. As they were usually very low it was customary to hinge the ends so that they could be dropped to leave a clear path round the deck. When they were raised they were held by a pin in a small casting on the rail. With iron and steel tugs came iron and steel towing rails. These were generally of an inverted 'T' section and were capped with wood to reduce chafing on the tow rope, a capping which could be readily replaced (213). On many of the smaller tugs a towing rail which spans the full width of the hull is not used but instead the fittings which project above the deck are protected by means of towing bows which are iron bars curved over the top of the skylight, hatch or companionway (100). These must be arranged in such a way as to prevent the rope from catching even if it drops to deck level when it slackens off.

In connection with the protection of the superstructure some form of stop is required to prevent the rope from causing damage if the tug is "girted". This means that the tug has swung across the rope at right-angles and is being pulled bodily sideways (214). The rope may bear heavily against the stop and it must be strongly made. On the old deep-sea tugs the stops might take the form of heavy wooden brackets which stiffened the superstructure and also supported the after end of the boatdeck. Some paddle tugs had round bars stepped in the bulwarks and curved backwards to prevent the rope from riding up. Screw tugs have stops at either side of the after end of the boat deck in the form of back-curving bars.

Towing Hooks: There is nothing to indicate when the hook was first introduced for towing. We can imagine that at first a variety of different bollards or bitts were used. Watkin's **Monarch** of 1833 shows a plain hook supported on pivot and resting on a curved bar to prevent it from dropping (14). In the early hooks there was no mechanism for tripping the hook and releasing the towrope if the tug got into difficulties. The only means of release available was an axe with which to cut the rope. the "Liverpool" hook was one of the first attempts to provide a quick-release arrangement on the hook (215). The hook was arranged to pivot and was kept in place by a tumbler which in its turn was held by a tripping lever. The tripping lever could be released by pulling on a rope or in other designs by striking it with a big mallet. If you look closely at photographs of the North East Coast paddle tugs you will often see the mallet lying beside the hook. Many older tugs were fitted with two hooks, one plain and one tripping type.

The Victorians were great inventors and they even found ways to change the shape of a towing hook. The 'Challenge towing hook' was used by McKie & Thomson of Govan and J. Fullerton of Paisley (215). The support for the hook was provided by an angle iron fastened to the boiler casing drilled with several holes to allow the position of the hook to be altered athwartships. The **Plato** (181) has a similar type of support but has a standard "Liverpool" type of hook.

Some owners consider that it is an advantage to have some form of shock absorber on the towing hook to take some of the stresses caused by a jerk on the towrope. A patent was taken out as early as 1859 for a sprung hook where the shocks were taken up by rubber discs sandwiched between iron plates. Nowadays steel springs are used - on the paddle tug **Eppleton Hall** now preserved in America there are three springs in a massive frame resting on a greased table which forms part of the casing over the boilers (45). The old "Liverpool" hook served its purpose but with the strains put on it by the pull of the rope it was found that after a time the release mechanism no longer operated. More complex hooks were therefore designed which could be tripped easily even with a heavy load on the hook (153).

Almost all the early tugs carried their hooks on a short curved bar. The deep sea tugs **Great Britain** and **Great Western** of 1876 had the bar supported on two stanchions braced for and aft and braced athwartships to take the strain (76). On the paddle tug **Lingdale** the load on the hook was transmitted to the keelson by a chain. More usually it was placed on the after end of the boiler casing and either the casing was heavily braced internally or there were tie rods which transferred the strain to the deck beams. The trouble with this arrangement was that when the tug put herself across the rope, which she often did when she wished to act as a brake on the movement of the tow, she was subjected to a tremendous heeling force. When this occurred the tug was said to be "girted" and sometimes she would be capsized if the rope did not break. In London, in February 1897, the Cory tug **Realm** (1890, 68.5ft. 50 tons. 42 n.h.p.) was girted and pulled over while assisting a ship. At the inquiry the owners were criticised for using a tug which was too small for the ship which she was towing, a ship 172ft. long carrying 400 tons of coal. The **Realm** was a craft tug intended for the towing of lighters.

From time to time designers have tackled this question and the answer had always been the same. Put the hook on the end of a long arm and secure that arm in such a way that it is forced to pivot only in the horizontal plane. In this way the heeling moment is greatly reduced and so is the danger to the tug. The original versions had a fixed channel section arranged in a curve nearly the beam of the tug and the arm which carried the hook was "tied" to the girder with rollers which both guided it and held it down. The modern version has a strong deep arm which is pivotted vertically on the main superstructure so that it can only swing in the horizontal plane and of such a length that it is nearly half the beam of the boat. The tripping mechanisms which are incorporated are now released pneumatically or hydraulically.

Not all tugs are equipped with towing hooks. The tug owners on the Continent favour a huge double cruciform bollard to which the towrope is fastened. On the **Vanguard** which was operated by Steel and Bennie of Glasgow, purchased as the **Du Guesclin**, the bollard also incorporated a

This 'Cock' tug photographed at Liverpool by John Clarkson was 'girted' and under the strain the towrope broke. The tug has moved bodily sideways about six feet. The crew have wisely moved to the higher side of the tug and forward to be clear of the flailing end of the rope.

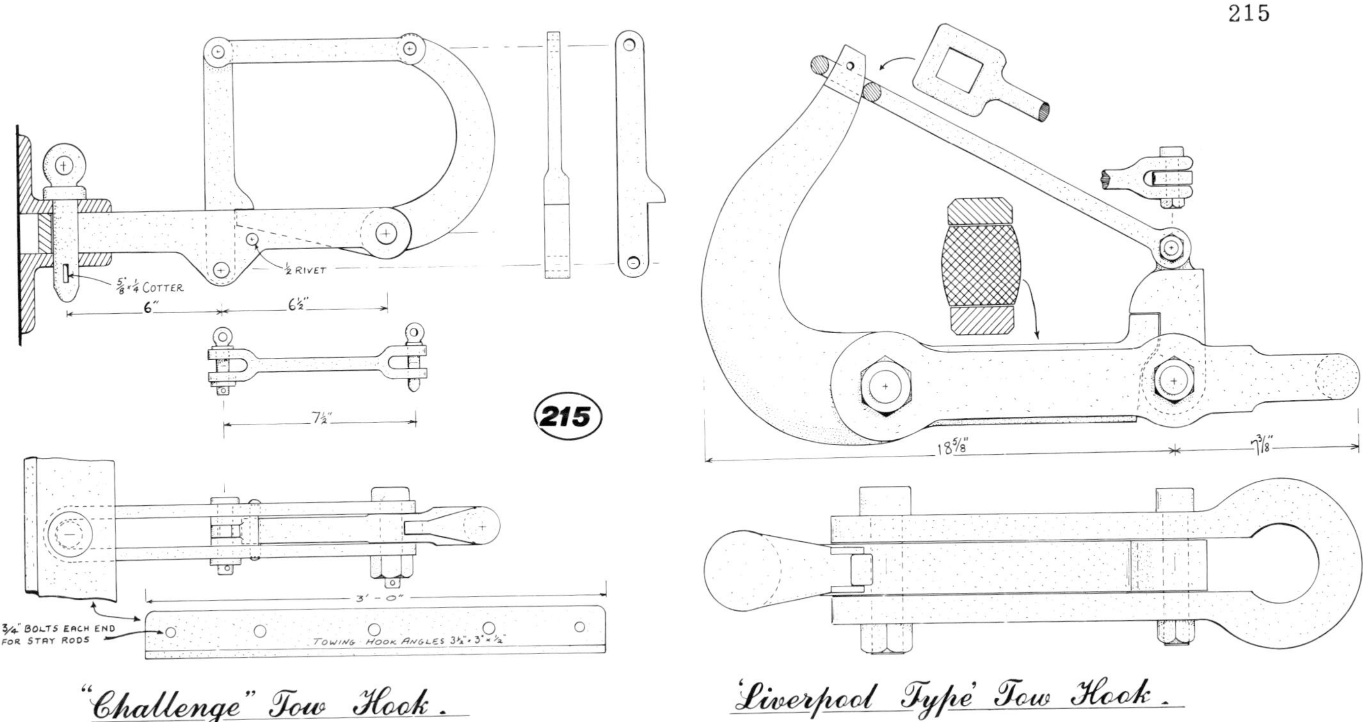

"Challenge" Tow Hook. 'Liverpool Type' Tow Hook.

sprung towing hook. The **Reliant** now in the National Maritime Museum has a similar arrangement on her foredeck and many other paddle tugs had a towing hook at the fore end, usually on a sampson post. The tugs of the Manchester Ship Canal Company normally work bow on to the tow when working as stern tug and they fix the towrope to a double cruciform bollard on the foredeck. The **Craigleith** of Leith had a towing hook on the fore end of the superstructure, an almost unique arrangement.

As an alternative to the towing hook the automatic towing winch was introduced in America in 1888 but it has never featured on British steam tugs to any extent except on the ocean-going tugs of later years. However, a number of the World War I "H.S." type tugs were equipped with towing winches for towing barge trains across the Channel. The ocean-going tug used to rely on the great length of towrope with its attendant sag to act as a 'spring' if undue stresses came on the rope. However, the automatic winch is the ideal arrangement where the winch is set for a given pull. If the pull is exceeded due to the tow sheering off to one side the winch pays out the rope to ease the strain and when the rope slackens again the winch winds in the rope once more. This type of winch is usually fitted with warping drums which are very necessary when recovering a tow rope of the size needed for deep sea work.

Cant Hooks: Another hook on a tug which is less familiar is the 'cant hook', though it was common enough on the old paddle tugs. In the early chapters the difficulty of manoeuvring a single engined paddle tug was mentioned. The bogie loaded with scrap had a relatively short life being superseded by the cant hook. This was a plain hook on a swivel at the edge of the sponsons aft of the paddle boxes; sometimes additional cant hooks were fitted forward.

When the tug was towing and required to alter direction drastically, the engine was throttled down and when the towrope slackened, the eye of the rope was transferred from the towing hook to the cant hook. The tug then went ahead and in doing so swung round the end of the towrope. When she was pointing in the right direction the rope was slackened off once more, the eye was put back on the main hook and the tug went ahead again. An alternative method was to have a short 'messenger' lashed to the towrope which pulled the towrope towards the side of the tug when it was slipped over the cant hook. Although the cant hook was intended to overcome the disadvantage of the single engined tug it was often found on the sponsons of the twin engined paddle tugs.

Towropes: The tow rope is the most important item of a tug's equipment. Generally manilla rope has been used but this is now being replaced by nylon ropes or ropes of other man-made fibres. The following are typical examples of the towropes carried aboard tugs in the past:

1865	P.T. **Conqueror**	(Coastal tug)	60 fathoms 5" manilla
1897	T.S.T. **Hotspur**	(Harbour tug)	75 fathoms 6" manilla
1918	S.T. **Saint Abbs**	(Salvage tug)	120 fathoms 9" manilla
		2x	60 fathoms 6" manilla
			75 fathoms 7 ½" hemp.
			115 fathoms 12" manilla cordage, cable laid.
1915	**Mt. George V**	(Modernised coastal tug)	100 fathoms 4" steel wire
			75 fathoms 7" manilla
			75 fathoms 5" manilla

Typical for harbour and river work a few years ago was a 12" manilla rope of about 11 fathoms, shackled to 16 to 30 fathoms of 3" to 3 ½" steel wire, the rope being attached to the hook and the wire to the bollards on the foredeck of the tow. For coastal work the towrope would be 14" manilla about 100 fathoms in length.

Nylon has many advantages despite its high cost. It weighs about half the weight of the equivalent manilla rope, as an 8" nylon hawser will stand the same strain as a 12" manilla, around 58 tons breaking load. It is easier to handle as it 'relaxes' as soon as the strain comes off and may be winched in and stored in a far shorter time. For tows on a long rope, which is common practice in deep sea work, manilla was generally used. Wire lacks weight and elasticity whereas manilla is heavier and it stretches. The sag and the stretch act as a kind of spring to absorb shocks and jerks.

Towropes are carried in a special store below the after deck and only the ready-use ropes are kept on deck. On the earlier tugs there was a cage-like cradle for the towrope just in front of the stern grating set up off the deck on blocks and sparred to allow free circulation of air to dry off the wet towropes (216). It is not so usual to see the towrope cradle nowadays with so much nylon rope in use. Nylon does not hold the water and in any case does not rot if left in a wet state. The ropes are either coiled on a flat grating or merely coiled on the deck.

The towing capacity of a tug is usually rated in terms of 'bollard pull'. The towrope is attached to a dynamometer which is fixed on the quayside, the tug goes full ahead and the pull is read off the dial in cwt. or tons. In the days of the steam tug the average bollard pull expected was about one ton per 100 i.h.p. of the engine and was around 8 to 10 tons. Deep sea salvage tugs with bollard pulls of 40 to 50 tons are not unusual. On the smaller tugs higher pulls for a given engine power have been achieved by the introduction of the Kort nozzle.

Whistle: To anyone who frequented harbours where ships were handled by tugs the operation must have seemed a very noisy one. Every now and again a syren would make you jump as it sounded off almost in your ear. It was all part of the control of the docking operation. From the ship's bridge the pilot gave instructions to the tugs, to the bow tug with a whistle (like a referee's whistle), and to the stern tug with the ship's syren:

One short blast.........	Stop towing.
Two short blasts........	Tow ahead.
Three short blasts......	Tow astern.
One long, one short blast.......	Tow to starboard.
One long, two short blasts.......	Tow to port.

These signals indicated in which direction the ship was to be towed and they were repeated by the appropriate tug to confirm that the instruction has been received and would be carried out. Some could only manage a feeble 'bleat', others would deafen you. The paddle tug **Elie** of Methil made a sound like the 'whoop' of a destroyer.

On the other hand it was possible to see a docking being carried out in complete silence and you had to marvel at the way in which the tugs eased the ship into position without any instructions from the pilot. This is becoming more common these days with the introduction of the radio telephone with which the pilot can give his orders verbally.

216

The sparred tow rope cradle of the paddle tug ***Eppleton Hall****. See also Plate 19 and page 45.*

Index

Engines of the paddle tug ***Clyde*** *of 1851 preserved at Renfrew (see page 198).*

Tugs and other vessels.

*The paddle tug **Defiance** was built in 1884 (101.0 ft, 115 tons, 80 n.h.p.) for Duncan McKellar who is seen aboard with some of his associates.*

INDEX: Tugs.

INDEX: *SHIPBUILDERS.*

The names of ships built by the yards and illustrated by a plan, are shown in brackets after the page number.

TUG OWNERS.

(See also page 187).

Towage Receipts.
Courtesy Steven Lang.

CARDIFF STEAM TOWING COMPANY.

12 October 1861

The Owners of the "Antioch"

To the Cardiff Steam Towing Co.,

577 Tons at

ST. GEORGE STEAM TUG COMPANY,
OFFICES, No. 5, GEORGE'S DOCK,

Liverpool, Sept 24 1862

Captain and Owners of the "Antioch"

Drs. to H. J. WARD & CO.,

OWNERS OF THE STEAMER "SEA KING."

For Towing from Prince Dock to Collingwood Dock 3.0.0
Sept 30th From Dk to River 3.0.0
& from River to sea 7.0.0